# Policy Responses to Tax Competition

NATIONAL BUREAU of ECONOMIC RESEARCH

National Bureau of Economic Research
Conference Report

NBER
NATIONAL BUREAU *of* ECONOMIC RESEARCH

# Policy Responses to Tax Competition

Edited by **David R. Agrawal, James M. Poterba, and Owen M. Zidar**

**The University of Chicago Press**

Chicago and London

The University of Chicago Press, Chicago 60637
The University of Chicago Press, Ltd., London

Published 2025
Printed in the United States of America

34 33 32 31 30 29 28 27 26 25 1 2 3 4 5

ISBN-13: 978-0-226-83859-5 (cloth)
ISBN-13: 978-0-226-84478-7 (ebook)
DOI: https://doi.org/10.7208/chicago/9780226844787.001.0001

Library of Congress Cataloging-in-Publication Data

Names: Agrawal, David R. editor | Poterba, James M. editor | Zidar, Owen M. editor
Title: Policy responses to tax competition / edited by David R. Agrawal, James M. Poterba, and Owen M. Zidar.
Other titles: National Bureau of Economic Research conference report
Description: Chicago ; London : The University of Chicago Press, 2025. | Series: National Bureau of Economic Research conference report | Includes papers from a hybrid conference of the same name held 16–17 March 2023, at Cambridge, MA and on Zoom. | Includes bibliographical references and index.
Identifiers: LCCN 2025009542 | ISBN 9780226838595 cloth | ISBN 9780226844787 ebook
Subjects: LCSH: Taxation—Congresses | Tax incentives—Congresses | Competition—Congresses | Economic policy—Congresses | Intergovernmental fiscal relations—Congresses | Interstate relations—Economic aspects—Congresses | Interstate agreements—Economic aspects—Congresses | LCGFT: Conference papers and proceedings | Conference papers and proceedings
Classification: LCC HJ2330 .P65 2025 | DDC 336.24/316—dc23/eng/20250512
LC record available at https://lccn.loc.gov/2025009542

Authorized Representative for EU General Product Safety Regulation (GPSR) queries: **Easy Access System Europe**—Mustamäe tee 50, 10621 Tallinn, Estonia, gpsr.requests@easproject.com

Any other queries: https://press.uchicago.edu/press/contact.html

♾ This paper meets the requirements of ANSI/NISO Z39.48-1992 (Permanence of Paper).

## Relation of the Directors to the Work and Publications of the NBER

1. The object of the NBER is to ascertain and present to the economics profession, and to the public more generally, important economic facts and their interpretation in a scientific manner without policy recommendations. The Board of Directors is charged with the responsibility of ensuring that the work of the NBER is carried on in strict conformity with this object.

2. The President shall establish an internal review process to ensure that book manuscripts proposed for publication DO NOT contain policy recommendations. This shall apply both to the proceedings of conferences and to manuscripts by a single author or by one or more co-authors but shall not apply to authors of comments at NBER conferences who are not NBER affiliates.

3. No book manuscript reporting research shall be published by the NBER until the President has sent to each member of the Board a notice that a manuscript is recommended for publication and that in the President's opinion it is suitable for publication in accordance with the above principles of the NBER. Such notification will include a table of contents and an abstract or summary of the manuscript's content, a list of contributors if applicable, and a response form for use by Directors who desire a copy of the manuscript for review. Each manuscript shall contain a summary drawing attention to the nature and treatment of the problem studied and the main conclusions reached.

4. No volume shall be published until forty-five days have elapsed from the above notification of intention to publish it. During this period a copy shall be sent to any Director requesting it, and if any Director objects to publication on the grounds that the manuscript contains policy recommendations, the objection will be presented to the author(s) or editor(s). In case of dispute, all members of the Board shall be notified, and the President shall appoint an ad hoc committee of the Board to decide the matter; thirty days additional shall be granted for this purpose.

5. The President shall present annually to the Board a report describing the internal manuscript review process, any objections made by Directors before publication or by anyone after publication, any disputes about such matters, and how they were handled.

6. Publications of the NBER issued for informational purposes concerning the work of the Bureau, or issued to inform the public of the activities at the Bureau, including but not limited to the NBER Digest and Reporter, shall be consistent with the object stated in paragraph 1. They shall contain a specific disclaimer noting that they have not passed through the review procedures required in this resolution. The Executive Committee of the Board is charged with the review of all such publications from time to time.

7. NBER working papers and manuscripts distributed on the Bureau's web site are not deemed to be publications for the purpose of this resolution, but they shall be consistent with the object stated in paragraph 1. Working papers shall contain a specific disclaimer noting that they have not passed through the review procedures required in this resolution. The NBER's web site shall contain a similar disclaimer. The President shall establish an internal review process to ensure that the working papers and the web site do not contain policy recommendations, and shall report annually to the Board on this process and any concerns raised in connection with it.

8. Unless otherwise determined by the Board or exempted by the terms of paragraphs 6 and 7, a copy of this resolution shall be printed in each NBER publication as described in paragraph 2 above.

# Contents

# Introduction

David R. Agrawal, James M. Poterba,
and Owen M. Zidar

## I.1 Introduction

Nations, states, and localities compete for mobile individuals, firms, and transactions when designing their tax systems. The capacity to move away from a high-tax jurisdiction is a key behavioral response for taxpayers, whether households or firms, and this response can be an important determinant of the location and scale of economic activity, as well as the fiscal capacity of governments. Rising economic integration, both within and across nations, is associated with higher mobility between jurisdictions. It places growing pressure on tax structures that were designed for a world with less economic mobility.

News accounts periodically claim that taxes are responsible for the migration of high-profile individuals and firms. For example, members of the band ABBA's time living outside of Sweden, when that country had top marginal income tax rates of more than 80 percent, was broadly attributed to tax issues. When Amazon was searching for a location for its second headquarters, many states and localities offered multi-billion-dollar subsidy deals to lure the online retail giant. Large corporations such as Lufthansa, Deutsche Bank, and Unilever had subsidiaries in the small German town Norderfriedrichskoog, with a population of about fifty, to benefit from its

David R. Agrawal is a professor of economics at the University of California, Irvine, and a fellow of CESifo.

James M. Poterba is the Mitsui Professor of Economics at the Massachusetts Institute of Technology, and president and CEO of the National Bureau of Economic Research.

Owen M. Zidar is a professor of economics and public affairs at Princeton University, and a research associate of the National Bureau of Economic Research.

zero-rated local corporate business tax rate.[1] These examples illustrate the more general point that tax-driven mobility can place constraints on the tax rates that jurisdictions can set.

Cross-jurisdiction mobility of the tax base can drive a wedge between the optimal tax policy for a single jurisdiction and the optimal policy for a collection of jurisdictions taken together. Although each jurisdiction may find it individually rational to offer lower taxes, because in-migration will increase the tax base and potentially offset the revenue loss from lower rates, the relocation of economic activity from another jurisdiction reduces its tax revenues and economic activity. The net effect on the tax-cutting jurisdiction is positive, but it is possible that the net losses to the other jurisdictions will exceed this benefit and make the aggregate impact negative.

This possibility is illustrated by the so called check-the-box rules that allow US multinationals to create entities that are treated differently in the United States and in foreign countries. These rules, described in Altshuler, Boller, and Suárez Serrato (2024), permit hybrid structures that reduce tax payments both in the United States and in foreign countries. Introduced in 1997, these rules allow US multinationals to enjoy lower effective taxes at the expense of some non-tax-haven foreign jurisdictions. Part of the initial motivation of the OECD's Base Erosion and Profit Shifting initiative (BEPS) was to reduce the abuse of these types of hybrid entities as well as the inefficiencies created by tax competition.

On the other hand, tax competition can provide a discipline on the tax rates levied by jurisdictions. It can generate benefits by facilitating sorting among diverse communities, taming the excessive taxation of Leviathan governments, and enhancing efficiency from better matching of firms to locations. Some individuals may be better off because of it.

Tax competition also crease two types of inefficiencies. First, when competition is responsible for tax rate disparities across jurisdictions, it results in resource misallocation across jurisdictions. The marginal product of production factors will be higher in high-tax jurisdictions. Second, when jurisdictions decide the size of their public sectors, if they equate the marginal benefit of spending to their inhabitants with the marginal own-jurisdiction cost of raising revenue, but do not consider interjurisdictional fiscal externalities, they may choose an inefficient spending level. A policy change in one jurisdiction can impact revenues and spending elsewhere, as the tax base or the beneficiaries of policies move across jurisdictions. Besides tax externalities, there can be spending externalities: nonresidents often consume public services outside of their home jurisdiction, but governments do not account for those expenditure spillovers when setting policy.

1. Further details on ABBA may be found at https://abbaarticles.blogspot.com/2012/04/1977-pop-group-abba-wants-to-leave.html. For corporate incentives, see the 2018 *Slate* article by Aaron Mak, "Here Are the Outrageous Incentives That Losing Cities Offered Amazon for HQ2," https://slate.com/technology/2018/11/amazon-hq2-incredible-incentives-losing-cities-offered.html, and von Schwerin and Buettner (2016).

In federal systems of government, national governments sometimes take actions to reduce tax competition. In addition, in countries including Germany, Switzerland, and the United States, subfederal governments have often engaged in interjurisdictional cooperation. One example is the Kansas-Missouri pact of 2019 in the US. There are also wider-ranging international initiatives such as the BEPS project at the OECD and the recent global minimum tax proposal. At the international level, the absence of an overarching tax authority has confounded cross-country tax coordination. Despite the political challenges, several recent policy initiatives—most notably the agreement by nearly 140 countries in 2021 on the G20/OECD's inclusive framework on global minimum taxation—have sought to limit tax competition. While there are many different policies designed to limit tax competition, there is no systematic catalogue of them, nor a comparative assessment of the extent to which they have affected jurisdictional behavior. This introduction describes a comprehensive menu of policy responses to interjurisdictional tax competition, along with framework for analyzing these responses. It also summarizes the research studies in this volume that present new evidence on some of these policies.

Policy responses to tax competition are sometimes widely accepted by jurisdictions, but sometimes they are highly contentious. States with cross-border metropolitan areas, such as New Jersey-Pennsylvania, have historically entered into reciprocity agreements that shift income taxes away from the location of work to the location of residence. Despite the long-standing agreement, New Jersey Governor Christie initially promised to abolish the NJ-PA agreement, but then reversed this decision. With respect to corporate profits, the 2017 Tax Cuts and Jobs Act exempted multinational foreign-sourced income from US taxes. But, worried this change would result in increased profit-shifting incentives, the US unilaterally passed the global intangible low-taxed income (GILTI) tax. Other policies such as state aid rules in the EU, formulary apportionment in the US states and Pillar 1 of BEPS, minimum taxes as in Pillar 2 of BEPS, and exit taxes represent prominent responses to competitive forces.

The policies we consider range from complete tax harmonization to more flexible structures that involve partial harmonization among a subset of jurisdictions or that force low-tax jurisdictions to enforce a minimum rate while allowing higher-tax jurisdictions tax autonomy. Many questions arise when considering policy responses to tax competition: What structures have been tried? Do they rely on an external actor like an overarching institutional authority? Do they require cooperation or do they allow for unilateral action? Do these institutions have staying power? What are the necessary preconditions to implement them? How effective are they at improving tax revenues and welfare? Beyond formal tax treaties, we also consider changes in auditing, mobility restrictions and border controls, and changes to apportionment formulas and sourcing rules. Within federal systems, we explore the tools available to state and federal governments, such as intergovernmental grants, intermunicipal cooperation, constitutional restrictions on taxing instruments, and jurisdictional amalgamation.

The distinction between unilateral and multilateral implementation of a policy response is critical because policies that can be adopted unilaterally may not internalize any interjurisdictional externalities and may instead be used as new strategic tools by their adopters. Further, the distinction between multilateral adoption without the involvement of an external actor (such as a bilateral treaty) and multilateral adoption with delegation to an external actor (such as the European Union) has important implications for the extent of the welfare improvements. If the taxed factor is locally mobile, then bilateral efforts between nearby jurisdictions may be sufficient. In cases where the tax base is globally mobile, however, bilateral arrangements run the risk of improving the well-being of the participating jurisdictions while imposing costs on those that do not participate. In these cases, an external actor—such as an overarching jurisdiction—may need to intervene to achieve the welfare optimum, but involving such an actor may place added constraints on the feasible policy interventions.

The substantial literature on the economic effects of tax competition finds that in many settings, it is not possible to determine whether a policy action is efficiency enhancing without a careful empirical assessment. There are a few general theoretical results that have nevertheless emerged. First, as noted in Keen and Konrad (2013), "if the decentralized solution suffers from externalities between the players, it generically holds that an appropriately chosen central planner's solution exists that yields strictly higher welfare in every country, relative to the decentralized outcome." Although this result implies that a possible Pareto improvement exists, it may be very difficult to implement and is likely to be politically infeasible. Second, when reaction functions slope upward, so that an increase in the tax rate of one jurisdiction raises the tax rate in another, minimum tax rates are more likely to increase the tax revenues of all jurisdictions than tax harmonization to a weighted average of the uncoordinated tax rates. Third, tax harmonization to a weighted average of the tax rates that prevail under competition will not yield an efficient outcome, because those rates were likely set inefficiently low. Fourth, tax rates and welfare generally increase as the number of competing jurisdictions decreases, meaning that consolidations, mergers, and cooperation that lead to fewer taxing jurisdictions will raise revenues. Fifth, making the tax base more inelastic by changing sourcing rules or enforcements will raise tax rates. Finally, when governments have many possible taxing instruments, tax coordination on one instrument can become Pareto worsening because jurisdictions compete more aggressively on other tax instruments. Taken together, there exist policies that can be Pareto improving, but how to design those policies to achieve those improvements requires careful empirical analysis, which we attempt to guide in this chapter.

## I.2 Defining "Tax Competition"

There are a number of excellent surveys of prior research on tax competition, and we highlight only a few of the many insights that emerge from this body of work.[2] Wilson and Wildasin (2004) define tax competition as "noncooperative tax setting by independent governments, under which each government's policy choices influence the allocation of a mobile tax base among 'regions' represented by these governments." This definition excludes a range of policy interdependencies between governments, including yardstick competition, expenditure spillovers, and policy learning. By requiring the tax base to be mobile among governments, this definition rules out any vertical competition that might occur between a higher-level government and a lower-level government that share the same tax base, discussed in Keen (1998). This is the situation that arises, for example, when a federal government as well as state governments apply sales taxes to the same transactions. While competition for a mobile tax base usually creates pressures that make taxes too low, vertical tax competition usually results in pressures that make taxes too high. The potential policy responses to vertical tax competition differ from the responses to horizontal tax competition between governments; we focus on the latter.

Tax competition can take many forms. Anything that changes the effective tax rate in a jurisdiction can be used as a competitive tool, such as the statutory tax rate, the definition of the tax base, the level of tax enforcement, and the availability of firm-specific or individual-specific subsidy deals as studied in Slattery and Zidar (2020). A jurisdiction may not be able to change only one policy instrument in isolation, as a feasible change in a statutory tax rate, for example, may require a change in the tax base, in expenditures, or in debt policy. The breadth of instruments that can be used to engage in tax competition implies that policies solely aimed to address competition in tax rates are at best a partial constraint on government competition.

The foregoing definition of tax competition allows for both strategic and nonstrategic tax competition. A large empirical literature has tested for tax policy competition estimating the slope of strategic reaction functions between the tax rates or other choices of different jurisdictions. Finding that the slope of the reaction function is zero does not imply the absence of tax competition; it only implies the absence of *strategic* interactions.[3] Even

2. Surveys include Agrawal, Hoyt, and Wilson (2022), Brülhart, Bucovetsky, Schmidheiny (2015), Keen and Konrad (2013), Brueckner (2003), and Wilson (1999).

3. To illustrate this point, consider a variant of the Zodrow and Mieszkowski (1986) and Wilson (1986) model in which infinitely many small localities levy a source-based tax on freely mobile capital and use the revenue to finance a local public good that benefits completely immobile residents. With infinitely many small governments, none can affect the world rate of return of capital. Governments are price takers: they compete with each other in a perfectly competitive market. The governments are not strategic, as they would be in a world of oligopolistic competition. Although a tax change in any one jurisdiction does not change the

when the reaction function has a zero slope, equilibrium tax rates are still inefficient due to interjurisdictional fiscal externalities.

Tax competition is evident at many levels of government. With respect to statutory tax rates, local governments complete for mobile capital via the property tax while states or provinces around the world have access to personal income tax rates on earnings or capital income that can be used to lure high-income individuals. States and local governments can compete for cross-border shoppers and businesses that can locate in different places by changing the retail sales tax or value-added tax rate. The sales tax case is one in which the tax base is locally mobile, so strategic interactions are expected to arise. And of course, at the international level, interjurisdictional differences in corporate tax rates have led to profit-shifting opportunities.

There are many examples of jurisdictions using specific policy levers such as bidding for firms or offering R&D tax credits. US cities compete to attract corporate offices, such as Amazon HQ2 and General Electric's headquarters. States compete for manufacturing facilities such as the 2008 Volkswagen plant that was ultimately located in Tennessee or the BMW or Boeing facilities that were located in South Carolina. Nations like Ireland, the Netherlands, and the United Kingdom compete to attract the intellectual property income of large multinational firms. Bartik (2020) estimates that in 2015, annual state and local business tax incentives in the US amounted to more than $45 billion, an amount that is roughly comparable to state corporate tax revenues.

## I.3 Tax Coordination and Policies Designed to Limit Competition

Tax coordination is a response to tax competition. Policies that promote coordination limit the noncooperative tax setting authority of independent governments, reduce the mobility of the tax base among these governments, or induce each government actor to internalize externalities imposed on other governments. Wildasin (2002) observes that tax coordination can occur by delegation to external actors, by mutual explicit agreements among a set of jurisdictions, or by a single jurisdiction unilaterally altering its policy.

This definition of tax coordination includes both policies that directly limit the tax setting of governments and those that indirectly limit the tax responsiveness of governments. For example, agreements that require the same tax rates in multiple jurisdictions, or that require minimum tax rates,

tax rate of other jurisdictions, the equilibrium is still subject to tax competition forces and is inefficient. The perfect mobility of the tax base implies that a tax change in one jurisdiction imposes a fiscal externality on all other jurisdictions. Taxes and spending are therefore too low. In contrast, as Wildasin (this volume) emphasizes, with strategic competition between a small number of jurisdictions, which might arise due to linkages from commuting from local labor markets, governments explicitly react to other jurisdiction's policies. Both the strategic and nonstrategic equilibrium are inefficient.

place direct limits on the tax-setting authority of each jurisdiction. Policies like these limit the potential competitive or strategic responses of jurisdiction to changes in the tax policies of other jurisdictions. Constitutional restrictions on local governments can also place tax rate restrictions on subnational governments.

Indirect limits to the competitive forces among governments are numerous. Policies that restrict the mobility of the tax base among governments can also allow jurisdictions to raise their tax rates. More intense auditing or changes in the sourcing rules may also implicitly reduce the mobility of the tax base, potentially reducing the incentive to cut rates. Indirect policies that induce local governments to internalize their external spillovers—for example, corrective transfers as in Agrawal, Hoyt and Ly (2023)—can also mitigate or even eliminate the inefficiencies from tax competition. Such "carrots" do not limit the authority of government or the mobility of the tax base, but instead incentivize the government to internalize those effects, perhaps through a system of matching grants. These policies do not place restrictions on tax rates directly, but they are part of the broad menu of policies that address tax competition.

With the foregoing definitions in mind, we now present a nonexhaustive summary of various policy responses that governments have adopted or proposed to limit tax competition. We describe sixteen policies, some available to any jurisdiction, others available only to groups, that can reduce the incentive to lower taxes to attract mobile components of the tax base. We describe how each policy works and its potential effects.

### I.3.1 Tax Harmonization (All Jurisdictions)

This policy, in its strictest form, eliminates tax rate differentials by forcing jurisdictions adopt a common tax rate. In practice, however, most harmonization initiatives involve significant flexibility. For example, the European Commission previously proposed that commodity tax rates in the European Community should not deviate by more than plus or minus 2.5 percentage points from a prescribed norm. Regardless of whether the policy is complete harmonization or adoption of a common tax rate target that jurisdictions are moving toward, reduction in tax rate differentials reduces tax base mobility—there is less incentive to move—and lowers the tax externalities that any one jurisdiction imposes on other jurisdictions.

Kanbur and Keen (1993) show that in a setting with two jurisdictions that maximize tax revenues, both jurisdictions may object to full harmonization. For a small jurisdiction, harmonization is certain to lower tax revenues by preventing it from lowering its rate and thereby expanding its small tax base. For a large jurisdictions, harmonization will only raise revenue if the harmonized rate is very close to its uncoordinated rate, which was set to maximize revenue in a Nash equilibrium. Intuitively, if the harmonized rate is set exactly at the uncoordinated rate, the large jurisdiction gains revenue through the limitation of tax arbitrage. However, forcing it to set a rate that is very low means the foregone tax revenues on its originally loyal base do not outweigh the gains from the base expansion. These results, while model based, indicate why building political consensus for harmonization may be challenging.

### I.3.2 Partial Tax Harmonization (Some Jurisdictions)

Partial harmonization involves a subset of countries or states within a country coordinating tax rates. Such harmonization might result, for example, from jurisdictional connections with a preexisting trade block. Within federal systems, state governments might force local governments within their territory to cooperate and set common tax rates. Partial harmonization has the advantage, relative to full harmonization, of requiring a consensus among a smaller set of jurisdictions. This may make the determination of the harmonized tax rate easier. However, it comes at the cost of not internalizing the spillovers to other jurisdictions that still set their tax rates noncooperatively, and vice versa. The importance of this cost depends on the factors being taxed; Conconi, Perroni, and Riezman (2008) show that in some cases partial harmonization can welfare dominate both full harmonization and tax competition.

### I.3.3 Interjurisdictional Cooperation and Supranational Institutions

Another way to mitigate competition is through the formation of interjurisdictional cooperatives or the creation of supranational institutions such as the European Union that dictate specific tax rules for their members. In some cases, the supranational institution may completely centralize taxation authority and assign it to the cooperative body. In the subnational setting, partnerships between municipalities or other subfederal jurisdictions can either be forced by the central government or can arise naturally from mutual interjurisdictional consultation. In the latter case, a jurisdiction opts into the coalition, deciding whether to cooperate and with whom. The extent of powers delegated to the cooperative can also vary. Some cooperatives are only allowed to engage in "consultation" with each other, while others have tax and spending authority that almost completely subsume local taxes. In other cases, they may operate in conjunction with local tax policies. France has one of the strongest forms of intermunicipal cooperation in the world, with substantial variation in how taxing powers are delegated to the cooperative.

A tax cooperative cannot internalize any externalities outside of the cooperative. But, when substantial taxing powers are delegated to the cooperative, Hoyt (1991) points out that the reduction in the number of competing jurisdictions reduces the extent of tax competition. However, with the formation of tax cooperatives, tax policy coordination typically is not the only government authority that is consolidated—cooperatives and supranational institutions are often designed to achieve economies of scale in public good provision or to catalyze the economic benefits from market integration. Empirical analyses of the effect of tax cooperatives on tax rates, such as Breuillé, Duran-Vigneron, and Samson (2018), typically identify the combined effects from limiting competition and achieving economies of scale.

### I.3.4 Minimum Tax Rates

A minimum tax rate is a lower bound on the tax rate that a jurisdiction may set. Recent corporate tax proposals of the global minimum tax have spurred new research on the use of tax floors as a means to reduce tax competition; see, for example, Hebous and Keen (2023), Janeba and Schjelderup (2023), and Johannesen (2022). A combination of both a minimum and a maximum tax rate is a weak form of harmonization that forces convergence toward a target rate. Unlike complete harmonization, minimum tax rates force low-tax jurisdiction to raise their tax rates, but do not force high-tax jurisdictions to lower theirs. With the minimum tax in place, the gap between the high- and the low-tax country will decline. In the presence of strategic competition, the high-tax country may find it in its best interest to raise its rate, but it will do so by less than the increase in the tax rate of the low-tax jurisdiction. Even if jurisdictions are price takers, they may raise their tax rates if the minimum tax policy forces a sufficiently large number of jurisdictions to raise their tax rate.

Minimum tax rates have been widely studied. Kanbur and Keen (1993) show that a minimum tax rate will increase the revenues of both small and large jurisdictions. Intuitively, because the slope of the best-response function is less than unity, taxes rise in the high-tax jurisdiction by less than the forced increase in the low-tax one. Thus, tax base leakages from the high-tax location fall, which combined with its higher rate raises revenue. The low-tax jurisdiction has a higher rate but now has a smaller base, but the authors show that its revenues are increasing in the minimum tax rate.

### I.3.5 Controlled Foreign Corporation Rules like GILTI

In 2017, the United States unilaterally introduced the GILTI provision, which requires firms to pay US taxes on low-taxed foreign income exceeding 10 percent of foreign tangible income when this income would otherwise be taxed at a low rate. Devereux (2023) points out that this provision is akin to a controlled foreign corporation rule that makes profit diverted to low-tax places subject to taxation in the parent country. One benefit of this type of policy is that it can be implemented unilaterally, but a cost is that it may encourage firms to leave or invert.

### I.3.6 Bans on Taxes and Centralization

Federal systems have some policy options that are not available at the international level. One is for higher-level governments to restrict the set of tax instruments that lower-level governments may use. For example, in some

US states, local governments can levy local sales taxes, while in other states they cannot. The same is true for local income taxes. While some of these differences may be a result of historical policy decisions that are hard to change, some could be a result of differences in the perceived costs of mobility of various factors across different states. Although harmonization can be facilitated by governments centralizing both expenditure and tax policies, the recent trend in many federal systems has been toward decentralization. Gadenne and Singhal (2014) note that this may be a reaction to some positive aspects of decentralization, particularly in developing countries where it is often seen as a way to reduce corruption or political rent seeking.

### I.3.7 Constitutional Restrictions and Tax and Expenditure Limitations

Constitutions may entirely ban some local taxes or they may place other restrictions on local (or even state) taxes. They may also restrict the amount by which taxes can change from one period to the next. For example, several US states have supermajority requirements to pass tax increases. These restrictions can apply to the repeal of existing tax breaks and to the enactment of new tax increases. At the local level, restrictions often require special referendums or higher thresholds to raise property tax revenues beyond a certain rate of growth. Knight (2000) studies supermajority rules that restrict governments' capacity to raise taxes. These rules typically do not prohibit lowering taxes or changing spending, so they may simply shift tax burdens toward user fees like higher education tuition payments. Budget rules relating to deficit reduction can also be used as a tool to restrict government competition, although such rules may be irrelevant if politicians can find simple work-arounds to avoid compliance with them—for example, by declaring a state of emergency.[4] A particular type of fiscal rule—a tax and expenditure limitation—is often used to limit the growth of government or of certain tax revenue streams, such as that from the property tax.

### I.3.8 Sourcing Rules

A sourcing rule determines where consumption, corporate profits, or personal income is taxed. Consumption taxes can be levied according to either the origin principle, levying the tax where things are purchased, or the destination principle, levying the tax where they are consumed. Income taxes can follow either source (where things are made) or residence (where the recipients of income live) principles. A source-based tax on mobile capital raises the required rate of return on capital in the jurisdiction levying the tax, and it results in capital flight.

In the case of commodity tax competition in the Kanbur and Keen (1993) model, the origin principle results in wasteful cross-border shopping and tax

4. Eliason and Lutz (2018), Poterba (1997), and Poterba and von Hagen (1999) explore these issues.

competition. If taxes are levied under the destination principle, however, then cross-border has no tax benefit and there is no tax competition, because households are assumed to be immobile. This illustrates that shifting the sourcing rule from the more mobile tax principle to the less mobile one can reduce tax competition. Rork and Wagner (2012) show that tax rates are higher when states tax personal income under the residence principle than under the source-based principle. The elasticity of residence appears to be lower than the elasticity of employment, especially in cross-border metropolitan areas.

While sourcing rules can be dictated by central governments for all states, they may also be chosen and agreed upon by the state and local governments within fiscal unions. Differences in sourcing rules across states may result in complex tax rules or double taxation. Of course, for a sourcing rule to be effective, governments must be able to enforce it. Some corporate tax reformers, including Devereux et al. (2020), have focused on shifting to a destination-based tax due in part to the difficulties of tracking where products are produced and the challenges of tracking the location of businesses as a result of inversions and other maneuvers.

### I.3.9 Formula Apportionment

While best known for its use by US states to allocate corporate tax bases, formula apportionment is also used in other contexts. Professional athletes, for example, apportion their personal income across states based on the number of games played in each state, and Pillar 1 of BEPS puts more weight on countries where goods and services are sold. Under formula apportionment, a company's profits are apportioned to a given location according to a weighted average of the share of sales, payroll, and capital there. States, for example, tax a shared tax base, which reduces the incentives for companies to engage in profit shifting. Formula apportionment creates incentives to shift sales, payroll, and capital toward low-tax states. Like the sourcing rules discussed above, an important question is whether those factors are more or less mobile than the corporate profits that are the ultimate object of taxation. Suárez Serrato and Zidar (2018) report that states have steadily increased the weight they place on sales in the apportionment formula. This may reflect a view that sales are the least mobile of the factors. It could also, however, reflect a policy choice that is being used to gain strategic advantage by some states in the tax competition game.

### I.3.10 Auditing and Enforcement

Tax enforcement is a potential policy response to competitive reduction of the tax base when that reduction is in part due to evasion. For example, with residence-based income taxation, a high-income taxpayer who owns two homes in different states may shift the taxable location to the lower-tax jurisdiction by falsely reporting the number of days spent in the secondary residence. In the case of US state sales taxes, a consumer may not file a use tax return in her resident state to pay taxes on out-of-state purchases. If this illegal misreporting could be easily identified and enforced via tax auditing, then tax base mobility due to evasion would be reduced, lowering tax competition. The efficacy of heightened enforcement in lowering inter-jurisdictional evasion is an open question. One scheme might be replaced by another in response to a new enforcement initiative, and if greater enforcement succeeds in raising the effective tax rate, it may induce more actual mobility of the tax base, rather than evasion. Stöwhase and Traxler (2005) observe that audit probabilities can be used as a strategic variable by states in a federal system.

### I.3.11 Mobility Restrictions

One way to limit the mobility of the tax base is for jurisdictions to impose regulatory constraints on the mobility of people and resources, such as immigration restrictions or domestic content rules for goods along with border checks at ports or international borders. Controls on the location of firms are common at the subfederal level. Many localities use exclusionary zoning laws to keep certain types of businesses from opening in their jurisdiction. Other regulatory policies, such as occupational licensing, may also reduce the mobility of businesses and labor by creating costs to moving across state lines. While policies like these may limit factor mobility and correspondingly reduce the incentive for jurisdictions to compete with regard to taxes, they may have substantial efficiency costs for economic activity that may outweigh the potential jurisdiction gains from reduced tax competition. There are also important examples of policies that are designed to prevent mobility-reducing policies. The Bretton Woods system is a prime illustration; it limited capital controls at the national level.

One type of mobility restriction used at the international level by some countries is an exit tax on individuals. Organ (2024) notes that these taxes do not regulate or ban international mobility, but make it costlier. If a high-income American taxpayer gives up US citizenship and moves to another country, that taxpayer must pay a 23.8 percent tax on the fair market value of all assets in excess of a $767,000 exemption level. Galle et al. (2021) discuss another type of tax rule that operates in a manner similar to an exit tax: "claw back" provisions that require a taxpayer who leaves a jurisdiction to pay taxes to the former tax home for several years after departure.

### I.3.12 Tax Treaties

Tax treaties are agreements between jurisdictions concerning the operation of their tax systems. They are often quite complex and address detailed tax issues. Many treaties include income sourcing rules. For example, states in the US can adopt tax treaties that include reciprocity agreements, whereby the employment state surrenders its taxing rights on the income of non-resident workers to the state in which the workers reside. Tax treaties are especially common with regard to foreign direct investment, where a capital-exporting country may allow for either a deduction of taxes paid in the host country, or a credit up to that amount under domestic taxation, or complete exemption from taxation. These provisions are described in Janeba (1995). Tax treaties can also apply to the use of preferential tax regimes, information sharing among countries, and interjurisdictional withholding. Because these agreements are often bilateral, they are especially useful in cases where base mobility is predominantly between two jurisdictions, perhaps due to substantial cross-border economic activity.

### I.3.13 Limitations on Bidding for Firms and Subsidy Deals

Many state and national tax codes have preferential provisions designed to attract or retain large firms or high-income individuals. These provisions can be viewed as a form of tax competition. Some governments have recently sought to limit preferential tax regimes for certain industries or preferential subsidy deals to win new firms. For example, there have been proposals for a national interstate compact to eliminate bidding for firms, but they have not received enough state signatories to go into effect. There are some bilateral limits on subsidy deals, such as that between Kansas and Missouri.

Whether bilateral agreements to limit subsidy deals or preferential tax regimes enhance efficiency is the subject of debate. Keen (2001) argued that preferential regimes could reduce the overall extent of tax competition by enabling jurisdictions to confine their most aggressive tax competition to a few subparts of the tax system. Limiting subsidy deals could intensify tax competition because jurisdictions could no longer lower tax rates only for a specific subgroup of firms or individuals, but would now need to change tax rates more broadly with effects on the entire tax base.

### I.3.14 Amalgamations and Mergers

Federal systems are often composed of many small subnational jurisdictions. Several countries have implemented sweeping reforms to reduce the number of municipalities by forcing or incentivizing municipalities to merge. For example, recent administrative reforms in Greece reduced the number of municipalities by about one-third. Mergers can be viewed in a similar light as intermunicipal cooperation, but without the requirement to create a new tier of governments in the federal system. Hoyt (1991) found that reducing the number of jurisdictions could reduce tax competition and increase welfare. Just as in product markets, where a single firm can mark up its price above marginal cost but many perfectly competitive firms will compete prices down to marginal cost, with government competition, decreasing the number of jurisdictions reduces competition and allows tax rates to rise.

### I.3.15 Public-Private Partnerships

Governments may privatize the provision and financing of public services, thereby removing them from the realm of tax competition. A private firm charging user fees, however, may discover some of the same competitive pressures that would face a government, and this could affect their choice of user fee. If these fees equal the value of the services to consumers, then households should not have any reason to move. But, in practice, private firms may not price at cost or be able to provide the demanded services as a result of market failures. Privatization may simply replace tax competition among governments with price competition among firms. Sinn (1997) noted that governments are usually involved in the provision of goods and services where there are market failures, which makes it more likely that firms providing these services will also encounter them.

### I.3.16 Intergovernmental Grants

The inefficiency of tax competition is a result of a fiscal externality: when one jurisdiction increases its tax rate, it causes an increase in the tax base elsewhere and generates higher revenues for one or more other jurisdictions. Wildasin (1989) shows that this inefficiency can be corrected by an intergovernmental subsidy. A Pigouvian solution exists where the federal government pays the policy-enacting jurisdiction a subsidy equal to the tax revenue that flows into other jurisdictions as a result of its tax rate increase. Appropriately designed intergovernmental grants can incentivize governments to set tax policy recognizing the externalities they impose on others. Of course, calculating the Pigouvian subsidy is empirically challenging. The general point, however, is that intergovernmental grants can be used to achieve a tax rate equilibrium that is efficient from the perspective of the entire system of jurisdictions. Similar objectives could also be pursued by allowing deductions for state or local taxes against federal taxes.

Agrawal, Hoyt, and Ly (2023) explain how to calculate the marginal corrective transfer that could achieve efficiency. This is a matching grant on each dollar of local spending that induces the local government to internalize both interjurisdictional fiscal externalities and externalities on the willingness to pay of nonresidents. This marginal corrective transfer can remedy all inefficiencies and spillovers from tax competition, and unlike a Pigouvian subsidy, can be calculated without knowing the optimal policy. It can also be implemented at the margin, drawing on the marginal value of public funds framework described in Hendren (2016) and Hendren and Sprung-Keyser (2020). Using intergovernmental grants to correct for externalities allows taxes to differ across local governments, reflecting their informational advantages in revenue collection while also internalizing spillovers from a federal perspective. A key disadvantage of such grants is that while they may be feasible, within nations, they may be almost impossible to implement in an international setting.[5]

## I.4 A Menu of Policies That Seek to Limit Tax Competition

The foregoing list of policies illustrates the rich set of options that policymakers can consider when trying to reign in tax competition. To organize these policies, we stratify them according to whether they can be implemented unilaterally or if they require the agreement of multiple jurisdictions, possibly with external delegation to an outside authority such as a federal government. We draw on Wildasin (2002) in considering three broad ways that governments can reduce tax competition: by explicit agreement, by involving an external actor, and by taking unilateral action. In some cases, the distinctions among these three categories are not clear.

Policy responses by explicit agreement require the joint action of two or more governments. For example, a subset of jurisdictions could jointly agree to set the same tax rate, while allowing each to still administer its tax system independently. Alternatively, two jurisdictions could adopt bilateral tax treaties that specify how income will be sourced for cross-border workers from either one. Policies that can only be adopted by explicit agreement are only likely to be observed when the cooperative outcome is in the best interest of both jurisdictions.

Policies that involve some delegation of functions to an external actor could involve a federal government, a supranational institution such as the European Union, or a new government structure such as an intermunicipal cooperative or a trade group. When policy actions are assigned to an external actor, that higher-level authority may also administer taxes and collect revenues and then return revenue to the local jurisdictions via grants. The centralized authority may also keep some or all of the revenue. Alternatively, tax rate harmonization could be imposed by the federal government, but jurisdictions could still administer their tax systems and determine how to deploy the resulting revenue. Because central authorities may face political challenges coordinating across many jurisdictions, suprajurisdictional institutions may be less likely to be adopted than bilateral agreements between two jurisdictions. It is important to recognize that an overarching federal government could act in the joint interest of all member states, while bilateral solutions are likely to improve the well-being of treaty signatories at a cost to other jurisdictions.

The third category of policy response includes policies that can be adopted

5. Wilson (2015) and Clemens and Veuger (this volume) survey the existing literature on the design of intergovernmental grants, touching on issues that relate to the type of grants considered here.

by jurisdictions unilaterally. Such policies could include a rule that one state is going to index its income tax rate or sales tax rate to that of a neighboring jurisdiction, or a policy that if an adjoining state's sales tax rate falls below a certain level, the enacting state would declare a tax-free zone for all businesses within some distance of the state border. Many sourcing rules and weights in allocation formulae for tax base apportionment can be set unilaterally. Policies that could be adopted unilaterally could also be adopted multilaterally. Some might view unilateral actions, such as a commitment to index state tax rates to other states' rates, as just another form of tax competition. A unilateral shift in the apportionment rule might be viewed as a way to obtain an advantage in the tax competition game.

Our three-part typology is helpful in determining the extent to which each policy option internalizes spillovers. Unilateral policies are the least likely to internalize spillovers, and may amplify them. The distinction between multilateral adoption without the involvement of an external actor, such as a bilateral treaty, and multilateral adoption with delegation to an external actor, such as the European Union, can determine whether the benefits are localized or more global, but it may also predict the difficulty of achieving agreement among all of the relevant jurisdictions. Agreement is likely to be more difficult to obtain when the policy involves ceding some power to an external actor.

Because the externalities associated with different taxes are different, issues of competition with distinct tax bases may be resolved by different policies in different settings. For example, tax base shifting under commodity taxation was historically likely to take the form of cross-border shopping with neighboring jurisdictions; bilateral treaties among neighboring jurisdictions could be an approach to internalizing the spillovers. However, in the case of globally mobile capital, an external actor may be necessary to coordinate across thousands of local governments. At the same time, unilateral actions by a single government might be more appropriate when loopholes in high-tax countries allow for tax base leakage.

Table I.1 categorizes the policies we have described in this three-part typology. Some policy options are difficult to fit into just one category. Some policies that we indicate could be carried out without delegation, for example, could also be carried out with delegation.

## I.5 Economic Analysis of the Policies

Evaluating each of the sixteen policies described in the previous section is a complex task that requires not only careful theoretical modeling but also empirical analysis, as in many cases both efficiency and distributional impacts are situation dependent. This section describes several key economic inputs to such policy evaluation.

**Table I.1** **Policy responses to tax competition**

| Policy response | Delegation to external actor | No delegation, but multilateral | Unilateral |
|---|---|---|---|
| Tax harmonization | X | X | |
| Partial harmonization | X | X | |
| Intermunicipal cooperation and supranational institutions | X | | |
| Minimum tax rates | X | | |
| Controlled foreign corporation rules (e.g., GILTI) | | | X |
| Bans on taxes and centralization | X | | |
| Constitutional restrictions and TELs | X | X | X |
| Sourcing rules | | X | X |
| Formula apportionment | | X | X |
| Auditing and enforcement | | X | X |
| Mobility restrictions | | X | X |
| Tax treaties | | X | |
| Limitations on bidding for firms and subsidy deals | X | X | |
| Amalgamations and mergers | | X | |
| Public/private partnerships | X | | |
| Intergovernmental grants | X | | |

### I.5.1 Elasticity of the Tax Base

The elasticity of the relevant tax base is critical to determining not only the revenue consequences of different policies but also their efficiency implications. Absent other distortions, tax coordination is likely to matter the most for taxes on factors, people, or firms that have large mobility elasticities. One stylized pattern is that mobility elasticities are decreasing in jurisdiction size: localities generally have larger elasticities than countries. Elasticities also differ across factors, and they are likely to be specific to consumption, capital, individuals, and firms. The extent of tax base mobility is a key determinant of the intensity of tax competition, and also of the impact of policies that are designed to respond to it.

Some policies that are designed to affect the competitive landscape for one tax base may also affect other tax bases. Cutting wealth taxes may influence the location choices of wealthy individuals and shift the geographic pattern of wealth holdings. It may also affect the location of some workers and consequently alter the labor income tax base. When tax bases are interrelated, recognizing cross-tax base elasticities can be key, particularly when one of the nontargeted tax bases is a large source of revenue or when reducing competition for one tax base triggers additional competition for another.

In some cases, the elasticity of the tax base exhibits an important geographic component. A tax base could be locally mobile among a small number of neighboring jurisdictions, or it could be globally mobile. In the case of limited local mobility, bilateral measures may be sufficient to internalize interjurisdictional externalities. For example, in the Kansas-Missouri context, the policies of both states were influencing the location decisions of firms within the cross-state Kansas City metropolitan area. When tax bases are globally mobile, addressing the inefficiencies that result from tax competition may be difficult without multilateral agreements or external actors. While historically capital was presumed to be more globally mobile than goods, the rise of digital commerce and the presence of capital mobility restrictions in some countries may call this presumption into question. Ultimately, the degree of tax base mobility is an empirical issue.

### I.5.2 Distributional Effects

While policies that respond to tax competition are largely designed to achieve economic efficiency, they also have distributional consequences. Two equity issues may arise: intrajurisdictional (how the policy affects different residents of the jurisdiction) and interjurisdictional (how it affects individuals, and even governments, in other jurisdictions). Jurisdictions differ in their productivity, amenities, trade costs, as well as location, size, productivity of the public sector and preferences for public services. These fundamental factors shape the level and distribution of economic activity in the absence of tax competition, as well as the distributional effects of policies that are designed to address competition.

Within a jurisdiction, policies may affect residents differently. For example, harmonizing tax rates at a low rate could benefit high-income residents more than low-income residents. Complex issues can arise when considering multijurisdictional policies. Tax rate harmonization, for example, forces some jurisdictions to raise rates but others to lower them. Depending on the income distribution across and within jurisdictions, such a policy could have important equity effects. Consider mobility restrictions that are designed to reduce tax competition. If the European Union enacted such restrictions, incumbent residents might benefit while immigrants trying to enter the community would be less well off. Muñoz (2024) explores issues related to this policy. As a general rule, policies that are implemented tend to benefit the residents of coalitions, often at the expense of nonresidents.

While some of the policies we describe may raise worldwide tax revenues, the revenue effects are unlikely to be equal across jurisdictions and some jurisdictions may see a revenue decline. Haufler (1996) uses a stylized model to explore the welfare effects of such revenue changes, pointing out that they depend on differences in the preferences for public goods and incomes across jurisdictions. A central message is that when assessing a potential policy intervention, it is important to determine whether it will benefit all jurisdictions or only a subset of jurisdictions, whether it will yield welfare gains for all households or only for some, and whether intergovernmental transfers are required to generate Pareto improvements.

### I.5.3 Political Economy and Capacity to Reach a Consensus

In the absence of delegation to an external actor, implementing bilateral or multilateral agreements requires an agreement among multiple jurisdictions. The capacity to reach such agreements may depend on political as well as economic characteristics of the jurisdictions. It is more likely the US and Canada could reach an agreement than the US and Russia, and more generally, agreements are more likely between relatively similar jurisdictions. Although a small theoretical literature exists on coalition formation to mitigate tax competition—see Konrad and Schjelderup (1999) and Burbidge et al. (1997)—there is limited empirical evidence on how cooperative agreements emerge and the nature of potential benefits. Rich data on voluntary intermunicipal organizations could inform this issue more broadly; Tricaud (2025) is an example of such analysis, focusing on which jurisdictions are holdouts to intermunicipal cooperation.

Location fundamentals may also influence the ability to reach a political consensus. In the case of subsidy competition, the jurisdictions most likely to advocate for the abolition of tax deals are those with the most attractive location fundamentals. Intuitively, jurisdictions with high productivity and high amenities are less on subsidy deals to attract firms.

### I.5.4 Strength of Federal Versus Subfederal Institutions and Fiscal Autonomy

Like the capacity to reach a multilateral consensus, the ability to reach a consensus with external delegation may depend on the relative strength of federal and subfederal institutions. In the US, municipal governments are "creatures of the state," meaning that state governments can grant or withdraw powers to municipalities. States differ in how strongly they constrain the actions of local governments and in the degree of fiscal autonomy that they grant them. In more decentralized states, the state government may struggle to implement coordinated responses to tax competition.

### I.5.5 Strategic Reaction Functions

Jurisdictions are likely to respond in different ways to tax coordination initiatives and other policy interventions. The slopes of strategic reaction functions describe one type of response, but there are others. In the case of a minimum tax, this slope is critical for determining whether and by how much high-tax jurisdictions will react to low-tax jurisdictions being forced to raise their tax rates. The reaction function slope determines how large a tax differential remains after a policy initiative, but not the welfare consequences of lessening tax competition. Jurisdictions may react to policy changes in many ways, which expands the set of potential reaction functions. If one jurisdiction unilaterally changes its sourcing rules or enforcement, its competitors could respond by altering their sourcing rules, or by changing tax rates, or by altering their enforcement activities, or by shifting other policy levers. In the case of unilateral changes in policy, the reactions of other jurisdictions are key determinants of welfare effects and in particular of whether limiting competition in one domain results in greater competition along another margin.

## I.6 New Evidence: Contributions in This Volume

The research project that culminated in this volume had three parts. The first involved a review of existing theoretical and empirical research on the determinants of and consequences of tax competition. Three of the papers in this volume were prepared in this context; they summarize a strand of existing research and offer directions for future investigation. The second brought together researchers who were studying various aspects of tax competition, documenting the extent of such competition and creating metrics for understanding its welfare effects. The third, which led to seven of the chapters in this volume, focused on policies that have been adopted in an effort to reduce tax competition. Each of the research teams presented an in-depth summary of a particular institution, along with an assessment of its effect on tax competition and an assessment of its consequences for economic efficiency. Where possible, these studies also address distributional considerations. Together, these seven studies provide important new evidence on the effect of public policies that are designed to reduce tax competition. They offer empirical evidence from four different countries and consider local as well as national policies.

The first three chapters are critical summaries of existing research. In chapter 1, Wildasin describes the classic theoretical framework for analyzing tax competition, noting the critical role of the degree of resource mobility, which is summarized by the elasticity of the tax base. He also highlights how political economy considerations, other institutional factors, and the available set of tax instruments affect the nature and degree of tax competition.

In the next chapter, Slattery develops an auction-based framework for analyzing how jurisdictions decide whether to make reduced-tax bids to attract a mobile firms to locate within their borders. The auction framework is particularly helpful for analyzing tax competition that centers on a particular firm, or in some cases a particular individual, who is evaluating the net-of-tax return to locating a nondivisible project in a single jurisdiction.

Chapter 3 focuses on how various policy responses to tax competition affect the distribution of tax revenues. Agrawal points out that while a minimum tax rate at any level can raise revenues for all jurisdictions, tax harmonization can only improve revenues in all jurisdictions if the rate is sufficiently high. This is because for initially high-tax jurisdictions, harmonization has two effects. It reduces their revenue because they are required to cut their tax rates, but it can also raise their revenue as taxable activity flows in, now that previously low-tax jurisdictions that attracted mobile activity have been forced to raise their tax rates. Unless the second effect is large—which requires a highly elastic tax base—high rate jurisdiction will see revenues contract. This chapter also discusses when coalitions are likely to emerge among governments, noting that the odds are higher when potential coalition partners are of similar size than when they are of very different sizes.

The next seven chapters describe various policies that have been at least in part an antidote to tax competition. Chapters 4 through 7 focus on policies that have been adopted in the US, while chapters 8 through 10 describe policies from other nations. In chapter 4, Bruce, Fox, and Shute examine the effects of a US Supreme Court decision that enabled states to collect sales tax on their residents' Internet purchases from out-of-state sellers. This court decision eliminated an opportunity for consumers in many US states to avoid sales taxation on easily shipped goods. The authors show that there were differences across locations in the impact of this ruling, with a larger increase in the tax burden on residents of rural areas who relied more on online shopping. They also demonstrate that cross-border in-person shopping became more important after the effective tax rate on internet purchases was increased.

The next chapter develops a model that can be used to quantify the gains from limiting tax competition, and applies it to a case study of the Kansas-Missouri tax competition compact. Kim addresses not only the economic consequences of moving from competition to cooperation but also the factors that helped build bilateral agreement. The political economy of cooperation is a theme that emerges in multiple chapters.

Gordon explores in chapter 6 a potential federal response to the externalities associated with state income tax competition: allowing state and local income taxes to be deducted from the federal income tax. By making the net-of-federal-taxes rate of state income taxes lower than the pretax rate, an income tax deduction reduces the distortions associated with interstate tax differentials. The deduction also reduces the cost of state and local spending in a way that may increase total subfederal expenditures. The paper also analyzes another policy—disallowing moving expenses as an income tax deduction—which raises the cost of moving, and thereby reduces the mobility of the individual income tax base.

In the next chapter, Clemens and Veuger analyze the role of intergovernmental grants in affecting incentives for tax competition. A key finding is that the way grants programs are designed, in particular the conditions that US federal grants impose on the states that receive them, can affect incentives for tax competition. The study does not find any evidence that intergovernmental transfers during the COVID-19 pandemic, which boosted state reserve funds, encouraged states to cut their corporate income tax rates. Implicit or explicit requirements associated with federal grants may explain this finding.

In chapter 8, Breuillé and Duran-Vigneron analyze how tax base elasticities and tax structure can affect intermunicipal cooperation. Their study focuses on French municipalities. There are more than 34,000 of them, and there are also a wide range of intermunicipal cooperative agreements that range from shared service provision compacts to nearly complete mergers that share taxing authority as well as spending decisions. They find that whether powers to tax different bases are shared between municipalities and cooperatives affects the degree of tax competition. A long institutional history of cooperation across jurisdictions played a key part in overcoming political economy concerns related to shared governance and municipal cooperation.

In the next chapter, Lyytikäinen analyzes minimum taxes, using a property tax reform in Finland that raised the minimum and maximum tax rates as a case study. He highlights the interaction between minimum tax rates and federal fiscal equalization rules, and illustrates the key role of strategic response functions in determining how jurisdictions respond to the federal requirement for a minimum property tax rate.

The closing chapter, by Brülhart, Köthenbürger, Krapf, Parchet, Schmidheiny, and Staubli, describes corporate taxation within Switzerland and the challenges associated with allocating tax rights, coordinating among subnational governments, and implementing equalization payments in a high-trust setting. The analysis illustrates the importance of easy coordination across jurisdictions when fashioning multilateral responses to tax competition. In the Swiss setting, federal grants serve a dual purpose, improving efficiency while also redistributing across jurisdictions.

## I.7 Conclusions and Directions for Future Work

The decline of mobility costs for households, firms, and factors, coupled with a long-term trend toward increased economic integration within and across nations, creates challenges for governments seeking to raise revenues from mobile factors. Although competition among governments can have both positive and negative consequences, nations and subnational governments have sought to limit competitive pressures. This volume draws on existing research on tax competition to offer some insights on the consequences of tax and on the effect of policies designed to mitigate it.

Although the literature on tax competition is vast, there are relatively few clear conclusions about when government intervention to limit tax competition promotes efficiency, and even fewer analyses that consider distributional consequences. This lack of clarity may be due to models and analyses that often focus on a single tax rate and a single policy response. Tax systems and the policy responses to tax competition are complex, as are the reactions of jurisdictions to those policies. A major goal of this volume is to point out the *collection* of potential policy responses across multiple tax bases, setting the stage for comparisons of the efficacy of the policy responses and of how potential interventions might interact with each other.

We classify policy responses based on whether they can be adopted unilaterally, can be launched by bilateral or multilateral agreement, or require the presence of an external actor such as a federal government. This classification is important because although unilateral policy changes could improve economic efficiency, they might also be viewed as a new form of competition. The need for an external actor can be an advantage as it allows for a level of government or an institution to evaluate what is best for the totality of its submembers, but it is also likely to create added constraints on the set of policies that can be implemented relative to bilateral or multilateral responses.

A key lesson from our review of policies is that their effects depend on a number of key economic parameters, such as the elasticity of the tax base with respect to the jurisdictional tax rate, and the cross-effects of changing one tax rate on other tax bases. We also note that both efficiency and distributional effects are important, in part because the distributional effects may be critical determinants of whether particular policies can secure political support and be adopted.

There are many ongoing policy discussions, at many levels of government, concerning the best ways to respond to tax competition. This makes it likely that the next several years will provide researchers with new policy experiments embodying different approaches to limiting tax competition. Two suggestions for future work emerge from the research presented in this volume. First, much of the prior literature has focused on a *single* tax instrument and a *single* policy response to limit competition. This level of detail often abstracts from the much broader complexity of the tax system as a whole and the large set of policy responses often used in combination with each other to address tax competition. The presence of multiple tax bases may necessitate nuanced policy responses, and multiple policy responses can interact, such that the totality of the intervention may have larger effects than the sum of the individual parts.

Second, it is important to move beyond static and partial equilibrium models to consider a wider set of potential responses to policies that may be directed at reducing tax competition. Bruce, Fox and Shute (this volume) suggest there may be unintended multimarket effects of tax harmonization initiatives on sourcing rules. Shifts of tax bases in response to changes in tax rates are not instantaneous. Although studying effects over multiple years following a policy change raises the risk of confounding effects from other policy changes, it also provides an important means to document the longer-term impacts of these interventions.

**Acknowledgments**

The editors are very grateful for funding from Arnold Ventures, which supported the research project on which this volume is based. They also wish to thank three NBER staff members for their superb assistance: conference director Carl Beck, who supported the research meetings at which the papers in this volume were presented; director of development Denis Healy, who served as the grant manager for this project; and coordinator of book publishing Helena Fitz-Patrick, who oversaw the entire editorial and production process. For acknowledgments, sources of research support, and disclosure of the authors' material financial relationships, if any, please see https://www.nber.org/books-and-chapters/policy-responses-tax-competition/introduction-policy-responses-tax-competition.

## References

Agrawal, David R., William H. Hoyt, and John D. Wilson. 2022. "Local Policy Choice: Theory and Empirics." *Journal of Economic Literature* 60 (4): 1378–455.

Agrawal, David R., William H. Hoyt, and Tidiane Ly. 2023. "A New Approach for Evaluating the Welfare Effects of Decentralized Policies." Working paper. https://papers.ssrn.com/sol3/papers.cfm?abstract_id=4009872.

Altshuler, Rosanne, Lysle Boller, and Juan Carlos Suárez Serrato. 2024. "Tax Planning and Multinational Behavior." Working paper. https://www.irs.gov/pub/irs-soi/24rptaxplanningmultinationalbehavior.pdf.

Bartik, Timothy J. 2020. "Using Place-Based Jobs Policies to Help Distressed Communities." Journal of Economic Perspectives 34 (3): 99–127.

Breuillé, Marie-Laure, Pascale Duran-Vigneron, and Anne-Laure Samson. 2018. "Inter-municipal Cooperation and Location Taxation." *Journal of Urban Economics* 107: 47–64.

Brueckner, Jan K. 2003. "Strategic Interaction among Governments: An Overview of Empirical Studies." *International Regional Science Review* 26 (2): 175–88.

Brülhart, Marius, Sam Bucovetsky, and Kurt Schmidheiny. 2015. "Taxes in Cities." *Handbook of Regional and Urban Economics* 5: 1123–96.

Burbidge, John B., James A. DePater, Gordon M. Myers, and Abhijit Sengupta. 1997. "A Coalition-Formation Approach to Equilibrium Federations and Trading Blocs." *American Economic Review* 87 (5): 940–56.

Conconi, Paola, Carlo Perroni and Raymond Riezman. 2008. "Is Partial Harmonization Desirable?" *Journal of Public Economics* 92: 254–67.

Devereux, Michael P. 2023. "International Tax Competition and Coordination with a Global Minimum Tax." *National Tax Journal* 76 (1): 145–66.

Devereux, Michael P., Alan J. Auerbach, Michael Keen, Paul Oosterhuis, Wolfgang Schön, and John Vella. 2020. *Taxing Profit in a Global Economy*. Oxford University Press.

Eliason, Paul, and Byron Lutz. 2018. "Can Fiscal Rules Constrain the Size of Government? An Analysis of the 'Crown Jewel' of Tax and Expenditure Limitations." *Journal of Public Economics* 166: 115–44.

Gadenne, Lucie, and Monica Singhal. 2014. "Decentralization in Developing Economies." *Annual Review of Economics* 6: 581–604.

Galle, Brian, David Gamage, Emmanuel Saez, and Darien Shanske. 2021. "The California Tax on Extreme Wealth (ACA 8 & AB 310): Revenue, Economic, and Constitutional Analysis." Indiana Legal Studies Research Paper No. 461. https://papers.ssrn.com/sol3/papers.cfm?abstract_id=3924524.

Haufler, Andreas. 1996. "Tax Coordination with Different Preferences for Public Goods: Conflict or Harmony of Interest?" *International Tax and Public Finance* 3 (1): 5–28.

Hebous, Shafik, and Michael Keen. 2023. "Pareto-Improving Minimum Corporate Taxation." *Journal of Public Economics* 225: 104952.

Hendren, Nathaniel. 2016. "The Policy Elasticity." *Tax Policy and the Economy* 30 (1): 51–89.

Hendren, Nathaniel, and Ben Sprung-Keyser. 2020. "A Unified Welfare Analysis of Government Policies." *The Quarterly Journal of Economics* 135 (3): 1209–1318.

Hoyt, William H. 1991. "Property Taxation, Nash Equilibrium, and Market Power." *Journal of Urban Economics* 30: 123–31.

Janeba, Eckhard. 1995. "Corporate Income Tax Competition, Double Taxation Treaties, and Foreign Direct Investment." *Journal of Public Economics* 56 (2): 311–25.

Janeba, Eckhard, and Guttorm Schjelderup. 2023. "The Global Minimum Tax Raises More Revenues than You Think, or Much Less." *Journal of International Economics* 145: 103837.

Johannesen, Niels. 2022. "The Global Minimum Tax." *Journal of Public Economics* 212: 104709.

Kanbur, Ravi, and Michael Keen. 1993. "Jeux Sans Frontières: Tax Competition and Tax Coordination when Countries Differ in Size." *American Economic Review* 83 (4): 877–92.

Keen, Michael. 1998. "Vertical Tax Externalities in the Theory of Fiscal Federalism." *IMF Staff Papers* 45 (3): 454–85.

Keen, Michael. 2001. "Preferential Regimes Can Make Tax Competition Less Harmful." *National Tax Journal* 54 (4): 757–62.

Keen, Michael, and Kai A. Konrad. 2013. "The Theory of International Tax Competition and Coordination." *Handbook of Public Economics* 5: 257–328.

Konrad, Kai, and Guttorm Schjelderup. 1999. "Fortress Building in Global Tax Competition." *Journal of Urban Economics* 46 (1): 156–67.

Knight, Brian G. 2000. "Supermajority Voting Requirements for Tax Increases: Evidence from the States." *Journal of Public Economics* 76: 41–67.

Muñoz, Mathile. 2024. "Trading Non-tradeables: The Implications of Europe's Job Posting Policy." *The Quarterly Journal of Economics* 139 (1): 235–304.

Organ, Paul R. 2024. "Citizenship and Taxes." *International Tax and Public Finance* 31: 404–53.

Poterba, James. 1997. "Do Budget Rules Work?" In *Fiscal Policy: Lessons from Economic Research*, edited by A. Auerbach. MIT Press.

Poterba, James, and Jürgen M. von Hagen. 1999. "Introduction." In *Fiscal Institutions and Fiscal Performance*, edited by J. M. Poterba and J. von Hagen. University of Chicago Press.

Rork, Jonathan, and Gary Wagner. 2012. "Is There a Connection Between Reciprocity and Tax Competition?" *Public Finance Review* 40 (1): 86–115.

Sinn, Hans-Werner. 1997. "The Selection Principle and Market Failure in Systems Competition." *Journal of Public Economics* 66 (2): 2470274.

Slattery, Cailin, and Owen Zidar. 2020. "Evaluating State and Local Business Incentives." *Journal of Economic Perspectives* 34 (2): 90–118.
Stöwhase, Sven, and Christian Traxler. 2005. "Tax Evasion and Auditing in a Federal Economy." *International Tax and Public Finance* 12: 515–31.
Suárez Serrato, Juan Carlos, and Owen Zidar. 2018. "The Structure of State Corporate Taxation and Its Impact on State Tax Revenues and Economic Activity." *Journal of Public Economics* 167: 158–76.
Tricaud, Clemence. 2025. "Better Alone? Evidence on the Costs of Intermunicipal Cooperation." *American Economic Journal: Applied Economics* 17 (1): 160–207.
von Schwerin, Axel, and Thiess Buettner. 2016. "Constrained Tax Competition—Empirical Effects of the Minimum Tax Rate on the Tax Rate Distribution." Paper presented at the Verein für Socialpolitik Annual Conference, Augsburg. https://www.econstor.eu/handle/10419/145642.
Wildasin, David E. 1989. "Interjurisdictional Capital Mobility: Fiscal Externality and a Corrective Subsidy." *Journal of Urban Economics* 25 (2): 193–212.
Wildasin, David E. 2002. "Tax Coordination: The Importance of Institutions." *Swedish Economic Policy Review* 9: 171–94.
Wilson, John D. 1986. "A Theory of Interregional Tax Competition." *Journal of Urban Economics* 19: 296–315.
Wilson, John Douglas. 1999. "Theories of Tax Competition." *National Tax Journal* 52 (2): 269–304.
Wilson, John Douglas, and David E. Wildasin. 2004. "Tax Competition: Bane or Boon." *Journal of Public Economics* 88: 1065–91.
Wilson, John D. 2015. "Tax Competition in a Federal Setting." In *Handbook of Multilevel Finance*, edited by Ehtisham Ahamad and Giorgio Brosio, 264–90. Edward Elgar.
Zodrow, George R., and Peter Mieszkowski. 1986. "Pigou, Tiebout, Property Taxation, and the Underprovision of Local Public Goods." *Journal of Urban Economics* 19: 356–70.

# 1

# Open Economy Public Finance
## Competition Among Governments

David E. Wildasin

### 1.1 Introduction

Many readers are likely to have heard the phrase "tax competition," which is one aspect of competition among governments that has garnered a great deal of attention in political and popular discussion.[1] The general idea of tax competition is that low taxes attract (and high taxes repel) people, businesses, and/or associated resources such as financial capital. There is an element of truth in this characterization, but it is seriously incomplete and misleading, especially when the term *competition* is laden with ideological overtones, favorable or unfavorable, and when debates about "tax policy" are really normative debates in disguise about the size and role of government—more properly described as expenditure policy. Those ideological connotations are to be entirely put aside here.

Like the blind men and the elephant, there are many ways to describe the forms and channels of "competition among governments"; there may be no comprehensive definition that suits all purposes, nor, perhaps, is one needed. The present chapter provides an overview of competition in (or among) "open economies," defined here to mean the economies of jurisdictions small or large (cities, states and provinces, and countries) or groups of jurisdictions (such as the EU) that are linked by the mobility of human and nonhuman resources, especially labor and capital. By tradition, an "open

David E. Wildasin is the Endowed Professor of Public Finance (Emeritus), Martin School of Public Policy and Administration and Professor (Emeritus) at the University of Kentucky.

1. Using a popular Internet search tool, the phrase "tax competition" yields about 1.2 million results—much greater than the modest 75,000 results from searching "fiscal competition," a term that is used preferentially below, or the still fewer 17,000 results obtained from a search on "intergovernmental competition." One may be tempted to hypothesize an inverse relationship between Internet search visibility and numbers of syllables, although this cannot be the whole story, judging by n. 6 below.

economy" is commonly understood to refer to a national economy that engages in trade in goods and services with the "rest of the world." As a broad generalization, in Heckscher-Ohlin-Samuelson (HOS) trade theory, each open economy is endowed with exogenously fixed amounts of primary factors of production (usually just labor and capital), domestic economic policies amount to lump-sum taxes or transfers, and attention is focused on policies that apply directly to international trade, such as tariffs and quotas. (Much the same applies to post-HOS models of international trade that postulate departures from perfectly competitive industries, such as oligopoly or monopolistic competition.) Also by tradition, much of public finance is a "closed-economy" branch of economics, focusing, almost in mirror-image fashion, on the domestic economic policies of a single government, downplaying international trade and trade policy, but sharing the HOS assumption of exogenously fixed endowments of people and other resources. (Closed-economy intertemporal public finance analysis typically endogenizes consumption/savings behavior and capital accumulation, but still starts with a single government, a single economy, fixed initial resource endowments, and an exogenously determined initial population.) For the study of open economy public finance and competition among governments, by contrast, it is precisely the mobility of human and nonhuman productive resources, and the (primarily) "domestic" economic policies that influence them, that are at the center of attention.

As already noted, government tax policies may influence the locations of mobile resources in open economies, but so may many other policies. For present purposes, an exclusive focus on tax policy is inappropriate, primarily because there is no sound economic reason to expect that people, businesses, and related resources that (potentially) flow into or out of an economy should be affected solely by tax policies, insofar as they are affected by policies at all. Indeed, as a first approximation, the expenditure side of a government's fiscal accounts are of the same order of magnitude as its revenues and, for that reason alone, the expenditure side deserves a comparable level of consideration. To a second order of approximation, in view of ineluctable accounting identities that arise from government budget constraints, one should also consider borrowing, intergovernmental transfers, and other nontax sources of revenue, all of which are components of the fiscal accounts that go beyond tax policy narrowly conceived. At least on a priori grounds, these aspects of fiscal policy certainly warrant attention in the discussion of "competition" for mobile resources. Secondarily, but also importantly, the boundary between "tax" policy and "expenditure" policy is often indistinct and arbitrary, as encapsulated in the concepts of "tax expenditures" or "tax incentives."[2] At least to the ear of the contemporary

2. The concept of "tax expenditures" is quite familiar to tax scholars; it generates an Internet search yield of 910,000 hits. But "tax incentives" are apparently far more widely known (or sought after), with more than 21 million hits—more evidence, perhaps, in support of the syllable-minimization hypothesis of Internet visibility.

economist, the expression "fiscal competition" (though still etymologically rooted in taxation) is less specifically linked to tax policy per se. Recognizing that fiscal policies are often intimately connected to regulations and legal interpretations (for example, in determining which natural or legal persons are subject to tax or qualify for access to public benefits and services in a given jurisdiction), "competition" among governments is also intended here to include these aspects of "regulatory policy" as well.

By creating economic linkages among locations (at least two and perhaps many hundreds of thousands of them), interjurisdictional flows of productive resources simultaneously depend upon and help to determine economic and fiscal conditions in multiple jurisdictions. The movements of people and capital from one economy to another directly affect the markets for labor, capital, and other goods and services in both locations, altering prices (wage rates, rates of return on capital, housing prices, and others), quantities (capital stocks, employment, production), and derived magnitudes (earnings, profits, and the functional and size distributions of incomes). The quantitative importance of such resource flows, their responsiveness to government policy choices, and their impacts on markets are questions that naturally invite economic analysis. But the movements of productive resources also directly and indirectly influence demographic, financial, social, and political conditions in both origin and destination jurisdictions and thus the policies that they choose. The joint and simultaneous operation of market forces and policymaking institutions ultimately combine to determine the efficiency, distributional, and social welfare implications of resource mobility in open economies and, importantly, the structure of governmental institutions themselves. The study of "open-economy public finance" thus presents a broad and challenging range of analytical issues in economics and political economy.

To introduce and motivate interest in the study of competition among governments, section 1.2 provides an informal overview of cases in which the movement of people and capital among localities, states and provinces, and nations has been affected by government tax, public expenditure, and regulatory policies. Although far from comprehensive, this sample of illustrative cases highlights the many dimensions of competition among governments and some of the important and difficult research questions that it raises, relevant in all regions of the world and all historical periods.

Section 1.3 reviews some of the basic theoretical approaches and key findings that have shaped research on open-economy public finance and competition among governments. This discussion emphasizes economic intuition and interpretations, but also provides sufficient formal analysis so that readers new to the field can see how key results are derived and how they depend on critical simplifying assumptions. Sections 1.4 and 1.5 sketch the analysis of successively more complex models, showing how and why they lead to findings that strengthen, extend, or perhaps overturn findings from more classical cases; these sections also highlight some of the many open research questions that await future study.[3] The concluding section 1.6 provides a short summary, highlighting the fact that the study of competition among governments presents opportunities for important contributions by many researchers, from many different perspectives.

## 1.2 Competition among Governments: Some Motivating Illustrations

Drawing selectively upon academic, policy, and popular literature, sections 1.2.1 and 1.2.2 provide some concrete examples, contemporary and historical, of competition for mobile resources and related policy issues. Competition among local, state/provincial, and national governments are each discussed in turn. Section 1.2.3 draws attention to a number of institutional issues related to the organization, administration, and evolution of the public sector, especially federalism and intergovernmental fiscal relations. Section 1.2.4 discusses external and internal border controls, their (often imperfect) enforcement, and some important instances in which they have been eased or eliminated, sometimes by the dissolution of the governments that imposed them. Section 1.2.5 identifies several themes that have come to characterize research on competition among governments and that will likely continue to motivate future research. This overview will also alert readers to the potential for cross-fertilization with others working in what may at first seem to be unrelated areas and help them to avoid potential misunderstanding, misapplication, or simple unawareness of relevant branches of research.

### 1.2.1 Subnational Governments, New and Old

#### *1.2.1.1 Local Governments*

Tiebout's 1956 paper on *local* public expenditure asserts (in deliberate contrast to Samuelson's classic 1954 and 1955 papers on the "pure theory of public expenditure") that the movement of people among local jurisdictions can "solve" the problem of preference revelation for local public goods. A reader may search Tiebout's paper in vain for any formal demonstration

3. It must be emphasized that this essay does not reference all relevant strands of research nor does it cite all relevant studies within its broad scope. Rather, in touching upon many different topics, it is intended, first, to highlight the relevance of an open economy perspective for public policy analysis; second, to indicate the important role of "system-wide" or "general equilibrium" considerations in open economy settings; third, to illustrate the value of research contributions from many branches of scholarship—theoretical, empirical, historical, legal, economic, and others—in understanding the factors that underlie public policy analysis in open economy contexts; and, finally, to provide at least a few signposts to pertinent literature for readers who may wish to explore further. A full bibliography of relevant works would consume many pages, and many important references can only be cited indirectly through the works mentioned here, some of which provide surveys of related literature. For any interested readers, a thematically organized listing of the author's own works, a selection of which are cited in this essay, may be found in an online appendix to Wildasin (2021).

of this claim, but the "Tiebout Model"—in quite a few different guises—has become a staple in the economics literature dealing with local government public finance. Following earlier work on local property tax capitalization, a seminal contribution by Oates (1969) focuses attention on one interpretation of the "Tiebout hypothesis," namely, the linkage between household mobility, residential property values, and local fiscal policies, emphasizing the need to account for both taxes *and* public expenditure (in this instance, local property taxes and public education spending) as determinants of property values. Oates's contribution exemplifies a very large literature, already rooted in the work of Adam Smith in its early manifestations (see also, e.g., Oates 2006 and Albouy 2009, 2016), which applies hedonic pricing theory to ascertain monetized valuations of locational attributes, including taxes, public goods and services, and other policy variables. As explained in Rosen (1979) and others, standard hedonic pricing models are built upon the maintained hypothesis that mobility—among occupations, job assignments, locations, or consumption choices—is "perfect" in the sense that prices (of housing, of labor, automobiles, and other commodities) adjust so that no agent can enjoy a higher level of utility by switching from one option to another. Many empirical studies using hedonic methods have provided convincing evidence that location-specific prices reflect the valuations that mobile households and workers place not only on local fiscal policies but also on environmental quality, crime, and other locational attributes.

A key element in Oates's work and throughout the literature of local public finance is that people do not care exclusively about taxes, public services, housing costs, or employment and income, but about all of these together. At least since Oates, this *linkage between the tax and expenditure sides of public fiscal systems* and *the role of locationally fixed resources*, often in the form of housing or land, has been a distinguishing characteristic of theoretical and empirical investigations of competition among governments.

Whereas research in the Tiebout tradition emphasizes the mobility of *people* among local governments, a substantial and complementary literature on local government property taxation (again, see Smith and Marshall, among other early writers) highlights the fact that investments in buildings in any one location—whether for residential or business uses—must offer *net* rates of return comparable to those available elsewhere. Such a hypothesis implies that *capital* is a mobile resource and that its location is affected by local government policies. Following the seminal work of Mieszkowski, Zodrow, and others referenced in section 1.3 below, the mobility of capital among local governments has become a thoroughly standard assumption. A portion of this literature also connects the mobility of capital to the mobility of labor.

Sorting out which resources are mobile and immobile in the context of local government finance is complicated by the fact that capital, being durable, is plausibly viewed as a fixed resource in some situations. Land, of course, is intrinsically immobile (although it may "migrate" from one jurisdiction to another if boundaries change.) Urban areas consist primarily of developed residential, commercial, and industrial properties—plots of land plus some type of building (durable capital)—that are typically bought and sold as a unit, making it difficult to disentangle (or to impute) the separate values of immobile land and "somewhat immobile" capital.[4] In any event, in view of the fact that housing is a principal source of wealth for many households, one may hypothesize (Fischel 2001) that voters and local policymakers seek to promote local government policies that protect and enhance the value of residential properties—a hypothesis that blends the immobility of land, the (relative) immobility of durable capital, and the mobility of households in a political economy framework.[5] These considerations suggest the potential usefulness of explicitly dynamic modeling in the analysis of endogenous policymaking by governments that compete for mobile resources (see section 1.5.4 below).

Though now strongly associated with Tiebout's name, the idea that households are mobile among local jurisdictions, and that households alter their places of residence in response to local policies, has much earlier antecedents. Stigler (1957), who stresses that household mobility places serious limitations on the ability of local governments to engage in redistributive policies, also draws attention to Cannan's (1912) discussion of local property taxation in England. The mobility of the poor was a recurring concern when responsibility for the relief of the poor, and its associated property tax burden, fell to local parishes. Cannan (p. 54) describes how a long series of statutes sought to restrict the movement of the poor from one parish to another: beginning in 1388, "it was enacted that certain persons dependent on charity should be confined to particular places." This was followed by similar acts (known alternatively, and revealingly, as "Poor laws" or "Settlement laws") in 1495, 1503, 1530, 1547, 1572, and still others after that. As might be expected, such "confinement" (which, at times, included enslavement as well as other less drastic enforcement mechanisms) was not easily achieved. The 1662 "Act for

4. Davis and Heathcote (2007) describe the problem of direct observation of residential land values as "potentially intractable," instead decomposing house values into the value of structures measured at replacement cost and inferring land values as the residual. They find that land values constitute between 30 percent (in 1982) and 45 percent (in 2005) of the value of residential properties in the US during the period 1975–2005. Further analysis by Davis (2009) extends these estimates back to 1955 and includes the value of commercial properties. Land values vary substantially over time and by sector.

5. Some studies hypothesize that local policies are chosen so as to maximize the values of property. Such a hypothesis is not inconsistent with voting mechanisms, though it may also accommodate nonvoting forms of political influence on the part of commercial property owners, property developers, and others. Brueckner and Joo (1991) propose a theoretical model in which households sell their properties as they progress through the life cycle, with maximization of property value becoming more important to them as they near the age at which they sell, paying more attention to personalized benefits and costs from local policies when they are young and far from the point of sale. See also Hilber and Mayer (2009).

the better Releife of the Poore of this Kingdom," also (revealingly) known as the "Act of Settlement" or "Act of Settlement and Removal" (see, e.g., Feldman 2003; Rose 1976) reflects the tensions between economically productive use of human resources and poor relief in a multijurisdictional setting. This statute sought to prevent the poor from relocating from one parish and becoming a burden on another, but it also established what amounted to temporary worker visas "to work in Time of Harvest with [a] Certificate" issued by "the Minister of the Parish [a] Churchwarden and [an] Overseer for the Poore." These certificates were intended to confirm that the worker maintained a dwelling in his home parish, would be received there upon the completion of his work assignment, and could thus be expelled from his harvest-time abode. The act further spells out that the relevant authorities would be punished if they failed to enforce these policies, an indication that its provisions were not self-enforcing. Indeed, whether in historical or contemporaneous settings, lower-level governments commonly possess and exercise some degree of policy autonomy, which means that higher-level governments must utilize suitable incentive mechanisms when enlisting their services in policymaking. With specific reference to contemporary poverty policies, central governments have relieved local governments of much of the *financial* responsibility for the support of the poor, an illustration of a public sector function that has been "upwardly reassigned" over time. It remains true, however, that local policies continue to affect the well-being of the poor and that they may thus enhance or impede the policy initiatives of central governments.

One fascinating aspect of the historical studies by Cannan and many others on "local government redistribution" is that they link the *taxation* of property (the predominant source of local government revenues in earlier eras and, in the US and many other countries, still today) with the *expenditure* of funds for public purposes. The contemporary relevance of these linkages is well illustrated by the large economics, policy, and legal literatures on local public education policy in the US, in which the distributional aspects of education—expenditures on schools and the taxes and intergovernmental transfers that finance them—have played a fundamental role.

Summing up, Tiebout's early contribution touches upon one important way in which the mobility of people matters for government policy, but it is noteworthy primarily for the deeper subsequent investigations that it has stimulated—it is better appreciated not as the last word on local public finance and household mobility, but as one of the first words. As Fischel (2006, 18) writes in his engaging and wide-ranging overview of research in local public finance, "the" Tiebout model (one might prefer to say the very broad *class* of models that have sprung up subsequent to Tiebout) "is now the accepted benchmark," attributable to a "new way of looking at economic and political problems. Instead of assuming a stationary population . . .

the world Tiebout envisioned is one of people in motion. . . . The Tiebout perspective, rather than the original model, is what is so attractive."

*1.2.1.2 State/Provincial Governments*

Localities are not the only subnational governments for which resource mobility is potentially important. In the US, policy debates regarding the taxation of personal and business income by state governments usually raise concerns—founded or unfounded—about the potential gains or losses of investment or people, especially high-income taxpayers and the low-income beneficiaries of redistributive policies. (As mentioned in section 1.1, the term "tax incentives" is often used for these special tax preferences, also known as "tax expenditures," for businesses.) These may take the form of very targeted—even firm-specific—tax relief, often purportedly as part of state "economic development" initiatives. Sometimes, states use explicit subsidies to encourage (inward) or discourage (outward) firm relocations. In general, such policies may span both state and local governments, supposedly aiming to attract or retain human as well as capital resources. They often include an ensemble of tax, expenditure, and regulatory policy interventions that extend over many years, highlighting the fact that "competition" often involves the use—simultaneous and sequential—of many policy instruments. (See, e.g., Chirinko and Wilson 2008, 2017, 2022; Slattery and Zidar 2020; and further discussion in section 1.5.1). Appendix A briefly discusses two recent high-profile episodes involving large US corporations that illustrate these features.

Migration—both internal and migration from abroad—has played a prominent, well-documented, and ongoing role in interstate (and interregional) demographic and economic change in the US since its founding. Annually, roughly 1.5 percent to 3.5 percent of the US population has moved from one state to another since World War II, with somewhat lower rates in more recent decades, during which time immigration from abroad has typically been 20 percent to 30 percent of total internal interstate migration. About 60 percent of the US population resides in its state of birth, ranging from 21 percent in Nevada to 79 percent in Louisiana in 2000. These figures indicate that many people change locations over the course of their lives.

Quite aside from simple head count measures, migration can be highly important for population subgroups.[6] The social, economic, and policy causes and consequences of the "Great Migration" of Black Americans during the early 20th century, mainly from the rural South to urban areas in

6. Research on international immigration by labor economists emphasizes the fact that not all immigrants are identical nor are all native workers. Holzer (2019) reviews this literature and some of its policy implications.

the rest of the country, have been extensively analyzed (Boustan 2016). The migration of poor beneficiaries of social safety net policies (especially Temporary Assistance for Needy Families and Medicaid) has generated interest and controversy in policy and academic circles, for instance with reference to "welfare magnets" (e.g., Borjas 1999; Figlio et al. 1999; Peterson and Rom 1990), echoing, at a distance of six centuries, some of the same concerns that appear in the English "settlement" laws. Highly skilled and better educated workers have traditionally exhibited differentially high rates of migration, pay higher levels of taxes, and are less dependent on income-conditioned social benefits.[7] As already noted, whereas support for the poor was once principally carried out at the local level, US state governments are now largely responsible for the administration of such support and, to some degree, for its financing. Particularly for the past half-century, however, the federal government has played an increasing role in the financing of social services, and, to a lesser extent, in their provision and administration—another case of institutional change resulting in an upward reassignment of governmental functions.

The fact that gross internal migration rates far exceed net migration rates (often by an order of magnitude) is a sometimes neglected feature of internal migration in the US (and elsewhere) that highlights the heterogeneity of the population. At least since Ricardo, economists have recognized that trade in goods can be very important for a pair of countries, even if there are no bilateral trade imbalances. Likewise, *gross* migration flows between two regions, even if accompanied by zero *net* flows, affect labor markets, industrial development, economic growth, the distribution of incomes, and, one might add, interregional trade. (As an example, the movement of a thousand chemists from one region to another, accompanied by the movement of a thousand bankers, medical technicians, or construction workers in the reverse direction, does not simply constitute wasteful cross-hauling of perfect substitutes.) This observation highlights the issue of *resource disaggregation*. Should "labor" be disaggregated by skill levels, race, age, marital status, country of origin, college major, native tongue, or in still other ways? What economic factors trigger gross migration flows? What are the fiscal implications of gross flows that far exceed net flows? Do (or should) governments choose policies that target demographic subgroups so as to attract or repel them?

The process of urbanization and the shifting mix of employment in agricultural and industrial occupations, from the beginning of the Industrial Revolution to the present, has similarly given rise to substantial interre-

7. Agrawal and Foremny (2018, 2019), Agrawal et al. (2020), Brülhart et al. (2022), and Moretti and Wilson (2017) examine income and wealth taxation by regional governments, particularly at the higher end of the income and wealth distributions.

gional demographic shifts with their attendant economic and fiscal impacts. Of course, one can hardly speak of rural–urban migration, urbanization, and industrialization without also speaking of capital mobility. Population growth is accompanied by investments in residential, commercial, and industrial property where people can live, shop, and work. State and provincial government policies that operate on investment margins are thus also linked to demographic change. The *simultaneous movement of multiple productive resources among regions throughout the world occurs at present and is well documented in historical experience.*

### 1.2.2 National Governments and Supranational Institutions

The mobility of people and capital at the international level has gained increased popular attention, especially in high-income countries, in recent years. The taxation of the incomes of multinational corporations involves complex interactions among the economic, financial, accounting, and legal dimensions of multinational enterprise and has attracted considerable attention from students of public finance from several disciplines. Efforts to constrain "harmful tax competition" and "tax havens" have given rise, in the political sphere, to multinational negotiations and agreements, notably those sponsored by the OECD, to coordinate national corporation income tax policies, as briefly discussed in Appendix A. In the absence of a powerful world government, the establishment of a global minimum corporation income tax rate and the regulations needed to implement it requires international treaties and other agreements that, inherently, reduce the policy autonomy of national governments.

In some cases, efforts to facilitate international commerce, including the movement of capital and people, have resulted in the creation of entirely new governmental institutions. From its inception in the Treaty of Rome in 1958 with six member states, the European Union has expanded through successive enlargements to encompass more than 20 countries, with further accessions from additional countries presently under consideration. In its early stages, the EU reduced national barriers to internal trade by establishing a common external tariff, but it has also always included the free internal movement of labor and capital among its basic principles. The implementation of these principles has given rise to continued institutional adaptations, including the Schengen Agreement of 1985, under which all but a few EU countries have now eliminated passport controls for travel within the Schengen zone—a trend notably punctuated by a step in the reverse direction by Brexit. Similar arrangements exist among the (non-EU) member states of the European Free Trade Association.

Whatever the formalities may be, international migration flows have become major determinants of demographic change in the developed world over the past several decades, increasing in magnitude at the same time that rates of "natural change" have fallen to historically low levels. The demographic importance of international migration is partly the consequence of prolonged declines in total fertility rates, which, since about 1980, have generally fallen well below the "replacement rate" of 2.0 births per woman in most OECD countries.[8] This "fertility bust" has been accompanied by a "migration boom" (Wildasin 2009); since the mid-1980s, for instance, the rate of immigration to the (then) 15 EU member states has exceeded the rate of natural population change. The UN (2019) reports that for Europe as a whole, net immigration since 1990 has exceeded natural change.

The cumulative effects of such prolonged flows have by now changed the demographic landscapes of many countries. As of 2021, the foreign-born population (OECD 2023a) constitutes more than 10 percent of the population of virtually all West European countries, amounting to 15 percent to 20 percent in Norway, Germany, Ireland, Austria, and Sweden; for the US and UK, this figure exceeds 13 percent.[9] In this regard, it is important to note that demographic trends tend to be highly inertial (UN 2017), even if they can in principle be controlled to some extent. For instance, barring forced population relocations or catastrophic mortality due to wars or other causes, the population shares of the foreign born in affluent countries is certain to increase for many years to come, even if all immigration flows were stopped immediately. This is a simple consequence of the fact that today's foreign-born populations are younger than the stock of native born, who will age out of the population relatively quickly.[10]

Since World War II, redistributive and social programs have grown steadily.[11] The 15 OECD countries (all West European) with the highest levels of *direct* social expenditures spend between one-fourth and one-third of GDP on a wide range of programs such as means-tested income support, health care, public pensions (that is, old-age support provided by the public sector, such as the US Social Security system), unemployment insurance, and child care. These direct expenditures, however, provide an incomplete and misleading perspective on the overall size of public social expenditures and redistribution. First, to the extent that these programs are financed from current government revenues, social expenditures are supported by taxes and social insurance contributions, generally paid by the working age population, through assessments on earnings, personal incomes, and consumption (especially value-added taxes, or VATs). These sources of revenue often con-

8. The "rate of natural change" is a term now commonly used in demography, substituting, tellingly, for what was more traditionally called the "rate of natural increase." Over time, "natural increase" has become "natural decrease" in many countries.

9. According to the latest US Census estimate, the foreign-born population is 13.9 percent of the total 2022 population, up from 13.6 percent in 2021.

10. In OECD countries, 80 percent of immigrants are of working age, compared to only 64 percent of the native-born (OECD/EU 2018).

11. The precise definitions of "redistribution" and "social welfare policy" are debatable, but typically do not include public expenditures for education, transportation, and many other public services that nevertheless have significant distributional impacts.

tain redistributive elements, exemplified by (but hardly limited to) features such as progressive tax rates on incomes. Furthermore, redistributive transfer policies also depend on interactions, sometimes in highly implicit forms, between public expenditure and revenue systems. For instance, net social expenditures are significantly reduced when cash payments are directly taxed and when their use by recipients is subject to indirect tax, an especially important element for countries that rely on VATs or other consumption-based taxes. Furthermore, social expenditures are effectively augmented by tax preferences that promote private expenditures for social purposes and by regulations that mandate such expenditures. Total social expenditures—including "private" social expenditures mandated or supported by the public sector—amount to about 20 percent of GDP in OECD countries on average. This figure is substantially higher, at 25 percent to 30 percent, in Western European countries, the US, and Canada.[12]

Official social expenditure measurements seldom take an intergenerational perspective, but a large fraction of cash expenditures take the form of public pensions and a large fraction of in-kind social expenditures take the form of health-care benefits that are utilized by the old. In addition, redistribution between old and young is substantially increased due to explicit and implicit government borrowing. The aggregate debt/GDP ratio for OECD countries is around 121 percent, and many policies, such as the underfunding of social insurance programs, the depreciation of publicly owned capital, and insufficient accumulation of reserves for contingencies, result in large amounts of implicit borrowing (Auerbach et al. 1999; Kotlikoff 1993). On the assumption that debt obligations will be repaid in some future periods, today's young populations, and those to follow, will face some combination of reduced public expenditures and higher taxes as a consequence. In short, the fiscal systems of many countries are very much influenced by the age structures of their populations. These (and other) demographic characteristics, in turn, have already been (and, simply as a matter of demographic inertia, will in future decades continue to be) substantially affected by international migration.

As is true for subnational governments, national governments often directly or indirectly control or influence population flows. In the case of border formalities, this control is direct, to the extent that it is enforced. Such policies often involve selective controls that facilitate the admission of people with desired attributes (such as educational attainments, specific skills, wealth, age, or cultural characteristics) while excluding others.[13] As in the literature on "welfare magnets" and interstate mobility in the US, there is

12. The US, at 29 percent, is approximately tied with France (at 30 percent) for the highest share of net social expenditures among OECD countries (OECD 2023c). See Adema (2000), Adema et al. (2014), and OECD (2023b) for details of estimation.

13. Forced relocations have also been employed, both within and among countries, particularly (but not only) during or in the aftermath of wars.

a parallel literature that examines the extent to which fiscal incentives affect international migration. For instance, Giulietti (2014) and Agersnap et al. (2020) provide recent—and conflicting—discussions of "welfare induced" migration, while others (e.g., Akcigit et al. 2016; Kleven et al. 2013, 2020) find evidence that fiscal policies affect migration of high-income workers. (Kleven et al. 2020 provide an overview of research on taxation and migration at multiple levels of government.)

### 1.2.3 Federalism, Institutional Change, and Competition

All large nations and most small ones contain multiple units of government, often numbering in the tens or hundreds of thousands, brought about through the explicit and implicit implementation of constitutions and legislative actions.[14] Rarely are the administrative and fiscal functions of these units of government neatly separated; shared (or contested) responsibilities are the norm. Systems of intergovernmental fiscal transfers are a major aspect of public finance in virtually all countries. In the US, aggregate federal government transfers to states consistently amount to 25 percent to 30 percent of state general revenues, while state government transfers to localities account for about 30 percent of state expenditures and about one-third of local revenues, showing that such transfers are mainstays of state and local fiscal systems.[15] Intergovernmental transfer programs in the US are extremely numerous and diverse, but, in aggregate, federal transfers to states have amounted to about 80 percent to 100 percent of state transfers to localities for the past half-century. State governments thus appear to serve, to some degree, as "conduits" or "pass-through entities" that connect the federal government to the local governments (Wildasin 2010b).[16]

To illustrate how intergovernmental fiscal relations evolve, consider means-tested programs of cash and in-kind support in the US. Over time, the federal government has assumed growing responsibility ("upward reassignment") for the financing of cash and in-kind assistance to the poor (see Wallis 1984 for the history of these policies), but state governments continue to exercise significant discretion over program benefits and administration. Federal transfers to the states pay for at least half of total expenditures for Temporary Assistance for Needy Families (cash and other benefits) and Medicaid (health benefits), with a maximum of about three-fourths granted to states with low per capita incomes, arrangements that plausibly reduce the incentives for states to limit inflows or increase outflows of poor residents.

14. One might also remark that many constitutional changes have been effectuated through the use of force in revolutions, coups, wars, and alliances.

15. These figures are drawn from the Census of Governments from 1977 to present. Federal transfers to localities and "upward" transfers from lower-level to higher-level governments are comparatively very small.

16. Saunoris (2012) estimates that a $1 increase in federal aid to states produces a long-run ($\approx$ 9–10 years) increase in state aid to local governments of about $0.60.

The precise form of these transfers and the federal regulations that accompany them, however—especially the permitted degree of policy discretion open to state governments—have changed significantly over time.

In addition to Temporary Assistance for Needy Families and Medicaid, the federal government provides means-tested cash and in-kind benefits through other programs (e.g., the Supplemental Nutrition Assistance Program, Supplemental Security Income, and housing assistance), sometimes administered through local government agencies, even as state and local governments pursue many other policies that (at least superficially) have redistributive impacts. For instance, local governments are the principal loci for the delivery and administration of public education, a sphere of policy in which distributional objectives are frequently asserted. On the financing side, local schools are heavily supported by fiscal transfers from state governments, accompanied by an overlay of regulatory requirements that (purportedly) ensure that recipient local governments use their funds to achieve desired or state-mandated policy objectives.[17] In different ways, then, both the federal and state governments can and do pursue policies that seem to be designed to promote distributional objectives.

Local governments exercise significant autonomy in setting their own policies, including local tax rates and land-use controls (limitations on multifamily housing, minimum lot-size requirements, development restrictions, and others). These local policies exemplify the original Tiebout insight that mobility permits people to "shop" (and pay for) varying levels of public services by establishing "prices" for local schooling and public safety, among others, plausibly enhancing efficient resource allocation compared with more uniform systems.[18] Price-like mechanisms also tend, however, to limit the access of lower-income households to high-quality school systems, possibly working in a direction contrary to the equity objectives of state fiscal transfers to local school systems.[19]

The overall efficiency and distributional performance of this system of thousands of jurisdictions, entangled by large fiscal transfers and complex regulatory structures, hinges on the locational decisions of households, the businesses that serve and employ them, and the interdependent policy

17. These transfers are often imposed or guided by court directives based on state constitutions. Courts may, for example, require—with varying degrees of specificity, up to and including detailed judicial management of school districts—that state governments provide sufficient funding for local schools to ensure that all students obtain an "adequate" education.

18. The same may also be said of the private provision of many other services that co-occupy spheres of local government policy, such as education, transportation, utilities, crime, and recreation.

19. Local governments can in principle be fully controlled by state governments, in accordance with "Dillon's Rule" (Dillon 1872). In practice, however, no state attempts to do so; instead, each has created its own somewhat distinctive governance arrangements, within which many types of local governments exercise independent control over some aspects of public policy.

choices made by governments themselves. As a conceptual device, it is often useful to consider hypothetical policy changes that could be made to one facet or another of this system, such as a change in the federal government grant formulae through which Medicaid assistance is offered to the states. If implemented, however, such a policy reform would initiate a complex chain of adjustments of state and local policies, in addition to market responses, the totality of which constitute the ultimate impact of the federal policy. The policies of the federal, state, and local governments thus operate through deeply entangled constitutional, legislative, executive, and bureaucratic systems. It is easy to understand, therefore, why much research has focused on understanding the "political economy" (that is, the *endogenous determination*) of policy choices at the state and local government levels. This undertaking has naturally built upon and fostered the further development of insights from many fields of scholarship, including economics, law, public administration, political science, and history.

Research in fiscal federalism attempts to understand the workings of governance and fiscal systems involving multiple governments, tackling the complex issues illustrated in the preceding remarks. Oates's classic *Fiscal Federalism* (1972) has stimulated much subsequent work and remains a valuable reference. Given the crucial role of fundamental institutional structures, including national and subnational constitutions and associated legal and social norms, research in this field naturally focuses on detailed country-specific issues. Interest in institutional change has been enhanced by the transformation of governance structures throughout the world in the past half-century, exemplified by the dissolution of the Soviet Union, the restructuring of political systems in the former Warsaw Pact nations, and the development of the EU and other European and international institutions. There has been a concomitant search for basic principles to guide analysis and policy in multigovernmental systems. Mature federations, such as the US and Canada, have served as reference points for the formulation and testing of models of fiscal federalism. It is not possible here to discuss fiscal federalism at greater length, but it is essential at least to be aware that the competition among governments for mobile resources occurs within multigovernmental systems and that these systems plausibly arise, in part, from the economic linkages that result from resource mobility. For additional discussion and references, see, e.g., Agrawal et al. (2023), Boadway and Shah (2009), Oates (2008), and Wildasin (2004).

### 1.2.4 Mobility and Restrictions on Movement: Evidence of Absence or Absence of Evidence?

The preceding discussion illustrates why the movement of resources warrants attention in policy analysis. But which resources are "mobile"? Are some more mobile than others? Historical experience tells us that people can be quite mobile, even on a global scale, and even during times when relocation was far more difficult than it is today.[20] On the other hand, there have certainly been occasions where such movement is far more limited, as happened in the US when immigration declined substantially prior to World War I and remained relatively low until after World War II. Are people internationally mobile, or not? More generally, how is "resource mobility" to be defined? If it is a matter of degree, how can this be quantified? And how does the degree of resource mobility matter for markets, public policy, and political economy?

Some resources, such as land, forests, or mineral deposits, are intrinsically immobile, so long as jurisdictional boundaries remain fixed. Furthermore, technological conditions may create insuperable barriers to resource mobility, as was true with regard to labor and capital mobility between the Old and the New Worlds prior to Columbus's voyages. Improvements in technology can reduce barriers to resource mobility—sometimes rather gradually, but nevertheless profoundly, as with transatlantic shipping after 1500, and sometimes more rapidly, as with the development of electronic communications during the past century. Thus, to make a clean and permanent determination as to whether any particular resource is mobile is not always possible.

The relocation of people is commonly defined by a change in a person's place of residence. It should be remembered, however, that people frequently change locations without changing their places of residence, whether for their daily commutes, recreation and tourism, or work-related travel. The fiscal and other impacts of commuting are topics of long-standing and continuing interest (e.g., Agrawal and Hoyt 2017; Greene et al. 1974), as is so-called tax exporting through taxes on accommodations, restaurants, and other services in tourist areas (Bonham et al. 1995), the taxation of transport-sector workers in interstate commerce (Wildasin 2007), and, more recently, the taxation of workers who work from home (Agrawal and Brueckner 2023).

So far as changes of residence are concerned, governments can and do impose policies that impede or even prohibit such migration. Controls on international migration are the most obvious case in point, whether applied in a measured, orderly, and controlled manner, through harsh and brutal means, or by lax or haphazard enforcement of border regulations. In affluent countries, immigration restrictions are the most conspicuous forms of migration controls, but the cases of the Iron Curtain, North Korea, and Cuba show that emigration restrictions can also be important.[21]

Similar instruments have been used to control internal migration, as was

20. See O'Rourke and Williamson (1999) and Williamson (1998), who emphasize transatlantic migration, and Hanson et al. (2023), who focus on migration in the western hemisphere.

21. US citizens whose income and wealth exceed certain thresholds are subject to taxation of unrealized capital gains if they renounce their citizenship. This policy, which may be viewed either as a kind of "exit tax" or, alternatively, as a recapture of deferred gains, does not limit

the case in the US with respect to fugitive slaves or in apartheid South Africa. According to Tian (2024), some 22.5 percent of the world population, in more than a half-dozen countries, is (or has recently been) subject to internal migration restrictions. Of particular note, China's *hukou* (household registration) system, which especially restricted rural/urban migration in pre-reform China, has been relaxed—significantly but unevenly—during the period of rapid growth of the Chinese economy. Zi (2017) discusses how interactions between trade expansion and *hukou* liberalization have differentially affected regional factor markets, income distribution, and welfare. Tian (2024) examines the endogenous adjustments of local policies by regions that have had greater or lesser gains from increased trade opportunities. Deng and Schoeb (2024) highlight the fact that local redistributive policies apply differentially to people with different *hukou* status, affecting the distributions of income and social well-being both locally and nationally. Because it restricts access by migrants to local social services, this system reflects some of the same tensions between resource mobility and redistributive policy that have already been mentioned above in connection, for instance, with the English Poor Laws and the "welfare magnets" controversies in the US.

In addition to policies imposed within the context of "stable" jurisdictional configurations, changes in jurisdictional structures themselves can drastically affect resource mobility. For instance, the Iron Curtain created serious impediments to movements of both labor and capital after World War II, but these were drastically reduced (German unification offers one dramatic and economically important illustration) after the collapse of the Soviet Union in 1991.[22] The breakup of the former Yugoslavia and the former Czechoslovakia, the potentially unstable division of the Korean peninsula, ongoing conflicts in Africa, and other historical and prospective changes in jurisdictional boundaries throughout the world have altered (or may in the future alter) the potential for resource movements.

Whether at the international or subnational levels, policies that impede or, in the extreme, completely obstruct migration serve as "silent witnesses" to the mobility of people who would otherwise change locations. By contrast, forced expulsions and population exchanges (as occurred, for example, after World War I and World War II, within the former Soviet Union, or at the

emigration per se, but may discourage it to some degree. Analysis by Organ (2022) suggests that such effects are modest.

22. Although formal restrictions on East-West migration in Germany ended when the Berlin Wall fell, migration flows were limited by a complex ensemble of regulatory (including labor-market regulations, which extended West German bargained wage structures to industries in the East) and fiscal policies (capital subsidies to industry in the East) that grossly distorted factor prices and factor markets, resulting in East German wages that were about 200 percent (!) of manufacturing value added in 1991–1993 (Sinn 1995). Sinn (1995, 2002) describes the political pressures from several interest groups (including West German labor unions) that resulted in these policies, which in turn resulted in very large transfer payments (not formally designated as such) to workers in the East, greatly reducing East-West migration incentives, but at a high efficiency cost.

time of Indian independence) stand as "vocal" witnesses to the heavy costs that result from policies that dictate population movement. At either of these extremes, observed migration flows are, to some extent, the consequences of policy choices.

Turning to capital mobility, various policies and institutions may regulate and, to a greater or lesser degree, limit the international mobility of capital. The post–World War II Bretton Woods system is perhaps the most conspicuous recent example of controls on international capital mobility, but many other bilateral and multilateral international agreements regarding the establishment and licensing of business enterprises can also affect the movement of capital on an international scale. On smaller geographical scales, the locations of business activities are heavily dependent upon subnational government laws and regulations governing the incorporation and operation of businesses. In the US, as mentioned above, local governments impose land-use regulations that affect overall economic development within their jurisdictions, thereby affecting the amounts and types of residential housing, commercial and industrial development, and related capital flows.

In view of the many factors that affect the movement of resources, when should one treat people or capital as mobile or immobile? Consider the analogous case of tariff policies. Increases in a tariff on some traded commodity generally reduce the volume of trade between two trading partners, and trade vanishes altogether if the tariff is sufficiently high. This usually means that the welfare cost of a tariff increases as the tariff rate goes up, and it reaches a maximum when the tariff becomes prohibitively high. Commodities that are exchanged between countries are said to be "tradeable," understood to be a property (conditional on technology or other "fundamentals") of the commodity, not the policies that regulate its exchange. Accordingly, when a prohibitive tariff is imposed on a commodity, it becomes "nontraded" but remains "tradeable." Similarly, for resources like people and capital, policies that may effectively prohibit them from moving do not make them "immobile": "movement" (which is often observable) is not synonymous with "mobility." Observed movement of a resource thus confirms its mobility, but absence of movement does not confirm its immobility. Indeed, as the prohibitive tariff example illustrates, policies that restrict the movement of mobile resources can be of the utmost importance precisely when they make movement unobservable.[23]

Quite aside from the effects of policy interventions, observed migration and capital flows within an economic system depend upon underlying market conditions. These may be conducive either to "very large" or "very small" resource flows. As a thought experiment, one might postulate some drastic

23. Although incidental to the terminological distinction just made, it seems apt and perhaps suggestive here to recall Mundell's (1957) classic paper arguing that "trade and factor mobility are substitutes."

hypothetical rearrangement of human or nonhuman resources, far from what is presently observed. If, for instance, all residents of Europe west of the Rhine River were relocated to its east, or if all residents of North America were relocated west of the Rocky Mountains, powerful economic incentives would produce very large migration flows that would tend to restore the preexisting population distributions. The fact that current migration flows fall far short of such amounts indicates not that labor is immobile but rather that existing population distributions are not far from equilibrium or steady-state values.

For these reasons, a "mobile resource" is understood in this essay to refer to a resource that can feasibly be relocated, irrespective of whether it is observed to move between any given locations in any particular period. This seems to be most appropriate because many kinds of policies, alone or in combination, may discourage, encourage, or stop resource movements altogether, and the magnitude of observed resource movement—including sometimes the complete absence of movement—is a joint consequence of market conditions and policy choices (by all relevant governments). It can still be useful, in the interest of analytical clarity, to postulate and compare extreme polar cases in which (say) capital is completely immobile or costlessly mobile. Such stylized comparisons may shed light on the implications of technological change (steamships, telegraphs, or the Internet), changes in policy (*hukou* reform, German unification, or the imposition of uniform tax rates on corporation incomes), or market conditions (differences in rates of return or quantity perturbations due to changes in production technologies, incomes, or preferences). But it is important, in different applications, to distinguish between hypothetical extremes and to ascertain empirically the imperfect (but not zero) degree of (joint) mobility of labor, capital, and other productive resources in varying historical and geographical contexts.

### 1.2.5 Recurring Themes and Research Questions

The preceding discussion could be augmented almost ad infinitum, and readers can adjoin to it their own favorite illustrations. Its primary goal is to show that resource mobility, notably the mobility of people and capital (or, if one prefers, of businesses), raises important economic and public policy issues over essentially all time scales and at all geographical scales. No single modeling framework can capture every relevant aspect of competition among governments for mobile resources, but the foregoing illustrations suggest several desiderata in analyses of competition among governments. As an incomplete summary, these include the following.

#### *1.2.5.1 Endogenous Location of Mobile Resources in Multiple Locations*

At least one resource must be presumed not to be intrinsically immobile, and there must be more than one location where it may be situated. Although the movement of resources among locations may be costly and time consuming, it is not entirely destructive: resources that leave one location arrive at some other location(s), thus necessarily affecting conditions in both (or all) places. These are obvious preconditions for the study of competition among governments, generally precluded in "closed economy" modeling frameworks.

#### *1.2.5.2 Multiplicity of Mobile Resources*

The mobility of both "labor" and "capital" (i.e., of human and non-human productive resources) warrants analysis at all geographical scales. Furthermore, economic analysis has amply demonstrated that the markets for mobile and immobile resources do not operate independently of one another. The earnings of workers evidently depend on the employment decisions of firms; the prices of land, housing, and industrial property depend on the incomes and preferences of households and on the levels and composition of business activity; and business profits and the returns on capital investments depend on labor market conditions, consumer demands, and site availability. Consequently, governments do not compete for any one mobile resource in isolation, but must instead compete for all mobile resources simultaneously.

#### *1.2.5.3 The Degree of Resource Mobility*

Some resources may reasonably be viewed as completely immobile. As matters of analytical convenience, either labor, capital, or particular categories of each are often viewed as "perfectly" or "costlessly and instantaneously" mobile or as intrinsically immobile. Practically speaking, however, many productive resources can in fact be relocated, but not immediately and without incurring some costs. The time periods involved range from hours or days to decades, and the costs involved can be pecuniary, psychic, and informational. Resource mobility is thus "imperfect."

#### *1.2.5.4 Multiplicity of Public Policy Instruments*

Many policy instruments, including taxes, expenditures, and regulations, affect the location of productive resources. These instruments are themselves multidimensional, and they are used simultaneously. For example, a government may derive revenues from taxes on value added, wages, profits, interest, and property. It may spend the proceeds on social insurance and redistributive transfers (with benefits that are available only to eligible recipients), defense, transportation, and education, while relying on borrowing to pay for expenditures in excess of revenues. All of these policies are potentially time-varying, so that competition for mobile resources involves not just current policies but also those that have been utilized in the past and those that may be utilized in the future. Because of political, legal, and financial constraints, not all of these policies can be freely chosen, independently of each other.

#### *1.2.5.5 The Role of Political Economy and Governmental Institutions*

The (many) public policies that simultaneously affect the locations of (many) productive resources in (many) locations are determined by (many) governments. Government policy choices are the results of collective decision-making mechanisms that emerge from governmental institutions. Because resource movements sometimes occur gradually and are not easily reversible and because they can affect economic conditions for long periods of time, they depend upon the durability and predictability of policy decisions and the institutions that produce them.

As will become evident in the following sections, the current state of research on competition among governments is relatively well developed along some of these dimensions, but substantially less so in other respects.

## 1.3 A Simplified Model of Competition for Productive Resources

This section describes a model of an economic system with many (or at least two) jurisdictions, each with its own fiscal policy. Keeping the technical formalities to a minimum, it emphasizes the "simple economics" of the model and some of its most important results.

Section 1.3.1 outlines the "open economy" structure of the model, which appears in the equilibrium conditions that link the markets of multiple jurisdictions. These conditions, or variants of them, are simple but fundamental. Using them, section 1.3.2 sketches the distributional and efficiency analysis of *exogenously given* fiscal policies in this open economy context, showing how the effects of policies in open economies differ, sometimes drastically, from those in more traditional closed-economy settings. Section 1.3.3 discusses the *endogenous* determination of fiscal policies by independent decisionmakers in each jurisdiction, bringing political economy considerations into the picture. Section 1.3.4 turns to the concepts of "movement" and "mobility" and to the implications of regulatory controls on the movement of productive resources.

### 1.3.1 Market Equilibrium

In order to present the model with a minimum of clutter, while preserving some of the economic and policy motivation for its development and use, let us imagine an economy with $n$ jurisdictions (we may call them "localities"), within each of which is located a set of perfectly competitive firms that utilize two inputs in production processes that yield a single homogenous output, taken as numéraire. One of these inputs, which we may refer to as "capital" (but could just as well be called "labor"), is homogeneous and costlessly mobile throughout the economy; let $k_i$ denote the amount of capital employed in locality $i$. The total amount of this input in the economy as a whole is exogenously fixed at some amount $\bar{k}$. The other input in each locality is fixed in amount and is completely immobile.[24] The total amount of output in locality $i$ is assumed to be a twice-differentiable and increasing function of the amount of capital, with a diminishing marginal product, i.e., $f_i'(k_i) > 0 > f_i''(k_i)$.[25]

All productive resources are privately owned by households who seek to earn the highest possible return ("income") from them. Capital is freely traded throughout the economy and, in equilibrium, it must earn the same net rate of return for its owners, denoted by $r$, in all locations. This equilibrium condition, which is of fundamental importance for the analysis, may be viewed as a spatial arbitrage condition. The other productive input in each locality is also competitively traded, but, being completely immobile, no such spatial arbitrage condition is a necessary feature of equilibrium. Competitive factor pricing dictates that the *gross* return to capital in locality $i$ is $f_i'(k_i)$ and (by a standard product-exhaustion argument) the gross return to the immobile resource in $i$ is $w_i = f_i(k_i) - k_i f_i'(k_i)$.

But for the specification of the public sector, the model is now complete. Each locality has a government that collects a tax from the owners of one of its productive resources and uses the proceeds to pay a subsidy or transfer $L_i$ to the owners of the other resource. To be specific, let $t_i$ represent a per-unit tax imposed on capital in locality $i$, so that the net return to capital in $i$ is $f_i'(k_i) - t_i$. Total tax revenue is then $t_i k_i$, the local government budget constraint is

(1) $$t_i k_i = L_i,$$

and the net return to the immobile resource is thus (by budget balance) $w_i + L_i = w_i + t_i k_i$.

The essential equilibrium conditions for the model are

(2) $$\sum_{i=1}^{n} k_i = \bar{k} \quad \textit{(capital market clearing / resource conservation)}$$

(3) $$f_i'(k_i) - t_i = r \ \forall i \quad \textit{(spatial arbitrage)},$$

which together constitute a system of $n + 1$ equations in the $n + 1$ unknowns $(r, k)$ (where $k = (k_1, k_2, \ldots, k_n)$ is the capital allocation vector).

These simple conditions provide a foundation for the analysis of fiscal policies imposed by more than one (perhaps many) jurisdictions in an economic system in which there is a single mobile resource, partially satisfying several of the modeling desiderata outlined in section 1.2.5.

24. This input is homogeneous within each locality, and hence its quantity may be normalized at unity. It need not be the same resource in each locality. If $k$ is called capital, it may be suggestive to call the immobile resource "labor" or "land," or to think of it as an aggregate of many types of immobile labor and natural resources.

25. When desired, these properties may be augmented with Inada-type conditions to ensure interior solutions.

### 1.3.2 The Incidence and Allocative Effects of Local Taxes on Capital

The basic model just outlined has been applied in influential analyses of local property tax incidence by Mieszkowski (1972) and others. As is typical in incidence analysis, public policies are taken as exogenously given, and the goal is to investigate the impact of policy changes on equilibrium prices, quantities, incomes, welfare, and other variables of interest.

A first step in this direction is to note that each of the equations (3) can be solved for the local demand for capital as a downward-sloping function of the cost of capital $(r + t_i)$ with a derivative $k_i'(r + t_i) = 1/f_i'' < 0$ and an elasticity of demand $\epsilon_i = d\ln k_i / d\ln(r + t_i) = (r + t_i)/(k_i f_i'') < 0$, with all expressions evaluated where (3) holds. Substituting from these demand functions into the capital-conservation equation (2), we may solve implicitly for the equilibrium net rate of return $r$ as a function of the vector $\mathrm{t} = (t_1, \ldots, t_n)$ of local tax rates. It follows immediately that

$$\text{(4)} \qquad \frac{\partial r}{\partial t_i} = -\frac{k_i'}{\sum_{j=1}^{n} k_j'} \in (-1,0),$$

from which it also follows that

$$\text{(5)} \qquad \frac{dk_i}{dt_j} = k_j' \frac{\partial r}{\partial t_i} > 0 \quad \forall j \neq i$$

$$\text{(6)} \qquad \frac{dk_i}{dt_i} = k_i' \frac{d(r + t_i)}{dt_i} < 0.$$

In words, *an increase in any locality's tax rate (i) depresses the economy-wide net return to capital, though by less than the increase in the tax rate itself; (ii) reduces the equilibrium stock of capital in that locality; and (iii) increases the equilibrium stock of capital in every other locality*. In this model, a "conservation law," embodied in (2), implies that the reallocation of capital in response to a change in any tax rate is nondestructive, so that the loss of capital from a locality that raises its tax rate is equal to the aggregate increase in capital for all other localities. These simple results, which have no counterparts in closed-economy models, show that each locality is linked to every other through the common capital market.[26]

As a convenient reference point, observe from (4) that $\partial r / dt_i = 1/n$ in the special case where all jurisdictions are identical. (If they are heterogeneous, but not "too" different, a unit increase in $t_i$ reduces $r$ by approxi-

26. The *directions* of the effects in (4), (5), and (6) are unambiguous, but their *magnitudes* can range from "small" to "large." One can immediately see that $dr/dt_i$ can be a very small number when $n$ is large—what one might consider to be a "typical" case—though it can be a much larger number when $n$ is small, as in many models of strategic competition built upon two-person game theory. More detailed remarks follow immediately below. The importance of the number and size of competing jurisdictions for strategic modeling are discussed further in sections 1.5.1 and 1.5.2.

mately $1/n$.) To a first approximation, then, an increase of $t_i$ by a discrete amount $\Delta t_i$ reduces the economy-wide net return to capital by approximately $\Delta t_i/n$, with better approximations to be had by adjusting for differences in locality-specific attributes (as captured in their production functions $f_i$). Note, however, that *if all localities—identical or not—increase their tax rates by the same amount, say* $\Delta t$, *the equilibrium net return to capital falls by* $\sum_{i=1}^{n} \partial r / \partial t_i = \Delta t$ *that is, by the amount of the common tax increase*. Such a common change in policy also has no effect on the equilibrium allocation of capital: no locality's capital stock increases or decreases as a result. In effect, *when all local policies are coordinated, the situation effectively reverts to the closed economy in which a single government sets policies for the entire economic system.*

The assumption that capital is privately owned means that the aggregate net income accruing to capital owners is $r\bar{k}$. These owners may be situated anywhere—all concentrated in one locality, equally distributed among localities, or even located outside of the entire system of all $n$ localities ("absentee ownership"). However capital ownership is distributed, a unit increase in the tax rate in locality $i$ reduces the net incomes of capital owners by $|\partial r / \partial t_i| \bar{k}$, that is, by an amount on the order of (in the symmetric case, equal to) $\bar{k} / n$. The tax revenue collected in locality $i$, $t_i k_i$, changes by $k_i(1 + \partial k_i / \partial t_i)$, and the aggregate tax revenues of all other localities increase by $\sum_{j \neq i} t_j \, dk_j / dt_i$. If all tax rates are (approximately) identical, as is true in particular when all tax rates are initially 0, the increase in total tax revenue for all localities is (approximately) $k_i$. Accordingly, the *total loss in income to all capital owners, per unit of tax revenue collected, is approximately* $\bar{k} / (nk_i) \approx 1$.

The results of this analysis may seem to be either obvious or impossible. To understand them clearly, recall that the number of localities has so far been left indeterminate. In particular, $n$ may be very large, and individual localities may accordingly be very small—so small that one might suppose that the effects of their policies on the economic system are "negligible."[27]

In one respect, this is indeed true. Just as any single idealized purely competitive firm acts as though its production and input choices have zero effect on product and input prices, so a change in capital tax policy by a single small locality would have a minute and undetectable effect on the net rate of return on capital within its jurisdiction as well as economy-wide: $\partial r / \partial t_i$ is of the order of $1/n$, or "nearly" 0. And yet an increase in any one locality's tax does reduce the aggregate net rate of return *slightly*, and it does so for *all* capital owners "in the world," that is, in the entire economic system encompassed by the model. The upshot is that the owners of capital in aggregate suffer a loss of net income approximately equal to the amount of additional tax revenue collected by this small locality: the product of a small

27. For many practical purposes, as discussed further below, this should perhaps be seen as the standard case, as the tax policy changes of very few (if any) jurisdictions, including even quite large nations, are likely to have large impacts on the economy-wide or world-wide net rate of return to capital.

number, $\partial r / \partial t_i$, when multiplied by a large number, $\bar{k}$, is not "negligible." And, following the remarks above, we confirm this by observing that if $n$ very small jurisdictions all impose taxes at some average rate $\bar{t}$, the effect of these taxes is to reduce the net rate of return to capital in the entire economy by approximately $\bar{t}$, thus reducing the aggregate incomes of capital owners by approximately $\bar{t}\bar{k}$. To conclude otherwise is to fall prey to a "fallacy of composition"; in exact analogy, it would be fallacious to infer that a 1 percent reduction in output by every one of a multitude of very small competitive firms, no one of which perceptibly influences total output, would have no effect on market supply or on the equilibrium product price. In short, the sum of very many very small numbers need not be small.

This line of reasoning highlights the importance of a "system-wide," "multimarket," or "general equilibrium" approach to the problem of tax incidence. Mieszkowski (1969), Bradford (1978), and others attribute the basic insight to Brown (1924).[28]

### 1.3.3 From Incidence to Political Economy: Endogenous Policy Choices and System-Wide Equilibrium

There are multiple possible interpretations of competition among governments, but central to this concept in most cases is the *endogeneity* of policy; instead of taking policy as exogenously or parametrically given, one postulates that policies are *chosen* by governments and then seeks to understand the implications of those choices for outcomes of interest. In the case of fiscal policies, these outcomes include tax rates, public expenditures, and, perhaps most importantly, allocative efficiency and distributional equity (aka "social welfare").[29]

There are many conceivable hypotheses about how localities choose their fiscal policies. One simple and commonly employed approach is to suppose that each jurisdiction contains a single and completely immobile group of identical households, or a single "representative" household, and that the government chooses policies that maximize the welfare of that one agent.[30]

Suppose, then, that a single household resides in locality $i$, and that this

28. The presentation above draws largely upon Bradford (1978). Brown (1929) was concerned with the impacts of *sector-specific* policies in a multisectoral rather than multijurisdictional economy. (As an example, Brown analyzes the effect of a tax on bricklayers, arguing that it affects the wages of workers employed in other occupations.) Harberger's classic 1962 study of the incidence of the corporation income tax, which was grounded on the standard two-sector general equilibrium model, may also be viewed from this perspective. It has long been recognized by Mieszkowski, McLure (1969), and others, however, that this approach is readily adapted to a multijurisdictional setting.

29. In the preceding analysis of tax incidence, governments compete for the mobile resource, but their policy "decisions" consist of exogenously imposed tax perturbations, with redistributive transfers adjusting endogenously, and passively, to achieve budget balance.

30. As strong as it may seem, the representative agent assumption is certainly less objectionable when applied to the case of, say, municipal governments than to larger entities, such as nations or groups of nations, as is often done in macroeconomics, international economics, and other fields. In any case, it offers a convenient starting point; some simple alternatives are considered later.

household owns the total stock of the immobile resource there as well as a share $\sigma_i \geq 0$ of the aggregate capital stock $\bar{k}$. Assuming that the locality is small, a change in its tax policy has an imperceptible effect on the economy-wide net return to capital, so that $\sigma_i \bar{k}\, \partial r / \partial t_i \approx 0$. Although the effect of $t_i$ on $r$ is minute, its effect on $k_i$ is not, nor is its effect on the *gross* return $w_i = f_i(k_i) - k_i f_i'(k_i)$ received by the immobile resource: $dw_i / dt_i = -k_i f_i''(\cdot) k_i' = -k_i < 0$. A change in $t_i$ also changes local tax revenue $t_i k_i$, which, in our simple base specification, is received by the immobile household as a transfer payment: $dt_i k_i(\cdot) = k_i + t_i k_i' = k_i[1 + t_i \epsilon_i / (r + t_i)]$. Putting these results together, the *net* income of the immobile household thus changes by

$$\frac{d(w_i + t_i k_i)}{dt_i} + \sigma_i \bar{k} \frac{\partial r}{\partial t_i} \approx \frac{d(w_i + t_i k_i)}{dt_i} = \frac{t_i}{r + t_i} k_i \epsilon_i . \tag{7}$$

This central result says that *the welfare of a representative agent in a small locality is increased if the local tax rate on capital is decreased (in absolute value)*. That is, if the tax rate is positive, the local resident benefits from a reduction in the tax rate. Also note, however, that this result does *not* suggest that local welfare increases if the locality applies a net *subsidy*—corresponding to values of $t_i < 0$—to local capital. In this model, "attracting capital investment" is not an end in itself for a welfare-maximizing locality. On the contrary, local welfare is enhanced by *reductions* in *net* subsidies to capital, even recognizing that a reduction in the local subsidy would "drive away" some of the local capital stock. A reduction in a capital subsidy would indeed reduce the demand for the (complementary) immobile resource, and thus (given the assumption of a neoclassical production function) its equilibrium gross return. But because any capital subsidy is necessarily financed by taxation of the immobile resource ($t_i < 0$ means that the net transfer payment $t_i k_i$ is negative), a reduction in the subsidy also reduces the fiscal burden imposed on the immobile resource. This tax reduction necessarily outweighs the increase in the gross income of the representative agent. Hence, the key condition for *optimal* local policy is that

$$\frac{d(w_i + t_i k_i)}{dt_i} = \frac{t_i}{r + t_i} k_i \epsilon_i = t_i = 0. \tag{8}$$

In summary, *when local capital tax revenues are used to finance transfer payments to an immobile local resident, the optimal fiscal policy for a small locality is neither to tax nor subsidize local capital investment.*

In an economy containing many such small localities, none (if acting in the interests of their immobile residents) would tax or subsidize mobile capital, so that, in equilibrium, $t_i = 0$ for all $i$. Accordingly, the spatial-arbitrage condition (3) implies that

$$f_i'(k_i) = r = f_j'(k_j) \quad \forall i, j, \tag{9}$$

that is, *in an equilibrium with competition among many small localities, the marginal productivity of capital is equated in all locations*. This is, of course, the necessary condition for the maximization of total output (the sum of GDP in all localities) in the economy, that is, for the efficient allocation of the mobile resource. In fact, it is obvious from (3) that this condition is met whenever all localities impose identical taxes; with "perfect" competition among many small localities, the identical local taxes are all *chosen* to be equal to 0.[31]

Note that efficient resource allocation is necessarily an issue that must be evaluated from a system-wide or general-equilibrium perspective: it is not possible to ascertain whether any one locality's policy, considered in isolation, is efficient. For instance, suppose that all localities but the first choose a uniform "tax" rate of $\bar{t} \neq 0$, positive or negative. In this situation, if locality 1 sets $t_1 = 0$, the allocation of capital is distorted: because the spatial-arbitrage condition (9) implies that $f_1'(k_1) = r < (>) f_i'(k_i) \quad \forall i \neq 1$, as $\bar{t} > (<) 0$, the equilibrium allocation of capital cannot be efficient. What matters for efficiency is not the *levels* but the *uniformity* of net fiscal burdens, positive or negative, for mobile productive resources; because competition among small localities drives these net burdens to a uniform value of 0 everywhere (a particular type of uniformity), the resulting equilibrium is efficient.

From the viewpoint of social welfare, the zero-tax equilibrium need not be fair or equitable: the distribution of income is dependent upon the amounts and productivity of the immobile resources (in the model, these are embedded in the production functions $f_i$), the distribution of capital ownership (the shares $\sigma_i$), and the interactions of these endowments and technologies through the pricing of productive resources in competitive markets. There is an entire $n$-dimensional frontier or envelope of attainable net incomes, which, in this simple model, is equivalent to the utility-feasibility frontier. The fiscal-competition equilibrium with zero taxes and subsidies yields an outcome at one point on this frontier. If, for some reason, one or more "disobedient" local governments were not to pursue the policies desired by their representative immobile resource owners, it is possible that they could select asymmetric policies that create an inefficient capital allocation and, in doing so, would move the system to the interior of the utility frontier, that is, to a Pareto-inefficient outcome. Depending on "distributional preferences," such an inefficient outcome might nevertheless be preferred, from an overall social welfare perspective, to the efficient zero-tax outcome that emerges as the decentralized policy equilibrium.

As one illustration of this last remark, suppose that the resident of locality 1 has a small capital ownership endowment ($\sigma_1$ is small). The imposition of higher taxes on capital in other localities would increase $k_1$ (as shown in (5)),

31. The phrase "race to the bottom" is sometimes used to describe the equilibrium policies of competitive governments, as discussed more thoroughly in section 1.4.3 below. Here, let us simply observe that, at least with respect to the use of fiscal instruments, no true "bottom" exists, as a tax rate can always be reduced below 0 by replacing it with a subsidy ($t_i < 0$). There is no lower bound on subsidy rates (other than the complete exhaustion of the other revenue sources that may be used to finance the subsidy). Because perfectly competitive localities do not offer any subsidies at all, their "tax" rates do not even approximate a lower bound.

and thus the income of the resident of locality 1, holding fixed the value of $t_1$ (whether at zero or at any other value, positive or negative). If this household is "ethically deserving," such policies would increase social welfare even while introducing inefficiency in the system-wide allocation of capital. This kind of equity-efficiency tradeoff is commonplace in public finance, although it can be avoided in some cases. In principle, it may be possible to achieve distributional objectives while simultaneously avoiding inefficient capital allocation by using lump-sum "interpersonal" transfers from the owners of immobile resources in one locality to, say, the representative agent in locality 1. In the present context, such transfers would be interjurisdictional in nature, which would require the existence of a suitable higher-level government (or some other equivalent institutional arrangement) that could extract revenues from less-deserving jurisdictions (i.e., from their representative immobile residents) with which to finance lump-sum transfers to a more-deserving one (such as locality 1 in this illustration). In this respect, the situation is quite different from the closed-economy public finance context, as the implementation of a first-best policy requires not simply the existence of ideal tax and subsidy instruments (and the information needed to utilize them), but an added *institutional structure*, as mentioned in the discussion of federalism in section 1.2.3.

An interesting and underinvestigated question is whether the large and durable systems of intergovernmental transfers seen in many federations have contributed to more efficient allocations of mobile resources than would otherwise have been the case. As remarked earlier (section 1.2.3), state governments in the US receive around one-third of their general revenues in the form of transfers from the federal government, and local governments likewise receive about one-third of their revenues as transfers from the state governments. (Canada and Germany have similarly well-established programs that transfer central government funds to their subnational governments.) A hypothetical expansion, contraction, or complete elimination of such direct or implicit transfers would change the fiscal policies of lower-level governments, with associated alterations in the allocation of productive resources among regions and efficiency effects of generally unknown magnitudes.[32] In systems with multiple governments, efficient taxation generally necessitates either direct intergovernmental transfers or equivalent tariffs and subsidies applied to interjurisdictional trade (including international capital flows), if governments cannot utilize lump-sum revenue sources (see Keen and Wildasin 2004 and Wildasin 1977).[33]

Let us conclude this section by noting how the market linkages empha-

32. Although intergovernmental transfers play a more modest role in the international sphere, they have gradually become more prominent in Europe since the foundation of the EU, and international financial assistance to developing countries is sometimes significant in magnitude.

33. The potential efficiency gains from intergovernmental transfers when lower-level governments use distortionary taxes are also discussed in Wildasin (1983, 1984).

sized in the incidence analysis of section 1.3.2 not only help to determine the gainers and losers from local policy changes but also provide a foundation for the study of endogenous policymaking. In particular, capital mobility constrains the ability of *small* localities to affect the system-wide net return to capital, which, as we have seen, shows that capital owners need not be explicitly represented in the local political process in order to ensure that they need not pay taxes in any one locality: competition does that work for them. (Observations in this spirit are central elements in the discussion of "open economy" public finance in Brennan and Buchanan 1980.) These political economy implications of resource mobility, which are elaborated further in section 1.4.2, stand in stark contrast to a closed-economy model where, with the same menu of tax and subsidy instruments, the owners of all local resources are trapped in potential conflict and stand to gain or lose through the manipulation of local policies.

### 1.3.4 Mobility vs. Movement: "No Trade" Equilibria and Artificial Barriers to Mobility

The preceding discussion has explicitly postulated that the mobile productive resource can be freely situated in any of the $n$ localities, with no cost of "relocation." One may add to the model any arbitrary "initial assignment" of the mobile resource, $k^0 \equiv (k_1^0, \ldots, k_n^0)$, to each of the localities (or even to "absentee" owners, not located in any of the $n$ localities), provided only that the aggregate initial amount adds up to the fixed aggregate amount $\bar{k}$. For any given vector of policies $t$, the equilibrium allocation of the mobile resource $k(t)$ is independent of this initial assignment, and the same is true for all other equilibrium values (factor prices and incomes, tax revenues, and public expenditures) of interest. For this reason, the "initial assignment" of the mobile resource is not economically important for the analysis. For the same reason, it cannot, properly speaking, be used to analyze the implications of the *movement* of this resource from one location to another (what might be called "investment flows" if $k$ is "capital" or "migration" if $k$ is "labor"): the implications of resource mobility (incidence, efficiency of equilibrium, and other results cited above) are unaffected by any discrepancy between the "initial" and "final" allocations.

To be even more explicit, one could, if desired, postulate that the initial assignment vector $k^0$ is just equal to the equilibrium allocation $k(t)$. In this special case, although the resource is freely *mobile*, no *movement* of this resource need take place for the equilibrium to be achieved, a formal verification of the remarks in section 1.2.4. In standard models of exchange or trade, such an outcome is customarily called a "no-trade equilibrium," and a similar term could also be applied here. At least within the context of this model, observed resource movement says nothing about the extent of competition among governments; rather, in a very loose sense, high rates of observed resource flows would simply be interpreted as an indication that the economic system is in "disequilibrium," that is, that the initial or current allocation of resources must be substantially changed in order to satisfy the spatial arbitrage condition (3).

As observed in section 1.2.4, many jurisdictions throughout history have applied regulatory constraints to the movement of productive resources. These regulatory interventions can directly affect resource movement, and they interact in important ways with fiscal policies. As the simplest possible illustration, consider what happens in the model described above when any one locality imposes and strictly enforces a constraint that prevents the movement of a productive resource. What would otherwise be an open local economy now becomes closed (as a matter of policy), its linkage to the external factor market is severed, local fiscal policies have no effect on the allocation of resources, and factor mobility no longer prevents local redistributive policies from achieving any desired distribution of net income. This is essentially the standard analytical framework of public finance, which disallows the linkage to external markets (and which, of course, accommodates many other margins of behavioral adjustment that have been suppressed here).

In practice, quantitative controls over resource mobility may or may not be binding. If they are not binding, then the basic model operates much as before.[34] If, on the other hand, they are binding, the free-mobility equilibrium condition (3) does not hold, which is to say that net income differentials among localities may persist in equilibrium. The condition (9) for efficient resource allocation may conceivably still hold, but, in general, restrictions on mobility preclude the equalization of gross returns required for efficiency. Thus, the imposition of binding controls affects both the distribution of income and the efficiency of resource allocation. When binding constraints are imposed, cross-border resource flows cannot be observed empirically, but, as in the case of no-trade equilibria, the fact that a resource cannot move does not necessarily indicate that it is immobile.

As discussed earlier, resource owners naturally seek, if possible, to influence local policies to protect and advance their own interests. Let us now consider how the political economy of fiscal policy is affected by restrictions on resource mobility. Suppose that a small locality 1 possesses an "initial" assignment of $k_1^0$ units of the mobile resource and that it institutes a restriction that ensures that only $\hat{k}_1 - k_1^0$ units may enter the locality. This means that the locality can have a total stock of the mobile resource no greater than $k_1^0 + (\hat{k}_1 - k_1^0) = \hat{k}_1$. For the constraint to be binding, it is necessary that the local net return on this resource must equal or exceed $r$, that is, $f_1'(\hat{k}_1) - t_1 > r$. In this circumstance, the locality has *two* policy instruments at its disposal: its fiscal policy $t_1$ and its regulatory policy, represented by

34. By restricting the set of feasible policy choices, however, constraints that are nonbinding at equilibrium can nevertheless have significant effects on strategic interactions among small numbers of competing jurisdictions.

$\hat{k}_1$. How do small changes in either of these policies affect the distribution of income within the locality? What policies best serve the interests of the owners of the immobile resource?

At this point, the analysis of income distribution, policy incidence, and policymaking becomes more complex. The owners of the units of the mobile resource within the locality may earn a higher net return than is available on external markets because arbitrage is restricted. Owners of the mobile resource who succeed in gaining entry to the locality enjoy a rent, or quasi-rent, relative to those remaining outside. These quasi-rents may, however, be dissipated; for instance, firms situated within the locality may still be able to obtain the resource from outside sources at a net return of $r$ (their reservation price) and thereby earn higher profits, which are then part of the incomes of their (the firms') owners. Following the outline of the previous analysis, it may be natural to assume that these profits accrue to the local "representative household" that owns the immobile resources within the locality, although other specifications are possible. Under this assumption, the net income $Y_1$ of the representative household consists, as before, of its gross income $f_1(\hat{k}_1) - k_1 f_1'(\hat{k}_1)$ plus the transfer payments that it receives, $t_1\hat{k}_1$, plus the quasi-rents earned on the potentially mobile resource, $\hat{k}(f_1'(\hat{k}_1) - t_1 - r)$, or, simply, $Y_1 = f_1(\hat{k}_1) - r\hat{k}_1$.[35] Recalling that the regulatory restriction is assumed to be (strictly) binding, $dY_1 / d\hat{k}_1 = f_1'(\hat{k}_1) - r - t_1 > 0$, that is, *a small easing of a binding constraint on the importation of the mobile resource increases the net income of the representative local household.* Because it reduces the amount of capital used elsewhere in the economy, such a policy change results in a small increase in $r$, with distributional impacts in other jurisdictions similar to those described in section 1.3.2. Following the logic of section 1.3.3, it is evident that the optimal local policy is always to increase $\hat{k}_1$, that is, *the owners of the immobile resource in a small locality are harmed by binding constraints on the entry of a mobile productive resource.* Similar remarks would apply, mutatis mutandis, in the case of upward-binding limitations on the utilization of a mobile resource (as in the case of forced emigration).

## 1.4 Efficient and Inefficient Provision and Financing of Pure and Impure Local Public Goods

In the simplest model, local governments use only two fiscal instruments, one, a tax on a mobile resource, and the other, a lump-sum transfer payment to the immobile resource owners. One interpretation of this model has "capital" as the mobile resource and, perhaps, "labor" (or households) employed

35. If a fraction $\gamma_1$ of the rents accrue either to absentee capital owners or absentee owners of firms, $Y_1 = [f_1(\hat{k}_1) - r\hat{k}_1] - \gamma_1[\hat{k}(f_1'(\hat{k}_1) - t_1 - r)]$; the following results must be amended accordingly in this case.

in the local economy as the immobile resource. The only purpose of the public sector is to redistribute incomes between the two. At first glance, this is a poor description of observed government policies, for at least two reasons. First, not all government policies are purely redistributive in nature. Second, governments are not generally restricted to using just two fiscal instruments. These two issues are not unrelated.

This section examines, first, the possibility that localities may provide public goods and services that may be financed by some combination of taxes on (or subsidies to) a mobile resource (denoted by $t_i$, as before) and a transfer to (or tax on) an immobile resource (denoted explicitly by $L_i$). As will become clear, the tax mix chosen by competitive localities can vary drastically, depending on the nature of the public goods in question. Specifically, when public expenditures are used to provide "impure" public goods and services that are "congested" by the presence of the mobile resource, taxation of the mobile resource provides a means by which a locality can recover the added costs imposed upon it. In fact, in important cases, localities rely solely on taxation of the mobile resource to provide the totality of their tax revenues. This is very different from the case in which localities provide "Samuelson pure" or "uncongestible" public goods; in this case, small competitive localities impose no tax at all on the mobile resource, just as in the simplest model of section 1.3.3. These results do not depend on what levels of public services the localities provide, which may be determined exogenously or endogenously. In the latter case, small competitive localities, acting on behalf of local interests, adhere to the Samuelson condition for public good provision, and this is so, whether local public goods are pure or impure.

### 1.4.1 Competition with Pure Local Public Goods

As an initial step, and to provide a concise illustration of how the formal model can be modified, consider the possibility that local governments provide a *Samuelson pure public input*, i.e., a public service for which the cost of providing $G_i$ units in locality $i$, $c_i(G_i)$, is invariant to the amount of the productive input $k_i$. One may then generalize the production function $f_i(k_i)$ to one that explicitly reflects this input, say $F_i(k_i, G_i)$. Provided that governments retain the capacity to make (positive or negative) lump-sum transfers $L_i$ to the owners of the immobile local resource, the local government budget constraint takes the slightly more complex form

$$(1') \qquad t_i k_i = L_i + c_i(G_i).$$

The local government now has two potential degrees of policy freedom rather than just one; that is, of the three instruments $(t_i, L_i, G_i)$, any pair may be modified, with the third determined by the budget constraint. The added dimension of policy choice raises new questions about the implications of changes in $G_i$ regarding the incidence of local policies and especially about endogenous local policy choice, but it does not obviate the findings from the simpler model. Formally speaking, whether $G_i$ is determined exogenously or endogenously, each locality still faces a tradeoff subject to (1′). For any given value of $G_i$, the incidence of a small change in $t_i$, accompanied by a small change in $L_i$ affects the allocation of capital, the equilibrium net return on capital $r$, and the net incomes of the owners of the immobile resources, as before. It follows, in particular, that *the optimal local policy for a small locality is to impose no tax on the mobile resource*; hence, *freely mobile capital is efficiently allocated in a system with many small competing localities that provide pure local public goods*. Now, however, the modified local government budget constraint (1′) implies not that $L_i = 0$, as in the simplest model with purely redistributive policies, but rather that $L_i = -c_i(G_i)$, that is, *a small locality maximizes the welfare of the owners of the immobile resource by imposing lump-sum taxes on this resource sufficient to finance all local expenditures on a pure local public input*. This result substantially simplifies the analysis of the optimal local choice of the public input, which—because $t_i = 0$—is financed by a local lump-sum tax.

Of course, although public inputs (infrastructure and the like) are important, many public goods and services may primarily (or even exclusively) benefit households. In one common specification, households are completely immobile, and their labor constitutes the local productive resource. Following the same reasoning as in the case of public inputs, the analysis of the incidence of local taxes on the mobile resource is unaltered. Furthermore, it follows that *to maximize the welfare of immobile local residents, small localities finance the provision of pure local public goods entirely by lump-sum taxes on their residents, with no taxes or subsidies on freely mobile productive inputs*.

If the freely mobile resource consists of households ("labor") rather than capital, it is again possible to incorporate household preferences for local public goods with minimal formal changes. In this case, however, it is necessary to recognize that spatial arbitrage cannot be characterized simply in terms of the equalization of after-tax factor returns. Rather, households may willingly accept lower after-tax net incomes (and correspondingly lower levels of private consumption) in order to enjoy higher amounts of public services, thereby achieving higher welfare or utility. For mobile households in locality $i$, utility may be represented by a function $u_i(f_i'(k_i) - t_i, G_i)$ that depends both on consumption of the numéraire private good and the level of public services $G_i$, and the free mobility of households implies that, in equilibrium, utility levels in all localities must be equalized at some common value $v$, so that

(10) $$u_i(f_i'(k_i) - t_i, G_i) = v \ \forall i. \quad (\textit{spatial arbitrage}).$$

Despite its slightly more complex form, this condition is exactly analogous to (3); together with the resource-conservation condition (2), the formal model provides a system that determines the equilibrium allocation of mobile households to jurisdictions (the vector $k$) and the equilibrium level of utility (denoted by $v$). The analysis of the incidence of changes in the rate of tax $t_i$ on the mobile resource is not affected by the presence of pure local public goods, provided that the lump-sum instrument $L_i$ may still be used to finance the local public good. The condition for the efficient assignment of households to localities is now slightly modified due to the presence of local public goods, but the most important implications of government competition for the mobile resource are unchanged. Specifically, *if a locality provides a pure (congestion-free) local public good that is valued by mobile households, and if it chooses its policies to maximize the welfare of the owners of immobile resources within its jurisdiction, it is optimal to impose no tax on the mobile households and to finance its public expenditures using a lump-sum tax imposed on the owners of the local immobile resource, that is, the locality sets* $t_i = 0$ *and* $L_i = -c_i(G_i)$. *In a system with many small localities, mobile households are allocated efficiently in equilibrium.*

Note that the presence of exogenously fixed ("pure" or uncongested) local amenities and disamenities, in addition to (or in lieu of) local public goods and services, does not alter the preceding results. Formally speaking, such amenities have already been captured in the specification of the local production functions $F_i(\cdot)$ and utility functions $u_i(\cdot)$, which are locality-specific in general (because of the $i$ subscripts). Thus, despite a slightly more complex notational burden, the key findings of the basic model are essentially preserved in the presence of pure or uncongestible local public goods and inputs, provided that lump-sum taxes are still accessible local policy instruments.

### 1.4.2 Competition with Impure Public Goods

As just shown, a small competitive locality that provides pure local public goods can only harm the owners of fixed local resources by taxing mobile resources. The simple reason for this is that the addition of new units of mobile resources entails no extra cost for the locality.

Matters are more complex when local public goods and services are "impure," "rival," or congestible, i.e., when a locality must increase its public expenditures to provide public services as the population (or the stock of capital) increases. This is a very important case empirically, as may be verified casually, but not misleadingly, by comparing the absolute size of the public transportation, police, or education budgets of highly populous cities with those of small cities and towns. The same is true for population-dependent social expenditures that, as described in section 1.2.2, often account for a very large share of the budgets of national governments.

In terms of the model presented above, it is possible that congestion effects for public services arise from the presence of mobile resources, from the presence of immobile resources, or both. In one interpretation of the model, the immobile resource could be one category of households (perhaps low-skilled workers or the elderly) and the mobile resource could be another category of households (perhaps high-skilled workers or the young). Because their numbers cannot vary, the cost to a locality of providing a given level $G_i$ of congestible public services to immobile residents is fixed and may be ignored for the remainder of this subsection, but the cost of providing such services to mobile households varies with their number.

To analyze this situation, a momentary change to a more suggestive notation will be helpful. Let us label the mobile resource "population" rather than "capital" and denote the population in locality $i$ by $N_i$ rather than $k_i$. Congestion effects in the provision of local public goods mean that the cost of providing a level of public service $G_i$ depends not only on $G_i$ itself but also on the size of the population being served, so that the cost function should be written as $c_i(G_i, N_i)$. The "marginal cost of the public service" is now an ambiguous term because the cost depends both on the level of the service $G_i$ and on the population size $N_i$. To be precise, for any given level of public service $G_i$, the "marginal congestion cost" is $\partial c_i(G_i, N_i) / \partial N_i$, that is, the cost of increasing the population by one unit. As an illustration, the "level of education" in a locality $G_i$ would increase if its schools were to offer more years of schooling, smaller class sizes, an enhanced curriculum, or improved school safety or facilities—enhancements that might commonly be described as "quality improvements." However described, the crucial distinction is that such features of an educational system are different from the number of students in the schools, which is linked to population size and is the crucial determinant of congestion effects.

As one simple and frequently used reference case, the cost of providing $G_i$ units of a public service could be proportional to population, in which case the cost function takes the form $c_i(G_i, N_i) = \gamma_i G_i N_i$ for some unit cost $\gamma_i > 0$. In this special case, the local "public" good—sometimes termed a *quasi-private* public good—is similar to an ordinary private good like bread, where consumption of the good or service by one member of the population reduces the amount available for others by the amount $\gamma_i G_i$ unless total expenditures are increased by an offsetting amount. This special case, or some variant of it, is often assumed in the context of elementary and secondary education, where "expenditures per pupil," i.e., $\gamma_i G_i$, is widely used as a measure of the amount of education provided.

In the presence of congestion effects, the local government budget constraint becomes

$$(1'') \qquad t_i N_i = L_i + c_i(G_i, N_i) \quad (\textit{congestible public goods, general case})$$

$$(1''') \qquad t_i N_i = L_i + \gamma_i G_i N_i \quad (\textit{congestible public goods, quasi-private case}).$$

It is clear that (1″) and (1‴) reduce to the pure local public good case (1′) when (marginal) congestion costs are 0.

Using now-familiar reasoning, hold $G_i$ fixed and consider the effects of a change in $t_i$, both for an individual locality $i$ and for the entire economic system. The spatial arbitrage condition (10) continues to hold (substituting the new notation $N_i$ for the old $k_i$), and a change in $t_i$ affects both locality $i$ and other localities as previously shown. More importantly, holding $G_i$ fixed, what is the optimal choice of $t_i$ for a locality that seeks to maximize the net income (or utility) of the owners of the local immobile resource? Using the new government budget constraint to substitute for $L_i$, the net return to the immobile resource is maximized when $t_i = \partial c_i(G_i, N_i) / \partial N_i$. Thus, *the optimal policy for a small locality is to impose a tax on the mobile resource equal to the marginal congestion cost that is produced by an additional unit of that resource*. In particular, *when local public goods are quasi-private, the optimal policy is to finance all public expenditures by such congestion tolls and to impose no tax or subsidy on the immobile resource.*

Analyzing how competitive local governments choose the "level of public good provision," $G_i$, in order to maximize the welfare of the owners of immobile resources is now straightforward. The problem decomposes into two parts: first, the choice of financing for any arbitrarily given level of $G_i$, which we have just analyzed, and second, the choice of $G_i$ itself. Taking the pure public good case initially, the fact that the locality chooses $t_i = 0$ means that any changes in $G_i$ are financed by incremental lump-sum taxes on the immobile resource. Whether the public good is one that benefits the immobile resource owners, benefits the mobile resource owners, is a public intermediate input that increases the productivity of firms, or is any combination of these, the optimal local choice is to choose $G_i$ at the level that satisfies the appropriate version of the classical Samuelson condition. If the local public good is congestible, essentially identical reasoning establishes the same result. Because the locality sets $t_i = \partial c_i(G_i, N_i) / \partial N_i$, any impact of $G_i$ on the amount of the mobile resource has no first-order effect on the optimal local policy.

To summarize this part of the discussion, we have seen that there is no "one size fits all" local tax policy that best serves the interests of immobile resource owners in all cases, irrespective of the types of public services that are provided. The taxation of a mobile resource provides a policy tool with which a locality can alter the amount of that resource, and it is optimal to use it to recover any added costs of public service provision that result from the presence of the mobile resource. This may or may not be sufficient to finance the optimal level of local public expenditures. If not, it is then optimal to tax (or subsidize, as the case may be) the local immobile resource in order to balance the local budget.

In the end, these findings in essence confirm those obtained in the simplest model of competition, presented in sections 1.3.2 and 1.3.3. A redistributive cash transfer is certainly one example of an impure public good—in fact, one that is quasi-private. As shown in section 1.3.3, the owners of immobile resources in competitive localities benefit from setting $t_i = 0$. Failing that, they benefit from moving $t_i$ toward 0: decreasing it, if positive, and increasing it, if negative. In other words, the optimal "congestion toll" on a mobile resource should entirely neutralize or offset any tax imposed upon it or any subsidy afforded to it. Applying this result to the case of in-kind transfers for public services, such as health, education, housing, or other congestible public services, a locality should optimally impose charges sufficient to recover the (marginal) cost of providing any of these services that can be accessed by mobile households.

There are many variations on these basic ideas. In some cases, it may be possible for a government to impose differential charges or taxes on mobile and immobile households who use specific congestible public services (e.g., by charging lower tuition for in-state students at a public university.) In other cases (e.g., in setting per-trip charges for rides on public transportation), such differential pricing may be infeasible. In this latter case of "imperfect excludability," a locality can impose a uniform congestion toll on *all* households that use the public service in order to recover the congestion costs created by mobile households, adjusting other instruments in an offsetting manner so as to achieve the mix of taxes and public service provision that maximizes the welfare of immobile residents (Vickrey 1965). Such variations highlight the importance of careful (perhaps imaginative) interpretation of the formal analysis for policy applications.

### 1.4.3 Restrictions on Instruments: Underprovision of Local Public Goods and the "Race to the Bottom"

The situation is quite different when the revenue instruments of localities are restricted. Such a case has, in fact, been almost paradigmatic in the literature on fiscal competition and has shaped much of the policy discussion on this subject, in which competition is said to result in a "race to the bottom" in public policies. This evocative (but not well-defined) phrase is sometimes taken to mean that local public goods are underprovided, relative to some efficient levels, that government redistributive policies are undesirably constrained, that regulatory policies are undesirably lax, that local tax policies are distorted in some manner, or perhaps several or all of these.

It is a now-standard result in the literature of fiscal competition (see, e.g., Zodrow and Mieszkowski 1986, and further references in Wilson 1999 and Agrawal et al. 2022) that local public goods may indeed be underprovided when (a) local governments can finance public goods only by taxing a mobile resource and (b) when there are no congestion effects associated with the presence of the mobile resource. It is easy to see why this should be the case under such conditions. Recall from the government budget constraint (1′) that public expenditures in the absence of congestion effects are just equal to the sum of revenues from the taxation of the mobile ($t_ik_i$) and immobile ($L_i$) resources, and that competitive localities choose fully efficient policies by setting $t_i = 0$, relying solely on the taxation of the immobile resource to finance public expenditures (so that $G_i = L_i$). If the latter source of revenues is ruled out ($L_i = 0$), it is impossible to provide any public services other than by taxing the mobile resource. Intuitively, public good provision is less attractive to localities that are constrained to use this second-best funding source, and it is therefore not surprising that underprovision of public goods occurs under these conditions.

The concept of a "race to the bottom" resulting from competition among governments may be traced to a US Supreme Court opinion by Louis D. Brandeis in the case of *Liggett Co. v. Lee* (288 U.S. 517). As discussed in more detail in Appendix B, Brandeis rues the fact that competition among state governments can lead them to liberalize their laws of incorporation—what he calls a "race to laxity"—and to reduce the taxes imposed upon corporations (especially chain stores, which Brandeis sees as potentially pernicious). The "race" in question, according to Brandeis, started as early as 1890—more than four decades prior to *Liggett Co. v. Lee*—when New York liberalized its laws in an ultimately unsuccessful attempt to forestall migration of corporations to New Jersey, after which New Jersey itself lost out in competition with Delaware. Although one might facetiously remark that, as races go, this one seems to have been a rather drawn-out affair, the "race" metaphor highlights the question of dynamics in competition among governments—in this instance, the dynamics of policy adjustment by competing governments. The subject of dynamics in fiscal competition is discussed further in section 1.5.3 below. Here, let us simply observe that static or atemporal models, such as those presented above, are intrinsically ill suited to the analysis of dynamic questions.

The underprovision (or, if one prefers, the "race to the bottom") result has featured very prominently in academic, policy, and popular discussions of fiscal competition. Its formal derivation can be traced to early works that were motivated by issues related to property taxation and the provision of public education by local school districts in the US. These are important units of government in the US fiscal system, but they are not representative of all localities in the US, state governments in the US, or, needless to say, central governments in the US and throughout the world. At least since the 1960s, local school districts, whose expenditures are of course dedicated to "educational" uses, have obtained nearly 100 percent of their tax revenues and more than 75 percent of all of their own-source revenues from property taxes.[36] It is quite plausible to view such governments as the providers of just one type of public service financed by just one source of revenue, and to view local property taxes as primarily taxes on mobile capital. By contrast, municipal governments obtain only about half of their tax revenues from property taxes. Furthermore, municipalities derive about 30 percent of

36. "Own-source" means "exclusive of intergovernmental transfers"; in the present context, these are mainly transfers from state governments.

their own-source revenues from a very wide range of nontax sources. State governments also utilize a very diverse array of revenue sources, including taxes on both individual and corporation incomes, general retail sales, many specific sales taxes (on fuels, tobacco, alcohol, utilities, and other commodities and services), as well as many nontax sources, which they use to finance many different types of public goods and services. Likewise, national governments utilize numerous sources of tax and nontax revenues (including government borrowing) to finance a wide array of public goods and services.

It should be obvious from these descriptive remarks that a model that is perhaps well suited to the analysis of local school districts in the US may not be equally well suited to the analysis of other subnational and national governments in the US and elsewhere in the world. In particular, as we have seen, a conclusion that competition among governments results in the underprovision of public services (or, more dramatically, a "race to the bottom") depends critically on the numbers and types of policy instruments that competing governments can utilize, and that, with relatively rare exceptions, governments can and do make use of multiple sources of revenues. It may well be true that competition for mobile resources affects the choice of tax rates imposed by governments. As demonstrated above, competitive governments may impose *no* taxes at all on mobile resources, relying instead solely on the taxation of immobile resources, but they may, *as a consequence*, achieve *fully efficient* levels of public service provision. Proper benefit-cost analysis may or may not support the conclusion that the expenditure levels of states and national governments are inefficiently low, but a finding that competition for business enterprise affects their corporation income tax policies need not by itself suggest that competition makes their overall fiscal systems less efficient; it may, instead, indicate just the opposite.

## 1.5 Multiple Mobile Resources, Market Areas, Large Jurisdictions, and the Degree of Resource Mobility

The previous sections have discussed many of the economic and policy implications of competition among governments under a relatively wide range of conditions. This section considers several extensions and modifications of the simplest models that address some of their limitations. In some cases, these changes do not alter the key findings of the analysis, but, in other cases, they have much more substantial impacts.

### 1.5.1 Multiple Mobile Resources

Economists often treat broad commodity categories as if they can be aggregated into single commodities. For example, familiar macroeconomic models treat all human resources as a single homogeneous productive factor of production ("labor") and all nonhuman productive resources as homogeneous "capital." The models of fiscal incidence and endogenous policy choice presented in sections 1.3.2 and 3.3 have followed this common practice by treating mobile and immobile resources as homogeneous aggregates. Such aggregation assumptions, which must generally be viewed as approximations made for the sake of tractability, are least misleading when the relative prices of the aggregated commodities do not change (the Hicks aggregation theorem).

Unfortunately, this assumption is frequently unjustified and can be misleading in analyzing competition among governments,. To begin with, the aggregate of "immobile resources" within a jurisdiction may be quite heterogeneous. The previous discussion has frequently referred to labor or households as "the immobile" resource. Land and other natural resources are intrinsically immobile but, in much of the literature, are commonly ignored—perhaps a justifiable assumption for some purposes, but potentially highly questionable.[37]

As an example, consider a hypothetical "rust belt" region, stereotypically consisting of intrinsically immobile natural resources, a large stock of long-ago installed and now substantially depreciated public infrastructure and private industrial capital, and a population of relatively old workers whose experience and skills are adapted to the requirements of declining industries. "Old" capital can leave this region over time but only gradually, at a rate dictated by the depreciation of public capital, housing, and the industrial base. The labor force can likewise decline over time, as old workers retire, their offspring relocate to other regions, and few young workers enter. Suppose that the government(s) of this region attempt to formulate tax, expenditure, and regulatory policies that attract new business investment and younger workers with skills and educational backgrounds that increase the profitability of such investments. What form would such policies take? What would the distributional effects of these policies be?

One could attempt to address these questions by treating "new" capital and labor as a composite mobile input and by treating "old" capital, "old" labor, "old" housing, and natural resources as a composite immobile resource. The preceding analysis suggests that a policy reform designed to attract the mobile resource would offer reduced tax burdens on new businesses; increased or targeted provision of public services attractive to younger workers; and amendments to land use, employment, environmental, and other regulations that facilitate the entry of mobile resources. As a

37. Land is far from a negligible resource in agriculture, of course, and economists of preindustrial eras naturally devoted considerable attention to it. In urban areas, the utilization and valuation of land is often (but perhaps quite erroneously) seen as far less important than the industrial, commercial, and residential capital investments ("improvements") built upon it. Although the valuation of urban land is not a straightforward undertaking, recent estimates place the land value share of urban property in large cities at levels on the order of 30 percent to nearly 50 percent, which are far from negligible. See section 1.2.1 above.

corollary, the inevitable costs of these policies would fall on the immobile resource owners.[38] Such a reform could not easily be achieved by across-the-board changes in policy, such as changes in tax rates for all businesses or residents, because these would fail to discriminate between mobile and immobile resources. Better suited for this purpose would be "temporary" or "targeted" tax breaks and favorable regulations for businesses (perhaps even individual firms) that locate in specific zones, reductions in social services or cash benefits for older workers, the establishment of amenity-rich residential zones, or regulations that facilitate the disposition and redevelopment of abandoned properties or those that are heavily depreciated. Such policies, which discriminate in favor of "new" capital, may well benefit the owners of immobile resources, including "old" capital (see (7)), provided that the fiscal burdens on new capital remain sufficient to recover the (marginal) congestion costs incurred in providing associated public services, as discussed in section 1.4.2.[39]

It is clear from this hypothetical exercise that the labeling of resources as separate homogeneous aggregates of "labor," "capital," and "land," where the units of each are treated uniformly by fiscal and regulatory policies, is inadequate for the purposes at hand. The hypothesized policy instruments, much like those seen in practice, apply differentially to superficially identical units of mobile and immobile resources. Treating businesses, labor, and natural resources as homogeneous aggregates may obscure important distributional impacts of policy. From the perspective of political economy, the owners of distinct immobile resources may disagree about how the costs of attracting mobile resources should be distributed and which are the best ways to attract them. There are two reasons for this. First, just as in traditional closed-economy public finance analysis, each category of immobile resource owner (for example, incumbent older workers) would prefer for these costs to be paid by the owners of other immobile resources (such as old industrial or residential properties). Second, in contrast to closed-economy analyses, policies that increase the stocks of heterogeneous mobile resources (capital and some types of labor) differentially affect the productivity of immobile resources, as incoming capital and workers exhibit different complement/

38. To simplify this example, let us ignore the possibility, surely relevant in practice, that some of these costs would be shifted to others outside of the region in the form of direct or indirect subsidies from higher-level governments and to future residents and taxpayers within the region through the use of debt, deferred maintenance, and preservation of public infrastructure and natural resources that serve immobile (but not mobile) resources.

39. Chirinko and Wilson (2006), in an analysis of state corporation income taxation in the US, show that investment tax credits increased markedly over the period 1990–2006 but that average statutory tax rates were relatively stable, so that the effective tax rate (or "wedge") fell sharply. This could be viewed as an effort to reduce tax burdens on "marginal" units of "new" capital without relinquishing tax revenues from sunk investments in "old" capital (Wildasin 2006), a theme developed further in Chirinko and Wilson (2017).

substitute relationships with old capital, old workers, and natural resources. For both of these reasons, immobile resource owners have incentives to advance their conflicting interests by influencing the local political process.

These distributional impacts, their political implications, and even the descriptions of public policies themselves cannot be illuminated if resources and public policies are improperly aggregated. The preceding remarks have used the specific example of a rust-belt region by way of illustration, but it is not difficult to see how similar considerations arise in the many other contexts described in section 1.2 and Appendix A. Indeed, there is a significant body of research in labor economics that examines the impact of (international) immigration on the wages of native workers, much of which draws attention to (and seeks to control for) the potential differences between immigrants and natives.[40]

The foregoing considerations show some of the hazards of factor aggregation in the analysis of competition among governments. Not all of the analysis and results presented in earlier sections, which distinguish only between highly aggregated mobile and immobile resources, must necessarily change drastically in a more disaggregated approach; in substantial part, they need not change at all. The simplest way to see this is to reinterpret the mobile resource $k$ in the basic model as a *vector* $k_i \equiv (k_i^1, \ldots, k_i^m)$ of $m$ distinct types of resources, with $r$, $t_i$, and $\bar{k}$ denoting the corresponding $m$-vectors of factor prices, tax rates, and aggregate endowments of mobile resources. The production functions $f_i(k_i)$ may be interpreted as depending on $k_i$ and on any number, say $M$, of immobile resources. In this case, the gross returns of all resources are given by the vector of first derivatives of $f_i$. The distributional effects of public policies depend upon the Hessian matrices of second-order derivatives. The fundamental equilibrium conditions (2) and (3) of the simplest model remain valid as written, as do the government budget constraints. The incidence analysis of section 1.3.2 can easily be generalized, and many of results that build upon that analysis in sections 1.3 and 1.4 thus also remain valid.

It is worth noting, however, that local policy changes can now produce "cross effects" involving substitution among mobile resources that have no counterpart when $m = 1$. Specifically, depending on the properties of the local production functions, an increase in (say) $t_{i1}$ generally changes the local demand for all of the mobile resources. If resource 1 is highly complementary with some other resource $j$, then $\partial k_{ij} / \partial t_{i1} < 0$; this is obvious in the

40. Dustman et al. (2016) provide an overview of some of the diverse findings in this literature, noting especially the heterogeneity of both native and nonnative workers, the elasticities of substitution among workers with different skills and experience, capital/labor substitution, and the time-varying effects of immigration. They also emphasize the impacts of immigration on the wages of native and nonnative workers, considered as aggregates. For examples of related literature that draw attention to the labor-market, fiscal, and political-economy implications of immigration, see, e.g., Borjas (2003), Dustman and Frattini (2014), Dustman et al. (2016), Preston (2014), and Scheve and Slaughter (2001).

extreme case of perfect complementarity (a Leontief production function) in which these two inputs are used in fixed proportions. The reverse is true when the two inputs are highly substitutable, as is obvious, again, in the extreme case of perfect substitutes (a small increase in the tax on input 1 drives that resource out of the locality entirely, and other inputs take its place). These allocative effects of local policy changes have corresponding impacts on the composition of local revenues (an increase in $t_{i1}$ can increase, decrease, or leave unchanged $t_{ij}k_{ij}$ depending on the substitutability/complementarity relationship between input 1 and input $j$). They also produce corresponding changes in the equilibrium factor price vector $r$. All of these effects are "small" if locality $i$ is small, but, as before, they add up to system-wide effects on factor incomes that are of the same order of magnitude as the amount of tax revenue collected, so that (for example) the incidence of a tax on highly skilled workers in one small locality may fall partially on the owners of (complementary) capital throughout the entire economy. Such effects are of interest when evaluating policies, perhaps those of a higher-level government, that may affect local policymaking.[41]

Factor heterogeneity also necessitates potentially important qualifications to the representative-agent prediction in (8) that each of many small localities optimally chooses $t_i = 0$ (or, more precisely, that $t_i$ is set equal to marginal congestion cost for each mobile resource), producing an efficient system-wide allocation of productive resources. Such a policy configuration would still be efficient and would yield the maximum net incomes for the totality of immobile resource owners in each locality, but would not generally yield maximum net incomes (or utilities) for each group individually. Hence, depending on the political process through which $t_i$ is selected, the equilibrium policy configurations and the system-wide efficiency of the equilibrium may be disturbed, even with many small jurisdictions. These complications suggest ways that further analysis of competition among governments in open economy settings can help to illuminate the efficiency and distributional implications of political institutions.[42]

### 1.5.2 The "Extent of the Market": Small Economies, Large Jurisdictions?

The underlying economic model of resource allocation and factor pricing presented in section 1.3.2 requires that there be two or more localities. The

41. As one example, a national or international policy that regulates the taxation of corporation incomes would affect the demand for capital by corporations in all jurisdictions. The incidence and welfare effects of such an agreement would depend on complement/substitute relationships between corporate capital and other mobile resources.

42. Although not directly focused on intergovernmental competition, studies by Hiscox (2001, 2002), Rogowski (1990), and others have explored how production technologies and resource mobility with heterogeneous productive resources can influence political coalition building. Similar approaches may also have much to reveal about policymaking at subnational levels.

discussion of endogenous policymaking presented in section 1.3.3, however, focuses on the case in which there are many such governments, each small or "atomistic" relative to the economy-wide capital market. Whether this is an economically important case, or whether jurisdictions are instead so "large" that changes in their policies have substantial effects on market prices in the "rest of the world," is perhaps debatable. As indicated in sections 1.2.2, 1.2.3, and 1.2.4, Appendix A, and the discussion immediately above, many economic and policy analyses presuppose that capital, labor, or both are "internationally mobile." Depending on the context, this may be taken to mean that resources can flow throughout the entire world, possibly with the exception of a limited number of isolated nations. Alternatively, labor, capital, or both might be mobile within large regions of the world that are isolated from the rest of the world (perhaps Europe or the Western Hemisphere), or, yet again, among just a handful of nations. In other contexts, one might suppose that competition involves only subnational governments (states within the US, say) or localities within a single state or province.

If the "market area" within which resources are mobile contains only a few jurisdictions, each of which is "large" relative to the market(s) for one or more mobile resources, the analysis of endogenous policy choice becomes far more complex than in the atomistic case, just as the analysis of oligopolistic/oligopsonistic competition among firms is much more complex than is the case with pure competition. The essence of the analytical difficulty can easily be seen from a consideration of the conditions for the preferred policy choices for each jurisdiction (8) and the system-wide equilibrium conditions (1), (2), and (3). When there are only a few large jurisdictions, each has a substantial effect on the equilibrium return to mobile resources (as shown in (4)), and the joint satisfaction of the conditions for a Nash noncooperative equilibrium in which each (large) jurisdiction chooses its most preferred policies is far from guaranteed and can only be assured under additional restrictions. Generally, theoretical models assume that there is only a single mobile resource, a single policy instrument, a single immobile representative agent in each jurisdiction, and only two (or perhaps several identical) jurisdictions. In addition, such models must also impose additional conditions on functional forms for preferences (often quasi-linear) or technologies (such as quadratic production functions that yield linear demand curves for mobile factors of production).[43]

Putting aside these theoretical hurdles, a substantial empirical literature analyzes strategic interactions among small numbers of governments (typically more than two, however), often focused on the estimation of policy reaction functions. Of course, by virtue of the government budget constraint,

43. See, e.g., Wildasin (1991), as well as Keen and Konrad (2013), who provide a wide-ranging survey. Rota-Graziosi (2019) and Taugourdeau and Ziad (2011) have demonstrated existence of equilibria under notably more satisfactory assumptions about production technologies.

even the very simplest models of fiscal competition must allow, whether implicitly or explicitly, for at least *two* policy instruments. For example, a major branch of literature on "tax competition" postulates that governments choose tax rates as strategic variables, viewing observed tax rates as a Nash noncooperative equilibrium in which each government optimizes its own policy, taking the policies of other governments as given.[44] These analyses assume, explicitly or implicitly, that public expenditures or other fiscal variables adjust "passively" to changes in tax rates. But this approach is not universal. Many studies postulate instead that governments choose *public expenditures* as strategic variables, with tax or other fiscal variables adjusting passively to ensure budget balance.[45]

The choice between these alternative modeling approaches (and others, not discussed here) is quite analogous to choosing between prices (Bertrand competition) and quantities (Cournot competition) as strategic variables in the analysis of duopolistic (or, more often, oligopolistic) competition among firms. As explained in standard textbooks in intermediate microeconomics, Bertrand and Cournot equilibria are quite different from one another. For essentially the same (technical) reasons, the same is true in the "duopolity" (or "oligopolity") context: Nash equilibria in tax rates are not the same as Nash equilibria in public expenditures (Wildasin 1988, 1991). Given a set of localities whose (possibly) strategic interactions are to be examined, one may postulate that strategy spaces consist either of tax rates or expenditures (or, in the spirit of conjectural variations, still more exotic possibilities), but it is (logically) impossible to postulate both.[46] For this reason, in order not to prejudge this important question, general terms such as "fiscal competition" may be preferred to more specific terms like "tax competition" or "welfare competition."

This analytical difficulty is most easily revealed in very simple models in which governments have only two policy instruments that are jointly subject to a government budget constraint. It by no means disappears, however—in fact, it becomes even more problematic—if one recognizes that almost

44. Brueckner and Saavedra (2001) analyze strategic tax rate setting by local governments in the Boston metropolitan area in a pioneering contribution to a literature that is now very large. See Agrawal et al. (2022) for a recent survey.

45. Case et al. (1993) and Williams (1966) follow this approach in analyzing benefit or other spillovers among governments. Studies of "welfare competition" (e.g., Brueckner 1991; Figlio et al. 1999) similarly treat welfare benefits as strategic variables. The history of local government redistribution in the UK, discussed earlier in section 1.2.1, continues to inspire new research; Brueckner (2023) finds evidence of strategic interaction among localities in 19th-century Britain.

46. There has been ongoing debate in the theoretical literature about the precise formulation of models of strategic interactions among governments, not only concerning the choices of strategic variables but also many other complicating features, usually in two-player games. See, for instance, Lockwood (2004) (comparing per-unit and ad valorem taxes); Hindriks and Nishimura (2017) and Ogawa (2013) (comparing Stackelberg and simultaneous-move games); and Keen and Konrad (2013) for still other game-theoretic considerations.

all governments have very many policy instruments at their disposal, as emphasized in section 1.4.3. Because governments exist for more than one period, one should also recognize that policy choices in one period are linked to those in other periods through intertemporal budget constraints. With so many policy instruments, distinguished by type of policy and date, what is the most meaningful way to define the strategy space? This question can be safely sidestepped when market areas are large and no individual government can influence the equilibrium prices of mobile resources—that is, the case of "perfect competition." How it should be resolved in cases of "imperfect competition" is a question that seems central to the analysis of competition for mobile resources among small numbers of governments, but one that so far eludes consensus.

There has been relatively little systematic consideration of how to define a market area (or, equivalently, a set of competing jurisdictions), other than on some a priori basis. (An analogous issue also arises in industrial organization in defining the "industry.") One might suppose that if "capital" and "labor" are internationally mobile, as has seemingly been confirmed in many policy contexts (section 1.2) and empirical analyses (section 1.5.1), then market areas are worldwide in scope. In this case, one might speculate that at most a handful of nations—the US, China, the EU nations collectively, or perhaps India—could be considered sufficiently large that their policies, individually, have "nonnegligible" effects on the worldwide equilibrium prices of at least some mobile resources. All subnational governments would then be "small jurisdictions" whose policies do not significantly affect equilibrium factor prices within their nations, much less the world economy, and they would not compete strategically with each other. In view of the many empirical studies that provide evidence of strategic interactions among subnational governments, whether in tax rates, public expenditures, or other policy instruments, this presents a puzzle that warrants further theoretical and empirical attention.[47]

47. The size of a "market area" need not be identical for every mobile resource. If capital is mobile throughout the world, virtually every national and subnational jurisdiction is "small" relative to the world capital market. However, some subset of jurisdictions, such as a group of local governments situated within a metropolitan area, may constitute a "local labor market" within which workers may switch places of employment relatively easily even if there are large hurdles to finding employment in other metro areas. In this case, one locality, such as a central city, may act as a monopsony buyer of labor from neighboring localities. If labor and capital are complementary inputs in production, taxation of central-city capital may drive down the "import price" of labor, to the benefit of central city residents. See Agrawal et al. (2022) and Wildasin (2014) for further discussion of this type of model. There are many other possibilities for such interjurisdictional interactions. For instance, the incidence of taxes on capital within a region that is small relative to the world capital market may nevertheless be borne (or "exported") to another "small" region if the two are linked through interindustry trade (e.g., Canada and the US, US states with upstream/downstream manufacturing linkages, or EU countries with high levels of interindustry integration [Wildasin 1993]).

### 1.5.3 Imperfect Resource Mobility: Moving Costs in Static Models

The determination of the size of the markets for mobile resources (or their degree of "integration") is closely related to what may seem at first to be rather different issues, such as the "costs" of resource mobility, the numbers and types of mobile and immobile resources (the factor aggregation problem), and the dynamic mechanisms through which the movement of resources takes place over time. If mobility costs are "sufficiently low," spatial arbitrage is perfect, and (net) factor prices must always be identical in all places at every instant of time, as shown in (3). Because this is clearly not literally true, one might infer that there is no spatial arbitrage and no resource mobility whatsoever, as is assumed in much of traditional closed-economy public finance. Of course, in that case, there is nothing to say about competition among governments, insofar as it is related to the mobility of productive resources.

The convenient polar extremes of perfect mobility (of at least one productive resource) and complete immobility have tended to dominate theoretical research, but few would wish to take too literally either of these idealized cases. Naturally, some degree of resource mobility is a sine qua non for the analysis of competition among governments, but this leaves open the meaning of "degree." The simplest way to incorporate mobility costs into a model of fiscal competition is to suppose that the movement of each unit of a mobile resource from one jurisdiction to another entails a uniform cost $c$. In this case, the spatial equilibrium condition (3) is altered slightly, and an economically meaningful distinction can (and must) now be made between initial and equilibrium allocations of mobile resources. Letting $k^0$ denote the former, and given a vector of policies $t$, the equilibrium allocation $k(t)$ and the return to the mobile resource $r$ on the external market must satisfy the market clearing/resource conservation condition (2) and, for all $i$,

(11) $k_i(t) - k_i^0 > 0 \rightarrow r = f_i'[k_i(t)] - t_i - c$ (open: inflow of mobile resource)

(12) $f_i'[k_i(t)] - t_i + c \geq r \geq f_i'[k_i(t)] - t_i - c$ (closed: zero flow of mobile resource)

(13) $k_i(t) - k_i^0 < 0 \rightarrow r = f_i'[k_i(t)] - t_i + c$ (open: outflow of mobile resource).

These conditions simply state that resource flows into or out of a jurisdiction only take place if net return differentials exceed the cost of relocation. Depending on the initial allocations, fiscal policies, and production technologies, satisfaction of these conditions may occur with resource flows between some but not all jurisdictions. Starting from any arbitrary policy vector $t$, small policy perturbations can readily be analyzed, just as in section 1.3.2. The main difference is simply that some jurisdictions are "isolated" from external markets by mobility costs. For them, small policy changes have no effect on their equilibrium stocks of the mobile resource or gross factor returns.[48]

The analysis of the political economy of fiscal competition becomes more complex in this case because otherwise-mobile resources may be "trapped" in their initial locations by the cost of moving. The returns to these resources are then no longer fixed (net of *c*) by perfect spatial arbitrage, and their owners therefore have incentives to influence local policies. As in the closed-economy case, the endogenously determined policies of all localities in a fiscal competition equilibrium depend upon how the political process resolves the conflicting interests of the owners of immobile and imperfectly mobile resources. If such an equilibrium exists, every locality is, at the margin, either "open," with inflows or outflows of the mobile resource, as shown in (11) and (13), or "closed," with no movement of the mobile resource, as shown in (12). If *c* is sufficiently small, the properties of an equilibrium with fiscal competition approximate those of the idealized case of costless mobility ($c = 0$).

A more general specification of moving costs or "attachment to place" relaxes the assumption of a uniform cost *c* and postulates instead that these costs differ idiosyncratically among individuals. Depending on the distribution of these idiosyncratic costs, a given utility or real-income differential between any pair of locations results in the relocation of some proportion of the population. Provided that the cost of moving is sufficiently high for some people, the equilibrium distribution of population among jurisdictions does not degenerate to a "corner solution" in which some jurisdictions are entirely empty. This remains true, even if changes in the distribution of population have no effect at all on market prices (wages, housing costs, or rates of return on capital and immobile resources). From the viewpoint of analytical simplicity, such an approach obviates the need to rely on market linkages to determine the equilibrium allocation of mobile resources via spatial arbitrage, as discussed in preceding sections, and it likewise suppresses consideration of the associated distributional, political economy, and other issues that arise with endogenous pricing. Which approach is preferable (and they are not mutually exclusive) may depend upon the questions under investigation. The key determinants of equilibrium locations in one case are distributions of unobservable idiosyncratic attributes whereas endogenously determined market prices play that role in the other. As a matter of interpretation, it is worth noting that measures of welfare or real incomes should, in either approach, treat moving costs, whether pecuniary or psychic, observable or unobservable, as real costs for those who incur them.

48. As described previously, it is formally straightforward to allow for many mobile resources by interpreting *k*, *r*, *t*, and *c*, as well as the amounts of immobile resources implicitly embedded in the production functions, as vectors of any desired dimensionality.

### 1.5.4 Imperfect Resource Mobility: Adjustment Costs in Dynamic Models

Although the introduction of moving costs allows meaningful comparisons to be made between initial and equilibrium allocations of mobile resources, they are not necessarily well-adapted to the analysis of interjurisdictional migration and investment *flows*. Such flows, by their nature, are measured by the amounts of resources (units of capital, units of human resources) that change locations *per unit of time*. Recalling the examples discussed in section 1.2, these resource flows may well take place over periods of years or even decades. In other instances they may occur much more rapidly. Liquid financial asset flows may take no longer than the duration of a proverbial mouse click, a modern manifestation of the impact of technological change on financial markets already thoroughly documented and analyzed by economic historians studying intercontinental gold markets at the advent of telegraphy (see, e.g., Hoag 2006 and O'Rourke and Williamson 1999). On the other hand, the process of site selection, regulatory approvals, and construction of major industrial plants takes years. The employment, output, wage, profit, and fiscal impacts of such investments may persist for decades, possibly (and presumably) varying at different rates over time.[49] The same is likely to be true for many other situations involving resource movements.[50] Comparative-statics analysis, which some would call "comparative steady state" analysis, can certainly be used to suggest some of the possible effects of resource mobility, but cannot come directly to grips with the intrinsically dynamic nature of complex and lengthy processes of adjustment.

To move toward dynamic modeling, recall that static equilibrium models, as in section 1.3, generally rely on some version of the spatial arbitrage condition (3) to characterize the demands for mobile resources in different locations. If the variable $k_i$ in a condition like (3) is interpreted literally as the amount of capital in locality $i$, it means that there is a single equilibrium quantity of capital that depends upon the system-wide equilibrium net rate

49. Construction of the Toyota Motor Manufacturing, Kentucky, Inc. plant in Georgetown, Kentucky, begun in 1986, is presently "Toyota's largest vehicle manufacturing plant in the world." (See details on Toyota's Kentucky plant at https://pressroom.toyota.com/facility/toyota-motor-manufacturing-kentucky-tmmk/.) This plant has subsequently been expanded, an example of a capital installation with ongoing net investment and long-term economic and fiscal impacts.

50. The Mariel boatlift of 1980 has been studied intensively by labor economists (Borjas 2017; Card 1990); the effect of a labor supply shock on wages, generally within the immediate aftermath of the boatlift, has been the primary focus of their attention. Recently, however, St. Clair (2024) has examined the impacts of the boatlift on local governments (Miami city, schools, and county) and their finances. This analysis indicates that the boatlift resulted in persistent (a decade and possibly longer in duration) and significant (20 percent or greater) increases in school district expenditures, accompanied by comparable increases in property tax revenues and intergovernmental transfers.

of return $r$ and the tax rate $t_i$. None of the variables that appear in this condition are explicitly time dependent, nor is the production function $f_i(k_i)$. Hence, $k_i$ is determined once and for all as a *time-independent* function of the *time-independent* variables $r$ and $t_i$ (or, in fact, of $r + t_i$). Properly speaking, then, this equation cannot be used to determine investment (whether gross or net of depreciation) in a durable input, which, to repeat, is a magnitude that is measured as a *flow* over time. Comparative-statics analyses based on equilibrium conditions like (3) thus cannot explain how *investment* depends on variables like $r$ or $t_i$: such conditions can only be used to determine the "long run" equilibrium *stock* of capital in an economy with unchanging policies and market conditions. Explicit distinctions between stocks and flows have of course long been a central elements in the theory of investment. It is now standard to postulate that changes in the stock of capital are costly and that this cost is an increasing function of the rate at which it changes, that is, of the *rate* of investment. Such modeling approaches naturally produce gradual (rather than instantaneous) adjustments to equilibrium stocks in response to changes in exogenous variables.[51]

Dynamic analysis of fiscal competition allows the study of several issues that cannot arise in static or atemporal models. First, and most obviously, a change in fiscal policy in any one small locality (as before, a locality whose policy choices have only very small effects on the system-wide net return to mobile resources) produces gradual rather than instantaneous changes in the allocation of mobile resources. For instance, if capital is the only mobile resource in the economy, a permanent increase in the tax rate $t_i$ in locality $i$ causes an outflow of capital that begins at the initiation of the policy change but extends through time.[52] As a result, the gross and net returns to capital and the immobile resources in that locality (given by their marginal productivities, which depend on factor stocks) and the flow of government revenue must also change gradually. The *rates of adjustment* for all of these variables are governed especially by the adjustment cost technology.[53]

The political-economy analysis of endogenous policymaking must also change in a dynamic model. When stocks of mobile resources can only

51. For readers not familiar with investment modeling, it is still instructive to review early contributions, such as the discussion found in Griliches (1967), Jorgenson (1967), and Tobin (1967). See Hayashi (1982) for analysis and valuable discussion of neoclassical adjustment-cost models.

52. Needless to say, "permanent" policy changes are theoretical devices, useful simplifications in dynamic analysis but no more realistic, if taken literally, than policy changes in comparative-statics/comparative steady-state analyses. In a pioneering study, Kehoe (1989) shows how competition for mobile capital can result in welfare-improving capital tax policies when governments cannot commit to future policies. In addition to time consistency, other issues naturally arise in dynamic models that have no static counterparts, but these are not discussed here for the sake of brevity.

53. In particular, the rate of capital outflow can vary from extremely rapid to very slow. In the former case, the results approximate those from the earlier comparative-statics analysis, whereas they approximate those from a closed-economy model in the latter case.

adjust gradually to policy changes, the owners of mobile resources are no longer indifferent to changes in the policies of small jurisdictions. Although the net return to the mobile resource must ultimately converge to the system-wide return $r$, a tax increase in a given locality can depress the net return for the mobile resource there for a possibly protracted period. Such an outcome bears some similarities to the section 1.5.3 analysis of imperfect mobility in static models: policy disagreements may arise similar to those in closed-economy settings, but exit options limit the degree to which local policies can burden the owners of imperfectly mobile resources. The static and dynamic cases differ in that exit choices occur within a single period (effectively, the only period) in the static case, whereas the exit choices occur gradually in the dynamic case.

To illustrate some of the implications of dynamic adjustments in fiscal competition, let us restrict attention to a single small jurisdiction $i$, which may impose a (positive, negative, or zero) tax on a single mobile resource, "capital." In order not to confuse notations, let $t$ denote time, a continuous variable, and let $\tau_t$ denote the tax rate imposed on capital at time $t$; because we are focusing on just one locality, we may ignore the $i$ subscript. To maintain comparability with the preceding static analysis, let us assume that the locality initially (i.e., at an arbitrary time $t = 0$) has a stock of capital $k_0$ that satisfies the spatial arbitrage condition (3), where, as before, $r$ is the externally given net rate of return on capital. This means that $r + \tau_0 = f'(k_0)$. An unanticipated change in the tax rate produces a long-run or steady-state equilibrium in which the spatial arbitrage condition is again satisfied, but at a new capital stock $k_\infty$. The spatial arbitrage condition can be used, just as before, to study the comparative-steady-state effects of local policy changes.

When changes in the stock of capital entail adjustment costs, however, a (permanent) change in fiscal policy at some arbitrary time $t = 0$ moves the local economy gradually toward a new steady state. The change in the capital stock at any time $t$, $\partial k_t / \partial \tau$, is initially very small (equal to 0 at time $t = 0$), but the *rate* of change—that is, the change in the *rate of investment*—is initially very high.[54] Consequently, the gross return to the immobile resource is unaffected at $t = 0$, but it falls as the capital stock (the complementary input) is reduced, declining in the long run as described in section 1.3.2. If at least some portion of the initial capital stock is owned by nonresidents of the locality, the immobile resource owners benefit, in present-value terms, from the imposition of some positive tax on (imperfectly) mobile capital: the "short run" gains from a local redistributive tax/transfer policy outweigh the "long run" losses, so that (8) no longer holds.

The analysis can be extended to allow for two imperfectly mobile resources, such as labor (possibly of a particular type, such as high-skilled or low-skilled workers) and capital, in addition to one immobile resource

54. The analytical details underlying this discussion appear in Wildasin (2003) and (2010a).

(or possibly more). Still focusing on just one locality, it remains true that an unanticipated policy change has no effect on resource stocks at the moment that it is initiated, and its impact on steady-state stocks still correspond to those that can be derived via comparative-statics analysis. The net return to both mobile resources is ultimately unaffected (strictly speaking, affected only negligibly) by the policy change, in accordance with (3). The long-run allocative effect of the policy depends on the substitute/complement relationships emphasized above (section 1.5.1).

However, from the viewpoint of "redistributive political economy," the comparative statics analysis is seriously misleading. To provide a concrete example, suppose that a new and permanent tax is imposed on capital and that the proceeds of the tax are redistributed to the other mobile resource, labor. The static analysis indicates that the owners of the mobile resources are indifferent to this policy but that the owners of the immobile resource are harmed by it and therefore would oppose it. The preferred local policy (the one chosen by the only party that is affected by it) is to set the tax, and the transfers that it finances, at zero. In a dynamic context, however, the situation is very different. For some period of time after this policy is instituted, the capital stock is not reduced by very much. For this reason, the gross returns to both capital and labor are also not affected very much during this period. If, as in the Cobb-Douglas case, capital and labor are complements, the outflow of capital that results from the tax would reduce gross wages somewhat, but only slightly; if instead capital and labor are sufficiently substitutable, the policy would raise the gross wage slightly. Most important, in the early stages of the policy, are the burdens imposed on capital and the transfers paid to labor, as these dominate any impacts on gross factor prices. Thus, this redistributive policy definitely harms capital owners and helps workers for some period of time. Gradually, the capital stock falls sufficiently to raise the gross return to capital by the amount of the tax and the gross wage falls by the amount of the transfer payments to labor, so that net factor returns approach their (unchanged) steady-state values. Because the owners of the mobile resources cannot adjust instantaneously to changes in policy, they now can gain or lose from policies about which they would otherwise be indifferent; the magnitude of these gains or losses are increased if adjustment costs are high and result in protracted periods of adjustment.

In this dynamic setting, the political economy of local policymaking with multiple, imperfectly mobile resources shares features suggested by the comparative-statics analysis of the open economy but it also shares features similar to those that arise in closed-economy models. Relatively little research has so far been undertaken in this direction, but further investigation may provide valuable guidance for the modeling of competitive policy setting, perhaps especially for the hundreds of thousands of "small" jurisdictions throughout the world.

## 1.6 Conclusion

In this chapter, the discussion of competition among governments has ranged widely, and readers will have seen that the subject, broadly conceived, touches upon many specialized branches of inquiry.

The policy-oriented overview of section 1.2 emphasizes that competition for mobile resources is not a matter that uniquely involves Tiebout-type movement of households searching for desired local public services at low cost, nor one that only relates to the movement of capital and business activities at the subnational or international levels, but also the movement of people among and within large regions, including nations and groups of nations. Resource flows among regions and their effects—on markets, incomes, and public finances—are far from a new phenomenon. They are associated with changes in tax, expenditure, debt, and regulatory policies and the evolution of the institutions of government through which policies are made.

Amid the multitude of complexities that arise in studying competition among governments, there is useful scope for many perspectives and types of analysis. Justifiably or not, economics traditionally places the operation of markets at center stage in the analysis of resource allocation, price determination, income distribution, welfare, and public policy. Section 1.3 follows this tradition by focusing on resource movements as (simultaneously determined) responses to and determinants of market conditions in different locations, a distinguishing feature of "open-economy" public finance and policy analysis. The very simplest of economic models shows how a policy change in one jurisdiction affects an entire system of open economies: their policies matter for the efficiency of resource allocation and the distribution of incomes. When individual jurisdictions are very "small" relative to the entire economic system, their policies individually are of small consequence but of great importance in aggregate. Furthermore, by creating economic linkages between markets within a jurisdiction and those external to it, resource mobility affects the distribution of economic rewards from local public policies. Insofar as economic payoffs are relevant for the actions of voters, business interests, landowners, politicians, and others involved in policymaking, openness to external markets affects desired policies and thereby the outcomes that emerge from the political process. In the highly simplified setup of section 1.3, this means that small jurisdictions opt to impose no net burden on freely mobile resources, nor do they offer any net subsidy to such resources. In brief, "perfect competition" among numerous small jurisdictions eliminates redistribution, cross-subsidies, or other forms of transfers between mobile and immobile resources or their owners.

The bare-bones model of section 1.3 can be modified and extended in several important directions, as shown in section 1.4. Many of the basic insights from section 1.3 continue to hold in more complex settings that allow for government provision of public goods and services, which may range from "purely public" (uncongestible) to "quasi-private" (provision of a unit of the service to one user precludes its use by another). In these contexts, it is possible that competition can result in "underprovision" of public services if governments are limited in the tax or other policy instruments at their disposal. On the other hand, if governments can apply suitable combinations of taxes, fees, charges, subsidies, regulations, and other policies, perfect competition may support efficient outcomes. The situation changes markedly when there are small numbers of jurisdictions, each sufficiently large that its policies perceptibly influence the market returns to mobile resources in the entire economic system. In such cases, game-theoretic strategic interactions must be considered in determining the policies chosen by individual governments and their efficiency and distributional consequences.

Needless to say, blanket assertions about the implications of competition among governments cannot rest simply on the analysis of idealized economic models. If taken too literally, idealized models—whether of the open-economy variety or the more traditional closed-economy types used in much of public finance and many other branches of economics—lend themselves to "demolition by caricature": it is often almost trivially easy, but not very useful, to find circumstances, empirically and in theory, in which their strongest implications fail to hold exactly. Meaningful assessments of the role and importance of competition among governments must be grounded on sophisticated interpretation and application of appropriate models. Section 1.5 draws attention to several fundamental questions that demand careful consideration: What does "competition" mean when there are many types of potentially mobile resources? Are the movements of these resources interdependent, and therefore jointly dependent on the multiple policies that apply to each, or do they proceed independently of one another? How does one determine the set of relevant policy instruments over which competing governments have control? How does one determine the geographical scope of the markets for mobile resources, and thus the set of competing jurisdictions? Are the market areas for each mobile resource identical or do they differ? Are some resources immobile in the "short run" but not in the "long run"? What are the fundamental determinants of the dynamic processes of resource movement, and over what time horizons do the policies of competitive governments extend? What are the determinants of the dynamics of policy adjustments, and how, if at all, are these related to the "degree of mobility" of productive resources?

Many additional questions are suggested, explicitly or implicitly, throughout this chapter. Relative to their closed-economy counterparts, "open-economy" perspectives on public economics and, more generally, on public policy analysis, require different analytical approaches, necessarily involving the consideration of multiple jurisdictions linked through external markets for productive resources. To an extent that varies over time, perhaps due to technological change and other fundamental factors, these markets may be global in some cases, possibly smaller in geographical scope in other cases, and in some cases entirely localized. The multiplicity of jurisdictions raises questions of an institutional nature that cannot be analyzed in frameworks that allow for only a single unit of government; these include not only "horizontal" interactions among governments but also "vertical" interactions. Indeed, competition for mobile resources may well affect the organizational structure of the entire public sector, as historical experience suggests, with different levels of government shedding, acquiring, and sharing revenue tools and programmatic functions, often within constitutional systems that are sometimes brittle, sometimes flexible, and of varying degrees of durability. An open-economy approach to public policy reveals issues for research that are highly relevant, timely, and deep.

**Acknowledgments**

This chapter is a substantially expanded version of "Open Economy Public Finance," a presentation at a 2021 NBER conference on Interjurisdictional Tax Competition. I am grateful to many colleagues and students for assistance in my research on this topic and to the editors for guidance in the preparation of this chapter. I retain responsibility for all errors. For acknowledgments, sources of research support, and disclosure of the author's material financial relationships, if any, please see https://www.nber.org/books-and-chapters/policy-responses-tax-competition/open-economy-public-finance-competition-among-governments.

## Appendix A

### *Some Illustrative Popular Accounts of Competition for Business*

The taxation of the incomes of multinational corporations has been the subject of considerable attention and debate and may serve as a first example of the issues that have arisen with respect to tax competition. For many years, some countries have opted for tax policies that afforded corporations the opportunity to reduce their tax burdens through carefully crafted investments, organizational structures, and accounting procedures (Hines 2010). These countries (both high income and less developed) have sometimes been characterized as potential "tax havens" that opportunistically (and perhaps unscrupulously) facilitate tax avoidance by businesses that engage in "tax-driven" transactions. Many policymakers and analysts have advocated reforms of corporate income tax policy so as to limit the scope and magnitude of such practices; for the past decade, many of these reform efforts have coalesced under the umbrella of the "base erosion and profit shifting" initiative of the OECD. The OECD plan is structured in two major parts or "pillars." Under Pillar One, a portion of the income of corporations can be taxed by countries from which they derive revenues, even if they are not "physically present" in those countries, an approach quite different from the OECD's previous and longstanding "permanent establishment" rule. Under Pillar Two, countries would impose a minimum tax rate of 15 percent on corporation income. Much of the motivation for the OECD plan seems to be to mitigate "harmful tax competition and a damaging 'race to the bottom' on corporate tax rates." At the same time, it is also supposed to support the use of "tax incentives" (a term similar in meaning to "tax expenditures") to describe purportedly "beneficial" targeted alterations of tax policies to promote economic and other policy objectives for specific purposes: "Jurisdictions will . . . be able to use the tax system to attract investment . . . , but the rules will discourage the use of damaging tax incentive policies." (OECD 2022, p. 6).[55]

As of 2021, some 130 countries had formally agreed to participate in at least some parts of the OECD program (see Joint Committee on Taxation [2023, Appendix] for the current state of play). The Netherlands, whose past policies have provided significant opportunities for multinational corporations to minimize their tax liabilities (e.g., the "Dutch sandwich" arrangement) has signed on to the OECD plan; in 2021, Dutch Deputy Finance Minister Vijlbrief remarked, "When the Americans initiate such a proposal . . . and get backing from big countries like Germany and France, it would be surprising if a deal isn't reached. Tax competition is becoming something of the past" (Baazil 2021). Others are more skeptical. For instance, also in 2021, Finance Minister Donohoe of Ireland (home of the "Double Irish" method) expressed the view that countries should be able to use tax policies to enhance investment, employment, and innovation. US President Biden endorsed a 15 percent minimum tax rate in 2021 (scaled back from an initial US position in favor of a 21 percent rate), but the US has yet to amend its tax laws to comply with the OECD plan. Some commentators (e.g., Stiglitz and Faccio 2023) have expressed serious doubts as to whether the US will ultimately sign on to it.

At the subnational level, the recent efforts of US municipalities to attract the second corporate headquarters of Amazon provide an interesting example of competition for large businesses. Some "238 U.S. cities sub-

55. A proper description of the base erosion and profit shifting project would necessitate an extensive discussion of many technical accounting and legal issues, largely avoided here in order to maintain a focus on more general economic policy questions. Of course, in this, as in all other policy settings, the regulatory implementations, procedures for adjudication of disputes, and judicial interpretations of treaties, statutes, and regulations can be of major importance.

mitted detailed bids" to the company (Jensen 2019), which, in 2018, had announced its intention to find a suitable location for its new facility; cities declared their eagerness to host the new headquarters by offering a rich mixture of tax reductions, regulatory relief, and publicly financed expenditure packages (e.g., infrastructure investments). In the end, Amazon chose to build its new headquarters ("HQ2") in Arlington, Virginia, in accordance with multiyear plans that involve undertakings by both the company and several local governments. The first phase of the construction was completed in 2023. (Due to the post-COVID-19 slowdown and ongoing reconsideration of remote work in the technology and other sectors, the second phase has been postponed.) The Amazon project has drawn criticism from various quarters.[56]

The Amazon project is merely one of the more visible illustrations of the intermingling of private and public activities and priorities that characterize many such "economic development" projects, which have become commonplace in the past several decades. It is noteworthy that they often entail fiscal and regulatory policy changes involving not only local governments but also state governments. In the Amazon case, the municipality of Arlington, the Arlington County government, and the state of Virginia all committed to supporting the project. It is noteworthy that the subsidies and tax relief that they have offered are contingent upon the company's attainment of key multiyear metrics, highlighting the intertemporal policy issues that often arise in fiscal competition.

Almost by their nature, large economic development projects must be targeted at specific locations, even if supported or initiated by higher-level governments. As one illustration, the state of New York, via its Empire State Development Corporation, has used its tax, expenditure, and regulatory policy instruments to support numerous projects in specific cities and regions within the state. One such project is a Tesla solar panel factory on a "brownfield" site in the "rust belt" city of Buffalo. As part of this project, beginning in 2014, the state built a large factory, which it leases to Tesla for $1 annually, and it also purchased $240 million of manufacturing equipment for use by Tesla. As of 2023, this project, part of the state's "Buffalo Billion"

56. Two (of many possible) critical statements convey the flavor of these criticisms, as seen contemporaneously. Jensen (2019) states, "For critics of the HQ2 process, or economic development practices in general, these bids offer clear evidence that businesses dominate the 'growth machine' in cities, with little role for the rest of civil society." Florida (2018) states that "the mayors and civic leaders of America's most liberal and economically dynamic cities have played right into the company's hands, rushing to subsidize one of the world's largest corporations and its richest man rather than building up their own local economic capacities and investing in pressing social needs. . . . It's time for residents and leaders of America's great cities to resist this kind of extortion, which ultimately undermines their own efforts at more inclusive and equitable development." On the positive side, supporters cite the potential benefits of the project, such as new opportunities (supported by public funds) for employment, educational facilities for a state university, and contributions by the company for "investments in affordable housing, education programs in schools and local nonprofits around Washington, DC" (Calvert 2023).

plan to improve the economy of the Buffalo region, has fallen far short of expectations for output, employment, and ancillary private sector development (Bykowicz and Mann 2023), and project auditors (KPMG 2018) wrote down the value of project assets by more than $1 billion. Such experiences naturally reinforce the opinions of critics of "fiscal competition," including the use of "tax incentives" and similar "industrial policy" initiatives generally, whether by subnational governments or at the national level.

# Appendix B

## *Brandeis, Liggett Co. vs. Lee, the "Race to the Bottom," and the Autonomy of "Courageous States"*

Commentators frequently allude to a so-called race to the bottom.[57] According to the *Oxford English Dictionary* and Bebchuk and Hamdani (2002), Cary (1974) was the first to use this phrase, which has now taken on a number of different meanings.

One aspect of competition among US states, emphasized by Cary and many other legal scholars, involves the competition for corporate charters, that is, a competition for business incorporations. Because laws of incorporation are regulatory policies, first and foremost, the competition for charters is not exactly equivalent to "tax competition." As discussed in the legal literature, there was significant liberalization in state laws governing business incorporations during the late 19th and early 20th centuries. Previously, states had commonly promulgated special statutes on a case-by-case basis, but they gradually shifted to "general" incorporation laws, which, in the words of Conard (1973, 632), "were introduced in the nineteenth century to permit people to organize themselves without the necessity of a special legislative act." The rapid growth of corporations in the early twentieth century made many uneasy, however, and some states acted to limit their expansion. Florida, in particular, imposed a system of graduated corporation annual license fees intended to curtail the growth of chain stores. Specifically, under Section 5 of the Florida statute, a corporation with 2 to 15 stores in any county would pay an annual fee of $10 per store, whereas a corporation with more than 75 stores would pay $40 per store. Moreover, if the corporation had 2 to 15 stores in different counties, it would pay not $10 but $15 per store, and a corporation with more than 75 stores located in different counties would have to pay $50 per store.

57. In 2023, the search phrase "race to the bottom" returned over 13 million references in a general Internet search and approximately 7,200 references on the JSTOR digital library of scholarly content, a number that many authors would be flattered to obtain.

A group of chain store owners challenged the constitutionality of these graduated fees, notably claiming that they were arbitrary and discriminatory. Upon reaching the Supreme Court, the majority rejected most of their arguments, but did agree that the state could not impose "unreasonable and arbitrary" differential fees on companies with establishments in multiple counties. In particular, the majority opinion stated that higher levies based on "the mere physical fact that . . . one [store] lies a few feet over a county line finds no foundation in reason or in any fact of business experience. There is no more reason for adopting the county line as the measure of the tax than there would be for taking ward lines in cities, or arbitrary lines drawn through the state regardless of county boundaries" (288 US 517).

Justice Brandeis dissented from this latter element of the majority opinion, declaring the entirety of Florida's "Anti-Chain Store Law" to be constitutional. According to Brandeis, "Whether the corporate privilege shall be granted or withheld is always a matter of state policy." States have the authority to address the "harm apprehended or experienced" due to business incorporations, whether by "revoking the corporate privilege . . . [or] by imposing . . . the handicap of higher, discriminatory license fees" such as those in Florida. Furthermore, "Whether the citizens of Florida are wise in seeking to discourage the operation of chain stores is, obviously, a matter with which this Court has no concern. Nor need it . . . consider whether the differences in license fees employed to effect such discouragement are inherently reasonable, since [firms] are at liberty to refuse to pay the compensation demanded for the corporate privilege and withdraw from the state, if they consider the price more than the privilege is worth."

These statements, which highlight the tradeoffs faced by states as they compete for capital, are very much in the spirit of sections 1.3 and 1.4 above. Brandeis here indicates not only that states are free to tax and regulate corporations as they see fit, but that the freedom to relocate affords the owners of capital all the protection they need from whatever burdens states may impose upon them. For their parts, it is up to the states to weigh the benefits and costs of alternative policies, recognizing that corporations can locate elsewhere if desired. In short, competition among the states is built into the Constitution, and it is up to the states and corporations to live with the consequences.

These remarks are interesting enough, but even more striking is the analysis employed by Brandeis in his further discussion of the prerogatives of states to "regulate" corporations. As he views the US experience, "Incorporation for business was commonly denied long after it had been freely granted for religious, educational, and charitable purposes. It was denied because of fear. Fear of encroachment upon the liberties and opportunities of the individual. Fear of the subjection of labor to capital. Fear of monopoly. Fear that the absorption of capital by corporations, and their perpetual life, might bring evils similar to those which attended mortmain. There was a sense of some insidious menace inherent in large aggregations of capital, particularly when held by corporations."

In Brandeis's view, states established general laws of incorporation not because "the apprehension of corporate domination had been overcome," but rather to avoid "the scandals and favoritism incident to special incorporation" and as "an expression of the desire for equality of opportunity." To his regret, however, states progressively relaxed previous restrictions on incorporation,

> due not to their conviction that maintenance of the restrictions was undesirable in itself, but to the conviction that it was futile to insist upon them, because local restriction would be circumvented by foreign incorporation. Indeed, local restriction seemed worse than futile. Lesser states, eager for the revenue derived from the traffic in charters, had removed safeguards from their own incorporation laws. Companies were early formed to provide charters for corporations in states where the cost was lowest and the laws least restrictive. The states joined in advertising their wares. *The race was one not of diligence, but of laxity*. [Emphasis added.] Incorporation under such laws was possible, and the great industrial states yielded in order not to lose wholly the prospect of the revenue and the control incident to domestic incorporation.

Here we see at its inception the use of the term "race"—if not literally "to the bottom"—to characterize competition among governments.

Brandeis evidently disapproves of undue liberalization of state laws of incorporation, and, accordingly, is sympathetic to state policies that bring corporations under tighter control. In *Liggett*, he sees the state of Florida acting on behalf of

> the individual retailers of Florida [who] are engaged in a struggle to preserve their independence—perhaps a struggle for existence. The citizens of the state, considering themselves vitally interested in this seemingly unequal struggle, have undertaken to aid the individual retailers by subjecting the owners of multiple stores to the handicap of higher license fees. They may have done so merely in order to preserve competition. But their purpose may have been a broader and deeper one. They may have believed that the chain store, by furthering the concentration of wealth and of power and by promoting absentee ownership, is thwarting American ideals; that it is making impossible equality of opportunity; that it is converting independent tradesmen into clerks, and that it is sapping the resources, the vigor, and the hope of the smaller cities and towns. . . . The purpose of the Florida statute is not, like ordinary taxation, merely to raise revenue. Its main purpose is social and economic. The chain store is treated as a thing menacing the public welfare. The aim of the statute, at the lowest, is to preserve the competition of the independent stores with the chain stores; at the highest, its aim is to eliminate altogether the corporate chain stores from retail distribution.

Brandeis's opinion continues in this vein, citing the many and profound evils of chain stores and large corporations in general:

> There is a widespread belief that the existing unemployment is the result, in large part, of the gross inequality in the distribution of wealth and income which giant corporations have fostered; that, by the control which the few have exerted through giant corporations, individual initiative and effort are being paralyzed, creative power impaired, and human happiness lessened; that the true prosperity of our past came not from big business, but through the courage, the energy, and the resourcefulness of small men; that only by releasing from corporate control the faculties of the unknown many, only by reopening to them the opportunities for leadership, can confidence in our future be restored and the existing misery be overcome, and that only through participation by the many in the responsibilities and determinations of business can Americans secure the moral and intellectual development which is essential to the maintenance of liberty. If the citizens of Florida share that belief, I know of nothing in the federal Constitution which precludes the state from endeavoring to give it effect and prevent domination in intrastate commerce by subjecting corporate chains to discriminatory license fees. To that extent, the citizens of each state are still masters of their destiny.

In the pursuit of these goals, Brandeis finds that Florida is free to tax corporations as it sees fit, even (contrary to the majority opinion) by applying differentially higher taxes on multicounty chain stores.

It is pertinent to note that only one year prior to *Liggett v. Lee*, Brandeis had delivered an opinion in *New State Ice Co. v. Liebmann*, 285 U.S. 262 (1932), which saw the birth of another resonant phrase. Here, Brandeis championed state autonomy on the grounds that states ought to have great latitude to "experiment" with different policies, that "denial of the right to experiment may be fraught with serious consequences to the nation," and that "a single courageous State may, if its citizens choose, serve as a laboratory; and try novel social and economic experiments without risk to the rest of the country." The concept of states as "laboratories of federalism" has subsequently become very familiar to students of federalism. It may thus be unsurprising that Brandeis, as an acknowledged defender of policy experimentation by "courageous" states, was disinclined to curtail Florida's autonomy in the regulation of corporations in the Florida chain-store case, even as he may have been dismayed by the policy choices of other "experimenting" states who engaged in a "race to laxity."

Taking these two opinions together, Brandeis clearly finds a high degree of state policy autonomy to be justified under the US Constitution. Prepared as he was to recognize the freedom of states to chart their own policy paths, would he also have supported their freedom to coordinate policies, if desired? Such coordination could, after all, curtail the "liberty [of corporations] to refuse to pay the compensation demanded for the corporate privilege and withdraw if they consider the price more than the privilege is worth." As noted in Appendix A, the OECD (2022) cites "harmful tax competition, and a damaging 'race-to-the-bottom' on corporate tax rates" as a justification for its Pillar Two global corporate income minimum tax rate. Because the US has maintained one of the highest statutory tax rates of any OECD country, Brandeis, one can only suppose, would have strongly defended "rate autonomy" for the US today, so that its citizens could remain "masters of their own destiny." But he would presumably also have sympathized with the OECD and other observers that such autonomy is less welcome when states or countries use it to offer lower tax rates. It is intriguing to ponder whether Brandeis would have approved of international agreements to set minimum tax rates and whether he would have been concerned to protect the freedom of corporations from such "cooperation" (some would say "collusion") by taxing authorities. How would he have assessed the right of any nation, one of the world's "laboratories," to pursue its own path by setting low corporation income tax rates?

## References

Adema, W. 2000. "Revisiting Real Social Spending Across Countries: A Brief Note." *OECD Economic Studies* 30: 191–97.

Adema, W., P. Fron, and M. Ladaique. 2014. "How Much Do OECD Countries Spend on Social Protection and How Redistributive Are Their Tax/Benefit Systems?" *International Social Security Review* 67: 1–25.

Agersnap, O., A. Jensen, and H. Kleven. 2020. "The Welfare Magnet Hypothesis: Evidence from an Immigrant Welfare Scheme in Denmark." *AER: Insights 2020*: 527–42.

Agrawal, David R., and Jan K. Brueckner. 2023. "Taxes and Telework: The Impacts of State Income Taxes in a Work-from-Home Economy." Working paper.

Agrawal, D. R., J. Brueckner, and M. Brülhart. 2023. "Fiscal Federalism in the 21st Century." Working paper.

Agrawal, D. R., and D. Foremny. 2018. "Fiscal Decentralisation and Mobility: Evidence from Spain's Income Tax System." *Ifo Dice Report* 10: 38–44.

Agrawal, D. R., and D. Foremny. 2019. "Relocation of the Rich: Migration in Response to Top Tax Rate Changes from Spanish Reforms." *The Review of Economics and Statistics* 2019: 214–32.

Agrawal, D. R., D. Foremny, and C. Martinez-Toledano. 2020. "Paraisos Fiscales, Wealth Taxation, and Mobility." World Inequality Lab Working Paper 2020–26.

Agrawal, D. R., and W. H. Hoyt. 2017. "Commuting and Taxes: Theory, Empirics and Welfare Implications." *Economic Journal* 128: 2969–3007.

Agrawal, D. R., W. H. Hoyt, and J. D. Wilson. 2022. "Local Policy Choice: Theory and Empirics." *Journal of Economic Literature* 60: 1378–455.

Akcigit, U., S. Baslandze, and S. Stantcheva. 2016. "Taxation and the International Mobility of Inventors." *American Economic Review* 106: 2930–81.

Albouy, D. 2009. "The Unequal Geographic Burden of Federal Taxation." *Journal of Political Economy* 117: 635–67.

Albouy, D. 2016. "What Are Cities Worth? Land Rents, Local Productivity, and the Total Value of Amenities." *The Review of Economics and Statistics* 98: 477–87.
Auerbach, A. J., L. J. Kotlikoff, and W. Leibfritz, eds. 1999. *Generational Accounting Around the World*. University of Chicago Press.
Baazil, D. 2021. "Global Tax Gains Momentum with Dutch Minister Seeing Summer Deal." *Bloomberg*, April 20.
Bebchuk, L. A., and A. Hamdani. 2002. "Vigorous Race or Leisurely Walk: Reconsidering the Competition over Corporate Charters." *Yale Law Journal* 112: 553–615.
Boadway, R. W., and A. Shah. 2009. *Fiscal Federalism: Principles and Practice of Multiorder Governance*. Cambridge University Press.
Bonham, C., E. Fujii, E. Im, and J. Mak. 1995. "The Impact of the Hotel Room Tax: An Interrupted Time Series Approach." *National Tax Journal* 45: 433–41.
Borjas, G. 1999. "Immigration and Welfare Magnets." *Journal of Labor Economics* 17: 607–37.
Borjas, G. 2003. "The Labor Demand Curve is Downward Sloping: Reexamining the Impact of Immigration on the Labor Market." *The Quarterly Journal of Economics* 118: 1335–74.
Borjas, G. J. 2017. "The Wage Impact of the Marielitos: A Reappraisal." *ILR Review* 70: 1077–110.
Boustan, L. P. 2016. *Competition in the Promised Land: Black Migrants in Northern Cities and Labor Markets*. Princeton University Press.
Bradford, D. F. 1978. "Factor Prices May Be Constant but Factor Returns Are Not." *Economics Letters* 1: 199–203.
Brennan, G., and J. M. Buchanan. 1980. *The Power to Tax: Analytical Foundations of a Fiscal Constitution*. Cambridge University Press.
Brown, H. G. 1924. *The Economics of Taxation*. Holt.
Brueckner, J. K. 1991. "Voting with Capitalization." *Regional Science and Urban Economics* 21: 453–67.
Brueckner, J. K. 2023. "Is Strategic Interaction Among Governments Just a Modern Phenomenon? Evidence on Welfare Competition under Britain's 19th-Century Poor Law." *International Tax and Public Finance* 30: 879–912.
Brueckner, J. K., and M. S. Joo.1991. "Voting with Capitalization." *Regional Science and Urban Economics Urban Economics* 21: 453–67.
Brueckner, J. K., and L. A. Saavedra. 2001. "Do Local Governments Engage in Strategic Property-Tax Competition?" *National Tax Journal* 54(2): 203–30.
Brülhart, M., J. Gruber, M. Krapf, and K. Schmidheiny. 2022. "Behavioral Responses to Wealth Taxes: Evidence from Switzerland." *American Economic Journal: Economic Policy* 14: 111–50.
Bykowicz, J., and T. Mann. 2023. "New York State Built Elon Musk a $1 Billion Factory. 'It Was a Bad Deal.'" *Wall Street Journal*, July 6.
Calvert, S. 2023. "Amazon HQ2 Delay Isn't a Concern, Northern Virginia Officials Say." *Wall Street Journal*, March 4.
Cannan, E. 1912. *The History of Local Rates in England*. P.S. King & Son.
Card, D. 1990. "The Impact of the Mariel Boatlift on the Miami Labor Market." *ILR Review* 43: 245–57.
Cary, W. L. 1974. "Federalism and Corporate Law: Reflections Upon Delaware." *Yale Law Journal* 83: 663–705.
Case, A. C., H. S. Rosen, and J. R. Hines Jr. 1993. "Budget Spillovers and Fiscal Policy Interdependence: Evidence from the States." *Journal of Public Economics* 52: 285–307.
Chirinko, R., and D. Wilson. 2006. "State Investment Tax Incentives: What Are

the Facts?" *National Tax Association: Proceedings of 99th Annual Conference on Taxation*, 36–44.
Chirinko, R., and D. Wilson. 2008. "State Investment Tax Incentives: A Zero-Sum Game?" *Journal of Public Economics* 92: 2362–84.
Chirinko, R., and D. Wilson. 2017. "Tax Competition Among US States: Racing to the Bottom or Riding on a Seesaw?" *Journal of Public Economics* 155: 147–63.
Chirinko, R., and D. Wilson. 2022. "Fiscal Policies for Job Creation and Innovation: The Experiences of US States." CESifo Working Paper 10158.
Conard, A. F. 1973. "An Overview of the Laws of Corporations." *Michigan Law Review* 71: 621–90.
Davis, M. A. 2009. "The Price and Quantity of Land by Legal Form of Organization in the United States." *Regional Science and Urban Economics* 39: 350–59.
Davis, M. A., and J. Heathcote. 2007. "The Price and Quantity of Residential Land in the United States." *Journal of Monetary Economics* 54: 2595–620.
Deng, P., and R. Schoeb. 2024. "Group-Specific Redistribution, Inequality, and Subjective Well-Being in China." *The Review of Income and Wealth* 70: 862–82.
Dillon, J. F. 1872. *Treatise on the Law of Municipal Corporations*. James Cockcroft & Co.
Dustman, C., U. Schönberg, and J. Stuhler. 2016. "The Impact of Immigration: Why Do Studies Reach Such Different Results?" *Journal of Economic Perspectives* 30: 31–56.
Dustman, C., and T. Frattini. 2014. "The Fiscal and Welfare Effects of Immigration: Introduction." *Economic Journal* 124: F565–F568.
Feldman, D. 2003. "Migrants, Immigrants, and Welfare from the Old Poor Law to the Welfare State." *Transactions of the Royal Historical Society* 13: 79–104.
Figlio, D. N., V. W. Kolpin, and W. Reid. 1999. "Do States Play Welfare Games?" *Journal of Urban Economics* 46: 437–54.
Fischel, W. A. 2001. *The Homevoter Hypothesis: How Home Values Influence Local Government Taxation, School Finance, and Land-Use Policies*. Harvard University Press.
Fischel, W. A. 2006. "Footloose at Fifty: An Introduction to the Tiebout Anniversary Essays." In *The Tiebout Model at Fifty: Essays in Public Economics in Honor of Wallace Oates*, edited by W. A. Fischel, 1–20. Lincoln Institute of Land Policy.
Giulietti, C. 2014. "Welfare Benefits Are Not a Key Determinant of Migration." *IZA World of Labor*, 1–10.
Greene, K. V., W. B. Neenan, and C. D. Scott. 1974. *Fiscal Interactions in a Metropolitan Area*. Heath.
Florida, R. 2018. "The Hypocrisy of Amazon's HQ2 Process." *Bloomberg*, May 10.
Griliches, Z. 1967. "Comment." In *Determinants of Investment Behavior*, edited by R. Ferber, 160–62. National Bureau of Economic Research.
Hanson, G., P. Orrenius, and M. Zavodny. 2023. "US Immigration from Latin America in Historical Perspective." *Journal of Economic Perspectives* 37: 199–222.
Harberger, A. C. "The Incidence of the Corporation Income Tax." *Journal of Political Economy* 70: 215–40.
Hayashi, F. 1982. "Tobin's Marginal *q* and Average *q*: A Neoclassical Interpretation." *Econometrica* 50: 213–24.
Hilber, C. A. L., and C. Mayer. 2009. "Why Do Households Without Children Support Local Public Schools? Linking House Price Capitalization to School Spending." *Journal of Urban Economics* 65: 74–90.
Hindriks, J., and Y. Nishimura. 2017. "Equilibrium Leadership in Tax Competition Models with Capital Ownership: A Rejoinder." *International Tax and Public Finance* 24: 338–49.

Hines, J. R. Jr. 2010. "Treasure Islands." *Journal of Economic Perspectives* 24: 103–26.
Hiscox, M. J. 2001. *International Trade and Political Conflict: Commerce, Coalitions, and Mobility*. Princeton University Press.
Hiscox, M. J. 2002. "Commerce, Coalitions, and Factor Mobility: Evidence from Congressional Votes on Trade Legislation." *American Political Science Review* 96: 593–608.
Hoag, C. 2006. "The Atlantic Telegraph Cable and Capital Market Information Flow." *The Journal of Economic History* 66: 342–53.
Holzer, H. 2019. *Immigration and the US Labor Market: A Look Ahead*. Migration Policy Institute.
Jensen, N. M. 2019. "Five Economic Development Takeaways from the Amazon HQ3 Bids." Brookings Institution, March 4.
Joint Committee on Taxation. 2023. *Possible Effects of Adopting the OECD's Pillar Two, Both Worldwide and in the United States*. Joint Committee on Taxation.
Jorgenson, D. W. 1967. "The Theory of Investment Behavior." In *Determinants of Investment Behavior*, edited by R. Ferber, 129–55. National Bureau of Economic Research.
Keen, M., and K. Konrad. 2013. "The Theory of International Tax Competition and Coordination." In *Handbook of Public Economics*, vol. 5, edited by A. J. Auerbach, R. Chetty, M. Feldstein, and E. Saez, 257–328. Elsevier.
Keen, M., and D. E. Wildasin. 2004. "Pareto Efficient International Taxation." *American Economic Review* 94: 259–75.
Kehoe, P. J. 1989. "Policy Cooperation Among Benevolent Governments May Be Undesirable." *The Review of Economic Studies* 56: 289–96.
Kleven, H., C. Landais, M. Munoz, and S. Stantcheva. 2020. "Taxation and Migration: Evidence and Policy Implications." *Journal of Economic Perspectives* 34: 119–42.
Kleven, H. C. Landais, and E. Saez. 2013. "Taxation and International Migration of Superstars: Evidence from the European Football Market." *American Economic Review* 103: 1892–924.
Kotlikoff, L. J. 1993. *Generational Accounting: Knowing Who Pays and When for What We Spend*. Free Press.
KPMG. 2018. "Fort Schuyler Management Corporation: Consolidated Financial Statements, June 30, 2018." http://www.ftsmc.org/annual-audited-financial-statements.
Lockwood, B. 2004. "Competition in Unit vs. Ad Valorem Taxes." *International Tax and Public Finance* 11: 763–72.
McLure, C. M. "The Inter-Regional Incidence of General Regional Taxes." *Public Finance/Finances Publiques* 24: 457–83.
Mieszkowski, P. M. 1969. "Tax Incidence Theory: The Effects of Taxes on the Distribution of Income." *Journal of Economic Literature* 7: 1103–124.
Mieszkowski, P. M. 1972. "The Property Tax: An Excise Tax or a Profits Tax?" *Journal of Public Economics* 1 (1): 73–96.
Moretti, E., and D. Wilson. 2017. "The Effect of State Taxes on the Geographical Location of Top Earners: Evidence from Star Scientists." *American Economic Review* 107: 1859–930.
Mundell, R. A. 1957. "International Trade and Factor Mobility." *American Economic Review* 47: 321–35.
Oates, W. E. 1969. "The Effects of Property Taxes and Local Public Spending on Property Values: An Empirical Study of Tax Capitalization and the Tiebout Hypothesis." *Journal of Political Economy* 77: 957–71.

Oates, W. E. 1972. *Fiscal Federalism*. Harcourt, Brace, Jovanaovich.
Oates, W. E. 2006. "The Many Faces of the Tiebout Model." In *The Tiebout Model at Fifty: Essays in Public Economics in Honor of Wallace Oates*, edited by W. A. Fischel, 21–45. Lincoln Institute of Land Policy.
Oates, W. E. 2008. "On the Evolution of Fiscal Federalism: Theory and Institutions." *National Tax Journal* 61 (2): 313–34.
OECD (Organisation for Economic Co-operation and Development). 2022. *Tax Incentives and the Global Minimum Corporate Tax: Reconsidering Tax Incentives after the GloBE Rules*. OECD Publishing.
OECD (Organisation for Economic Co-operation and Development). 2023a. Foreign-Born Population (indicator). Accessed on October 14, 2023. doi: 10.1787/5a368e1b-en.
OECD (Organisation for Economic Co-operation and Development). 2023b. *Social Expenditure (SOCX) Update 2023: Private Social Expenditure and the Influence of Tax Systems*. https://web-archive.oecd.org/temp/2024-06-24/63248-expenditure.htm.
OECD (Organisation for Economic Co-operation and Development). 2023c. Social Spending (indicator). Accessed on October 15, 2023. https://doi.org/10.1787/7497563b-en.
OECD/EU (Organisation for Economic Co-operation and Development/European Union). 2018. *Settling In 2018: Indicators of Immigrant Integration*. OECD Publishing.
Ogawa, H. 2013. "Further Analysis on Leadership in Tax Competition: The Role of Capital Ownership." *International Tax and Public Finance* 20: 474–84.
Organ, P. R. 2022. "Citizenship and Taxes." *International Tax and Public Finance* 31: 404–53. https://doi.org/10.1007/s10797-022-09767-5.
O'Rourke, K. H., and J. G. Williamson. 1999. *Globalization and History*. MIT Press.
Peterson, P. E., and M. C. Rom. 1990. *Welfare Magnets: The Case for a New National Standard*. Brookings Institution.
Preston, I. 2014. "The Effect of Immigration on Public Finances." *Economic Journal* 124: F569–F592.
Rogowski, R. 1990. *Commerce and Coalitions: How Trade Affects Domestic Political Alignments*. Princeton University Press.
Rose, M. 1976. "Settlement, Removal and the New Poor Law." In *The New Poor Law in the Nineteenth Century*, edited by D. Fraser, 25–44. MacMillan.
Rosen, S. 1979. "Wage-Based Indexes of Urban Quality of Life." In *Current Issues in Urban Economics*, edited by P. Mieszkowski and M. Straszheim, 74–104. Johns Hopkins University Press.
Rota-Graziosi, G. 2019. "The Supermodularity of the Tax Competition Game." *Journal of Mathematical Economics* 83: 25–35.
Saunoris, J. W. 2012. "Three Essays on Fiscal Federalism and the Role of Intergovernmental Transfers." PhD diss., University of Kentucky.
Scheve, K., and M. Slaughter. 2001. "Labor Market Competition and Individual Preferences over Immigration Policy." *The Review of Economics and Statistics* 83: 133–45.
Sinn, H. W. 1995. "Staggering Along: Wages Policy and Investment Support in East Germany." *Economics of Transition* 3: 403–26.
Sinn, H. W. 2002. "Germany's Economic Unification: An Assessment after Ten Years." *Review of International Economics* 10: 113–28.
Slattery, C., and O. Zidar. 2020. "Evaluating State and Local Business Incentives." *Journal of Economic Perspectives* 34: 90–118.
St. Clair, T. 2024. "The Fiscal Effects of Immigration on Local Governments: Revisiting the Mariel Boatlift." *Regional Science and Urban Economics* 109: 104053.

Stigler, G. J. 1957. "The Tenable Range of Functions of Local Government." In Joint Economic Committee, US Congress, *Federal Expenditure Policy for Economic Growth and Stability*, 213–19. USGPO.
Stiglitz, J. E., and T. Faccio. 2023. "The Global Minimum Corporate Tax Needs More Work." Roosevelt Institute.
Taugourdeau, E., and A. Ziad. 2011. "On the Existence of Nash Equilibria in an Asymmetric Tax Competition Game." *Regional Science and Urban Economics* 41: 439–45.
Tian, Y. 2024. "International Trade Liberalization and Domestic Institutional Reform: Effects of WTO Accession on Chinese Internal Migration Policy." *The Review of Economics and Statistics* 106: 794–813.
Tiebout, C. M. 1956. "A Pure Theory of Local Expenditures." *Journal of Political Economy* 64 (5): 416–24.
Tobin, J. 1967. "Comment." In *Determinants of Investment Behavior*, edited by R. Ferber, 156–60. National Bureau of Economic Research.
UN (United Nations). 2017. *The Impact of Population Momentum on Future Population Growth*. United Nations.
UN (United Nations). 2019. *International Migration 2019*. United Nations.
Vickrey, W. W. 1965. "General and Specific Financing of Urban Services." In *Public Expenditure Decisions in the Urban Community*, edited by H. G. Schaller. Routledge.
Wallis, J. J. 1984. "The Birth of the Old Federalism: Financing the New Deal, 1932–1940." *Journal of Economic History* 44: 139–59.
Wildasin, D. E. 1977. "Production Efficiency in Tax-Distorted Economies with Multiple Revenue Constraints." Working paper.
Wildasin, D. E. 1983. "The Welfare Effects of Intergovernmental Grants in an Economy with Independent Jurisdictions." *Journal of Urban Economics* 13: 147–64.
Wildasin, D. E. 1984. "The Welfare Effects of Intergovernmental Grants with Distortionary Local Taxes: A Simple General Equilibrium Analysis." *Journal of Public Economics* 25: 103–25.
Wildasin, D. E. 1988. "Nash Equilibria in Models of Fiscal Competition." *Journal of Public Economics* 35: 229–40.
Wildasin, D. E. 1991. "Some Rudimentary 'Duopolity' Theory." *Regional Science and Urban Economics* 21: 393–421.
Wildasin, D. E. 1993. "Fiscal Competition and Interindustry Trade." *Regional Science and Urban Economics* 23: 369–99.
Wildasin, D. E. 2003. "Fiscal Competition in Space and Time." *Journal of Public Economics* 87: 2571–88.
Wildasin, D. E. 2004. "The Institutions of Federalism: Toward an Analytical Framework." *National Tax J.* 57: 247–72.
Wildasin, D. E. 2006. "Comments." *National Tax Association: Proceedings of 99th Annual Conference on Taxation*, 45–49.
Wildasin, D. E. 2007. "Pre-emption: Federal Statutory Intervention in State Taxation." *National Tax Journal* 60: 649–62.
Wildasin, D. E. 2009. "Public Finance in an Era of Global Demographic Change: Fertility Busts, Migration Booms, and Public Policy." In *Skilled Immigration Today: Problems, Prospects, Policies*, edited by J. Bhagwati and G. Hanson. Oxford University Press.
Wildasin, D. E. 2010a. "Fiscal Competition for Imperfectly-Mobile Labor and Capital: A Comparative Dynamic Analysis." *Journal of Public Economics* 95: 1312–21.
Wildasin, D. E. 2010b. "Intergovernmental Transfers to Local Governments." In *Municipal Revenue and Land Policies*, edited by G. K. Ingram and Y.-H. Hong, 47–76. Lincoln Institute of Land Policy.

Wildasin, D. E. 2014. "Strategic Interactions Among Atomistic Governments in Small and Open Metropolitan Areas." Working paper.
Wildasin, D. E. 2021. "Open Economy Public Finance." *National Tax Journal* 74 (2): 467–90.
Williamson, J. G. 1998. "Globalization, Labor Markets and Policy Backlash in the Past." *Journal of Economic Perspectives* 12: 51–72.
Wilson, J. D. 1999. "Theories of Tax Competition." *National Tax Journal* 52 (2): 269–304.
Zi, Y. 2017. "Trade Liberalization and the Great Labor Reallocation." *American Economic Review*.
Zodrow, G. R., and P. M. Mieszkowski. 1986. "Pigou, Tiebout, Property Taxation, and the Underprovision of Local Public Goods." *Journal of Urban Economics* 19 (3): 356–70.

# 2

# Subsidy Competition as an Auction

Cailin Slattery

In 2008, Volkswagen decided to locate a new assembly plant in Chattanooga, Tennessee. Volkswagen received a subsidy of over $550 million, the result of a fierce competition between multiple states to win the new plant and associated jobs and investment—the neighboring state of Alabama offered at least $400 million. This practice of competing for plants and headquarters locations is prevalent in the United States, where there have been hundreds of large discretionary deals in the past 15 years, with notable recent examples including Amazon HQ2, the GE headquarters in Boston, and Tesla's gigafactories in Nevada and Texas.

Is subsidy giving good policy? Researchers want to be able to evaluate the practice of offering discretionary subsidies and compare this to counterfactual regimes with regulations on subsidies. Two challenges make this a particularly difficult exercise. First, there are data limitations. Ideally, the researcher would observe the set of subsidy offers a firm receives, and then use that information to study the firm's location choice. These data are rarely available, and instead the researcher will observe the subsidy in the winning location, if that. The second issue is that the subsidy is an equilibrium outcome. State and local governments compete with subsidies and the firm makes a location decision, which is a function of the subsidy offers and the location characteristics. The location the firm would have chosen in absence of a subsidy is unknown.[1]

Cailin Slattery is an assistant professor of business and public policy at UC Berkeley's Haas School of Business.

1. In many ways this is similar to classic models of tax competition. The essential difference is that the government chooses a firm-specific tax (subsidy), instead of setting the tax for all firms in the jurisdiction. However, some of the core tensions remain: tax rates are in equilibrium and the tax base in absence of tax differentials is not observable.

Consider the Volkswagen deal in 2008. The researcher observes the corporation locating in Chattanooga for $550 million. This is the result of Volkswagen's location decision: some function that includes the final subsidy offer but also the local characteristics that dictate how profitable the company will be at that specific site. The observed subsidy is also a function of Tennessee's willingness to pay for attracting Volkswagen to that location, the number of other competitors there were for the plant, and the payoffs the competitors would be able to provide to Volkswagen. The researcher does not know Volkswagen's location in some no-subsidy counterfactual, or whether Volkswagen creates more surplus in Tennessee than in that counterfactual choice.

Therefore, researchers need a framework in order to be able to evaluate how subsidies affect firm location choice and how governments determine how much they are willing to pay for any given firm. I will argue that the appropriate framework is an auction. The press already describes subsidy competitions as "bidding wars," an apt characterization of the process by which states and cities compete for an individual firm.[2] For the remainder of the chapter, I will make the argument that the auction framework is not only appropriate but a very useful framework to study subsidy giving.

There are a few key benefits to the auction approach. The first is that it is realistic. An auction closely approximates what happens in real life, which is a negotiation between a firm and multiple governments. Second, it is relevant. In the empirical auctions literature, the objective is to recover the valuation of bidders. This is a policy-relevant object in the subsidy competition—how much is a government willing to pay for a firm? If we have the distribution of government valuations, we can start answering questions about how governments determine willingness-to-pay, and whether this willingness-to-pay aligns with realized benefits. Therefore, we can rely on the empirical auctions toolkit to recover the distribution of willingness-to-pay.

Third, the auction toolkit is not data intensive: researchers can learn a lot from limited data. In an auction, the transaction price is usually sufficient to recover the full distribution of bidder's valuations. Therefore, it is a good fit for the subsidy competition setting, where researchers only observe winning subsidies, not the full set of offers.

Last, once the researcher estimates a structural auction model, they are able to evaluate policy counterfactuals. This is an area where there is little policy experimentation. Every state in the US allows subsidy giving, and although regional or nationwide subsidy "truces" are often proposed, they are rarely realized (see Kim, this volume, for an exception). Therefore, policy counterfactuals are of great interest to policymakers: How would the distribution of economic activity change if the federal government limited states'

2. For example: Nick Wingfield and Patricia Cohen, "Amazon Plans Second Headquarters, Opening a Bidding War Among Cities," *The New York Times*, September 7, 2017.

abilities to offer subsidies? What if a set of neighboring states agreed to stop competing for firms—how far would that go? Studying these types of policy proposals necessitates a structural model.

I am not the first to propose an auction framework as a useful tool to study subsidy competition. Black and Hoyt (1989) and Martin (2000) explicitly model subsidy competition as an auction, and provide theoretical motivation for my approach (Slattery 2022). In contemporaneous work, Kim (2020) estimates a subsidy competition game using a first-price private value sealed-bid auction. Similarly, Mast (2020) estimates a model in which New York counties compete for mobile establishments, and models the bidding process as a first-price scoring auction with common values.[3]

The chapter proceeds as follows. First, I will review some background on auctions, and use that framework to motivate the type of model that I find best fits the institutional details of subsidy competition between states in the US (Slattery 2022). Next, I provide more details on that model, and then show two approaches to estimation, discussing drawbacks and benefits to each. Lastly, I conclude with a discussion of feasible counterfactual analyses and thoughts for future work.

## 2.1 Auction Framework

In an auction, bidders compete for a good (or service). Each bidder has some information on how much they value the good. They use that information to formulate their bids, and the specific auction rules allocate the winner and determine the payment.

The objective of the empirical auction literature is to recover the bidders' valuations. The auction rules, or the game, give way to an optimal bidding strategy that is dependent on the private information each bidder has about their valuation. Therefore, equilibrium theory gives us a way to map private information to bids. Then, once we recover bidders' valuation, we can infer welfare and predict changes in the equilibrium if we changed the environment of the game.

### 2.1.1 Choosing an Auction Type

The tools from the empirical auction literature are dependent on auction type. Auctions can differ in both their format and their information structure. Therefore, the first thing we must do is to determine the appropriate auction to approximate subsidy competition.[4]

3. The auction framework is far from the only useful approach. For example, Ossa (2018) applies a quantitative trade model to study state government incentives to offer subsidies, in the aggregate.

4. Readers interested in learning more about empirical auctions will find the Handbook of Industrial Organization (Hortaçsu and Perrigne 2021) to be a useful starting point.

### *2.1.1.1 Standard Auction Formats*

An auction format is generally defined by an allocation and payment rule. In a first-price sealed-bid auction, everyone writes down their bid and submits it to the auctioneer, and then the person with the highest bid wins, paying the price they wrote down. In a second-price sealed-bid auction, again all the participants write down their bid and submit to the auctioneer, and the person with the highest bid wins, but pays the price of the second highest bid.

Other common formats include descending- and ascending-price open-outcry auctions. The descending-price auction (Dutch) starts at a very high price, and the price descends until the first bidder agrees to the price, winning the auction. Alternatively, in the ascending-price open-outcry (English) auction, the auctioneer starts at a low price and then accepts increasingly higher bids from bidders. Bidders are able to bid multiple times, and the auction ends when there is only one bidder remaining willing to pay the price.

In some auctions, it is not the highest price that wins, but the highest score. The scoring auction is used when the bids are multidimensional. For example, if a contractor bids on a project, the bid could have a price component as well as some quality components, like their history of completing similar projects and their estimated time horizon. In that case, the contractor with the highest score would win.

### *2.1.1.2 Information Structure*

The other important piece that will govern equilibrium strategy in auctions is the assumption about bidders' valuations. In an independent private value model, a bidder's valuation of the good is only a function of their own, independent, information. Therefore, a bidder's valuation is *private* as it does not affect its competitors' valuations.

Alternatively, in a common value auction, all of the bidders have the same valuation for the good, but have only an imperfect signal of what that value would be. The typical example here is an auction for an oil lease—each company has an estimate of the amount of oil in the tract, but this is only an estimate. The actual amount of oil in the tract does not change depending on the winner and is unknown until the land is drilled.

### *2.1.1.3 Bidding for Firms*

So now, with that background, I will show you what I think the appropriate model is for the subsidy competition for large plants and headquarters in the United States. I use institutional details to inform my modeling approach.

First, we know that firms care about not only the subsidy offer but also the location characteristics. So, it is as if there is a price and a quality component to the bid. We need a scoring auction. In other words, the auction is not a competition over subsidies but rather over location payoffs, where the payoffs are the sum of the subsidies and the location profits. The subsidies are just the lever that the state can control—it cannot instantaneously change the location characteristics.

Second, we know that there are multiple bids submitted by the same government. So, the state puts in one offer, hears back from the firm, and updates the subsidy package to make it more generous. This is an ascending auction.

Third, we know that states have some information on each others' offers. For example, North Carolina's internal report for the Job Creation Investment Grant describes how many other states were considered for a project and the details of those states' incentive packages. This is because the firm is letting North Carolina know when another state has a more attractive offer, giving North Carolina a chance to respond. This approximates the open-outcry auction.

Last, we need to take a stand on the information structure. I think that the private values paradigm is appropriate: each state or city has a location-specific benefit of winning the firm. This can be private value conditional on observable firm characteristics, so that all states can agree, for example, that more jobs are better. An alternative approach would be to model it as a common value auction. That assumption would mean that the firm creates the exact same amount of value in each location it could enter, and the only reason we observe different subsidy offers is because each city has different guesses of what that value would be.[5]

Taken together we have a private-value open-outcry ascending scoring auction. The open-outcry ascending auction is known as the "English auction," and I will use that terminology. The English auction is now a common way to model markets with negotiated prices. Recent work on consumer loans and mortgage markets takes this approach to model consumers shopping across banks for the best contract offer (Allen et al. 2019; Cuesta and Sepúlveda 2019). The consumer will sign the contract with the lowest-cost bank, at the interest rate that leaves the second-lowest-cost bank with zero profits. Basically, they pay the second price, which is the outcome of the English auction. In a subsidy competition the firm is "shopping" across locations for the highest payoff, where the payoff is the location-specific profit plus the subsidy offer. The firm can then use other locations' offers to negotiate better subsidy deals.

The bargaining analogy is illuminating because it highlights other realms of intergovernmental competition and cooperation where the English auction may be useful. Certainly this is not only a tactic that is used by indi-

5. Kim, this volume, has an interesting extension that allows for spillovers between jurisdictions. The valuation for winning a firm is private to the state, but they capture some of the valuation even if the firm does not choose that state, but locates in the neighboring jurisdiction.

vidual firms; trade associations, for example, may lobby local governments for preferential tax regimes or changes in regulations for a specific type or group of firms, using other states' existing regulations as leverage.

## 2.2 Model, Identification, and Estimation

In this section I will formalize the model to set ideas and aid in the discussion of identification and estimation. This is a slightly simplified version of the model in Slattery (2022).

### 2.2.1 Model

There are two types of agents in the model: state governments that compete with subsidies and firms that receive discretionary subsidies. The timing of the game is as follows:

**($t = 0$)** *Firm i* decides to expand or relocate, and contacts a short list of $n$ sites, $s \in \mathcal{N}_i$, about locating in $s$.
**($t = 1$)** *State governments*, $s \in \mathcal{N}_i$, bid for firm $i$.
**($t = 2$)** *Firm i* locates in the site with highest payoff.

Each location, $s \in \mathcal{N}_i$, independently draws a profit level and a private valuation for firm $i$, $\{\pi_{is}, v_{is}\}$, from the joint distribution $H_{\Pi,V}(\pi, v \mid z)$. The sum of profit and valuation, $w_{is} = \pi_{is} + v_{is}$, represents the total welfare created if firm $i$ locates in location $s$.

Locations that are on the firms' short list, $\mathcal{N}_i$, compete for the firm in a private-valuation English auction. The English auction is an open-outcry ascending auction, which means that a state can announce a bid and then *increase* their bid once another state makes a more attractive offer. The optimal strategy for states in the auction is to drop out of the bidding when the subsidy reaches their valuation for winning the firm.[6]

The firm's objective is to maximize payoffs. This means that the winning state is not always the one with the highest subsidy offer. Instead the firm will locate in the state that gives them the highest payoff, which is the sum of their profit in the state and the subsidy offered by the state.

I model firm $i$'s payoff from locating in state $s$ as the sum of subsidies and profits: $\text{subsidy}_{is} + \pi_{is}$. Here, $\text{subsidy}_{is}$ is the final bid (subsidy offer) of state $s$, and $\pi_{is}$ is the profit of firm $i$ in state $s$. The profit can include the existing tax structure, local wages, regulations, and other location characteristics that the firm values. Firm $i$ locates in $s$ if it gives the highest payoff of all states in $\mathcal{N}_i$.

6. The English auction is strategically equivalent to the sealed-bid second-price auction: the optimal strategy is to bid (or bid up to) your valuation. If you bid more than your valuation, then you receive a negative payoff upon winning the auction. If you bid (or drop out) below your valuation, there is a chance that you will lose the auction at a price you would have been willing to pay.

The outcome of the model is a set of equilibrium subsidies and firm locations, $\{\text{subsidy}^*_{is}, y^*_{is}\}$, such that:

$$\text{losing subsidy offers:}\quad \text{subsidy}_{ij} = v_{ij}(x_j, z_i)$$

$$\text{winning subsidies:}\quad \text{subsidy}^*_{is} \leq v_{is}(x_s, z_i)$$

$$\text{locations:}\quad y^*_{is} = \mathbb{1}[\pi_{is} + \text{subsidy}^*_{is} \geq \pi_{ij} + \text{subsidy}_{ij}\ \forall\ j \in \mathcal{N}_i].$$

### 2.2.2 Auction Example

Consider the case where two states compete for a firm. State A values winning the firm at \$80 million, and State B values winning the firm at \$100 million. However, the firm is more profitable in State A, where it would make \$50 million, instead of \$40 million in State B. Therefore, in absence of any competition, the firm would locate in state A. Total welfare sums state and firm payoffs to \$130 million.

The outcome changes when the states can compete with subsidies. State B could start off the bidding by making an offer to dominate State A, offering \$11 million and giving a total payoff of \$51 million to the firm. State A can respond when they learn they have been overbid, and so can State B. The two states will go back and forth, making offers until one of the states arrives at their *stopping rule*. This occurs when State A offers a subsidy of \$80 million. They are not willing to go over \$80 million; this is how much they value the firm. So, the best offer State A can make to the firm is a payoff of \$130 million (\$80 million in subsidy plus \$50 million in profits).

State B then responds with a slightly more attractive offer: offering a subsidy of slightly more than \$90 million and leaving the firm with a payoff of \$130 million and change. Therefore, under subsidy competition, the firm makes a different location choice, choosing State B, and total welfare is \$140 million.

What is important here? We should compare the two outcomes. Without subsidy competition the firm's location choice results in a total welfare of \$130 million, with \$100 million going to State A and the \$30 million in going to the firm. Subsidy competition slightly increases the size of the pie, resulting in a total welfare of \$140 million. However, in the subsidy competition case, State B captures less than \$10 million of the surplus, and the firm receives more than \$130 million. So, in the aggregate, state payoffs are higher without competition.

This example highlights the importance of the distribution of valuations and profits for policy analysis. If State B had a higher value for winning the firm, so a more negative correlation between valuation and profits, we could have aggregate state payoffs increase. If instead State B had a smaller value for winning the firm, we would be in a zero sum game case, where the firm would still locate in State A with a subsidy, so we would just transfer rents from the state to the firm with no change in location choice. Here, the welfare results will depend on the distribution of these two objects, which we will be able to estimate with the help of the auctions framework.

### 2.2.3 Estimation and Identification

Estimation of the model depends on the data the researcher has available and the assumptions the researcher is willing to make. This of course will vary, and reasonable researchers often come to different conclusions on the correct assumptions—or the assumptions can depend on the institutional details in the setting. I will discuss two approaches to estimation of the model, given different sets of assumptions.

Suppose that researchers were to observe the realized subsidies in the places that the firm located, the runner-up location in the competition, and the number of bidders (or the number of states that were in the running for the new plant or headquarters). This is what I observe in Slattery (2022). If firms did not care about differences in profitability across locations and just chose the highest subsidy location, then data on winning bids and the number of bidders are sufficient to recover the distribution of valuations (Athey and Haile 2002).[7]

However, we do think that firms do care about profits. That is why I specified this as a scoring auction. Given that it is a scoring auction, we need to recover the scoring rule (the firm's profit function). To this end, I parameterize the firm profits and the government's valuation function.

**Assumption 1**: Profits of firm $i$ in state $s$ are a linear function of a set of observed location characteristics, $x_s$: $\pi_{is} = x_s\beta$.[8]

**Assumption 2**: The valuation is a function of a set of observed location and firm characteristics, $z_{is}$, and an unobserved location-firm specific match, $\epsilon_{is}$. The unobservable portion of the valuation is additively separable, mean zero, and independent of location observables that affect profits: $v_{is} = \alpha z_{is} + \epsilon_{is}$.

Given the model, and these basic assumptions over the parameterization of profits and valuations, we can proceed to the discussion of identification and estimation. I will discuss two approaches, which each require different assumptions.

7. The intuition here is that in the English auction, the winning bid is equivalent to the valuation of the second-place bidder, because the second-place bidder would have bid all the way up to their valuation for the good. Therefore, winning bids represent the second-highest valuations; this is an order statistic for the distribution of valuations, and if we know the number of bidders, we can recover the parent distribution.

8. This is a simplification of Slattery (2022), where I specify profits as a random coefficients model, estimating $\beta_i$, where $\beta_i = \beta + z_i\beta^o + \sigma\eta_i$ and $\eta_i \overset{iid}{\sim} N(0, 1)$. The random coefficients model allows firms that are similar on observables to have different preferences over location characteristics, for reasons that are unobservable to the econometrician.

### 2.2.3.1 *Order Statistic Approach*

The first approach starts with the outcome of the English auction, and proceeds in three steps.

*Step 1.* The model tells us that the winning location will offer a subsidy that makes the firm indifferent between locating in the winning or runner-up location. Therefore, the payoffs in the winning and runner-up locations should be roughly equivalent, where superscript (1) denotes the winning location and (2) the runner-up:

$$\pi_i^{(1)} + \text{subsidy}_i^{(1)} = \pi_i^{(2)} + \text{subsidy}_i^{(2)}. \quad (1)$$

Any location that does not win the auction will end up bidding up to their valuation for winning the firm, which means that $\text{subsidy}_i^{(2)}$ is equivalent to the runner-up's valuation, and I can follow the parameterization specified above in Assumptions 1 and 2 to plug in for $\pi$ and $v$ and rearrange terms, giving a functional form for winning subsidies:

$$\text{subsidy}_i^{(1)} = (x^{(2)} - x^{(1)})\beta + z_i^{(2)}\alpha + \epsilon_i^{(2)}. \quad (2)$$

Therefore, profit parameters are identified with variation in the difference between the two characteristics, and winning bids. To see the intuition for this approach, imagine two subsidy deals for automobile manufacturing facilities of identical size. One plant locates in Alabama with a subsidy of $100 million and the other locates in Ohio with a subsidy of $140 million. In both cases, the runner-up in the subsidy competition is South Carolina, so the runner-up valuation and profit are held constant. Now suppose Alabama and Ohio have almost all of the same location characteristics: the same tax rate, the same wages, the same skilled workforce. The only difference between the two states is that Alabama is a right to work state and Ohio is not. Then, the $40 million difference in the two observed subsidy deals can be attributed to how much automobile manufacturers prefer to locate in a right to work state.

*Step 2.* Given the estimates of $\hat{\beta}$ and $\hat{\alpha}$, as well as residual $\hat{\epsilon}$, I predict total welfare (payoffs) in the runner-up location. The estimates of welfare in the runner-up locations give way to the distribution of the second order statistic of welfare. The last assumption that I need to make before proceeding to the estimation is on the distribution of welfare:

**Assumption 3**: Welfare across locations, $w$, is distributed i.i.d. $F(w|z)$.

This assumption precludes bidder types—strong versus weak locations. It is a strong assumption, given the observed differences across bidders, and therefore I also propose an alternative estimation approach in the next subsection. I can nonparametrically identify the distribution $F(w|z)$, using the distribution of runner-up welfare, $F(w|z)^{(n-1:n)}$. Identification of $F(w|z)$

comes from the order statistic identity. The $i$-th order statistic from an i.i.d. sample of size $n$ from an arbitrary distribution $F$ has distribution (Athey and Haile 2002; Arnold et al. 1992):

$$F^{(i:n)}(w|z) = \frac{n!}{(n-i)!(i-1)!}\int_0^{F(w|z)} t^{i-1}(1-t)^{n-i}dt, \tag{3}$$

where $n$ is the number of bidders. Therefore the distribution of welfare in all states, $F(w|z)$, is identified from data on the second-order statistic of welfare, $w_i^{(n-1:n)}$.

*Step 3.* Finally, I invert this welfare distribution to recover the marginal distribution of state valuations. I have this representation of welfare being the sum of the valuation of the state and the profit of the firm. I know the distribution of profits of the firm from Step 1, and the distribution of welfare from Step 2, so I can back out the distribution of valuations.

### *2.2.3.2 Extreme Value Approach*

Given the same model, an alternative approach relies on an assumption on the error term, $\epsilon$.

**Assumption 4**: The unobservable state valuation, $\epsilon_{is}$, independently distributed according to an extreme-value distribution with location and scale parameters $(0, \sigma_\epsilon)$.[9]

Given this assumption, welfare also has an extreme-value distribution with location and scale parameters $(x_s\beta + z_{is}\alpha, \sigma_\epsilon)$. Therefore, I can write the probability of observing the winning location, $y_i^{(1)}$, among the set of locations considered, $\mathcal{N}_i$, with the usual logit formula:

$$P(y_i^{(1)}|\mathcal{N}_i) = \frac{\exp\left(\frac{x^{(1)}\beta + z_i^{(1)}\alpha}{\sigma_\epsilon}\right)}{\sum_{k\in\mathcal{N}_i}\exp\left(\frac{x_k\beta + z_{ik}\alpha}{\sigma_\epsilon}\right)}. \tag{4}$$

Given the set of locations on the short-list, $\mathcal{N}_i$, this is a standard logit that I can estimate to recover $\beta/\sigma_\epsilon$ and $\alpha/\sigma_\epsilon$ with variation in the characteristics of the winning and nonwinning locations (Fox et al. 2012).[10] This is similar to the approach that Brülhart et al. (2012) take to study the effect of agglomeration and tax differentials on firm locations.

However, I only observe the choice set, $\mathcal{N}_i$, for half of the sample. This

9. This is a common approach to modeling auctions with asymmetric value distributions (Allen et al. 2019; Brannman and Froeb 2000).

10. I also have another piece of information: the second-choice locations (the runners-up). Therefore, I can instead maximize the probability I observe the winning ($y_i^{(1)}$) and runner-up ($y_i^{(2)}$) locations out of the set of potential locations $\mathcal{N}_i$. This follows the same logic as (4) but provides more variation for identifying $\beta$ and $\alpha$.

is the second assumption needed for this approach. I simulate potential short list locations, using observables. Therefore, I can proceed by simulated maximum likelihood to estimate $\hat{\beta}$ and $\hat{\alpha}$. Given $\hat{\beta}$ and $\hat{\alpha}$, I can predict profits and the observable portion of valuation in each location. However, we also have the unobservable part of the valuation, $\epsilon_{is}$, which will dictate the added heterogeneity in state valuations, and therefore the welfare results.

I identify $\sigma_\epsilon$ using data on winning bids and the outcome from the model that I use in the previous approach. Therefore, given $\hat{\beta}, \hat{\alpha}$, and simulations of $\epsilon_i$, I can use (2) to predict subsidies. The only remaining unknown, $\sigma_\epsilon$, is pinned down by matching the distribution of model predicted subsidies to observed subsidies (data).

### 2.2.4 Counterfactual Analysis

Given that we finally have our main objects of interest, the distributions of state valuations and profits, we can move to the counterfactual analysis. I want to discuss three counterfactuals that would be feasible given the estimation model and estimation I detail above. Then, in the next section, I will discuss more ambitious models and the associated counterfactuals.

The first, which is what I do in Slattery (2022), is a subsidy ban that restricts states and local governments from offering discretionary subsidies or any tax credits. This is a partial equilibrium analysis because I do not have states also choosing tax rates in the model, so I cannot to allow the states to change their tax rate, which we might think would happen if we restricted incentives. In order to implement this counterfactual, I predict where each firm would be most profitable, using the estimated profit parameters. Given that profit, I simulate the valuation of the winning location from the joint distribution. Then I compare the total welfare with and without subsidy competition.

Another interesting and potentially more realistic counterfactual would be a regional truce. In this case, a subset of regions, perhaps neighbors, agree not to compete for firms. Using the same technique as the total ban, one could predict the resulting firm locations, welfare, and, interestingly, how the distribution of winning subsidies would change under the new regime.

Lastly, as a complement to the subsidy game, we can use the estimates from the model to study the effect of investments in location characteristics, as opposed to changes in subsidy regimes. For example, if a state invested in infrastructure, one could estimate how this would change the number of firms the state attracted and the equilibrium subsidy offers needed to attract them.

## 2.3 Closing Thoughts

If bidding for firms reduces welfare, what should be done to limit it? Although there is a long history of subsidy giving in the US, evaluating subsidy competition has been difficult due to limited data and a lack of exogenous variation in the policy space. Auctions provide a convenient framework, allowing researchers to learn about the primitives of interest even with limited amounts of data. Importantly, the auction is necessary for the policy counterfactuals—how do different restrictions on bidding affect firm locations and other economic outcomes of interest?

Interested researchers can do even more with the auction framework. For example, if you are interested in the dynamic interaction between subsidy contests, a sequential auction would allow you to factor in the fact that some states have a binding budget constraint or that their willingness to pay may be affected by past performance. Another idea that I am excited about is incorporating entry. In past work I find that subsidy competition does not do much to improve allocative effficiency because the locations that would benefit the most from winning a subsidy contest are never even considered as a potential location (Slattery 2022). One could incorporate the entry decision of the states and regions to engage in the competition, which would allow a counterfactual where there are some sort of matching subsidies or preferences for disadvantaged regions, just as government procurement auctions have programs that prefer disadvantaged bidders.

This is not a US-specific phenomenon. This chapter is framed around a competition between states, but one can think of competition between countries, or, at an even more local level, competition between municipalities within a state or region. It happens, with more regulations, in the European Union and is quite common in other large countries like Canada, Brazil, and India. There is much more to learn about competition and economic development policy in these contexts. I am optimistic that future work can continue to leverage the auction and other models used in empirical industrial organization to study competition between governments and the potential policy responses to limit that competition when it is harmful.

### Acknowledgments

For acknowledgments, sources of research support, and disclosure of the author's material financial relationships, if any, please see https://www.nber.org/books-and-chapters/policy-responses-tax-competition/subsidy-competition-auction.

## References

Allen, Jason, Robert Clark, and Jean-François Houde. 2019. "Search Frictions and Market Power in Negotiated-Price Markets." *Journal of Political Economy* 127 (4): 1550–98.

Arnold, Barry, N. Balakrishnan, and H. N. Nagaraja. 1992. *A First Course in Order Statistics*. SIAM.
Athey, Susan, and Philip Haile. 2002. "Identification of Standard Auction Models." *Econometrica* 70 (6): 2107–40.
Black, Dan A., and William H. Hoyt. 1989. "Bidding for Firms." *The American Economic Review* 79 (5): 1249.
Brannman, Lance, and Luke M. Froeb. 2000. "Mergers, Cartels, Set-Asides, and Bidding Preferences in Asymmetric Oral Auctions." *The Review of Economics and Statistics* 82 (2): 283–90.
Brülhart, Marius, Mario Jametti, and Kurt Schmidheiny. 2012. "Do Agglomeration Economies Reduce the Sensitivity of Firm Location to Tax Differentials?" *The Economic Journal* 122 (563): 1069–93.
Cuesta, José Ignacio, and Alberto Sepúlveda. 2019. "Price Regulation in Credit Markets: A Trade-Off between Consumer Protection and Credit Access." Working paper.
Fox, Jeremy T., Kyoo il Kim, Stephen P. Ryan, and Patrick Bajari. 2012. "The Random Coefficients Logit Model Is Identified." *Journal of Econometrics* 166 (2): 204–12.
Hortaçsu, Ali, and Isabelle Perrigne. 2021. "Chapter 11: Empirical Perspectives on Auctions." In *Handbook of Industrial Organization, Volume 5*, edited by Kate Ho, Ali Hortaçsu, and Alessandro Lizzeri, 81–175. Elsevier.
Kim, Donghyuk. 2020. "Government Incentives and Firm Location Choices." Working paper.
Martin, Laurent. 2000. "Bidding for Firms: An Asymmetric Auction Model of Interjurisdictional Competition." Working paper, University of Washington.
Mast, Evan. 2020. "Race to the Bottom? Local Tax Break Competition and Business Location." *American Economic Journal: Applied Economics* 12 (1): 288–317.
Ossa, Ralph. 2023. "A Quantitative Analysis of Subsidy Competition in the U.S." *Journal of Public Economics* 224. https://doi.org/10.1016/j.jpubeco.2023.104919.
Slattery, Cailin. 2025. "Bidding for Firms: Subsidy Competition in the U.S." *Journal of Political Economy* 133 (5). https://www.journals.uchicago.edu/doi/10.1086/735509.

# 3

# Limits to Competition
## Strategies for Promoting Jurisdictional Cooperation

David R. Agrawal

### 3.1 Introduction

Technological change, economic integration, and globalization pose challenges for decentralized fiscal systems, spurring calls for policy coordination among jurisdictions to mitigate harmful tax competition. Tax competition is the process by which independent jurisdictions noncooperatively set taxes and where each government's tax policies influence the allocation of mobile tax bases among competing jurisdictions.[1] The noncooperative setting of tax policies in an open economy setting results in interjurisdictional tax differentials that create incentives for interjurisdictional tax avoidance by people, factors, firms, profits, and shoppers. This tax-induced mobility imposes interjurisdictional fiscal and economic externalities on other jurisdictions—a tax increase in one jurisdiction expands the tax base of other jurisdictions and may expand economic activity in other jurisdictions—possibly resulting in strategic interactions among governments. These externalities on other jurisdictions imply that the tax competition equilibrium will be inefficient, as the jurisdiction enacting the policy will not account for the externalities. As a result, there generally exists a coordinated equilibrium that would be chosen by a social (federal) planner that yields strictly higher welfare in *every* jurisdiction.

Within federal systems, the inefficiencies from local tax competition—*usually* viewed as resulting in tax rates that are too low—may result in a

David R. Agrawal is a professor of economics at the University of California, Irvine, and a fellow of CESifo.

1. See Wilson and Wildasin (2004).

central governments seeking to limit competition.[2] The tools that central governments have to limit competition among subnational jurisdictions are abundant, ranging from complete tax harmonization of local tax rates to minimum taxes. In addition, federal systems may facilitate intermunicipal cooperation where taxes and services are delegated to a higher level of government, allowing for partial harmonization of taxes among a subset of jurisdictions. More generally, at the state level, jurisdictions may enter into tax treaties or interstate compacts that change how taxes are sourced or enforced. Despite how common these policy limits are in federal systems, cooperation and coordination remains understudied. In this chapter, I review the existing theoretical and empirical evidence on these limits, derive new results for interjurisdictional cooperation using a simple model that allows me to compare a wide *variety* of policy limits on competition, and reflect on possible future research on the topic. The recent debate on the global minimum tax highlights both the policy importance of the topic, as well as the need for additional research concerning the topic.

Despite the policy importance of potential limits to tax competition, many unanswered questions in open economy public economics remain. How diverse are tax rates in an increasingly globalized and "border-free" world when there is no central coordination of tax policies across jurisdictions? What forms of coordination could benefit *all* jurisdictions? Benefit *some* jurisdictions? If allowed to cooperate in setting fiscal policies, with whom will jurisdictions form coalitions, and how do these coalitions influence the patterns of tax rates set across jurisdictions? Does coordination raise or lower tax rates and revenues? Does coordination influence the location of firms, factors, people, and economic activity? What coordination policies improve worldwide total revenue the most? Improve welfare the most? Should we have more or less decentralization of tax policy?

Although many questions remain, a significant literature and many surveys have been devoted to the study of tax competition and coordination (Agrawal, Hoyt, et al. 2022; Brueckner 2003; Brülhart et al. 2015; Keen and Konrad 2013; Wildasin 2021; Wilson 1999; Wilson and Wildasin 2004). However, a major challenge facing the literature on policy limits to tax competition is that most theoretical models of tax coordination are designed to focus on either a *particular* tax (corporate tax, consumption tax, etc.) or a *particular* policy remedy (harmonization, minimum tax rates, cooperation, etc.). As a result, the ability to make generalizations across various taxes, and perhaps more importantly across various remedies to tax competition, is limited. But governments often debate which coordination policies are

2. Of course, there are reasons one would want to encourage competition among governments. For example, if governments are Leviathan, then tax competition can be useful to discipline the Leviathan (Brülhart and Jametti 2019).

best and for which tax bases, so a framework that is broadly applicable is necessary. A major goal of this chapter is to propose a general model that is applicable to the study of many types of taxing instrument and across many types of policy responses.

To do this, I build on the Kanbur and Keen (1993) model—which, while designed to study commodity tax competition, has been shown by Keen and Konrad (2013) to be applicable to any tax policies where the tax base can be *shifted* across jurisdictions at some cost to the taxpayer. The generality of the shifting behavior—profit shifting, migration, capital flight, cross-border shopping—allows for potential applications to corporate taxes, capital taxes, commodity taxes, or income taxes, among others. Jurisdictions in the model maximize tax revenues and interact strategically—game theoretically—when setting equilibrium tax rates. The general model is then used to compare various policy responses to tax competition, including tax harmonization, minimum tax rates, forced cooperation (resulting in partial harmonization), voluntary cooperation with endogenous coalition formation, and tax treaties on sourcing rules. The comprehensive scope of the policies considered allows for novel comparisons of the pros and cons of various policy responses that were not possible in the prior literature. Of course, any such general model must make some assumptions and simplifications. I believe the model is general enough to capture the central features of tax competition and tax base mobility, but *simple* enough that it yields *sharp* insights into the policy debates to limit competition. The simplifications made here can be relaxed in future research.

The model, featuring two symmetrically sized jurisdictions and a single jurisdiction that may be larger or smaller, yields several key insights:

1. If most jurisdictions are small, harmonization will only increase tax revenues in all jurisdictions if harmonization is to a tax rate that is sufficiently close to the highest uncoordinated tax rate. If instead most jurisdictions are large, tax harmonization may harm the smaller jurisdictions while benefiting the larger ones.

2. If most jurisdictions are small, a binding minimum tax rate will improve tax revenues in all jurisdictions *regardless* of the level of the minimum tax rate. If instead most jurisdictions are large, a binding minimum tax rate will only improve tax revenues in all jurisdictions if the size differences between the jurisdictions are sufficiently small.

3. If a subset of jurisdictions is forced to cooperate, regardless of the combination of the jurisdictions forced to cooperate, tax rates rise in all jurisdictions relative to the uncoordinated equilibrium, but tax revenues may fall in some jurisdictions. There exist scenarios where revenues increase in all jurisdictions, including nonmembers of the coalition, under cooperation.

4. If jurisdictions can choose with whom to cooperate, assuming that side

payments are not possible, a coalition between two asymmetric jurisdictions can only arise if the jurisdictions are sufficiently similar in their sizes.

5. From the perspective of total (combined) tax revenue in all jurisdictions, a coalition setting a common tax rate within the coalition revenue-dominates minimum tax rates, which in turn, dominate complete harmonization. If there are more smaller jurisdictions than larger jurisdictions, then a coalition between an asymmetric and symmetric jurisdiction revenue-dominates any other coalition, while if the reverse is true, a coalition of two symmetric jurisdictions revenue-dominates all alternative policies.

Comparing across policies, the model suggests a clear dominance of minimum tax rates over complete harmonization. However, with minor caveats, interjurisdictional cooperation (partial harmonization among a subset of jurisdictions) also dominates both harmonization and minimum tax rates. The reason for this dominance of partial harmonization is important for policy: with cooperation, the coalition government harmonizes tax rates to its best value—taking as given the taxes of nonmembers—without any centrally imposed constraints. With minimum tax rates or centralized harmonization, policy proposals usually restrict the set of coordinated tax rates to be in *between* the uncoordinated equilibrium tax rates. But if tax competition results in taxes being too low in the uncoordinated equilibrium, a reform that uses those low rates to limit competition will be less effective than those reforms that do not constrain the coordinated equilibrium tax rates to be between the observed equilibrium rates. Indeed, there are a whole host of coordinated tax rates that are revenue-superior to the noncooperatives equilibrium and also revenue improving for *all* jurisdictions, suggesting that there exist many policies limiting tax competition that may be welfare improving.

After detailing the theoretical model and its results, I selectively survey the empirical evidence on the efficacy of policies limiting tax competition. In particular, I emphasize empirical studies that use mobility elasticities to construct counterfactual exercises following the implementation of various policy reforms. I also discuss the empirical evidence on the effects of intermunicipal cooperation, commonly used around the world, on the level of tax rates, the costs imposed on municipalities from joining, and the effect of cooperation on strategic tax competition. Overall, the empirical literature generally confirms the predictions of the theoretical model.

Finally, I conclude with directions for future research. While the model I present is stylized, it represents a starting point for researchers seeking to systematically compare different policy interventions. Given the increase in data availability for subnational taxing policies and the advances in spatial empirical designs, the empirical future for studying the efficacy of these policies is ripe for further study.

## 3.2 Policies to Limit Cooperation

Fiscal federations and supranational institutions such as the European Union have numerous tools at their disposal to limit tax competition.[3] And more recently, the global minimum tax (Johannesen 2022) highlights the possibility that these policy tools may be implementable at the international level. In this section, I classify various types of policy responses into various intervention categories and qualitatively describe them.

### 3.2.1 The Level of Government

Within federal systems, which level of government should be assigned particular spending and tax policies? A state or federal government could limit tax competition by granting taxing rights to a higher level of government—in the most extreme case, this would involve centralizing the tax base entirely.[4] Some of these rules may be codified in state constitutions. The argument for centralization is that tax base mobility is more limited across international borders than across state and local borders. However, centralization comes at the cost of limiting local autonomy.

There are many examples of taxes or expenditures that have been centralized over time. For example, departments in France have taken over many function of the French communes and Dutch regional police forces were centralized. Sometimes, however, the responses to centralization are unpopular and may lead to a renewed wave of decentralization (for debate on the topic, see Donahue 1997; Inman and Rubinfeld 1997; Musgrave 1997; Qian and Weingast 1997). Other examples of the extent of centralization from the United States are that local sales taxes are allowed in over 30 US states, but the remainder of states have outright bans on localities levying local sales taxes on the same base taxed by the state. Of course, there are varying degrees to these types of restrictions and the extent of decentralization: some states might allow (or not allow) municipalities to set the rates, while in other states the rates might be set by the higher-level county rather than the municipality. Delegating tax authority to a higher level of government may mitigate tax competition by reducing the number of competitors. Hoyt (1991) shows that as the number of jurisdictions decreases, tax rates rise. Loosely speaking, decreasing the number of jurisdictions acts to reduce the tax base externality produced by a single jurisdiction's policy on other

3. Of course, as in the tradition of Tiebout (1956), an argument can be made that we want to facilitate rather than limit tax competition in the same way we want to facilitate competition between private firms. When thinking about limits to tax competition, policymakers address the parasitic effects arising from interjurisdictional fiscal externalities.

4. For a complete discussion of the assignment problem, see Boadway and Shah (2009) and Agrawal, Brueckner, et al. (2024). Janeba and Wilson (2011) discuss the tradeoffs of centralization and decentralization.

jurisdictions in the federal system (for example, the shifting of capital to other jurisdictions from a tax change).

Federal systems might also reduce the externality produced by a single jurisdiction's policy by forcing local governments to amalgamate. Municipal mergers may reduce tax competition, but may also come with economies of scale in the provision of public services. Amalgamations are sometimes forced upon lower-level governments by higher-level governments seeking to consolidate the number of jurisdictions, but some mergers arise voluntarily. Amalgamations were a key part of 1970s reforms in the UK, which were aimed at increasing the population sizes of municipalities. To a lesser extent, amalgamations were common in Sweden and Germany, but are perhaps less common in the United States (Epple and Romer 1989).

### 3.2.2 Tax Coordination

"Tax coordination" broadly refers to policies that place limitations on the tax rates that governments can set. These policies include harmonization, minimum tax rates, maximum tax rates, or tax and expenditure limitations.

#### *3.2.2.1 Harmonization*

One common policy proposal is that jurisdictions harmonize tax rates to a single, centrally determined tax rate. Harmonization effectively "closes" borders to tax-induced avoidance schemes, which benefits high-tax jurisdictions but may come with a revenue cost of lowering tax rates for these jurisdictions. Proposals for tax harmonization usually stipulate that the single harmonized rate is a weighted average of the tax rates that arise in the noncooperative equilibrium (Keen 1987, 1989; Keen et al. 2002). As will become clear in the analysis below, such a harmonization proposal, however, fails to entirely eliminate the negative consequences of tax competition. In particular, tax competition distorts taxes, perhaps downward, in a way that taking an average of these observed taxes may not actually move some jurisdictions to a more efficient tax rate. Indeed, harmonization might move some jurisdictions away from their efficient rate.

A simple way to see this is that in a standard tax competition model, if all jurisdictions are symmetric, all taxes will be equalized in the noncooperative equilibrium. But the presence of fiscal externalities still implies that coordination could be welfare improving, but as there are no tax differentials, uncoordinated tax rates are already harmonized. As a result, there are no gains from harmonization to a weighted average of the noncooperative rates if we do not consider other rates. Thus, in an ideal world, harmonization proposals would best be to a weighted average of the optimal tax rates in the *absence* of tax competition. But these rates are unobserved, making such a hypothetical rate nearly impossible to discern. Thus, in practice, uncoordinated equilibrium rates act as a proxy for this ideal rate, but using this proxy misses the *level* effects that tax competition has on all jurisdictions' tax rates. Harmonization also comes with the challenge that jurisdictions need to agree on the tax rate—or the weights determining that rate—to which to harmonize.

### *3.2.2.2 Minimum Tax Rates*

A possible alternative might be that jurisdictions establish a minimum tax rate (or perhaps alternatively depending on whether taxes are "too high" or "too low," a maximum tax rate).[5] The global minimum tax on corporate profits is one such prominent example (Hebous and Keen 2023; Janeba and Schjelderup 2023; Johannesen 2022). Minimum tax rates force low-tax jurisdictions (potentially tax havens) to raise their tax rates. These minimum tax rates then hopefully reduce interjurisdictional tax differentials, reducing mobility of the tax base. But unlike harmonization, the minimum tax rate places no restriction on high-tax jurisdictions, potentially allowing high-tax jurisdictions to reoptimize their tax rates by strategically responding to the higher tax rates in the haven countries.

Another form of coordination includes restrictions either on the levels or the growth of tax instruments via tax or expenditure limitations.[6] One challenge with these rules as a tool to limit tax competition is that they are usually implemented as a means to constrain the size of governments. Thus, these policies might be effective at mitigating tax competition if tax competition makes taxes "too high" rather than "too low" or if fiscal competition occurs in expenditures rather than taxes (Wildasin 1988).

## 3.2.3 Cooperation and Partial Harmonization

Tax harmonization among the entire set of countries in the world or among all localities in a country is likely hard to achieve. However, harmonization among a subset of jurisdictions may be more feasible. I call this *partial harmonization*, which occurs through the formation of coalitions among a subset of jurisdictions. A theoretical literature on coalition formation and partial harmonization exists (Abidi and Taugourdeau 2024; Burbidge et al. 1997; Konrad and Schjelderup 1999). One common form of such coalition formation is intermunicipal cooperation (Breuillé and Duran-Vigneron in this volume; Hulst and van Montfort 2007). Intermunicipal cooperation may occur on a single fiscal policy or multiple fiscal policies, with localities ceding one or several taxes to the cooperative. In more informal cases, the cooperation simply involves consultation on setting policies (without any

5. The use of both a maximum or a minimum tax rate might be viewed as government agreeing upon a "range" of tax rates that would be appropriate, and thus requires a less stringent agreement to harmonize taxes to a single rate. See Luna et al. (2007) for an example of a maximum tax rate and Lyytikäinen (2012, 2023) for examples of both a minimum and maximum rate.

6. For example, Poterba and Rueben (1995) discuss limits on property taxation and Eliason and Lutz (2018) study fiscal rules more generally.

transfer of formal powers, but simply consisting of advising each other). But there are many examples around the world where the cooperative actually conducts joint operations and the provision of services with intermunicipal agencies and tax revenues. Finally, and the focus of subsequent theory, cooperation may be forced (statutory obligation under federal law) or may be a result of voluntarily established cooperative bodies where jurisdictions decide with whom to cooperate.

Local policymaking is an especially opportune area for jurisdictions to engage in cooperation: municipalities are small, with a median population less than 1,000 people in many countries. One reason for cooperation in public services is that the presence of many small jurisdictions does not allow for municipalities to exploit economies of scale. Second, perhaps more relevant on the revenue side of the budget, a very large number of competing jurisdictions can foster intense competition for mobile factors, which yields an inefficient equilibrium of policies. Thus, reducing the number of jurisdictions can mitigate the effects of harmful tax competition (Hoyt 1991).[7]

Examples of municipal cooperation are extensive, such as detailed in Hulst and van Montfort (2007). France has one of the longest and most comprehensive histories of intermunicipal cooperation. The French establishment for intermunicipal cooperation (EIMC) commonly provides some public services across all member municipalities using a common tax or several shared taxes, which it has the authority to set independent of the individual municipal governments. In France, municipalities can levy tax rates on four main tax bases: business, residence, developed property, and undeveloped property. But, after agreeing to cooperate, some taxing powers are surrendered to the EIMC.[8] EIMCs were historically preceded by syndicates, which were a weaker form of cooperation over public service provision but without tax authority. In Finland, the 1995 Finnish Local Government Act allowed local governments to perform their functions either alone or in cooperation with other local governments. In Germany, one possible form of informal cooperation is via regional conferences (*Regionalkonferenzen*). In Belgium, 2001 reforms allowed for municipal cooperation. The most extensive forms of cooperation are the service association (*dienstverlenende vereniging*) and the mandated association (*opdrachthoudende vereniging*). In the Netherlands, the 1950 Joint Provisions Act explicitly allowed towns the power to cooperate and for provinces to promote the joint interests. The act allows municipalities, with restrictions, to transfer decision-making powers of local government to the cooperative bodies. Italy has several different forms of purely intermunicipal cooperation in single- and multipurpose service delivery (conventions, agreements, consortia, unions) and mixed public-

7. Of course, reducing the number of jurisdictions may reduce Tiebout sorting benefits across municipalities.

8. See Breuillé and Duran-Vigneron (chapter 8 in this volume) for a survey of the institutional details of EIMCs.

private cooperation in social economic development (area pacts). Finally, the US allows for the formation of special districts (Goodman 2020). While many of these cooperative groups focus on public services provision, suggesting economies of scale are the primary reason for their formation, some of the cooperative structures also allow for tax authority to be delegated to the tier. Finally, town twinning is an example where towns may even cooperate across international borders through informal agreements. Mainly, this form of cooperation is aimed at benefiting businesses working across international borders.

While the focus of this chapter is on the effect on horizontal tax competition (Wilson 1999; Wilson and Wildasin 2004), some forms of intermunicipal cooperation such as the French case create a new tier of government in the federalist hierarchy. Although municipalities cede some taxing authority to the EIMC, they also maintain some local taxing autonomy. As a result, although intermunicipal cooperation may affect the intensity of horizontal tax competition, it may also create a new form of vertical tax competition (Hoyt 2017; Keen 1998; Keen and Kotsogiannis 2002). Vertical tax competition is the strategic interactions between higher and lower levels of government resulting from both tiers of government cohabitating the tax base. Even if the municipality and the newly formed cooperative are prohibited from taxing the same bases, distinct tax bases may still overlap in real terms or have interdependencies. However, horizontal tax competition usually places downward pressure on tax rates and vertical tax competition places upward pressure on tax rates. Intuitively, with horizontal fiscal externalities, a tax increase expands the tax base elsewhere; however, a higher-level government's tax increase reduces the tax base of lower-level governments via changes in demand for labor, goods, or factors. Thus, intermunicipal cooperation may raise tax rates due to reductions in horizontal competition but also because of the vertical tax externalities resulting from a new tier of government. A concern arises if this results in taxes being too high. These vertical tax competition forces are absent from the subsequent model.

### 3.2.4 Tax Rules and Tax Treaties

Another possible way that jurisdictions can mitigate the effects of tax competition is by entering into a bilateral tax treaty or an interstate compact.[9] The surge of subsidy competition for large firms has recently spurred state agreements banning subsidy deals, along with a recent proposal for an interstate compact on the issue (Kim in this volume).[10]

One common example of tax treaties arises in the personal income tax. There is great debate over how to tax nonresident income, and as a result,

9. Voit and Nitting (1999) identify interstate compacts and agreements in the United States.

10. See Brülhart et al. (in this volume) for the agreements in Switzerland defining a common corporate tax base and instruments.

states resort to tax treaties to allocate taxing rights on multijurisdictional income. In the US, the default is to tax nonresident earnings in the state where it is physically earned, with the resident state then asserting taxing rights on the income as well, but offering a tax credit to eliminate double taxation. However, if states enter into bilateral tax treaties—reciprocity agreements (Agrawal and Hoyt 2018; Coomes and Hoyt 2008; Rohlin et al. 2014)—then the states agree that nonresident workers only need to pay and file taxes in the resident state. Beyond US state income taxes, bilateral tax treaties govern the taxation of cross-border workers in the international setting. These tax treaties, which often concern sourcing rules over where income is taxed, have important implications for tax competition. Intuitively, if taxes bases are differentially mobile under the source rather than under the residence principle, tax competition will be less intense under rule that makes the tax base more inelastic. At a basic level, for the taxation of personal income, the difference is between these two principles involves employment versus worker mobility. If jobs/firms are more mobile than people, the residence principle is preferred to a source principle based on the location of the job.

As a result, the tax rules governing where income, sales, or factors are taxed—at source/residence or at origin/destination—are critical determinants of the extent and existence of tax competition (Fox et al. in this volume). Beyond sourcing rules, rules governing the enforcement of these sourcing principles have the potential to also influence the extent of tax competition. In particular, if a strict sourcing rule cannot be enforced, then the tax base will remain mobile.

Finally, institutional rules and intergovernmental relationships also influence tax competition. For example, state constitutional restrictions may limit taxing authority by requiring municipalities to obtain supermajorities on tax increases. Such political constraints have important implications for tax competition, though the implications for tax competition are ambiguous. Beyond constitutional issues, intergovernmental grants are a feasible way to influence the extent and existence of tax competition (Clemens and Veuger in this volume; Köthenbürger 2002; Wildasin 1989) and the state and local tax deduction may also mitigate the fiscal externalities of states taxing high income earners (Cullen and Gordon 2008).

## 3.3 A Simple Fiscal Competition Model

The prior literature is filled with numerous examples of models to study minimum tax rates, tax harmonization, sourcing rules, tax treaties, and interjurisdictional cooperation. However, a limitation of the literature is that it often studies only a single type or a few types of tax coordination. Further, the diversity of modeling strategies used to study each policy and type of tax makes it challenging to compare the outcomes and feasibility of various tax coordination policies, as it is unclear whether the differences are driven by the policies or the model structures. Moreover, with the exception of the literature on coalition formation and intermunicipal cooperation, the prior literature on tax coordination often focuses on two jurisdictions. The focus on two jurisdictions then prevents a comparison of complete tax coordination policies with partial harmonization or policies that require jurisdictions to endogenously cooperate with other jurisdictions.

In this section, I sketch a simple model of tax competition, originally developed to study commodity tax competition in the context of cross-border shopping. The model originates with Kanbur and Keen (1993), but I sketch a simpler variant proposed by Nielsen (2001).[11] Despite its initial application to commodity taxation, Keen and Konrad (2013) and Agrawal and Wildasin (2019) show the Kanbur and Keen (1993) model can be extended to characterize many different types of fiscal competition with tax base shifting—profit shifting, real relocation/migration, capital flight, or commuting. The model originally featured two jurisdictions, but I extend it to multiple jurisdictions following Agrawal, Bagh, and Mardan (2025), allowing me to study partial harmonization and coalition formation.

For simplicity, consider three jurisdictions, indexed by $i$. The three jurisdictions set tax rates $T_i$ to maximize tax revenues in a Nash game. Jurisdictions have some market power and thus interact strategically with other jurisdictions when setting tax rates. The assumption of revenue maximization is obviously a simplification of reality, where governments may actually maximize welfare of residents, property values, and political economy objectives.[12] The assumption that governments are Leviathan, as in Kanbur and Keen (1993), can be viewed as a political economy model of tax setting or can be interpreted as a welfare-maximizing government where there is a very high marginal value of public services financed by tax revenues. The Leviathan assumption allows me to focus on tax rates and revenues, but misses issues related to economies of scale in public services, as well as any effects on resident and firm surplus. And unlike many models of welfare maximization, tax competition can help discipline the Leviathan to prevent taxes from being too high. For the purposes of this chapter, I think of revenue maximization as a way to understand the provision of public services and consider ranking policies simply on the basis of tax revenues. Although I cannot make welfare conclusions, most models of tax competition imply that public good provision is too low. Studying tax revenues therefore allows

11. See also Haufler (1996) and Trandel (1994). If the convex transportation costs in Haufler are quadratic, the cutoff rules in Haufler are the same as in the model of Nielsen (2001), with costs that are linear in distance to the border. Haufler, however, is more general along many other dimensions including welfare-maximizing governments rather than revenue-maximizing governments.

12. Trandel (1994) shows that many of the Kanbur and Keen (1993) results are robust to welfare-maximizing governments.

me to make claims as to whether revenues (and thus public services) can be made more efficient by limiting tax competition.

Jurisdictions are asymmetric in size. If borders are closed, the sizes of the tax bases of the jurisdictions are $\Theta_i$. This parameter determines the relative sizes (residents, profits, etc.) of the jurisdictions. I assume that tax changes do not change the total amount of economic activity in the world. Thus, in the presence of closed borders, the tax base is fixed even if the jurisdiction increases its tax rate. But, open borders allow for some shifting of economic activity to low-tax jurisdictions and thus the tax base across jurisdictions. The amount of shifted activity from jurisdiction $i$ to jurisdiction $j$ is denoted $s_{ij}$ where $s_{ij} \geq 0$ if $T_i \geq T_j$ and $s_{ij} < 0$ if $T_i < T_j$. In this model, all shifting is tax driven so the shifting variable is positive if the shifting is outward and negative if the shifting is inward. The total tax base of a country is given by its initial base net of any activity shifted out of the jurisdiction plus any activity shifted into the jurisdiction:

$$(1) \qquad B_i = \Theta_i - \sum_{j \neq i} s_{ij}.$$

If, for example, jurisdiction 2 sets a tax rate lower than jurisdiction 1, but higher than jurisdiction 3, its tax base is $B_2 = \Theta_2 - s_{23} - s_{21}$ where $s_{23} > 0$ and $s_{21} < 0$. As noted previously, taxes only affect the location of the activity, but do not influence the total amount of economic activity in the jurisdictions, so mobility is the only response to taxation.

Shifting activity comes at some cost to the firm or individual doing it. I assume that shifting costs are bilateral and are convex in the amount of shifting.[13] I assume that the cost functions are identical in each jurisdiction, so that shifting the first unit to any jurisdiction incurs the same marginal and total cost regardless of where it is shifted from. For tractability, I assume this cost function is quadratic. This implies a cost function for outward shifting from a jurisdiction:

$$(2) \qquad c(s_{ij}) = \frac{\delta(s_{ij})^2}{2},$$

where $\delta$ is a cost parameter and the cost function is defined for values of $s_{ij} \geq 0$. Several points are in order. First, the quadratic cost function is standard in spatial models such as Kanbur and Keen (1993). Second, shifting costs are bilateral, meaning that for a resident of jurisdiction $i = 1$, the cost function of shifting into $i = 2$ is a function of the amount of activity shifted into 2 and not a function of the total amount of shifting into both jurisdiction 2 and 3. In the case of cross-border shopping, bilateral shifting costs correspond to transport costs being border specific (e.g., related to the distance from each border). In the case of profit shifting, this assumption

13. Under an alternative framing, individuals may be heterogeneous in the cost of shifting activity into each other jurisdiction.

means that the cost of profit shifting to one jurisdiction is independent of the amount of shifting to other jurisdictions.[14] If relaxing the quadratic assumption, in a more general model such as Haufler (1996), the cost function would need to be continuously differentiable with properties that satisfy $c'_{ij} > 0$ and $c''_{ij} > 0$ if $s_{ij} > 0$; $c_{ij}(0) = c'_{ij}(0) = 0$; and $c''_{ij}(0) > 0$, $\forall i$.

In the presence of open borders, an arbitrage condition will determine the amount of tax-base shifting. In particular, the marginal benefit of shifting must equal the marginal cost of shifting. The marginal benefit of shifting another unit is simply equal to the tax savings, while the marginal cost is determined by differentiating (2). Solving the arbitrage condition for the amount of shifting then yields

(3) $$s_{ij} = \frac{T_i - T_j}{\delta},$$

which is positive if $T_i > T_j$ and negative if $T_i < T_j$. Armed with this optimality condition, which solves the shifting problem of the economic agents, government revenues can easily be constructed as

(4) $$R_i = T_i B_i = T_i\left(\Theta_i - \sum_{j \neq i} \frac{T_i - T_j}{\delta}\right),$$

where the first term, $\Theta_i$, indicates larger jurisdictions have a larger base, all else equal. And the second term with the summation captures both the inflows of shifted activity, as well as outflows of shifted activity. Notice that when the sign of the tax differential is positive, the shifting is outward, but when it is negative, the shifting is inward.

Some discussion of what is meant by the shifted tax base is in order. The phenomenon of tax competition, especially in the area of international capital income taxation, features many different types of shifting behavior. The distinction between base shifting in the form of shifting real investment and production versus the virtual shifting of the tax base through various "tax havens" or institutional structures is of great importance. Both types of shifting are closely intertwined and the two are not independent of each other, depending on the tax argument considered. For the purposes of this chapter, I make no distinction between whether the activity shifted is real economic activity or tax evasion or avoidance, and, more generally, the model features standard jurisdictions and not jurisdictions featuring the special features of tax havens. In the context of a federation and competition between subnational entities, which is focal in this chapter, the issue is much less relevant but would merit more distinctions in the international tax setting. For a survey of these issues, see Keen and Konrad (2013).

A model with three jurisdictions, each differing in size, allows for a wide

14. See Huizinga et al. (2008) and van't Riet and Lejour (2018) for empirical evidence that multinational firms base their decisions on bilateral costs.

**Table 3.1** **Notation: Asymmetries in the model**

| Case | Asymmetries |
|---|---|
| $\theta > 0$ | $a$ is larger than $s$, $\sigma$ |
| $\theta = 0$ | $a$, $s$, $\sigma$ are symmetric |
| $\theta < 0$ | $s$, $\sigma$ are larger than $a$ |

This table summarizes the notation concerning jurisdictional asymmetries.

range of tax equilibria. To simplify the model, and to express taxes as a function of a single relative size parameter, I consider the case where two jurisdictions are symmetric in their sizes, but one jurisdiction is smaller or larger. This corresponds to the axially symmetric case in Agrawal, Bagh, and Mardan (2025). To simplify notation, let the jurisdictions now be indexed by $i = a, s, \sigma$ where $a$ stands for the asymmetric jurisdiction and $s$ and $\sigma$ stand for the symmetric jurisdictions. The asymmetric jurisdiction ($i = a$) has a different size—possibly smaller or larger than the other two jurisdictions. To implement this, suppose that the total amount of taxable economic activity in the world is fixed and is normalized to 3 units, such that if all three jurisdictions were the same size they would have one unit of activity. To model the asymmetries, let $-1 < \theta < 1$ denote the relative size advantage (or disadvantage) of jurisdiction $a$. Thus, in the absence of shifting $\Theta_a = 1 + \theta$. As the total amount of activity in the world is fixed, then the sizes of the two symmetric jurisdictions are $\Theta_s = \Theta_\sigma = 1 - \theta/2$. Critically, if $\theta < 0$ jurisdiction $a$ is smaller, while if $\theta > 0$ jurisdiction $a$ is larger, and if $\theta = 0$, all jurisdictions are symmetric.

All subsequent proofs to solve this model are in Appendix A. As the $\theta$ parameter is critical to the analysis below, table 3.1 summarizes the asymmetries in the model.

### 3.3.1 The Uncoordinated Nash Equilibrium

Because of the finite number of jurisdictions, the jurisdictions have some market power in this closed system and thus are strategic—game theoretic—in their tax-setting behavior. The existence of strategic interactions are common in many models of tax competition and arise naturally in models of commodity tax competition where the tax base is locally mobile. If jurisdictions do not have market power, perhaps because they are atomistic in size or there are infinitely many jurisdictions, then jurisdictions are not strategic in their tax-setting behavior. But, even jurisdictions that are not strategic engage in tax competition—of the perfectly competitive form—and as a result the tax competition equilibrium is inefficient even if jurisdictions are not strategic. The strategic model here is best suited for competition within a metropolitan area, but even at the international level, jurisdictions may be strategic in their tax setting behavior. Differentiating the revenue functions yields the best response functions:

(5)
$$T_s = \frac{1}{4}\delta\left(1 - \frac{1}{2}\theta\right) + \frac{1}{4}T_a + \frac{1}{4}T_\sigma$$
$$T_\sigma = \frac{1}{4}\delta\left(1 - \frac{1}{2}\theta\right) + \frac{1}{4}T_a + \frac{1}{4}T_s$$
$$T_a = \frac{1}{4}\delta(1 + \theta) + \frac{1}{4}T_s + \frac{1}{4}T_\sigma .$$

The slopes of these functions indicate that for a one unit increase in a competitor's tax rate, a jurisdiction will strategically match that increase with a one-quarter unit tax increase. Thus, as in all models of revenue maximization, tax rates are strategic complements.

And solving for the uncoordinated Nash equilibrium yields uncoordinated equilibrium tax rates of

(6)v
$$T^U \equiv T_s^U = T_\sigma^U = \frac{1}{2}\delta - \frac{1}{10}\delta\theta$$
$$T_a^U = \frac{1}{2}\delta + \frac{1}{5}\delta\theta,$$

where the superscript $U$ denotes the uncoordinated Nash tax rates. This implies a tax differential of

(7)
$$T_a^U - T^U = \frac{3}{10}\delta\theta,$$

which indicates that the larger of the jurisdictions always sets the higher tax rate. This result is consistent with the prior literature: starting from equal tax rates, a larger jurisdiction perceives a smaller elasticity because its base is larger. Then, following a Ramsey rule, the lower elasticity implies a higher tax rate. Total equilibrium revenues are then given by

(8)
$$R^U \equiv R_s^U = R_\sigma^U = \frac{1}{50}d(\theta - 5)^2$$
$$R_a^U = \frac{1}{50}d(2\theta + 5)^2 .$$

Under the assumptions of the model, such a Nash equilibrium is guaranteed to exist because the best response functions slope upward and therefor the game is supermodular (Topkis 1979). The equilibrium has the standard properties in the literature: the larger jurisdiction sets a higher tax rate and taxes are increasing in the shifting cost parameter. The existence of tax differentials in the Nash equilibrium then implies that shifting occurs from the big jurisdiction(s) to the smaller jurisdiction(s). Moreover, the bigger jurisdiction realizes more tax revenue.

It is clear that the uncoordinated equilibrium is inefficient. To see this, I can solve the social (joint maximization) problem,[15] which maximizes aggregate tax revenues of all three jurisdictions:

$$R_{joint} = \sum_i T_i\left(\Theta_i - \sum_{j \neq i} \frac{T_i - T_j}{\delta}\right) = \sum_i T_i \Theta_i. \tag{9}$$

The second equality follows because one jurisdictions gain from shifting is another jurisdiction's loss ($s_{ij} = -s_{ji}$). Then maximizing (9), because the tax base is inelastic except for shifting, would result in governments setting a tax rate that is so high that it extracts all private surplus from the taxed individuals or firms. Calling this tax rate $T^*$, it is then clear that $T_a^U < T^*$ and $T^U < T^*$. In other words, the tax competition equilibrium is inefficient, not socially optimal: it will yield lower government spending than in the absence of tax competition.

### 3.4 Tax Coordination

Having solved for the uncoordinated equilibrium, in this section I consider various policies that are designed to limit the effects of tax competition: harmonization, minimum tax rates, partial harmonization with forced cooperation, partial harmonization with coalition formation, and sourcing rules. I analyze what happens to tax rates, whether tax revenues improve in all jurisdictions, and subsequently whether tax revenues improve for the entire system of jurisdictions.

#### 3.4.1 Harmonization

One commonly discussed policy intervention is tax harmonization, which requires all jurisdictions to set a common tax rate. Harmonization might be achieved by a federal mandate within a country or within a supranational institution such as the European Union. While the harmonized rate could conceivably be to any tax rate, a common proposal—and the focus of this chapter—is to harmonize to a weighted average of the Nash equilibrium (uncoordinated) tax rates:

$$\tau = \omega T_a^U + (1 - \omega)T^U, \tag{10}$$

where weight $\omega \in [0,1]$ is given to the asymmetric jurisdiction—potentially the higher or lower tax jurisdiction depending on its size—and equal weights of $(1 - \omega)/2$ are given to each of the symmetric jurisdictions.

15. Note that in this model, maximizing joint revenues is equivalent to maximizing each jurisdiction's closed economy tax revenues separately, if the reservation value for the economic activity to occur is the same across all jurisdictions.

Before proceeding to the formal analysis, there are two policy relevant points to note about this type of harmonization. First, in the perfectly symmetric case where all three jurisdictions are identical ($\theta = 0$), harmonization to a weighted average of Nash tax rates would not be an actual policy intervention because the weighted average is simply equal to the uncoordinated rate set by all three jurisdictions. Second, harmonization to a weighted average of the Nash tax rates may not achieve the socially optimal tax rates. In particular, if tax competition results in inefficiently low tax rates, it is possible that the Nash tax rates of *all* jurisdictions are less than the socially optimal lowest tax rate. Thus, there is no value of $\omega$ that can achieve that desired outcome. Further, if the socially optimal tax rates are differentiated across jurisdictions, then harmonization does not allow for any of this diversity in tax rates.

What are the effects of harmonization in the simple shifting model presented previously? Under the assumptions above, proving the effects of harmonization follows closely Kanbur and Keen (1993), but as will become apparent, the results become more nuanced. Because harmonizing tax rates results in the elimination of tax differentials, no tax base shifting will occur after the policy is implemented. As a result, the tax bases of each jurisdiction are simply equal to their "closed" economy bases. Then, tax revenue in each jurisdiction is $\tau\Theta_i$ and is increasing in $\tau$. Thus, each jurisdiction would achieve the most tax revenue by harmonizing to the highest possible tax rate. But, for various weights $\omega$, the question remains as to if the harmonized amount of revenue is better than the Nash tax revenue. Evaluating $\tau\Theta_i$ using (10) and comparing it with the uncoordinated revenues in (8) implies a cutoff rule in $\omega$ for which harmonization lowers or raises revenues.

For the two jurisdictions of a similar size, $s$ and $\sigma$, the revenue under tax harmonization is greater than the revenue earned in the uncoordinated equilibrium if

$$(11) \qquad \omega \begin{array}{c} > \\ < \end{array} \frac{\theta - 5}{5(\theta - 2)} \quad \begin{array}{l} \text{if } \theta \geq 0 \\ \text{if } \theta < 0 \end{array}.$$

Critically, if these jurisdictions are smaller than the other ($\theta > 0$), then the weight on the higher tax jurisdiction $a$ needs to be sufficiently large. Intuitively, if the harmonized rate is too low, then the smaller jurisdictions lose by foregoing revenue from activity shifted into their jurisdiction but gain little additional revenue from their home base of economic activity. Only if the added revenue from their home base outweighs the losses of revenue from foregoing the inward shifted economic activity do they gain. If $s$ and $\sigma$ are the larger ($\theta < 0$) jurisdictions, the weight on the other smaller jurisdiction needs to be sufficiently low. Intuitively, a high-tax jurisdiction can always gain from harmonization to its own tax rate: it gains revenue from economic activity previously shifted out of the jurisdiction while maintaining its same tax rate.

Now turning to jurisdiction $a$, the asymmetric jurisdiction requires

$$\omega \begin{matrix} > \\ < \end{matrix} \frac{3\theta}{5(\theta+1)} \quad \begin{matrix} \text{if } \theta \geq 0 \\ \text{if } \theta < 0 \end{matrix}, \tag{12}$$

in order for harmonization to revenue-dominate the uncoordinated equilibrium. Critically, the second branch makes it clear that if the asymmetric jurisdiction is the smaller one ($\theta < 0$), there exist no (positive) weights that will result in tax coordination improving the revenue of the jurisdiction. However, if the asymmetric jurisdiction is the larger one ($\theta > 0$), then $\omega$ must be sufficiently large for the jurisdiction to benefit from harmonization. In other words, tax harmonization that is too close to the lower uncoordinated Nash tax rate, $T^U$, will harm the larger country because it loses revenue from its previously loyal base, which is not fully compensated by a reduction in shifting.

Combining this evidence, if $\theta < 0$, harmonization will not be able to find a political consensus on purely revenue grounds. But if $\theta > 0$, all jurisdictions will agree to harmonize *if* the harmonized rate is sufficiently high. In particular, it is clear that (11) is always larger than (12) for all relevant values of $\theta$. Thus, (11) determines the minimum feasible weight for which revenue will improve in all jurisdictions—using the language of Kanbur and Keen (1993), a Pareto-improving policy. For example, if $\theta = 0.50$, the weight must exceed $\omega = 0.60$. At the same time, if the weight is too low rather than too high, then both jurisdictions may lose tax revenue. For example, $\omega = 0$ will result in the low-tax jurisdiction keeping the same rate, but losing activity shifted into its jurisdiction, while the high-tax jurisdiction will apply a much lower rate to its home base. Thus, despite the existence of Pareto-improving harmonization policies, all jurisdictions might fear harmonization if they worry the harmonized weight is too low.

**Proposition 1**: In a world with two small jurisdictions and one large jurisdiction, tax harmonization will improve tax revenues in all jurisdictions if the weight on the larger jurisdiction is sufficiently high, but if that weight is too low, both jurisdictions will lose revenue. If instead, there are two large jurisdictions and one small jurisdiction, tax harmonization will surely harm the smaller jurisdiction and will only benefit the larger jurisdictions if the weight on the smaller jurisdiction is sufficiently low.

The proposition stands in contrast to the stark result in Kanbur and Keen (1993). In their model with only two countries, tax harmonization to any tax rate between the Nash tax rates will *always* harm the small country and may harm the large country if harmonization is to a rate that is too low. Intuitively this occurs because revenue in the small jurisdiction (using small/large letters now to distinguish quantities for the small/large jurisdiction in their model) in the uncoordinated Nash equilibrium is $r(t^U, T^U)$. Under a harmonized equilibrium, at the harmonized rate where revenue would be its highest, revenue is $r(T^U, T^U)$. But in Kanbur and Keen (1993), a simple revealed preference argument rules out this yielding higher revenue: the small jurisdiction did not choose $T^U$ as its Nash tax rate when the big jurisdiction choose $T^U$; thus harmonization must make it worse off. In my model, harmonization may improve the outcomes of smaller jurisdictions if there are multiple of them. The intuition is clear. When there are now three jurisdictions, the Nash revenues in the small jurisdictions are $R_s(T^U, T_a^U, T^U)$. Why is harmonization to the higher tax rate revenue improving in this case? Notice with $\omega = 1$, the harmonized tax revenue in the smaller jurisdiction is $R_s(T_a^U, T_a^U, T_a^U)$. Unlike the case of two jurisdictions, a revealed preference argument no longer applies because harmonization changes rates for multiple jurisdictions. In particular, the harmonized rate forces all other small jurisdictions to also raise their rates, leaving the possibility that each one is now better off. The presence of multiple jurisdictions implies that jurisdictions compete with more competitors (Hoyt 1991). The increase in the number of competitors heightens tax competition and the extent of tax base externalities in the uncoordinated equilibrium. As a result, small jurisdictions may gain revenues because harmonization mitigates this fiercer form of tax competition.

Under complete harmonization, the tax rate is imposed by a supranational institution or by a federal government on all of its states. In other words, harmonization is not modeled as a result of a grand coalition from which exit could occur, but rather is a result of a mandate. Thus, I do not consider the possibility that jurisdictions will explicitly defect in this section; coalition formation will be considered subsequently. But the above proposition indicates which jurisdictions would politically support harmonization from a tax revenue perspective.

### 3.4.2 Minimum Tax Rates

Minimum tax rates differ from harmonization because they only bind for jurisdictions setting taxes below the imposed minimum rate.[16] As a result, a minimum rate forces low-tax jurisdictions to raise their rates, but unlike harmonization, does not require high-tax jurisdictions to lower their rates—and indeed, may even allow them to raise their rates. I consider the interesting case where the minimum tax rate binds for some jurisdictions but not for others. In other words, the minimum tax rate is given by (10) with weight $\omega \in (0,1]$ given to the asymmetric jurisdiction's equilibrium tax rate.

#### *3.4.2.1 Minimum Tax Rate Binds for Multiple Jurisdictions*

First, consider the case where $\theta > 0$ so that the asymmetric jurisdiction is the larger of the three. In this case, the symmetric jurisdictions, $s$ and $\sigma$, will be forced to set a minimum tax rate $\tau$ given by (10). The larger jurisdiction is not constrained by this tax rate, and given its best response function

16. See Konrad (2009) for a case with a nonbinding minimum tax rate.

slopes upward, will find it in its interest to raise its tax rate. In this case, its best response becomes:

$$T_a = \frac{1}{4}\delta(1+\theta) + \frac{1}{2}\tau, \tag{13}$$

which is also the new equilibrium tax rate, $T_a^M$, as a function of the exogenous parameters.

In this case, the minimum tax rate increases revenues of both jurisdictions. The proof of the effect of the minimum tax rate on revenues follows Nielsen (2001). Tax revenues in the smaller jurisdictions are then $[\tau\delta(5-\theta) - 2\tau^2]/4\delta$, which are concave in the minimum tax rate. If the minimum were set to $T^U$, revenues would clearly be unchanged. But at this point, the derivative with respect to $\tau$ is positive, as it is for all possible values of $\tau$. If on the other hand, the minimum were set to $T_a^U$, the jurisdiction clearly collects higher tax revenues than the uncoordinated equilibrium, so the same must be true for all intermediate values of $\tau$. As for the bigger jurisdiction, its tax revenue is $[\delta(1+\theta) + 2\tau^2]/8\delta$, which are clearly higher than $R_a^U$ for all values of $\omega > 0$.

### *3.4.2.2 Minimum Tax Rate Binds for a Single Jurisdiction*

Second, consider the case where $\theta < 0$ so that the asymmetric jurisdiction, $a$, is the smaller of the three and thus sets the lower rate in the uncoordinated equilibrium. Then, the jurisdictions for which the minimum tax rate does not bind ($i = s, \sigma$) can adjust their tax rates in response. Evaluating the best response functions (5) at the minimum tax rate and solving for the new equilibrium tax rates, denoting it with a superscript $M$, yields

$$T_s^M = T_\sigma^M = \frac{1}{3}\left(1 - \frac{\theta}{2}\right) + \frac{1}{3}\tau. \tag{14}$$

In this case, the minimum tax rate may harm some jurisdictions while benefiting others. As for these bigger jurisdictions, tax revenues are $[\delta(\theta-2) - 2\tau]^2/18\delta$, which are clearly higher than $R^U$ for all values of $\omega > 0$. Thus, again, the minimum tax helps the jurisdictions set higher tax rates than the uncoordinated tax equilibrium, allowing them to raise more revenue. Matters are more complex for the lower-tax jurisdiction for which the minimum tax rate binds. Tax revenues are $[\tau\delta(5+2\theta) - 4\tau^2]/3\delta$, which are concave in the minimum tax rate. At the lowest possible value of the minimum tax rate, the jurisdiction is clearly unaffected, but the derivative of revenues with respect to the minimum tax rate is positive. However, at the highest possible value of the minimum tax rate, revenue may yield higher or lower revenue than the uncoordinated case. In particular, at its highest possible value, the minimum tax rate regime will yield higher revenues in this case where $\theta < 0$ if:

$$-\frac{1}{50}\delta(8\theta + 5)\theta > 0 \Leftrightarrow \theta > -\frac{5}{8}. \tag{15}$$

Obviously, a similar value can be solved for involving intermediate weights $\omega$. Keeping in mind that $\theta < 0$ in this case, the prior expression says the minimum tax rate will only be revenue improving if the size asymmetries between jurisdictions are sufficiently small. Otherwise, the jurisdiction would have been better off in the uncoordinated equilibrium, where its much smaller size allowed it to aggressively undercut the larger jurisdictions and capture a large amount of economic activity shifted into the jurisdiction. But if size asymmetries are sufficiently small, the minimum tax rate raises revenues on its own tax base in a manner that offsets any loss from inward shifting.

**Proposition 2**: *In a world with two small jurisdictions and one large jurisdiction, a binding minimum tax rate will improve tax revenues in all jurisdictions regardless of the level of the minimum tax rate. If instead there are two large jurisdictions and one small jurisdiction, a binding minimum tax rate will improve tax revenues in all jurisdictions if the size differences between the jurisdictions are sufficiently small.*

Unlike tax harmonization, strategic responses still occur with a minimum tax rate. In the new Nash equilibrium, the small jurisdiction sets the minimum tax rate, still undercutting the large jurisdiction. But the higher tax rate that it sets then allows the larger jurisdiction to strategically respond. As shown above, the minimum tax rate can raise revenue for the smaller jurisdiction. Even though the small jurisdiction will gain revenue from being forced to raise its tax rate, it would not have raised the tax on its own because doing so would induce the large jurisdiction to respond.

In contrast to harmonization, ignoring the case where size differences are very large, revenue is higher in both jurisdictions. All jurisdictions now set higher tax rates, but the increase is greater in the small jurisdiction—the effect on the large jurisdiction's tax is dampened by the slope of best response function. Thus, interjurisdictional tax differentials fall. Because the minimum tax rate reduces tax differentials, revenue therefore certainly increase in the larger jurisdictions. But similar to harmonization, the effect on the small jurisdiction is initially unclear: revenue is gained from taxing the loyal base as a higher rate, but lost through diminished tax shifting into the jurisdiction. The former effect can be shown to dominate under most conditions because the minimum tax rate mitigates tax competition. This is a remarkably strong result that establishes a clear dominance of the minimum-tax strategy over that of harmonization. Harmonizing to any tax rate between the unconstrained Nash equilibrium will likely harm the small jurisdiction and may also harm the large jurisdiction, but imposing that same rate as a minimum will be to the benefit of all.

### 3.4.3 Forced Cooperation: Partial Harmonization

As an alternative to complete harmonization, a central government could "force" two jurisdictions to cooperate with each other and set a common tax rate. I label this type of coordination as *partial harmonization*, meaning that the tax rates of a subset of jurisdiction are harmonized. With partial harmonization, the government could either force the two symmetric jurisdictions to cooperate or force the asymmetric jurisdiction to cooperate with one of the symmetric jurisdictions.

### 3.4.3.1 Cooperation Between Two Symmetric Jurisdictions

Initially, assume that cooperation is forced upon the two symmetric jurisdictions, similar to the setup of Konrad and Schjelderup (1999). Jurisdictions $s$ and $\sigma$ then set a common tax rate denoted $T_{s\sigma}$ and raise common (total) revenue of $R_{s\sigma}$. This coalition then chooses its tax rate $T_{s\sigma}$ in a Nash game with jurisdiction $a$. The tax revenue function for the coordinated jurisdiction and the uncoordinated jurisdiction are

$$(16)\qquad \begin{aligned} R_{s\sigma} &= 2 - \theta - \frac{2(T_{s\sigma} - T_a)}{\delta} \\ R_a &= 1 + \theta - \frac{2(T_a - T_{s\sigma})}{\delta}, \end{aligned}$$

where the tax base in the coordinated jurisdictions is twice their closed border sizes plus a shifting term. Critically, the shifting term appears twice in the revenue functions. The reason for this is that the cost of shifting is jurisdiction pair specific, and I assume this pair-specific shifting remains for each member after the coalition forms. Tax coordination does not eliminate the two jurisdictions, but rather just forces them to set a common tax rate. Thus, there is a shifting rule that determines the amount of shifting between $s$ and $a$ along with another rule that determines shifting between $\sigma$ and $a$; in other words the cost of shifting is unchanged. Given the common tax rate, the same cutoff rule hold for both pairs. Its useful to think of this using the example of the commodity tax setting: coordinating tax rates still imply the cooperative has two borders from which it loses cross-border shoppers.[17] However, there is no shifting between $s$ and $\sigma$ as the tax rate is harmonized.

Differentiating the revenue functions and solving obtains the Nash tax rates, superscripted by $C$ for cooperation, with the forced coalition members in parenthesis:

$$(17)\qquad \begin{aligned} T_{s\sigma}^{C(s\sigma)} &= \frac{1}{6}\delta(5 - \theta) \\ T_a^{C(s\sigma)} &= \frac{1}{6}\delta(4 + \theta), \end{aligned}$$

17. As an alternative example, firms in $s$ and $\sigma$ still have incentives to shift profits to $a$ with the same cost function.

implying a tax differential between the cooperative and the noncooperating jurisdiction of:

$$(18) \qquad T_{s\sigma}^{C(s\sigma)} - T_{a}^{C(s\sigma)} = \frac{1}{3}\delta\left(\frac{1}{2} - \theta\right).$$

From this tax difference between the cooperating jurisdiction and the noncooperating jurisdiction, notice that if the cooperating jurisdictions are sufficiently similarly sized as the other jurisdiction ($0 < \theta < 1/2$) or initially larger than the other jurisdiction ($\theta < 0$), the cooperative will set a higher tax rate than the noncooperating jurisdiction. But if the jurisdiction outside the cooperative is sufficiently large ($\theta > 1/2$), the noncooperating jurisdiction will set a higher tax rate. Intuitively, joining two larger jurisdictions will make them even larger in their common base. And if these jurisdictions are not too small initially, their combined size will still be larger than the other jurisdiction. Then, starting from equal tax rates, the cooperative will perceive a smaller elasticity and mark up its tax rate. However, if the jurisdictions are initially very small, their combined tax base will not exceed that of the larger jurisdiction, and they will still perceive the larger elasticity and set the lower tax rate.

Next, despite this ambiguity in the tax differential, it is easy to show that for all values of $\theta$, taxes in the cooperative and the noncooperative are higher than the uncoordinated equilibrium: $T_{s\sigma}^{C(s\sigma)} > T^{U}$ and $T_{a}^{C(s\sigma)} > T_{a}^{U}$. Partial harmonization allows the cooperating jurisdictions to set higher tax rates by reducing the intensity of tax competition; because taxes are strategic complements, the outside member also raises its tax rate.

What about tax revenues? Although tax rates are rising in all jurisdictions, the tax differential will generally change in response to cooperation. As a result, the equilibrium tax bases of the jurisdictions change relative to the noncooperative equilibrium. As a result, some jurisdictions will see a reduction in inward shifting of activity. This possibly negative effect is offset by less intense tax competition, due to a smaller number of competing jurisdictions, and higher tax rates on the loyal base. Despite the possibility of counteracting effects, it is also easy to show that in the presence of equally splitting tax revenues within the cooperative, $R_{s\sigma}^{C(s\sigma)}/2 > R^{U}$.[18] The cooperative sets a higher tax rate and tax competition between the two jurisdictions is eliminated, both raising revenues. The same holds true for the noncooperating jurisdiction, $R_{a}^{C(s\sigma)} > R_{a}^{U}$: it sets a higher tax rate and benefits from less intense tax competition. This result is consistent with Hoyt (1991), who shows that the smaller the number of jurisdictions, tax competition becomes

18. In this case, because both jurisdictions are equally sized, it is reasonable to believe that tax revenues are split equally among them. Equal splitting would be identical to splitting tax revenues proportional to the equilibrium bases in this case.

less intense, which raises tax rates. Thus, these channels dominate any loss of shifting into initially the low-tax jurisdiction.

### 3.4.3.2 *Cooperation Among Asymmetric Jurisdictions*

Next, assume partial harmonization involves a coalition of two jurisdictions that differ in size. Without loss of generality consider the possibility that jurisdictions $a$ and $\sigma$ cooperate, but jurisdiction $s$ does not. Then, the tax base in the absence of shifting of the cooperative is $2 + \theta/2$ while it is $1 - \theta/2$ in the noncooperating jurisdiction. As in (16), there are similar cutoff rules for shifting that enter into the tax base, allowing me to construct the revenue function. Solving for the Nash equilibrium in tax rates yields:

$$(19) \qquad T_s^{C(a\sigma)} = \frac{1}{6}\delta\left(4 - \frac{1}{2}\theta\right)$$

$$T_{a\sigma}^{C(a\sigma)} = \frac{1}{6}\delta\left(5 + \frac{1}{2}\theta\right),$$

implying a tax differential of

$$(20) \qquad T_{a\sigma}^{C(a\sigma)} - T_s^{C(a\sigma)} = \frac{1}{6}\delta(\theta + 1) > 0.$$

Critically, unlike the prior case, notice the tax differential is always positive. This indicates that when two jurisdictions that differ in size cooperate, the tax rate in the cooperative is surely to be higher than the tax rate in the other jurisdiction. This result follows because $2 + \theta/2$ is always larger than $1 - \theta/2$ so that, starting from equal taxes, the cooperative always perceives the smaller elasticity and raises its tax rate. Simply put, the cooperative will always have a size advantage relative to the other jurisdiction. Notice that this even holds true if the asymmetric jurisdiction is the smallest: combining one large jurisdiction with a very small one still means the cooperative is largest.

Given the above statement, then it is clear that the equilibrium tax rates of the cooperating jurisdictions are always higher than those in the uncoordinated Nash equilibrium ($T_{a\sigma}^{C(a\sigma)} > T_a^U$; $T_{a\sigma}^{C(a\sigma)} > T_\sigma^U$). For the jurisdiction external to the cooperative, it can be verified that its tax rate also rises relative to the uncoordinated case. Intuitively, tax competition is dampened, which places upward pressure on its tax rate. Revenues in the noncooperating jurisdiction unambiguously increase as well, as tax rates are higher and tax competition dampened ($R_s^{C(a\sigma)} > R_s^U$).

In this case, cooperating jurisdictions differ in size. Thus, comparing tax revenues of jurisdictions within the cooperative to their uncoordinated values requires further assumptions about how revenues are split among the jurisdictions in the cooperative. In a comprehensive model, the split of tax revenues would be modeled via a formal bargaining process such as

Nash bargaining (Nash 1950). However, in this chapter, I take two stylized approaches, leaving more formal analysis for future research. This simple approach might be justified as an exogenous rule determined by the federal government that determines how revenues are split in coalitions.

One simple possibility is that revenues are equally divided within the cooperative, while an alternative possibility is that revenues are allocated proportional to the declared equilibrium tax bases within each member jurisdiction. Under equal splitting, if $\theta$ is sufficiently negative, then revenues will fall in jurisdiction $\sigma$ relative to the noncooperative equilibrium; otherwise, revenues increase. The opposite is true for jurisdiction $a$: if $\theta$ is sufficiently large (and positive), revenues will fall for this jurisdiction relative to the noncooperative equilibrium.[19] Intuitively, equal splitting of revenues advantages the small jurisdiction at the expense of the large jurisdiction. On the other hand, if tax revenues are allocated proportional to their tax bases in each local jurisdiction, then if $\theta$ is of an intermediate value, tax revenues will rise in both jurisdictions relative to the noncooperative case ($R_a^{C(a\sigma)} > R_a^U$; $R_\sigma^{C(a\sigma)} > R_\sigma^U$).[20] Intuitively, the larger jurisdiction benefits from less tax competition even though it gives up some of its size advantage, while the smaller jurisdiction of the two gives up its ability to undercut.

**Proposition 3**: *Regardless of the two jurisdictions cooperating, partial harmonization raises tax rates in all jurisdictions relative to the uncoordinated Nash equilibrium. If two symmetric jurisdictions cooperate, tax revenues also rise in all jurisdictions. But, if two jurisdictions of different sizes are forced to cooperate, while revenues unambiguously increase in the noncooperating jurisdiction, revenues may rise or fall in the cooperative member jurisdictions. If revenues are allocated proportional to the coordinated equilibrium tax bases or equally shared, then there exist scenarios where revenues increase in both cooperative members relative to the noncooperative setting.*

The proposition has some similarities to Konrad and Schjelderup (1999). In their model, all jurisdictions are symmetric. They then show that if a subset of jurisdictions coordinate on a tax rate marginally higher than the uncoordinated equilibrium and if taxes are strategic complements, the welfare of each jurisdiction (both inside and outside of the jurisdiction) increases. Further, in the coordinated Nash equilibrium, they show the coordinating jurisdictions receive higher welfare. These results have parallels to the result above, showing that revenues rise relative to the uncoordinated equilibrium. However, the asymmetry of jurisdictions present in my model, but not in

19. The precise condition for revenue to increase in jurisdiction $a$ requires $-263\theta^2 - 940\theta + 700 > 0$ or $\theta$ needs to be smaller than approximately 0.63. For jurisdiction $\sigma$ to increase its revenue requires $-47\theta^2 - 1220\theta - 700 > 0$ or $\theta$ needs to be larger than approximately $-0.56$.

20. The precise condition for revenue to increase in jurisdiction $a$ requires $\theta > -10/19$. For jurisdiction $\sigma$, it requires $\theta < 10/17$.

theirs, allows for a richer array of outcomes for the individual jurisdictions, showing that the precise coalition of jurisdictions matters.

### 3.4.4 Voluntary Cooperation: Partial Harmonization

The prior section considered forced cooperation, but in many countries, intermunicipal cooperation or the signing of tax treaties is voluntary. In these cases, jurisdictions have flexibility to determine with whom to cooperate with. As a result, the decision to cooperate—and with whom—is endogenous to the tax competition game. As a result, coalition formation becomes a necessary part of the game, similar to the setup of Burbidge et al. (1997). I consider coalition formation in this section.

In stage one, jurisdictions decide with whom to cooperate, if anyone. The rules are as follows. There is no preplay or precommunication in this model.[21] Each of the three jurisdictions declares a possible partner. Each jurisdiction has three strategies that they may declare. For example, jurisdiction $s$ may play $\sigma$, $a$, or $s$, where the first two strategies denote possible coalition partners and the last strategy indicates an intent to go it alone. If two of the jurisdictions declare a strategy that results in both wanting to be in the same coalition, then that coalition is formed regardless of the third player's strategy. If no two jurisdictions declare each other, the jurisdictions then act in an uncoordinated game. In stage two, taxes are set in a Nash game. The game is solved backwards and simply requires comparing tax revenues under the different combinations of coalitions to solve for the equilibrium coalition.

When thinking about coalition formation, the equilibrium concept is important. For purposes of this chapter, I use the standard Nash equilibrium concept. This concept is intuitive, but likely a weak equilibrium concept for a noncooperative game of this form. To see this, note that in a Nash equilibrium, each jurisdiction takes as given the strategies of the other players. Thus, the Nash game does not consider mutually beneficial deviations by possible coalitions of players. For coalition games, it would instead be reasonable for players to discuss their strategy in a preplay stage, though without making a binding commitment. In this case, it must be that any agreement is self-enforcing. The Nash concept is a necessary requirement for any agreement to be self-enforcing, but it is not sufficient. Given this, Bernheim, Peleg and Whinston (1987a, 1987b) define a coalition-proof Nash equilibrium, which are the Pareto efficient strategies that are self-enforcing: if no coalition of players, given a fixed action of its complement, can agree to deviate such that all members of the coalition are better off. While such an equilibrium concept is more realistic, it is more demanding, and given the overview purpose of this chapter, I focus on the weaker Nash concept. The Nash concept sheds light on the possible set of equilibrium, ruling out

21. See Konrad and Thum (2021) for a model of tax coordination with negotiations.

some possibilities, even if it is less realistic than the coalition-proof Nash equilibrium. An alternative to the coalition-proof Nash concept would be a strong Nash equilibrium (Aumann 1959), but such an equilibrium often does not exist.

The Nash equilibrium concept is applied by considering all possible combinations of declarations of strategies ($\sigma$, $a$, or $s$) by all three jurisdictions ($\sigma$, $a$, or $s$). The Nash equilibrium is obtained by taking as given the other two players' declarations and determining whether there exists a unilateral deviation by one jurisdiction. It does not require I check coordinated deviations by two jurisdictions. Keep in mind that the Nash concept has been applied to solve for all tax rates; the Nash equilibrium solved for here can be viewed as a two-stage coordinated Nash equilibrium, which differs from the single-stage uncoordinated Nash equilibrium above.

To determine the payoff of each jurisdiction in each regime, the revenue splitting rule is important. I proceed by considering both the scenario where taxes are distributed proportional to the size of the equilibrium tax base in each jurisdiction and, alternatively, the case where tax revenues are split equally. Furthermore, for simplicity, I also assume that there cannot be a grand coalition that would form or that the federal government exogenously prohibits such a coalition, in which case the tax base would be completely captive and taxes and revenues would be excessively high. In a model of welfare maximization, allowing for the grand coalition would be important. But, even then, there are plausible explanations to rule out a grand coalition. One possibility at the national level is that it is nearly impossible to implement tax coordination across all countries in the world. An obvious example is an EU versus US story, where coordination incentives are stronger within the EU than between European and North American countries. Another possible justification at the local level is that municipal cooperation across state borders is challenging due to institutional differences in the rules governing local policymaking. Even beyond those institutional arguments, there are economic reasons to believe that larger coalitions with more members may entail substantial costs that may outweigh the gains of coordination (Alesina and Spolaore 2005).

With two symmetric jurisdictions cooperating, the revenue distribution to each member state is invariant to the splitting rule. When two symmetric jurisdictions cooperate, then equilibrium revenues for each member state, denoted with a superscript $C$ for cooperation, under voluntary partial cooperation are

(21)
$$\frac{R_s^{C(s\sigma)}}{2} = \frac{R_\sigma^{C(s\sigma)}}{2} = \tilde{R}_s^{C(s\sigma)} = \tilde{R}_\sigma^{C(s\sigma)} = \frac{1}{36}\delta(\theta - 5)^2$$
$$\tilde{R}_a^{C(s\sigma)} = \frac{1}{18}\delta(\theta + 4)^2$$

where the subscript denotes the jurisdiction receiving the revenue and the term in parenthesis of the superscript is the coalition. The tilde denotes that the revenue under an allocation rule that is proportional to the tax base.

But when two asymmetric jurisdiction cooperate together, the revenue distribution method is important. With revenues allocated proportional to the tax bases, revenues under cooperation are:

$$(22) \qquad \begin{aligned} \tilde{R}_s^{C(a\sigma)} &= \frac{1}{72}\delta(\theta - 8)^2 \\ \tilde{R}_a^{C(a\sigma)} &= \frac{5}{72}\delta(\theta + 10)(1 + \theta) \\ \tilde{R}_\sigma^{C(a\sigma)} &= \frac{1}{72}\delta(\theta + 10)(5 - 4\theta). \end{aligned}$$

Equilibrium revenues for the coalition between *as* can be derived similarly by flipping the revenues for jurisdiction $s$ and $\sigma$. When the splitting rule is governed by equal splitting, tax revenue in each jurisdiction is one-half the coalition's tax revenue, with formal expressions given in Appendix A, section Derivation: Voluntary Cooperation.

Then, pairwise revenue comparisons of each regime indicate that the preferred strategies for each jurisdiction depend on the value of $\theta$. The revenue hierarchy for each jurisdiction, conditional on a value of $\theta$, can then be used to construct the Nash payoff matrices. These matrices in Appendix A, section Derivation: Voluntary Cooperation, allow me to solve for the Nash equilibrium coalitions. All formal derivations are relegated to the appendix.

As discussed above, the Nash concept is relatively weak so multiple equilibria often exist, so I only focus only on equilibria where a coalition will form, ignoring those where the game reduces to its uncoordinated form.

**Proposition 4**: *Regardless of whether tax revenues are split proportional to the jurisdiction's tax bases or equally split, a coalition between one of the symmetric jurisdictions and the asymmetric jurisdiction is only an equilibrium if the size asymmetries are of intermediate values. On the other hand, regardless of whether tax revenues are split proportional to the tax bases or equally split, a coalition between both symmetric jurisdictions is an equilibrium for all size differentials.*

The proposition states that if tax revenues are split proportional to the tax base, then, *a* partnering with one of the other two jurisdiction will only arise if $\theta$ is sufficiently close to zero. If $\theta$ is too far away from zero, then coalitions *as* and *aσ* can never arise in equilibrium. Intuitively, if the asymmetric jurisdiction is too small ($\theta \to -1$), it prefers to deviate to be alone: when a very small jurisdiction is alone, it can set a low tax rate but attract a very large tax base due to shifting into the jurisdiction. If the asymmetric jurisdiction is too large ($\theta \rightarrow 1$), then the symmetric jurisdictions either prefer their own coalition or the uncoordinated game because, with base-splitting, their very small size means they only receive a negligible amount of the coalition's tax revenue.

On the other hand, a coalition between symmetric members will arise for all values of $\theta$. Intuitively, when $\theta > 0$, two smaller jurisdictions join together. However, the smaller jurisdictions have no incentive to deviate to be with the large jurisdiction—in fact, they wish the other small jurisdiction were in a coalition with $a$. Any deviation to be with $a$ thus results in very low payoffs for the jurisdiction deviating because the base is allocated proportional to relative equilibrium sizes. If $\theta < 0$, the equilibrium with a coalition among symmetric jurisdictions arises only if player $a$ declares that it wants to go it alone, in which case the coalition of $s$ and $\sigma$ is better than the uncoordinated equilibrium. However, if $a$ does not declare $a$, then the coalition of symmetric jurisdictions cannot emerge when $\theta < 0$.

With equal splitting, $s\sigma$ is similarly a Nash equilibrium for all values of $\theta$, as equal splitting is identical to base splitting if the members are symmetric. But, matters are more nuanced for coalition $as$ or $a\sigma$. Again, like base splitting, $a$ partnering with one of the other two jurisdictions will only arise if $\theta$ is in an intermediate range. Intuitively, if the asymmetric jurisdiction is too small ($\theta \rightarrow -1$), forming a coalition with $a$ always yields the lowest payoff for the larger symmetric jurisdiction, as the gains from combining only result in a slightly higher tax rate, but require the larger jurisdiction to give up a substantial amount of revenue to the smaller due to the unfavorable splitting rule. If the asymmetric jurisdiction is too large ($\theta \rightarrow 1$), then that jurisdiction prefers to go it alone rather than be in a coalition where it has to share a large share of its revenues with the much smaller.

The results in this proposition have some parallels to Burbidge et al. (1997). That paper shows that if there are two jurisdictions, the grand coalition is the equilibrium. However, the authors show that if there are more than two jurisdictions, then a coalition structure other than the grand coalition is the unique equilibrium. Given the complexity of the model, the authors prove this result using an example: two states that are symmetric and large in size will form a coalition. Unfortunately, the authors do not characterize all potential equilibrium coalitions for different parameter constellations, highlighting the value in the simplicity of the model that I have proposed.

A richer model than mine might consider additional cases, such as three entirely asymmetric jurisdictions. Under the completely asymmetric case, one could answer the following question, Does a central planner prefer joining the two largest jurisdictions to joining the two smallest jurisdictions? In particular, a central planner's preferred coalition may differ from the endogenously chosen coalition among the the jurisdictions, possibly creating a conflict of interest between the central government and decentralized governments. But this simple model, even with a Nash equilibrium concept, suggests that a wide range of coalitions may be possible—but that there are also many parameter constellations for which some coalitions will not emerge. Critically, a key message is that if jurisdictions are sufficiently asymmetric, it is never in the interest of those asymmetric jurisdictions to form a coalition.[22]

Finally, a key simplification in this model is that when a coalition forms, all tax authority is ceded to the coalition. In practice, intermunicipal cooperation coexists with its members maintaining some municipal tax autonomy. The cohabitation of taxes bases by the municipality and the the cooperative creates incentives that can make tax rates too high (Hoyt 2001, 2017; Keen and Kotsogiannis 2002, 2004). Whether this force moves the equilibrium closer toward the optimal solution or moves it too far past the optimal is an empirical question. This "vertical" channel is not in the model, but worthy of future study.

### 3.4.5 Sourcing Rules

As an alternative to minimum tax rates, tax harmonization, or cooperation, governments may change whether taxes are based on a source or residence principle. In the context of commodity taxes, this would be the origin versus the destination principle (Lockwood 1993, 2001). If goods are taxed at origin, then revenue accrues to the jurisdiction where the sale occurs. If goods are taxed at destination, then revenue accrues to the jurisdiction where the consumer lives. Of course, the corporate tax and the capital tax literatures also have long discussed the difference between source-based and residential-based capital taxes (Auerbach and Devereux 2018). More generally, the taxation of cross-border labor income requires clear sourcing rules, as the rise of telework now could result in states taxing remote workers either in the state where the firm is located or in the state where the worker resides (Agrawal and Brueckner 2025).

In the above model, jurisdictions tax mobile factors in the jurisdiction where the economic activity is "shifted to" but could tax the activity in the location where the activity is "shifted from." Suppose that governments change the sourcing rule to tax it where the activity is shifted from. In this case, tax revenue then becomes proportional to the initial "closed" economy bases of each jurisdiction:

$$R_i = T_i B_i = T_i \Theta_i. \tag{23}$$

Then, because this simple model assumes Leviathan governments and features no other behavioral responses, the tax base becomes perfectly inelastic, allowing governments to set tax rates that are as high as possible. As the

22. See Fleurbaey et al. (2022) for a discussion of moral motives in the competitive context along with the issue of cooperation.

maximization becomes similar to (9), all tax rates are thus set to $T^*$.[23] In the case of consumption taxes, this would be the tax rates such that the government extracts all of the surplus from the consumers of the taxed commodities. While such a model is a bit extreme, it provides some useful intuition.

**Proposition 5**: *Equilibrium tax rates will be higher under the sourcing rule where taxes are levied on the more inelastic base.*

To gain some intuition, it is useful to consider the example of cross-border workers and personal income taxes. The typical US state levies a (personal) income on all income earned within the state, a source-based tax.[24] However, some US states have entered into reciprocity agreements, which turn their income tax systems into residence-based taxes, with no taxation of nonresident earnings, but taxing resident income resulting from cross-border commuting. Thus, reciprocity agreements are a form of a tax treaty that shifts the state personal income tax away from a source-based taxed toward a residence-based tax (Agrawal and Hoyt 2018; Coomes and Hoyt 2008; Rohlin et al. 2014). The results above suggest that reciprocity can reduce tax competition if firms and employment are more elastic then residential locations. Rork and Wagner (2012) write, "States may have less incentive to engage in income tax competition with neighboring states, as nonresident workers no longer contribute to the tax base." Intuitively, sourcing rules change the elasticity of the tax base. As a Leviathan government follows a simple Ramsey rule when setting its Nash tax rates, sourcing rules that lower the elasticity will raise tax rates.

Finally, consider an extreme case. If residential decisions are completely immobile, but the employment location can easily be shifted across borders, then switching to tax the activity at the residential location away from employment location entirely eliminates tax competition. In practice, this is too extreme, but it suggests that there are intermediate cases.

In the context of capital income taxation, standard models again predict that taxes should be levied on the more immobile factors. The optimal rate of a source-based capital income tax is zero in a small open economy. Auerbach and Devereux (2018) elegantly state the intuition: "Imposing a positive tax rate raises the required rate of return, reducing the domestic capital stock and causing deadweight loss. The incidence of the tax is on immobile domestic residents—who could be taxed directly without creating the deadweight loss." As I discuss in Agrawal and Brueckner (2025), with capital mobility and cross-country tax differentials, capital taxes either distort international savings (when residence-based) or international produc-

23. I assume the reservation value for the activity to occur at all is the same across all jurisdictions.

24. In the US, matters are slightly more complex, as the state of residence also may tax the income. To avoid double taxation, tax credits are provided.

tion (when source-based). The international version of the production efficiency theorem states that, in the absence of pure profits, and with a full set of taxes, only residence-based taxes are used and source-based taxes are zero in the optimum. This is true not only in a small open economy but also for a set of symmetric countries that are all "large" (Eggert and Haufler 1999).[25]

### 3.4.6 Other Policy Responses

Of course, there are many other tools—especially in fiscal federations—that allow governments to potentially limit tax competition and that could possibly be introduced in the context of the theoretical model. These policies might involve outright bans of local taxes on particular bases, might involve restrictions on the rates jurisdictions are able to set (e.g., only integers), or place limits on the rate of growth of particular taxes. Other possible restrictions may include tax and expenditure limitations, intergovernmental grants, and tax enforcement. While I omit formal modeling of these policies, I discuss a few issues briefly here.

Intergovernmental grants have long been used to equalize tax bases across jurisdictions. However, they also have an important effect on fiscal competition, as discussed by Köthenbürger (2002). In particular, he shows that in a small open economy, tax base equalization yields the efficient tax rates by helping to internalize fiscal externalities.

Further, the discussion on the role of sourcing rules raises the possibility that governments could use enforcement tools to mitigate tax competition. If shifting behavior could be eliminated via perfect enforcement rather than a change of sourcing rules, then the optimal tax rates would still be derived from maximizing (23) when shifting responses are fraudulent. But, as discussed above, the ability to use enforcement as a tool requires distinguishing between real shifting and tax evasion in the model. However, if enforcement is not done by the higher-level governments, then it is possible that enforcement policies also become strategic choice variables (Stöwhase and Traxler 2005). Perhaps competing in tax rates is too politically obvious, in which case governments might not change the statutory rate and instead lower the effective tax rate via more lax enforcement. In Stöwhase and Traxler (2005), the enforcement decisions interact with the fiscal equalization rules in place. These authors show that without regional transfers, fiscal competition leads to audit rates that are inefficiently low for revenue-maximizing governments.

Although the chapter considers interjurisdictional cooperation, another possible way to reduce the number of jurisdictions are via municipal mergers and annexations. These municipal mergers differ from the intermunicipal cooperation because following a merger, a jurisdiction surrenders the entirety of its tax and spending policy to the merged jurisdiction. With intermunicipal cooperation, however, local governments may maintain autonomy over

25. See also Bucovetsky and Wilson (1991), Gordon (1986), and Keen and Piekkola (1997).

some policies, with others ceded to the cooperative. Thus, absent federal requirements to do so, mergers and annexations may be politically more challenging, perhaps not happening simply because municipalities could not agree on the merged municipality's name. Perhaps this explains why such mergers have been infrequent in the US (Epple and Romer 1989), though other countries have forced mergers in an effort to reduce the number of jurisdictions. Further, mergers are often more about exploiting economies of scale in the provision of public services rather than tax harmonization.

Finally, what is the role of preferential tax regimes where jurisdictions provide advantaged tax treatment to some firms, individuals or factors? These preferential regimes are often seen as a wasteful form of tax competition. But Keen (2001) shows that preferential regimes may allow jurisdictions to confine their most aggressive tax competition to particular parts of the tax system, and therefore, banning them may actually worsen tax competition. Of course, counterarguments exist. The issue of preferential regimes has recently gained attention in the context of bidding for firms, where states create preferential policies to attract a large firm to the state (Black and Hoyt 1989; Slattery 2024; Slattery and Zidar 2020). Modeling all of these potential policies in the context of the model presented above is left for future research.

## 3.5 Comparing Revenues Across Policies

While the above analysis indicates that there are a vast array of policy mechanisms that can improve tax revenues of all jurisdictions relative to the uncoordinated case, an important question is which of the policies improves total (combined) tax revenues the most. The answer to this question then sheds light on which policy would be preferred from a "social" or federal planner's perspective. Of course, in a model of Leviathan governments, there are some philosophical questions that need addressing. In particular, certain assumptions are necessary to conclude that the socially optimal policy would be the one that maximizes tax revenues of all region. Under one view, revenue-maximizing governments have a traditional welfarist interpretation if residents place a very high marginal valuation on the public good financed by the tax revenues (Kanbur and Keen 1993). In this setting, the policy that increases tax revenues the most would be better. Under an alternative view, revenue-maximizing governments can be viewed from a public choice perspective as governments that seek to extract surplus from residents. In this latter setting, tax coordination may fuel the Leviathan and, as such, tax competition yielding lower tax rates and revenues would be preferred—if the social planner were not a Leviathan—as an attempt to tame the Leviathan (Brülhart and Jametti 2019). For purposes of this chapter, I take a simple view that both the local and social planners maximize tax revenue, and thus evaluate the policies on the basis of which one yields higher tax revenues, which in a more general model might remedy inefficiencies of public good provision.

### 3.5.1 Aggregate Tax Revenues

To provide a systematic comparison across policies, tax revenues can be summed over all three jurisdictions under each regime. This combined revenue can then be used by the social planner to determine which policy yields the most total revenue. It is clear from the above analysis that appropriately enforcing taxes via appropriate sourcing rules achieves the highest tax revenues. But given that this partially derives from several of the assumptions of the model, such as inelastic demand, my focus is on comparing across all the other policies other than sourcing rule changes.

I proceed by summing tax revenues for all three jurisdictions for each policy regime. In the case of the uncoordinated Nash strategy, denoting combined revenues with the subscript "total," yields:

$$R_{total}^{U} = \delta\left(\frac{3}{2} + \frac{3}{25}\theta^2\right). \tag{24}$$

Under the policy of tax harmonization, tax revenues depend on the weights given to the jurisdictions' tax rates. Then total tax revenues are

$$R_{total}^{H} = \delta\left(\frac{3}{2} + \frac{9\omega - 3}{10}\theta\right), \tag{25}$$

which is clearly increasing in $\omega$ if $\theta > 0$ and decreasing in $\omega$ if $\theta < 0$.

Under a minimum tax rate, the weights also matter. Total tax revenues are now piecewise in $\theta$:

$$R_{total}^{M} = \begin{cases} \delta\left(\frac{3}{2} + \frac{3\omega\theta}{4} + \frac{3(8 + 2\omega - 3\omega^2)\theta^2}{200}\right) & \theta \geq 0 \\ \delta\left(\frac{3}{2} + \frac{(\omega - 1)\theta}{2} + \frac{(4\omega^2 - 6\omega - 4)\theta^2}{50}\right) & \theta < 0 \end{cases}, \tag{26}$$

because the minimum differentially influences tax competition depending on if it binds for one or two jurisdictions.

With partial harmonization via coalitions, total revenue if coalitions *as* or *aσ* form is:

$$R_{total}^{C(as)} = R_{total}^{C(a\sigma)} = \delta\left(\frac{\theta^2 + 2\theta + 82}{36}\right), \tag{27}$$

while if *sσ* is the equilibrium coalition, then

$$R_{total}^{C(s\sigma)} = \delta\left(\frac{2\theta^2 - 2\theta + 41}{18}\right). \tag{28}$$

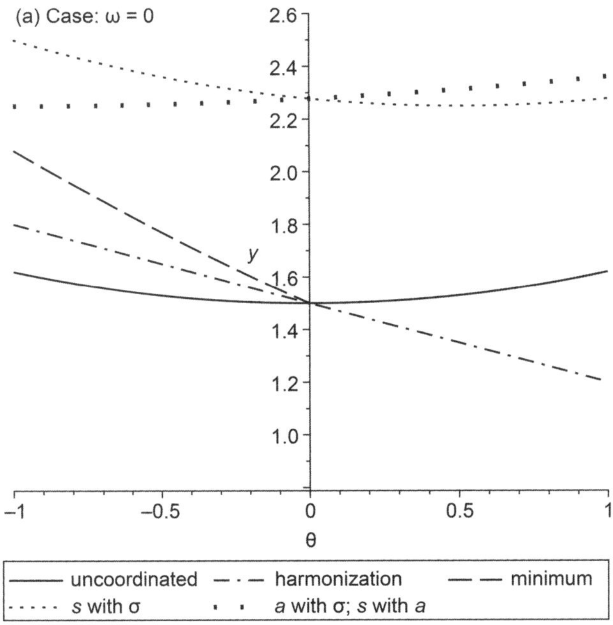


**Fig. 3.1 Total (combined) revenue of all jurisdictions**
This figure shows total (combined) revenue as a function of θ. As the harmonized tax revenues and minimum tax revenues are a function of the weight ω, I display revenues for three different values of ω across the three panels, which are split across two pages. In panel (a), for θ > 0, the lines for the uncoordinated and minimum tax revenues are coincident lines. In panel (c) they are coincident lines when θ < 0.

### 3.5.2 Which Regime Revenue Dominates?

Figure 3.1 shows the level of total revenue for each policy for all values of θ. Given some policies depend on the parameter ω, I depict three graphs where this weight takes on a low, medium, and high value.

First, compare the minimum tax rate and harmonization. Differencing total revenues $R^M_{total}$ and $R^H_{total}$, it is easy to see that the minimum tax rate always delivers higher tax revenues for a given value ω.[26] The intuition is clear: harmonizing, even to the highest possible tax rate, constrains the tax rate of the bigger jurisdiction. However, setting the same rate as the minimum allows the bigger jurisdiction to raise its tax rate above and beyond the minimum. Although this results in tax base shifting, some of the tax base is taxed at a higher rate under the minimum and the shifted base is taxed at a rate no lower that what would have been harmonized to.

Further, it is also easy to show that the minimum tax rate dominates

26. If θ = 0, the two regimes are equivalent to each other and to the uncoordinated equilibrium.

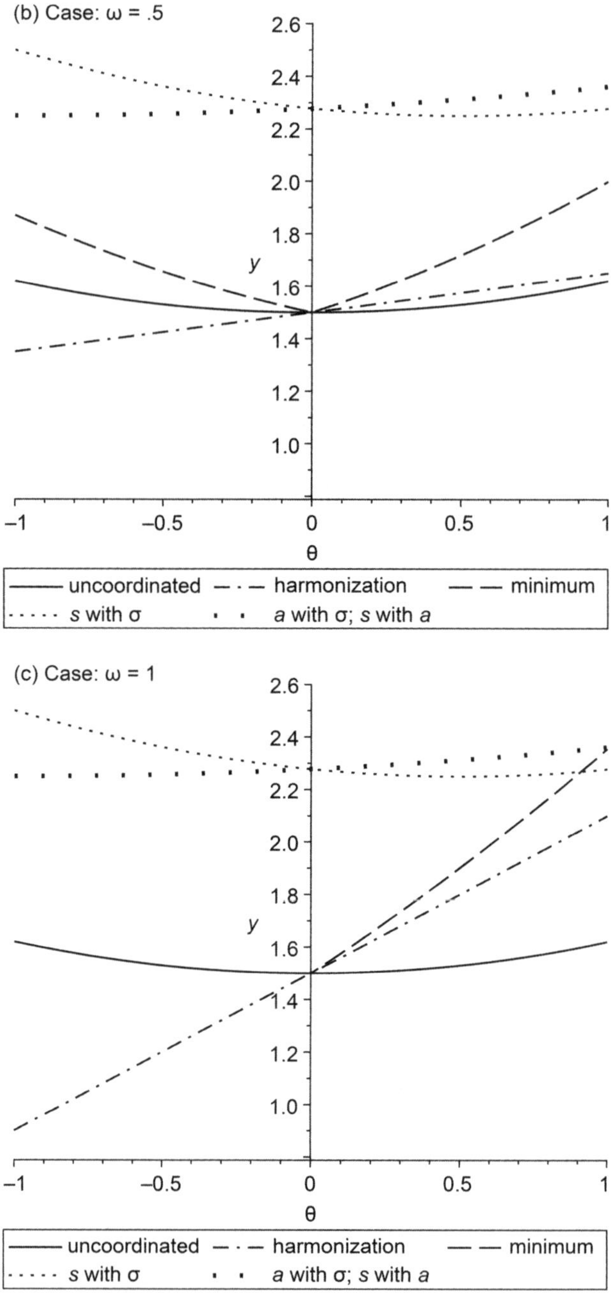
(b) Case: ω = .5
2.6
2.4
2.2
2.0
1.8
y
1.6
1.4
1.2
1.0
–1
–0.5
0
0.5
1
θ
uncoordinated
harmonization
minimum
s with σ
a with σ; s with a
(c) Case: ω = 1
2.6
2.4
2.2
2.0
1.8
y
1.6
1.4
1.2
1.0
–1
–0.5
0
0.5
1
θ
uncoordinated
harmonization
minimum
s with σ
a with σ; s with a

**Fig. 3.1 (cont.)**

the uncoordinated equilibrium. These results, combined with the possible existence of Pareto improvements discussed above, mean that there is ample reason to prefer minimum tax rates over harmonization to an identical tax rate.

Next, consider the case of partial harmonization. It can easily be verified that the total tax revenue from either coalition exceeds the total tax revenue from the uncoordinated equilibrium, as is evident from the figure. But which coalition yields more tax revenues? Comparing the two coalitions from a total revenue perspective, yields:

$$R_{total}^{C(as)} - R_{total}^{C(s\sigma)} = \frac{(2-\theta)\theta\delta}{12}, \tag{29}$$

such that $R_{total}^{C(as)} > R_{total}^{C(s\sigma)}$ if $\theta > 0$ and $R_{total}^{C(as)} < R_{total}^{C(s\sigma)}$ if $\theta < 0$.

Given the minimum tax rate revenue dominates harmonization, I can then compare partial harmonization with the minimum rate. Does the coalition yield more revenue than the minimum tax rate? First consider the coalition *as* or $a\sigma$. Then, equation (27) minus (26) is always positive for both branches of (26) regardless of the value of $\omega \in [0,1]$. The same is true for coalition $s\sigma$, with one minor exception: the minimum tax rate regime dominates if $\omega$ is close to one and $\theta$ is close to 1.[27] Thus, the revenue-preferred solution from a central planner's perspective is coalition $a\sigma$ or *as* if $\theta > 0$ and coalition $s\sigma$ if $\theta < 0$. These coalition arrangements dominate all other possible policy responses for most parameter values. Intuitively, for most parameter constellations, the coalition of jurisdictions allows them to raise their tax rates above the minimum tax rate, even if the minimum tax rate is set to its highest possible value. Then the combined bases of those jurisdictions are taxed at a higher tax rate. Because taxes are strategic complements, the tax rate in the jurisdiction outside the coalition is also slightly higher, resulting in revenue gains.

**Proposition 6**: *A minimum tax rate revenue-dominates harmonization to the same tax rate. A minimum tax rate regime also revenue-dominates total revenues in the uncoordinated equilibrium. However, there always exists a coalition under partial harmonization where total revenues dominate the total revenues from the minimum tax regime. When the asymmetric jurisdiction is the larger, the revenue preferred outcome is a coalition between one of the symmetric jurisdictions and the asymmetric jurisdiction; when the asymmetric jurisdiction is the smaller, the revenue preferred outcome is the coalitions with two symmetric jurisdictions.*

Interestingly, if $\theta$ and $\omega$ are sufficiently close to one, the minimum tax regime will dominate coalition $s\sigma$ even if it does not dominate coalitions

27. The precise condition for the minimum tax regime to yield more revenue is $(9\theta\omega + 2\theta - 10)(9\theta\omega - 8\theta - 140) > 0$, which for $\omega = 1$ implies $\theta > 10/11$.

*aσ* or *as*. Would coalition *aσ* or *as* emerge in equilibrium? Recall that under voluntary coalition formation, coalition *aσ* or *as* is only a Nash equilibrium if $\theta$ is not too close to one. Thus, unless the federal government forces cooperation, there exists a range of large values of $\theta$ where $\omega$ is sufficiently high such that the minimum tax regime revenue dominates any feasible voluntary coalition from the federal government's perspective. This result shows a tension between imposing coalitions on subnational governments versus letting those coalitions arise via their own free will. Obviously the central government prefers forcing a coalition on the subnational jurisdictions to implementing the minimum tax rate for these extreme parameter values. That said, this range of $\theta$ and $\omega$ only arises for very extreme values.

As emphasized earlier in the chapter, the proposition raises an interesting paradigm. Minimum tax rates clearly dominate complete harmonization both from a Pareto principle for each jurisdiction and from a total revenue principle. Intuitively, the minimum tax rate allows high tax jurisdictions to raise their tax rates, while harmonization does not. But minimum tax rate proposals also usually seek to set the minimum somewhere between the noncooperative taxes, thus imposing a maximum value for the lowest possible tax rate that is equal to the highest uncoordinated tax rate. This is especially noticeable when $\theta = 0$, because both harmonization and the minimum tax rate regime are equivalent to each other and to the uncoordinated equilibrium: if all jurisdictions set the same rate and the policy requires coordination to a rate in between, either policy cannot mitigate tax competition forces! Of course, the model presented here is static. In the long run, the federal government or supranational institutions may decide to change the harmonized rate. Perhaps, with time, they may increase it without regard to the historical uncoordinated tax rates.

Partial harmonization via a coalition, however, does not constrain the members of the coalition to set a tax rate less than or equal to the maximum noncooperative tax rate. Indeed, there are clearly cases where the coalition raises their tax rate above that Nash value, thus allowing the other jurisdiction to also raise its tax rate. Partial coordination thus mitigates tax competition by reducing the number of competitors, but does not impose any restriction on the resulting taxes. Thus, minimum taxes and harmonization suffer from an important fallacy: if taxes are too low due to tax competition, any policy intervention that relies on the Nash tax rates is utilizing taxes that are too low. Partial harmonization, by still allowing autonomous choice over all taxes, allows for a reduction of competitors but potentially lets *all* jurisdictions set taxes *above* the noncoordinated tax rates.

Interestingly, harmonization never revenue-dominates partial harmonization. The reason is that harmonization puts the most stringent restrictions on all jurisdictions to be constrained to set tax rates between the uncoordinated values. While a minimum tax rate only raises the lower tax jurisdiction rate in this range, it allows the higher tax jurisdiction to raise its rate above the equilibrium. Partial harmonization places no explicit restriction on jurisdictions to be between the equilibrium.

## 3.6 Empirical Evidence

In this section, I selectively review some empirical evidence on tax coordination. I focus on two strands of the literature: first, counterfactual exercises concerning minimum tax rates and harmonization, and second, empirical evidence on partial harmonization resulting from intermunicipal cooperation.

### 3.6.1 Minimum Tax Rates Versus Harmonization

As noted above, in many circumstances, there is a clear dominance of minimum tax rates over tax harmonization. Perhaps this—and the political challenges of harmonization across sovereign international countries—explains why recent policy efforts on reforming the international tax structure have focused on the global minimum tax rather than tax harmonization. But in federalist systems, central governments could consider passage of either minimum tax rates or tax harmonization. Despite this, the empirical evidence on harmonization and minimum tax rates remains limited.

Fajgelbaum et al. (2019) study the spatial distortions of tax dispersion and consider counterfactual exercises that reduce the dispersion in tax rates across jurisdictions. Using a more general welfare function than revenue maximization, eliminating tax dispersion could have ambiguous effects on tax revenues. The authors find that reducing tax dispersion across US states raises welfare. Their model does not incorporate tax competition forces explicitly, so adding endogenous policy determination to a model like theirs represents a promising avenue for future research.

In one recent example that links closely to the prior theory, Agrawal, Foremny, et al. (2025) study the mobility responses to regional wealth taxes within Spain. Tax-induced migration and mobility is a shifting behavior that can result in interjurisdictional fiscal externalities. A unique feature of the Spanish setting is that only the region of Madrid—the largest region within Spain—set a zero tax rate on wealth; all other regions within Spain set reasonably similar positive tax rates to each other. As a result, most all migration was from high-tax regions to Madrid. After estimating the elasticity of wealth-tax-induced mobility, the authors then conduct counterfactual simulations of various tax coordination policies. Given that Madrid is a relatively large region, representing approximately 15 percent of the entire population of Spain, it makes sense to think about the effects in the context of the model above where Madrid is a single large region.[28] From the theory

28. Obviously there are other larger regions in Spain, so this is a simplification. Further, Madrid is not revenue maximizing wealth tax revenues by setting a zero tax rate. An alternative

above, harmonization would need to be to a sufficiently high tax rate, while a minimum tax rate may benefit all regions.

The authors first estimate the elasticity of the number of wealth tax filers to regional wealth tax rates: Madrid's lower tax rate increases the number of wealth tax filers there by about 8 percent, which is a decline in the number of filers in other regions by about 2 percent. To shed light on the theoretical issues discussed above, the authors then consider various tax harmonization schemes. To do this, they exploit the fact that tax harmonization removes tax differentials, thus eliminating tax-induced migration. The amount of tax-induced migration can be determined from the estimated elasticities of mobility. Then for each tax rate in between that of the lowest tax region and the highest tax region, Agrawal, Foremny, et al. (2025) count the number of regions that see increases in tax revenue from harmonization. As with the theory above, abstracting from taxable wealth responses, there are two effects. Harmonization raises regional tax revenue by reducing migration to Madrid. But, if the harmonized rate is to a rate lower than the uncoordinated tax rate of the region, revenues mechanically fall due to the lower rate on the inframarginal tax base. Simulating these revenue effects using the causal mobility estimates to obtain the revenue gains from reduced mobility, the authors show that when harmonization is to a low rate, only a few regions realize increases in revenue. For tax harmonization to benefit all regions, the tax rate needs to be sufficiently close to the maximum decentralized region. Figure 3.2 shows the result. For all regions to benefit, the tax rate needs to be very high; for a majority of regions to benefit, the harmonized tax rate is (interestingly) very close to the default tax schedule that the central government requires go into effect if the region does not proactively change it. Consistent with the theoretical propositions above, Agrawal, Foremny, et al. (2025) provide new empirical evidence documenting that harmonization needs to be to a sufficiently high rate to benefit all regions, highlighting the political difficulty of finding a consensus for harmonization.

Then, the authors compare tax harmonization to minimum tax rates.[29] Counterfactual simulations are a bit more challenging because the authors cannot explicitly model strategic tax competition and do not know if eliminating a tax haven will result in mobility simply shifting to the region setting the minimum tax rate. Nonetheless, assuming a partial equilibrium analysis, and that after the minimum tax rate is adopted, it is to a rate sufficiently high that it eliminates most shifting responses, allows the authors to make some progress. Figure 3.3 shows the revenue changes under two different scenarios: (1) a minimum tax regime with the minimum tax rate set at the

might be that more wealthy individuals in Madrid drives up personal income tax revenues, but even under such a story, it appears Madrid is not a Leviathan government.

29. See Keen et al. (2022) for simulations related to the global minimum tax.

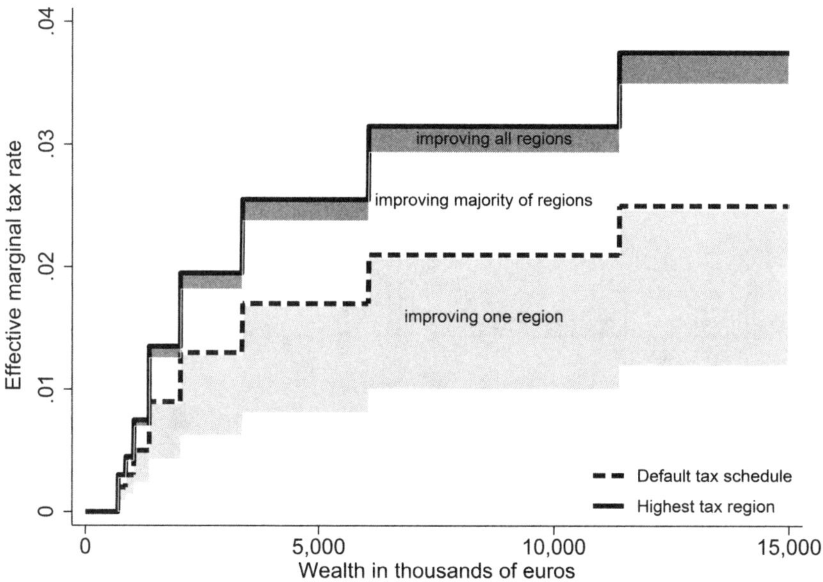


**Fig. 3.2 How many regions increase tax revenue from harmonization to different rates?**

This figure shows the number of regions benefiting from various harmonized wealth tax schedules in Spain. The dotted line is the recommended default schedule proposed by the national government, while the solid black line is the tax schedule of the highest tax region. The lower bound of each shaded area represents one region, a majority of regions, and all regions that would benefit from that harmonization to that tax rate. To construct this, the figure looks at only wealth tax revenue, but Agrawal et al. (2022) also consider spillovers to other tax based, such as capital income tax revenue.

national default schedule (dashed line on the prior figure) and (2) tax harmonization to the same rate.

Critically, under the (strong) assumption of the minimum tax rate eliminating all shifting behavior, the minimum rate and harmonization affect jurisdictions previously below the new rate in the same manner. If these minimum tax rate jurisdictions would still benefit from some inflows of wealthy tax payers from higher tax regions, then the minimum tax rate scheme might lead to higher revenues for them than harmonization. However, for jurisdictions with uncoordinated rates above the default schedule, harmonization lowers tax revenues, while the minimum tax rate raises revenues. This is because the minimum rate reduces shifting but does not force the jurisdiction to raise the rate. This effect might be mitigated if there were some revenue losses from shifting to jurisdictions adopting the minimum, but might also be amplified if the jurisdictions responded by raising their tax rates substantially. Given the assumptions, the precise magnitudes should not be the focus, but rater the emphasis is on the heterogeneity of responses

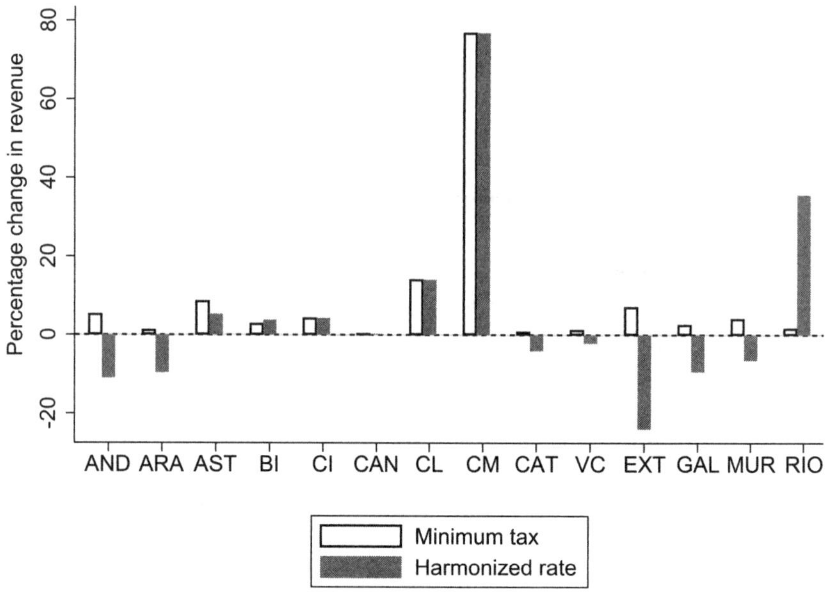


**Fig. 3.3 Tax harmonization versus minimum tax rates**
This figure shows the percent change in tax revenues for each region for a minimum tax rate and harmonization to the same minimum and harmonized rate (the recommended national default schedule). All changes here are for wealth tax revenues only. Agrawal et al. (2022) also consider spillovers to other tax based, such as capital income tax revenue.

by policy and region. These simulations clearly indicate the dominance of the minimum tax rate regime from a political economy perspective: minimum tax rates can raise revenues everywhere, while harmonization cannot.

### 3.6.2 Intermunicipal Cooperation

Many countries have various forms of intermunicipal cooperation, but I mainly focus on France. France has a very long history of intermunicipal cooperation, as discussed in Agrawal, Breuillé, et al. (2025). It dates back to the syndicates that were formally codified in the March 22, 1890 law, allowing jurisdictions to form cooperatives to provide necessary public services among municipalities (clean water, sewage treatment, waste collection, etc.), but without taxing authority. More extensive cooperation leading to the establishment of EIMCs arose in French laws of 1966, 1970, 1992, 1999, 2010, and 2015. EIMCs are an example of (voluntary) cooperation among municipalities of one's choosing—in fact, it was not even until 2010 that municipalities were required to join an EIMC. EIMCs can be viewed as another level in the fiscal federalism hierarchy, with municipal delegation of particular revenue and expenditure instruments, including taxing power, to the EIMC. But many fiscal instruments remain under municipal control.

Despite rich data on local public finance in France, it is difficult to study the effect of joining an EIMC empirically: municipalities select into EIMCs, and they select with whom to cooperate. Fiscal policies are then determined in an open economy setting, with fiscal competition persisting at the municipal level and also codetermined with the EIMC's fiscal policies.

After forming an EIMC, some tax policies remain under the control of the municipality. Given the theory above, partial harmonization seems to be unambiguously beneficial. But, as noted above, the presence of a new tier of government with vertical tax externalities creates other forces. The question then is whether joining an EIMC actually mitigates or amplifies strategic tax competition among municipalities within the EIMC relative to competition with those outside of it. Agrawal, Breuillé et al. (2025) study this issue, and I present their discussion of it here. On the one hand, an EIMC may reduce strategic tax competition as members of the cooperative share common policy goals on at least some dimensions. Moreover, any leakage of the tax base shrinks not only the tax base of the municipality, but also the cooperative, implying that any tax-induced shifting outside of the EIMC imposes a "double harm" to the municipality. As a result, competition with towns outside the cooperative may be more fierce. On the other hand, competition within a cooperative may be more intense with respect to remaining municipal tax instruments. This offsetting effect might arise if the tax base is locally mobile within the set of similarly situated municipalities and the common EIMC structure amplifies that local mobility, perhaps due to common institutions. Either way, the formation of EIMCs implies that the strategic responses to "peer" municipalities within the same EIMC may be different than with municipalities outside of the EIMC. This heterogeneity is not usually modeled in standard tests of the existence of strategic interactions.

Traditional tax competition researchers often estimate a strategic reaction function regressing a jurisdiction's tax rate on the spatial average of competitor tax rates (Brueckner 2003; Brueckner and Saavedra 2001):

$$T = \rho WT + X\beta + \varepsilon \tag{30}$$

where $T$ is a vector of tax rates for municipalities over time, $W$ is a block-diagonal weights matrix identifying competitor municipalities, and $X$ are any covariates and fixed effects. Then, the coefficient $\rho$ is the slope of the strategic reaction function. In words, it says if the weighted average of competitor tax rates rise by one unit, then the own-jurisdiction tax rate changes by $\rho$ units. If taxes are strategic complements—where reaction functions slope upward—then $\rho$ is positive. If taxes are strategic substitutes—where reaction functions slope downward—then $\rho$ is negative. A zero-sloped reaction function implies the lack of strategic tax interactions—but does not imply there is not tax competition at work. In particular, if jurisdictions are small and there are infinitely many of them, jurisdictions compete à la perfect competition, but not strategically. Even if jurisdictions are not strategic, a tax change in any one jurisdiction still imposes an interjurisdictional fiscal externality on the rest of the world.

A reaction function such as (30) assumes that a single parameter governs the intensity of strategic reactions. The question then is whether intermunicipal cooperation changes the extent of strategic reactions. Agrawal, Breuillé, et al. (2025) study whether EIMCs dampen tax competition among towns within the cooperative relative to towns external to the EIMC. To do this, (30) is modified to allow for different slopes for both groups:

$$T = \rho^{\mathrm{EIMC}} W^{\mathrm{EIMC}} T + \rho^{\mathrm{OUT}} W^{\mathrm{OUT}} T + X\beta + \varepsilon \tag{31}$$

where $W^{\mathrm{EIMC}}$ is the weight matrix for municipalities inside the EIMC and $W^{\mathrm{OUT}}$ is the weight matrix for those outside. Then, if $\rho^{EIMC}$ is significantly different from $\rho^{OUT}$, the strategic responses to each subgroup of towns are different. In addition to standard endogeneity of nearby jurisdiction tax rates, the spatial weight matrices are also endogenous because the decision of with whom to cooperate is a choice. The authors use new spatial econometric methods to address these concerns. The authors estimate that $\rho^{EIMC} < \rho^{OUT}$, with the difference between the coefficients statistically significant. The differential pattern of strategic responses suggests that municipalities react less intensely to change by municipalities in the same EIMC than they do to municipalities outside of the EIMC. Intermunicipal cooperation thus dampens strategic tax competition among municipalities. In the context of the theoretical model above, there is no tax competition within an EIMC, so this empirical evidence suggests that even allowing jurisdictions within a coalition to maintain some tax autonomy can still have beneficial effects.

Although the strategic responses are dampened by tax cooperation, the reaction function slope does not translate into a welfare metric (Agrawal, Hoyt, et al. 2022), and the prior results cannot be translated into the efficiency effects of cooperation. To shed some light on this, Breuillé et al. (2018) exploit a difference-in-differences design to identify the effect of cooperation on the total (EIMC plus municipal) tax rate of local jurisdictions. The authors compare tax rates in the treatment group (municipalities that form an EIMC) with a comparison group (municipalities that do not form a EIMC in their sample). In their setting, tax rates may change for numerous reasons: economies of scale in public good provision resulting from cooperation allow jurisdictions to reduce costs and cut taxes, or the effects on tax competition discussed above may arise, allowing them to raise taxes. If economies of scale were at work, this would suggest costs would fall ancd tax rates would fall to balance the budget. On the other hand, if tax competition becomes less intense, one might expect tax rates to rise. The authors find, as in figure 3.4, that total tax rates rise. Of course, other mechanisms may be at play.

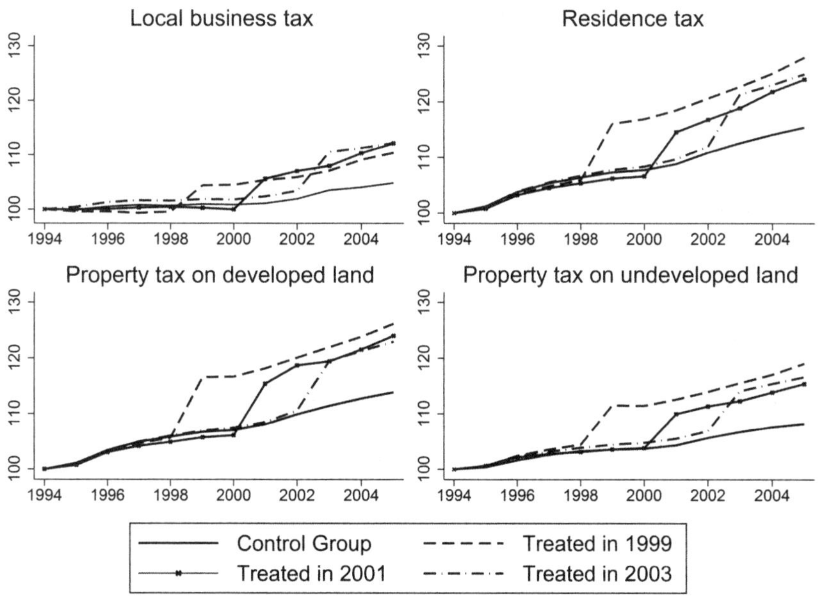


**Fig. 3.4 The effect of intermunicipal cooperation on total tax rates**
This figure is a modified figure from Breuillé et al. (2018) and shows the effect of joining an EIMC on total tax rates. Treated groups are towns joining an EIMC in a year, while the comparison group is towns that do not join an EIMC.

These results suggest that economies of scale are not the dominant force resulting from intermunicipal cooperation. While the authors cannot causally identify EIMCs dampening tax competition and can only identify the level effect on tax rate, the increase in tax rates combined with the evidence on reaction function slopes in Agrawal, Breuillé, et al. (2025) is consistent with it. The intuition follows Hoyt (1991), who shows that reducing competition by reducing the number of jurisdictions in a metropolis increases both tax rates and welfare.

Cooperating can be costly for municipalities, as they lose autonomy over local policies, reducing their ability to tailor policies to local preferences and protect local interests. Tricaud (2025) provides evidence on this by exploiting a 2010 reform in France that required holdout municipalities to join an EIMC. She classifies municipalities that were forced to join an EIMC as treatment municipalities and then compares them to municipalities that joined an EIMC voluntarily previously. She focuses on two costs to municipalities. First, EIMCs decide where and how much building can be allowed in each member municipality. New development can be costly for some municipalities that have been using local housing regulations to prevent outsiders from coming in—NIMBYism. Second, decisions over the location of public services can benefit some municipalities while harming others. EIMCs may concentrate resources for new facilities in high-density areas. As a result, low-density municipalities might end up with fewer facilities, increasing the distance to public services for their residents. Tricaud (2025) finds that after a municipality is forced to join an EIMC, the number of building permits increases in these towns relative to the comparison group. This evidence is consistent with municipalities not joining an EIMC in order to prevent development in the "backyard" of residents. With respect to the second cost, she finds that the number of daycare slots falls in rural municipalities, while it increases in urban municipalities. This suggests that joining an EIMC moves public services further away from smaller municipalities. Thus, cooperation can be costly for some municipalities in a way not captured by the purely tax-driven model above.

Overall, the empirical evidence on intermunicipal cooperation suggests that it has been successful at limiting the parasitic effects of tax competition. While this comes at some cost, which might be born by some municipalities more so than others, EIMCs may be a way to mitigate competitive tax competition while still allowing for Tiebout sorting benefits across EIMCs.

## 3.7 Directions for Future Research

Policy responses to tax competition are becoming increasingly common, but there are many open questions that remain. First, while there are many individual studies of *specific* policies to limit competition, like the goal of this chapter, more work is needed to compare across various forms of cooperation, such as minimum tax rates versus harmonization versus partial harmonization. When doing so, it is useful to know the effect on taxes and spending levels, but also the effects on the mobility of businesses/factors/individuals and any costs imposed on municipalities. Simple theory, like the one presented above, could be helpful by nesting different forms of cooperation in a single model, providing information on the parameters needed to conduct counterfactual exercises that shed light on welfare. It would be useful to make explicit comparisons of welfare across various policy responses so that governments can determine how to respond to heightened tax competition.

Second, the literature on federal or state interventions in local policy matters (Agrawal, Hoyt, et al. 2022) is much more developed than the literature with respect to voluntary forms of cooperation, such as intermunicipal cooperation and bilateral tax treaties. An important empirical challenge here is that both the decision to engage in cooperation and with whom to cooperate is endogenous because it is selected by the municipality. The data challenges of studying such forms of cooperation are numerous, especially in countries where local data are not tracked nationally, and where special districts often have vague fiscal authorities. Moreover, information on bilateral tax treaties is often not centralized, and understanding how the treaties work in practice often involves complex legal interpretations.

Third, when thinking about the effect of policy responses to tax competition, it is tempting to only look at tax rates as the outcome. However, more emphasis on the effect of cooperation and coordination on interjurisdictional fiscal externalities and public spending is necessary. As the inefficiencies resulting from tax competition are driven by fiscal externalities, and cannot be inferred by the slope of the reaction function per se, estimating the effect on fiscal externalities is critical for understanding whether taxes are too high or too low and whether the implemented policy responses move the equilibrium closer to the efficient level. A challenge is that it is difficult to measure fiscal externalities when governments are small. While the interjurisdictional effect on the world may be large, the effect any one other jurisdiction may be small. An alternative would be, perhaps, to estimate the fiscal externality of any one jurisdiction on the aggregation of all other municipalities in the federal system. These fiscal externalities are important because they have implications for the level of public services within the economy.

Fourth, there are many understudied limitations on fiscal instruments by state authorities. Although a large literature focuses on TELs and minimum tax rates in federal systems, some big picture restrictions—including the outright ban of local taxes by the state or constitutional prohibitions—remain understudied. Do outcomes differ when localities cannot levy local sales taxes but can levy municipal income taxes? When they cannot levy local income taxes but can levy local sales taxes? Do state constitutions affect tax competition? Are there restrictions on progressivity that may also influence whether or how governments cannot compete? Related to the literature on preferential tax rates (Keen 2001), a progressive income tax allows localities to have multiple policy levers (a rate for high-income individuals and a rate for low-income households) that potentially influences the nature of competition. But flat taxes lack this flexibility. Can preferential tax regimes be beneficial?

Fifth, sourcing rules and the remittance rules (Slemrod 2019) that enforce where taxes are due are important. This is well known in the capital tax and corporate tax literature, but personal income tax treaties such as reciprocity agreements and sourcing rules concerning consumption taxes are less well studied. Taxing rights over income and consumption are becoming increasingly controversial, especially with the dramatic increase in teleworkers and e-commerce. Telework allows individuals and firms to be located in different states; e-commerce allows individuals to consume goods from all over the world. How this "globalization" of labor and consumption increases tax competition may depend upon the sourcing rules in place that define the location of taxation.

Sixth, what political challenges do cooperation and coordination face?

Ultimately, any policy responses to tax competition need to be passed by governing bodies. At the international setting, this requires the agreement of many countries. Within federal systems, such reforms might come about voluntarily by agreement of municipalities or may be imposed by federal or state-level authorities. In the latter case, any policy reform forcing municipalities to cooperate requires a consensus in the state legislative bodies, made up of representatives who may be sensitive to their local—rather than state—interests. Thus, understanding the obstacles to adopting cooperation/coordination, including the political economy of adoption, is critical to increasing its usage. These political considerations might be especially important if the model were dynamic, such that governments were playing a repeated game.

Finally, the model developed in this chapter is stylized: it uses a single tax instrument, assumes Leviathan rather than welfare maximizing governments, has no role for public services, assumes a Nash equilibrium concept, assumes jurisdictions have market power that gives rise to strategic interactions, and does not have three fully asymmetric jurisdictions. Expanding on these simplifications represents a useful path for research. In practice, governments have access to multiple taxes; there is a budget constraint and governments offer a package deal of local services. This combination of taxes and services raises issues as to whether governments compete in taxes or expenditures (Wildasin 1988). Whether governments compete in taxes or expenditures is similar to the difference between Cornout and Bertrand competition, and just as firms cannot compete in both prices and quantities, governments pick one strategic variable with the other adjusting residually. Matters become more complex when there are multiple taxes and expenditure programs. If governments then have the choice to cooperate or coordinate some but not all policy instruments, we need to understand what taxes and expenditures governments choose to cooperate over. In other words, do governments chose to limit the instruments with the most intense competition? Or do they pick the ones for which a coordinated consensus can be politically achieved?

More generally, the model assumes a Nash game, but the prior literature indicates the results of a minimum tax may vary in a Stackelberg (Wang 1999) or repeated game setting. The Nash concept with coalition formation also faces limitations, and future work might utilize a coalition-proof Nash equilibrium. Researchers might also endogenize the splitting rules for coalitions using a Nash bargaining concept, or explicitly model the possibility of side payments.

Further, jurisdictions in the model above have some market power that gives rise to strategic interactions, but localities are small and any one locality likely cannot affect the world rate of return. Thus, it would be reasonable to focus on models of atomistic competition—where governments compete in the purest form of competition—perfect competition. In such models, jurisdictions would not interact strategically, but tax competition forces would still introduce inefficiencies: although the fiscal externality on any one jurisdiction caused by another small jurisdiction raising its tax rate is negligible, the fiscal externality on the system of jurisdictions is not. Of course, many systems of jurisdictions also have a federalist hierarchy, and future research might consider how tax coordination influences the externalities imposed by one level of government on other levels.

How does cooperation impact competition and economic outcomes in an increasingly complex world? Many generalizations of the model in this chapter abound, but I hope the framework sketched above is useful for researchers considering the welfare effects of policy responses to interjurisdictional competition.

**Acknowledgments**

I thank Marie-Laure Breuillé, Jan Brueckner, Dirk Foremny, John Hatfield, Andreas Haufler, William Hoyt, Kai Konrad, Tidiane Ly, Mohammed Mardan, Clara Martínez-Toledano, James Poterba, David Wildasin, Owen Zidar, and participants at the NBER meeting on Interjurisdictional Tax Competition. Any remaining errors are my own. For acknowledgments, sources of research support, and disclosure of the author's material financial relationships, if any, please see https://www.nber.org/books-and-chapters/policy-responses-tax-competition/limits-competition-strategies-promoting-jurisdictional-cooperation.

## Appendix A

### Derivation: Nash Equilibrium

The revenue functions are given by

(A.1)
$$
\begin{aligned}
R_s &= T_s\left(1 - \frac{\theta}{2} - \frac{T_s - T_a}{\delta} - \frac{T_s - T_\sigma}{\delta}\right) \\
R_\sigma &= T_\sigma\left(1 - \frac{\theta}{2} - \frac{T_\sigma - T_a}{\delta} - \frac{T_\sigma - T_s}{\delta}\right) \\
R_a &= T_a\left(1 + \theta - \frac{T_a - T_s}{\delta} - \frac{T_a - T_\sigma}{\delta}\right).
\end{aligned}
$$

Differentiating and solving the system of first order conditions presented in the main text yields the Nash equilibrium.

## Derivation: Harmonization

For the two jurisdictions of a similar size, the revenue under tax harmonization is greater than the revenue earned in the uncoordinated equilibrium if

$$[(1-\omega)T^U + \omega T_a^U]\left(1-\frac{\theta}{2}\right) - R^U > 0. \tag{A.2}$$

Evaluating at the uncoordinated Nash values and simplifying yields

$$-\frac{3}{100}\theta\delta(5\theta\omega - \theta - 10\omega + 5) > 0, \tag{A.3}$$

which implies the equation in the text, (11).

For the asymmetric jurisdiction $a$, the revenue under tax harmonization is greater than the revenue earned in the uncoordinated equilibrium if

$$[(1-\omega)T^U + \omega T_a^U](1+\theta) - R_a^U > 0. \tag{A.4}$$

Evaluating at the uncoordinated Nash values and simplifying yields

$$\frac{3}{50}\theta\delta(5\theta\omega - 3\theta + 5\omega) > 0, \tag{A.5}$$

which implies the equation in the text, (12).

## Derivation: Minimum Tax Rates

First consider the case where $\theta > 0$. In this case, the minimum tax rate exceeds $T^U$ but is below $T_a^U$. Then, the best response of the higher tax jurisdiction will be

$$T_a = \frac{1}{4}\delta(1+\theta) + \frac{1}{4}T_s + \frac{1}{4}T_\sigma = \frac{1}{4}\delta(1+\theta) + \frac{1}{2}\tau. \tag{A.6}$$

For the small jurisdictions, tax revenues—evaluated at $T_s = T_\sigma = \tau$ and $T_a = (1/4)\delta(1+\theta) + (1/2)\tau$—are given by

$$R_s^M = R_\sigma^M = \frac{\tau(5\delta - 2\tau - \delta\theta)}{4\delta}, \tag{A.7}$$

where the superscript $M$ denotes the minimum tax regime. The derivative with respect to $\tau$ is

$$\frac{(5-\theta)\delta - 4\tau}{4\delta}, \tag{A.8}$$

which evaluated at $\tau = T^U$ yields

$$-\frac{3}{20}\theta + \frac{3}{4} > 0. \tag{A.9}$$

This means that revenue is increasing as the small jurisdictions are forced to raise the tax rate marginally. Evaluated at the maximum value for which the minimum rate does not bind for both jurisdictions, $\tau = T_a^U$, also yields

$$-\frac{9}{20}\theta + \frac{3}{4} > 0. \tag{A.10}$$

Thus, tax revenue of the smaller jurisdiction is always increasing in $\tau$.

As for the bigger jurisdiction, its tax revenue—evaluated at $T_s = T_\sigma = \tau$ and $T_a = (1/4)\delta(1+\theta) + (1/2)\tau$—is

$$R_a^M = \frac{(\delta(1+\theta) + 2\tau)^2}{8\delta}. \tag{A.11}$$

Then (A. 11) minus $R_a^U$ yields

$$\frac{(9\delta\theta + 15\delta + 10\tau)(\delta\theta - 5\delta + 10\tau)}{200\delta}, \tag{A.12}$$

which is strictly increasing in $\tau$ and when evaluated at $\tau = T^U$, is equal to zero. Thus, revenue is increasing for all values of $\omega$.

Next, consider the case where $\theta < 0$. In this case, $T_s^U = T_\sigma^U > \tau$. Evaluating the best response functions (5) at the minimum tax rate yields

$$\begin{aligned} T_s &= \frac{1}{4}\delta\left(1 - \frac{1}{2}\theta\right) + \frac{1}{4}\tau + \frac{1}{4}T_\sigma \\ T_\sigma &= \frac{1}{4}\delta\left(1 - \frac{1}{2}\theta\right) + \frac{1}{4}\tau + \frac{1}{4}T_s. \end{aligned} \tag{A.13}$$

Solving for the new equilibrium yields

$$T_s = T_\sigma = \frac{1}{3}\left(1 - \frac{\theta}{2}\right) + \frac{1}{3}\tau. \tag{A.14}$$

As for the bigger jurisdictions, tax revenues are

$$R_s^M = R_\sigma^M = \frac{(\delta(\theta - 2) - 2\tau)^2}{18\delta}. \tag{A.15}$$

Then (A. 15) minus $R^U$ yields

$$\frac{(2\delta\theta + 5\delta - 10\tau)(8\delta\theta - 25\delta - 10\tau)}{450\delta}, \tag{A.16}$$

which is strictly increasing in $\tau$ and when evaluated at $\tau = T_a^U$, is equal to zero. Thus, revenue is increasing for all values of $\omega > 0$.

For the jurisdiction for which the minimum tax rate binds, tax revenues are

$$R_a^M = \frac{[\tau\delta(5 + 2\theta) - 4\tau^2]}{3\delta}, \tag{A.17}$$

which is concave in the minimum tax rate. At the lowest possible value of the minimum tax rate, the jurisdiction is clearly unaffected, but the derivative of revenues with respect to the minimum tax rate

$$\frac{(2\theta + 5) - 8\tau}{3\delta} = \frac{2\theta}{15} + \frac{1}{3} \tag{A.18}$$

is positive. However, at the highest possible value of the minimum tax rate, $T^U$, the difference in revenues with the uncoordinated case is

$$\frac{(2\delta\theta + 5\delta - 10\tau)(20\tau - 6\delta\theta - 15\delta)}{150\delta} = \frac{-\theta\delta(8\theta + 5)}{50\delta}. \tag{A.19}$$

This is positive if

$$-\frac{1}{50}\delta(8\theta + 5)\theta > 0 \Leftrightarrow \theta > -\frac{5}{8}. \tag{A.20}$$

**Derivation: Forced Cooperation**

Initially, assume that cooperation forces the two symmetric jurisdictions to cooperate. Then, the tax revenue functions are given by (16) yielding the Nash tax rates in the text. The tax differential is

$$T_a^{C(s\sigma)} - T_{s\sigma}^{C(s\sigma)} = \frac{1}{3}\delta\left(\theta - \frac{1}{2}\right), \tag{A.21}$$

which is positive for $\theta < 1/2$. To sign the pattern of taxes relative to the uncoordinated equilibrium, note that

$$\begin{aligned} T_{s\sigma}^{C(s\sigma)} - T^U &= \frac{1}{15}\delta(5 - \theta) > 0 \\ T_a^{C(s\sigma)} - T_a^U &= \frac{1}{30}\delta(5 - \theta) > 0. \end{aligned} \tag{A.22}$$

With respect to tax revenues, equilibrium revenues of the coalition and the nonmember are

$$\begin{aligned} R_{s\sigma}^{C(s\sigma)} &= \frac{1}{18}\delta(\theta - 5)^2 \\ R_a^{C(s\sigma)} &= \frac{1}{18}\delta(\theta + 4)^2. \end{aligned} \tag{A.23}$$

To sign the pattern of tax revenues in individual jurisdictions, one must determine how revenues are allocated within the cooperative. Given both jurisdictions are of equal size, a reasonable assumption is equal splitting. Then, differencing coordinated and uncoordinated revenues (after dividing the cooperative's revenue by two) yields

(A.24)
$$\frac{R_{s\sigma}^{C(s\sigma)}}{2} - R^U = \frac{7}{900}\delta(\theta - 5)^2 > 0$$
$$R_a^{C(s\sigma)} - R_a^U = \frac{1}{450}\delta(5 - \theta)(11\theta + 35) > 0,$$

Thus, cooperation yields higher tax revenues in both jurisdictions. With symmetric jurisdictions cooperating equally, splitting revenues are the same as if splitting proportional to the equilibrium bases.

Next, without loss of generality, consider the possibility that jurisdictions $a$ and $\sigma$ cooperate, but jurisdiction $s$ does not. Then tax revenues are

(A.25)
$$R_s = T_s\left[1 - \frac{\theta}{2} - \frac{2(T_s - T_{a\sigma})}{\delta}\right]$$
$$R_{a\sigma} = T_{a\sigma}\left[2 + \frac{\theta}{2} - \frac{2(T_{a\sigma} - T_s)}{\delta}\right]$$

and the equilibrium tax rates are given in the text. This implies a tax differential of

(A.26)
$$T_s^{C(a\sigma)} - T_{a\sigma}^{C(a\sigma)} = -\frac{1}{6}\delta(\theta + 1) < 0.$$

The equilibrium tax rates can be compared with the noncooperative equilibrium, noting that, in this case, because the members of the cooperative differ in size, three pairwise comparisons are necessary:

(A.27)
$$T_s^{C(a\sigma)} - T_s^U = \frac{1}{6}\delta\left(1 + \frac{1}{10}\theta\right) > 0$$
$$T_{a\sigma}^{C(a\sigma)} - T_a^U = \frac{1}{3}\delta\left(1 - \frac{7}{20}\theta\right) > 0$$
$$T_{a\sigma}^{C(a\sigma)} - T_\sigma^U = \frac{1}{3}\delta\left(1 + \frac{11}{20}\theta\right) > 0.$$

Turning to tax revenues, equilibrium tax revenues of the cooperative and nonmember are given by

(A.28)
$$R_s^{C(a\sigma)} = \frac{1}{72}\delta(\theta - 8)^2$$
$$R_{a\sigma}^{C(a\sigma)} = \frac{1}{72}\delta(\theta + 10)^2,$$

and the noncooperating jurisdiction sees an increase in revenues:

(A.29)
$$R_s^{C(a\sigma)} - R_s^U = \frac{1}{1800}\delta(\theta + 10)(70 - 11\theta) > 0.$$

Comparing tax revenues within the cooperative requires further assumptions about how revenues are split among the jurisdictions in the cooperative. With equal splitting in the cooperative, then the difference in tax revenues becomes

$$\text{(A.30)} \qquad \frac{R_{a\sigma}^{C(a\sigma)}}{2} - R_a^U = \frac{1}{3600}\delta(700 - 940\theta - 263\theta^2)$$

$$\frac{R_{a\sigma}^{C(a\sigma)}}{2} - R_\sigma^U = \frac{1}{3600}\delta(700 + 1220\theta - 47\theta^2).$$

The expression $(R_{a\sigma}^{C(a\sigma)}/2) - R_\sigma^U$ is positive if $700 + 1220\theta - 47\theta^2 > 0$, which is true if $(610/47) - (450/47)\sqrt{2} < \theta$. The expression $(R_{a\sigma}^{C(a\sigma)}/2) - R_a^U$ is positive if $700 - 940\theta - 263\theta^2 > 0$, which is true if $-(470/263) + (450/47)\sqrt{2} > \theta$.

An alternative proposal allocates revenues proportional to the equilibrium tax bases in each local jurisdiction. Letting the tilde denote revenues after base splitting, this means revenues will be allocated according to

$$\text{(A.31)} \qquad \tilde{R}_a^{C(a\sigma)} = T_{a\sigma}^{C(a\sigma)}\left[1 + \theta - \frac{(T_{a\sigma}^{C(a\sigma)} - T_s^{C(a\sigma)})}{\delta}\right]$$

$$\tilde{R}_\sigma^{C(a\sigma)} = T_{a\sigma}^{C(a\sigma)}\left[1 - \frac{\theta}{2} - \frac{(T_{a\sigma}^{C(a\sigma)} - T_s^{C(a\sigma)})}{\delta}\right],$$

where each jurisdiction has the same amount of shifting activity because they face the same tax differential, and where the terms in brackets are the asymmetric sizes of the jurisdiction in the absence of shifting net of any shifting. Evaluating (A.31) at the coordinated Nash tax rates, and subtracting revenues in the uncoordinated regime yields

$$\text{(A.32)} \qquad \tilde{R}_a^{C(a\sigma)} - R_a^U = \frac{1}{1800}\delta(35 - \theta)(19\theta + 10)$$

$$\tilde{R}_\sigma^{C(a\sigma)} - R_\sigma^U = \frac{1}{1800}\delta(10 - 17\theta)(8\theta + 35),$$

where I use a single jurisdiction subscript of a member in the coalition to denote split revenues in contrast to using both jurisdictions' subscripts to indicate combined revenues. The first expression is positive if $(35 - \theta)(19\theta + 10) > 0$ which is true if $\theta > -10/19$. The second expression is positive if $(10 - 17\theta)(8\theta + 35) > 0$, which is true if $\theta < 10/17$.

**Derivation: Voluntary Cooperation**

First, consider the case where tax revenues are split proportional to the tax bases in equilibrium. In the case where two symmetric jurisdictions cooperate, this amounts to equal splitting of revenues, where a single jurisdiction in the subscript indicates the revenue of a single member of the cooperative in the superscript:

(A.33)
$$\tilde{R}_s^{C(s\sigma)} = \tilde{R}_\sigma^{C(s\sigma)} = \frac{1}{36}\delta(\theta-5)^2$$
$$R_a^{C(s\sigma)} = \frac{1}{18}\delta(\theta+4)^2.$$

But when two asymmetric jurisdiction cooperated, taking the case *aσ* as representative, revenues under cooperation are

(A.34)
$$R_s^{C(a\sigma)} = \frac{1}{72}\delta(\theta-8)^2$$
$$R_a^{C(a\sigma)} = \frac{5}{72}\delta(\theta+10)(1+\theta)$$
$$R_\sigma^{C(a\sigma)} = \frac{1}{72}\delta(\theta+10)(5-4\theta).$$

Revenues in the case *as* can be similarly derived.

Under equal splitting, revenues in the asymmetric case need to be replaced with $R_a^{C(a\sigma)} = R_{a\sigma}^{C(a\sigma)}/2$ and $R_\sigma^{C(a\sigma)} = R_{a\sigma}^{C(a\sigma)}/2$. With equal splitting, there is no tilde, and it is known to be the jurisdiction revenue rather than the coalition revenue because of the single jurisdiction in the subscript. Under the symmetric coalition, equal splitting and base splitting yield the same revenues.

Having ruled out a grand coalition by assumption, it suffices to compare all unilateral deviations from a coalition. To facilitate this, I construct a matrix given in table 3A.1 where rows are all possible coalitions and columns give the payoff for the jurisdictions. The matrix shows all payoffs for each type of splitting rule. However, the splitting rules are exogenously

**Table 3A.1** **Jurisdiction payoffs by coalition**

| | Jurisdiction | | | |
|---|---|---|---|---|
| Coalition | *s* | *a* | *σ* | ID |
| uncoordinated | $\frac{1}{50}\delta(\theta-5)^2$ | $\frac{1}{50}\delta(2\theta+5)^2$ | $\frac{1}{50}\delta(\theta-5)^2$ | *A* |
| *sσ* | $\frac{1}{36}\delta(\theta-5)^2$ | $\frac{1}{18}\delta(\theta+4)^2$ | $\frac{1}{36}\delta(\theta-5)^2$ | *B* |
| *as* (base splitting) | $\frac{1}{72}\delta(\theta+10)(5-4\theta)$ | $\frac{5}{72}\delta(\theta+10)(\theta+1)$ | $\frac{1}{72}\delta(\theta-8)^2$ | $\tilde{C}$ |
| *as* (= splitting) | $\frac{1}{144}\delta(\theta+10)^2$ | $\frac{1}{144}\delta(\theta+10)^2$ | $\frac{1}{72}\delta(\theta-8)^2$ | *C* |
| *aσ* (base splitting) | $\frac{1}{72}\delta(\theta-8)^2$ | $\frac{5}{72}\delta(\theta+10)(\theta+1)$ | $\frac{1}{72}\delta(\theta+10)(5-4\theta)$ | $\tilde{D}$ |
| *aσ* (= splitting) | $\frac{1}{72}\delta(\theta-8)^2$ | $\frac{1}{144}\delta(\theta+10)^2$ | $\frac{1}{144}\delta(\theta+10)^2$ | *D* |

Rows indicate the coalition and the splitting rule. Columns are the jurisdictions. The cells are equilibrium tax revenues.

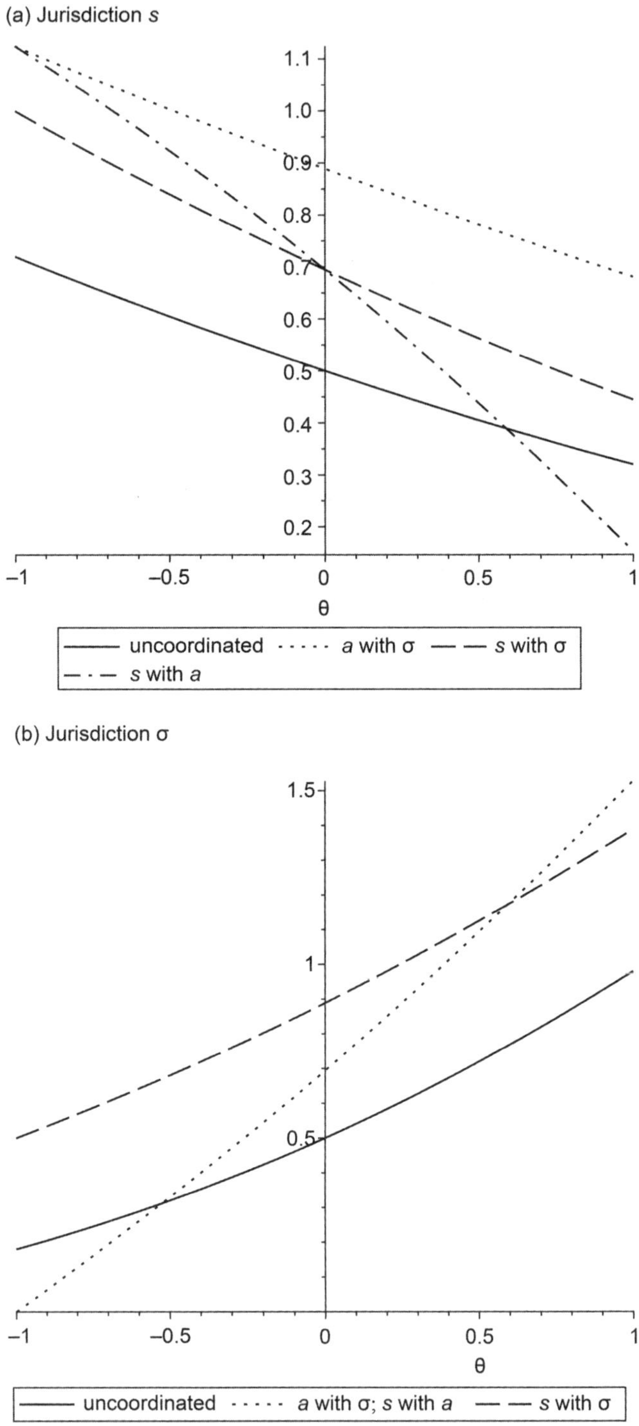


**Fig. 3A.1 Payoffs for each jurisdiction with base splitting**

This figure shows the payoffs (revenue) for each jurisdiction for all possible coalitions by values of θ. Within coalitions, tax revenues are split proportional to the tax bases.

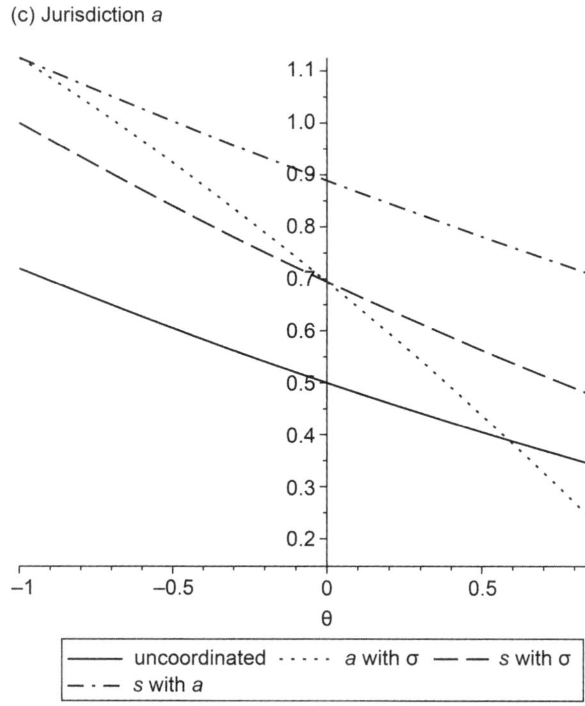


**Fig. 3A.1 (cont.)**

determined and thus, jurisdictions need to only consider deviations within regimes governed by the same splitting rules.

In order to visualize these payoffs for all values of θ, I normalize δ = 1 (or equivalently divide by δ) and then plot the payoff functions—with tax revenues on the vertical axis—separately for base splitting (figure 3A.1) and equal splitting (figure 3A.2).

While these figures visualize which strategies revenue-dominate each other, to determine the equilibrium I must check for all unilateral deviations taking as given and fixed the other player strategies. As noted in the text, the Nash equilibrium in a coalition game is likely too weak a concept, but for simplicity, I use this equilibrium concept. To determine the Nash equilibria, I write the payoff matrices in the following tables 3A.2 and 3A.3. Player *s* plays rows as strategies, player σ plays columns as strategies, and player *a* plays boxes as strategies. Each strategy is the jurisdiction that the player wishes to partner with. For example, if player *s* plays σ, they are declaring their intent to form a coalition with σ; if player *s* plays *s*, they are declaring their intent to go it alone. If any two players declare each other, then that coalition forms and they receive the revenue payoffs for that coalition. Note that under the rules of this game, if *s* plays σ, σ plays *s*, and *a* plays *a*,

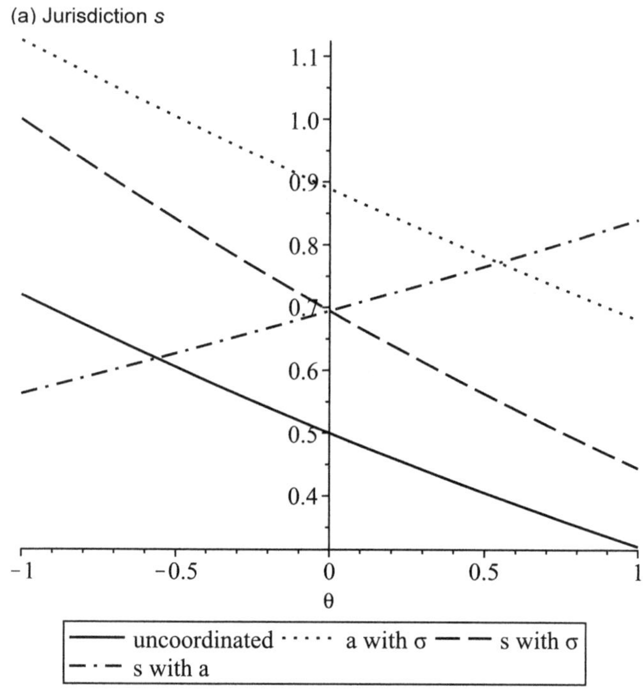


**Fig. 3A.2 Payoffs for each jurisdiction with equal splitting**
This figure shows the payoffs (revenue) for each jurisdiction for all possible coalitions by values of θ. Within coalitions, tax revenues are split equally within the coalition.

then *sσ* emerges as a coalition. But what if instead of *a* playing *a*, it plays *s*? Under the assumptions I have made, since both *s* and σ still agree, the payoffs remain unchanged as *sσ* still emerges as a coalition. Finally, consider the case where *s* plays σ, σ plays σ, and *a* plays σ. With these strategies, no two jurisdictions wish to form a coalition together. As a result, the payoffs default to the unccordinated Nash game (e.g., as if *s* plays *s*, σ plays σ, and *a* plays *a*). Of course, alternative rules governing the game could be specified.

Table 3A.2 shows the payoff matrices for base splitting, while table 3A.3 shows the payoffs for equal splitting. Note that the payoffs given in figure 3A.1 and figure 3A.2 are clearly a function of θ. However, conditional on a given value of θ, the payoff of each player can be ranked from 1 (lowest) to 4 (highest). In the payoff matrices, I use this rank rather than the precise revenue amount. Finally, the rankings differ on the basis of θ. Thus, I calculate the value of θ where any payoff curve intersects another curve, and then construct a different payoff matrix for each unique range of θ with the cutoff values of θ delineating the cases.

The Nash equilibria are then obtained by checking for unilateral profit-

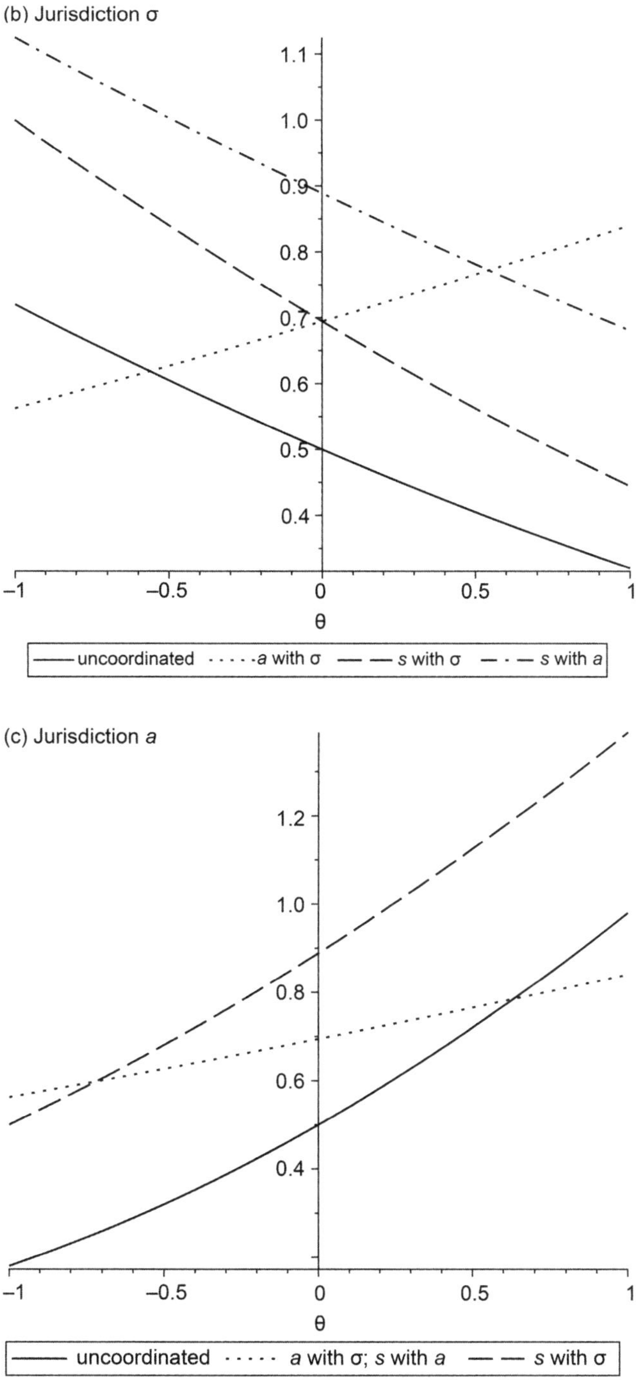

(b) Jurisdiction σ
1.1
1.0
0.9
0.8
0.7
0.6
0.5
0.4
–1
–0.5
0
0.5
1
θ
uncoordinated
a with σ
s with σ
s with a
(c) Jurisdiction a
1.2
1.0
0.8
0.6
0.4
–1
–0.5
0
0.5
1
θ
uncoordinated
a with σ; s with a
s with σ


**Fig. 3A.2 (cont.)**

**Table 3A.2** **Base splitting game: Nash equilibria**

$A.\left[\text{Case: } \theta \leq -\frac{10}{19}\right]$

| Player $a$: Strategy σ | | | | | Player $a$: Strategy $s$ | | | | | Player $a$: Strategy $a$ | | | | |
|---|---|---|---|---|---|---|---|---|---|---|---|---|---|---|
| | | Player σ | | | | | Player σ | | | | | Player σ | | |
| Player $s$ | Strategy | σ | $s$ | $a$ | Player $s$ | Strategy | σ | $s$ | $a$ | Player $s$ | Strategy | σ | $s$ | $a$ |
| | σ | 1,1,3 | 2,2,4 | 4,3,1 | | σ | 1,1,3 | 2,2,4 | 1,1,3 | | σ | 1,1,3 | 2,2,4 | 1,1,3 |
| | $s$ | 1,1,3 | 1,1,3 | 4,3,1 | | $s$ | 1,1,3 | 1,1,3 | 1,1,3 | | $s$ | 1,1,3 | 1,1,3 | 1,1,3 |
| | $a$ | 1,1,3 | 1,1,3 | 4,3,1 | | $a$ | 3,4,1 | 3,4,1 | 3,4,1 | | $a$ | 1,1,3 | 1,1,3 | 1,1,3 |

$B.\left[\text{Case: } -\frac{10}{19} < \theta \leq 0\right]$

| Player $a$: Strategy σ | | | | | Player $a$: Strategy $s$ | | | | | Player $a$: Strategy $a$ | | | | |
|---|---|---|---|---|---|---|---|---|---|---|---|---|---|---|
| | | Player σ | | | | | Player σ | | | | | Player σ | | |
| Player $s$ | Strategy | σ | $s$ | $a$ | Player $s$ | Strategy | σ | $s$ | $a$ | Player $s$ | Strategy | σ | $s$ | $a$ |
| | σ | 1,1,1 | 2,2,4 | 4,3,3 | | σ | 1,1,1 | 2,2,4 | 1,1,1 | | σ | 1,1,1 | 2,2,4 | 1,1,1 |
| | $s$ | 1,1,1 | 1,1,1 | 4,3,3 | | $s$ | 1,1,1 | 1,1,1 | 1,1,1 | | $s$ | 1,1,1 | 1,1,1 | 1,1,1 |
| | $a$ | 1,1,1 | 1,1,1 | 4,3,3 | | $a$ | 3,4,3 | 3,4,3 | 3,4,3 | | $a$ | 1,1,1 | 1,1,1 | 1,1,1 |

$C.\left[\text{Case: } 0 < \theta \leq \frac{10}{17}\right]$

| Player $a$: Strategy σ | | | | | Player $a$: Strategy $s$ | | | | | Player $a$: Strategy $a$ | | | | |
|---|---|---|---|---|---|---|---|---|---|---|---|---|---|---|
| | | Player σ | | | | | Player σ | | | | | Player σ | | |
| Player $s$ | Strategy | σ | $s$ | $a$ | Player $s$ | Strategy | σ | $s$ | $a$ | Player $s$ | Strategy | σ | $s$ | $a$ |
| | σ | 1,1,1 | 3,3,4 | 4,2,3 | | σ | 1,1,1 | 3,3,4 | 1,1,1 | | σ | 1,1,1 | 3,3,4 | 1,1,1 |
| | $s$ | 1,1,1 | 1,1,1 | 4,2,3 | | $s$ | 1,1,1 | 1,1,1 | 1,1,1 | | $s$ | 1,1,1 | 1,1,1 | 1,1,1 |
| | $a$ | 1,1,1 | 1,1,1 | 4,2,3 | | $a$ | 2,4,3 | 2,4,3 | 2,4,3 | | $a$ | 1,1,1 | 1,1,1 | 1,1,1 |

$D. \left[\text{Case: } -\frac{23}{2} + \frac{3\sqrt{65}}{2} < \theta \leq \frac{10}{17}\right]$

| Player *a*: Strategy σ | | | | | Player *a*: Strategy *a* | | | | | Player *a*: Strategy *a* | | | | |
|---|---|---|---|---|---|---|---|---|---|---|---|---|---|---|
| | | Player σ | | | | | Player σ | | | | | Player σ | | |
| Player *s* | Strategy | σ | *s* | *a* | Player *s* | Strategy | σ | *s* | *a* | Player *s* | Strategy | σ | *s* | *a* |
| | σ | 2,2,1 | 3,3,4 | 4,1,3 | | σ | 2,2,1 | 3,3,4 | 2,2,1 | | σ | 2,2,1 | 3,3,4 | 2,2,1 |
| | *s* | 2,2,1 | 2,2,1 | 4,1,3 | | *s* | 2,2,1 | 2,2,1 | 2,2,1 | | *s* | 2,2,1 | 2,2,1 | 2,2,1 |
| | *a* | 2,2,1 | 2,2,1 | 4,1,3 | | *a* | 1,4,3 | 1,4,3 | 1,4,3 | | *a* | 2,2,1 | 2,2,1 | 2,2,1 |

$E. \left[\text{Case: } \frac{10}{17} < \theta\right]$

| Player *a*: Strategy σ | | | | | Player *a*: Strategy *a* | | | | | Player *a*: Strategy *a* | | | | |
|---|---|---|---|---|---|---|---|---|---|---|---|---|---|---|
| | | Player σ | | | | | Player σ | | | | | Player σ | | |
| Player *s* | Strategy | σ | *s* | *a* | Player *s* | Strategy | σ | *s* | *a* | Player *s* | Strategy | σ | *s* | *a* |
| | σ | 2,2,1 | 3,3,3 | 4,1,4 | | σ | 2,2,1 | 3,3,3 | 2,2,1 | | σ | 2,2,1 | 3,3,3 | 2,2,1 |
| | *s* | 2,2,1 | 2,2,1 | 4,1,4 | | *s* | 2,2,1 | 2,2,1 | 2,2,1 | | *s* | 2,2,1 | 2,2,1 | 2,2,1 |
| | *a* | 2,2,1 | 2,2,1 | 4,1,4 | | *a* | 1,4,4 | 1,4,4 | 1,4,4 | | *a* | 2,2,1 | 2,2,1 | 2,2,1 |

Each table denotes the payoff matrix for the three jurisdictions in that range of θ. Player *s* plays rows, player σ plays columns, and player *a* plays boxes. The numerical values are the rank of revenue for the jurisdiction, with four denoting the most revenue. Best responses are in bold and Nash equilibria are underlined.

**Table 3A.3** **Equal splitting game: Nash equilibria**

*A.* $\left[\text{Case: } \theta \leq -\frac{22}{7} + \frac{12\sqrt{2}}{7}\right]$

| Player *a*: Strategy σ | | Player σ | | |
|---|---|---|---|---|
| Player *s* | Strategy | σ | *s* | *a* |
| | σ | 2,2,1 | 3,3,3 | 4,1,4 |
| | *s* | 2,2,1 | 2,2,1 | 4,1,4 |
| | *a* | 2,2,1 | 2,2,1 | 4,1,4 |

| Player *a*: Strategy *s* | | Player σ | | |
|---|---|---|---|---|
| Player *s* | Strategy | σ | *s* | *a* |
| | σ | 2,2,1 | 3,3,3 | 2,2,1 |
| | s | 2,2,1 | 2,2,1 | 2,2,1 |
| | *a* | 1,4,4 | 1,4,4 | 1,4,4 |

| Player *a*: Strategy *a* | | Player σ | | |
|---|---|---|---|---|
| Player *s* | Strategy | σ | *s* | *a* |
| | σ | 2,2,1 | 3,3,3 | 2,2,1 |
| | *s* | 2,2,1 | 2,2,1 | 2,2,1 |
| | a | 2,2,1 | 2,2,1 | 2,2,1 |

*B.* $\left[\text{Case: } -\frac{22}{7} + \frac{12\sqrt{2}}{7} < \theta \leq \frac{610}{47} - \frac{450\sqrt{2}}{47}\right]$

| Player *a*: Strategy σ | | Player σ | | |
|---|---|---|---|---|
| Player *s* | Strategy | σ | *s* | *a* |
| | σ | 2,2,1 | 3,3,4 | 4,1,3 |
| | *s* | 2,2,1 | 2,2,1 | 4,1,3 |
| | *a* | 2,2,1 | 2,2,1 | 4,1,3 |

| Player *a*: Strategy *s* | | Player σ | | |
|---|---|---|---|---|
| Player *s* | Strategy | σ | *s* | *a* |
| | σ | 2,2,1 | 3,3,4 | 2,2,1 |
| | *s* | 2,2,1 | 2,2,1 | 2,2,1 |
| | *a* | 1,4,3 | 1,4,3 | 1,4,3 |

| Player *a*: Strategy *a* | | Player σ | | |
|---|---|---|---|---|
| Player *s* | Strategy | σ | *s* | *a* |
| | σ | 2,2,1 | 3,3,4 | 2,2,1 |
| | *s* | 2,2,1 | 2,2,1 | 2,2,1 |
| | *a* | 2,2,1 | 2,2,1 | 2,2,1 |

*C.* $\left[\text{Case: } \frac{610}{47} - \frac{450\sqrt{2}}{47} < \theta \leq 0\right]$

| Player *a*: Strategy σ | | Player σ | | |
|---|---|---|---|---|
| Player *s* | Strategy | σ | *s* | *a* |
| | σ | 1,1,1 | 3,3,4 | 4,2,3 |
| | *s* | 1,1,1 | 1,1,1 | 4,2,3 |
| | *a* | 1,1,1 | 1,1,1 | 4,2,3 |

| Player *a*: Strategy *s* | | Player σ | | |
|---|---|---|---|---|
| Player *s* | Strategy | σ | *s* | *a* |
| | σ | 1,1,1 | 3,3,4 | 1,1,1 |
| | *s* | 1,1,1 | 1,1,1 | 1,1,1 |
| | *a* | 2,4,3 | 2,4,3 | 2,4,3 |

| Player *a*: Strategy *a* | | Player σ | | |
|---|---|---|---|---|
| Player *s* | Strategy | σ | *s* | *a* |
| | σ | 1,1,1 | 3,3,4 | 1,1,1 |
| | *s* | 1,1,1 | 1,1,1 | 1,1,1 |
| | *a* | 1,1,1 | 1,1,1 | 1,1,1 |

*D.* [Case: $0 < \theta \le 26 - 18\sqrt{2}$]

| Player *a*: Strategy σ | | | | |
|---|---|---|---|---|
| | | Player σ | | |
| Player *s* | Strategy | σ | *s* | *a* |
| | σ | 1,1,1 | 2,2,4 | 4,3,3 |
| | *s* | 1,1,1 | 1,1,1 | 4,3,3 |
| | *a* | 1,1,1 | 1,1,1 | 4,3,3 |

| Player *a*: Strategy *s* | | | | |
|---|---|---|---|---|
| | | Player σ | | |
| Player *s* | Strategy | σ | *s* | *a* |
| | σ | 1,1,1 | 2,2,4 | 1,1,1 |
| | *s* | 1,1,1 | 1,1,1 | 1,1,1 |
| | *a* | 3,4,3 | 3,4,3 | 3,4,3 |

| Player *a*: Strategy *a* | | | | |
|---|---|---|---|---|
| | | Player σ | | |
| Player *s* | Strategy | σ | *s* | *a* |
| | σ | 1,1,1 | 2,2,4 | 1,1,1 |
| | *s* | 1,1,1 | 1,1,1 | 1,1,1 |
| | *a* | 1,1,1 | 1,1,1 | 1,1,1 |

*E.* [Case: $26 - 18\sqrt{2} < \theta \le -\frac{470}{263} + \frac{450\sqrt{2}}{263}$]

| Player *a*: Strategy σ | | | | |
|---|---|---|---|---|
| | | Player σ | | |
| Player *s* | Strategy | σ | *s* | *a* |
| | σ | 1,1,1 | 2,2,4 | 3,4,3 |
| | *s* | 1,1,1 | 1,1,1 | 3,4,3 |
| | *a* | 1,1,1 | 1,1,1 | 3,4,3 |

| Player *a*: Strategy *s* | | | | |
|---|---|---|---|---|
| | | Player σ | | |
| Player *s* | Strategy | σ | *s* | *a* |
| | σ | 1,1,1 | 2,2,4 | 1,1,1 |
| | *s* | 1,1,1 | 1,1,1 | 1,1,1 |
| | *a* | 4,3,3 | 4,3,3 | 4,3,3 |

| Player *a*: Strategy *a* | | | | |
|---|---|---|---|---|
| | | Player σ | | |
| Player *s* | Strategy | σ | *s* | *a* |
| | σ | 1,1,1 | 2,2,4 | 1,1,1 |
| | *s* | 1,1,1 | 1,1,1 | 1,1,1 |
| | *a* | 1,1,1 | 1,1,1 | 1,1,1 |

*F.* [Case: $-\frac{470}{263} + \frac{450\sqrt{2}}{263} < \theta$]

| Player *a*: Strategy σ | | | | |
|---|---|---|---|---|
| | | Player σ | | |
| Player *s* | Strategy | | *s* | *a* |
| | σ | 1,1,3 | 2,2,4 | 3,4,1 |
| | *s* | 1,1,3 | 1,1,3 | 3,4,1 |
| | *a* | 1,1,3 | 1,1,3 | 3,4,1 |

| Player *a*: Strategy *s* | | | | |
|---|---|---|---|---|
| | | Player σ | | |
| Player *s* | Strategy | σ | *s* | *a* |
| | σ | 1,1,3 | 2,2,4 | 1,1,3 |
| | *s* | 1,1,3 | 1,1,3 | 1,1,3 |
| | *a* | 4,3,1 | 4,3,1 | 4,3,1 |

| Player *a*: Strategy *a* | | | | |
|---|---|---|---|---|
| | | Player σ | | |
| Player *s* | Strategy | σ | *s* | *a* |
| | σ | 1,1,3 | 2,2,4 | 1,1,3 |
| | *s* | 1,1,3 | 1,1,3 | 1,1,3 |
| | *a* | 1,1,3 | 1,1,3 | 1,1,3 |

Each table denotes the payoff matrix for the three jurisdictions in that range of θ. Player *s* plays rows, player σ plays columns, and player *a* plays boxes. The numerical values are the rank of revenue for the jurisdiction, with four denoting the most revenue. Best responses are in bold and Nash equilibria are underlined.

**Table 3A.4** **Nash equilibria with base splitting**

| Range of θ | Nash coalition | Other player's strategy | Asymmetric? |
|---|---|---|---|
| $\theta \le -\frac{10}{19}$ | *sσ* | *a* | |
| $-\frac{10}{19} < \theta \le 0$ | *sσ* | *a* | |
| $0 < \theta \le \frac{10}{17}$ | ***aσ*** | ***a,s,σ*** | Y |
| | ***as*** | ***a,s,σ*** | Y |
| | ***aσ*** | ***σ*** | Y |
| | ***as*** | ***s*** | Y |
| | *sσ* | *a,s,σ* | |
| $-\frac{23}{2} + \frac{3\sqrt{65}}{2} < \theta \le \frac{10}{17}$ | *sσ* | *a,σ* | |
| $\frac{10}{17} < \theta$ | *sσ* | *a,s,σ* | |

The splitting rule governing the results in this table is base splitting. This table lists the Nash equilibria coalitions for the complete range of θ. The uncoordinated equilibrium is omitted from the table. The first column is the range of θ. The second column lists the equilibrium coalition(s). And the third column lists the strategy (strategies) the noncoalition member must play for that coalition to be a Nash equilibrium. For example, in the first row *sσ* is a Nash coalition if θ is sufficiently small, but this equilibrium only arises if the nonmember of the coalition (*a*) plays strategy *a*. If *a* were to play any other strategy, the coalition members have incentive to deviate. The equilibrium coalitions that arise between asymmetric jurisdictions are marked with a "Y" in the final column and are highlighted in bold.

able deviations. The best responses to the other player strategies are highlighted in bold font. Then the equilibria are denoted in underline. Note that the equilibria are conditional on the values of θ. More generally, some equilibria can only arise if the other player uses a given strategy while others may arise regardless of the nonmember's strategy, which clearly is a result of the assumption regarding no preplay or communication. Tables 3.A4 and 3.A5 summarize these equilibria along with when they arise. The use of other, likely stronger, equilibrium concepts is discussed in the main text of the chapter.

### Derivation: Sourcing Rules

If taxes can be effectively sourced such that the tax base cannot be shifted to engage in tax arbitrage, the revenue functions become

$$R_i = T_i B_i = T_i \Theta_i. \tag{A.35}$$

As this does not depend on the tax rate, a Leviathan will set taxes to extract all the surplus.

**Table 3A.5** **Nash equilibria with equal splitting**

| Range of θ | Nash coalition | Other player's strategy | Asymmetric? |
|---|---|---|---|
| $\theta \leq -\frac{22}{7} + \frac{12\sqrt{2}}{7}$ | $s\sigma$ | $a,s,\sigma$ | |
| $-\frac{22}{7} + \frac{12\sqrt{2}}{7} < \theta \leq \frac{610}{47} - \frac{450\sqrt{2}}{47}$ | $s\sigma$ | $a,s,\sigma$ | |
| $\frac{610}{47} - \frac{450\sqrt{2}}{47} < \theta \leq 0$ | $s\sigma$ | $a,s,\sigma$ | |
| | $\boldsymbol{a\sigma}$ | $\boldsymbol{a,s}$ | Y |
| | $\boldsymbol{as}$ | $\boldsymbol{a,\sigma}$ | Y |
| $0 < \theta \leq 26 - 18\sqrt{2}$ | $\boldsymbol{a\sigma}$ | $\boldsymbol{a,s,\sigma}$ | Y |
| | $\boldsymbol{as}$ | $\boldsymbol{a,s,\sigma}$ | Y |
| | $s\sigma$ | $a$ | |
| $26 - 18\sqrt{2} < \theta \leq -\frac{470}{263} + \frac{450\sqrt{2}}{263}$ | $\boldsymbol{a\sigma}$ | $\boldsymbol{a,s,\sigma}$ | Y |
| | $\boldsymbol{as}$ | $\boldsymbol{a,s,\sigma}$ | Y |
| | $s\sigma$ | $a$ | |
| $-\frac{470}{263} + \frac{450\sqrt{2}}{263} < \theta$ | $s\sigma$ | $a$ | |

The splitting rule governing the results in this table is equal splitting. This table lists the Nash equilibria coalitions for the complete range of θ. The uncoordinated equilibrium is omitted from the table. The first column is the range of θ. The second column lists the equilibrium coalition(s). And the third column lists the strategy (strategies) the noncoalition member must play for that coalition to be a Nash equilibrium. For example, in the last row $s\sigma$ is a Nash coalition if θ is sufficiently large, but this equilibrium only arises if the nonmember of the coalition ($a$) plays strategy $a$. If $a$ were to play any other strategy, the coalition members have incentive to deviate. The equilibrium coalitions that arise between asymmetric jurisdictions are marked with a "Y" in the final column and are highlighted in bold.

## Derivation: Total Revenue Dominance

Recall the sum of revenues across all three jurisdictions for each scenario that are given in the text and restated here:

(A.36)
$$R^U_{total} = \delta\left(\frac{3}{2} + \frac{3}{25}\theta^2\right)$$

(A.37)
$$R^H_{total} = \delta\left(\frac{3}{2} + \frac{9\omega - 3}{10}\theta\right)$$

(A.38)
$$R^M_{total} = \begin{cases} \delta\left(\frac{3}{2} + \frac{3\omega\theta}{4} + \frac{3(8 + 2\omega - 3\omega^2)\theta^2}{200}\right) & \theta > 0 \\ \delta\left(\frac{3}{2} + \frac{(\omega - 1)\theta}{2} + \frac{(4\omega^2 - 6\omega - 4)\theta^2}{50}\right) & \theta < 0 \end{cases}$$

$$\text{(A.39)} \qquad R^{C(as)}_{total} = R^{C(a\sigma)}_{total} = \delta\left(\frac{\theta^2 + 2\theta + 82}{36}\right)$$

and

$$\text{(A.40)} \qquad R^{C(s\sigma)}_{total} = \delta\left(\frac{2\theta^2 - 2\theta + 41}{18}\right).$$

To show that $R^M_{total} \geq R^H_{total}$, note that

$$\text{(A.41)} \qquad R^M_{total} - R^H_{total} = \begin{cases} -\dfrac{2\theta\delta\left(\omega + \dfrac{1}{2}\right)(5 + \theta\omega - 2\theta)}{25} & \theta > 0 \\ -\dfrac{3\theta\delta(3\theta\omega + 4\theta + 10)(\omega - 2)}{200} & \theta < 0 \end{cases}$$

and equals zero when $\theta = 0$. However, the derivative of this difference with respect to $\theta$ is increasing if $\theta > 0$ but is decreasing if $\theta < 0$. Thus, $R^M_{total} - R^H_{total} \geq 0$ for all values of $\theta$. Conducting a similar exercise, yields $R^M_{total} - R^U_{total} \geq 0$.

As noted in the text,

$$\text{(A.42)} \qquad R^{C(as)}_{total} - R^{C(s\sigma)}_{total} = \frac{(2 - \theta)\theta\delta}{12},$$

such that $R^{C(as)}_{total} > R^{C(s\sigma)}_{total}$ if $\theta > 0$ and $R^{C(as)}_{total} < R^{C(s\sigma)}_{total}$ if $\theta < 0$.

Comparing total revenues under each coalition game with the revenues under tax harmonization, it is easy to show that $R^{C(as)}_{total} > R^H_{total}$ and $R^{C(s\sigma)}_{total} > R^H_{total}$ for all parameter constellations.

Finally, I compare the minimum tax rate regime with the coalition regime. Initially, I focus on the case where $\theta < 0$. I first check the relationship with the coalitions that yields the lowest revenue for $\theta < 0$:

$$\text{(A.43)} \quad R^{C(as)}_{total} - R^M_{total} = \frac{(72\theta^2\omega^2 - 108\theta^2\omega - 47\theta^2 - 450\omega\theta + 500\theta + 700)\delta}{900},$$

and it can be verified that this is positive in the relevant ranges. Given this is positive for the coalition yielding the lower revenues, it is also positive for the other coalition.

Then, repeating this exercise for $\theta > 0$, yields

$$\text{(A.44)} \quad R^{C(as)}_{total} - R^M_{total} = \frac{(81\theta^2\omega^2 - 54\theta^2\omega - 166\theta^2 - 1350\omega\theta + 100\theta + 1400)\delta}{1800},$$

and the derivative of this expression is decreasing in $\omega$. For $\theta > 0$ coalition *as* yields the highest revenue. Given the above expression evaluated at $\theta = 0$ is positive and the derivative with respect to $\omega$ is negative, if $R^M_{total}$ is larger, it will be the case for $\omega = 1$. Evaluating yields $R^{C(as)}_{total} - R^M_{total} > 0$ for all $0 < \theta < 1$.

Turning to the coalition yielding the lower revenues when $\theta > 0$:

$$(A.45) \qquad R^{C(s\sigma)}_{total} - R^{M}_{total} = \frac{(9\theta\omega + 2\theta - 10)(9\theta\omega - 8\theta - 140)\delta}{1800},$$

and the derivative is decreasing in $\omega$. Again, given the above expression evaluated at $\theta = 0$ is positive and the derivative with respect to $\omega$ is decreasing, if $R^{M}_{total}$ is larger, it will be the case for $\omega = 1$. Evaluating at $\omega = 1$ yields $R^{C(s\sigma)}_{total} - R^{M}_{total} = [(11\theta - 10)(\theta - 140)\delta]/1800\delta$, which is positive if $\theta < 10/11$. Thus, there exists a range of $\omega$ and $\theta$ sufficiently close to one where the minimum regime revenue dominates.

## References


Abidi, Zineb, and Emmanuelle Taugourdeau. 2024. "Tax Competition and Harmonization Where Tastes for Public Goods Differ." *International Tax and Public Finance* 31: 953–979.

Agrawal, David R., Marie-Laure Breuillé, and Julie Le Gallo. 2025. "Tax Competition with Intermunicipal Cooperation." *National Tax Journal* 78 (1), 5–43.

Agrawal, David R., and Jan K. Brueckner. 2025. "Taxes and Telework: The Impacts of State Income Taxes in a Work-from-Home Economy." *Journal of Urban Economics* 145, 103732.

Agrawal, David R., Jan K. Brueckner, and Marius Brülhart. 2024. "Fiscal Federalism in the Twenty-First Century." *Annual Review of Economics* 16: 429–54.

Agrawal, David R., Dirk Foremny, and Clara Martínez-Toledano. 2025. "Wealth Tax Mobility and Tax Coordination." *American Economic Journal: Applied Economics* 17 (1): 402–430.

Agrawal, David R., and William H. Hoyt. 2018. "Commuting and Taxes: Theory, Empirics and Welfare Implications." *The Economic Journal* 168 (616): 2969–3007.

Agrawal, David R., William H. Hoyt, and John D. Wilson. 2022. "Local Policy Choice: Theory and Empirics." *Journal of Economic Literature* 60 (4): 1378–455.

Agrawal, David R., Adib Bagh, and Moahmmed Mardan. 2025. "Sensitivity Versus Size: Implications for Tax Competition." *Theoretical Economics*, forthcoming.

Agrawal, David R., and David E. Wildasin. 2019. "Technology and Tax Systems." *Journal of Public Economics* 185: 104082.

Alesina, Alberto, and Enrico Spolaore. 2005. *The Size of Nations*. MIT Press.

Auerbach, Alan, and Michael P. Devereux. 2018. "Cash-Flow Taxes in an International Setting." *American Economic Journal: Economic Policy* 10 (3): 69–94.

Aumann, Robert. 1959. "Acceptable Points in General Cooperative n-Person Games." In *Contributions to the Theory of Games IV*, edited by A. W. Tucker and R. D. Luce. Princeton University Press.

Bernheim, B. Douglas, Bezalel Peleg, and Michael D. Whinston. 1987a. "Coalition-Proof Nash Equilibria I. Concepts." *Journal of Economic Theory* 42 (1): 1–12.

Bernheim, B. Douglas, Bezalel Peleg, and Michael D. Whinston. 1987b. "Coalition-Proof Nash Equilibria II. Applications." *Journal of Economic Theory* 42 (1): 13–29.

Black, Dan A., and William H. Hoyt. 1989. "Bidding for Firms." *American Economic Review* 79 (5): 1249–56.

Boadway, Robin, and Anwar Shah. 2009. *Fiscal Federalism: Principles and Practice of Multiorder Governance*. Cambridge University Press.
Breuillé, Marie-Laure, and Pascale Duran-Vigneron. 2025. "Intermunicipal Cooperation in France and Related Tax Issues" In *Policy Responses to Tax Competition*, edited by David R. Agrawal, James M. Poterba, and Owen M. Zidar. University of Chicago Press.
Breuillé, Marie-Laure, Pascale Duran-Vigneron, and Anne-Laure Samson. 2018. "Inter-municipal Cooperation and Local Taxation." *Journal of Urban Economics* 107: 47–64.
Bruce, Donald, William F. Fox, and Alannah M. Shute. 2023. "Wayfair: A Step Toward the Destination, but Sales Tax Competition Remains." In *Policy Responses to Tax Competition*, edited by David R. Agrawal, James M. Poterba, and Owen M. Zidar. University of Chicago Press.
Brueckner, Jan K. 2003. "Strategic Interaction Among Governments: An Overview of Empirical Studies." *International Regional Science Review* 26 (2): 175–88.
Brueckner, Jan K., and Luz A. Saavedra. 2001. "Do Local Governments Engage in Strategic Property-Tax Competition?" *National Tax Journal* 54: 203–30.
Brülhart, Marius, Sam Bucovetsky, and Kurt Schmidheiny. 2015. "Taxes in Cities: Interdependence, Asymmetry, and Agglomeration." In *Handbook of Regional and Urban Economics*, vol. 5B, edited by Gilles Duranton, J. Vernon Henderson, and William Strange. North Holland.
Brülhart, Marius, and Mario Jametti. 2019. "Does Tax Competition Tame the Leviathan?" *Journal of Public Economics* 177: 104037.
Brülhart, Marius, Marko Koethenbuerger, Matthias Krapf, Raphael Parchet, Kurt Schmidheiny, and David Staubli. 2025. "Competition, Harmonization, and Redistribution: Corporate Taxes in Switzerland." In *Policy Responses to Tax Competition*, edited by David R. Agrawal, James M. Poterba, and Owen M. Zidar. University of Chicago Press.
Bucovetsky, Sam, and John Douglas Wilson. 1991. "Tax Competition with Two Tax Instruments." *Regional Science and Urban Economics* 21 (3): 333–50.
Burbidge, John B., James A. DePater, Gordon M. Myers, and Abhijit Sengupta. 1997. "A Coalition-Formation Approach to Equilibrium Federations and Trading Blocs." *American Economic Review* 87 (5): 940–56.
Clemens, Jeffrey, and Stan Veuger. 2023. "Intergovernmental Grants and Policy Competition: Concepts, Institutions, and Evidence." In *Policy Responses to Tax Competition*, edited by David R. Agrawal, James M. Poterba, and Owen M. Zidar. University of Chicago Press.
Coomes, Paul A., and William H. Hoyt. 2008. "Income Taxes and the Destination of Movers to Multistate MSAs." *Journal of Urban Economics* 63 (3): 920–37.
Cullen, Jullie Berry, and Roger H. Gordon. 2008. "Deductibility of State and Local Taxes: Is There a Case for Continuing This Tax Expenditure?" Working paper.
Donahue, John D. 1997. "Tiebout? Or Not Tiebout? The Market Metaphor and America's Devolution Debate." *Journal of Economic Perspectives* 11 (4): 73–81.
Eggert, Wolfgang, and Andreas Haufler. 1999. "Capital Taxation and Production Efficiency in an Open Economy." *Economics Letters* 62: 85–90.
Eliason, Paul, and Byron Lutz. 2018. "Can Fiscal Rules Constrain the Size of Government? An Analysis of the "Crown Jewel" of Tax and Expenditure Limitations." *Journal of Public Economics* 166: 115–44.
Epple, Dennis, and Thomas Romer. 1989. "On the Flexibility of Municipal Boundaries." *Journal of Urban Economics* 26 (3): 307–19.
Fajgelbaum, Pablo D., Eduardo Morales, Juan Carlos Suárez Serrato, and Owen

Zidar. 2019. "State Taxes and Spatial Misallocation." *Review of Economic Studies* 86 (1): 333–76.
Fleurbaey, Marc, Ravi Kanbur, and Dennis J. Snower. 2022. "An Analysis of Moral Motives in Economic and Social Decisions." Working paper.
Goodman, Christopher B. 2020. "Patterns in Special District Creation and Dissolution." Working paper.
Gordon, Roger. 1986. "Taxation of Investment and Savings in a World Economy." *American Economic Review* 76 (5): 1086–102.
Haufler, Andreas. 1996. "Tax Coordination with Different Preferences for Public Goods: Conflict or Harmony of Interest." *International Tax and Public Finance* 3 (1): 5–28.
Hebous, Shafik, and Michael Keen. 2023. "Pareto-Improving Minimum Corporate Taxation." *Journal of Public Economics* 225: 104952.
Hoyt, William H. 1991. "Property Taxation, Nash Equilibrium and Market Power." *Journal of Urban Economics* 30 (1): 123–31.
Hoyt, William. 2001. "Tax Policy Coordination, Vertical Externalities, and Optimal Taxation in a System of Hierarchical Governments." *Journal of Urban Economics* 50: 491–516.
Hoyt, William H. 2017. "The Assignment and Division of the Tax Base in a System of Hierarchical Governments." *International Tax and Public Finance* 24 (4): 678–704.
Huizinga, Harry, Luc Laeven, and Gaätan Nicodème. 2008. "Capital Structure and International Debt Shifting." *Journal of Financial Economics* 88 (1): 80–118.
Hulst, Rudie, and André van Montfort. 2007. *Inter-Municipal Cooperation in Europe*. Springer.
Inman, Robert P., and Daniel Rubinfeld. 1997. "Rethinking Federalism." *Journal of Economic Perspectives* 11 (4): 43–64.
Janeba, Eckhard, and Guttorm Schjelderup. 2023. "The Global Minimum Tax Raises More Revenues Than You Think, or Much Less." *Journal of International Economics* 145: 103837.
Janeba, Eckhard, and John Douglas Wilson. 2011. "Optimal Fiscal Federalism in the Presence of Tax Competition." *Journal of Public Economics* 95 (11–12): 1302–11.
Johannesen, Niels. 2022. "The Global Minimum Tax." *Journal of Public Economics* 212: 104709.
Kanbur, Ravi, and Michael Keen. 1993. "Jeux Sans Frontières: Tax Competition and Tax Coordination When Countries Differ in Size." *American Economic Review* 83 (4): 877–92.
Keen, Michael. 1987. "Welfare Effects of Commodity Tax Harmonization." *Journal of Public Economics* 33 (1): 107–14.
Keen, Michael. 1989. "Pareto-Improving Indirect Tax Harmonisation." *European Economic Review* 33 (1): 1–12.
Keen, Michael. 1998. "Vertical Tax Externalities in the Theory of Fiscal Federalism." *IMF Staff Papers* 45 (3): 454–85.
Keen, Michael. 2001. "Preferential Regimes Can Make Tax Competition Less Harmful." *National Tax Journal* 54 (4): 757–62.
Keen, Michael, and Kai A. Konrad. 2013. "The Theory of International Tax Competition and Coordination." In *Handbook of Public Economics*, vol. 5, edited by Alan J. Auerbach, Raj Chetty, Martin Feldstein, and Emmanuel Saez, 257–328. North Holland.
Keen, Michael, and Christos Kotsogiannis. 2002. "Does Federalism Lead to Excessively High Taxes?" *American Economic Review* 92 (1): 363–70.

Keen, Michael, and Christos Kotsogiannis. 2004. "Tax Competition in Federations and the Welfare Consequences of Decentralization." *Journal of Urban Economics* 56: 397–407.
Keen, Michael, Li Liu, and Hayley Pallan. 2022. "Tax Spillovers in Cross-Border Real Investment: Evidence from a New Dataset on Multinationals." Working paper.
Keen, Michael, Sajal Lahiri, and Pascalis Raimondos-Möller. 2002. "Tax Principles and Tax Harmonization Under Imperfect Competition: A Cautionary Example." *European Economic Review* 46: 1559–68.
Keen, Michael, and Hannu Piekkola. 1997. "Simple Rules for the Optimal Taxation of International Capital Income." *Scandinavian Journal of Economics* 99 (3): 447–61.
Kim, Donghyuk. 2025. "Interjurisdictional Competition and Coordination: Evidence from Kansas City." In *Policy Responses to Tax Competition*, edited by David R. Agrawal, James M. Poterba, and Owen M. Zidar. University of Chicago Press.
Konrad, Kai A. 2009. "Non-binding Minimum Taxes May Foster Tax Competition." *Economics Letters* 102 (2): 109–11.
Konrad, Kai A., and Marcel Thum. 2021. "The Better Route to Global Tax Coordination: Gradualism or Multilateralism?" *Canadian Journal of Economics* 54 (2): 793–811.
Konrad, Kai, and Guttorm Schjelderup. 1999. "Fortress Building in Global Tax Competition." *Journal of Urban Economics* 46 (1): 156–67.
Köthenbürger, Marko. 2002. "Tax Competition and Fiscal Equalization." *International Tax and Public Finance* 9 (4): 391–408.
Lockwood, Ben. 1993. "Commodity Tax Competition Under Destination and Origin Principles." *Journal of Public Economics* 52 (2): 141–62.
Lockwood, Ben. 2001. "Tax Competition and Tax Coordination Under Destination and Origin Principles: A Synthesis." *Journal of Public Economics* 81: 279–319.
Luna, LeAnn, Donald J. Bruce, and Richard R. Hawkins. 2007. "Maxing Out: An Analysis of Local Option Sales Tax Rate Increases." *National Tax Journal* 60 (1): 45–63.
Lyytikäinen, Teemu. 2012. "Tax Competition Among Local Governments: Evidence from a Property Tax Reform in Finland." *Journal of Public Economics* 96 (7–8): 584–95.
Lyytikäinen, Teemu. 2025. "Minimum Tax Rates and Tax Competition: Evidence from Property Tax Limits in Finland." In *Policy Responses to Tax Competition*, edited by David R. Agrawal, James M. Poterba, and Owen M. Zidar. University of Chicago Press.
Musgrave, Richard A. 1997. "Devolution, Grants, and Fiscal Competition." *Journal of Economic Perspectives* 11 (4): 65–72.
Nash, John F. Jr. 1950. "The Bargaining Problem." *Econometrica* 18 (2): 155–62.
Nielsen, Søren Bo. 2001. "A Simple Model of Commodity Taxation and Cross-Border Shopping." *The Scandinavian Journal of Economics* 103 (4): 599–623.
Poterba, James M., and Kim S. Rueben. 1995. "The Effect of Property-Tax Limits on Wages and Employment in the Local Public Sector." *American Economic Review* 85 (2): 384–89.
Qian, Yingyi, and Barry R. Weingast. 1997. "Federalism as a Commitment to Reserving Market Incentives." *Journal of Economic Perspectives* 11 (4): 83–92.
Rohlin, Shawn, Stuart S. Rosenthal, and Amanda Ross. 2014. "Tax Avoidance and Business Location in a State Border Model." *Journal of Urban Economics* 83: 34–49.

Rork, Jonathan C., and Gary A. Wagner. 2012. "Is There a Connection Between Reciprocity and Tax Competition?" *Public Finance Review* 40 (1): 86–115.

Slattery, Cailin. 2024. "Bidding for Firms: Subsidy Competition in the U.S." *Journal of Political Economy*, forthcoming.

Slattery, Cailin, and Owen Zidar. 2020. "Evaluating State and Local Business Incentives." *Journal of Economic Perspectives* 34 (2): 90–118.

Slemrod, Joel. 2019. "Tax Compliance and Enforcement." *Journal of Economic Literature* 57 (4): 904–54.

Stöwhase, Sven, and Christian Traxler. 2005. "Tax Evasion and Auditing in a Federal Economy." *International Tax and Public Finance* 12 (4): 515–31.

Tiebout, Charles. 1956. "A Pure Theory of Local Expenditures." *Journal of Political Economy* 64 (5): 416–24.

Topkis, Donald M. 1979. "Equilibrium Points in Nonzero-Sum *n*-Person Submodular Games." *SIAM Journal on Control and Optimization* 17: 773–87.

Trandel, Gregory A. 1994. "Interstate Commodity Tax Differentials and the Distribution of Residents." *Journal of Public Economics* 53 (3): 435–57.

Tricaud, Clemence. 2025. "Better Alone? Evidence on the Costs of Intermunicipal Cooperation." *American Economic Journal: Applied Economics* 17 (1), 160–207.

van't Riet, Maarten, and Arjan Lejour. 2018. "Optimal Tax Routing: Network Analysis of FDI Diversion." *International Tax and Public Finance* 25 (5): 1321–71.

Voit, William Kevin, and Gary Nitting. 1999. *Interstate Compacts & Agencies 1998*. Council of State Governments.

Wang, You-Qiang. 1999. "Commodity Taxes under Fiscal Competition: Stackelberg Equilibrium and Optimality." *American Economic Review* 89 (4): 974–81.

Wildasin, David. 1988. "Nash Equilibria and Models of Fiscal Competition." *Journal of Public Economics* 35: 229–40.

Wildasin, David E. 1989. "Interjurisdictional Capital Mobility: Fiscal Externality and a Corrective Subsidy." *Journal of Urban Economics* 25 (2): 193–212.

Wildasin, David E. 2021. "Open-Economy Public Finance." *National Tax Journal* 74 (2): 467–90.

Wilson, John Douglas. 1999. "Theories of Tax Competition." *National Tax Journal* 52 (2): 268–304.

Wilson, John D., and David E. Wildasin. 2004. "Capital Tax Competition: Bane or Boon." *Journal of Public Economics* 86 (6): 1065–91.

# 4

# *Wayfair*
# A Step Toward the Destination, but Sales Tax Competition Remains

Donald Bruce, William F. Fox, and Alannah M. Shute

## 4.1 Introduction

Sales taxes remain the second largest contributor to state tax revenues and are viewed as an important way to link an individual's tax burden to their ability to pay for public services. Sales tax structures have changed dramatically in the US during the past four decades. Perhaps the strongest motivation for the evolving sales tax landscape has been the erosion of the sales tax base, which has fallen from 51.0 percent of personal income in 1979 to 31.4 percent in 2020.

Two factors in this gradual erosion have been explicit policy decisions to exempt items from the taxable base and a lack of policy decisions to include untaxed items. For example, most states have exempted food for consumption at home, with only six retaining it fully in the base and five providing preferred rates. Also, many states have failed to expand their sales taxes to evolving consumption, such as digitized transactions and two-sided platforms (see Agrawal and Fox 2021).

Another cause of base erosion involves the shift in consumption patterns away from generally taxable goods toward generally untaxed services. The rapid growth in services such as health care and education, which are generally not sales-taxable, has eroded the base relative to total income or

Donald Bruce is the Randy and Jenny Boyd Distinguished Professor at the Haslam College of Business at the University of Tennessee with a joint appointment as director of the Boyd Center for Business and Economic Research and professor in the Department of Economics.

William F. Fox is the Boyd Distinguished Professor Emeritus at the Haslam College of Business and special advisor to the UTK Chancellor at the University of Tennessee.

Alannah M. Shute is a PhD candidate in economics at the University of Tennessee.

consumption.[1] Finally, and most importantly for our purposes in this chapter, sales tax base erosion has stemmed from greater tax competition from untaxed jurisdictions and remote sales. Rapidly expanding remote sales often led tax compliance to move from sellers in storefronts to buyers purchasing from out-of-state firms.

Perhaps in response to the shrinking base, states have raised their rates consistently over this window, with the median rate rising from 3.0 percent in 1970 to 6.25 percent today, though the pace of increases appears to have slowed recently. The narrowing sales tax base and higher sales tax rates have likely increased behavioral responses to the tax on the part of buyers and competitive measures from state and local governments to preserve or enhance their sales tax bases and revenues.

While the statutory incidence of sales taxes typically falls on the vendor (which can be origin taxation, depending on the sourcing rules), the ideal economic incidence would be on the buyer who is the primary beneficiary of those public services (destination taxation). Origin-based sales taxes foster tax competition as shoppers move around (or shop online) to reduce their tax burden and vendors move around to avoid having to collect and remit sales taxes. States have undertaken significant efforts to better enforce destination taxation of remote sales to reduce harmful, unfair, and revenue-reducing tax competition. The most prominent mechanism for this has been more extensive definitions of nexus for sales tax purposes, beginning with more expansive physical presence concepts and then economic nexus as a result of recent court cases.

Are states seeking to maintain revenues or are they seeking to protect domestic firms from untaxed out-of-state remote competition? Do the specific policy choices result from the fact that it is easier politically to enhance compliance rather than to broaden the base? Parsing out the causal determinants of the policy changes is beyond the scope of this chapter. Instead, we focus on how the structural changes have impacted intrastate and interstate tax competition and how buyers have responded to the sales tax transitions.

The institutional details of the sales tax are integral to how behavior is affected, so we first provide a detailed discussion of state and local sales tax features and the extent to which they have fostered sales tax competition in recent decades. We then explore the extent to which greater destination taxation has influenced the location of (a) consumer purchases and (b) business locations using two different empirical approaches. First, we analyze county-level data for Tennessee and select surrounding states to provide suggestive evidence that sales tax collections have grown more in rural Tennessee counties and less in Tennessee border counties since *Wayfair* legislation was adopted in the state. Additionally, we show that collections have grown

1. Merriman and Skidmore (2000) find that failure to sales tax services is one explanation for why services consumption has risen more rapidly than goods.

more since *Wayfair* in North Carolina counties along the Tennessee border, where the tax rate differential is on the order of 2.85 percentage points lower. Second, we examine state-level data to show that business applications have grown at much faster rates after *Wayfair* in states with the highest sales tax rates. We attribute this to the removal of the significant disincentive to establish sales tax nexus that dominated the pre- *Wayfair* environment. We conclude with a discussion of options for future policy and research surrounding sales tax competition.

## 4.2 Sales Taxes in the US

Sales taxes are imposed by 45 states and thousands of local governments in 36 states.[2] State governments raised $340.6 billion and local governments generated $102.9 billion in 2020 sales tax revenues.[3] Three broad policy decisions determine characteristics and economic effects of sales taxes: where sales are sourced for tax purposes, the tax rate, and which sales are included in the base.[4] As will be seen in this brief summary of these institutions, states differ widely in many elements of their sales tax, so generalities do not necessarily fit each state.

State general tax rates range from 7.25 percent in California and 7.0 percent in Indiana, Mississippi, Rhode Island, and Tennessee to 0 percent in five non-sales-taxing states: Alaska (which has local sales taxes), Delaware, Montana, New Hampshire, and Oregon.[5] States also impose differential tax rates on certain transactions, such as the six states that tax food for consumption at home at a preferential rate. State rates rose relatively rapidly for decades, with the median rate rising from 3 percent in 1970 to 5 percent in 1990 and 6.25 percent today. Rate hikes were particularly prevalent in the years around the 1980s and 1990s recessions. Increases have been less common since the Great Recession, and no state sales tax rate has been increased since 2019.

Local tax rates often vary widely within and across states. The revenue may be available for spending at the city, county. or district level, with states also differing as to whether the rate is levied at the state or local level and in

2. Afonso (2019) reports that 40 states allow local governments to have a local sales tax, but only 36 states, including the District of Columbia, report local sales tax revenues in the 2020 Census State and Local Government Finance database. Also, Indiana, Maine, and Oregon report less than $300,000 each in local sales tax revenue. See 2018 State & Local Government Finance Historical Datasets and Tables from US Census Bureau, https://www.census.gov/data/datasets/2018/econ/local/public-use-datasets.html.

3. See 2020 State & Local Government Finance Historical Datasets and Tables from the US Census Bureau, https://www.census.gov/data/datasets/2020/econ/local/public-use-datasets.html.

4. Sales taxes can be differentiated using other criteria as well, such as the required mechanism to change the rate or other policy options. See Afonso (2019) and Agrawal (2014).

5. See State Sales Tax Rates and Food & Drug Exemptions from the Federation of Tax Administrators, https://taxadmin.org/wp-content/uploads/resources/tax_rates/sales.pdf.

the mechanism for setting the rate.[6] These differences may have important implications for tax competition. Local rates in some states are low and add little to the combined state and local tax rate but are higher than state rates in other states. Agrawal (2014) observes that local tax rates are higher and more dispersed in states with low state tax rates than in states with high state tax rates. Eleven states, including Idaho, Minnesota, Pennsylvania, and Wisconsin, have local rates that average less than 1 percent.[7] Colorado, which has the lowest state sales tax rate among states with the tax (2.9 percent), has the highest maximum local rate (8.3 percent). Alabama, Colorado, Louisiana, and New York have higher average local rates than the state rate. Except for two areas with higher rates, Virginia state government sets a flat local rate for all local governments. California sets the local rate as well. Tennessee and Louisiana have the highest combined average state and local sales tax rate at 9.55 percent.

Sales tax bases differ widely across states but are generally much narrower than consumption with limited imposition on services (health care, education, many digital transactions, and so forth are generally untaxed) by many states and specific exemptions for certain goods (food, prescription drugs, and so forth). Hawaii, with a base that exceeds 100 percent of personal income, is an exception. New Mexico, South Dakota, Wyoming, and Washington are the only other states where the base is at least 50 percent of personal income. The average state sales tax base is less than one-third of personal income and, as noted above, has fallen dramatically as a share of personal income since 1979 (see figure 4.1). Further, sales taxes are frequently levied on intermediate transactions, which raises the possibility of tax pyramiding. Base differences mean that consumption decisions are frequently influenced by differential taxation across jurisdictions and between taxable and nontaxable items, which incentivizes both government tax structure decisions and buyers' consumption decisions.

Local tax bases may differ from their respective state bases. For example, parishes have some independence in setting tax bases in Louisiana, six states tax food at the local but not state level, and Tennessee has modest definitional differences between state and local taxation of utilities. Many states limit local government tax structures to lessen competition. Some states set the rate for local government (Virginia). Others place an upper limit on the local rate (Tennessee) or limit the total local tax per item (Tennessee). As noted, a number of states allow remote vendors to collect an average local tax rate for the state rather than use the destination tax rate (Alabama and Texas). States can also limit tax competition through other policies, such as reducing the size of government (Proposition 13 legislation in California and TABOR in Colorado).

6. Agrawal (2014) illustrates the level of government in each state which levies sales tax rates.
7. See The Sales Tax Clearninghouse, https://thestc.com/strates.stm.

**Fig. 4.1 Sales tax base as a share of personal income, 1979–2021**

*Sales tax sourcing* refers to whether transactions are taxed at the origin or the destination of where the sale takes place. Sourcing rules are often in the background or implicit when tax competition or effects of taxes are analyzed, but the role that tax rates and base definitions play in decisions often depends on the sourcing. Several papers have examined theoretical outcomes of destination versus origin taxes. For example, Lockwood (1993) concludes that (1) the tax equilibrium is generally not invariant to origin versus destination taxation and (2) we cannot a priori know how tax rates and tax revenue will be affected by changes in origin versus destination taxation. Keen and Lahiri (1998) argue that the presumed superiority of the destination principle may be incorrect in certain circumstances with imperfect competition. They conclude that "optimal taxation in the presence of imperfect competition may well include both origin and destination elements." Below we note that the sales tax has both origin and destination components, but there is no reason to presume that these have developed in an optimal configuration.

The decision of whether to source the sales tax where the vendor is located (origin) or where the item will be enjoyed (destination) is key to much of the economic effects of the sales tax. The choice affects the economic incentives that influence consumer decisions about where and how to purchase goods and services and what to buy. In many cases, origin and destination occur in the same jurisdiction, such as when a purchase is made in a store by a resident of the jurisdiction who takes possession of the item immediately.

In these cases, the distinction is unimportant. Origin and destination are separable for many remote sales, however, such as numerous digital transactions and much e-commerce, but also for cross-border purchases. Consumers often purposefully make decisions to separate origin and destination to limit tax liabilities or enforcement.

States generally levy sales taxes on a destination basis, but as described below, they often fail to enforce them effectively, which creates significant influences on behavior and provides the variation studied in much of the empirical research. State legislation following the landmark *Wayfair* ruling focuses on enhancing enforcement of destination taxation by altering the remittance rules, but has also changed some aspects of sourcing, particularly for local governments.[8] Either origin or destination at the local level can exist regardless of whether the state or the local government administers the tax, levies the rate, or uses the revenue. Both before and after *Wayfair*, local governments differ across states as to where transactions are sourced, though as a rule the sourcing decisions are the same for all local governments within each state. Sales are frequently sourced to the origin local government if the buyer is in state (Tennessee and Texas are examples). Sales into the state from out of state are often sourced to the destination, such as in Tennessee, even though they are sourced at origin for in-state transactions. Conversely, out-of-state sales into Alabama are simply sourced to the state at a fixed 8.0 percent state and local rate, with the local component shared by formula. Texas allows the seller to decide whether to use a fixed rate for local taxes or collect and source at the destination rate. In-state sales in these three states, on the other hand, are generally subject to the origin local tax rate (particularly for cross-border shopping) and revenues are retained at origin, but sales delivered from a marketplace warehouse (even if in state) would be taxed at destination. Implications of these differences for competition are discussed further below.

Similar issues arise for taxation of cross-jurisdictional activity with other tax instruments. As one example, states have been transitioning the corporate income tax from origin to destination for many years (Fox and Yang 2016; Suárez Serrato and Zidar, 2018). The traditional three-factor formula includes payroll, property, and sales, with the first two sitused at origin of production and the latter sourced at destination for goods. Most states have significantly increased their weight on the destination factor, with 32 using 100 percent sales apportionment.[9] Also, states traditionally sitused goods at destination and services at source, though many states recently transitioned services to destination as well (Fox and Yang 2016).[10] The explicit or

8. *South Dakota v. Wayfair, Inc.*, No. 17–494. 585 U.S. (2018).

9. See State Apportionment of Corporate Income from the Federation of Tax Administrators, https://taxadmin.org/wp-content/uploads/resources/tax_rates/apport.pdf.

10. Until recently, states generally sourced services where the greater cost of performance took place, but many have moved to destination sourcing of services as well during the past 15 years.

implicit justification for moving to destination sourcing has been competitive forces to reduce tax on production in states (Edmiston 2002).

These changes have moved the corporate income tax toward a destination sales tax, though there are significant differences. Many years ago, McLure (1980)[11] observed that the formula for the single sales factor corporate tax can be written as $t_i(I_j / S_j)S_{ij}$ where $t_i$ is state *i*'s CIT rate, $I_j / S_j$ is firm *j*'s national margin on sales, and $S_{ij}$ is firm *j*'s sales in state *i*. This evidences that firm *j*'s tax payment in state *i* depends on the state tax rate and the firm's national margin, with the sales in the state being the only state specific element for firm *j*. Thus, the corporate tax can be thought of as a sales tax at a rate that varies across firms based on each firm's national sales margin. States differ regarding the rules that determine which sales are sitused to the state ($S_{ij}$) and how profits ($I_j$) are defined. For example, some states impose combined reporting, some use water's edge rules, and so forth in determining $I_j$. Sourcing sales at origin versus destination requires similar decisions to those with the sales tax. The Supreme Court made clear prior to *Wayfair* that physical presence rules applicable for the general sales tax did not apply to the corporate tax. So corporate taxes were often collected based on economic presence prior to *Wayfair*, though Congress preempted some economic presence through PL 86-272.[12]

Three key differences between the single sales factor corporate tax and the sales tax distinguish how they work and will likely create very different incentives and incidence. First, the corporate tax is closer to a gross receipts tax since the sales factor includes essentially all sales for taxable firms with no deductions for intermediate transactions. The sales tax allows significant tax on intermediate sales, but there are also important deductions, such as sales for resale and exemption for inputs that become component parts of manufactured goods. These deductions for some intermediate transactions move the sales tax toward a consumption tax. Second, the taxes have different treatment for business structures and different exemptions and exclusions. The corporate tax applies only to sales by *profitable corporations*, but not pass-through entities (in many states), not-for-profit firms, and nonprofitable firms. The sales tax applies to all businesses regardless of business structure that sell sales-taxable goods and services, including pass through firms and in many cases not-for-profit firms. The sales tax also has wide exemptions for certain types of goods and buyers and has not been expanded to many services. Third, as a rule, whether the tax is remitted by the buyer or seller, which is a key element of the sales tax, is seldom an issue for corporate taxes. It is possible to imagine remittance of the corporate tax by the company or the shareholder, though normally shareholders do not have the information necessary to file the tax, but not by the consumer.

11. Also, see Gordon and Wilson (1986).

12. PL 86-272 precludes states from taxing firms whose only connection with a state is that the firm solicited in the state for the sale of tangible personal property.

Digital services taxes (DST) that were levied by a number of countries are also frequently destination based. Hines (2023) summarizes 21 countries that have adopted some form of DST since 2016 and observes that VAT registration and remittance was the first step. More recently, DSTs are destination-based gross receipts taxes (the most common approach), withholding taxes on payments to foreign digital providers, or imposition of the corporate income tax based on the argument that the foreign digital firms have physical presence in the country. Though generally revenue based rather than profits based, DSTs are intended to alter the sourcing of tax revenues on international transactions, moving away from traditional corporate income tax physical presence concepts of permanent establishments.

VATs are imposed on a destination basis, though tax was not levied on imports into the EU with a value under €22 until July 1, 2021, when this exemption was removed. Elimination of the exemption potentially has effects much like the *Wayfair* decision by erasing the zero-tax option (though in this case it only existed for low-priced transactions) and altering the relative price of cross-border transactions, though small remote vendors (as opposed to low-priced items) are not required to collect and remit in the US.

On a similar note, sourcing has also been integral to discussion of personal income taxation of commuters (Agrawal and Stark 2022). States have traditionally taxed the income either at origin of where the work occurs (nonreciprocity states) or at residence (reciprocity states) of the workers. While some states have entered into reciprocity agreements to ensure that income is only taxed in one state, growing remote work is causing reconsideration of the best approach.

### 4.3 Limitations on Enforcing Destination Taxation Prior to *Wayfair*

Better enforcement of destination taxation has been the main competitive response by states over the past several decades, with the likely goals of greater control over the tax rate and expanded revenues. Specifically, states have sought to change the remittance rules from compliance by buyers, who have been subject to often uncollected use tax, to remittance by vendors. Other policy changes have focused on broadening the base to services and digitized content (to a limited extent), narrowing taxation of selected goods, and some rate increases.

The US Supreme Court ruled in the *Wayfair* case that states could require remote firms that meet minimum activity thresholds to collect and remit their sales tax even if the firms do not have physical presence, effectively creating an economic presence nexus standard.[13] Two earlier Supreme Court decisions had determined states could only require firms with physical presence to collect their sales tax, which allowed ample opportunity for many

13. *South Dakota v. Wayfair, Inc.*, No. 17–494. 585 U.S. (2018).

remote firms to compete around taxes.[14] The physical presence constraint on remittance rules became much more apparent and impactful as remote sales grew rapidly, though remote sales grew rapidly in part because the physical presence standard enabled many buyers to act as if they had a zero-tax option. While states responded by broadening their definitions of physical presence to several things such as whether firms were listed in telephone books, whether buyers clicked through from in-state sites to out-of-state vendors, and many other modest measures of physical presence to enhance enforcement of destination tax, the inability to collect destination tax remained apparent (Bruce et al. 2009).

Several states, including Colorado and Oklahoma, enacted legislation requiring remote vendors to provide information on sales into the state in cases where the firm could not be required to collect sales tax. This third-party information was intended to enhance enforcement of destination taxation. The Direct Marketing Association sued to prevent enforcement of the Colorado legislation, but the US Supreme Court sided with Colorado in a decision that preceded *Wayfair*.[15] Perhaps most importantly, this decision included a statement by Justice Anthony Kennedy that the Court should reconsider the *Quill Corp. v. North Dakota* case, which prompted many states to develop legislation that appeared in violation of the *Quill* decision. A number of states including Alabama and Tennessee were sued, but the South Dakota suit was decided quickly at the state level and taken up by the US Supreme Court.

Ultimately, the Supreme Court in *Wayfair v. South Dakota* overturned the earlier precedents and allowed states to require larger remote vendors to collect and remit the tax if they have a sufficient economic nexus in the state. All sales-taxing states responded to the *Wayfair* decision by passing two forms of legislation. The first imposed economic nexus on large vendors selling into the state, and the second required marketplace facilitators to collect their tax. The legislation is new, and many issues remain, such as what constitutes a marketplace.[16] The legislation permits states to levy destination taxes more successfully, since vendor compliance is much more effective than buyer compliance (use tax).

Fox et al. (2022) demonstrate that greater vendor remittance of destination taxes increased tax receipts, particularly from higher income consumers, which suggests that the tax became less regressive as enforcement

14. *National Bellas Hess v. Department of Revenue*, 386 U.S. 753 (1967) and *Quill Corp. v. North Dakota*, 504 U.S. 298 (1992).

15. Brohl, 575 U.S. 1 (2015).

16. For example, the Texas Comptroller of Public Accounts provided a response to frequently asked questions about what constitutes a remote seller and a marketplace for Texas sales tax purposes. See Remote Sellers and Marketplace Frequently Asked Questions from the Texas Comptroller of Public Accounts, https://comptroller.texas.gov/taxes/sales/remote-sellers-marketplace-faq.php. See Ferrante and George (2023) for discussion of some issues surrounding marketplace facilitator laws.

improved. Further, collections are higher in states that require more vendors to comply—those states with a lower sales threshold above which firms are required to collect and remit the tax. Agrawal and Fox (2021) and Agrawal and Shybalkina (2022) provide evidence that growing remote sales during the COVID-19 window (which reduced cross-border origin taxes in larger retail centers) and better enforcement of tax at destination shifted revenues from larger to smaller jurisdictions.

Agrawal (2021) argues that increased online sales in a jurisdiction puts downward pressure on state and local tax rates unless online firms collect the sales tax. Using pre-*Wayfair* data, he finds lower sales tax rates in most municipalities as online sales rise, but higher rates in places where online firms are more likely to collect the tax (i.e., jurisdictions where destination taxation is better enforced).

## 4.4 Tax Competition

Tax structure decisions and effects of taxes on consumption choices presumably are endogenously determined, though broad structural decisions on sourcing and tax bases are infrequent (detailed base decisions are more commonly made). Tax rate decisions, particularly at the local level, are made much more regularly as reported by Baker et al. (2021), who show that rates were changed 3,000 times between 2004 and 2014. Buyers choose what and where to buy along a number of margins that are affected by tax rate, tax base and sourcing decisions. Baker et al. (2021) found that consumers make short-run and long-run decisions, with purchasing affected much more in the short run than in the long run because of stocking up in anticipation of rate changes (particularly for durable goods). Interestingly, Baker et al. (2021) found that buyers often behaved similarly for taxable and tax-exempt purchases, suggesting that the purchasing decisions were more nuanced than simple responses to prices or tax-inclusive prices. They link the behavior to high fixed costs of shopping and not to lack of salient tax bases. Still, it seems possible that buyers often act with generalized knowledge of what is taxable.[17] The cross-jurisdiction differentials and structural changes offer identification strategies for studying many aspects of tax policy and competition.

State and local governments compete around sales tax structures as they set tax rates, tax bases, and sourcing rules, though what they are maximiz-

17. Tax base discussions and knowledge are likely generalized for most people, but legislative and administrative distinctions are very precise and can be difficult for taxpayers to know without considerable time investment. For example, Iowa's Department of Revenue (Rule 701-26.24(422)) recently issued guidance that taxable recreational services include physical fitness activities, cooking and music classes, hunting and fishing ranges, and cycling classes, based on the definition of recreation. On the other hand, music and art classes taught at elementary or secondary schools are exempt.

ing may not be articulated and ranges from well-being to tax revenue to productive activity within their borders. Both Mintz and Tulkens (1986) and Kanbur and Keen (1993) recognize that totally enforced destination taxation of all consumption in a setting where neither residents nor businesses can move allows states to tax away all consumer surplus for marginal consumers and precludes the need to compete to maximize tax revenues. With this recognition, both papers focus on tax rate competition with origin taxes and consumers residing differing distances from the border. Consumer surplus may be taxed away for some consumers, but not for inframarginal consumers (those closer to the border) or those farther from the border who will shop entirely at home). In their model, competition with origin taxation results in the government setting tax rates that are much lower than what a Leviathan government would set under destination taxation.

State sales taxes lie between the extremes of origin and destination taxation, because of administrative inability to enforce destination taxation and legal tax structures having both origin and destination characteristics. Further, as noted above, the structures may not be salient to buyers, which can also change how buyers respond. This section identifies specific reasons why and how state and local taxes differ from purely origin or destination based and how these differences can alter behavioral responses compared with theoretical constructs. First, unlike as discussed by Kanbur and Keen (1993), governments may not be maximizing tax revenues but instead optimizing over a range of political and economic factors that influence the size of government, choice of tax rates, selection of the base and choices between tax instruments including personal income taxes, corporate taxes, and property taxes (see Hettich and Winer 1988). As a result, tax structures may differ from the revenue-maximizing levels. But, even in these more general settings, it is likely that tax rates will be lower under origin-based than under destination-based taxation because the tax base is more mobile under the former.

Second, even though most components of state sales taxes have historically been levied on a destination basis, practical limitations on enforcement of destination mean the tax has many characteristics of an origin tax. Several examples of how destination taxation is not enforced are provided here. States require collection and remittance by sellers with taxable nexus in the state, which prior to *Wayfair* meant some version of physical presence. After *Wayfair* it means economic presence, though small remote sellers remain exempt in every state. In addition, buyers are required to remit the "use tax" in cases where tax is not collected by the seller.[18] Use taxes are defined very similarly to the sales tax, so the state liability is normally the same, but use tax compliance is broadly thought to be very weak, as evidenced by the Fox et al. (2022) result. People generally do not understand or are unaware

18. Agrawal (2014) observes that use taxes are not always in place for local governments.

of the tax, and there was seldom any third-party information to enhance enforcement (Manzi 2015) so the overall tax compliance fell well short of enforcement on destination.[19]

Further, even with 100 percent compliance with the rules, the structure is unable fully to enforce destination taxation. As practically implemented, but different from what economists would view as ideal, destination is presumed to occur where possession of goods is taken, but this is not destination for many cross-border sales. Taxes along state or local borders often operate more like they are origin sourced since buyers in high-tax jurisdictions can cross into low-tax jurisdictions, purchase items, take possession, and pay taxes at the lower rate. States can expand destination taxation by requiring out-of-state vendors near the border who meet the sales tax thresholds included in post-*Wayfair* legislation to collect tax on cross-border shipments, but buyers can limit these efforts by taking possession of the goods where purchased or by having goods separately shipped. Identification of buyers' addresses by vendors would be necessary to collect at destination or state use taxes[20] would impossibly need to be enforced.[21] This information is not required by any state, and it seems unlikely that states would impose this burden.

Vendors are not required to collect either selling state or delivery state tax on items shipped out of state by common carrier (unless the vendor has nexus in the recipient state), causing reliance on the use tax. Use of the sellers' trucks for delivery would likely create nexus in the delivery state, but nexus is not triggered if common carriers are used. The selling state often requires some information on where goods are delivered as evidence that tax is not due in the selling state, and in some cases these data have been shared by the selling state tax authorities with the delivery state authorities. Use tax has been assessed in some of these cases based on the third-party information.

Base and sourcing differences across states open opportunities to avoid tax. Buying in states that exclude specific purchases from their base offers an extreme example of cross-border shopping with a zero-tax option for the buyer. Better-enforced destination taxes on remote transactions may make these differences more salient in the future and increase the buyers' cross-border responsiveness. Also, residents of origin-taxing states may benefit from buying in a state that taxes at destination since no tax may be due in either state. While this is not the general case, in any state it arises for certain

19. The Washington State Department of Revenue (2018) finds that use tax compliance is the weakest of any state tax, though it has been improving in recent years. Bruce et al. (2009) estimate significant revenue shortfalls from e-commerce alone that arise because of inability to enforce destination taxation.

20. The use tax is due in an amount equal to the tax differential if the home state rate is higher, but as previously noted, the tax is seldom remitted.

21. Vendors have buyers' addresses in cases where they ship items to the buyers.

services, such as repairs. Behavioral responses could alter where these services are produced as well as where they are purchased since vendors have the incentive to locate in a low tax rate destination state.

Origin sourcing still exists for local jurisdictions in many states regardless of whether items are shipped (see Tennessee and Texas, for example). In some cases, Texas local governments have agreements with large vendors to reduce the tax rates and collect at origin. Tennessee limits the possibility for competition by placing a maximum $44 local tax per transaction. These provisions have no implications for state tax liabilities.

Third, sales taxes are levied on many intermediate purchases, both because of the administrative challenge of identifying when an intermediate sale is occurring (the key advantage of VATs is that businesses are defined) and the political goal of keeping tax rates low. Taxes on intermediate purchases can pyramid and create differential effective tax rates across goods and services for both in-state and out-of-state purchases, creating a series of competitive opportunities. Better enforcement of destination taxes may increase taxes on intermediate purchases and raise production costs in the destination state. Of course, pyramiding makes effective tax rates and tax burdens less salient to voters.[22] Tax on intermediate transactions may not be inefficient in cases where the final product goes untaxed, as can often occur with health care, for example.

Considerable quantitative research has been conducted on consumer responses to sales tax differentials. Mikesell (1970) and Fox (1986) found substantial responsiveness of sales tax differentials along state borders. Fox et al. (2014) found that goods shipments were much larger across long distances when states imposed higher tax rates, consistent with efforts to evade destination taxation. Further, they found that state revenue department membership in multistate associations appeared to expand the ability to enforce destination taxation and reduce the propensity to ship goods further to evade taxes. E-commerce research (Baugh et al. 2018; Einav et al. 2014; Ellison and Ellison 2009) found purchases were also highly responsive to tax differentials. E-commerce should be more responsive to tax differentials than the cross-border research since (a) the cross-border analyses examined responses to tax differentials (home state versus neighbor state) from driving across state borders and (b) the e-commerce research generally considers the home tax rate versus the zero-rate option, meaning a larger tax differential often existed. The cost of ordering items may also be significantly reduced by purchasing online rather than crossing the border to shop.

Limited research exists on competitive effects on state tax structures, though more has been undertaken on local tax structures. For example, Agrawal (2016) studied sales tax rate policy and determined that buyers

22. States generally exempt purchases for resale and of inputs used directly in the manufacturing process. States have a range of other exempt intermediate transactions as well.

behave as though they are considering county and city taxes as a package. The governments respond by considering the other level of government and neighboring tax rates in their tax policy decisions. City tax rates are lower in counties with higher county tax rates and vice versa. Further, cities closer to the county border are more likely to reduce their tax rates when home county tax rates are high than are cities in the interior of counties. Bruce et al. (2007) examine how imposition of state maximum rates impacts local tax policy.

## 4.5 Investigating Responses to Enhanced Destination Taxation

The above discussion motivates myriad empirical explorations, most of which will require more time to pass and more data to be accumulated. For example, will the Agrawal (2021) result hold as every jurisdiction enforces destination taxes better on remote sales, but with the many other limitations on destination-based consumption taxation discussed above? This section takes first steps to quantitatively measure the extent to which sales tax competition is still occurring even after states have adopted many policies to expand destination taxation. We are able to pursue two interesting topics: one addresses demand-side responses and the other addresses supply-side responses to the shift toward greater destination taxation.

## 4.6 Destination Taxation and the Location of Taxable Sales: Empirical Evidence

Many who purchased taxable goods from online vendors prior to the *Wayfair* decision and subsequent state legislation paid zero tax on the remote transactions and now face destination enforcement. Better enforcement of destination taxes raises the effective tax rate for taxable transactions relative to exempt transactions and can reduce or eliminate zero-tax options. Still, buyers either pay no tax (e.g., by buying online or cross-border shopping with delivery from vendors that do not remit the tax), or they pay the state and local tax on one side or the other of the border.[23]

Importantly for our purposes, diminished opportunities to avoid taxes through online purchases may increase the propensity to cross-border shop (either across state boundaries or within state across local boundaries) for those seeking lower tax/after tax price options. We now consider the extent to which reduction in zero-rate options for e-commerce transactions has affected the propensity to cross-border shop. *Wayfair* may have partially returned local governments to pre-Internet tax competition between jurisdictions, but likely with the greater salience to tax differences that was devel-

23. Evasion could occur by the selling vendor understating the value of a transaction or the buyer understating the value for use tax purposes, both of which would lower the effective tax rate.

oped in the years before the *Wayfair* decision. At the same time, expanding online shopping could reduce cross-border shopping. Thus, the remaining extent of sales tax competition is an empirical question. Consumer responses to changed enforcement of destination taxation, if observed in the data, will inform future policy responses to restore lost bases or gain new bases.

We use a simple model to illustrate how *Wayfair* changed relative prices for consumers. The lowest of three prices[24] determines where consumers in state $H$ buy: cost of purchasing at home, cost of traveling across the border to shop, and cost of buying online. We focus on taxes and transactions costs by assuming that identical products are available in each market, the net of tax price for goods is 1 in all places, and no transactions costs exist for purchasing at home.[25] Consider then three categories of sales: (1) local sales where origin tax equals destination tax; (2) cross-border sales where origin differs from destination, the origin tax rate is lower than the destination rate (since consumers would not cross-border shop unless the rate is lower), and the buyer can pay the origin rate when cross-border shopping; and (3) Internet sales where origin differs from destination and the origin tax rate was zero before *Wayfair*. The price of purchasing at home is then the domestic tax rate ($tH$). The price of purchasing across the border is $T(d) + tA$, where $T(d)$ is travel costs that are directly related to distance in state $H$ to the border and proportional to the price of goods, and $tA$ is tax in the neighboring state. The price of purchasing online is $I + tH$, where $I$ is the transactions costs for online purchases. The home state (destination) tax is included in the online purchase now, but $tH$ was not collected on online sales prior to *Wayfair*, so the transactions cost was the only price. Before *Wayfair*, purchases were made online when $I$ was less than both $TH$ and $T(d) + tA$. *Wayfair* did not change the price (tax) of purchasing in either state so it did not alter prior decisions to buy in the home or cross-border state, but it could change decisions to purchase online where the price is now $I + tH$. Online shopping would no longer occur in this model if $I > 0$ since $tH$ is imposed on both home and online shopping. Previous online purchases are replaced with shopping at home if $tH < tA + T(d)$ and with cross-border shopping if $T(d) + tA < tH$. In both cases the change comes at the expense of online shopping, so the tax choice reverts to border tax competition, as in Kanbur and Keen (1993), and consumers appropriately near the border will cross-border shop if $tH > tA$.

By focusing on taxes, the model fails to account for online sales after *Wayfair*. The model could be adapted to include this, but as structured it highlights the key issue from our perspective: the rate of tax. Outside the simple conceptual model, cross-border shopping or online shopping can occur

24. We thank David Agrawal and Alan Auerbach for motivating this framework.

25. This is equivalent to interpreting the transactions costs of cross-border and Internet shopping as relative to the minimal costs of shopping locally.

under other conditions, several of which include additional roles for tax rates in influencing behavior. For example, consumers would cross-border shop if goods can be shipped home without paying $tA$ in the bordering state (as discussed above) and $T(d) < tH$ so cross-border shopping will take place if the home tax exceeds travel costs without considering the neighbor's tax rate. People could shop online or cross-border shop for goods that are not available at home. Online shopping could also occur if the net of tax price is lower for online shopping, if the transactions' cost is lower online than at home, or if the purchase is made from an online vendor that does not collect the home state sales tax (either through tax evasion or because the vendor is too small to trigger taxable presence).

We look for early post-*Wayfair* evidence of shifting consumer patterns by examining county-level monthly sales tax collections in Tennessee and selected bordering states. While our focus on Tennessee is driven by the availability of useful data, the state's relatively constant tax rates, due in part to many counties setting the maximum allowed local rate, and tax base definitions allow us to isolate consumer behavioral responses to better enforcement of destination taxation through changes in the remittance rules and changes in the extent of origin (or non-) taxation as cross-border taxes are affected. Figure 4.2 shows the monthly year-over-year growth in combined state and local sales tax collections in Tennessee for 2017 through 2022. Economic nexus and marketplace facilitator legislation was adopted in 2019

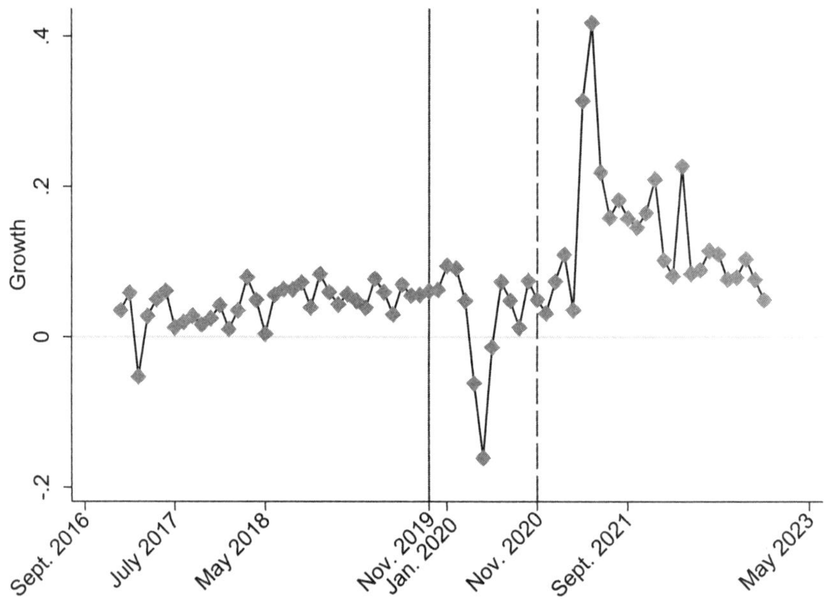


**Fig. 4.2 Monthly year-over-year growth in state and local sales tax collections in Tennessee, 2017–2022**

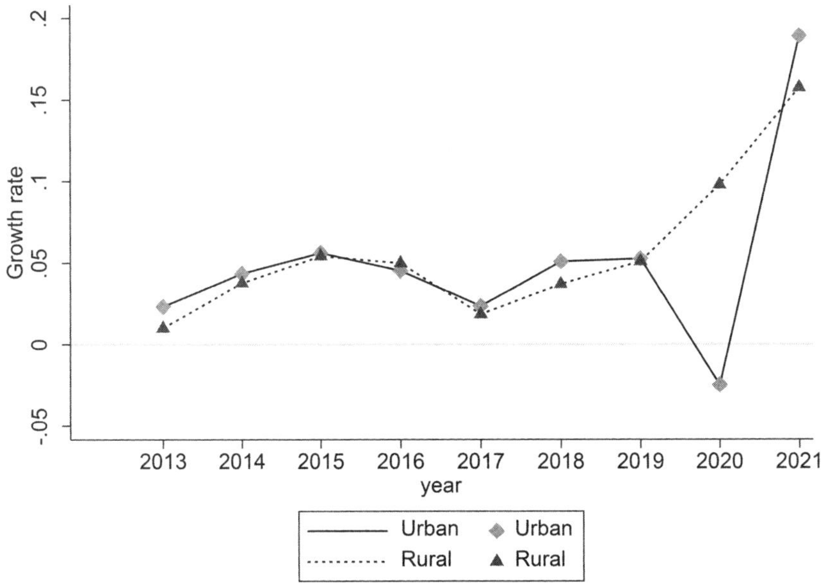


**Fig. 4.3 Year-over-year state and local sales tax growth for urban versus rural Tennessee counties, 2013–2021**

and 2020, respectively, and both contributed to the recent growth in collections, which remained positive in 2020 despite the COVID-19 pandemic. The revenue impact of these two pieces of legislation is clear in figure 4.2, which includes vertical bars for the first effective months of economic nexus legislation (November 2019) and marketplace facilitator legislation (November 2020). Total sales tax growth fell significantly in early 2020 as a result of the pandemic but quickly rebounded thanks in large part to the effects of these two pieces of legislation. The severe spike in 2021 evidences effects of the sharp temporary decrease in 2020.

Additional impacts of the economic nexus and marketplace facilitator legislation in Tennessee can be found in figure 4.3, which plots average annual state and local sales tax collections growth for urban and rural counties separately. For the purposes of our analysis, urban counties (and their largest cities) include Shelby (Memphis), Davidson (Nashville), Hamilton (Chattanooga), and Knox (Knoxville). Despite similar growth paths before 2020, sales tax collections in rural counties grew while those in the four urban counties fell in 2020, perhaps because of the emergence of greater destination taxation coincident with the pandemic and more online shopping. The pattern in figure 4.3 is the net result of better enforcement of destination taxes on online sales (which should benefit all counties) and the reduction in cross-border sales (and the origin tax on these sales) as these consumers buy more online where the revenues accrue to their home (destination) counties.

To get a more granular look at the impact of economic nexus legislation on sales tax collections growth, we estimate a series of linear regressions in table 4.1. The dependent variable is the year-over-year monthly growth rate of total state and local sales tax collections in a county. Key independent variables include an indicator for the enactment of economic nexus legislation (econ_nexus), an indicator for urban counties (urban), the total state and local sales tax rate in the county (rate), an indicator for counties situated along the state border (border) and various fixed effects.

Columns (1) and (2) include these variables and are identical except that standard errors are clustered at the county level in column (2). Columns (3) and (4) mirror the first two specifications but also include fixed effects for county and year (which results in the loss of the urban and border indicators in the results). Columns (5) through (8) mirror the first four specifications but also include an interaction between the economic nexus indicator and the urban indicator. Results are quite robust throughout the table, so we focus on our preferred specifications in columns (6) and (8). The first common result is that economic nexus legislation appears to have had a positive impact on county-level sales tax collections regardless of our specification.[26] That said, the combined effect is much lower or even negative in urban counties, even after controlling for the sales tax rate (which has a positive effect) and border-county status (which has a negative effect). The negative border effect is consistent with lower growth on the higher tax rate Tennessee side of the border and the negative urban nexus variable is accounting for slower urban sales as the e-commerce/store front mix changed during the COVID-19 window. Tennessee has higher tax rates than all eight states on the Tennessee border, with an average 3.03 percent state and local tax rate differential.[27] The difference is very small relative to states such as Arkansas and very large relative to states such as Kentucky and Virginia. The cross-state tax rate differences are often much greater than the cross-county border differences within Tennessee.

We also analyzed a sample truncated in February 2020 to see if the table 4.1 results were driven by COVID-19, which could impact the data beginning March 2020.[28] The truncated sample shortened the post-*Wayfair* response time and eliminated the window that included marketplace facilitator legislation in Tennessee, which began in October 2020. The economic nexus and border variables remain highly significant, though the economic nexus coefficient fell approximately in half when the border variable was included in the equations (parallel to columns (1), (2), (5), and (6)). The lower economic nexus variable provides some evidence that the sharp rise in tax collections resulted from COVID-19-related behavior. On the other

26. To be sure, effects on total sales may be greater than on taxable sales as a result of complementary sales (see Baker et al. 2021), but the elasticities need not be larger.

27. Alabama data were unavailable for this calculation.

28. These additional results are available from the authors upon request.

**Table 4.1** **Economic nexus legislation and county-level sales tax collections in Tennessee**

| VARIABLES | (1) | (2) | (3) | (4) | (5) | (6) | (7) | (8) |
|---|---|---|---|---|---|---|---|---|
| econ_nexus | 0.083*** | 0.083*** | 0.017** | 0.016*** | 0.085*** | 0.085*** | 0.019*** | 0.019*** |
| | (0.003) | (0.003) | (0.007) | (0.006) | (0.003) | (0.003) | (0.007) | (0.006) |
| urban | −0.007 | −0.007* | | | 0.005* | 0.005 | | |
| | (0.004) | (0.003) | | | (0.003) | (0.007) | | |
| econ_nexus × urban | | | | | −0.047** | −0.047** | −0.046*** | −0.046*** |
| | | | | | (0.019) | (0.017) | (0.011) | (0.017) |
| rate | −0.001 | −0.001 | 0.034** | 0.034* | −0.001 | −0.001 | 0.032** | 0.032* |
| | (0.003) | (0.005) | (0.014) | (0.018) | (0.003) | (0.005) | (0.014) | (0.018) |
| border | −0.006*** | −0.006** | | | −0.006*** | −0.006** | | |
| | (0.002) | (0.003) | | | (0.002) | (0.003) | | |
| Constant | 0.041*** | 0.041*** | −0.032 | −0.032 | 0.040*** | 0.040*** | −0.028 | −0.028 |
| | (0.008) | (0.012) | (0.035) | (0.044) | (0.008) | (0.012) | (0.035) | (0.046) |
| FE | No | No | County<br>Year | County<br>Year | No | No | County<br>Year | County<br>Year |
| Clustered | No | County | No | County | No | County | No | County |
| Observations | 10,222 | 10,222 | 10,222 | 10,222 | 10,222 | 10,222 | 10,222 | 10,222 |
| R-squared | 0.1170 | 0.1170 | | | 0.1185 | 0.1185 | | |
| Within R-squared | | | 0.0012 | 0.0012 | | | 0.0029 | 0.0029 |

Notes: Results in this table are from separate regressions. The dependent variable is the year-over-year growth rate in state and local sales tax collections at the county level. A total of 38 county-months of data are omitted due to missing data. Standard errors are in parentheses. *** $p < 0.01$, ** $p < 0.05$, * $p < 0.1$.

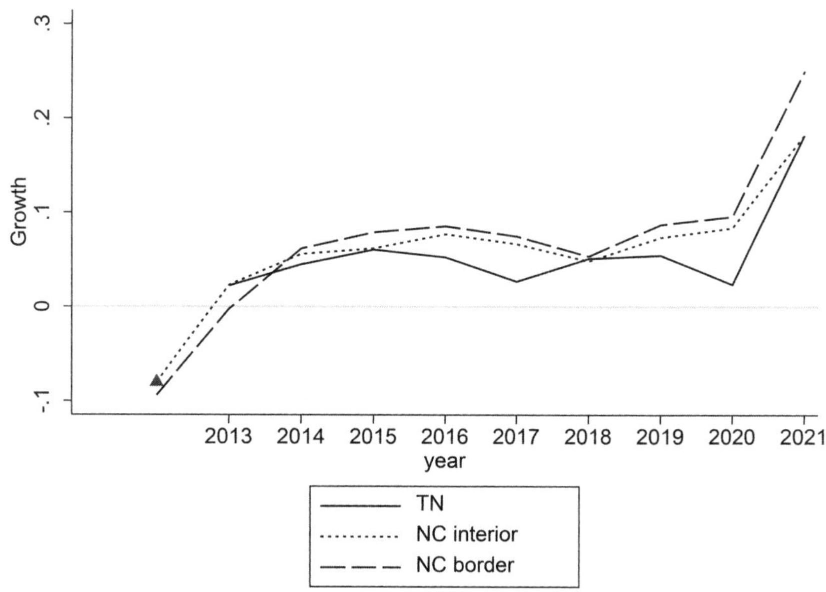


**Fig. 4.4 Growth in sales tax collections for Tennessee and North Carolina, 2012–2021**

hand, the border variable rose slightly in size, consistent with significant increase in cross-border shopping after the *Wayfair* decision. The urban variables were statistically insignificant in the shorter window, suggesting that COVID-19 drove much of the subsequent relative reduction in cross county sales into urban counties.

To get a better sense of the cross-border impact of Tennessee's economic legislation, figure 4.4 compares annual growth in sales taxes for counties in Tennessee and North Carolina, a border with an average sales tax rate differential of about 2.85 percentage points.[29] North Carolina counties experienced faster growth than Tennessee counties after 2018, with border counties in North Carolina seeing faster growth than interior (nonborder) counties in North Carolina.[30] The graph is consistent with better collection of tax on remote sales (likely in both North Carolina and Tennessee) and expanded sales on the low tax North Carolina side of the border, suggesting more direct competition between states for sales. Baker et al. (2021) see intertemporal substitution as the short-run response to rate changes, with

29. Our decision to focus this part of our analysis on the Tennessee–North Carolina border is driven primarily by its relatively large tax rate differential and by the lack of useful county-level sales tax collections data for most other border states.

30. Tennessee required large remote vendors to begin collecting sales tax in November 2019 and marketplaces in November 2020, and North Carolina required large remote vendors to begin collecting tax in November 2018 and marketplace facilitators in February 2020.

**Table 4.2** **Economic nexus legislation in Tennessee and county-level sales tax collections in North Carolina**

| VARIABLES | (1) | (2) | (3) | (4) |
|---|---|---|---|---|
| econ_nexus | 0.083*** | 0.083*** | −0.027*** | −0.027*** |
| | (0.002) | (0.004) | (0.008) | (0.008) |
| border | −0.001 | 0.001 | | |
| | (0.004) | (0.005) | | |
| econ_nexus × border | 0.040*** | 0.040*** | 0.040*** | 0.040*** |
| | (0.011) | (0.012) | (0.008) | (0.012) |
| rate | 0.031*** | 0.031*** | 0.037*** | 0.037 |
| | (0.006) | (0.009) | (0.010) | (0.023) |
| Constant | −0.170*** | −0.170*** | −0.186*** | −0.186 |
| | (0.039) | (0.063) | (0.065) | (0.155) |
| FE | No | No | County Year | County Year |
| Clustered | No | County | No | County |
| Observations | 12,000 | 12,000 | 12,000 | 12,000 |
| R-squared | 0.0809 | 0.0809 | | |
| Within R-squared | | | 0.0040 | 0.0040 |

Notes: Results presented in this table are from separate regressions. The dependent variable is the year-over-year growth in county-level collections. Robust standard errors are in parentheses. *** $p < 0.01$, ** $p < 0.05$, * $p < 0.1$.

more cross-border shopping a longer-run reaction. So, effects could grow with time.

The availability of monthly collections data at the county level in North Carolina allows us to measure the impact of nexus legislation on cross-border shopping along the Tennessee border. North Carolina is of particular interest because the rate differential along the border is about average compared to the other seven states that border Tennessee. Compelling evidence of a resurgence in cross-border shopping is found in the regression results in table 4.2.[31] Focusing on our preferred specifications in columns (3) and (4), we see a generally negative impact of economic nexus legislation in Tennessee on county-level sales tax growth in North Carolina counties, but that impact turns positive for North Carolina counties along the Tennessee border. The propensity of Tennessee buyers to cross the border and shop in North Carolina appears to grow as the zero-tax option is limited by *Wayfair*-related legislation and tax-sensitive Tennessee shoppers buy more in North Carolina. We only investigate counties along the border, without seeking to determine how much distance from the border affects buyers, but the cross-border shopping gradient could be relatively steep for many products.

Again, we reestimated the equations with a sample truncated in February

31. We do not find similar evidence for Arkansas and Virginia counties, and regression results for those states are available upon request. Unique events, such as the temporary closure of the main highway connecting Arkansas and Tennessee (I-40), surely affected these results.

2020.[32] All variables remained statistically significant and were quantitatively larger. The economic nexus-border interaction coefficient rose nearly 25 percent in magnitude, suggesting that cross-border shopping from Tennessee to North Carolina was enhanced by better enforcement by Tennessee of tax on Internet transactions.

## 4.7 Destination Taxation and the Location of Business Activity: Empirical Evidence

The reemergence of cross-border shopping as the best means for tax avoidance might also affect business location decisions about where to produce or sell.[33] Both rate and base differences (e.g., in the tax treatment of food) can potentially impact business geographic choices. Business location/development is affected through three avenues. First, before *Wayfair*, vendors had a significant interest in avoiding the establishment of physical presence nexus (particularly in large or high-sales-tax-rate states) so they would not be required to collect and remit sales taxes on sales into a state, and this disincentive is eliminated. Second, better enforcement of destination taxes on purchases of intermediate goods raises production costs in the taxing states. Ernst & Young (2022) estimates that the sales tax on business purchases is 20.4 percent of the total state and local business tax burden, which is much greater than the 11.7 percent of the burden that comes from corporate income taxes. This suggests that the dislocation effects could be larger than with corporate taxes. Third, incentives to locate on the low-tax side of borders can be altered by more cross-border shopping.

*Wayfair* unwound significant inequities in the sales tax landscape by sharply reducing the tax disadvantage faced by in-state retailers who had to collect and remit sales taxes in the face of essentially untaxed Internet commerce. Beem and Bruce (2021) provide evidence that the steady erosion of state sales tax bases between 1979 and 2014 (resulting in part from growth in untaxed remote sales) resulted in fewer new firms and establishments and less employment. These findings from pre-*Wayfair* data suggest that *Wayfair* and related policy changes should have resulted in more new businesses (firms and/or establishments) and more employment.

We should see faster growth in new firm formation in states that did more to restore lost sales tax bases, though effects on intermediate sales and cross-border shopping can offset this to some extent. Given that these policy responses have thus far been at the state level, it is appropriate to explore this possibility using state-level data over time.

The data shown in figure 4.5 are compiled from the US Census Bureau's

32. These additional results are available from the authors upon request.

33. Houde et al. (2023) determine that Amazon experienced significant shipping cost savings and economies of scale as it expanded its distribution network and physical presence prior to the *Wayfair* decision.

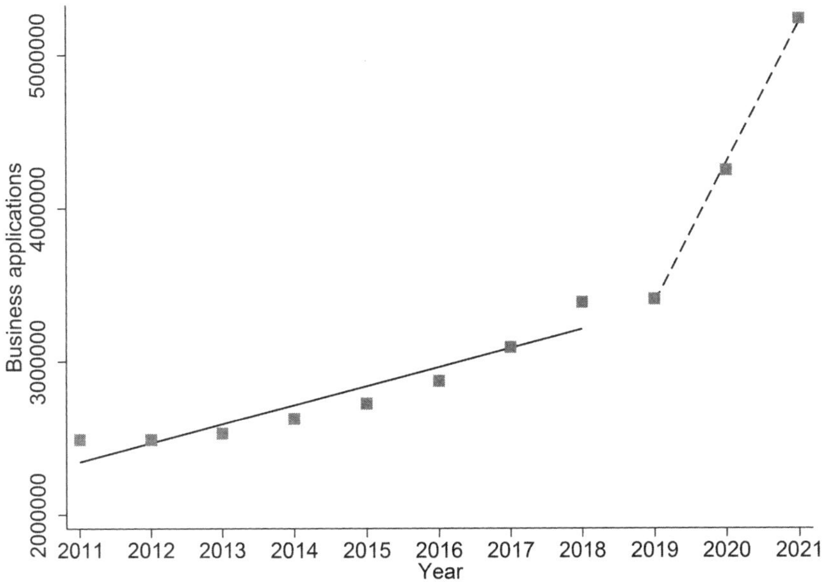


**Fig. 4.5 Trends in business applications before and after *Wayfair***

Business Formation Statistics and show trends in the total number of business applications before and after 2018. The number of business applications has been steadily increasing since 2011 but has grown much more rapidly in the most recent data. From 2019 to 2021, the number of business applications in the US increased by nearly two million.[34]

We further explore the influence of economic nexus legislation on business applications using a series of panel regressions in table 4.3, which covers ten years of annual data for sales-taxing states. The dependent variable for these regressions is the state's year-over-year growth rate of business applications. Key independent variables include an indicator for the presence of economic nexus legislation (econ_nexus, which varies across states and time), the average combined state and local sales tax rate (rate), and a measure of sales tax base breadth (breadth, or the sales tax base as a percentage of personal income in the state). The various columns in table 4.3 differ as above with the inclusion of clustered standard errors, state and year fixed effects, and an interaction between economic nexus and the sales tax rate.

We focus the discussion on our preferred results in columns (7) and (8) of table 4.3. We find that the effect of economic nexus on business applications depends on the sales tax rate, with economic nexus lowering the growth rates. Generally speaking, economic nexus reduced the growth rate of busi-

34. The annual data employed here preclude truncating the data because of COVID-19 as was done in the sales tax analysis above.

**Table 4.3** **Economic nexus and business applications**

| VARIABLES | (1) | (2) | (3) | (4) | (5) | (6) | (7) | (8) |
|---|---|---|---|---|---|---|---|---|
| econ_nexus | 0.073*** | 0.073*** | −0.008 | −0.008 | −0.012 | 0.005 | −0.109*** | −0.109** |
| | (0.011 ) | (0.008) | (0.015) | (0.020) | (0.062) | (0.040) | (0.038) | (0.042) |
| rate | 0.003 | 0.003 | −0.006 | −0.006 | −0.001 | −0.001 | −0.017 | −0.017 |
| | (0.003) | (0.003) | (0.011) | (0.018) | (0.003) | (0.003) | (0.012) | (0.019) |
| econ_nexus × rate | | | | | 0.012 | 0.012** | 0.014*** | 0.014*** |
| | | | | | (0.008) | (0.005) | (0.005) | (0.005) |
| breadth | 0.000 | 0.000 | −0.001 | −0.001 | 0.000 | 0.000 | −0.002* | −0.002 |
| | (0.000) | (0.000) | (0.001) | (0.001) | (0.000) | (0.000) | (0.001) | (0.001) |
| Constant | 0.027 | 0.027 | 0.163* | 0.163 | 0.058** | 0.058** | 0.250*** | 0.250* |
| | (0.028) | (0.023) | (0.090) | (0.135) | (0.024) | (0.023) | (0.094) | (0.144) |
| FE | No | No | State<br>Year | State<br>Year | No | No | State<br>Year | State<br>Year |
| Clustered | No | State | No | State | No | State | No | State |
| Observations | 450 | 450 | 450 | 450 | 450 | 450 | 450 | 450 |
| R-squared | 0.1332 | 0.1332 | | | 0.1385 | 0.1385 | | |
| Within R-squared | | | 0.0059 | 0.0059 | | | 0.0264 | 0.0264 |

Notes: Results presented in this table are from separate regressions. The dependent variable is the year-to-year growth in state-level business applications. Alaska, Delaware, New Hampshire, Montana, Oregon, and District of Columbia are omitted due to the absence of a state sales tax. Standard errors are in parentheses. *** $p < 0.01$, ** $p < 0.05$, * $p < 0.1$

ness applications most for states without a sales tax (about 10 percent) and became positive for states around the median combined state and local sales tax rate. States with higher than median tax rates experience faster growth in business applications, with the largest impacts in the states with the highest sales tax rates. A tax rate increase of one percentage point raises the total effect of economic nexus on business applications by 1.4 percentage points. The result is consistent with pre-*Wayfair* growth rates having been affected most by firms not choosing to locate establishments in high tax rate states, and this effect being reversed by economic nexus. As with the sales analysis in the previous section, firm locations are likely to be a longer-run response with greater effects over time.

These results are consistent with the idea that business location decisions are heavily influenced by sales tax policies. Prior to economic nexus legislation, businesses had an incentive to locate in states with no sales tax because they were not required to collect sales taxes from consumers unless they had a physical presence in the state. Firms were also incentivized to locate warehouses and other facilities in low tax rate and low population states. After economic nexus standards were adopted by sales taxing states, firms no longer had a disproportionate incentive to locate in states without a sales tax and could locate freely based on other factors such as access to supply chains and consumer markets. Decomposing effects on firms into those arising because nexus becomes less of a concern, those from cross-border shopping, those from more effective tax on business inputs, and other factors offers very interesting potential for further research.

## 4.8 Discussion, Policy Options, and Areas for Future Research

The landmark 2018 Supreme Court ruling in the *Wayfair* case has certainly enhanced state governments' ability to enforce destination taxation. That said, significant barriers to full destination taxation remain, and those continue to present opportunities for harmful tax competition. For example, considerable variation exists in the economic nexus legislation across the states, especially when it comes to the various size thresholds above which a collection obligation can exist. Additional variation remains in both the extent to which origin and destination basis coexist within states and state-level definitions of remote sellers and marketplaces. Wide cross-state differences also remain in the set of sales-taxable transactions. Importantly, on the heels of this key sales tax enforcement victory, some states have increased their efforts to enhance enforcement of preexisting destination-based taxes.

States can and will continue to compete for mobile economic activity and tax bases in a variety of ways, and indeed movement toward more cross-border shopping may narrow but intensify the competition. Nexus thresholds are unnecessarily arbitrary and complex, suggesting the need for a federal solution. Nonetheless, the existence of variable sales tax rates and base definitions will continue to encourage at least some degree of cross-border shopping, both in the physical sense and in the online sense since some remote vendors do not exceed the size-based nexus thresholds, or some firms that lack visibility may seek to play the audit lottery by failing to collect tax even if it is due. The tradeoff between efforts to streamline or harmonize state and local sales tax systems and the benefits from competing for mobile activity are not likely to disappear soon. States may also enhance destination further by imposing compliance rules on cross-border neighbors that parallel those imposed on remote firms.

To be sure, it is not clear that simply limiting sales tax competition is necessarily socially optimal. Variation in taxation and expenditure policies across jurisdictions can create important efficiency gains from the appropriate sorting of individuals and businesses. And competitive forces can provide an important constraint against Leviathan-style maximization of the size of the public sector. Discussions about policy options to further reduce sales tax competition should go beyond rates, bases, and sourcing rules to include consideration of voting thresholds for policy changes, equalization grants or other mechanisms to offset competition, and a host of other limitations on the setting of rates or the uses of revenues.

Regardless of the evolving sales tax policy landscape, the ongoing economic and technological shifts create a wide range of significant research opportunities. It will be important for scholars to continue to explore how better-enforced destination taxes affect e-commerce sales, the extent of cross-border shopping, sales of taxable versus nontaxable items, residential locations, and business location and development. Effects of destination enforcement on state and local tax rates and bases also call for new analysis, but also how legal tax and expenditure limits affect state and local tax rates and bases in the changing environment.

The post-*Wayfair* legislation discussed above, which reduced buyers' ability to find zero tax options but potentially expands cross-border shopping, alters incentives for governments to compete and could significantly change the behavioral elasticities found in earlier research. But the combination of differential imposition of the sales tax on consumer purchases, inability to fully enforce destination taxes, and taxes on intermediate purchases can still place downward pressure on tax rates as described by Agrawal (2021).

Consumers can still shop across borders and take possession in lower rate jurisdictions or purchase from smaller remote vendors or vendors that are failing to comply with tax collection requirements (since it is likely very difficult for states to determine which small vendors across the country meet their sales thresholds). Current incentives to cross-border shop are similar to those that existed prior to the rapid growth in e-commerce. Earlier analysis finds that destination sourcing allows rural areas to experience more rapid growth in sales tax revenue after *Wayfair*, but revenues may also grow faster on the low tax side of state or local borders, creating a second set of revenue adjustments.

Research that addresses similar topics to those conducted in the past but using post-*Wayfair* data allows the opportunity to determine the effects of better-enforced destination taxes on taxpayer responsiveness to tax differentials. For example, analysis could be conducted on how government tax structures are affected. Post-*Wayfair* data may find that effects of online sales on tax rates have diminished with better enforcement, but the relative effects of cross-border sales on tax rates have grown since the *Wayfair* legislation will affect enforcement of online sales more. Thus, Agrawal's (2021) findings about the extent to which e-commerce sales affect tax rate policy may be lessened and the role of cross-border sales increased (Agrawal 2016). Distance to the border could become increasingly important to buyers looking to evade taxes, and also to state and local governments as they set tax policy. Rates could be higher as tax rates are less impacted by the zero-tax option from online sales and lower near the border because of cross-border shopping. Also, research on the responsiveness of local rates to competition in origin versus destination states and along state borders appears to offer good potential.

Research on how state limitations on local tax rate setting affects cross-border shopping elasticities and local tax rate policy also appears to be promising. Most if not all previous research ignores these constraints. Empirical analysis of which policies are most effective would improve precision of behavioral elasticities and expand our understanding of how competition affects policy decisions. Agrawal (2014) and Baker et al. (2021) demonstrated that local tax rate changes were frequent in the decade of data that each analyzed, evidencing that governments are willing to shift certain aspects of their tax structure.

The relative price effect for exempt versus taxable transactions could become larger for those previously avoiding the tax by purchasing online. Of course, no one pays the effective average tax rate (which has risen because of better enforcement) since they either pay no tax or the tax on one side of the border. Consumers will be more likely to pay at some tax rate after *Wayfair*, so the measured elasticities for taxable versus exempt items and cross-jurisdiction tax elasticities will be larger, presumably for those for whom the tax is more salient. Research to identify characteristics of those for whom the tax is more salient (for example, younger or higher-income households) remains an interesting issue. The slow pace at which states broaden their bases as new goods and services develop also arises here. Many states have failed to expand their bases to digitized transactions and two-sided platforms, and failure to collect or impose tax on these items becomes more important when tax is fully enforced on substitutes and complements. Destination sourcing of these transactions is ever more challenging and raises both technical and measurement issues.

Incentives to avoid taxes by moving to jurisdictions with a tax/expenditure bundle more consistent with consumers' tastes can grow with better enforcement of destination taxes. Enhanced enforcement of destination taxes moves the sales tax closer to an income tax, though large exemptions from the tax and pyramiding distort this relationship. Still, it opens the opportunity for research on whether personal income or sales taxes have larger effects on mobility choices, one component of which is the differential salience of the two taxes. Martinez (2022) shows that local income taxes affect mobility across Swiss cantons, but effects of sales taxes on mobility have been studied less.[35] Both sales and personal income taxes are dominated by the property tax at the local level but are the largest tax sources at the state level. These averages hide significant cross-state differences that could be exploited for analysis. Again, cross-border shopping provides an important limitation on destination taxation of sales, perhaps causing responsive residents to move closer to the border or to other jurisdictions.

To be sure, there is no shortage of interesting and important avenues for empirical research. The passage of time and availability of better and more recent data will enable a completely fresh look at some of the classic theoretical and empirical results from the sales tax competition literature.

### Acknowledgments

The authors are thankful to David Agrawal, Alan Auerbach, James Poterba, Owen Zidar, and participants in the NBER Conference on Policy Responses to Tax Competition for comments on an earlier draft. For acknowledgments, sources of research support, and disclosure of the authors' material financial relationships, if any, please see https://www.nber.org/books-and-chapters/policy-responses-tax-competition/wayfair-step-towards-destination-sales-tax-competition-remains.

## References

Afonso, Whitney B. 2019. "The Barriers Created by Complexity: A State-by-State Analysis of Local Sales Tax Laws in Light of the Wayfair Ruling." *National Tax Journal* 72 (4): 777–800.

Agrawal, David. 2014. "LOST in America: Evidence on Local Sales Taxes from National Panel Data." *Regional Science and Urban Economics* 49: 147–63.

Agrawal, David. 2016. "Local Fiscal Competition: An Application to Sales Taxation with Multiple Federations." *Journal of Urban Economics* 91: 122–38.

35. Fox et al. (1989) provide an early look at how state and local taxes affect migration decisions.

Agrawal, David. 2021. "The Internet as a Tax Haven?" *American Economic Journal: Economic Policy* 13 (4): 1–35.
Agrawal, David, and William F. Fox. 2021. "Taxing Goods and Services in a Digital Era." *National Tax Journal* 74 (1): 257–301.
Agrawal, David, and Julia Shybalkina. 2023. "Online Shopping Can Redistribute Local Tax Revenue from Urban to Rural America." *Journal of Public Economics* 219: 104818.
Agrawal, David, and Kirk Stark. 2022. "Will the Remote Work Revolution Undermine State Progressive Income Taxation?" *Virginia Tax Review* 42 (1).
Baker, Scott R., Stephanie Johnson, and Lorenz Kueng. 2021. "Shopping for Lower Sales Tax Rates." *American Economic Journal: Macroeconomics* 13 (3): 209–50.
Baugh, Brian, Itzhak Ben-David, and Hoonsuk Park. 2018. "Can Taxes Shape an Industry? Evidence from the Implementation of the Amazon Tax." *The Journal of Finance* 73 (4): 1819–55.
Beem, Richard, and Donald Bruce. 2021. "Failure to Launch: Measuring the Impact of Sales Tax Nexus Standards on Business Activity." *Journal of Public Economics* 201: 104476.
Bruce, Donald, William F. Fox, and LeAnn Luna. 2009. "State and Local Government Sales Tax Revenue Losses from Electronic Commerce." *State Tax Notes* 52 (7): 537–57.
Bruce, Donald, LeAnn Luna, and Richard Hawkins. 2007. "Maxing Out: An Examination of Local Option Sales Tax Rate Increases." *National Tax Journal* 60 (1): 45–63.
Edmiston, Kelly. 2002. "Strategic Apportionment of the State Corporate Income Tax." *National Tax Journal* 55 (2): 239–62.
Einav, Liran, Dan Knoepfle, Jonathan D. Levin, and Neel Sundaresan. 2014. "Sales Taxes and Internet Commerce." *American Economic Review* 104 (1): 1–26.
Ellison, Glenn, and Sara Fisher Ellison. 2009. "Tax Sensitivity and Home State Preferences in Internet Purchasing." *American Economic Journal: Economic Policy* 1 (2): 53–71.
Ernst & Young. 2022. "Total State and Local Business Taxes: State-by-State Estimates for 2021." https://www.ey.com/en_us/tax/total-state-and-local-business-taxes-for-fy21.
Ferrante, Lauren A., and Steffi N. George. 2023. "Good Idea Gone Wrong? Evaluating Marketplace Facilitator Laws." *State Tax Notes*, May 8.
Fox, William F. 1986. "Tax Structure and the Location of Economic Activity Along State Borders." *National Tax Journal* 39 (4): 387–401.
Fox, William F., Enda Hargaden, and LeAnn Luna. 2022. "Statutory Incidence and Sales Tax Compliance: Evidence from Wayfair." *Journal of Public Economics* 213: 104716.
Fox, William F., Henry Herzog, and Alan Schlottmann. 1989. "Metropolitan Fiscal Structure and Migration." *Journal of Regional Science* 29 (4): 523–36.
Fox, William F., LeAnn Luna, and Georg Schaur. 2014. "Destination Taxation and Evasion: Evidence from U.S. Inter-State Commodity Flows." *Journal of Accounting and Economics* 57 (1): 43–57.
Fox, William F., and Zhou Yang. 2016. "Destination Taxation: Road to Economic Success?" *National Tax Journal* 69 (2): 285–314.
Gordon, Roger, and John D. Wilson. 1986. "An Examination of Multijurisdictional Corporate Income Taxation Under Formula Apportionment." *Econometrica* 54: 1357–73.
Hettich, Walter, and Stanley Winer. 1988. "Economic and Political Foundations of Tax Structure." *American Economic Review* 78 (4): 701–12.

Hines, James R. Jr. 2023. "Digital Tax Arithmetic." *National Tax Journal* 76 (1): 119–43.
Houde, Jean-François, Peter Newberry, and Katja Seim. 2023. "Nexus Tax Laws and Economies of Density in E-Commerce: A Study of Amazon's Fulfillment Center Network." *Econometrica* 91 (1): 147190.
Kanbur, Ravi, and M. Keen. 1993. "Jeux Sans Frontières: Tax Competition and Tax Coordination When Countries Differ in Size." *American Economic Review* 83 (4): 877–92.
Keen, Michael, and Sajal Lahiri. 1998. "The Comparison Between Destination and Origin Principles Under Imperfect Competition." *Journal of International Economics* 45 (2): 323–50.
Lockwood, Ben. 1993. "Commodity Tax Competition Under Destination and Origin Principles." *Journal of Public Economics* 52 (2): 141–62.
Manzi, Nina. 2015. "Use Tax Collection on Income Tax Returns in Other States." Policy Brief, Minnesota House of Representatives, Research Department. https://www.house.mn.gov/hrd/pubs/usetax.pdf.
Martínez, Isabel Z. 2022. "Mobility Responses to the Establishment of a Residential Tax Haven: Evidence from Switzerland." *Journal of Urban Economics* 129: 103441.
McLure, Charles. 1980. "The State Corporate Income Tax: Lamb in Wolves' Clothing." In *The Economics of Taxation*, edited by H. Aaron and M. Boskin, 327–46. Brookings Institution.
Merriman, David, and Mark Skidmore. 2000. "Did Distortionary Sales Taxation Contribute to the Growth of the Service Sector?" *National Tax Journal* 52 (1): 125–42.
Mikesell, John L. 1970. "Central City and Sales Tax Rate Differentials: The Border City Problem." *National Tax Journal* 23 (2): 206–13.
Mintz, Jack, and Henry Tulkens. 1986. "Commodity Tax Competition between Member States of a Federation: Equilibrium and Efficiency." *Journal of Public Economics* 29 (2): 133–72.
Suárez Serrato, Juan Carlos, and Owen Zidar. 2018. "The Structure of State Corporate Taxation and Its Impact on State Tax Revenues and Economic Activity." *Journal of Public Economics* 167: 158–76.
Washington State Department of Revenue. 2018. *2018 Compliance Study*. https://dor.wa.gov/sites/default/files/2022-02/compliancc_study_2018.pdf.

## Comment Alan J. Auerbach

This interesting chapter provides a very helpful introduction to the changing US sales tax landscape and presents intriguing new evidence regarding the impact of the landmark 2018 Supreme Court ruling in *South Dakota v. Wayfair*, which reversed a long-standing limit on the ability of states and local governments to collect sales taxes on the purchases by their residents from remote out-of-state vendors. Prior to *Wayfair*, there had been a general sense that state sales taxes would become less and less viable with the growth

Alan J. Auerbach is the Robert D. Burch Professor of Economics and Law, and director of the Robert D. Burch Center for Tax Policy and Public Finance at the University of California, Berkeley, and a research associate of the National Bureau of Economic Research.

in remote sales. Post-*Wayfair*, this pessimism has perhaps been lifted, but state and local sales taxes remain very imperfect representations of the ideal destination-based consumption tax. As the chapter discusses, sales tax bases have been declining over the years, reflecting both active and passive policy choices—carving out large categories of consumption to be exempt from tax, and failing to include in the tax base the growing share of services in overall consumption. The *Wayfair* decision, in itself, had no direct implications for these policies, as it applied to goods that governments already were attempting to tax. But it could have other, indirect effects, several of which this chapter considers. It also might have effects beyond those treated in the chapter, an issue to which I will return after reviewing what the chapter does cover.

Strictly speaking, *Wayfair* did not expand the set of transactions subject to tax. State and local governments restricted from requiring remote vendors to collect sales taxes on residents' purchases typically attempted to impose use taxes on purchasers at the same rate as the sales tax, but these use taxes were typically very hard to enforce and had very low compliance rates, at least for household purchasers. Hence, one can think of the pre-*Wayfair* environment as being one with a zero rate of tax on remote purchases, which gave them a significant advantage over purchases from vendors with a physical presence in the taxing jurisdiction. Post-*Wayfair*, this route to tax avoidance was sharply curtailed, remaining only to the extent that vendors fall below taxpaying size thresholds or simply evade collecting the taxes now due. That leads to a number of predictions from the authors, including:

1. An increase in sales tax collections, reflecting an effective expansion of the sales tax base to include remote sales;
2. An increase in purchases of tax-exempt commodities, to the extent that these serve as substitutes for the remote purchases now effectively subject to tax;
3. An increase in cross-border shopping in low-tax states, to take advantage of the main remaining way for consumers to lower the sales taxes that they pay;
4. An increase in tax revenues in low-tax border areas, reflecting the switch from remote sales to cross-border shopping;
5. An increase in taxes collected by rural versus urban locations, as residents of the former, having fewer local shopping opportunities, would be more likely to rely on remote purchases (a phenomenon at least as old as the Sears Catalog);
6. A shift in the location of remote vendors, away from jurisdictions made attractive largely by the pre-*Wayfair* ability to avoid taxes on remote sales; and
7. Possibly other shifts in production activity, occasioned by increased taxes on remote business-to-business sales.

Concerning the last two points, the attractiveness of selling from states with low tax rates, with low populations of consumers subject to tax, or both, was diminished by the taxation of remote sales. But the attractiveness of locating a business in a high-tax state would depend on the profile of the business. Those conducting remote sales might now be more likely to locate in a high-tax state, but those making remote *purchases* might be less likely to do so, to the extent that those purchases had previously been partially untaxed—probably a much smaller issue than the nontaxation of household purchases, but possibly still relevant. This is because, as the authors note, state and local sales taxes typically include a lot of business-to-business sales in their tax bases, providing only spotty exemptions for particular types of purchases (e.g., for immediate resale or as direct inputs into production). The persistence of this defect in the sales tax model, a standard feature in the United States, is somewhat hard to understand, given the steady shift toward sales apportionment for the corporate income tax. That is, if states have recognized the competitive advantage of shifting taxes away from production and toward consumption, why has this insight not extended to the design of the sales tax? One possible explanation is that states need the money, and lack the political will to expand the sales tax base in other directions. To the extent that *Wayfair* increases the bite of sales tax on business inputs, this could provide an impetus to reform, but I am skeptical that the impact will be large enough for this reform to happen.

Using data, mostly from Tennessee but also for North Carolina and the country as a whole, Bruce, Fox, and Shute address many of these questions empirically. In doing so, they face several econometric challenges. First, *Wayfair* is a recent decision, and so there are few years of data in the succeeding years, a particular problem if states were slow to adopt conforming legislation. (In Tennessee, we learn, the two relevant pieces of legislation occurred in November 2019 and November 2020.) Second, the *Wayfair* decision affected all states and localities. There is no simple control group against which the *Wayfair* "treatment" can be measured. Finally, the COVID-19 pandemic hit the US economy less than two years after the Supreme Court issued its decision, leaving a short window during which to distinguish the effects of *Wayfair* from the effects of the pandemic, which had very strong effects on the level and patterns of consumer purchases and on the level of business activity.

Recognizing these challenges, the authors look selectively and creatively for patterns consistent with the above predictions. Figure 4.2 shows a large spike in Tennessee sales tax collections during 2021, which the authors interpret as consistent with prediction 1 listed above. Figure 4.3 shows a relative increase in rural versus urban sales tax receipts in 2020. Both of these effects could be due at least in part to the COVID-19 pandemic (a drop in sales in 2020 followed by a rebound in 2021; a less pandemic-impacted economy in rural areas), and the authors consider a shorter pre-COVID sample when moving on to their econometric analysis. In table 4.1, we learn that urban areas' revenues grew more slowly than rural revenues after *Wayfair* implementation, even apparently (in unpublished results) for the shorter pre-COVID sample.[1] In table 4.2, we see that border areas in North Carolina (a neighboring state with a much lower sales tax rate) had higher sales tax revenues in the post-*Wayfair* period, consistent with increased cross-border shopping. Presumably, at least some of these revenues came at the expense of border areas of Tennessee, confirming the authors' prediction that the *Wayfair* decision could heighten government incentives to engage in tax competition, at least among neighboring states. In table 4.3, we see that the *Wayfair* decision had a heterogeneous impact on the level of business applications, with these falling in low-tax states and rising in high-tax states. This is precisely what prediction 6 above would have forecast: businesses selling to high-tax states would no longer have a tax advantage from locating in a low-tax state.[2]

With more time we will have an opportunity to uncover more results about the effects of the *Wayfair* decision. Of particular interest is how states respond to the new environment in a post-COVID setting. I have already expressed skepticism that they will be induced to reform their treatment of business-to-business purchases. But will the apparent response to cross-border shopping incentives lead to lower or more uniform tax rates in border regions? Will the effective increase in their sales tax bases lead states to reduce sales tax rates overall, or will the added revenue show up somewhere else in state budgets? Will states use the extra revenue on offsetting reductions in sales tax bases, or will the higher effective rate on taxed commodities relative to exempt commodities lead to base broadening instead?

With substantial variation across states in sales tax rates, and (as the authors note) with states in the past appearing willing to change their sales taxes periodically, we have the hope of addressing these and other questions in the coming years, and can appreciate the initial insights and evidence that Bruce, Fox, and Shute have provided to help shape our thinking.

For acknowledgments, sources of research support, and disclosure of the author's material financial relationships, if any, please see https://www.nber.org/books-and-chapters/policy-responses-tax-competition/comment-wayfair-step-towards-destination-sales-tax-competition-remains-auerbach.

1. I would have found it interesting to see the "border" and "rate" variables in table 4.1 interacted with the post-*Wayfair* indicator (econ_nexus x border and econ_nexus x rate), to see whether the predictions of increased cross-border shopping and particular revenue improvements in high-tax-rate areas were supported.

2. I am not sure how this finding squares with the big jump in national business applications in 2020 and 2021 depicted in figure 4.5. The latter result could be due to a change in size composition of businesses across states or to COVID-related changes in the business sector, but this is just speculation.

5

# Interjurisdictional Competition and Coordination
## Evidence from Kansas City

Donghyuk Kim

### 5.1 Introduction

When do jurisdictions compete to attract firms and when do they coordinate? This chapter studies how jurisdictions' gains from coordination depend on the economic spillovers, competitive externalities, and the political payoffs from winning firms. A simple model of interjurisdictional competition and firm location choice describes that the potential gains are large when one of the two externalities is dominant. To gain from addressing the freeriding problem, weak competitive externalities must allow firms to be diverted from elsewhere. On the other hand, to gain from internalizing the competitive externalities, weak economic spillovers must create room for incentive spending to be reduced. Coordination can also result in the loss of political payoffs, hurting elected officials but benefiting the residents.

The model is applied to study the competition between the states of Kansas and Missouri for relocating existing Kansas City firms across the border during 2009–2019. This competition has received much public attention due to the two states' large spending on relocation incentives. Evidence suggests that Kansas City firms were unlikely to move out of the metropolitan area, implying high competitive externalities between the two states. The economic linkage between the two states within Kansas City also appears to be strong. The model prediction that the two states would substantially freeride given these circumstances is inconsistent with the observed intensity of the border war. Large political payoffs from relocating firms is one possible explanation.

Donghyuk Kim is an assistant professor of economics at Iowa State University.

Evidence suggests that the Republican Kansas Governor Sam Brownback faced high political gains from relocating Kansas City firms from the Missouri side of the border. Brownback had implemented large tax cuts, known as the Kansas Experiment, to advance his fiscally conservative agenda. One key indicator of success for Brownback was the number of jobs created in the Kansas side of Kansas City since the Missouri side formed a suitable comparison group. The Democratic Missouri Governor Jay Nixon opposed tax cuts and pursued streamlining government functions to balance the budget. Nixon faced heavy resistance from the Republican state legislators that favored tax cuts to compete against Kansas.

The growing unpopularity of the border war pushed the two states to coordinate on reducing the relocation incentives. The first two coordination attempts in 2014 and 2016 failed. Brownback rejected Missouri's truce offer likely because he still needed to prove that the Kansas Experiment worked. It was only when there was near consensus that Brownback's policies had failed that he made a counteroffer. The new Democratic Kansas Governor Laura Kelly that replaced Brownback was politically charged to undo Brownback's policies, one of which was aggressive recruiting of Kansas City firms from Missouri. The third coordination attempt in 2019 to end the border war between Kelly and the new Republican Missouri Governor Michael Parson was successful. However, the agreement appears tenuous when the two states are presented with major firm relocation opportunities.

Some features of the Kansas City case are relevant for studying interjurisdictional competition and coordination in other regions. Jurisdictions in a common metropolitan area or regional industry cluster are likely to exert high competitive externalities and economic spillovers on each other, especially when competing for the area's existing firms.[1] For example, in the New York metropolitan area, Connecticut relocated two financial firms, UBS in 1994 and RBS in 2005, from New York to nearby Stamford. On the other hand, the political payoffs from winning firms are more likely to vary over time for idiosyncratic reasons, affecting the chances of interjurisdictional coordination. For example, Maryland, Virginia, and Washington, DC, initially failed to coordinate on a joint incentive offer to attract Amazon HQ2 but later supported each other when all three were shortlisted, writing to Amazon CEO Jeff Bezos: "In many ways, our jurisdictions have embraced a shared vision for the future."[2] Similarly in 1991, jurisdictions in the New York metropolitan area signed a nonaggression pact to end soliciting firms from each other, but the agreement stopped at stating the common goals. The latest efforts to achieve interjurisdictional coordination

1. See Agrawal and Hoyt (2018)'s Table A1 for a complete list of multistate metropolitan statistical areas.

2. See the letter dated March 2, 2018: https://www.mwcog.org/file.aspx?D=HwLseJ7aJHsBmH1naLNzSfAQwhlk2O6%2Buxivt6jdcls%3D&A=PItT8K8AWtIE77N5a2EWKtkmQVPVN9pZMoCtSsVuQLo%3D.

are being made by state legislators across the nation in response to heightened public criticism of incentives. Since 2019, 15 states have introduced bills and one state has passed the bill to join the Phase Out Corporate Giveway Interstate Compact to end poaching firms from other signatory states with firm-specific incentives.

### 5.1.1 Related Literature

The extensive literature on interjurisdictional competition for firms with business incentives documents the rapidly intensifying competition in the US (Bartik 2020) and finds mostly small welfare impacts of the competition due to the insensitivity of firms' decisions to incentives (Bartik 2005; Jensen 2017; Kim 2020; Mast 2020; Patrick 2014; Slattery 2020; Slattery and Zidar 2020). The large payoffs from attracting firms would explain why jurisdictions are willing to offer large sums of incentives, but the literature's findings imply that a substantial part of those payoffs are transferred to firms as incentives. In this chapter's regional setting, interjurisdictional competition has further distributional consequences if a considerably larger share of the payoffs are derived by the elected officials than by the residents and if the competitive externalities and economic spillovers are strong. As Jensen et al. (2014), Jensen and Malesky (2018), and Slattery (2022) find, politicians use business incentives to claim credits for job creation, often around reelection, to signal their success in promoting economic growth. The political gains from relocating firms with incentives also appear to have been strong in Kansas City, especially in the middle of the Kansas Experiment. This chapter's case study suggests that the political payoffs can sometimes shift to elicit interjurisdictional coordination.

The rest of the chapter proceeds as follows. Section 5.2 provides a model of interjurisdictional competition and firm location choice and discusses jurisdictions' potential gains from coordination. Section 5.3 presents a case study of the state competition in Kansas City, focusing on the conditions that likely contributed to the state coordination. Section 5.4 concludes.

## 5.2 Model

I model incentive offer decisions of three jurisdictions, $s \in \{K, M, O\}$ and location decisions of $J$ number of firms, $j \in \{1 \cdots J\}$. Jurisdictions $K$ and $M$ belong to the same metropolis, standing for Kansas and Missouri in Kansas City. Jurisdictions and firms make decisions sequentially in the order described below.

### 5.2.1 Interjurisdictional Competition

I consider two cases with and without coordination between jurisdictions $K$ and $M$. The following discussion is conditional on a firm, so I suppress the firm subscript $j$ for brevity.

### 5.2.1.1 No Coordination Between Jurisdictions K and M

Jurisdictions compete to host the firm by simultaneously offering incentives. Jurisdiction $s$ chooses its incentive offer, $b_s$, to maximize the expected payoff:

$$(1)\quad \max_{b_s}(v_s^e + v_s^p - b_s)\Pr(s \text{ wins}\,|\,b_s) + 1[s \in \{K,M\}]\gamma v_s^e \Pr(\{\text{K,M}\}(s \text{ wins}\,|\,b_s).$$

Jurisdiction $s$ derives $v_s^e + v_s^p - b_s$ if it wins the firm. $v_s^e + v_s^p$ captures the gross payoff from winning and consists of two additively separable components. First, $v_s^e$ captures the economic payoff from the firm's job creation, retention, and investment that contribute to the income of jurisdiction $s$'s residents. Second, $v_s^p$ captures the political payoff that jurisdiction $s$'s elected official derives by claiming credits for $v_s^e$ and also through possible political contributions of the firm receiving incentives (quid pro quo), both contributing to the reelection chances. The political payoff is assumed to be strictly increasing in economic payoff: $(\partial v_s^p / \partial v_s^e) > 0$. The motivation for this assumption is that a politician would likely earn more credits if she delivers larger economic benefits to her constituents.

Jurisdiction $s \in \{K,M\}$ derives $\gamma v_s^e$ even if the other jurisdiction in the metropolis wins. The motivation for this assumption is that if the economic linkage between jurisdictions $K$ and $M$ is strong, the economic benefit of one of those two jurisdictions hosting a firm is likely to spill over to the other jurisdiction. $\gamma \in [0,1]$, governs the magnitude of such economic spillover between jurisdictions $K$ and $M$ and, for simplicity, is assumed symmetric.

The first-order condition for the optimal incentive offer, $b_s$, is

$$(2)\quad b_s = v_s^p + v_s^e\left(1 + 1[s \in \{K,M\}]\gamma\frac{\Pr'(\{K,M\}s \text{ wins}\,|\,b_s)}{\Pr'(s \text{ wins}\,|\,b_s)}\right) - \frac{\Pr(s \text{ wins}\,|\,b_s)}{\Pr'(s \text{ wins}\,|\,b_s)},$$

where $\Pr'(\cdot|\cdot)$ denotes the first derivative of the probability function with respective to the conditioning variable.

The optimal incentive offer is increasing in the gross payoff, $v_s^e + v_s^p$, but decreasing in the economic spillover magnitude, $\gamma$, for jurisdictions $s \in \{K,M\}$, since they shade their offers to freeride on each other's win. This freeriding effect also depends on the diversion ratio, $-1 \le [\Pr'(\{K,M\}\ s\ wins\,|\,b_s)]/[\Pr'(s\ wins\,|\,b_s)] \le 0$, whose magnitude captures the competitive externality that jurisdiction $s \in \{K,M\}$'s marginally higher offer exerts on the other jurisdiction in the metropolis. The magnitude of the diversion ratio increases with the firm's substitutability between locations $K$ and $M$. The final term captures the strategic markdown, a function of the firm profits and competing jurisdictions' incentive offers. In the extreme case with maximum spillover and competitive externalities (i.e., $\gamma = 1$ and $[\Pr'(\{K,M\}\ s \text{ wins}\,|\,b_s)/[\Pr'(s\ wins\,|\,b_s)] = -1$), incentive offers would be driven only by political payoffs.

#### 5.2.1.2 *Coordination Between Jurisdictions **K** and **M***

Jurisdictions $K$ and $M$ coordinate by choosing a joint incentive offer, $b_{KM}$, maximizing the sum of their economic payoffs. The political payoff is assumed to not matter but the model may be extended to include positive political payoffs if elected officials share credits for delivering economic payoffs to the constituents. The maximization problem is

$$\max_{b_{KM}} \sum_{s\in\{K,M\}} (v_s^e + \gamma v_{\{K,M\}s}^e - b_{KM})\Pr(s\,wins\,|\,b_{KM}). \tag{3}$$

The first-order condition for the optimal joint incentive offer is

$$b_{KM} = \frac{\sum_{s\in\{K,M\}}(v_s^e + \gamma v_{\{K,M\}s}^e)\Pr'(s\text{ wins}\,|\,b_{KM}) - \Pr(s\text{ wins}\,|\,b_{KM})}{\sum_{s\in\{K,M\}}\Pr'(s\text{ wins}\,|\,b_{KM})}. \tag{4}$$

The optimal joint offer internalizes the economic spillover, exerting an upward pressure. The competitive externalities are also internalized, exerting a downward pressure through increasing the amount of strategic markdown.

### 5.2.2 Firm Location Choice

Upon receiving incentive offers, the firm chooses the location that maximizes its profit, assumed to equal the location's incentive offer plus the scalar base profit that depends on exogenous characteristics. To close the model, the firm's location choice probability is

$$\Pr(s\text{ wins}\,|\,b_s) = \int\!\!\int\!\!\int \prod_{s'\neq s} G_{b_{s'}}(b_s + \overline{\pi}_s - \overline{\pi}_{s'})dH_{\overline{\pi}}, \tag{5}$$

where $(\overline{\pi}_K, \overline{\pi}_M, \overline{\pi}_O) \sim H_{\overline{\pi}}$ denotes base profits, and $G_{b_s}$ denotes jurisdiction $s$'s offer distribution.

### 5.2.3 Expected Payoff from Coordination

The change in jurisdictions $K$ and $M$'s combined expected payoffs from coordination is

$$\sum_{s\in\{K,M\}} \overbrace{\Pr(s\text{ wins}\,|\,b_{KM}) - \Pr(s\text{ wins}\,|\,b_s)}^{\Delta\text{winningprobability}}(v_s^e + \gamma v_{\{K,M\}s}^e - b_s) \tag{6}$$

$$+ \Pr(s\text{ wins}\,|\,b_{KM})\overbrace{(b_s - b_{KM})}^{\Delta\text{payment}} - \Pr(s\text{ wins}\,|\,b_s)v_s^p.$$

There are two sources of gains from coordination. First, jurisdictions $K$ and $M$ can raise their winning probabilities through coordinating on an offer higher than what they would have individually offered without coordination. This channel operates through countering the freeriding problem and hence

**Table 5.1** **Jurisdictions *K* and *M*'s potential gains from coordination**

| | Competitive externality | |
|---|---|---|
| Economic spillover | Low | High |
| Low | Small gain | Large gain from payment ↓ |
| High | Large gain from win probability ↑ | Small gain |

is important when the economic spillovers between the two jurisdictions are significant. Second, the jurisdictions can avoid competing against each other and decrease the incentive payments. This channel is important when the competitive externalities between the two jurisdictions are significant.

The two sources of gains from coordination are also at a race against each other. For jurisdictions $K$ and $M$ to benefit from addressing the freeriding problem, the competitive externalities between them need to be small so that there is scope for firms to be diverted from jurisdiction $O$. On the other hand, for jurisdictions $K$ and $M$ to benefit from internalizing the competitive externalities, the economic spillovers between them need to be small so that they are not extensively freeriding, creating room for the incentive offers to go down. In the extreme case with maximum economic spillovers and competitive externalities and minimum political payoffs,[3] jurisdictions $K$ and $M$ cannot benefit from coordination. This is because the joint winning probability cannot go up when firms never choose jurisdiction $O$, and the incentive payments also cannot go down when they are already zero due to maximum freeriding. The above arguments are summarized in table 5.1 and also illustrated using simulations of the parameterized model in Kim (2023).[4]

One obstacle to coordination is the commitment problem: the jurisdictions' potential disagreement over how to divide the total payoffs after competition takes place. For instance, suppose the jurisdictions make a high joint offer and divert a firm from outside the metropolis. Would a jurisdiction still be willing to contribute to the joint offer if it finds out that the firm is coming to the metropolis but going to the other jurisdiction? Similarly, suppose the jurisdictions make a low joint offer and reduce their incentive spendings. Would the winning jurisdiction still be willing to share its incentive savings with the other jurisdiction that cooperated in softening the competition? These motives to deviate from coordination resemble a prisoner's dilemma and are stronger after firms' location decisions are made when one jurisdiction is in a position to hold up the other.

Another obstacle to coordination is the loss of political payoffs, which this

3. I.e., $\gamma = 1, [\Pr'(K, M)(s \text{ wins} \mid b_x)] / [\Pr'(s \text{ wins} \mid b_x)] = -1$, and $v_s^p = 0$.

4. The simulated model assumes that jurisdictions $K$ and $M$ offer separate but jointly optimal incentives $b_k$, $b_M$. The gains from coordination articulated above are illustrated.

chapter argues is important for the Kansas City context. In the model, coordination weakly benefits the residents as shown in table 5.1 but prevents the elected officials of jurisdictions *K* and *M* from deriving the political payoffs. If this distributional consequence is severe and if the competitive externalities between jurisdictions *K* and *M* are large, the elected officials may fail to coordinate on lower incentives and rather compete more intensely, hurting the residents. In this case, the gains from coordinating on lower incentives would be amplified for the residents, but the politicians would not be willing to deliver those gains. To address this principal-agent problem, voters would need to substantially shade the credits they give to their elected officials for winning firms.

The model may be modified to approximate settings with positive political payoffs from coordination. When competitive externalities are low and economic spillovers are high, jurisdictions *K* and *M* would combine forces to attract firms from outside the metropolis. In this case, the metropolis residents may reward their elected officials for a successful coordination, without which firms would have been unlikely to choose the metropolis. On the other hand, when the competitive externalities are high and economic spillovers are low, the metropolis residents may be more reluctant to reward their elected officials, since while coordination reins in the within-metro competition, it is unlikely to attract new firms from outside the metropolis. How political payoffs from coordination vary with economic spillover and competitive externalities needs to be further studied.

### 5.2.4 Special Form of Coordination: Truce

A special form of coordination relevant for the Kansas City context is setting the joint incentive offer to zero ("truce") when competing for existing firms in jurisdictions *K* and *M* that have zero chance of choosing jurisdiction *O*. In this case, since jurisdictions *K* and *M* exert maximum competitive externalities on each other, a truce would be optimal in presence of either small economic spillovers or large political payoffs. In the latter case, the elected officials would be uninterested in a truce even though the residents face substantial gains from coordinating on lower incentives. The degree of the principal-agent problem may also vary across the two jurisdictions if the political payoffs from retaining firms are different from those of relocating new firms. For example, suppose voters reward a relocation more than a retention and punish a failed relocation less than a failed retention. In this case, the politician with more opportunities to relocate firms, perhaps because her jurisdiction is less economically developed, would be less willing to agree to a truce since she expects more to gain politically from relocations. The politician in the other jurisdiction would be far more interested in a truce since she has less to gain politically from fighting for retentions.

The disparity in jurisdictions *K* and *M*'s economic strengths also highlights the commitment problem as a potential obstacle to coordination. The

Table 5.2 **Kansas and Missouri's relocation incentive spendings in Kansas City, 2009–2019**

| | Kansas | Missouri |
|---|---|---|
| Incentive spending | $199 million | $212 million |
| # Jobs relocated | 7,449 | 6,565 |
| # Firms relocated | 76 | 35 |
| Incentive spending per job | $21,000 | $23,000 |
| Incentive spending per capita | $20 | $14 |

Note: Data from the Hall Family Foundation. Kansas's incentives are provided through the Promoting Employment Across Kansas (PEAK) program, and Missouri's incentives are provided through the Missouri Works program. Three firms that relocated to Missouri are excluded due to missing job information.

weaker jurisdiction facing ample opportunities to relocate firms would have less to gain from a truce limiting those opportunities. Hence, the stronger jurisdiction that has more to gain from the incentive savings would have to credibly commit to share its savings to elicit the weaker jurisdiction's coordination.

## 5.3 Kansas City Case Study

I use the model to study Kansas and Missouri's competition for relocating existing firms within the Kansas City metropolitan area. This competition has received much public attention for its remarkable intensity. Table 5.2 shows that each state spent nearly $200 million to relocate firms from each other in Kansas City during 2009–2019, according to the data collected by the Hall Family Foundation. These are sizable amounts considering the fact that Kansas and Missouri collected about $334 and $510 million respectively in corporate income taxes in an average year during the sample period. Kansas attracted about 1,000 jobs more than Missouri for a total of 7,449 jobs. Kansas and Missouri spent about $21,000 and $23,000 per job respectively.[5] In per-capita terms, the two states spent about $20 and $14 in an average year during the sample period, comparable to Slattery and Zidar's (2020) finding that the average state tax credits per capita amount to $19 in 2014.[6]

The numbers reported in table 5.2 include the incentives paid under the two states' flagship job creation programs. Kansas's Promoting Employment Across Kansas (PEAK) program allows firms with at least 10 (100) new employees to retain up to 95 percent of the payroll withholding taxes up to 7 (10) years. On the other hand, the Missouri Works program allows firms with at least 10 new employees to retain up to 100 percent of the state withholding

5. These numbers are lower than the average state spending of $46,000 per job found by Slattery and Zidar (2020), who focus on subsidies worth more than $5 million.

6. The total incentive spending reported in the first row of table 5.2 is divided by each state's population in Kansas City metropolitan area times the number of sample years.

taxes up to 5–6 years and 6–7 percent of new payroll of at least 100 new employees up to 5–6 years. The total incentives spent on relocating existing Kansas City firms across the border would further increase if local incentive payments that mostly consist of local property tax abatements are included.

I study three aspects of the Kansas City competition using the model.

### 5.3.1 Competitive Externality

Kansas and Missouri competed for existing firms in Kansas City that were unlikely to move out of the metropolitan area at the time.[7] Anecdotal evidence suggests that most firm relocations were initiated by firms threatening to move to the other side of the border or the economic development agencies recruiting firms.[8] The firms would have also faced relatively low cost of moving across the state border due to the physical proximity and the access to the same pool of workers and suppliers. Press coverage frequently emphasizes how the firm relocations would have only changed the workers' commuting patterns. Jensen (2017) finds that Kansas's PEAK program had little impact on Kansas firms' employment and relocation decisions, suggesting that they were unlikely to move without the incentives. If the firms that Kansas and Missouri fought for were unlikely to move out of the city, competitive externalities between the two jurisdictions would have been high, implying the model's diversion ratio, $[\Pr'(\{K,M\}\,s \text{ wins} \mid b_s)]/[\Pr'(s \text{ wins} \mid b_s)]$, is close to $-1$.

### 5.3.2 Economic Spillover

The economic spillovers that Kansas and Missouri would have derived when each other hosts firms would have been substantial given the tight economic linkage within the metropolitan area. One piece of supporting evidence is the large share of residents that commute across the state border: job opportunities are open to all residents regardless of which jurisdiction hosts firms. The likelihood ratio of a Kansas resident working in Missouri relative to in Kansas is 0.18, while the likelihood of a Missouri resident working in Kansas relative to in Missouri is 0.25, according to the commuting flows data from the 2011–2015 American Community Survey.[9] The job opportunities would further increase when considering the local multiplier effects generated by the entry of complementary businesses. It must be noted that these effects may change in the long run as workers move their residences to optimize commute times and tax payments, as studied by Agrawal and

7. One well-known exception is Applebee's relocation to California in 2015. Prior to this move, however, it relocated twice across the state border in Kansas City.

8. The Kansas Commerce Department was reported to have sent mass recruitment mails to Missouri businesses in 2016, including Missouri's Downtown Council Community Improvement District (Vockrodt 2016).

9. These statistics are computed by dividing the share of Missouri (Kansas) workforce residing in Kansas (Missouri) by the share of Kansas (Missouri) workforce residing in Kansas (Missouri).

Hoyt (2018). Although the tax revenues generated from hosting firms would not spill over, the incentives also limit the amount of tax revenues that can be generated. In sum, Kansas and Missouri would have derived considerable economic spillovers from each other's wins, implying high $\gamma v_K^e, \gamma v_M^e$ in the model.

If ignoring the political payoffs from the analysis, the above discussion suggests that Kansas and Missouri's gains from coordination are small, as the model predicts that Kansas and Missouri would voluntarily shade their incentive offers in competition against each other due to the economic spillovers and competitive externalities. In this case, a formal coordination would be unnecessary. However, this model prediction is inconsistent with the observed intensity of the competition between Kansas and Missouri, and the analysis needs to incorporate the political payoffs from relocating firms.

### 5.3.3 Political Payoff

The political payoffs from relocating firms appear to have been high during the 2010s. Sam Brownback, the Republican governor of Kansas during 2011–2018, aggressively cut individual income taxes and eliminated pass-through income taxes. These policies, the Kansas Experiment, appear to have been impacted by the nationwide buildup of the Tea Party movement and its demand for fiscally conservative policies. The media portrays Brownback as having had ambitions for a second presidential bid. Brownback initially enjoyed extensive support, winning his first gubernatorial race with a wide margin (31.1 percentage points) and backed by the Republican-controlled state legislature. However, his popularity quickly waned due to the state's fiscal crisis and poor economy. Brownback won the second race with a narrow margin (3.7 percentage points) and resigned in 2018 to serve an ambassadorial role after the Kansas Experiment was repealed despite his veto.

The success of the Kansas Experiment, which appears to have been pivotal for Brownback's political ambition, was measured by key economic indicators such as job creation and business growth. Brownback framed his economic policies as a winning strategy to compete for firms against other states, among which Missouri was singled out. Brownback underscores his success in relocating firms from the Missouri side of Kansas City in his 2017 State of the State Address: "As new businesses decline nationally, we boast a record number of new businesses here. Businesses from Missouri are moving across the border, making Kansas City more of a Kansas city. . . . Other states, most notably Missouri, are looking at how to create an economic atmosphere for private sector job growth" (Brownback 2017).

Brownback's choice of Kansas City to showcase his policy effects is likely related to the fact that Missouri's Democratic governor during 2009–2017, Jay Nixon, opposed aggressive tax cuts and pushed for streamlining government functions to balance the budget and invest in job creation. Nixon won both of his gubernatorial elections with considerable margins (18.9 and 12.2 percentage points) but still faced strong resistance from the Republican-controlled state legislature to cut taxes similar to Kansas. Nixon vetoed the tax cut bill in 2013, but the state legislature overrode the veto in 2014. Pitching the new Missouri Works program as a streamlined program to incentivize high-quality job creation, Nixon describes his policies as superior to those of Kansas and other states in the 2012 State of the State Address:

> Because of our focus on fiscal responsibility and efficiency, Missouri is one of the few states with a Triple-A credit rating from all three rating agencies. Kansas can't say that. Neither can Arkansas, Illinois, Kentucky, Nebraska or Tennessee. . . . We know how to manage our money—better than our neighboring states, and much better than Washington. . . . From our low taxes to our strong workforce, Missouri is well positioned for job creation. To keep our economy growing, we must build on these strengths. That's what our Missouri Works strategy will do. (Nixon 2012)

In sum, Brownback and Nixon took competing approaches to economic development and were mindful of their performances relative to each other. The competition was fueled by the partisan nature of the policies. The political payoffs from relocating firms in Kansas City thus would have been high if the city were perceived as a battlefield for the competing policies and if the job numbers in the city were used to keep scores. This would have been especially true for Brownback, who had a bigger point to prove.

Assuming high $v_K^p, v_M^p$, the model predicts that Kansas and Missouri would have offered high incentives, mostly driven by political payoffs if the competitive externalities and economic spillovers are high as argued in the previous subsections. The first-order condition (equation 1) that captures this intuition can be used to quantify the minimum political payoffs that explain the observed incentive spendings. In an empirical exercise with further structure on firm profits and economic payoff distributions, Kim (2023) finds a substantial share of incentive spendings to be politically driven: at least 10 percent of Kansas's total median payoff net of spillovers is political when relocating a firm with less than 20 jobs. On the other hand, at least 10 percent of Missouri's total median payoff net of spillovers is political when relocating a firm with at least 100 jobs.

The model further predicts that the political payoffs generate distributional consequences from coordination: the residents gain from coordinating on lower incentives while the politicians lose the expected political payoffs. In result, as discussed below, a significant reduction in political payoffs was needed for the elected officials to coordinate.

### 5.3.4 Failed Coordination Attempts

Declining political payoffs from firm relocations contributed to the multiple coordination attempts between Kansas and Missouri. Growing skepticism about the effects of incentives is documented in the local media. At least twelve editorials criticizing the border war are found in the local newspaper, *Kansas City Star*, during 2012–2016. Academic research has also shown that the incentive programs deliver little benefits to the residents not only in Kansas City but also in other areas (e.g., Bartik 2005; Jensen 2017). The competition between Kansas and Missouri also received the national spotlight and was satirized in a late night talk show on national television. A group of about twenty civic and business leaders in Kansas City played a leading role in urging Brownback and Nixon to end the border war. In 2011, they wrote to the two governors:

> The Kansas City community is experiencing an economic border war. State incentives are being used to lure businesses back and forth across the state line with no net economic gain to the community as a whole and a resulting erosion of the area's tax base. We are asking that you direct your Departments of Commerce to develop parallel legislation to reduce this unproductive use of tax incentives. While your departments work on this legislation, we ask that you both mutually agree to a bilateral halt to the issuance of incentives for business relocations between the two states within the Greater Kansas City area.[10]

As a result, both governors openly expressed the need to tame the competition and engaged in dialogues that continued for more than a year. Kansas launched the Kansas Border Challenge Advisory Committee, and Missouri legislators started working on a bill. In 2014, Nixon signed Missouri Senate Bill No. 635, which proposed to Kansas a moratorium on incentive provision to Kansas City firms relocating across the border without new job creation.[11] However, this proposal failed to elicit an agreement from Kansas for at least three reported reasons.

First, Kansas raised the concern that firms would leave Kansas City if the two states did not provide relocation incentives. Kansas wanted to use discretionary incentives for firms likely to move out of the city, but Nixon did not have the discretion to pick particular firms to incentivize, as the Missouri Quality Jobs program (predecessor to Missouri Works program) worked by entitlements. Missouri Republican legislators were unlikely to hand over the discretion to Nixon for the fear of his "micro-managing tax credit programs" (Hanna 2013). The two states also disagreed over the degree of their competitive externalities. Missouri Republican Senator Ryan Silvey, who filed the moratorium, stated in 2014 that Kansas City firms were unlikely to leave the city even if the relocation incentives were banned:

> The chances of a (Kansas City-area) company relocating to another region because we wouldn't allow cross-border competition is exceed-

10. See https://web.archive.org/web/20110429053237/http://www.kansascity.com/2011/04/11/2793596/letter-from-kc-area-business-leaders.html.

11. Senate Bill No. 635, https://www.senate.mo.gov/14info/pdf-bill/intro/SB635.pdf.

ingly slim. The fact is, they're just not interested in doing anything. I think it's because Kansas is worried about their ability to attract businesses from outside the region. Once they're in the region, they feel like they can bring them across the border. But they want to use us to get them here. (Roberts 2014)

Second, Kansas wanted Missouri to lower its local tax abatements to the same level as Kansas, while Missouri was concerned that Brownback's tax cuts were already creating an uneven playing field. Finally, Kansas expressed that Missouri's proposal was coercive, especially when Missouri Senator Silvey threatened with a retaliatory "Kansas recruitment act" if Kansas did not accept the offer. Blake Schreck, president of the Lenexa Chamber of Commerce and a member of the Kansas Border Challenge Advisory Committee, replied in 2014 that Missouri's proposal "made it feel to many that Kansas was being dictated to rather than being negotiated with" (Roberts 2014).

In 2016, Kansas offered a proposal of its own to Missouri just before the official time was up for responding to the first proposal. The main difference in Kansas's proposal was that the state incentives could still be awarded to Kansas City firms relocating across the border if they invested at least $10 million in a new building. Brownback's intention was to support the construction industry and to limit the use of incentives for the "lease jumpers" that relocate from one leased space to another just across the border. This time, Missouri legislators brushed off the offer stating that the $10 million capital exemption rule would require an amendment to the Missouri Works program and that the offer was less comprehensive than the first one Missouri made (Hudnall 2016). Kansas's offer did not address dealing with firms likely to move out of the city, a concern that Kansas reported was keeping it from agreeing to Missouri's first offer.

The disparity in Brownback's and Nixon's political payoffs likely also played a role in the failed coordination attempts. It is evident that Brownback had a large stake in delivering positive results of the Kansas Experiment. Kansas City firm relocations were framed as a measure of success, and Brownback would have wanted the border war to continue. On the other hand, Nixon was on the defensive, having to compete against increasingly aggressive Kansas. Losing the border war or increasing relocation incentives to keep up with Kansas's tax cut would have bolstered the Missouri Republican's demand for a similar tax cut, which ran counter to Nixon's platform. It is also worth pointing out that failing to retain firms is likely more politically costly than failing to relocate firms, since the former entails worse economic outcomes whereas the latter maintains the status quo. Being on the defensive thus would have meant that Nixon faced a higher political cost of the border war.

The disparity in Kansas's and Missouri's economic strengths would have further implied that Kansas had more to gain both economically and politically from the border war. As the Missouri side of the Kansas City is more developed and dense, Kansas would have faced more opportunities to relocate existing firms from Missouri. The truce offer limiting those opportunities would have hence appeared unattractive to Kansas unless Missouri credibly committed to share its incentive savings with Kansas.

It was only when Brownback was confronted with the fiscal crisis that he offered to reduce relocation incentives, albeit partially. In 2016, Brownback's approval rating hovered around 20 percent, and he was labeled the least popular governor in the country. Brownback's political payoffs from firm relocations would also have fallen dramatically, as the consensus was that the Kansas Experiment had failed and was about to be repealed. Missouri Republicans hence would have been less worried about losing the border war. Nixon was also term limited and his second term was about to end.

Although the first two coordination attempts may have failed due to the disparity in political payoffs, it was the growing unpopularity of the border war that pushed them to actively consider coordination in the first place. The strong leadership of Donald Hall, the CEO of Hallmark, in unifying the voices of local civic and business leaders and mediating the dialogues between Brownback and Nixon also was a catalyst in eliciting the coordination proposals.

### 5.3.5 Successful Coordination

The third coordination attempt succeeded. Kansas elected a new Democratic governor, Laura Kelly, while Missouri elected a new Republican governor, Michael Parson. In 2019, Parson signed Senate Bill No. 182 similar to the original one that Nixon signed in 2014, and Kelly signed an executive order agreeing to stop paying state incentives to Kansas City firms relocating from one border county to another unless net new jobs are created.[12]

There are three notable factors that likely contributed to the fruition of the third attempt. First, Kelly was motivated to undo the effects of the Kansas Experiment and resolve the fiscal crisis, which would have presented her with substantial political returns to ending the border war. Writing to a local newspaper after the signing of the executive order, Kelly describes her success in ending the border war as a part of reversing Brownback's policies: "The Brownback-Colyer administration's lack of interest in ending the border war was emblematic of economic recklessness on their watch that extended well beyond a failed tax experiment. The fiscal fallout was unprecedented. The process of rebuilding state operations—including the important work of fueling job growth—began the day I took office" (Kelly 2019).

Second, in 2019, a coalition of state legislators from the two states helped attract USDA's two research agencies (about 550 jobs) to Kansas City in

12. Missouri Bill: https://www.senate.mo.gov/19info/pdf-bill/House/HCS-SB/SB0182.pdf; Kansas Executive Order: https://governor.kansas.gov/wp-content/uploads/2019/08/EO-19-09_Executed.pdf.

competition against other states. This incident reflects a change in mood for a regional cooperation. Speaking of the two governor's agreement, Tim Cowden, president and CEO of the Kansas City Area Development Council, notes that the bi-state cooperation on USDA "has no doubt contributed to this watershed moment in our region's history" (Shorman and Kite 2019). Third, Mayor Quinton Lucas of Kansas City, Missouri, also backed the state-level coordination by agreeing to Kelly's request to limit the local property tax abatements to ten years to level with the limit in Kansas.

Zero relocation incentives are consistent with the model's predicted outcome if there were no political payoffs but high competitive externalities and economic spillovers. The model explains the ramping up of the border war and its eventual end with the changing political payoffs. However, changing economic payoffs as an explanation of the phenomenon cannot be ruled out. For this argument to hold, significantly large changes in economic payoffs are necessary since some are assumed to spill over to the neighboring jurisdiction. It could be that in the wake of the Great Recession, the economic payoffs from relocating firms rose substantially, escalating the border war. On the other hand, it is less clear how the economic payoffs could have declined to end the war.

The state cooperation that attracted the USDA jobs is a telling example of how interjurisdictional coordination depends on competitive externalities and economic spillovers. The two states both recognized the need to combine forces when their competitive externalities were low: USDA had received 136 proposals from 36 states. However, once the USDA officially selected Kansas City, the competitive externalities reached the maximum, and the two states intensely fought each other. It appears that the political payoffs drove the competition. Missouri Representative Emanuel Cleaver recalls calling Kansas Representative Sharice Davids after hearing the news of USDA's selection of Kansas City: "I told her, 'Either side that wins, both sides win.' You look at Sprint, for example, I have a large number of constituents who work at Sprint in Johnson County, so I'm not going to be that disappointed if the USDA picks Kansas. . . . Nevertheless, I prefer that it be relocated to Kansas City, Missouri, and I'm going to work very hard to get that done" (Lowry et al. 2019).

The ceasefire agreement appears tenuous when the two states are presented with opportunities to poach firms from each other. Just after the agreement, Missouri attracted a financial firm, Waddell and Reed, from Kansas with $62 million in state incentives and $35 million in local incentives. Missouri defended this deal as having been grandfathered in before the ceasefire agreement. After a merger, the company decided not to relocate in the end. Kansas similarly defended its relocation offer of $20 million to Bluescope Construction in 2020. More recently, Kelly, just before her reelection in 2022, expressed intention to use incentives to attract the Kansas City Chiefs' Arrowhead Stadium from Missouri.

## 5.4 Conclusion

This chapter has studied the state competition for firm relocations in Kansas City, focusing on the role political payoffs likely have played in shaping the transition from competition to coordination. The current coordination puts the two states in a situation similar to what the model predicts with strong competitive externalities and economic spillovers but no political payoffs. Political gains from firm relocations continue to tempt politicians. Future research can study what conditions makes informed voters more likely to credit politicians for attracting firms with business incentives. Specifically, how the political returns to coordination and incentive usage differ between Kansas City and other nonaffected areas can be explored. The political economy of two policy instruments—taxes and firm-specific incentives—played an important role in the Kansas City context. The nature of interaction between the two instruments needs to be studied in a unified framework as noted by Agrawal et al. (2022). Finally, how political payoffs shape regional coordination when the competitive externalities are weak (e.g., Kansas and Missouri's cooperation to attract the USDA and host World Cup games) can also be studied further.

**Acknowledgments**

I thank David Agrawal, Jim Poterba, Cailin Slattery, Owen Zidar, and the conference participants for their insightful comments that improved the chapter. I thank the Hall Family Foundation for providing the incentives data. The views expressed in this chapter are those of the author. All errors are my own. For acknowledgments, sources of research support, and disclosure of the author's material financial relationships, if any, please see https://www.nber.org/books-and-chapters/policy-responses-tax-competition/interjurisdictional-competition-and-coordination-evidence-kansas-city.

# References

Agrawal, David R., and William H. Hoyt. 2018. "Commuting and Taxes: Theory, Empirics and Welfare Implications." *The Economic Journal* 128 (616): 2969–3007.

Agrawal, David R., William H. Hoyt, and John D. Wilson. 2022. "Local Policy Choice: Theory and Empirics." *Journal of Economic Literature* 60 (4): 1378–455.

Bartik, Timothy J. 2005. "Solving the Problems of Economic Development Incentives." *Growth and Change* 36 (2): 139–66.

Bartik, Timothy J. 2020. "Using Place-Based Jobs Policies to Help Distressed Communities." *Journal of Economic Perspectives* 34 (3): 99–127.

Brownback, Sam. 2017. "2017 State of the State Address." January 10, 2017. https://

web.archive.org/web/20240915052709/https://governor.kansas.gov/wp-content/uploads/2017/01/2017-State-of-the-State.pdf.
Hanna, John. 2013. "Analysis: Wariness Greets Call for K.C.-Area Truce." *The Topeka Capital-Journal*, November 17, 2013. https://www.cjonline.com/story/news/politics/state/2013/11/17/analysis-wariness-greets-call-kc-area-truce/16377955007/.
Hudnall, David. 2016. "Missouri Lawmakers Rebuff Kansas Gov. Sam Brownback's 'Border War' Peace Offering." *The Kansas City Star*, April 20, 2016. https://www.kansascity.com/news/local/news-columns-blogs/the-buzz/article72852702.html.
Jensen, Nathan M. 2017. "Job Creation and Firm-Specific Location Incentives." *Journal of Public Policy* 37 (1): 85–112.
Jensen, Nathan M., and Edmund J. Malesky. 2018. *Incentives to Pander: How Politicians Use Corporate Welfare for Political Gain*. Cambridge University Press.
Jensen, Nathan M., Edmund Malesky, Mariana Medina, and Ugur Ozdemir. 2014. "Pass the Bucks: Credit, Blame, and the Global Competition for Investment." *International Studies Quarterly* 58 (3): 433–47.
Kelly, Laura. 2019. "Reaching Across the Aisle to End the Kansas-Missouri Border War." *The Kansas City Star*, August 19, 2019. https://www.kansascity.com/opinion/readers-opinion/guest-commentary/article234101222.html.
Kim, Donghyuk. 2020. "Government Incentives and Firm Location Choices." Working paper, Iowa State University.
Kim, Donghyuk. 2023. "Economic Spillovers and Political Payoffs in Government Competition for Firms: Evidence from the Kansas City Border War." *Journal of Public Economics* 224: 104941.
Lowry, Bryan, Jonathan Shorman, Allison Kite, and Steve Vockrodt. 2019. "Kansas, Missouri Teamed Up to Lure USDA Jobs to KC. Now, the Competition Begins." *The Kansas City Star*, June 16, 2019. https://www.kansascity.com/news/politics-government/article231523378.html.
Mast, Evan. 2020. "Race to the Bottom? Local Tax Break Competition and Business Location." *American Economic Journal: Applied Economics* 12 (1): 288–317.
Nixon, Jay. 2012. "Text of Mo. Gov's State of the State Address," January 17, 2012. https://www.newstribune.com/news/2012/jan/17/text-mo-govs-state-state-address.
Patrick, Carlianne. 2014. "Does Increasing Available Non-tax Economic Development Incentives Result in More Jobs?" *National Tax Journal* 67 (2): 351–86.
Roberts, Rob. 2014. "Kansas Shoots Down Missouri Truce Bill; Silvey Fires Back." *Kansas City Business Journal*, March 11, 2014. https://www.bizjournals.com/kansascity/news/2014/03/11/kansas-shoots-down-missouritruce-bill-silvey-fires.html.
Shorman, Jonathan, and Allison Kite. 2019. "Kelly Plans Action to End Kansas-Missouri Border War, After Parson Signed Truce Bill." *The Wichita Eagle*, June 15, 2019. https://www.kansas.com/news/politics-government/article231580593.html.
Slattery, Cailin Ryan. 2020. "Bidding for Firms: Subsidy Competition in the U.S." Working paper.
Slattery, Cailin. 2022. "The Political Economy of Subsidy Giving." Working paper, University of California, Berkeley.
Slattery, Cailin, and Owen Zidar. 2020. "Evaluating State and Local Business Incentives." *Journal of Economic Perspectives* 34 (2): 90–118.
Vockrodt, Steve. 2016. "Kansas Continues Trying to Bring Missouri Businesses across State Line." *The Kansas City Star*, August 23, 2016. https://www.kansascity.com/news/business/article97243862.html.

## Comment Cailin Slattery

Subsidy giving has many potential drawbacks: cost per job estimates are often high, spillover effects are uncertain, politics may influence subsidy decisions, and competition drives up the subsidy size. However, there is also a clear allocative efficiency argument for allowing subsidies. Locations that would benefit the most from attracting a firm, but where the firm is less profitable, can express this benefit with a subsidy. In effect, these less attractive locations can use the subsidy to compensate the firm for locating where it is less profitable, thereby increasing total welfare.

The allocative efficiency argument is not as compelling when subsidy competition occurs within a single metro area. In this case, two states that share a metro area compete to attract the same firm, or one state spurs a competition by offering subsidies to poach a firm from the other side of the border. When a firm relocates from one side of the metro area to the other, very little new economic activity is generated. Instead, the most salient change is the commuting pattern of the firm's employees. Therefore, local coordination or harmonization—limiting subsidy competition between neighbors—may have large welfare gains. In fact, past work has found that regional tax harmonization can achieve most of the gains of national tax harmonization, given that the regions are sufficiently homogeneous (Fajgelbaum et al. 2018). Kim's chapter studies local coordination in the subsidy competition context, with a specific focus on the fierce subsidy competition, and subsequent truce, in the Kansas City metro area.

Consider subsidy competition with three competitors: Kansas City, Kansas; Kansas City, Missouri; and another location outside Kansas City. These three locales are competing for a single firm, and the firm has a simple decision to make—which location offers the highest profit? This profit is a function of the location-specific characteristics and the subsidy offer. The cities have a more complicated problem—what subsidy should they offer the firm? The benefit from attracting the firm is the sum of the economic and political payoff, less the subsidy payout. Kim specifies the subsidy competition as a first price auction: cities privately submit bids (subsidy offers), and the city that offers the highest profit for the firm wins the auction. Therefore, the city trades off between maximizing benefit with a lower subsidy and maximizing the probability it wins the competition with a higher subsidy. With the auction, the model can predict optimal incentive offers and the firm's location choice when all three localities compete.

The model incorporates spillovers by allowing for economic linkages between jurisdictions. For example, if a firm locates in Kansas City, Missouri, then Kansas City, Kansas, might also benefit from job creation.

Cailin Slattery is an assistant professor of business and public policy at UC Berkeley's Haas School of Business.

This economic linkage allows for free riding between neighbors and effects equilibrium bids. Neighboring locations are also linked via the competitive externality—neighbors are more likely to be close substitutes. A marginally higher subsidy offer from Kansas City, Missouri, for example, is more likely to divert a firm to choose that location instead of Kansas City, Kansas, thus affecting the Kansas bid.

Given the baseline model, Kim then demonstrates how incentive offers would change if Kansas and Missouri coordinated to compete against the "outside" location. The two sides of the state border could internalize the economic payoffs in the whole metro area—there is no free riding, which would allow for a larger incentive offer, all else equal. Also, the two states would no longer compete against each other, which would put downward pressure on the incentive offer. Therefore, the predictions on the changes in equilibrium bids, and hence gains from coordination, hinge on the economic spillover and the competitive externality (Table 5.1).

Table 5.1 shows that there are very little gains to coordination when the competitive externality and the economic spillover are both high. This is exactly the case in Kansas City. Often there is no "outside" location, firms are choosing between either side of the border, the economic linkage is strong, and the locations are close substitutes. What can be done? Well, here there are gains to another type of coordination: a regional truce.

In 2019, Kansas and Missouri did just that. No subsidies would be offered to firms relocating from the other side of the border within Kansas City (Hardy 2019). This was an interesting development, because there were two previous attempts at a truce before the successful agreement in 2019. What changed to allow the governments of Kansas and Missouri to agree to the truce? Or, why did the previous attempts fail?

Kim argues that the political payoffs changed. In effect, in the setting where the competitive externality and economic spillovers are high, the two forces counteract each other and political payoffs drive the equilibrium bids. Therefore, due to the political gain from attracting firms, politicians do not have an incentive to agree to a ceasefire. Kim highlights two changes between the first attempt at the truce in 2014 and the agreement in 2019. First, both states saw a change in leadership: new governors, with new political incentives, were elected. Second, with the departure of Kansas's previous governor, Sam Brownback, the infamous "Kansas Experiment" came to an end. Therefore, Kansas no longer needed to offer generous incentives to buoy its job creation statistics.

I do not disagree that the political payoffs changed between 2014 and 2019, certainly with the added pressure of the Kansas Experiment. Kim also mentions a growing public distaste for the border war, which helped to motivate the opening of the negotiations in 2014. But I am still left with a puzzle. The competition between Kansas and Missouri was ongoing for at least 30 years before negotiations begun, according to NPR (Planet Money

2016). Was there public support for subsidy competition throughout this period, or did added media attention lead to the recent change? And if the subsidy competition was not salient in earlier years, what did the politicians have to gain? Moreover, in other metro areas that cross state borders, like the New York metro area, spanning New York, New Jersey, and Connecticut, why has there not been any coordination?

I propose an additional, complementary, theory: heterogeneity in firm profits. Consider the firm's problem in the model. In the case of the truce, the firms are only choosing between Kansas City, Kansas, and Kansas City, Missouri, and it will not see any incentives. Therefore, the firm will just locate at the side of the border that has the maximum profits. Even if the two sides of the border are close substitutes, it may be that one is more attractive, and importantly, is more attractive to most firms. Therefore, Kansas did not want to agree to a truce with Missouri because it predicted that all of the firms would prefer Missouri in the absence of incentives. In fact, Missouri, the more dominant side of the metro area, always instigated the truce. This also may partly explain why the truce has been so tenuous. Similarly, it is the states that I predict would do well in the absence of subsidy competition that propose national bans (Slattery 2022).[1]

For the remainder of my discussion I will consider the type of coordination that is the focus of the Kim model: coordination in incentive offers. I will go through a few real world cases, and consider reasons why it is not more commonly practiced. Then, I will consider whether there are gains to alternate strategies.

## Coordination in Subsidy Offers

### USDA and the Kansas City Metro Area

Kim's model illustrates how equilibrium subsidy offers change when localities can coordinate: Kansas City, Kansas, and Kansas City, Missouri, offer one incentive to attract a firm to the Kansas City metro area. As mentioned in the chapter, this is exactly what the two states did in 2019 when they submitted a joint bid to attract the USDA to Kansas City. The USDA was looking to relocate two research agencies outside of the Washington, DC, area.

The joint bid was successful, and the USDA chose to locate in the Kansas City metro area, over 135 other locations that competed. When the winner was announced, the USDA had not yet chosen which side of the state border, though feasibly it could have located one agency on each side. Four months later, the USDA signed a lease for a building on the Missouri side to house both teams—the Kansas side would not get either agency.

1. New York legislators drafted and circulated the End Corporate Welfare Act to try to gain traction for a national subsidy truce.

Again, Kansas's reluctance to coordinate with the "stronger" side of the metro may have been well founded. While certainly Kansas will receive some benefit from the influx of federal workers, Missouri will likely reap the majority of the gains. This opens some questions about the incentive offer.

According to the USDA, the incentive package from the Kansas City metro area amounted to about $26 million from state and local governments (Shurr 2019). What is not clear is how that incentive offer is split between the two jurisdictions. Does Kansas still have to contribute to the incentive, given that the final location is in Missouri? How do two jurisdictions share in the "indirect benefit" that is a large focus when governments calculate subsidy offers? It would be interesting to get some perspective from practitioners in the Kansas City area, as this type of information is not available in the press releases or reporting on the deal.

### Amazon HQ2 and the Detroit-Windsor Joint Bid

Another example comes from the infamous competition for Amazon HQ2 in 2017. Detroit, Michigan, and Windsor, Ontario, made a joint incentive offer to attract the retail headquarters. This seems like it could have been much more complicated than the Kansas City case, because the two jurisdictions are across the US-Canada border, not merely state lines. However, it may have been simpler in two ways.

First, it is not clear that Detroit and Windsor have a long history of competing for businesses, perhaps because relocating across countries is not as straightforward as across states. Therefore, when the opportunity arose to cooperate, both cities were favorable to the idea. The *Detroit Free Press* reported soon after the offer was announced: "The involvement of Windsor in the Detroit deal came early. Shortly after the Amazon contest was announced Windsor Mayor Drew Dilkens emailed Dan Gilbert to see if he had considered including the city across the river. According to Dilkens, Gilbert wrote back within an hour or two saying that the email was 'timely' and that he was just going to call Dilkens" (Gross 2017).

Second, the incentive offer was clearly demarcated across jurisdictions. While Michigan and Detroit offered exemptions to income, property, utility, and corporate taxes for employment and property in Detroit, Windsor offered real estate and tax credits for property across the border. Therefore, the incentive payment was targeted to a location and investment size. Specifically, Windsor offered to contribute incentives worth over $100 million if Amazon located 5,000 workers in Canada (Guillen and Reindl 2017). The split of workers between cities is feasible in the case of a megaproject like Amazon, which originally promised up to 50,000 workers associated with the headquarters. Therefore, there would be little need for ex-post negotiation on incentive payouts.

In the end, Amazon did not choose to locate in Detroit-Windsor, but the offer did make it through the first round of the competition. However, given the size of the headquarters proposed and the public nature of the competition, it is surprising that we did not see more joint offers from states and cities. In contrast, the original winning cities—Long Island City in New York and Arlington in Virginia—competed fiercely with their neighbors of Newark, New Jersey, and Montgomery, Maryland.

### Alternate Strategies

The paucity of coordination across jurisdictions may be due to the political payoff to attracting firms, the presence of a consistently "stronger" neighbor, the difficulties in splitting incentive payouts, and other administrative and political barriers to communication across jurisdictions. One might consider an alternative type of coordination for Kansas City, Kansas, and Kansas City, Missouri: explicit collusion via bidding ring.

With a bidding ring, bidders collude to suppress competition (McAfee and McMillan 1992). There are different bidding ring schemes, but generally a group of bidders arrange so that only one bidder from the group participates in each auction of interest. Sometimes it is as simple as assigning different dates in the calendar to different bidders, while in other schemes the colluding players hold a knockout auction that determines who will bid. Then, side payments are arranged to the bidders who did not participate but would have liked to (Asker 2010).

Kansas and Missouri should be able to find a way to rotate their participation in auctions—for some firms, Kansas offers an incentive and Missouri offers nothing, and vice versa. A calendar-based approach is the most simple and would allow for different shares: the Missouri side of the metro has a larger population, and perhaps the percentage of auctions that they can participate in should reflect that. Here, Kansas does not need to worry about being slightly less attractive than Missouri, because Missouri will not bid against Kansas when it is Kansas's turn to participate. Also, the two sides do not need to negotiate the incentive payout when putting together a joint bid, or renegotiate once the firm chooses one side of the metro. Moreover, if Kansas and Missouri are truly close substitutes for firms, this will have the effect of suppressing competition and lowering the incentive offers necessary to attract firms.

An important caveat is necessary: bidding rings are in violation of the Sherman Act. Therefore, it must be that cities receive some exemption, much like how the federal government allows for limited antitrust exemptions in the agriculture industry (US Department of Agriculture 1985). Perhaps the growing distaste for subsidy giving is consistent with this type of reform.

A final thought I have concerns the logistics of coordination. The issue of ex-post subsidy renegotiation is a sticking point for me in the USDA case study. Perhaps we do not see more jurisdictions coordinate on subsidy offers because it is hard to split the incentive offer across localities. If the USDA locates in Missouri, does Kansas still contribute to the incentive? Does that contribution account for the economic spillovers that it benefits from? And how do the states measure that spillover? One straightforward option is to tie incentive payments based on employment. Both states should be able to easily identify employees that work at the USDA in Missouri but live in Kansas.[2] In this scenario, Kansas would agree to some incentive contribution by employed Kansans. This is certainly more straightforward than measure ex-post economic "benefit" in each state.

In conclusion, Kim provides a helpful framework to study coordination between neighboring jurisdictions in subsidy competitions. The chapter also provides rich texture in light of the Kansas City border war and subsequent, but tenuous, truce. I hope this discussion provides some food for thought of why coordination is not more widespread, and some motivation for further exploration into possible obstacles and solutions.

For acknowledgments, sources of research support, and disclosure of the author's material financial relationships, if any, please see https://www.nber.org/books-and-chapters/policy-responses-tax-competition/comment-interjurisdictional-competition-and-coordination-evidence-kansas-city-slattery.

## References

Asker, John. 2010. "A Study of the Internal Organization of a Bidding Cartel." *American Economic Review* 100 (3): 724–62.

Fajgelbaum, Pablo, Eduardo Morales, Juan Carlos Suárez Serrato, and Owen Zidar. 2018. "State Taxes and Spatial Misallocation." *The Review of Economic Studies* 86 (1): 333–76.

Gross, Allie. 2017. "Gov. Rick Snyder Touts Detroit-Windsor Amazon Bid with Ontario Premier." *Detroit Free Press*. https://www.freep.com/story/news/local/michigan/detroit/2017/10/ 22/amazon-headquarters-rick-snyder-detroit-windsor/788602001/.

Guillen, Joe, and JC Reindl. 2017. "Detroit's Amazon Bid Pitches Big Tax Breaks, Cheap Labor Costs, Possible Ferry to Windsor." *Detroit Free Press*. https://www.freep.com/story/money/ 2017/12/20/detroit-amazon-headquarters/969602001/.

Hardy, Kevin. 2019. "'Sometimes Common Sense Does Prevail.' Missouri, Kansas Celebrate End of Border War." *Kansas City Star*, August 14. https://www.kansascity.com/news/business/article233725152.html.

McAfee, R. Preston, and John McMillan. 1992. "Bidding Rings." *The American Economic Review* 82 (3): 579–99.

Planet Money. 2016. "Episode 699: Why Did the Job Cross the Road?" https://www.npr.org/ sections/money/2016/05/04/476799218/episode-699-why-did-the-job-cross-the-road.

Shurr, Alisha. 2019. "Kansas City Selected as New Home for Two USDA Labs: What That Means for Missouri." *The Missouri Times*. https://themissouritimes

2. Notably, Kansas and Missouri do not have tax reciprocity.

.com/kansas-city-selected-as-new-home-for-two-usda-labs-what-that-means-for-missouri/.

Slattery, Cailin. 2025. "Bidding for Firms: Subsidy Competition in the U.S." *Journal of Political Economy* 133 (5). https://www.journals.uchicago.edu/doi/10.1086/735509.

US Department of Agriculture. 1985. "Understanding the Capper Volstead Act." https://www.rd.usda.gov/files/cir35.pdf/.

6

# Fiscal Federalism and the Role of the Income Tax

Roger Gordon

What is the role of the income tax in a federal system of government? The past literature on the income tax has largely assumed that the role of this tax is to redistribute income from rich to poor in order to maximize the (perhaps weighted) sum of individual utilities. Vickrey and Mirrlees shared a Nobel Prize for papers developing this model of the income tax, while among many other papers Gruber and Saez (2002) provided empirical estimates of key parameters yielding quantitative estimates for the implied optimal tax schedule.

Largely, this literature has focused on the role of a national government in such a redistribution of income. In practice, though, most notably in the US, individual states also impose income taxes on their residents, with tax rates that vary widely across states. Apparently, the implicit objective functions of state governments vary, with some desiring substantial redistribution and others much less so.

Surprisingly, this simultaneous use of the income tax by both federal and state governments seems hard to justify in the context of the fiscal federalism literature, as embodied in Oates (1972). In this literature, decentralization enables individuals with heterogeneous tastes to sort across locations based on these tastes. Those who have high demand for particular services choose locations spending a lot on these particular services, but in exchange need to pay more in taxes and fees to finance these services. Decentralized provision induces costly migration by households, but the gains from better matching government service provision to heterogeneous tastes can justify these costs,

Roger Gordon is Professor Emeritus and Research Professor of economics at the University of California, San Diego, and a research associate of the National Bureau of Economic Research enabling decentralized provision to raise national social welfare, compared to the setting where services are provided solely by the federal government.

In the case of the income tax, heterogeneous tastes refer not to heterogeneous household preferences but to heterogeneous implicit objective functions of the various state governments.[1] The puzzle, given longstanding decentralized use of the income tax, is that decentralized use seems to lower the implicit measure of social welfare used by the national government.[2] From the national perspective, social welfare would be higher if the income tax is the sole responsibility of the national government, with revenue potentially used to finance transfers to state and local governments.

What if individuals have heterogeneous behavioral elasticities, though, when responding to tax incentives? Could decentralization help in this setting, allowing those with high elasticities to sort into states with low tax rates, lessening overall misallocations due to tax distortions? Migration, though, should lead to those with high elasticities to sort into states with higher (rather than lower) tax rates, since these individuals are better able to avoid paying these high rates. Decentralized use of the income tax still results in worse outcomes.

The aim of this chapter is to explore an alternative hypothesis for the overall role of the income tax, in part to help explain the longstanding simultaneous use of the income tax by states as well as by the federal government. Given the large uncertainties particularly younger individuals face concerning their future earnings,[3] in principle individuals should value getting insurance to reduce the dispersion in their future earnings, paying into the system when they end up doing well to get help in exchange when they end up doing badly. Such insurance can be provided through use of an income tax, with revenue used to finance lump-sum transfers.

In spite of the risks people face concerning their future career prospects, we see little or no such income insurance provided in the private market. Apparently, adverse selection (those expecting high future earnings declining to buy such insurance) and moral hazard costs (in part from those who ex post have high earnings dropping future coverage) are too high to support such private coverage. However, if the national government uses an income tax to provide such insurance, there would be mandatory "participation" in the income tax, avoiding any adverse selection problems or ex post drop-

1. Self-interested individuals would always prefer higher net-of-tax income.

2. Here, we assume that the national government's implicit objective function depends solely on the distribution of individual utilities, as would be required if decisions are to lead to Pareto-efficient outcomes (as shown in Kaplow 1995).

3. For example, a Mincer-style regression forecasting individual earnings as a function of age, education, gender, and parental characteristics (much of the information available to an individual when entering the labor force) can explain only maybe a quarter of the observed variation in future earnings. In an older population, including past earnings in the regression helps in forecasting future earnings, but still leaves substantial residual variation.

ping of coverage, two key advantages of government provision of this type of insurance.[4]

Many years ago, Buchanan (1976) argued that this insurance role for the income tax was the key source of its strong political support, in an attempt to provide a more convincing positive explanation for the income tax. Based on their self-interest, individuals potentially gain from insuring against future risks through the income tax.[5]

The existing optimal income taxation models do talk about insuring individuals against the risk they face behind a "veil of ignorance," as argued in Rawls (1971). But redistribution based on outcomes from past risks would not per se be a source of political support for the income tax from self-interested voters. Insurance against future risks would be a source of support.

How does our model contrast with past optimal income taxation models? Past optimal taxation models trade off the resulting equity gains from the tax with the offsetting efficiency losses incurred due to tax distortions. This chapter instead focuses on potential efficiency gains from an income tax through insuring individuals against future risks. To more sharply distinguish our model from the past literature, we entirely ignore any equity gains from the income tax by assuming an equal social value of an ex ante dollar going to each individual. The efficiency gains from income insurance provided by the tax will then be traded off with the same types of efficiency costs as in the prior literature.

By focusing on an insurance role for the income tax, though, we also make salient the potential behavioral responses to the tax coming from increased risk taking, a response noted years ago in Domar and Musgrave (1944) but largely ignored in the optimal taxation literature. While an individual would be just indifferent to a marginal increase in risk taking, by the envelope condition, from a social perspective there would be efficiency gains arising from the sharing of individual idiosyncratic risks across the broader population.[6] Risk taking through the pursuit of new ideas can also generate positive informational externalities, given the limits of patent protection.

The extent of the uncertainty in future earnings that individuals face will vary dramatically across individuals, as can their degree of risk aversion. As

4. Insurance coverage would still create other costly distortions, through discouraging labor supply, effort, or full compliance with the tax code, limiting the optimal amount of insurance provision.

5. Hoynes and Luttmer (2011) and Stepner (2019) both provide empirical evidence that the insurance value to individuals from the income tax can be substantial.

6. Note that the variance of the sum of idiosyncratic risks in tax payments goes to zero relative to the sum of expected tax revenue by the law of large numbers. While individuals face potentially high risk-bearing costs from idiosyncratic risks in their own earnings, there should be no risk-bearing costs from idiosyncratic risks borne jointly through random tax revenue. The resulting efficiency gains from lowering the costs of risk bearing through taxation are then traded off with other distortions created by the tax system.

emphasized in the fiscal federalism literature (e.g., Oates 1972), one response is to allow decentralized provision of such a public "service," allowing individuals to sort across jurisdictions providing different degrees of insurance provision. Those facing high risks can sort into states that have high taxes and high transfers, while those facing low risks can sort into states with low taxes and transfers. This decentralized provision, with heterogeneous tax rates across states, then provides some important efficiency benefits relative to just federal use of an income tax.

The chapter then develops a formal model where states offer heterogeneous tax/transfer programs, each designed to best benefit their residents at the time, while each individual can then migrate (at a cost) if the plan offered by another state looks more attractive given their own personal expected earnings and degree of future uncertainty. For any given level of expected future income, individuals facing high risks in their future earnings would be more likely to move to a jurisdiction with higher taxes and transfers, while those with settled careers would gravitate instead to states with low income tax rates.

What types of households face high risk? Certainly younger workers face more risks than older workers, since their future career path is still unclear.[7] High-tax states should then have a younger population. Once individuals' careers are well established, the most successful ex post would have a propensity to migrate to low-tax states.[8]

Those working in start-up firms, particularly in more innovative firms, face substantial risk given the high failure rate of these firms, but also the huge potential payoffs when the firm is successful. High-tax states should then attract more innovative start-up firms. Once a firm is well established and has a stable niche, it may have an incentive to shift its operations to a low-tax state.[9]

This argument that the income tax provides insurance focuses on insuring idiosyncratic risks that each individual faces, but where there is no aggregate risk by the law of large numbers. As shown in Gordon (1985), proportional taxation of risky publicly traded securities would lead to no reduction in

7. Even older workers with a settled career face some uncertainty about when poor health or simply lack of vitality will push then to retire. Such risks of losing a few years of earnings, though, seem small, compared to the uncertainty faced by the young concerning their entire lifetime career path. As noted in Diamond (1977), an uncertain date of retirement could be partially insured through providing larger net transfers under the Social Security program to those who retire at a younger age.

8. The costs of moving, though, will limit such out-migration from high-tax states, costs that would not inhibit exit from any privately provided contract insuring future income risk.

9. That Elon Musk started his career in California (a high-tax state), but then moved personally and shifted his new plants from California to Texas, once his career became well established, fits well within this theory. The propensity of highly successful inventors to move from high-tax to low-tax countries documented in Akcigit et al. (2016) is also consistent with this choice to start a firm in a high-tax jurisdiction, then for the most successful to migrate to a low-tax jurisdiction once future risks are less.

risk-bearing costs and no change in risk taking, since these risks should already be efficiently allocated across individuals through the securities market. However, while the securities market helps insure risky returns to capital income, it does not do well in insuring risks to earnings, even when those risks arise from the business cycle, as documented in Schmidt (2022).[10]

Migration will be driven not only by differences in future risks but also simply by differences in expected future income: Individuals with high income would tend to migrate to low-tax states, while those with low expected future income would tend to migrate to high-tax (and high-benefit) states, for any given amount of future risks the individual faces. The costs of migrating to another state limit these adverse selection and moral hazard pressures with state provision, though they also limit the potential efficiency gains from sorting based on insurance demand.[11]

The choices states make about their tax/transfer programs will not be second-best efficient from a national perspective, however. In particular, a state's increase in its income tax rate generates positive "horizontal" externalities to other states, as some high-income individuals facing low future risks migrate toward low-tax states while some low-income individuals currently living in lower-tax states (and particularly those facing more future risks) leave to take advantage of the resulting increase in benefits in the state raising its tax rate. In both cases, this migration response adds to the tax base in other states. Due to these positive fiscal externalities, states choose too low tax rates (offer too little insurance) from a national perspective.

One possible federal response is to impose its own income tax, setting a floor for the overall insurance provided to residents in the country. Such a federal program would not be vulnerable to either adverse selection or ex post migration responses, giving it an advantage over state programs. However, a federal tax cannot provide the heterogeneity in provisions that would be appropriate given the heterogeneity in household circumstances.

The optimal federal tax rate should be at least as high as the optimal state tax rate would be in the state attracting households facing the least risks. A yet higher rate would imply a net efficiency loss for those households facing the least risk, but can take into account the positive externalities from a higher rate on the insurance programs in other states through weaker migration incentives faced by the most (least) successful households in high-

10. Schmidt (2022) provides evidence that even though the risk that an individual loses his or her job has a strong cyclical component, only a small idiosyncratic fraction of individuals in fact lose their job during a recession, limiting the ability of the stock market to hedge against this type of cyclical income shock.

11. The costs of migration are many, including costs of finding a new job and residence, paying realtor fees if the individual owned their prior residence, parting with friends in the prior community and trying to make friends in the new community, forcing children to adjust to a new school system, losing all the location-specific information acquired in their prior community about where to find particular goods and services, and of course paying to move one's belongings to a new location.

tax states (the lowest tax state), saving directly on migration costs and also allowing these states to provide a more generous insurance program.

A second potential federal response is to subsidize state use of the income tax, such as occurs through SALT deductions under the federal income tax. Due to the migration responses, having a more generous program creates positive externalities to other states and as a result leads to too little insurance provision. A subsidy can in principle help correct for such underprovision.[12]

A third potential federal response would be to treat moving costs less generously under the federal income tax. To the degree that people move in order to take advantage of a more attractive job offer in another location, then these moving costs should in principle be a deductible expense, so that the tax falls on net earnings. However, when individuals move for consumption reasons, such as a preference for a different climate, there would be no grounds to treat this form of consumption differently than other forms of consumption. To that extent, moving costs should not be deductible. Here, current tax law matches this reasoning, allowing a deduction only when the individual is moving to a new job. However, an important reason that individuals may choose to move to a new job is to relocate to a state with a more favorable tax rate, generating in the process negative fiscal externalities. Here, there would be grounds for adding to the costs of this choice (working to internalize these externalities), contrary to current law.[13]

In addition, we discuss some more detailed adjustments to the federal income tax, aimed directly at providing more insurance specifically for risky closely held firms. One possibility would be a higher tax rate, but more generous deductions. A second would be less aggressive enforcement of taxes on such activities. A third would be more generous loss offset provisions for such business ventures.

The outline of the chapter is as follows. Section 1 lays out key assumptions, made in an attempt to keep the model as simple and transparent as seemed feasible. For one, we assume that individuals live for two periods, facing on average high risks in period 1 but much lower risks in period 2. Section 2 will then derive equilibrium locational choices for both young and old, for any given set of state income tax rates, with a focus on the empirical regularities forecast by the model. Section 3 will then use this model to solve for each state's choice of the generosity of its income tax/transfer program given the characteristics of its residents and possible mobility responses, maximizing the sum of the resulting dollar-equivalent benefits received by its initial residents. Section 4 will then analyze each of the roles described

12. We will show, however, that this particular attempt at a subsidy worsens allocations, by reducing the implicit insurance available to residents, in a setting in which there is too little insurance due to migration pressures.

13. However, raising moving costs also discourages individuals from migrating to a state with a more appropriate implicit insurance plan, or even moving to a new location within the same state.

above for the federal government, while section 5 will note some surprising forecasts from the model.

### 6.1. Key Assumptions of the Model

We assume that each individual $i$ lives for two periods, and works in both periods.[14] In the previous period, they lived in some state $h$. If they remain in that state, the ex post earnings for those in period 1 of their life would equal $\tilde{Y}_i^{1p} = Y_i(1 + \tilde{\epsilon}_i)$, where $Y_i$ is their initial expected income,[15] and $\tilde{\epsilon}_i$ is an idiosyncratic random shock to income in period 1, with variance $\sigma_i^2$. The ex post earnings for those in period 2 of their life would equal $\tilde{Y}_i^{2p} = \tilde{Y}_i^{1p}(1 + \tilde{\eta}_i)$, where $\tilde{\eta}_i$ is an idiosyncratic random shock to income with variance $\alpha\sigma_i^2$, with $\alpha < 1$.

Each individual in period 1 has a child. Her offspring will face her own idiosyncratic shocks over her life. The child's values for $Y_i$ and $\sigma_i$ can be correlated with those of her parent. These values depend in part on educational and occupational choices that can easily be affected by the parent's characteristics.

The role of state and local governments to begin with is to provide goods and services to residents. The Tiebout model (1956) assumes these expenditures are financed with user fees. Given heterogeneous preferences for such services within a jurisdiction, though, use of benefit taxes can help generate more efficient political choices for the level and composition of public services. Those with higher private consumption would presumably have higher demand as well for the consumption of government-provided services, providing some justification for sales taxes and property taxes to help finance local public services.

Normally, we would then argue that the use of taxes on consumption comes at the cost relative to user fees of discouraging the labor supply needed to finance extra consumption. In our context, though, consumption as well as income taxes help provide insurance to individuals against random future income, in itself an efficiency gain lost when user fees are employed instead. Our focus will then be on the trade-off between efficiency gains provided through the combined use of consumption and income taxes providing insurance for earnings risk along with a combination of public services and lump-sum transfers, while imposing offsetting costs by distorting labor supply, work effort, and tax compliance.

14. Assume for example, that individuals are aged 20 to 45 in the first period and aged 45 to 70 in the second period. Following this interpretation, individuals are born when their parent is aged 25, making them aged 20 at the beginning of the next period.

15. Given that reported income can depend on the tax rate the individual faces, we interpret $Y_i$ as the expected income they report in their current state of residence under that state's current tax law. If they move and as a result face a different tax rate, their expected reported income can change.

In general, the timing of income and consumption differs, with consumption smoothed relative to income. In our setting with a two-period life cycle model, the timing would differ only to the degree that individuals shift income across periods. To simplify the discussion, we ignore any savings (or borrowing) across these two periods, so that consumption and net income are equal within each period, after taking into account tax and transfer provisions. Given our assumption that expected income in period 2 is the same as ex post income in period 1, the individual faces no reason to borrow against future income.[16] In addition, we ignore precautionary savings in period 1 to help cushion any risks that will be faced in period 2.[17]

Use of an income tax could still have an advantage over a sales tax if individuals face borrowing constraints within each of the two periods.[18] It also has the advantage that it taxes all earnings, whereas state sales taxes cover only roughly a third of household consumption, introducing distortions to consumption bundles. Evasion rates could also differ between income and consumption taxes, with consumption taxes vulnerable to cash sales and cross-border shopping, while income taxes are vulnerable particularly to evasion by closely held businesses, an issue we return to below.[19] For simplicity, though, we focus on the combined tax rate on earnings (both when earned and when spent), and will simply refer to this combined tax as an "income" tax.

Each state $s$ imposes a linear income tax at rate $t_s$,[20] with per capita revenue equal to $T_s \equiv t_s\bar{Y}_s$, where $\bar{Y}_s$ is the average reported income among those who choose to reside in that state. The tax base for this tax is individual earnings, with, say, a cash-flow tax on business income to capture earnings retained within one's firm. This tax base then shares risks from idiosyncratic income reported in closely held firms as well as risks in wage income.

This tax revenue is used to finance public services as well as transfer payments. We assume for simplicity that the value of public services to residents

16. Given this assumption, we ignore another possible gain through use of an income tax, through providing net transfers to individuals in period 1 when their income is relatively low financed by net taxes on individuals in period 2 when their income is relatively high, thereby weakening possible borrowing constraints.

17. As seen in Kimball (1990), individuals would choose not to engage in precautionary savings if the third derivative of their utility (as a function of income) equals zero, an assumption we implicitly make below from making use of a second-order Taylor expansion of the individual's utility function.

18. Borrowing constraints are more likely the greater is the variance in the individual's income.

19. Gordon and Nielsen (1997) examine the relative evasion rates in Denmark of their income tax compared to their VAT, and found very similar overall evasion rates, with just a slight advantage to the VAT. However, the Danish VAT covers roughly two-thirds of consumption, whereas US state sales taxes cover only roughly one-third of consumption.

20. Here, we define $t_s$ as the income tax rate equivalent to the combined consumption and income taxes used in the state. Note that we do not attempt to solve for the optimal nonlinear tax schedule. Doing so would be much more complicated in our setting than in the past optimal-tax literature, since a change in any marginal tax rate now distorts the behavior of all taxpayers ex ante, given risk, and not just those individuals earning a specific level of income ex post.

can be measured simply by the expenditures on these services, and will treat overall government expenditures as if it were entirely a lump-sum transfer.[21]

Individuals have the option to move across states at the beginning of each period, once they learn the tax and transfer rates chosen by each state, paying a moving cost of $m_i$, where $m_i$ is presumed to be much lower in period 1 than in period 2 of a person's life. If an individual chooses to live in some state $s$, her ex post consumption equals $\tilde{C}_{is} = \tilde{Y}_i^p(1 - t_s) + t_s\bar{Y}_s - m_i\iota_{s\neq h}$, where $m_i$ is the fixed cost of migrating. Here, $\iota_{s\neq h} = 1$ if the individual chooses to move out of her home state $h$, and equals zero otherwise.

We do allow individuals to change their labor supply, the riskiness of their career choice, their effort, and their tax compliance behavior in response to any change in the taxes and transfers they face. In each case, these behavioral responses affect state tax revenue, but to first-order these changes would leave utility unaffected by the envelope condition.

Other than differences in $t_s$ and in $T_s$, for simplicity we assume states are equivalent. In particular, we assume enough local communities in each state that an individual can find a location offering the desired package of public goods and services. We ignore any amenity differences across states that might differentially affect individual or firm preferences across location. We assume that market-clearing wage rates are equalized across states, as would occur if the factor-input proportions differ enough across industries that the industry composition in each state can adjust to equalize wage rates across locations.

To differentiate our model from the traditional optimal income taxation model, we also ignore any justification for these taxes as a form of income redistribution by assuming that the ex ante marginal utility of an extra dollar is viewed to be the same for all households.[22] The policy focus will then be on maximizing efficiency, given the challenges of insuring income.

For simplicity, we will also ignore the presence of any form of private insurance for income risks, even though we recognize that some such insurance can be present. Such insurance could in principle exist through various routes. For one, family members can insure each other.[23] Churches or other

21. Any explicit discussion of expenditures on public services would face the issue not only of the marginal benefit to residents of cash versus additional public services but also of the effects of the composition of these expenditures on migration patterns. For example, providing services of particular value to high-income residents (such as a higher-quality state university system) has the added benefit to the state of keeping more high-income residents in the state's tax base.

22. We do this not because we think distributional issues should play no role in the policy debate, but in order to learn more about the implications of insurance motives per se for the income tax.

23. See Altonji et al. (1992), however, for empirical evidence that does not support the presence of this type of insurance between parents and children. However, two-earner households do help insure each other by pooling their income. We will then presume that two-earner couples tend to face lower risk relative to their combined income than one-earner couples or single individuals.

social "clubs" can help insure their members against adverse events, to the extent that they can make exit from the club costly. Firms can partially insure workers by having wage rates vary less over time than does the marginal product of the firm's workers, a form of insurance that can survive due to a firm's control over hours of work, due to costs incurred following a layoff in the event of low marginal products arising from high fixed costs to the firm of finding and training a replacement worker once marginal products increase, and due to the high costs to workers of exiting the firm when their marginal product is unusually high.[24]

We also for simplicity ignore land as an input to housing, avoiding the need to solve for equilibrium land prices. Land prices would depend heavily on the supply versus demand for space in states offering each particular level of insurance—for example, pushing large states to choose a tax/benefit schedule that appeals to a broader range of individuals, whereas small states can focus on more specialized parts of the market. Given the omission of land from the model, individuals face no constraints on moving into a state, other than the costs of moving there and the need to pay the tax rate charged by that state.

The sequence of events in each period is as follows. First, states choose their tax rate, raising this rate as long as the sum of the net dollar-equivalent benefits to existing residents from this change to the state's tax/transfer program is positive. Then individuals choose whether to migrate (at a cost) to a different state. Next, individuals learn their random draw on income, and consume their resulting after-tax earnings plus their lump-sum transfer.

An individual's expected utility in any given period and chosen state of residence equals

$$(1) \quad EU(\tilde{C}_{is}) \approx U(\bar{C}_{is}) + U'(\bar{C}_{is})E(\tilde{C}_{is} - \bar{C}_{is}) + 0.5U''(\bar{C}_{is})E(\tilde{C}_{is} - \bar{C}_{is})^2$$

$$= U(\bar{C}_{is}) - .5\rho_i U'(\bar{C}_{is})E(\tilde{C}_{is} - \bar{C}_{is})^2 / \bar{C}_{is}.$$

Here, we took a second-order Taylor expansion of utility, recognize that $E(\tilde{C}_{is}) = \bar{C}_{is}$, and then denote the individual's coefficient of relative risk aversion by $\rho_i \equiv -U''(\bar{C}_{is})\bar{C}_{is} / U'(\bar{C}_{is})$. While we allow $\rho_i$ to vary across individuals, we assume it is a fixed parameter for each individual.

### 6.2. Equilibrium Location Choices of Individuals

In equilibrium, we assume that $T_s$ is simply a function of $t_s$: If $T_s$ differed (even slightly) among states charging the same $t_s$, then nobody would choose to move to the state with the lower value of $T_s$, leading to a dramatic fall in that state's population. Similarly, if a state charged a higher tax rate but offered the same or lower net transfer as some other state with a lower tax

24. See Chetty and Saez (2010) for an analysis of the complications that arise in the design of an optimal taxation program in the presence of private income insurance.

rate, then nobody would choose to move to the higher-tax state. We then summarize the equilibrium net transfer by the function $T_s = f(t_s)$ with $f' > 0$, and the individual's choice set by the function $f(t_s) - m_i \iota_{s \neq h}$.

Consider first each individual's locational choice in period 2, where they take as given their initial locational choice and their expected income in period 2, $\tilde{Y}_i^{1p}$. Here, they either choose to remain in their initial state, denoted by $h$, or else move to their best alternative among the other states. In order to characterize their preferences, we derive the shape of their indifference curves, trading off a higher $t_s$ with a higher $T_s$.

Differentiating their utility function with respect to $t$ and then allowing that individual's transfer, denoted $T_i$, to adjust to leave utility unaffected on net, we find that

$$(2) \qquad \frac{\partial T_i}{\partial t} = \tilde{Y}_i^{1p}\left[1 - \frac{\rho_i \tilde{Y}_i^{1p}\alpha^2\sigma_i^2(1-t)}{\bar{C}_i D_i}\right]$$

Here, $D_i = 1 + .5\rho_i(1+\rho_i)(\tilde{Y}_i^{1p})^2\alpha^2\sigma_i^2(1-t)^2 / \bar{C}_i^2$. At first glance, it would seem that $\partial T_i / \partial t$ need not be positive. However, if it were negative then the individual would gain from reducing their $Y_i$, so that this case would never be seen in equilibrium. The observed indifference curve must then have a positive slope. The expression in brackets captures the gains from reduced risk-bearing costs resulting from a higher tax rate, in itself making the indifference curve flatter.

Taking a second derivative, we find that the second derivative equals zero when $T = 0$, given that $C_i = \tilde{Y}_i^{1p}(1-t) + T$,[25] and is positive when $T > 0$.[26]

We then conclude that these indifference curves are steeper for those with a higher income, and shallower, given income, for those facing more risk or those who are more risk averse. We then expect those with higher income and facing little risk to have a higher propensity to move to a low-tax state in period 2, whereas those with lower income or facing more risk will tend to move to high-tax states.[27] Given high moving costs, though, many individuals are likely to remain in the state they chose in period 1.

We capture this choice problem in figure 6.1. Here, the dotted curve represents the function $f(t_s)$, describing the available choice set individuals face if they move, along with the point labeled $H$ (higher by the amount $m_i$) if they choose not to move. The solid curve represents the points providing the same utility as staying in the current state. As drawn, the individual, ignoring moving costs would move to a state with a lower tax rate, but given moving costs chooses to remain in the state they chose in period 1.

25. An implication of constant relative risk aversion is that the risk premium is a constant fraction of income when the risk is a constant fraction of income.

26. Note that an exempt income of $E$ under a state income tax is equivalent to an addition to $T$ of $tE$, at least for those with $Y > E$.

27. Firms with high inherent risk, such as entrepreneurial start-ups, should then concentrate in high-tax states in order to more easily attract employees.

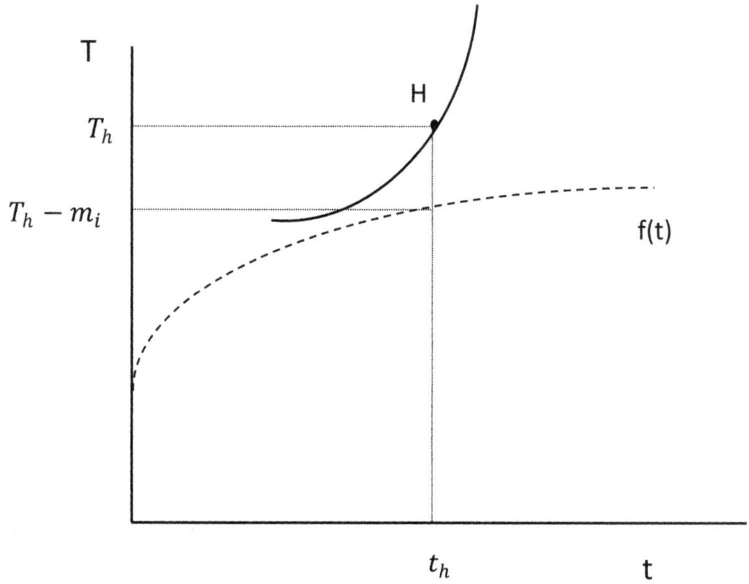


**Fig. 6.1 Individual location choice**

What about the individual's locational choice in period 1, assuming the individual was born in state $b$? Now, the individual is choosing a location to

$$\max_h \{EU(\tilde{C}_{i1} | b) + EU(\tilde{C}_{i2} | h, \tilde{\varepsilon}_i)\} \tag{3}$$

To begin with, ignore the option to move in period 2. In period 1, the individual faces much more risk than will be faced when making a locational decision in period 2, and also faces much lower moving costs. The young are therefore more likely than the old to locate in a high-tax state (buy more insurance).[28] In contrast, those with higher $Y$ and facing less risk could still choose to move to a lower-tax state.

The option to move in period 2 adds to the incentive to locate in a higher-tax state in period 1, since the individual can escape this high tax rate if their income turns out to be high enough to justify paying the migration costs of relocating.

One omission from the above expression, to avoid undue notation, is that an individual's choice of location in period 1 becomes the birth state of that individual's offspring. Given the correlation in incomes and risks across generations, the optimal choice for the offspring will be similar to that for

28. Since they were born in a state chosen by their young parents who also likely faced high risk when choosing where to live, they are likely already in a high-tax state and may well remain in that state rather than paying the moving costs to choose a somewhat different high tax rate. Those born in a low-tax state, in contrast, should have a greater propensity to move in period 1.

the parent. In any case, given low moving costs in period 1 this additional factor will likely be small.

The model then has some intriguing empirical forecasts, which are potentially testable. Among them:

Since the young face more uncertainty than those who are older about their future career paths, we would expect to see a differential propensity for the young to migrate to high-tax states for any given level of current income.

Young two-earner couples who choose to move, though, would have less incentive to move to high-tax states than one-earner couples or single individuals, for any given level of past income, given that they already pool risks within the family.

Innovative start-up firms should be particularly concentrated in high-tax states, since their employees as well as the entrepreneurs would particularly gain from having better insurance coverage.

Migrants from high-tax to low-tax states would tend to have high income and face relatively low risk.

High-tax states should then end up with a younger population, while low-tax states should have an older population, since those in period 2 have less need for insurance.

Those who choose to move to (stay in) a high-tax state should have greater dispersion in their future earnings than do otherwise identical individuals from the same initial state who chose not to move to (emigrate from) the high-tax state.[29]

High migration costs should discourage moves unless the resulting change in taxes and benefits is large enough. Migration rates should then be lower for residents in states with intermediate tax rates, while those who migrate would normally choose a substantial change in their tax rate (particularly for the old who are assumed to face much higher moving costs).

## 6.3. Equilibrium Choice of Tax Rate by Each State

Each state is assumed to raise its tax rate in a given period as long as the resulting dollar-equivalent benefits summed[30] across residents living in the state at the beginning of that period are positive.

29. This could occur due both to sorting and to behavioral responses in the amount of risk taking when more insurance is available.

30. Recall that we suppress any concern about distributional issues by giving equal weight to the dollar-equivalent ex ante benefits to each resident at each decision date. Note that under

Here, we preserve a feature of the optimal tax literature by taking as a social objective maximizing the sum of individual utilities. This focus on the average benefits to residents contrasts with the traditional focus in the political-economy literature on the median benefits to voters, where it is assumed that the median voter is decisive in any election. Our approach makes use of the income tax less appealing than it would be focusing on the preferences of the median voter, since the dollar impact of a marginal tax change on high-income residents can be dramatically larger than its dollar impact on even median-income residents. Use of a median voter model, though, is challenging in our context, since median preferences depend on the joint distribution of expected income, the degree of risk in income, and the degree of risk aversion, and not just the preferences of the individual with median income.

In solving for the tax rate that maximizes the sum of utilities, we need to take into account the labor supply and risk-taking incentives faced by each individual, as well as whether any of these individuals expect to migrate elsewhere in response to the choice of a state's tax rate, given the effects of these behavioral responses on the state budget and so on the equilibrium lump-sum transfer.[31]

There will be equal numbers of people entering period 2 and period 1 of their lives, given that those who had been in period 1 each had a child. Each cohort will then comprise half of the state's residents potentially impacted by a tax change.[32]

Here, we follow the assumptions made in the past optimal taxation literature, and ignore any altruistic preferences of parents (those in period 2 of their lives) toward their adult children (entering period 1 of their lives). In doing so, we deviate from Buchanan (1976), who argued that even quite wealthy parents could support use of the income tax because of the insurance benefits it provides to their children before their children's careers are well established. Under Buchanan's assumptions, support for the income tax would be considerably stronger.

For past residents, if they expect to migrate out of state given their current expected income and the future risks they face, then they will be unaffected by a marginal change in the state's tax rate.

the Von Neumann-Morgenstern assumptions, each individual's utility function is unique up to a linear transform. Here, we choose the units for each individual's utility function so that the expected marginal utility of income is equated across individuals.

31. One complication we ignore is that any migration that occurs in response to the choice of tax rate affects not only current tax revenue but also the set of individuals whose welfare affects the policy choice in the next period.

32. Note that our discussion, for simplicity, does not mention the children of those in period 1 of their life, who are also resident in the state for much of that period. Since the children are not working, they are impacted by state policy choices only due to changes in the lump-sum transfer. In our discussion below, we already take into account the aggregate lump-sum transfers in our measure of the sum of the benefits to state residents.

If a resident instead intends to remain in the state, then the dollar impact of a tax change on this individual depends on any impact on the lump-sum transfer they receive from the government minus its impact on the certainty-equivalent income they are left with after taxes:

$$(4) \qquad \frac{1}{U_i'}\frac{\partial U_i}{\partial t_s} = \bar{Y}_s\left(1 - e_s\frac{t_s}{1-t_s}\right) - Y_i\left(1 - \frac{\rho_i Y_i \alpha^2 \sigma_i^2 (1-t_s)}{\bar{C}_i D_i}\right)$$

Here $e_s$ denotes the elasticity of the state's average reported income with respect to the fraction of income left net of tax, $(1 - t_s)$. This average income can change due to changes in each resident's labor supply, effort, or tax compliance, the standard focus. It also changes due to migration in and out of the state of rich versus poor, and also due to changes in risk taking by existing residents. While $e_s$ would be positive due to the first effect,[33] the third effect pushes in the opposite direction (since more risk taking adds to an individual's expected income).[34] The strong presumption is that migration responses to a tax increase also impose a net cost on the state, as some rich residents leave and some poor individuals migrate in, attracted by the resulting higher transfer payments.[35]

Note that past empirical estimates for this elasticity of taxable income make use of national tax changes, thereby leaving out any migration response. In addition, they likely fail to capture well any resulting changes in risk taking.[36]

Adding up these dollar impacts on residents and setting this sum to zero to solve for the optimal tax rate, we find at the optimal tax rate that

$$(5) \qquad \bar{Y}_s\left(1 - e_s\frac{t_s}{1-t_s}\right) = \bar{Y}^{st}(1 - \Pi_s), \text{ or}$$

$$(5a) \qquad (\bar{Y}_s - \bar{Y}^{st}) + \bar{Y}^{st}\Pi_s = \bar{Y}_s e_s \frac{t_s}{1-t_s}.$$

Here, $\bar{Y}^{st}$ denotes the average expected income among past residents who decide to stay in the state, while $\Pi_s$ is the weighted average benefits from extra

33. Any drop in tax revenue due to a reduction in labor supply or effort implies an efficiency cost, while any drop due to increases in evasion are partially an efficiency cost (see Chetty 2009).

34. See Domar and Musgrave (1944) for an early recognition of this behavioral response to taxes. For empirical support for this forecast, see Bird (2001) and Cullen and Gordon (2007).

35. This strong presumption comes from a setting without risk. However, the migration from low-tax to high-tax states of individuals facing high future risks in itself likely leads to a net fiscal loss to these low-tax states. (This migration would be a form of brain-drain, as the most energetic and ambitious residents migrate elsewhere to pursue high-risk ventures, hoping to "make it big.")

36. Increased risk taking would result in an immediate fall in income when start-ups first enter, hoping to develop a new product/process, or when an individual first shifts to a riskier occupation, even though expected income should eventually be higher. Event studies would then systematically underestimate the longer-run impact of a tax change on state income, focusing on the discontinuity in reported income in the immediate period following a discrete change in tax rates.

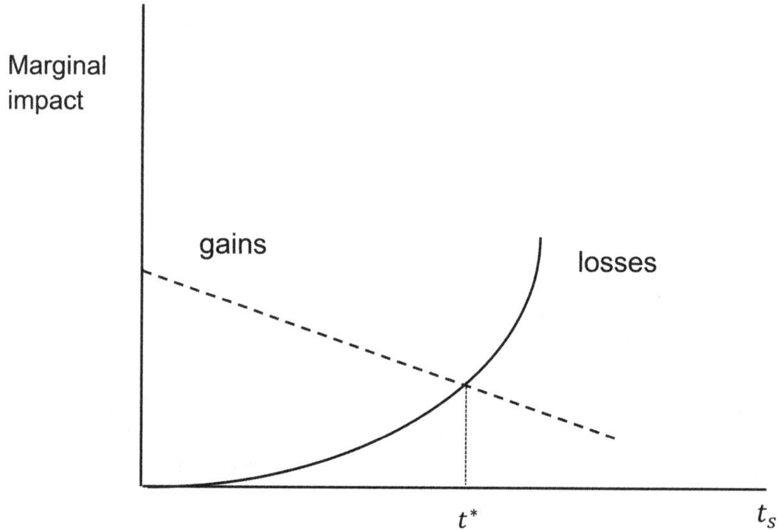


**Fig. 6.2 State choice of tax rate**

risk sharing among these stayers. As seen in this expression, individuals are trading off the gains from extra risk sharing due to a higher tax rate with the costs through added distortions to various dimensions of behavior. In addition, taxes are more attractive for initial residents to the extent that their expected tax payments are less than their expected lump-sum transfers, due to the difference between $\bar{Y}^{st}$ and $\bar{Y}_s$.

$\bar{Y}_s > \bar{Y}^{st}$ to the extent that the average income of those who migrate into the state exceeds the average income of those who stay in the state, and conversely. We expect that low-tax (high-tax) states attract individuals with unusually high (low) income, who are willing to pay the moving costs to face a lower tax rate (higher lump-sum transfer). We then expect $\bar{Y}_s > \bar{Y}^{st}$ in low-tax states, and conversely for high-tax states. This extra term then serves to reduce the dispersion in tax rates.[37]

In figure 6.2, we graph the expressions on the two sides of equation (5a). The curve reflecting the efficiency costs arising from the resulting drop in reported taxable income (as a function of $t_s$) is the solid curve. This curve starts at zero and is upward sloping and convex for a given value of $e_s$, due to the way $t_s$ enters the expression.

The curve reflecting the gains to those staying in the state from sharing more risk with the government as well as through preexisting migration

37. Note that the extra term $(\bar{Y}_s - \bar{Y}^{st})$ introduces a trade-off between efficiency and redistribution, now not redistribution between rich and poor but instead between remaining and new residents.

patterns on the average income is captured by the dashed curve, which is downward sloping since further marginal risk-sharing gains become smaller as individuals are left with less risk net-of-tax. Where the curves cross would be the optimal choice for $t_s$, denoted by $t^*$.

The extent of insurance provision is then limited by the range of behavioral responses captured by the parameter $e_s$. Among these responses is the effects of a higher tax rate in a state on the equilibrium sorting of individuals across states. A change in sorting patterns in response to a tax change implies positive fiscal externalities, with richer individuals fleeing to other states, and poor individuals in other states leaving, attracted by a now higher transfer payment in the state raising its tax rate. Because of these externalities, states will choose too low income tax rates from a national perspective. The next section focuses on possible federal policy responses.

## 6.4. Implications for Possible Federal Government Interventions

### 6.4.1. Use of the Federal Income Tax as a Base-Level Tax

One possible federal policy response, which of course we see, is to impose a federal income tax, at some tax rate denoted $t_F$, which in effect serves as a base level tax from which the states may choose to impose a supplementary income tax.[38]

Consider first the impact of a federal tax on the chosen state tax rates. Let $\tau \equiv t_F + t_s$ denote the combined tax rate affecting individuals in each state $s$.[39] Note that the value of $\tau_s$ that solves the equation

$$(\bar{Y}_s - \bar{Y}^{st}) + \bar{Y}^{st}\Pi_s = \bar{Y}_s e_s \frac{\tau_s}{1-\tau_s} \tag{5b}$$

equals the tax rate $t_s$ that solves equation (5a) if the other parameters remain the same.[40] If this were the equation determining state tax rates, then we find a one-for-one drop in state tax rates when a federal tax rate is imposed, leaving individual behavioral incentives unchanged.

The right-hand side of equation (5b), though, takes into account the drop in both state and federal tax revenue due to the elasticity of taxable income

38. The question analyzed in this section overlaps with that analyzed in Gordon and Cullen (2012). However, that paper focused on a setting where states are identical, contrary to the setting in this chapter.

39. Here, we ignore the possible deductibility from federal taxable income of state tax payments as an itemized deduction.

40. Note in particular that $\bar{Y}_s$ remains unchanged only if the federal income taxes collected from any given state are then used entirely to finance a lump-sum transfer to residents of that state, thereby avoiding any redistribution across states. If the federal government considered in addition possible lump-sum transfers between states, further improvements in allocations would be possible to the extent that transfers are targeted at states where residents have a greater propensity to undertake additional risks.

with respect to the income tax. Yet any state would have reason to take into account any resulting drop in federal tax revenue only to the extent that this drop is borne by residents in the state. Even a large state would bear only a small fraction of the federal tax loss resulting from an increase in that state's tax rate. Replacing the right-hand side of equation (5b) with the impact of changes in reported earnings on just that state's tax revenue, as in equation (5a), leads to higher equilibrium state tax rates than implied by a one-for-one offset.

Given that individuals already receive some insurance through the federal tax/transfer system, however, the marginal gains to state residents from further insurance through a state tax/transfer system are reduced. This drop in the size of $\Pi_s$ would be large in states where residents face significant risks, and would be zero (in the limit) in a state where residents faced no risk. The optimal state tax rate is reduced in response to the introduction of a federal tax, particularly in states where it had been higher, even if the fall in tax rate is not one-for-one.

As a result, the dispersion in state tax rates will be reduced. Tax rates in the low-tax state remain positive, since both terms on the left-hand side of equation (5b) are positive, while tax rates fall in the high-tax states due to the introduction of a federal tax. The reduced dispersion in state tax rates implies weaker migration incentives, in itself an efficiency gain, given the negative externalities generated by migration decisions. In addition, weaker migration incentives lead to lower elasticities $e_s$, pushing the differentials $(\bar{Y}_s - \bar{Y}^{st})$ toward zero. Each of these changes in themselves improve state allocations, conditional on federal tax revenue.

The initial problem motivating federal intervention was that state decisions on their tax rates generate positive externalities in other states, implying too low equilibrium tax rates. Now, however, state taxes impose negative fiscal externalities on the federal government to the extent that individuals in response report lower taxable income, a negative externality that is greater the higher the federal tax rate. Gordon and Cullen (2012) in a setting with many identical states, then argue that state incentives in setting their tax rates are efficient when the federal tax rate is high enough that the negative externality imposed on the federal government by an increase in any given state's tax rate just offsets the positive externalities this tax change creates for other states.

In our setting, in contrast, states are heterogeneous. At the optimal federal tax rate, the aim is instead to choose a federal tax rate such the sum of the costs from having net positive externalities generated by tax changes in some states and net negative externalities generated by tax changes in other states are minimized. Positive horizontal externalities will outweigh the negative vertical externalities in the states generating the largest spillovers (presumably the states with the most extreme tax rates, low and high), leading to too low tax rates from a federal perspective in these states. In contrast, states generating the smallest spillovers (presumably those with intermediate tax rates, where the benefits from migration will be low enough to discourage much migration) will generate negative net externalities, leading them to choose too high tax rates from a federal perspective. The optimal federal tax rate trades off the costs from having too high tax rates in some states, and too low tax rates in other states.

### 6.4.2. Allowing State Income Tax Payments as an Itemized Deduction

Even with the optimal use of a federal income tax, equilibrium tax rates in the states choosing the highest-tax rates will still be too low from a federal perspective, even if the chosen tax rates are too high in states with intermediate tax rates.

One other policy response that targets mainly higher-income individuals in high-tax states is the availability of state sales or income tax payments as an itemized deduction under the federal income tax. With this provision, an individual saves on taxes an amount equal to $t_F t_s \tilde{Y}_i$, assuming the individual's other itemized deductions are already larger than the standard deduction. The tax savings then are focused on individuals with high income living in states with a high tax rate.

Allowing state sales and income tax payments as an itemized deduction lowers the cost to a state of raising its tax rate, and raises the cost to an individual of moving from a high-tax to a low-tax state (and then having lower itemized deductions). In this section, we confirm that this provision leads to higher equilibrium state tax rates and lower migration rates. But we will then argue that this provision reduces equilibrium insurance provision, and on net is counterproductive.

Consider first the effects of this policy on migration decisions of high-income individuals in period 2, considering a move from a high-tax to a low-tax state. The tax savings from the itemized deduction equal $t_F t_s \tilde{Y}_i$, assuming all tax payments can be deducted. If the individual moves to a low-tax state, however, these deductions are much smaller due to the lower state tax rate. This differential tax savings will then lead fewer people to migrate.

Itemizers who remain in the high-tax state are partly those who would have stayed even without this itemization provision, plus those who choose to stay only because of it. Both groups benefit from the added itemized deduction, but only the second set of itemizers changed their migration decision, implying potentially large budgetary outlays for any given reduction in migration propensities. Financing these outlays has efficiency costs.[41] From its effects on migration alone, support for this provision would be unclear.

What about effects of this provision on the tax rates chosen by states? How do preferences of residents over the state's tax rate change in response to this

41. There would in general also be equity costs from a transfer focused on the highest-income individuals, costs we ignore in our focus on efficiency effects of insurance provision.

itemization provision? If individuals can always deduct their state income taxes under the federal tax, then an increase in the tax rate by $dt/(1 - t_F)$ now has the same effect on the distribution of after-tax income as would an increase in the tax rate by $dt$ without this provision. For those who itemize, the optimal state tax rate would then go up by the multiple $1/(1 - t_F)$. However, given that most individuals do not itemize, state tax rates would go up by much less than this multiple.

The policy concern, however, is not per se that tax rates are too low in high-tax states, but that insurance provision in these states is too limited. With this deductibility of state tax payments, individuals face a lower marginal tax rate, implying that they now bear greater risk. By introducing this itemized deduction, the efficiency gains that resulted from transferring risk from individuals to the government are then reduced. In addition, having to bear a larger fraction of any risks, individuals will choose to take on less risk, implying a further efficiency loss. The resulting increase in the state's chosen tax rate would not be enough to offset this impact on the allocation of risk. Allowing state tax payments as an itemized deduction as a result imposes efficiency losses through its effects on risk taking.

### 6.4.3. Policies That Affect Moving Costs

As seen in equation (5a), the provision of insurance through the income tax is limited because of the offsetting costs arising from the resulting tax distortions affecting both reported labor income and migration decisions. Migration decisions create positive fiscal externalities to the budgets of other states.

Even under the optimal federal tax rate, there would still be too much migration on efficiency grounds, leaving a potential role for interventions that reduce migration rates. In particular, the effects of an individual's migration from a high-tax state $b$ to a low-tax state $a$ implies a gain to the budget in state $a$ equal to $t_a(Y_i + \Delta Y_i) - T_a$ and a change in the budget of state $b$ equal to $T_b - t_b Y_i$. Here, $\Delta Y_i > 0$ to the extent that the individual reports higher earnings, now that the individual faces a lower tax rate.[42] In addition, the impact of this migration decision on the federal budget equals $t_F \Delta Y_i$.

If the individual were just indifferent to this move, then the combined fiscal externalities of this move equal the sum of these three terms:[43]

$$(6) \qquad t_a(Y_i + \Delta Y_i) - T_a + (T_b - t_b Y_i) + t_F \Delta Y_i$$

$$(6a) \qquad \approx (t_b - t_a)\left[\bar{Y}_b - Y_i\left(1 - e_i \frac{\tau_a}{1 - \tau_a}\right)\right] - t_a(\bar{Y}_a - \bar{Y}_b).$$

42. But expected reported earnings can also fall due to a choice to pursue a less risky career, now facing less insurance coverage.

43. To derive the second line, we made use of the definitions of price elasticity of income and of the $T_s$.

Given the presumption that the highest income individuals will be the ones most likely to migrate to save on taxes, we would expect $Y_i \gg \bar{Y}_b$, leading to a negative first term in equation (6a) for any plausible elasticity of reported taxable income. Given the migration of the high income to low-tax states and the low income to high-tax states, we would also expect $\bar{Y}_a > \bar{Y}_b$, implying that the second term in equation (6a) will also be negative. Together these imply a negative net externality from marginal migration decisions, leaving open an independent role for interventions to reduce migration.[44]

Consider then the treatment of moving costs under the federal income tax. Until the 2017 tax legislation, moving costs (under certain conditions) were a deductible expense under the income tax. This deduction has been suspended during 2017–2025 except for those moving to a new job. To what degree can this policy choice affect the efficiency of allocation decisions in our setting?

Restrictions on exit from an insurance plan play a major role in the survival of an insurance plan. Our model built in strong restrictions on migration by assuming individuals can move only twice in their lives. Without any restrictions or costs of migration, an insurance package can easily unravel, with only those residents in a state experiencing the worst outcomes in equilibrium remaining covered by any insurance plan, with others migrating to states with lower tax rates, causing a breakdown in any insurance coverage. The lack of any cost of exit from a plan insuring income risk explains the lack of a private market for such insurance.

Some restrictions on exit therefore raise efficiency, with more insurance being provided in equilibrium the higher these exit costs. If there were no other reason for moving other than to escape the high taxes faced in the state where one currently resides, if and when an individual learns that their future income will be high, then the most efficient policy choice would be arbitrarily high moving costs for the old in period 2.[45]

What about migration decisions made in period 1? Costs faced to enter a plan could improve allocations to the extent that they discourage people moving simply to claim a higher lump-sum payment, but worsen allocations to the extent they lead to a worse match between individuals and insurance plans. Individuals who grew up in a low-tax state *a* would choose to move to a high-tax state *b* whenever

$$T_b - T_a > (t_b - t_a)Y_i + m_i - Y_i(RP_a - RP_b). \quad (7)$$

44. The expression for the net externality from the migration of individuals from a low-tax state to a high-tax state will also be negative unless the migration is dominated not by the low income but by those facing substantial future risks.

45. When a high-income resident exits in response to a marginal increase in the state's tax rate, this decision has only a second-order effect on that individual's utility by the envelope condition. However, that state loses tax revenue, lowering the welfare of the remaining residents in the state.

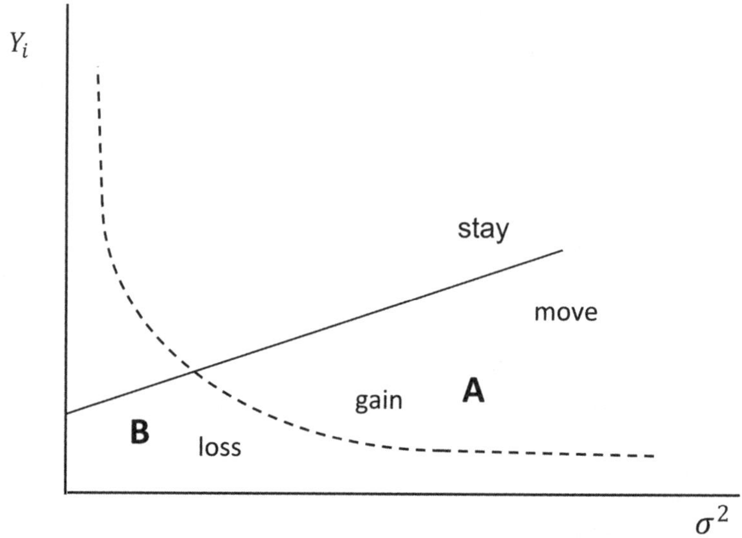


**Fig. 6.3 Migration patterns**

Here, $RP_s$ denotes the risk premium (as a fraction of expected income) if the individual chooses to live in state $s$. For any given level of risk an individual faces, equation (7) then implies that individuals move only if their expected income is below some level (a higher cut-off the more future risk they face).

The net fiscal impact of a move on the combined tax revenue in these two states equals $(t_b - t_a)Y_i - T_b + T_a + t_b\Delta Y_i$, where $Y_i$ measures the change in the individual's reported income due to the move to a high-tax state.[46] For an individual just indifferent to moving, the net social gain from the move then equals

$$(8) \qquad Y_i(RP_a - RP_b) - m_i + t_b\Delta Y_i.$$

Figure 6.3 describes both who chooses to move and then which moves imply a net social gain or loss. The solid line captures the implications of equation (7) characterizing which individuals choose to move, while the dashed line describes the set of individuals whose move would imply zero net social gain or loss based on equation (8). Individuals located in area A represent movers who provide a net social gain from moving through improved risk allocations dominating, while those in area B represent movers who impose a net social loss due to their moving costs dominating. The

46. $Y_i$ would be positive to the extent individuals shift to a riskier career due to better insurance protection, but negative to the extent that the higher tax rate discourages labor supply and effort, and leads to more evasion.

net social gain is more positive (more negative) the further individuals are to the northeast (southwest) of the dashed curve.

If the government were to use tax policy to either aid or discourage moves, this would affect equation (7) describing individual migration decisions, shifting this curve up or down, but not affect equation (8) since true mobility costs would not be affected. Whether an intervention helps or hurts is unclear in general, depending on the density functions for moving costs, expected income, and risk premia.

Deductibility of moving costs under the income tax has only minimal effects on the moving costs for the young (whose possessions likely fit in their car trunk), while facilitating moves by the old. From the perspective of our model, this policy would be counterproductive, leading to worse fiscal externalities and an undermining of the provision of income insurance.

An alternative policy that also discourages moves is the provision that imposes a capital-gains tax on owner-occupied housing at the time of sale, rather than, for example, an earlier policy that allowed a deferral of this tax if a new property of at least comparable value was purchased around the same time. Given the tax savings in present value resulting from deferral of capital-gains liabilities, taxing capital gains whenever the individual moves does discourage migration of the old without affecting migration of the young (who even if they owned housing would not have owned for long enough to have much capital gains).[47] Omitted from our model, though, is any other reason for a move, such as moving to a job that provides a better match for the individual's skills, or moving to be nearer to key friends and relatives.

A formal analysis could trade off these various offsetting effects of higher moving costs. Instead, we turn to other possible policy responses.

### 6.4.4. Tax Provisions Affecting Closely Held Firms

There are many sources of risky labor income. One important source of risky income is employment in a closely held firm, particularly in a firm engaged in innovative activity. Around two-thirds of start-up firms fail within a relatively short period of time, though a subset can be spectacularly successful. Often, employees in these firms are paid in part through stock options, implying risky income while employed in addition to any risk of continuing employment.

It is worth considering then the tax treatment of closely held firms, including sole proprietorships, partnerships, LLC firms, and to some degree subchapter S corporations, income in each case taxed under the personal income tax. Risks faced by publicly traded corporations, in contrast, should already be allocated efficiently across the economy through the stock market.

47. However, it also discourages within-state moves, a net cost.

There are various ways in which policy provisions can affect the allocation of risks generated by these firms, and their incentives to undertake further risks. One approach was tried in a dramatic fashion in Kansas during 2012–2017, when the income tax rate on closely held firms was set to zero. The 2017 federal tax reform also reduced the effective personal tax rate on income from a specified subset of closely held firms to 80 percent of the normal rate.

By imposing a lower tax rate on particular firms, these tax changes distorted the allocation of economic activity, in itself imposing efficiency costs. The main potential source of offsetting efficiency gains would be through increased risk taking. Yet as a result of these cuts in marginal tax rates, less of the risky income generated in these firms is offloaded onto the government, leaving higher risk-bearing costs to the owners and employees in these firms. Risk-bearing costs as a result are higher, and further risk taking is discouraged.

A contrasting approach would be to raise rather than lower the marginal tax rate on such activity, shifting more of the resulting risk to the government, but to complement this higher tax rate with more generous deductions in order to maintain the level of activity in this sector.[48] In combination, these policies can in principle maintain the level of employment and investment in this sector but lower the overall costs of risk bearing and encourage more risk taking in this sector.

Any differential tax treatment of closely held and publicly traded firms, though, opens up opportunities for tax avoidance through shifting profits between a closely held firm and a jointly owned publicly traded corporation.[49] If these same tax provisions (a higher marginal tax rate and more generous deductions) were offered to both corporate and closely held firms, these particular tax avoidance opportunities could be avoided. Corporate investment incentives can be preserved through the appropriate degree of generosity of various deductions. The main cost is likely to be income shifting by multinationals, now facing a higher tax rate on profits reported in the US, to their foreign subsidiaries.

Another important aspect of the taxation of closely held firms, ignored so far in the discussion, is the high rate of tax evasion among such firms. While closely held firms may aggressively pursue available opportunities to hide profits, though, they have every incentive to document any tax losses they experience. One policy choice is how much effort to expend to detect and penalize such tax evasion. By preserving the sharing of any losses with the government, but allowing these firms to retain a larger fraction of their

48. For example, the types of capital used in these firms could be granted more accelerated depreciation provisions.

49. The threat of this type of tax avoidance was likely a key reason why the 2017 federal tax reform lowered the tax rates on corporate and closely held firms in tandem.

profits, lax tax enforcement would still lead to risk sharing for the outcomes that would have been particularly costly for firms to bear while in the process encouraging greater risk taking. Of course, any efficiency gains through the resulting risk-taking incentives must be balanced against costs arising from the resulting differential taxation of closely held and publicly traded firms, but also taking into account the cost savings from less aggressive tax enforcement.

Yet another aspect of the tax treatment of closely held firms is the specific tax treatment of any losses they experience. One particular provision of the 2017 federal tax reform was the elimination of any deductibility of noncorporate business losses against other personal taxable income. The effects of this provision on risk taking is the reverse of the effects of weak tax enforcement. With this provision, firms bear all of any losses they experience, but receive only the after-tax share of any profits they generate. This provision therefore raises risk-bearing costs and discourages risk taking, in both cases generating an efficiency loss.

## 6.5. Some Surprising Implications of the Model

A key focus of this chapter dealt with the effects of the income tax both on the incentives to pursue jobs with riskier income and on the overall costs of bearing the risks in this income. There is a long-standing literature, dating back to Domar and Musgrave (1944), arguing that a higher income tax rate lowers the costs of bearing idiosyncratic earnings risk, and as a result encourages more risk taking.

While these effects of taxes have been recognized for a long time, their implications are often overlooked. This section will highlight two of them.

For one, there is a longstanding presumption that when a state raises its income tax rate, it induces a migration pattern that provides positive fiscal externalities to other states.[50] Higher-income individuals in the state may now find it worth the cost to migrate elsewhere, while lower-income residents elsewhere may now be tempted to move to the state that raised its tax rate and as a consequence raised its lump-sum transfer.

Yet, when a state raises its tax rate, it also makes the state a more attractive location for those residents living elsewhere who face high risks and would be willing to pay a higher tax rate in order to obtain better insurance against these risks. Individuals facing high risks in exchange must be earning higher expected income, to be willing to face these risks. Attracting the ambitious risk takers from other states, then, could well impose a negative fiscal externality on these other states, at least raising a question whether the overall fiscal externalities generated when a state raises its tax rate are positive.

50. I have followed this presumption throughout the chapter.

Another long-standing presumption is that when a state raises its tax rate, the resulting behavioral responses will inevitably lower the reported income in the state, through adverse migration responses as well as through fewer hours of work, less work effort, and greater tax avoidance activity.

Yet if we look at the data, per capita incomes are if anything higher in states with high tax rates (states such as California, Massachusetts, and New York). Yes, there can be many possible explanations for high per capita incomes specific to any given state. For example, the agglomeration economies generated by the concentration of activity in Silicon Valley, along Route 128, or on Wall Street may be so strong that long-standing activity in these locations continues even when tax rates in the state rise. Alternatively, high-income individuals are willing to spend a larger fraction of their income on having access to amenities, such as being able to live in a nice climate. This taste makes the rich relatively immobile, enabling a state in a nice climate to raise its income tax rate without inducing much exit, potentially explaining higher observed incomes in California (but maybe not in New York or Massachusetts).

The effects of taxes on migration patterns and risk-taking incentives, though, provide yet another potential explanation for the observed high incomes in states with high income tax rates. In particular, the counterfactual forecast that higher-income individuals concentrate in tax havens can be reversed if these individuals face enough risk relative to lower-income individuals. Certainty the fraction of the high-income individuals active in a closely held firm is dramatically higher than for lower-income residents. The variability of ex post lifetime income among college graduates is also high relative to that of the rest of the population. Even ignoring effects of taxes on migration patterns, those living in a high-tax state face greater incentives to engage in risk-taking activity, again in the process raising per capita income in the state. Our model provides then yet another explanation for the observed high incomes in high-tax states.

I hope this chapter encourages future researchers to undertake empirical work looking at risk-taking propensities among residents in high-tax compared to low-tax states, and also to look at migration patterns between states, to see if those who move to high-tax states are often high income and tend to work in risky sectors. Such research, looking at the effects of taxes on the variance of income as well as on expected income, would be a welcome addition to the literature.[51] That taxes should affect risk-taking propensities seems clear from the theory. Whether these effects are large or small, though, requires empirical work to document.

51. In particular, by the above theory, a state's tax increase should lead to an increase in individual risk-taking propensities. Given the costs of any induced changes in occupation or location, income would be expected to fall initially, but in the longer run expected income should be higher, and the variance of ex post income should be higher (and growing relatively over time) than in other states.

**Acknowledgments**

I would like to thank Julie Cullen, James Hines, and Michelle White, as well as participants in the Policy Responses to Tax Competition Conference for comments on an earlier draft of the paper that became this chapter. For acknowledgments, sources of research support, and disclosure of the author's material financial relationships, if any, please see https://www.nber.org/books-and-chapters/policy-responses-tax-competition/fiscal-federalism-and-role-income-tax.

## References

Akcigit, Ufuk, Salome Baslandze, and Stefanie Stantcheva. 2016. "Taxation and the International Mobility of Inventors." *American Economic Review* 106: 2930–81.

Altonji, Joseph, Fumio Hayashi, and Laurence Kotlikoff. 1992. "Is the Extended Family Altruistically Linked? Direct Tests Using Micro Data." *American Economic Review* 82: 1177–98.

Bird, Edward J. 2001. "Does the Welfare State Induce Risk-Taking?" *Journal of Public Economics* 80: 357–83.

Buchanan, James. 1976. "Taxation in Fiscal Exchange." *Journal of Public Economics* 6: 17–29.

Chetty, Raj. 2009. "Is the Taxable Income Elasticity Sufficient to Calculate Deadweight Loss? The Implications of Evasion and Avoidance." *American Economic Journal: Economic Policy* 1: 31–52.

Chetty, Raj, and Emmanuel Saez. 2010. "Optimal Taxation and Social Insurance with Endogenous Private Insurance." *American Economic Journal: Economic Policy* 2: 85–114.

Cullen, Julie Berry, and Roger H. Gordon. 2007. "Taxes and Entrepreneurial Risk-Taking: Theory and Evidence for the U.S." *Journal of Public Economics* 91: 1479–1505.

Diamond, Peter. 1977. "A Framework for Social Security Analysis." *Journal of Public Economics* 8: 275–98.

Domar, Evsey, and Richard Musgrave. 1944. "Proportional Income Taxation and Risk-Taking." *Quarterly Journal of Economics* 58: 388–422.

Gordon, Roger. 1985. "Taxation of Corporate Capital Income: Tax Revenues vs. Tax Distortions." *Quarterly Journal of Economics* 100: 1–27.

Gordon, Roger, and Julie Berry Cullen. 2012. "Income Redistribution in a Federal System of Governments." *Journal of Public Economics* 96: 1100–09.

Gordon, Roger, and Søren Bo Nielsen. 1997. "Tax Evasion in an Open Economy: Value-Added vs. Income Taxation." *Journal of Public Economics* 66: 173–97.

Gruber, Jon, and Emmanuel Saez. 2002. "The Elasticity of Taxable Income: Evidence and Implications." *Journal of Public Economics* 84: 1–32.

Hoynes, Hilary, and Erzo Luttmer. 2011. "The Insurance Value of State Tax-and-Transfer Programs." *Journal of Public Economics 95*: 1466–84.

Kaplow, Louis. 1995. "A Fundamental Objection to Tax Equity Norm." *National Tax Journal* 48: 497–514.

Kimball, Miles. 1990. "Precautionary Savings in the Small and in the Large." *Econometrica* 58: 53–73.

Oates, Wallace. 1972. *Fiscal Federalism*. Harcourt Brace Jovanovich.
Rawls, John. 1971. *Theory of Justice*. Belknap.
Schmidt, Lawrence. 2022. "Climbing and Falling Off the Ladder: Asset Pricing Implications of Labor Market Event Risk." http://dx.doi.org/10.2139/ssrn.2471342.
Stepner, Michael. 2019. "The Insurance Value of Redistributive Taxes and Transfers." Unpublished paper.
Tiebout, Charles. 1956. "A Pure Theory of Local Expenditures." *Journal of Political Economy* 64: 416–24.

## Comment James R. Hines Jr.

### Federalism and Tax Competition

Economic mobility forces governments to compete, both within and across federations. Not every jurisdiction openly acknowledges this competition or even necessarily understands that it is happening, nor do they all welcome it, but all feel its effects. Tax competition arises because economic activity gravitates to locations where it finds the best deals. Governments are eager to attract economic activity and loath to lose it, so they try to avoid policies that would drive valuable activity elsewhere. Economic actors with the most income at stake benefit from low tax rates. This inevitably puts downward pressure on tax rates, which is the basis of classic works on horizontal tax competition and the associated race to the bottom.[1]

Roger Gordon's intriguing chapter calls attention to a fascinating alternative possibility: that at least some governments might compete with others by offering higher tax rates. How is it possible to compete this way, given that nobody who pays taxes actually prefers to be subject to a higher tax rate, all other things equal? Naturally, it has to be the case that not all other things are equal. In particular, in the Gordon framework, governments imposing high tax rates use tax revenue to provide larger-than-average transfers to all residents. If governments differ in the taxes they exact and the transfers they offer, with higher tax rates accompanied by larger transfers, then taxpayers in choosing where to locate get to select whether they prefer socialism (high tax rates and generous government transfers) or capitalism (low tax rates and skimpy transfers). The point of the Gordon chapter is that many, including some with high expected incomes, will choose socialism—doing so strictly on the basis of self-interest. Tax payments by rich socialists pro-

James R. Hines Jr. is the Richard A. Musgrave Collegiate Professor of Economics at the University of Michigan and a research associate of the National Bureau of Economic Research.

1. See, for example, Baldwin and Krugman (2004); Black and Hoyt (1989); Bucovetsky (1991); Bucovetsky and Wilson (1991); Keen and Konrad (2013); Rota-Graziosi (2019); Wildasin (1988); Wilson (1986, 1999); Zodrow and Mieszkowski (1986).

vide much of the funding that makes it possible for governments to finance the promised transfer payments, and so a high-tax party is sustainable.

The governments in this model do not know that they compete with others, nor do they care; the model posits that governments choose policies designed to maximize outcomes for their existing residents, regardless of policy options elsewhere. The reality is that not everyone will continue to live in the jurisdiction once these governments adopt policies designed to help them, because taxpayer circumstances will change and they will discover even more attractive deals elsewhere; some existing residents of other places will move in to take their places. While government policies are therefore myopic, and as a result suboptimal from the standpoint of the people that the governments represent, these myopic policies are not *too* bad in this context, since the model assumes away the existence (or at least the importance) of land. Without land, the only things fixed in a location are the people who find it too costly to move. These less-than-fully-mobile residents would prefer their government to be a bit more forward looking, adopting policies that might draw in rich socialists who will help fund generous transfers for themselves and others. Governments do some of that without really trying, but of course if you try you can do even better. Tax policy is therefore not quite ideal from the standpoint of current residents, though arguably good enough for government work.

The Gordon model serves as a useful reminder that any time there is economic mobility of any kind, governments face a competitive setting. Indeed, even without mobility it is possible to have competition—residents of Maine might compete with Alaskans to produce the most elegant ice sculptures, even if neither the sculptures nor the sculptors ever move and nobody else cares—but mobility surely stiffens competition, a reality that governments ignore at their peril.

## Taxes as Insurance

The point of departure for the Gordon chapter is the insurance function of taxation. If individuals are risk averse, have uncertain incomes, and are unable to obtain private insurance, then government can provide a form of insurance through compulsory taxation. In the Gordon model, tax-based insurance takes the form of paying a fixed percentage of income to the government in return for a lump-sum transfer that is the same for all taxpayers in the jurisdiction. This is a stylized arrangement, and, viewed strictly as an insurance policy, would not be much of a deal for high-income taxpayers, because while their expected tax payments increase with their expected incomes, their expected transfer receipts do not. For the same reason, it is an excellent deal for low-income taxpayers. The analogy to a fire insurance policy would be one where homeowners pay insurance premiums that are proportional to the value of their homes, but in the event that a house burns down, the homeowner receives the average value of a house in his or her town. The problems of such policy terms are obvious: those in fancy homes would pay heavily for inadequate insurance, while those in low-value homes would have strong incentives to store kerosene in the basement.

A private market can do better, and so can governments. In the chapter's model, forward-looking governments would have incentives to condition their taxes and social insurance policies on any information they can glean about taxpayers. Second-period taxes and transfers would therefore be functions of first-period incomes, those who move into a jurisdiction would face taxes and transfers that are not the same as those facing first-period residents, and governments would also condition taxes and transfers on the prior locations of new arrivals. Furthermore, taxes and transfers would be nonlinear functions of taxable income.

In order to simplify the analysis and abstract from distributional concerns, the chapter assumes that governments are restricted to collecting taxes that are scalar functions of income. Such taxes, together with the transfers they finance, will indeed offer insurance, though not enough to tempt many high-productivity individuals to seek jurisdictions with higher tax rates. It would have to be a very risk-averse, high-productivity person who chooses to relocate to a jurisdiction that imposes high taxes in return for modest transfers. All that said, however, it is absolutely true that even a flat-rate income tax extracts more from taxpayers in states of the world when their needs for funds are less acute, and less when needs are more acute, so in that sense offers insurance.

One of the puzzling aspects of Silicon Valley is that it is located in California, where individual income tax rates on successful tech entrepreneurs are unusually high. Given how potentially mobile start-up firms appear to be, why do so many founders locate their companies in California and not, say, Nevada, where there is no state income tax?[2] The Gordon chapter posits that entrepreneurs who understand the riskiness of their business ventures will appreciate the relatively more generous social safety net that high-tax California can provide. In practical terms, this corresponds to California entrepreneurs reassuring themselves that just in case their start-up firms fail, they can live on government transfer payments, and that this justifies locating their potentially very profitable businesses in a high-tax state. This implication perhaps takes the model specification too literally. A slightly different, and perhaps more intuitive, interpretation is that entrepreneurs might for various reasons—including what the public sector offers—prefer

2. Anyone who has ever visited both California and Nevada may have noticed that these two states also differ in their nontax attributes. Rauh and Shyu (2024) offer evidence that the three-point hike in the marginal income tax rate of top bracket taxpayers introduced by the 2012 California ballot measure appears nonetheless to have prompted significant out-migration by high-income California residents.

to live in California, and ex ante they consider the expected probabilistic cost in present consumption terms of paying high tax rates in states of the world in which they are very rich to be very low.

## Which Taxes?

The chapter characterizes the taxes that it analyzes as "income taxes," even though tax obligations are scalar functions of income. While there exist flat-rate income taxes, the chapter's taxes might more naturally be classified as sales taxes or VATs, which are commonly applied at flat rates on broad ranges of consumption. There is no saving in the Gordon model, so all income is consumed, and would, therefore, be taxed by a sales tax or VAT. Income taxes, by contrast, apply to what the taxpayer earns, whether or not the taxpayer consumes the income that year. Income taxes are also commonly applied in progressive fashion, with average tax rates that rise with income. This progressive feature of most income taxes clearly illustrates their potential role in mitigating uninsured income risk, and makes it natural to think of governments designing income taxes with population risk sharing in mind.

One of the nice aspects of the Gordon model is that it illustrates that more than just income taxes can reduce idiosyncratic income risk, as sales taxes and other flat-rate consumption taxes will also serve this function. The same is largely true of property taxes, since they increase the cost of property ownership that is associated with higher incomes, though the details of property tax implementation and incidence can somewhat complicate this picture. The reality is that governments rely on higher income taxpayers to finance most public sector expenditures, and fiscal systems therefore inevitably introduce at least some risk sharing compared to outcomes in the absence of taxation. Of course systems will vary in their degrees of risk sharing, and governments can be purposeful in their actions and thereby attract high-income, risk-averse taxpayers who can contribute to the tax base.

## Equilibrium Diversity

The classic Tiebout (1956) model does not rely on any intrinsic differences among jurisdictions; instead, communities differentiate themselves by endogenously selecting different levels of taxes and expenditures. Of course, a realistic model acknowledges and incorporates genuine differences, and the original Tiebout model does so, but one of its implications is that such intrinsic differentiation is not necessary to produce ultimate jurisdictional heterogeneity. In the Tiebout model, two Florida towns with identical pristine beaches will offer widely different combinations of taxes and public services, thereby accommodating differences in demands for public services among those who also insist on proximity to warm water and sand. The analogy to private market differentiation is clear: companies that do not differ in any intrinsic characteristics nonetheless may choose different paths that ultimately, and in equilibrium, make them do very different things.

The Gordon model shares the feature of the Tiebout model that nothing relies on intrinsic differences between jurisdictions. In the Gordon model, jurisdictions differ only in their initial populations—and since populations are mobile, these differences endogenously change as governments adjust their fiscal policies. Differently situated taxpayers prefer different fiscal bundles, and governments choose policies to accommodate these preferences. As a result, government policies have the effect of doubling down on any differences between jurisdictions in the characteristics of their populations, since the process of accommodating the preferences of the current majority will make people with its attributes less likely to leave, and others like them more likely to arrive from outside.

The Gordon model has the feature that there exists an equilibrium in which all jurisdictions offer the same fiscal bundles and have the same population distributions. In such a setting, nobody will have a policy-based incentive to move, and governments—which ignore the possibility of population mobility—will not have incentives to change what they do. Lest one be concerned that our world will settle into bland uniformity, it may be reassuring to note that such a symmetric equilibrium is unstable. Any random population movement, any change in population characteristics, or any deviation from a government policy tailored ideally for the existing population will drive the asymmetric dynamics just mentioned, accentuating the differences.

**Fiscal Federalism as Insurance**

While insurance is valuable, not everyone wants the same policy, nor would private markets offer insurance to everyone on the same terms. To the extent that governments feel compelled to provide all residents the same social insurance, there is an obvious possible problem. Significant population differences in demands for social insurance, together with majoritarian decision making, almost inevitably means that those in unusual situations or with uncommon preferences will find that government policies do not conform to their preferences. And what is true of social insurance is also true of everything else that government does.

Fiscal federalism offers insurance against being in the minority. If I prefer that my town spend significantly more money on public libraries and am willing to pay for the libraries with higher taxes, but 90 percent of my community feels otherwise, then it is very unlikely that the town will budget any extra money. If 10 percent of US population agrees with me, then in a Tiebout world with population mobility, 5 states would offer excellent public libraries, and 45 would not. Despite my minority preferences, I would get to live in a town with the libraries that I want, not by having my town spend more money but by moving to a town that does.

The Gordon chapter identifies an important channel by which governments can provide insurance, where what the chapter models is a type of financial insurance against idiosyncratic shocks to income. Federalist governments are not generally thought to have much ability to offer social insurance that redistributes income, given the prevalence of horizontal externalities in tax setting and fiscal adverse selection introduced by population mobility. The chapter's model shows that this critique can easily be overstated, since there remains an important channel for insurance. It seems, however, that one might further broaden the framework of the Gordon model, and acknowledge that a federalist system itself provides a more fundamental type of insurance against being on the wrong side of the majority. Relying on population mobility together with government willingness to accommodate differences, a federalist system has the potential to get closer than any alternative to meeting the needs of all of its residents.

For acknowledgments, sources of research support, and disclosure of the author's material financial relationships, if any, please see https://www.nber.org/books-and-chapters/policy-responses-tax-competition/comment-fiscal-federalism-and-role-income-tax-hines.

## References

Baldwin, Richard E., and Paul Krugman. 2004. "Agglomeration, Integration and Tax Harmonisation." *European Economic Review* 48 (1): 1–23.

Black, Dan A., and William H. Hoyt. 1989. "Bidding for Firms." *American Economic Review* 79 (5): 1249–56.

Bucovetsky, Sam. 1991. "Asymmetric Tax Competition." *Journal of Urban Economics* 30 (2): 167–81.

Bucovetsky, Sam, and John Douglas Wilson. 1991. "Tax Competition with Two Tax Instruments." *Regional Science and Urban Economics* 21 (3): 333–50.

Keen, Michael, and Kai A. Konrad. 2013. "The Theory of International Tax Competition and Coordination." In *Handbook of Public Economics*, vol. 5, edited by Alan J. Auerbach, Raj Chetty, Martin Feldstein, and Emmanuel Saez, 257–328. North-Holland.

Rauh, Joshua, and Ryan J. Shyu. 2024. "Behavioral Responses to State Income Taxation of Higher Earners: Evidence from California." *American Economic Journal: Economic Policy* 16 (1): 34–86.

Rota-Graziosi, Grégoire. 2019. "The Supermodularity of the Tax Competition Game." *Journal of Mathematical Economics* 83 (1): 25–35.

Tiebout, Charles M. 1956. "A Pure Theory of Local Expenditures." *Journal of Political Economy* 64 (5): 416–24.

Wildasin, David E. 1988. "Nash Equilibria in Models of Fiscal Competition." *Journal of Public Economics* 35 (2): 229–40.

Wilson, John D. 1986. "A Theory of Interregional Tax Competition." *Journal of Urban Economics* 19 (3): 296–315.

Wilson, John Douglas. 1999. "Theories of Tax Competition." *National Tax Journal* 52 (2): 269–304.

Zodrow, George R., and Peter Mieszkowski. 1986. "Pigou, Tiebout, Property Taxation, and the Underprovision of Local Public Goods." *Journal of Urban Economics* 19 (3): 356–70.

7

# Intergovernmental Grants and Policy Competition
## Concepts, Institutions, and Evidence

Jeffrey Clemens and Stan Veuger

### 7.1 Introduction

In the literature on fiscal federalism, the sources and implications of strategic interactions both within and between layers of government have long been of interest (Agrawal et al. 2022; Dahlby 1996; Gordon 1983). Examples include bidding wars over firm location, tax or expenditure competition over mobile workers or capital, and issues that can arise when the same base is taxed separately by multiple layers of government. Intergovernmental transfer arrangements, which are our focus here, have the potential to affect these interactions or to correct for some of the distortions from which these strategic interactions may stem (Dahlby 1996; Gordon 1983). Additionally, we emphasize the role of the strings that can be attached to federal dollars, which take the form of implicit or explicit spending floors in key areas, including cash welfare assistance, Medicaid, and public education. By curbing "races to the bottom" or less severe forms of expenditure competition, these strings indirectly curb competition over the taxes through which a subnational government's share of these expenditures are financed.

Our purpose is threefold. First, we summarize core insights from both classic and more recent papers on the role of intergovernmental grants in systems of fiscal federalism. Second, we provide an updated look at some of the key institutions through which intergovernmental transfers are implemented in the United States. Third, we consider the rich environment of the COVID-19 pandemic in which new intergovernmental transfers were

Jeffrey Clemens is an associate professor of economics at the University of California, San Diego, and a research associate of the National Bureau of Economic Research.

Stan Veuger is a senior fellow in economic policy studies at the American Enterprise Institute, and a fellow at the IE School of Politics, Economics, and Global Affairs.

deployed, and present empirical evidence on how they affected state-level corporate tax policy. For a complementary review of the empirical literature on the downstream effects of intergovernmental transfer arrangements, organized by outcome category, see Lago et al. (2024).

Our analysis of corporate tax rates during the pandemic finds that states that received disproportionately large federal grants were less likely than other states to reduce their corporate tax rates. To avoid concerns associated with the endogeneity of federal grants as a response to poor economic conditions, we use only the variation in federal grants that is associated with the disproportionate representation of low-population states. The analysis suggests that state governments that were particularly flush with cash did not use that cash to lure companies through corporate tax competition.

We conclude by discussing productive directions for future research on the economics of fiscal federalism and the role of intergovernmental grants as policy instruments in federal systems. First, we discuss the additional research opportunities associated with the diversity of intergovernmental grant programs implemented during the COVID-19 pandemic. Second, we discuss the need for additional research on the roles played by the conditions (or "strings") that are often attached to federal grants and the mechanisms employed to deliver them. We also note that the literature on the responsiveness of subnational governments either to matching rates or to the strings attached to federal grants remains less developed than the purely theoretical literature on the structure those grants might optimally take. Finally, given that a core rationale for decentralization is to improve the extent to which public services cater to the preferences of the populations that finance them, we see substantial room for additional research on the ways in which decentralization shapes the level of taxation, the level of service provision, the targeting of public services across potential beneficiaries, and the politics of fiscal federalism.

## 7.2 Theory and Empirics of Intergovernmental Transfers

In this section we summarize insights from both the theoretical and empirical literatures on the potential role of intergovernmental transfers in improving outcomes and subnational policy within federal systems. We begin in section 7.2.1 by revisiting some of the canonical papers in the literature on fiscal federalism and discussing how their insights point to potential efficiency rationales for intergovernmental transfers. In section 7.2.2 we discuss how equity considerations enter the picture. In section 7.2.3 we discuss the basics of how intergovernmental grants alter the budget sets and behavior of state or local governments. Finally, in section 7.2.4 we highlight that strategic interactions between governments can shape the effects of intergovernmental transfers in ways that extend beyond the immediate income and substitution effects of those grants.

### 7.2.1 Efficiency Rationales for Intergovernmental Grants

Classic papers in the literature on fiscal federalism have described the conditions under which the decentralized provision of public goods can outperform federal provision, and perhaps even result in efficient allocations and delivery, as in Tiebout (1956) and Oates (1972). Subsequent research (e.g., Gordon 1983) has drawn attention to a number of channels through which decentralized revenue collections or public goods provision may yield inefficient outcomes. These later insights highlight the potential role for intergovernmental grants and other instruments of intergovernmental relations in combatting inefficiencies that can arise in federal systems.

As the literature has highlighted, intergovernmental transfer arrangements have the potential to better align the incentives of subnational governments with the preferences of the federation. As we discuss below, this may sometimes involve straightforward corrections to the misaligned incentives. However, it may require accounting for such considerations as the strategic interactions between governments or differences in preferences across the jurisdictions within a federation.

It is instructive to distinguish between three classes of inefficiencies in the provision of public goods: those associated with private objectives (e.g., agency problems) or constraints (e.g., imperfect information), or those which prevail even under the right private objectives and in the absence of such constraints (e.g., externalities).

In Tiebout (1956), residential choice across jurisdictions serves several functions that help to overcome these challenges. First, the classic "Tiebout sorting" mechanism emphasizes that mobility across jurisdictions gives individuals with similar preferences an opportunity to group themselves together. This sorting mechanism can be beneficial even under omniscient and benevolent government due to the "public" nature of local public goods consumption. That is, absent sorting across jurisdictions, the level of public goods could not be tailored to individual preferences. A related advantage is that by "voting with their feet," individuals effectively reveal the level of public goods consumption they desire, which can help alleviate the informational problems facing benevolent but constrained governance. Finally, the competitive pressures associated with mobility give politicians an incentive to produce those public goods efficiently even if their objective is to maximize rents.

Oates (1972) highlights the importance of informational and delivery constraints on the governance of benevolent, centralized authorities. In Oates's "decentralization theorem" the role of variations in local preferences for public goods takes center stage. In the absence of cross-jurisdictional externalities or additional economies of scale in production, it is more efficient for local governments to finance and supply the locally preferred levels of public goods consumption than for the federal government to provide the same level of public goods consumption to all localities. A key force underlying the recommendation to decentralize is the idea that local governments will tend to have superior information, as also highlighted by Tiebout (1956), for assessing the level of public goods consumption their constituents desire. Information asymmetries between central, and perhaps overburdened, principal authorities and their agents similarly play a prominent role in Aghion and Tirole's (1997) analysis of the trade-offs associated with delegating authority. Rogger and Somani (2023) provide evidence that in practice, information quality can indeed vary meaningfully across the levels of hierarchies. In their survey of Ethiopian government officials, officials at lower, more decentralized, levels of government hold more accurate beliefs about key variables such as the size of the population they serve.

While different models of electoral competition and of politician behavior have different implications for policy competition, there is empirical evidence that decentralization is particularly effective when local political actors face political competition and accountability. Basurto et al. (2020), for example, find that local chiefs in Malawi do a good job of targeting resources toward households that generate substantial returns on their farm inputs despite also engaging in a degree of nepotism on the side. Bianchi et al. (2023) find that effectiveness of a decentralization effort in Italy increased in the degree of local political competition. Janvry et al. (2012) also find positive effects of political competition in the context of a decentralized cash transfer program in Brazil. While this is speculative, it may be well be that reduced levels of electoral competition at the state level (Abramowitz and Webster 2016) have contributed to the lackluster administrative capacity of a number of state unemployment agencies in the United States as demonstrated, for example, by their inability during the COVID-19 pandemic to process unemployment insurance benefits that imply reasonable replacement rates (Ganong et al. 2020).

While the Tiebout (1956) model and decentralization theorem (Oates 1972) are sometimes read as arguments in favor of decentralization, they can also be read as statements of its limits. A complementary analysis from Olson (1969), for example, explicitly considered the optimal assignment of responsibilities across levels of government. Regarding externalities in the benefits of public goods, a key point in Olson's analysis is to emphasize that efficiency requires boundaries to be drawn so as to match the beneficiaries and financers of each public good.[1] Musgrave (1971) raises similar points.

1. A consequence of this insight, as Olson (1969) writes, is that "only if there are several levels of government and a large number of governments can immense disparities between the boundaries of jurisdictions and the boundaries of collective goods be avoided. There is a case for every type of institution from the international organization to the smallest local government." This insight thus provides a potential rationale for the large set of geographically overlapping governments found in the United States. Whether that patchwork is actually operating efficiently is another matter.

Shoag and Veuger (2018) demonstrate empirically that the extent to which local jurisdictional boundaries capture spillovers affects the extent to which policymakers target the externalities in question.

As summarized by Oates (2008), more recent theoretical developments layer in additional considerations. One strand of literature emphasizes that the performance of decentralized governments can suffer from the moral hazard of potential federal bailouts. That is, the cost of fiscal mismanagement may be borne in part, at least in expectation, by the residents of other jurisdictions, giving each jurisdiction a perverse incentive to "raid the fiscal commons." This suggests a role for balanced budget requirements and other institutional constraints on the behavior of subnational governments. Another strand of literature has relaxed the assumptions of benevolent governance and uniform public goods provision, inspired by the public choice and political economy literatures.

These theoretical extensions highlight that the forces at work in determining legislative outcomes at the federal level versus more localized levels need not imply that any one level of government is systematically preferred to others. Indeed, the analyses of Olson (1969) and Musgrave (1971) highlight that multiple, and potentially overlapping, layers of government may be necessary to map jurisdictions into the regions that capture the benefits of various public goods. Additionally, there are cases in which allowing multiple levels of government to tax the same base can be efficiency improving (Hoyt 2017).

Gordon (1983) can similarly be read as cautioning readers that decentralization is not a panacea. He illustrates several inefficiencies that can arise due to externalities associated with either the tax instruments deployed by local governments or through the provision of the public goods themselves. First, some tax instruments may generate revenues from nonresidents as well as residents. Second, if local policies shift economic activity across jurisdictions, the revenues of both the activity-losing and the activity-gaining jurisdiction will be affected. Wilson (1986) and Zodrow and Mieszkowski (1986) provide complementary analyses of the implications of local governments' use of distorting taxes on mobile capital.[2] Third, the policies of one jurisdiction may alter the resource costs faced by other jurisdictions. Fourth, the benefits from local public goods will not tend to vanish at the borders of the jurisdictions that have been drawn. Transportation networks, the incapacitation effects of incarceration, and the improvements in air or water quality that derive from local regulations will tend to have benefits that accrue in part to neighboring areas. Such spillovers need not be positive, as when policing generates displacement effects or when one jurisdiction's industrial development has negative environmental consequences for

2. Oates and Schwab (1988) consider the implications of local taxation of mobile capital accompanied by local standards associated with the environmental impacts of firms' activities.

its neighbors. Gordon notes, additionally, that decentralized "communities will tend to enact excessive tax rates on congestion producing activities, since they enjoy any gains from decongestion, but ignore the associated loss from extra congestion elsewhere."

Among the papers discussed above, the analysis of Gordon (1983) connects most directly to the remainder of the current chapter. Though he focuses primarily on developing an analysis of the inefficiencies that can be associated with interjurisdictional tax and expenditure externalities, Gordon also discusses potential remedies. Among those remedies are intergovernmental grants, which can be structured to effectively subsidize the provision of goods that are underprovided or penalize the provision of goods that are overprovided. This possibility is ultimately created by the separation across levels of government of, on the one hand, taxation and, on the other hand, spending and program administration. A subsequent paper by Dahlby (1996) helpfully provides a more comprehensive assessment of how such subsidies and penalties might optimally be set. In the subsections below, we turn to characterizing the potential structure of both corrective and purely redistributive grants, as well as discussing some of the empirical evidence on the effects of such efforts in practice.

### 7.2.2 Equity Rationales for Intergovernmental Grants

Equity considerations feature prominently in discussions or analyses of intergovernmental transfer arrangements. In early analyses, an argument for using intergovernmental grants for redistribution tended to arise from standard logic involving differences in marginal utilities across space. Equity considerations emerge in the Gordon (1983) classic, for example, as well as in the model of Wildasin (1984), who examines the welfare impact of intergovernmental transfers when recipient governments use distortionary taxes. An important question is whether such transfers would remain attractive even if individual-based redistribution has been fine-tuned according to social welfare considerations. Gaubert et al. (2021) provide an argument that the answer can be yes, with emphasis on the potential importance of concentrations of poverty among households with limited capacity to move.

The use of intergovernmental transfers to redistribute resources across regions raises standard political economy concerns. That is, the objective function of a federal legislature will include a desire to redistribute across politically defined constituencies in addition to, or perhaps in place of, redistributing out of purely equity-driven concerns. Studies finding that variations in political representation shape the distribution of federal funds across regions include Atlas et al. (1995), Cascio and Washington (2014), Clemens and Veuger (2021), Hauk and Wacziarg (2007), Knight (2008), Lee (1998), and Rodden (2002).[3]

3. Recent work in the context of the COVID-19 pandemic has shown, in turn, that the distribution of federal funds can have substantial impacts on subsequent electoral outcomes (Clemens, Payson, et al., 2024)

Fiscal assistance packages delivered on an ad hoc basis under emergency circumstances, as during the COVID-19 pandemic, can be especially ill designed with respect to both the magnitude of the assistance and its distribution across regions, which suggests potential value to designing such programs as automatic stabilizers (Clemens and Veuger 2023). Formula-based aid also has the potential to reduce policy uncertainty at the subnational level and to improve macroeconomic outcomes as a result (Shoag and Veuger 2016).[4]

Arguments for redistribution through intergovernmental grants may be at their strongest in the context of K–12 school finance, where the public service in question is an investment in human capital for which children are dependent on their parents and communities. In the US context, an important literature has considered the court-ordered equalization of school finances, which highlights the potential relevance of the distributional preferences of political actors at various levels of government. A number of papers have demonstrated that court-ordered school finance equalization reduces across-district spending inequality as measured using a variety of metrics (Baicker and Gordon 2006; Card and Payne 2002; Corcoran et al. 2004). Interestingly, Baicker and Gordon (2006) find additionally that states offset the increase in education resources sent to low-income districts by reducing grants targeted at other expenditure categories.

School finance interventions have varied in their effect on spending levels. Reforms that clawed back the high spending of wealthy districts have been found to "level down" by reducing school spending (Hoxby 2001). In contrast, reforms that increased the "foundation grants" to low-income districts without altering the effective price of spending by high-income districts have been found to increase spending (Jackson et al. 2016). Jackson et al. (2016) find that school finance equalizations (SFEs) stemming from rulings that districts were failing an "adequacy" standard spurred additional spending while "equity"-driven SFEs do not. The associated variations in spending are predictive of variations in children's subsequent education and labor market outcomes. LaFortune et al. (2018) provide additional evidence that SFEs driven by "adequacy" standards had substantial positive impacts on both the resources and test score outcomes of students in low-income districts. Shores et al. (2022) provide further evidence that there has been substantial heterogeneity in the effects of SFEs. Overall, the evidence on the effects of SFEs is mixed, suggests substantial heterogeneity, and suggests further that both the basis for a reform and the structure of the reform can play an important role in shaping its impacts. A key question for evaluating these school finance interventions is whether the objective is to equalize resources, equalize outcomes, raise the floor for outcomes in low-resource

4. Though the formulas have to be appropriate for stabilization purposes, which is not necessarily the case when apportionment is based on formulas used in normal times. We discuss this consideration in more detail in subsection 7.4.2.

districts, or something else altogether. This is a question on which there may be substantial disagreements across key stakeholders and across jurisdictions.

### 7.2.3 Intergovernmental Grants and Institutional Changes to Subnational Budget Sets

Moving from motivation to implementation, in this subsection we describe in broad terms how the policy levers associated with intergovernmental relations can alter the incentives and constraints facing state and local governments. The core policy instruments include matching grants, categorical block grants, general fiscal assistance, and a myriad of rules including balanced budget requirements, maintenance of effort requirements, and either floors or ceilings on either the level or growth of revenues or expenditures. We describe the basic structure of such instruments, their theoretical effects, and empirical evidence on their effects in practice.

#### *7.2.3.1 Matching Grants*

If the federal government's primary concern is that state or local governments may have an insufficient incentive to deliver a particular public good, or to engage in spending on goods, services, and transfers more generally, a natural remedy is to correct that incentive through a matching grant. By matching (or reimbursing) a state's expenditures at some fixed rate, the federal government can lower the effective price and induce state governments to increase the level at which the good, service, or transfer is provided. The optimal subsidy rate can be analyzed in the same vein as Pigouvian taxes for correcting environmental or other externalities.

One central choice the federal government can make is to subsidize the provision of a particular expenditure category or of state and local government spending in total. An interesting insight of Gordon (1983) is that the federal government can subsidize the overall revenue collections of state and local governments by making those tax payments deductible at the federal level. The deductibility of state and local tax payments is thus a tool that can be used to subsidize overall state and local government revenue collections and may thus correct for underprovision in aggregate. Cullen and Gordon (2008) and Hemel (2019) analyze arguments in favor of and against this approach. A program-specific matching grant, in contrast, can alter the relative prices of particular types of spending (e.g., education or highway construction versus health care) and are thus useful for correcting the over- or underprovision of one type of spending relative to another.

A moderately sized empirical literature has found evidence that matching grants are an effective tool for increasing expenditure on targeted categories. Baicker (2005a), for example, finds that both the number of US states' welfare beneficiaries and the generosity of the benefits those beneficiaries receive are sensitive to the generosity of the rates at which state welfare spending has been reimbursed by the federal government. In a pair of recent papers, both Bundorf and Kessler (2022), and Leung (2022) find evidence that higher matching rates in the federal subsidy for US states' Medicaid programs result in substantially higher spending per beneficiary.[5] Coyne (2017) estimates a substantial elasticity of deductible revenues to variations in the tax price generated by the deductibility of local taxes at the federal level. The spending of US school districts has also been found to respond to the implicit subsidy and taxation associated with SFE arrangements (Hoxby 2001).

The responsiveness of spending to the incentives created by matching grants raises the question of whether the induced spending is a corrective to an underprovision problem or a manifestation of a moral hazard problem. This question underlies a perennial debate over the desirability of converting matching grants into block grants, as occurred in the 1996 welfare reform through which the US federal government replaced the Aid for Families with Dependent Children (AFDC) program with the Temporary Assistance for Needy Families (TANF) program.

Similar changes in the structure of federal support for the Medicaid program have been proposed regularly but not adopted. A complication of such reform proposals is that they tend to bundle changes in incentives with changes in the long-run growth of federal support and substantial redistributions of federal funds across states (Clemens and Ippolito 2018). Notably, the Medicaid financing reform proposal included in the unsuccessful 2017 American Health Care Act converted federal support into a capped, fixed amount per enrollee, which was commonly referred to as a "per capita cap" (Adler et al. 2017). This is of interest because the per capita cap financing structure maintains an incentive for states to enroll additional beneficiaries while turning off the incentive to spend more per beneficiary. The latter margin, namely, spending per beneficiary, is in the margin along which recent estimates from Leung (2022) and Bundorf and Kessler (2022) find state spending to be highly elastic.

Matching grants formulas create a perverse incentive to "relabel" unmatched expenditures as matched expenditures in ways that can undermine the federal government's desired targeting. This phenomenon is illustrated by research on the Disproportionate Share Hospital (DSH) program, through which the federal government sought to incentivize the states to support hospitals that serve low-income populations (Baicker and Staiger

5. Bundorf and Kessler (2022) and Leung (2022) arrive at this conclusion using different sources of variation. Leung estimates that variations in the traditional Federal Medical Assistance Percentage, which delivers less-generous subsidies to relatively high-income states subject to floor match-rate of 50 percent. Bundorf and Kessler analyze variations in match-rates generated by the Affordable Care Act (ACA), which resulted in more generous overall match-rates for states that elected to expand coverage to childless, low-income adults, some of whom were eligible for states' Medicaid programs prior to the ACA expansions.

2005; Duggan 2000). It did so by including DSH payments from states to eligible hospitals as among the expenditures that received a federal match. A brazen strategy for increasing federal dollars without actually supporting these institutions was to target them with hospital-specific taxes, then return the money in the form of match-rate-eligible DSH payments.[6] A less transparent approach involved the wiring of funds back and forth between the state government and hospitals owned by local governments, where the state's "DSH payment" to the local public hospital would generate a match, creating a surplus to be shared between the entities via an upward transfer from the hospital to the state.[7] Hackmann et al. (2024) provide additional evidence that states engage in "creative financing schemes" in efforts to divert federal matching funds toward alternative purposes. Ensuring that matching grants hit their intended targets is thus nontrivial. State efforts to relabel various safety net expenditures as eligible for federal reimbursements are sure to continue; early in 2023, for example, California sought permission to use Medicaid dollars to finance housing support through "transitional rent" (Hart 2023).

#### *7.2.3.2 Categorical Block Grants and Maintenance of Effort Requirements*

The federal government can also provide funds to state and local governments in the form of block grants. Block grants can, in turn, be "unrestricted," such that the money is distributed as a form of general budgetary support, or "categorical," meaning that the money is earmarked for particular uses. In this subsection we focus on the latter.

A standard but important point regarding categorical (or targeted) block grants is that the recipient government may not use the funds for their intended purpose. When both state and federal funds are used to finance spending on the targeted good, service, or transfer, a categorical block grant may simply crowd out counterfactual own-source funding. Knight (2002), for example, finds that federal highway aid substantially crowds out state funds once the endogeneity of the distribution of federal grants is accounted for. Such grants are thus only assured to increase targeted spending if they

6. Baicker and Staiger (2004) write: "One such mechanism used in the early 1990s was the imposition of provider-specific taxes. For example, a state could impose a tax of $1 billion dollars on a particular hospital. It could then pay the hospital $1 billion dollars in DSH payments, which would be matched by the federal government with at least $500 million—a net increase in state resources, accompanied by no change in resources to the hospital."

7. Summarizing a rather transparent instance of such a scheme, Baicker and Staiger (2005) write: "For example, the GAO (1994) documented the transfer of a $277 million federal/state DSH payment to a Michigan county nursing facility, which wired $271 million back to the state *the same day*" (emphasis in original). Accounting for these financing schemes can be important for correctly accounting for the costs and benefits of incremental health care resources; Baicker and Staiger find that DSH funds are associated with substantial mortality improvements in states where the funds tend to reach their target, but not in the states that aggressively engage in efforts to capture the federal funds.

set a binding floor on a state's spending. For example, the TANF program (discussed further in subsection 7.3.2) combines categorical block grants with maintenance-of-effort requirements derived from 1994 state welfare spending levels.

The SFEs described earlier, whereby states with insufficient low-income school district spending are found by courts to fail an "adequacy" standard, function effectively as such a binding floor.[8] Although these standards do not tend to involve explicit spending floors (Corcoran et al. 2004), they generated substantial increases in per-pupil spending in low-income school districts, supported by increases in state government grants (Jackson et al. 2016). Cascio et al. (2013) emphasize that districts can vary substantially in their scope for offsetting funds from higher levels of government. In particular, they provide evidence that the low scope of some districts for offsetting federal aid was important for understanding the degree to which the 1965 introduction of Title I funds increased school spending and reduced dropout rates in southern states.

The literature on block grants has drawn attention to a "behavioral" phenomenon widely known as "the flypaper effect." This term is commonly used in two different ways. In the context of categorical blocks grants, it highlights a tendency to spend targeted funds disproportionately on the targeted spending category, even in the absence of binding requirements imposed on the lower level of governments. We discuss its usage in the context of unrestricted block grants in the next subsection.

#### *7.2.3.3 Unrestricted Block Grants and Balanced Budget Requirements*

A federal government can also provide unrestricted block grants, which provide a general form of support that augments a jurisdiction's own-source general revenue. Unrestricted block grants do not alter the incentives associated with the provision of any particular public good. They can be described as providing a foundation of fiscal capacity, which tends to have a redistributive motive, as discussed earlier in section 7.2.2.

As an empirical matter, it has long been observed that unrestricted block grants influence spending more than standard economic theory would predict. That is, an unrestricted federal grant increases the wealth of a jurisdiction's residents. In theory, the resulting increase in the demand for public goods will correspond with residents' marginal propensity to consume public goods out of an increase in their own wealth or income.

In practice, as discussed by Hines and Thaler (1995), it has often been estimated that each dollar in unrestricted block grants generates substantial increases in local government expenditure. Early estimates from Case et al. (1993), Feldstein, (1975), and Inman (1971) suggest, across a variety of settings, that a dollar in federal grants generates net spending increases

8. In this example the state is the "federal" or "higher" level of government.

that range from 60 cents to the full dollar. These results embody the aforementioned "flypaper effect," whereby federal dollars "stick" where they land rather than being sent to local taxpayers.

Evidence from more recent work has been mixed. Dahlberg et al. (2008), Feiveson (2015), and Köthenbürger and Loumeau (2023), for example, find evidence consistent with substantial flypaper effects. LeDuc and Wilson (2017) find an even larger effect from American Recovery and Reinvestment Act grants for highway spending, with net spending increasing more than dollar-for-dollar. In contrast, Knight (2002) finds evidence of almost perfect crowding out of federal transportation grants. Lutz (2010) similarly finds evidence of nearly perfect crowding out in the context of a court-ordered school finance reform in New Hampshire. Gordon (2004) presents interesting evidence on the dynamics of adjustments to school district finances. Specifically, she finds that an additional dollar in federal aid initially generates a dollar in net revenues, but that changes in local revenues adjust to offset federal aid within three years.

Carlino et al. (2023) provide evidence of an interesting source of heterogeneity. Specifically, they find that Democratic governors are faster to spend federal grants than are Republican governors, with corresponding differences in the associated stimulus impacts.

In light of this body of evidence, the distribution of federal dollars through unrestricted block grants can plausibly be viewed as a measure designed to increase state and local spending, even though it does not change the tax-price of state and local expenditures on the margin. Note that the flypaper effect does not necessarily indicate inefficiency: Allers and Vermeulen (2016) provide evidence from the Netherlands of full capitalization of grants into home prices in a context with significant flypaper effects. That said, there are some indications of inefficiencies. Carlino et al.'s (2023) finding of systematically different spending of federal funds by Democratic and Republican governors, for example, reveals that the intended impacts of federal funds tend not to be realized uniformly around the country.

A second rationale for unrestricted block grants is to provide revenue stability over the course of the business cycle (as in Clemens and Veuger 2023). This can be necessary in part due to subnational balanced-budget requirements, which may in turn be a response to moral hazard concerns (the raiding of the fiscal commons, etc.). In the US context, all states save Vermont have voluntarily adopted balanced budget requirements either through legislation or as provisions in state constitutions. In a number of cases, these rules were adopted in direct response to fiscal crises in the mid-19th century. These requirements vary in their effective stringency, and requirements that expressly limit the ex post carrying over of unexpected deficits into subsequent fiscal years have been found to exert their intended impact on the average size of state budget deficits as well as the pace at which states restore balance in the wake of negative shocks (Alt and Lowry 1994;

Bohn and Inman 1996; Clemens and Miran 2012; Poterba 1994).[9] These binding balanced-budget requirements can lead states to raise taxes or cut spending during recessions. Revenue stabilization grants may thus serve a purpose of limiting the extent to which state spending fluctuations would otherwise exacerbate the business cycle (Asdrubali et al. 1996). Local governments similarly face balanced-budget requirements, and are in addition restricted in the changes they can make to their tax codes without legislative action at the state level. Shoag et al. (2019) show that cities located in so-called home rule states, which enjoy greater levels of autonomy, respond to negative revenue shocks by raising other types of revenue more rapidly than cities in other states.

In the European context, the Stability and Growth Pact and its subsequent modifications impose restrictions on the size of allowable deficit and debt levels. Those restrictions were widely seen to have exacerbated the Great Recession in several member states, without necessarily ensuring their primary objective of fiscal sustainability. In response to the next economic crisis, triggered by the COVID-19 pandemic, not only were the budget rules waived but the European Union also developed, for the first time, significant countercyclical fiscal authority in the form of the Next Generation EU Agreement.

*7.2.3.4 Strings Attached*

An aspect of intergovernmental grants that is typically underemphasized in textbook treatments involves the restrictions that are often imposed as a condition for receipt. That is, both categorical and matching intergovernmental grants can and often do come with restrictions that, to varying degrees, limit the autonomy of subnational governments when it comes to using the funding. These restrictions are not just limited categorical restrictions of the kind mentioned in the previous subsection: they often go significantly further by mandating eligibility rules, delivery mechanisms, compliance with Civil Rights legislation, and other rules that, in some cases, have at best a tangential connection to the purpose of the funds in question.

Prominent examples of the strings attached to federal funds span the full range of the most prominent expenditure categories. First, to be eligible for federal matching funds, state Medicaid programs must be certified by the federal government as having met requirements that impose floors on the populations made eligible and on the medical benefits to which beneficiaries are entitled. Second, as noted above, a maintenance of effort requirement ensures that TANF spending remains at or above the 1994 spending

9. Stricter fiscal rules are also associated with lower interest rates (Bayoumi et al. 1995; Eichengreen 1992; Goldstein and Woglom 1992; Poterba and Reuben 1999). While the evidence is suggestive that bond markets may reward polities for adopting strict fiscal rules, research in this area has acknowledged the difficulty of isolating plausibly exogenous variation in fiscal rules that might enable a causal impact on interest rates to be established.

on states' cash welfare assistance programs. Third, the receipt of funding through Title I of the Elementary and Secondary Education Act is linked to compliance with academic standards and testing requirements, as implemented through the No Child Left Behind Act and subsequently revised by the Every Student Succeeds Act (Skinner 2022). Finally, the receipt of up to 10 percent of federal highway funds was famously linked to states' adoption of a prohibition on alcohol consumption by individuals below age 21 by the 1984 National Minimum Drinking Age Act. Baicker et al. (2012) discuss how the mid- to late 20th-century rise in state government spending as a share of total spending corresponded with a rise of mandates and other requirements of this sort.[10]

The discussion in section 7.3 of the current set of intergovernmental grant programs in the US context illustrates the wide range of restrictions at play here. Mauri (2024) emphasizes the distinction between subnational autonomy as measured by budgetary entries and their "effective" autonomy as measured by adjustments to their behavior in response to shocks to grant levels. But even the latter does not fully capture effective autonomy, as quantitative responses may not fully reflect the qualitative nature of many of the aforementioned federal rules and regulations. The extent to which such measures are binding in practice is an open question in need of empirical research.[11]

Conditions attached to intergovernmental aid are common in international contexts as well. Member countries that participate in IMF programs typically do not simply borrow money from the IMF but agree to implement sets of policies to accompany the loans they receive. In the European context, member states had to submit proposals for reform and investment in order to qualify for grants and loans from the Recovery and Resilience Facility set up in response to the COVID-19 pandemic.

### 7.2.4 Intergovernmental Grants and Policy Competition

Subnational governments do not sit quiescently, waiting for the federal government to send them and their peers instructions and to make tweaks to their budget sets. They also respond directly to the policies enacted by other subnational jurisdictions, as well as indirectly to federal policy to the

10. There are constitutional limits to the strings the federal governments may attach. While the Supreme Court in *South Dakota v. Dole* upheld the National Minimum Drinking Act's withholding of funding from noncompliant states, it struck down part of the Affordable Care Act for not leaving the states with a real choice in the matter of the expansion of the Medicaid program, as discussed below in subsection 7.3.2.

11. In the context of the COVID-19 pandemic, for example, Treasury Department guidance makes clear that the American Rescue Plan Act's transfers to state and local governments "may not be used for deposit into any pension fund (US Department of the Treasury 2022)." Analyses from both Clemens, Giesecke, et al. (2024) and Brang et al. (2024) find that this restriction was not binding in practice, as states that received more funding made larger contributions to their pensions.

extent that it affects policy decisions by other subnational governments. This combination of facts has given rise to a literature that studies how federal instruments, including the intergovernmental grants we are interested in, can correct for features of subnational policy competition that are deemed undesirable.

Agrawal et al. (2024) establish a framework to quantify the welfare effects of decentralized policies. Local policies result in benefit spillovers, mobility of households and firms, and interjurisdictional fiscal externalities that are not internalized by the government enacting the policy. They delineate and quantify these external benefits and costs. Their magnitudes are measured by a new metric, the "marginal corrective transfer" (MCT), that is, the grant a federal government should provide to induce a locality to internalize these interjurisdictional externalities. Formally, the MCT is estimated as the wedge between the marginal value of public funds of the locality enacting the policy and of the entire federation.[12]

Dahlby (1996) helpfully enumerates the various sorts of tax and expenditure externalities and the matching grants that correct for them. Externalities can be horizontal, when policy in one subnational unit affects other subnational units, or vertical, when policy in a subnational unit affects the federal budget constraint.[13] They can also be direct or indirect, where indirect externalities correspond to what are frequently referred to as "fiscal externalities." Appendix table 7A.4 reproduces his tables 1 and 2.

A number of theoretical papers analyze the effects of fiscal equalization transfers on tax competition specifically. For example, Buettner's (2006) model distinguishes two different ways in which such transfers can affect subnational tax policy. If the overall grant volume goes up, tax rates are likely to go down. On the other hand, if the federal grant declines with increases in the tax base, that likely leads to higher tax rates. This second finding is in line with work by Köthenbürger (2002) and can in fact lead to excess taxation (Bucovetsky and Smart 2006). Boadway (2004) reviews fiscal equalization in theory and practice. In a more recent paper, Chirinko and Wilson (2017) emphasize that tax policy response to windfalls depends crucially on whether private goods are necessities or luxuries.

On the empirical front, Egger et al. (2010) use evidence from Lower Saxony to show that capacity equalization grants raise equilibrium tax rates,

12. See Hendren (2016) and Hendren and Sprung-Keyser (2020) for elaboration on the concept of the marginal value of public funds and how it can be inferred through analyses of the effects of public policy.

13. A famous example of vertical externalities from the US context is the Maryland tax policy at the heart of the dispute in the 1819 Supreme Court case *McCulloch v. Maryland*. Maryland had attempted to impose a tax on notes issued by banks not charted in the state, of which there was only one: the Second Bank of the United States. The Court struck down the Maryland tax, explained that "the power to tax involves the power to destroy," and determined that the Necessary and Proper Clause of the US Constitution indicates that the federal government has implied powers in addition to its enumerated ones.

confirming the findings of Buettner (2006) for Baden-Wuerttemberg. On the international side of things, Devereux et al. (2002) study corporate income tax competition between EU and G7 countries.

Turning to the spending side, Calabrese et al.'s (2012) model and computations suggest the externality associated with low-income households entering high-income communities can make decentralization with property tax financing a welfare-reducing proposition. The idea is that Tiebout sorting, and the differing levels of public-good provision associated with communities of differing incomes, is undermined by free-riding in the housing market. This is similar to the logic of the "welfare magnet" hypothesis associated with Peterson and Rom (1989, 1990), and illustrates the "indirect horizontal effects" of antipoverty spending.

Early empirical work by Case et al. (1993) shows that subnational governments indeed appear to mimic each other's spending behavior, as Baicker (2005b) confirms for the policy decisions of the US states in the Medicaid context. Caldeira et al. (2015) develop complementary findings in an analysis of the spending decisions of local governments in Benin.

Berry et al. (2003) Brueckner (2000), Rom et al. (1998), Saavedra (2000), and Volden (2002), were part of a boomlet of work on these questions around the time AFDC became TANF (and a matching grant thereby became a block grant). The evidence for a "race to the bottom," that interstate competition has worked to reduce the generosity of redistribution in antipoverty programs, is relatively weak. This may be due to caseload shifting in what is ultimately a patchwork of different programs, as Bailey and Rom (2004) suggest. Goodman-Bacon and Schmidt (2020) find evidence for this in the context of the introduction of Supplemental Security Income.

Skupnik (2014) studies whether there is a race to the bottom in welfare generosity in the European Union, but does not find much evidence. This can be explained in the European context by the lack of response of migration flows to welfare levels.

To the extent that race-to-the-bottom or welfare-magnet-type effects exist, a binding floor on spending, whether mandated or financed by the federal government through categorical block grants, will tend to have spillover effects on the spending decisions of jurisdictions that were not bound directly by the floor. This implies that increases in spending on a particular public good can, in such cases, be achieved through less heavy-handed federal policy. In other settings, however, spillover effects might work in opposition to the goals of federal policy and thus require what looks like a more aggressive approach.

## 7.3 Intergovernmental Transfers in the United States

Most of the mechanisms analyzed in section 7.2 are features of the current system of fiscal federalism in the United States. In this section, we provide an

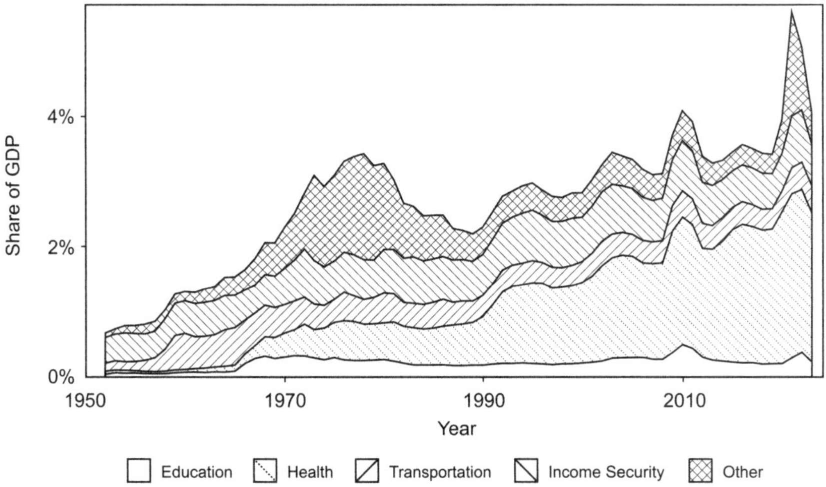


**Fig. 7.1 Federal intergovernmental spending as a share of GDP**

Note: This figure uses data from Office of Management and Budget (2022a, 2022b) to show federal grants to state and local governments as a share of GDP over time. A breakdown of the composition of each spending category shown can be found in table 7A.1.

overview of the key institutions through which intergovernmental transfers are implemented in practice. Our focus is mostly on transfers from the federal government to subnational jurisdictions; the states play a supplemental role in providing funding to cities, counties, and other local jurisdictions.

Figure 7.1 illustrates the evolution over time of federal grants by functional category. Federal grants to states and localities grew steadily between the 1950s and the Great Recession, from under 1 percent to over 3 percent of GDP. They were relatively stable at around 3.4 percent of GDP between the Great Recession and the start of the COVID-19 pandemic but hit an all-time high of 5.6 percent of GDP in 2021.

The composition of federal grants has changed dramatically over time. In 1959, transportation accounted for 41 percent of federal grants to state and local governments. It was just under 7 percent in 2021. Health-related federal grants, by contrast, rose from 5 percent to 15 percent of total grants with the 1965 introduction of the Medicaid program and continued to expand in importance thereafter.

Other components of the federal grants portfolio have not followed such stark trends. Education peaked at just over 25 percent of total federal grants with the rollout of the Great Society programs during the 1960s, but in the early 1980s the federal role in education finance declined. Recently education's share of total federal grants has drifted below 10 percent. Income security has been relatively steady over the last 70 years, with mild countercyclical fluctuations.

A visually striking episode in figure 7.1 is the dramatic rise in "other" transfers in the late 1970s. This increase consisted of funds from the General Revenue Sharing trust fund, funds associated with active labor market policies initiated by the Nixon administration, and transfers for community and regional development that peaked during the Carter administration.

The General Revenue Sharing episode has been analyzed by Feiveson (2015), who finds that "cities increased expenditures one-for-one with federal grants." This is suggestive of a large flypaper effect of the kind discussed in subsection 7.2.3.3. Characteristics of subnational jurisdictions played an important role in moderating the allocation of these resources. In states with pro-union collective bargaining laws, cities used more than half of the transfers for wage increases for public-sector workers. Cities in other states dedicated more of the funding to increased service provision.

Leading up to the COVID-19 pandemic, grants related to health care had become far and away the largest category of intergovernmental transfers. The health share reached just over 60 percent in the years prior to the pandemic.

Table 7.1 shows the main programs driving intergovernmental transfers

**Table 7.1** **Average annual grant outlays to state and local governments, FY 2015–2019**

| Category | Program name | Annual outlay | Category total |
|---|---|---|---|
| *Largest grants by category* | | | |
| Health | Grants to States for Medicaid | 353,628 | 377,092 |
| Health | Children's Health Insurance Fund | 13,927 | |
| Income security | Child Nutrition Programs | 20,847 | 100,341 |
| Income security | Tenant Based Rental Assistance | 19,071 | |
| Transportation | Federal-Aid Highways (Trust Fund) | 40,150 | 59,771 |
| Transportation | Urban Mass Transportation Grants (Trust Fund) | 9,046 | |
| Education | Education for the Disadvantaged | 14,679 | 38,912 |
| Education | Special Education | 11,721 | |
| Other | Children and Families Services Programs | 9,677 | 55,473 |
| Other | Disaster Relief Fund | 5,552 | |
| *Other large grants* | | | |
| Income security | Temporary Assistance for Needy Families | 14,872 | |
| Income security | SNAP, WIC, and CSFP | 11,562 | |
| Income security | Foster Care and Adoption Assistance | 7,460 | |
| Other | Community Development Fund | 5,485 | |
| Income security | Public Housing Operating Fund | 4,408 | |
| **Average annual total outlays for grants** | | | **631,588** |

Note: This table uses data from Office of Management and Budget (2022b) and US Bureau of Economic Analysis (2023). Average annual outlay expressed in real 2012 USD millions and are deflated using the BEA's implicit price deflator.

in the years 2015–2019: the two largest programs in each grant category and the five largest other programs. The table makes clear how health spending came to dominate intergovernmental transfers: it is largely a consequence of the size of the Medicaid program. Medicaid is currently the single largest source of transfers from the federal government to states and localities, accounting for about half of the total. In the following five subsections, we analyze this and other significant programs as they stood just prior to the COVID-19 pandemic, category by category. We discuss pandemic-era changes to the landscape in section 7.4, in particular subsection in 7.4.2.

### 7.3.1 Health Care

The Medicaid program was enacted in 1965 and provides health insurance primarily for individuals with low incomes. All states and territories have Medicaid programs. The federal government sets certain parameters, such as coverage and eligibility requirements, and provides matching funds, but each state administers its own program and can set coverage and eligibility levels above and beyond certain federal minima. The regular matching rate (federal medical assistance percentage, or FMAP) varies across states based on per capita income, but is in principle at least 50 percent and at most 83 percent. This means the states receive at least one dollar in federal support for each dollar spent on Medicaid.[14] It was by far the largest federal grant program in 2015–2019, with an average annual outlay of over $350 billion in real 2012 dollars.

The Medicaid program illustrates some of the key points discussed in section 7.2. First, it is an example of a program designed to incentivize higher spending levels on a specific service than would otherwise materialize. It does so by lowering the relative price, to each state, of spending on Medicaid. Note that there are limits on how far the federal government can go in its deployment of incentives along these lines. In the 2012 case of *NFIB v. Sebelius*, the Supreme Court struck down provisions of the Affordable Care Act that threatened the withdrawal of all Medicaid reimbursements from states that refused to expand their Medicaid program to all adults under the age of 65 with incomes up to 133 percent of the federal poverty level (FPL). This decision was rooted in the view that the threat of losing all Medicaid reimbursements did not leave the states with a "legitimate choice" and was a "gun to the head." The Court argued that effectively forcing the states to implement a new federal program would undermine political accountability; that "when the State has no choice, the Federal Government can achieve its objectives without accountability."

14. The matching rate, or federal share, is calculated as 1 minus the state share. The state share, in turn, equals 45 percent $*$ [(state per capita income)$^2$/(US per capita income)$^2$]. The federal share is increased for the colonies, certain services, and certain beneficiaries. The latter group includes individuals newly eligible for Medicaid under the Affordable Care Act of 2010, for whom the FMAP is 90 percent.

Second, the Medicaid program's lower bounds on the generosity of states' programs serves to limit policy competition. By placing a floor on the provision of health insurance to some of the most vulnerable groups in society, the program reduces the risk of a "race to the bottom" in the provision of the social safety net. And by providing significant subsidies to states that choose to run expansive Medicaid programs, it reduces the need for collection of own-source resources. This, in turn, reduces the scope for tax competition.

In addition, the FMAP illustrates a lesson that is relevant for the design of intergovernmental grants more generally. While its funding structure follows relatively straightforwardly from the motivations highlighted in the previous two paragraphs, federal policymakers have in recent decades relied repeatedly on this structure to shape the provision of grants for purposes of macroeconomic stabilization. Specifically, in response to the 2001 recession, the Great Recession, and the COVID-19 pandemic, the federal government has temporarily raised FMAPs as a mechanism for injecting additional funds into state governments' budgets (Clemens et al. 2021; Clemens and Veuger 2023; Leung 2022). We have observed elsewhere that this linking of macroeconomic stabilization to the size of states' Medicaid programs violates the Tinbergen rule, which holds that independent policy objectives are best met through the use of independent policy instruments (Clemens and Veuger 2023).

While much smaller than Medicaid, the second-largest health program in terms of intergovernmental grants is the Children's Health Insurance Program (CHIP) at $14 billion a year. CHIP complements the Medicaid program by providing federal matching grants to the states to provide health insurance for children in households with incomes that are modest but that nonetheless exceed the Medicaid limit. CHIP matching grants are calculated on the basis of a so-called enhanced FMAP (eFMAP) that is higher than the regular FMAP but otherwise relies on similar considerations.[15]

### 7.3.2 Income Security

During the 2015–2019 period, the two largest federal grant programs meant to provide income security to households, especially households with children, were the child nutrition (school breakfasts and lunches) and tenant-based rental assistance programs. Both involved federal grants of around $20 billion a year. Four other income security programs merit mention here for the relatively large amounts of grant money involved. The TANF program, which succeeded cash assistance through the AFDC program following the 1996 welfare reform, involves some $15 billion per year. In combination, federal food aid through the Supplemental Nutrition Assistance Program

15. The eFMAP is equal to FMAP plus 0.3 * (100%—FMAP), with a maximum value of 85 percent.

(SNAP, formerly food stamps), the supplemental food program for Women, Infants and Children (WIC), and the Commodity Supplemental Food Program (CSFP) generates about $11 billion in intergovernmental transfers.[16] Finally, the federal government provides $7.5 billion in annual Foster Care and Adoption Assistance grants.

The four food aid programs in this category (school breakfasts and lunches, SNAP, WIC, and CSFP) vary in both the groups of recipients they target and in their delivery. All of them are means tested and exist, in principle, to provide sufficient nutrition to vulnerable categories of individuals: low-income school-age children; low-income households; low-income women during pregnancy, postpartum, and while breastfeeding, as well as with children under 5; and low-income seniors. The states generally have some flexibility in how they deliver these benefits and who is eligible for them, within a set of federal parameters.

Delivery is an interesting aspect of these programs. The child nutrition programs are largely in-kind: the school system is deployed to deliver breakfast and lunch to school-age children. Similarly, CSFP benefits are typically delivered as a monthly package. As we move ever so slightly toward the cash benefit side of the spectrum, WIC benefits typically come in the form of vouchers or checks that can be used to purchase specific types of food, though some states deliver packages for this program as well. For such programs, the administrative burdens imposed on stores become relevant, as not all stores participate, which, in turn, imposes convenience costs on beneficiaries (Meckel et al. 2021). The store-based delivery mechanism creates a tension between antifraud measures, which reduce the profitability of store participation, and the value of the program to beneficiaries (Meckel 2020). Finally, SNAP benefits come in the form of electronic benefit cards that can be used to purchase a wide (but restricted) range of food products. This delivery mechanism raises questions involving the potential costs associated with high-frequency fluctuations in demand that arise due to the monthly benefit-deliver cycle (Goldin et al. 2021; Shapiro 2005; Wilde and Ranney 2000).

The relatively heavy reliance on in-kind delivery and restrictions on the use of benefits may reflect, besides a paternalistic impulse, the central role of the congressional agriculture committees and the US Department of

16. Note that some of these programs and other programs discussed later in this section are significantly larger than these numbers would seem to indicate, as the programs' primary benefits involve direct transfers to households and other third parties as well. For key programs including Unemployment Insurance, for example, federal grants primarily fund program administration as opposed to program benefits. Or take the Low-Income Housing Tax Credit (LIHTEC) program: while it is associated with an annual cost to the federal government of $13.5 billion, this cost overwhelmingly consists in a tax expenditure associated with tax credits that are allocated to the states (and by them to developers through a public bidding process) as opposed to conventional spending (Keightley 2023).

Agriculture in designing and administering these federal grant programs.[17] Either way, these aspects also embody significant restrictions on the use of funds by subnational governments compared to a counterfactual of unrestricted block or matching grants.

In addition to delivery mechanisms, the food aid programs also differ in how their funding is allocated procedurally by Congress. SNAP and the school breakfasts and lunch programs constitute so-called mandatory spending,[18] in the sense that the authorizing legislation has set their funding levels,[19] while the WIC and CSFP programs involve discretionary spending that is controlled by the annual appropriations process (Aussenberg and Billings 2020).

An interesting contrast involves appropriations for WIC and for tenant-based rental assistance. Most of the latter is distributed through the Section 8 Housing Choice Voucher Program (HCVP). While both WIC and the HCVP are subject to the annual appropriations process, the link between eligibility and ability to receive benefits is significantly more tenuous for the HCVP. Since the 1990s, the WIC program has been funded at a level that has allowed the states to provide benefits to everyone who applied (Aussenberg 2017). The HCVP, on the other hand, has been characterized by rationing in the form of years-long waiting lists of the sort one might more commonly associate with the immigration bureaucracy or the British national health care service, as eligibility standards and/or benefit levels are too generous relative to the amount of federal funding Congress makes available. While this has been useful to researchers as a source of econometric identification (see e.g., Jacob and Ludwig 2012), it is hard to square with conventional notions of horizontal equity.[20]

In addition to subsidizing housing provided by third parties, public housing agencies also operate their own developments, subsidized by the federal government through the Public Housing Operating Fund. A salient characteristic of these programs is the extent to which their effectiveness depends on the interaction of program generosity with state and local characteristics such as housing supply elasticities (Eriksen and Ross 2015), land use restrictions (Corinth and Irvine 2023), and the efficiency of agency operations (see e.g., Thompson 2022).

The programs discussed so far all involve in-kind transfers or transfers of cash that can only be spent on specific goods and services. This is a manifestation of the broader move away from cash benefits in the US safety net over the past several decades, at least for most families with little or no

17. Currie and Gahvari (2008) provide a wide-ranging discussion of the potential motivations for the use of in-kind transfers as an alternative to paying out benefits in the form of cash.

18. So do Medicaid and CHIP, discussed in the previous subsection.

19. Most recently the 2018 Farm Bill.

20. In response to this longstanding issue, Collinson et al. (2019) argue for shallower or time-limited subsidies.

earnings.[21] The main remnant of the traditional cash welfare system is the TANF program, which replaced the New Deal-era AFDC program in 1997. The current structure of the program is of a block grant to the states, the size of which is based on pre-TANF federal funding amounts. The block grants have not been adjusted for inflation or population growth since 1996 and have lost 45 percent of their real value over that period. To receive their full block grant, states must meet certain requirements, including a maintenance-of-effort requirement that sets minimum levels of spending from state funds, based on pre-TANF levels, on TANF and related activities.[22]

Finally, the federal government provides significant funds to states under the banner of Foster Care and Adoption Assistance, generally through the FMAP-based matching system discussed earlier for Medicaid. Recent research has found that the generosity of states' foster payments have little impact on the supply of homes for children in need of placement and may also have limited impact on child well-being, which contrasts with typical estimates of the effects of household income generated through other cash assistance program (Chorniy and Mills 2022).

### 7.3.3 Transportation

Transportation-related programs were the dominant category of federal grantmaking to the states in the late 1950s. Of the different categories of intergovernmental grants, it is arguably the area that has experienced the least amount of change in the postwar period. The Federal-Aid Highway Program (FAHP) continues to be the source of a large majority of federal funds allocated to the states in this category. Over time, highway funds started to be allocated through an increasing number of FAHP programs, with funding calculated on the basis of various formulas. Congress eliminated or consolidated many of these programs in 2012 and simplified the allocation mechanism. In recent years, federal highway aid has been allocated based on each state's share of funding in fiscal year 2015, with a floor equal to 95 percent of each state's contribution to the highway account of the Highway Trust Fund. Contributions to the trust fund come primarily from excise taxes on motor fuels (Kirk 2021), although Congress has increasingly had to supplement these revenues with general revenue over

21. This move has been offset to an extent—and to a large extent for low-income households with significant market income—by the expansion of the Earned Income Tax Credit and the (refundable portion of the) Child Tax Credit, and by the rapid growth, especially during the 1990s, in the number of nonelderly recipients of Supplemental Security Income.

22. Whether these funds reach their intended targets is a matter of governance. In a high-profile case that will probe some of the limits of how such funds can be used, Mississippi's Department of Health of Human Services has filed a lawsuit in an attempt to retrieve tens of millions of TANF dollars that were allegedly paid to former NFL quarterback Brett Favre and others in exchange for services that may not have been delivered and in connection with various projects, such as the construction of a university volleyball facility and the capitalization of a biotechnology startup, that may be incompatible with the objectives of the program (Baker 2022).

time.[23] There are two principal reasons for this. First, the excise taxes on both gas and diesel fuel have been eroded in real terms as they are not indexed to, and have not been raised otherwise to keep up with, inflation. Second, increasing fuel efficiency and growing adoption of electric vehicles have reduced the excise tax base. Note that the FAHP does not rely on congressional appropriations directly. Instead, the Federal Highway Authority has contract authority over the trust fund and enters into binding contracts to fund projects.

This "revenue sharing" structure, through which revenue is collected at the federal level but then returned almost directly to the states, illustrates perhaps most directly how fiscal federalism can reduce the scope for tax competition while leaving program administration and implementation up to the states. In that sense it stands in contrast with the previously discussed programs, which are also substantively concerned with avoiding a "race to the bottom" in the provision of services.

The second-largest, but significantly smaller, transportation program is the Federal Public Transportation Program, which OMB refers to as Urban Mass Transportation Grants. The federal government had limited involvement with public transportation until the mid-1960s, when reduced ridership triggered bailouts of public transit systems that in a sense have become permanent (Mallett 2022). In 2019, close to 90 percent of all public transportation trips were made by bus or heavy rail, though the program funds other types of public transit as well. The grants in question flow from the public transit account of the Highway Trust Fund. Funding is allocated through dozens of programs and on the basis of various formulas. The largest one of these, the Urbanized Area Formula Program, bases the allocation of funds on a mix of characteristics of urban areas that include population, population density, and the number of low-income individuals, plus various measures of public transit usage and cost.

### 7.3.4 Education

While the federal government's role in financing K–12 education is generally limited (federal funding accounts for less than 10 percent of education spending), it does have several programs that make grants to states or local school districts. The largest is the Title I program, which provides school districts with additional funding intended to support educationally disadvantaged children. Title I is authorized under the Elementary and Secondary Education Act of 1965, as amended, and allocates funding based largely on

23. Between September 2008 and 2021 a total of $157 billion was transferred to the Highway Trust Fund from Treasury general funds and the Leaking Underground Storage Tank (LUST) Trust Fund, including $125 billion to the highway account (Kirk 2021). The 2021 Infrastructure Investment and Jobs Act includes an additional $118 billion general revenue transfer, but also increases future contract authority levels. In combination these changes are projected to increase the trust fund's funding gap (Committee for a Responsible Federal Budget 2022).

the number or share of children living in poverty in the district. The formulas also incorporate elements such as the amount of spending per pupil from state and local revenue, a minimum amount for small states, and provisions that keep funding from declining rapidly year over year. The different formulas combine to produce allocations that may strike some as counterintuitive: districts with similar shares of formula children, for example, can receive wildly different allocations per child, and different states receive very different allocations per formula child (Gordon and Reber 2023). These types of discrepancies are typical for a system of matching grants, but they are exacerbated by specific details of the formulas.

The 1974 Individuals with Disabilities Education Act provides grants to school districts for special education. Kolbe et al. (2022) illustrate that the formulas for these grants, as revised in 1999, generate allocations that are more detached from the number of children with special needs than one might expect.

### 7.3.5 Other

The "Other" category naturally includes a grab bag of different programs, some of which are quite significant in terms of the associated federal grants to state and local governments. We discuss the Disaster Relief Fund, the second-largest line item in normal times, in more detail in the context of the COVID-19 pandemic (below in subsection 7.4.2). Here we will focus on Children and Families Services Programs and the Community Development Fund.

By far the largest of the Children and Families Services Programs, accounting for about 80 percent of total grants, is Head Start. Head Start funds early-childhood development services for low-income children below the age of compulsory school attendance (i.e., those ages 0–4). At least 90 percent of beneficiaries need to meet one of several criteria. They must come from families with incomes below the FPL, they must be categorically eligible because their families receive Supplemental Security Income or TANF, or they must be in foster care or homeless. There are limited exceptions for children from households between 100 percent and 130 percent of the FPL. The program facilitates a comprehensive set of educational, health, nutritional, and social services for close to 1 million children through nonprofit and for-profit providers. Kline and Walters (2016) find that Head Start draws about a third of its beneficiaries from competing programs, and that its positive effects are particularly large in places where services would not otherwise be provided. Accounting for this cross-program substitution effect reduces estimates of the net fiscal impact of the program and raises its benefit-cost ratio.[24]

24. Similar cost and benefit accounting issues arose previously in our discussion of Baicker and Staiger's (2005) research on the effects the DSH program.

The Community Development Fund provides block grants to state and (large) local governments to engage in a wide range of activities meant to improve the circumstances of low- and moderate-income people, prevent or eliminate blight, or address threats to the health or welfare of the community.[25] In this instance, the potential use of funds is purposefully broad. Money is allocated on the basis of two formulas, and to two categories of grantees: so-called entitlement communities (principal metropolitan cities, other cities with a population over 50,000, and other urban counties with over 200,000 residents) and the states, which then redistribute the funds to nonentitlement communities. Funding is allocated based on two different formulas (that in turn differ slightly for entitlement communities in states) that involve population, poverty, overcrowding, housing built before 1940, and lagged population growth. Supplemental funding is at times appropriated to in response to disasters and emergencies, as we will see in subsection 7.4.2.

## 7.4 The COVID-19 Pandemic

### 7.4.1 Intergovernmental Grants and Strategic Interactions During COVID-19

The COVID-19 pandemic has proven to be an important episode with respect to developments associated with the strategic interactions among governments as well as with respect to the role of intergovernmental grants as instruments of fiscal and social policy. Externalities associated with cross-border flows of COVID-19 itself, for example, raise important issues related to the costs of cross-border economic activity and the potential importance of cooperation among neighboring governments.

In the United States, an interesting development in this regard was the emergence of several interstate compacts: the Western States Pact, the Midwest Governors' Regional Pact, and the Eastern States Multi-State Council. While it is not entirely clear what purposes these compacts, the interstate equivalent of treaties, ultimately served, one of their ostensible purposes was to facilitate coordination on the eventual rolling back of restrictions on economic activity.[26] To the best of our knowledge, these pacts have not yet been the subject of economics research.

The pandemic gave rise to demand for novel sets of goods, services, and regulatory measures that pose considerable challenges linked to spillovers across jurisdictions. As an initial example, the development of vaccines pro-

25. 24 CFR § 570.200.

26. One might think these interstate compacts would require congressional authorization under the Compact Clause of the US Constitution (Article I, Section 10, Clause 3), but the Supreme Court in *Virginia v. Tennessee* and a series of subsequent cases decided to interpret this clause so as to make it less burdensome.

vides a case of a global public good for which international cooperation to achieve high levels of investment would have been attractive. Second, the pandemic's early stages provided an unusually clean case study in Gordon's (1983) point that one government's activities may alter the resource costs faced by others. When personal protective equipment, ventilators, and vaccine doses were in short supply, purchases secured by one government could alter the prices and availability facing others. Third, the continuation of economic activity in one jurisdiction could alter the flows of case counts into others through a classic pandemic disease externality. Fourth, shutdowns to economic activity impaired supply chains in ways that exerted negative externalities on the productivity of other jurisdictions. Notably, the opposing implications of considerations three and four make it difficult to sign the net direction of the externalities associated with any one jurisdiction's decision to shut down or maintain economic activity.

In addition to these spillovers and externalities, the pandemic generated a shock to both the types and amounts of spending in which state and local governments were expected to engage. Because contractions of economic activity threaten governments' tax bases and other sources of revenue (Clemens and Veuger 2020a and 2020b), this combination of factors contributed to widespread support for the use of large federal transfers to support the activities of state and local governments. In the US context, this led federal grants to state and local governments to reach historic highs, not only in absolute terms but also as a share of GDP, by a considerable margin. We now turn to discussing how these grants were designed and allocated.

### 7.4.2 COVID-19-Era Intergovernmental Grants in the United States

The federal government's response to the COVID-19 pandemic was wide ranging and involved dramatic changes to fiscal, monetary, healthcare, tax, immigration, housing, and public-health policy. Most relevant to us here is the component of the fiscal policy response that involved aid to state, local, tribal, and territorial governments, which amounted to some $900 billion.[27] We have discussed and analyzed the macroeconomic and public finance implications of this aid elsewhere (e.g., Clemens and Veuger 2023); here and in the next section we will concentrate on the specific programs and vehicles used to deliver the aid and its implications for policy competition.

Our discussion of how federal grants to the states were adjusted in response to the COVID-19 pandemic mostly follows the structure of section 7.3. Table 7.2 follows the same structure as table 7.1 and shows average

27. This number does not (and should not) correspond to the totals in table 7.2 below. Differences are due to a variety of factors, including that the current exercise focuses on fiscal years 2020 and 2021, that not all funds appropriated have been committed or disbursed, that we do not include aid to tribal and territorial governments here, categorization differences between OMB and the Committee for a Responsible Federal Budget, and that the amounts in the tables are in real 2012 USD.

Table 7.2 **Average annual grant outlays to state and local governments, FY 2020–2021**

| Category | Program name | Annual outlay | 2022 estimated outlay | Category total |
|---|---|---|---|---|
| *Largest grants by category* | | | | |
| Health | Grants to States for Medicaid | 425,364 | 450,581 | 455,828 |
| Health | Children's Health Insurance Fund | 14,360 | 13,323 | |
| Income security | Tenant Based Rental Assistance | 21,762 | 21,367 | 128,129 |
| Income security | Child Nutrition Programs | 21,052 | 24,678 | |
| Transportation | Federal-aid Highways (Trust Fund) | 39,024 | 37,203 | 67,562 |
| *Transportation* | *Urban Mass Transportation Grants* | 8,289 | 20,134 | |
| Education | Education for the Disadvantaged | 13,878 | 15,737 | 47,741 |
| *Education* | *Education Stabilization Fund* | 11,380 | 27,451 | |
| *Other* | *Coronavirus Relief Fund* | 103,032 | 87,933 | 198,562 |
| Other | Disaster Relief Fund | 36,866 | 29,042 | |
| *Other large grants* | | | | |
| *Income security* | *Emergency Rental Assistance* | 14,093 | 14,802 | |
| Income security | Temporary Assistance for Needy Families | 13,911 | 13,661 | |
| Income security | SNAP, WIC, and CSFP | 13,141 | 12,440 | |
| Education | Special Education | 11,002 | 14,724 | |
| Other | Children and Families Services Programs | 10,829 | 11,728 | |
| **Average annual outlays for grants** | | | | **897,823** |

Note: This table uses data from Office of Management and Budget (2022b) and US Bureau of Economic Analysis (2023). Average annual outlay expressed in real 2012 USD millions and are deflated using the BEA's implicit price deflator. Programs that were not included in Table 7.1 are rendered in italics.

outlays for 2020 and 2021, as well as estimated outlays for 2022. Many of the programs in table 7.2 were also included in table 7.1, though four new programs made the list during the pandemic: non-trust-fund Urban Mass Transportation Grants, the Education Stabilization Fund, the Coronavirus Relief Fund, and Emergency Rental Assistance. Additionally, many of the programs that did appear in table 7.1 were expanded significantly.

### *7.4.2.1 Health Care*

One of the very first measures Congress took in response to the COVID-19 pandemic, in the mid-March 2020 Families First Coronavirus Response Act, was to increase the FMAP by 6.2 percentage points[28] and the CHIP matching rate by 4.34 percentage points. This federal generosity—Medicaid grants in 2020–21 were 20 percent greater in real terms than in 2015–2019—did come with strings attached. Most importantly, the states had to comply with a continuous coverage requirement to keep people who lost eligibil-

28. This increase also triggered increased matching grants for Foster Care and Adoption Assistance, naturally.

ity enrolled in Medicaid and CHIP. As a result, enrollment grew by some 21 million people from February 2020 through November 2021.[29] While a principal goal of the FMAP increase was to stabilize state budgets, Clemens et al. (2021) find that the increases in matching funds were not correlated with variations in states' Medicaid enrollment increases due to the large variation in expenditures on the inframarginal, prepandemic beneficiary population. The late-2022 Consolidated Appropriations Act phases out the matching rate increases between April and December 2023.

*7.4.2.2 Income Security*

The federal government took dramatic steps to provide income security to households throughout 2020 and 2021. This happened not only through direct cash payments, increased unemployment insurance benefits,[30] and the Paycheck Protection Program, but also through increased spending on grants to state and local governments in this category.

A particularly large new program was the Emergency Rental Assistance (ERA) program, one of many aggressive interventions in housing markets during a period that perhaps most remarkably featured a nationwide eviction moratorium. Subnational governments enjoyed significant leeway in determining how to allocate funds, but Driessen et al. (2023) report that

> from the first quarter of 2021 through the second quarter of 2022 grantees had provided ERA to 5.35 million unique households, the majority of which had incomes at or below 30% of local area median income. Roughly 70% of those served received rental assistance and about 64% received assistance with rental arrears. About 14% received utility assistance and 27% received assistance with utility arrears.

A second program that merits mention here is SNAP. The federal government, which fully funds SNAP benefits and splits the cost of program administration with the states, waived all work requirements and raised benefit amounts in different ways over the course of the pandemic, including by 15 percent through the first three quarters of 2021. While these emergency allotments ended for all states after February 2023, a number of states had chosen to end them prior to that, starting with Idaho in March 2021 (Long 2023).

Finally, widespread school closures interfered with the delivery of school meals. In response, eligible school children received benefits through the

29. As pandemic policies unwind, this raises the question of how the insurance coverage status of these individuals will change as their Medicaid eligibility is reassessed (Dague and Ukert 2022).

30. While the states processed the bonus unemployment insurance benefits paid by the federal government through programs like the Federal Pandemic Unemployment Compensation, Pandemic Emergency Unemployment Compensation, and Pandemic Unemployment Assistance, we follow the OMB's classification here and consider these to be payments to individuals, not intergovernmental grants. Tastes may differ, but gotta draw the line somewhere!

Pandemic Electronic Benefit Transfer (P-EBT) program, which mimicked the approach of the SNAP program to the delivery of benefits.

*7.4.2.3 Transportation*

The public-health crisis and the associated changes in commuting patterns and work arrangements led to a steep drop-off in mass transit ridership. In response, Congress allocated large discretionary amounts of funding to transport systems, catapulting non-trust-fund Federal Public Transportation Program grants to the second position in our transportation category. Note that many of these funds are being disbursed after fiscal year 2021, as table 7.2 indicates. A key question is whether these grants will become permanent, similar to how permanent federal involvement in this area resulted from the negative shock to revenue from widespread car ownership, as discussed in subsection 7.3.3.

*7.4.2.4 Education*

The main vehicle for education-related COVID-19 grants to state and local governments is the Education Stabilization Fund. The two main components of this fund were the Elementary and Secondary School Emergency Relief (ESSER) Fund and the Higher Education Emergency Relief Fund. ESSER funds totaling nearly $200 billion were allocated proportional to existing Title I allocations. It is not obvious whether the distributional considerations underlying Title 1 grant formulas relate to the revenue and spending implications of the COVID-19 public health crisis.

*7.4.2.5 Other*

Two of the most significant sources of pandemic-era federal aid to state and local governments can be described as "Other" programs. The first is the Disaster Relief Fund (DRF), mentioned in subsection 7.3.5 above, which was supercharged during the pandemic. The DRF is managed by FEMA and is meant to serve as a source of funds as needed by the federal government to address domestic emergencies through disaster relief. Funding arrives from a combination of annual appropriations and discretionary supplemental appropriations. The fund's largest gross appropriations in history materialized in 2021 ($50 billion from the American Rescue Plan Act), though they were larger in real terms in 2005, the year of Hurricane Katrina (Painter 2022). While the DRF seems well suited to deal with unexpected disasters that strike specific parts of the country, its funding and operating models are less suited for the provision of macroeconomic stabilization funds (Clemens and Veuger 2023).

A large contribution to the stabilization objective was provided through the final program we discuss, the Coronavirus Relief Fund. This fund distributed general-purpose fiscal assistance grants to state, local, and tribal governments. As Clemens and Veuger (2023) emphasize, these grants would prove to be much larger than estimates of the shock to need. A straightforward potential explanation for this is that policymakers overlearned the lessons of the period following the Global Financial Crisis, when state and local governments were perceived to be a fiscal drag on the recovery (see e.g., Bernanke 2020).

### 7.4.3 Intergovernmental Grants and Tax Competition during COVID-19

During the COVID-19 pandemic, federal aid has placed the budgets of state and local governments on unusually favorable footing (Clemens and Veuger 2023). There is broad interest in the question of how state and local governments have utilized and will utilize their windfalls of federal fiscal assistance. A narrower question of interest is whether windfalls of federal fiscal assistance have been used to support states' efforts to lure capital through tax competition or, alternatively, through increased provision of public services that are of value to businesses. In this subsection we present new empirical results answering this question for the case of the corporate tax.

Whether windfalls encourage or discourage tax competition is theoretically ambiguous. The empirical evidence is mixed as well. Helm and Stuhler (2021) find evidence of tax increases in response to windfalls, triggered by revised census counts, for German municipalities. Berset and Schelker (2020) find the opposite effect of a sudden increase in fiscal equalization grants that befell municipalities in the Swiss canton of Zurich. Finally, Köthenbürger and Loumeau (2023) use a regression kink design to study the effect of federal transfers on tax rates in all of Switzerland and find null effects.

Perhaps most intuitively, a (temporary) loosening of the subnational budget constraint may trigger an across-the-board reduction in tax rates, especially in a context of restrictions on the size of budget surpluses. In fact, when this kind of tax reduction does not materialize, it is typically described as an anomaly (the flypaper effect discussed in subsection 7.2.3.3). Additionally, a business-destroying shock like the pandemic might temporarily elevate the stakes of tax competition as states compete over the new firms and the new (intangible) capital that will replace the old.

On the other hand, large windfalls may, in themselves, enhance a location's attractiveness to new capital. That is, windfall transfers to state governments imply public procurers flush with cash. Similarly, where state and local windfalls are passed onto taxpayers, local demand for private goods may be elevated as well. With respect to firm location decisions, the prospect of heightened demand and strengthened public-good provision may substitute for the benefits of a lower tax rate and insulate states with particularly large windfalls from tax competition.

To add to the ambiguity, the effects of a windfall on the corporate tax rate also depend on the income elasticity of public relative to private consumption, as modeled by Chirinko and Wilson (2017). Larger windfalls may lead to either a lower or higher corporate tax rate. In their model, the resulting slope is informative regarding the reaction functions that are central to traditional models of tax competition. Finally, different models of electoral competition also imply different responses to windfalls. In threshold models of retrospective voting, a politician who receives a small windfall will typically find it more attractive to set risky economic policies than a politician who receives a large windfall.

A key challenge to empirically estimating the effects of windfall fiscal assistance on tax policy is a standard endogeneity concern: fiscal assistance may tend to be targeted at areas in greatest need. Variations in economic prosperity and distress, rather than aid per se, may thus tend to underlie the observed correlation between aid and enacted tax rates. To overcome this and other potential sources of bias, we supplement a purely descriptive look at the data with an instrumental-variable estimator. In particular, we build on existing evidence showing that the overrepresentation of small states in the US Congress led federal legislation to send disproportionate relief to the state and local governments in those states (Clemens and Veuger 2021). Importantly, we confirm in our 2021 paper that variation induced by these predetermined, constitutionally anchored political factors was orthogonal to a rich set of measures of the COVID-19 crisis's direct impact on state-level public health and public finances. This strategy of instrumenting for federal aid with aid levels predicted by congressional representation has supported separate analyses of the effects of pandemic fiscal assistance packages on macroeconomic outcomes (Clemens et al. 2022; Clemens, Kearns, et al. 2023) as well as outcomes including population-wide vaccination and testing rates (Clemens, Hoxie, et al. 2023).

In the unadjusted data, we observe that among the 11 states to enact reductions in their top corporate rate between 2019 and 2022, for example, only 3 were among the top half of states with respect to the federal fiscal assistance they received in per capita terms. In a simple bivariate regression, as presented in Appendix table 7A.3, an additional \$1,000 in aid per capita, which is well within our empirical range, predicts a 13 percentage point lower likelihood of a decrease in the corporate tax rate; this estimate is statistically distinguishable from zero at the 99 percent confidence level. Similarly, an additional \$1,000 in aid per capita predicts a modest 0.15 percentage point increase in the corporate tax rate, an estimate that is statistically distinguishable from zero at the at the 95 percent confidence level. The map presented in figure 7.2 reveals that corporate tax cuts were enacted predominantly by relatively low- and mid-size population states and were not enacted by high-population states.

These simple correlations between aid and corporate tax policy may not be informative regarding the causal effect of a fiscal assistance windfall due

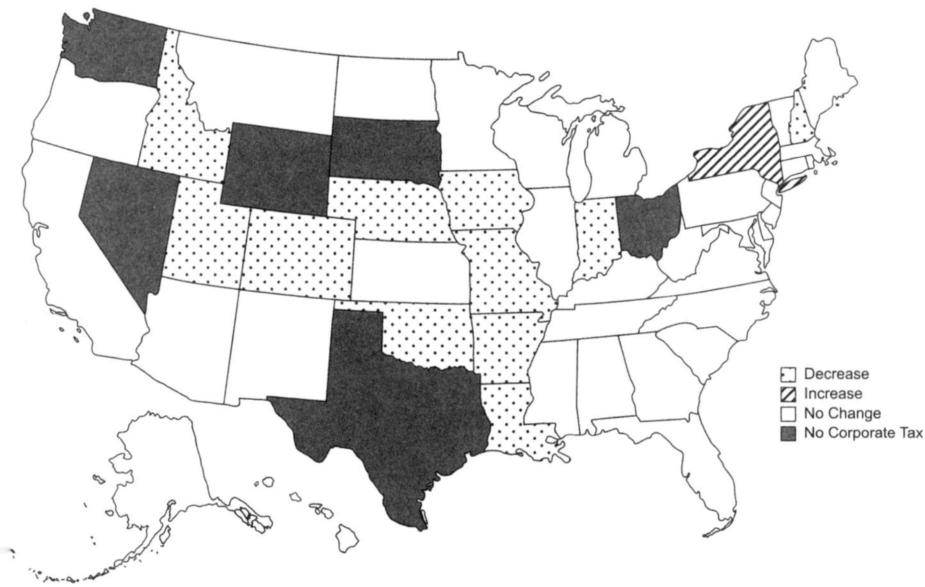


**Fig. 7.2 Changes to corporate tax rates, 2019–2022**

Note: This figure uses data from the Tax Policy Center (2019, 2020, 2021, 2022) to show the geographic distribution of changes to the maximum corporate tax rate between 2019 and 2022. States with "No Corporate Tax" include those with a gross receipts tax but no corporate tax rate (NV, OH, TX, and WA), as well as those with no gross receipts tax and no corporate tax rate (SD and WY).

to the endogeneity concerns discussed above. If federal aid is targeted at states that would otherwise have raised taxes due to their levels of budgetary distress, for example, the correlations discussed above would be biased toward positive values. Alternatively, if hard-hit states feel compelled by economic conditions to compete harder for firms via corporate tax competition, then these correlations would be biased toward negative values.

Our instrumental-variables estimation strategy is described by the two equations below:

$$\text{(1a)} \qquad \frac{TotalAid_s}{Pop_{s,y_{2020}}} = \alpha + \gamma_1 RepsPerMillion_s + \gamma_2 X_s + \varepsilon_s$$

$$\text{(1b)} \qquad Corporate\ Rate\ Reduction_s = \alpha + \beta_1 \widehat{\frac{TotalAid_s}{Pop_{s,y_{2020}}}} + \beta_2 X_s + u_s.$$

In the first-stage regression (1a), ($TotalAid_s\ /\ Pop_{s,y_{2020}}$) is regressed on the number of representatives and senators per million residents in 2020 and a vector of control variables, $X_S$, that differs across specifications. The first stage outcome, ($TotalAid_s\ /\ Pop_{s,y_{2020}}$), is the sum of the fiscal aid a state and the local governments therein received across the four major pieces of pandemic relief legislation: the Families First Coronavirus Response Act, CARES Act, Response and Relief Act, and American Rescue Plan Act.

Fitted values from the first stage (1a) are used to estimate the second stage (1b). Here the outcome is an indicator for whether a state enacted a corporate rate reduction in any year between 2019 and 2022. The coefficient $\beta_1$ is thus an estimate of the relationship between the variations in federal aid that were driven by variations in congressional representation and the likelihood that a state enacted a corporate rate cut. We also present estimates in which the outcome variable is an indicator for whether a state enacted an increase, as opposed to a reduction, in their corporate tax rate.

With respect to the covariates in $X_s$, in one specification, for example, we control only for the log of a state's population, such that our identifying variation relies solely on the unusual relationship between population and representation in the US Congress. In additional specifications, we include controls for factors including the prepandemic trend in the corporate tax rate, other features of the pandemic policy landscape, variations in political factors, and variations in the severity of the pandemic.

Estimates of the model described above are reported in tables 7.3 and 7.4. In our analyses of corporate tax declines (table 7.3), we observe that the use of the instrumental-variables strategy results in larger coefficients describing the effect of pandemic fiscal assistance on the likelihood that a state enacted a corporate rate cut. In models that include controls for the prepandemic trend in corporate tax rates as well as for variations in other features of the pandemic policy landscape, an additional $1,000 in aid per capita, which as noted above is well within our empirical range, predicts a 50 percent lower likelihood of a corporate rate reduction ($p < .01$). Across the specifications presented, the point estimates range from –0.21 to –0.53. An equivalent set of regressions that do not weight states according to their population yields point estimates ranging from –0.22 to –0.37 with similarly high levels of statistical significance (results not shown). The finding that greater aid is negatively related with the enactment of corporate rate cuts is thus strengthened as we move from bivariate regression to instrumental-variable estimation. As noted previously, 11 states enacted corporate rate decreases between 2019 and 2022. This was ultimately quite similar to the total of 10 states that enacted corporate rate decreases during the 2016 to 2019 period.

Our analysis thus finds that the small-state bias in federal grants is negatively correlated with corporate rate reductions. That is, larger aid allocations predict a greater likelihood that corporate tax rates held steady, while smaller aid allocations predict reductions in corporate tax rates.

Table 7.4 presents our analysis of the relationship between federal aid and the enactment of increases in corporate tax rates. Here we obtain null effects. Further, the point estimates tend to fall outside of the confidence intervals associated with the estimates presented in table 7.3, suggesting an

**Table 7.3 Pandemic-related intergovernmental grants and corporate tax decreases**

| | Baseline (1) | Political (2) | COVID (3) | Combined (4) | Simple (5) |
|---|---|---|---|---|---|
| Total aid per resident (USD thousands) | −0.525*** | −0.518*** | −0.386*** | −0.348** | −0.210** |
| | (0.159) | (0.157) | (0.132) | (0.148) | (0.107) |
| Log(Population) | −0.346*** | −0.338*** | −0.239*** | −0.154 | −0.158*** |
| | (0.0811) | (0.0929) | (0.0846) | (0.113) | (0.0477) |
| Share of population eligible for MLF | 0.388 | 0.531 | 0.425 | 0.385 | |
| | (0.361) | (0.411) | (0.321) | (0.362) | |
| Change corporate tax rate (2018–2019) | 2.367 | 1.781 | 1.154 | 5.591 | |
| | (3.526) | (4.520) | (3.687) | (4.312) | |
| Average OSI (March 2020) | 0.819 | 0.0629 | −0.651 | −0.779 | |
| | (1.037) | (2.440) | (0.877) | (2.076) | |
| Average OSI (January 2022) | 2.237** | 2.245*** | 3.102*** | 3.474*** | |
| | (0.885) | (0.870) | (0.685) | (0.662) | |
| Political controls | N | Y | N | Y | N |
| COVID-19 controls | N | N | Y | Y | N |
| Observations | 44 | 44 | 44 | 44 | 44 |
| R-squared | 0.327 | 0.340 | 0.448 | 0.519 | 0.204 |
| First-stage F-stat | 13.944 | 23.2207 | 43.5942 | 38.4523 | 73.824 |

Note: This table uses data from Chidambaram and Musumeci (2021), Committee for a Responsible Federal Budget (2021), Federal Reserve Board (2021), Google LLC (2021), Hale et al. (2020), Lewis et al. (2021), Medicaid and CHIP Payment Access Commission (2021), MIT Election and Data Science Lab (2017), Tax Policy Center (2018, 2019, 2020, 2021, 2022), US Census Bureau (2021), US Department of the Treasury (2021a, 2021b), US Federal Transit Administration (2021a), and US Office of Elementary and Secondary Education (2021) to estimate the following equations:

(1a) $$\frac{TotalAid_s}{Pop_{s,y2020}} = \alpha + \gamma_1 RepsPerMillion_s + \gamma_2 X_s + \varepsilon_s$$

(1b) $$Corporate\ Rate\ Reduction_s = \alpha + \beta_1 \widehat{\frac{TotalAid_s}{Pop_{s,y2020}}} + \beta_2 X_s + u_s$$

where $TotalAid_s$ is the total federal aid per resident to state and local governments (USD thousands) in state $s$ pooled across all four major bills. It is scaled by $Pop_{s,y2020}$, state $s$'s 2020 official census population. In first stage equation (1a), $(TotalAid_s \,/\, Pop_{s,y2020})$ is instrumented using $RepsPerMillion_s$, the number of representatives and senators per million residents for state $s$ in 2020. Estimates of equation (1b) are shown in Columns 1 through 5. $Corporate\ Rate\ Reduction_s$ is a binary variable indicating whether a state's maximum corporate tax rate decreased between 2019 and 2022. Column 1 reports the results of our baseline specification of equation (1b), which includes a set of state-level controls for state $s$ ($X_s$) including the log of 2020 official census population; the share of a state's population living in a town eligible for financing through the MLF; and the March 2020, end of March 2020, and January 2022 month averages of a state's Oxford Stringency Index. In Column 2, controls for share of votes cast for Donald Trump in the 2020 US presidential election in state $s$, and the percent change in retail mobility relative from January 2022 to a February 2020 baseline are added. In Column 3, controls for the number of new COVID-19 in January 2022, the cumulative number of COVID-19 deaths in January 2022, new COVID-19 cases in January 2022, and the cumulative number of COVID-19 cases in January 2022, are added. Column 4 presents results including both political and COVID-19 controls. Column 5 presents results of a simple specification controlling only for the log of 2020 official census population. Observations are weighted by area population of state $s$ and standard errors (in parentheses) are clustered by state $s$. States that do not have a corporate tax rate (South Dakota, Wyoming, Nevada, Ohio, Texas, and Washington) are excluded from this analysis.

**Table 7.4** **Pandemic-related intergovernmental grants and corporate tax increases**

| | Baseline (1) | Political (2) | COVID (3) | Combined (4) | Simple (5) |
|---|---|---|---|---|---|
| Total aid per resident (USD thousands) | −0.219 | −0.183 | −0.0574 | −0.116 | 0.0488 |
| | (0.246) | (0.153) | (0.101) | (0.124) | (0.0874) |
| Log(Population) | −0.0927 | −0.159 | −0.0142 | −0.149 | 0.0687 |
| | (0.125) | (0.102) | (0.0644) | (0.0907) | (0.0738) |
| Share of population eligible for MLF | 0.103 | 0.367 | 0.130 | 0.355* | |
| | (0.200) | (0.242) | (0.175) | (0.214) | |
| Change corporate tax rate (2018–2019) | 2.123 | −1.549 | −5.588 | −7.107 | |
| | (4.412) | (5.419) | (3.916) | (5.147) | |
| Average OSI (March 2020) | 2.122 | 4.442** | 1.027 | 3.430** | |
| | (1.954) | (2.253) | (0.863) | (1.453) | |
| Average OSI (January 2022) | 1.394 | 0.505 | 1.618 | 0.813* | |
| | (1.265) | (0.358) | (1.014) | (0.443) | |
| Political controls | N | Y | N | Y | N |
| COVID-19 controls | N | N | Y | Y | N |
| Observations | 44 | 44 | 44 | 44 | 44 |
| R-squared | N/A | 0.511 | 0.388 | 0.660 | 0.146 |
| First-stage F-stat | 13.944 | 23.221 | 43.5942 | 38.4523 | 73.824 |

Note: This table uses data from Chidambaram and Musumeci (2021), Committee for a Responsible Federal Budget (2021), Federal Reserve Board (2021), Google LLC (2021), Hale et al. (2020), Lewis et al. (2021), Medicaid and CHIP Payment Access Commission (2021), MIT Election and Data Science Lab (2017), Tax Policy Center (2018, 2019, 2020, 2021, 2022), US Census Bureau (2021), US Department of the Treasury (2021a, 2021b), US Federal Transit Administration (2021a), and US Office of Elementary and Secondary Education (2021) to estimate the following equations:

(2a) $$\frac{TotalAid_s}{Pop_{s,y2020}} = \alpha + \gamma_1 RepsPerMillion_s + \gamma_2 X_s + \varepsilon_s$$

(2b) $$Corporate\ Rate\ Reduction_s = \alpha + \beta_1 \widehat{\frac{TotalAid_s}{Pop_{s,y2020}}} + \beta_2 X_s + u_s,$$

where $TotalAid_s$ is the total federal aid per resident to state and local governments (USD thousands) in state $s$ pooled across all four major bills. It is scaled by <<EQt069.pdf>>, state $s$'s 2020 official census population. In first stage equation (1a), <<EQt070.pdf>> is instrumented using $RepsPerMillion_s$, the number of representatives and senators per million residents for state $s$ in 2020. Estimates of equation (2b) are shown in Columns 1 through 5. *Corporate Rate Increase$_s$* is a binary variable indicating whether a state's maximum corporate tax rate increased between 2019 and 2022. Column 1 reports the results of our baseline specification of equation (1b), which includes a set of state-level controls for state $s$ ($X_s$) including the log of 2020 official census population; the share of a state's population living in a town eligible for financing through the MLF; and the March 2020, end of March 2020, and January 2022 month averages of a state's Oxford Stringency Index. In Column 2, controls for share of votes cast for Donald Trump in the 2020 US presidential election in state $s$, and the percent change in retail mobility relative from January 2022 to a February 2020 baseline are added. In Column 3, controls for the number of new COVID-19 in January 2022, the cumulative number of COVID-19 deaths in January 2022, new COVID-19 cases in January 2022, and the cumulative number of COVID-19 cases in January 2022, are added. Column 4 presents results including both political and COVID-19 controls. Column 5 presents results of a simple specification controlling only for the log of 2020 official census population. Observations are weighted by area population of state $s$ and standard errors (in parentheses) are clustered by state $s$. States that do not have a corporate tax rate (South Dakota, Wyoming, Nevada, Ohio, Texas, and Washington) are excluded from this analysis.

asymmetry in the relationship between federal aid and the decision to reduce versus increase corporate rates. We also note, however, that the confidence intervals for the estimated effects of federal aid on increases in corporate rates are wider than the intervals for the estimated effects on decreases in corporate rates. This is related to the fact that increases in corporate rates were exceedingly rare during our sample period. In an environment of sizable surpluses, the comparative irrelevance of the rate increase margin may be the source of the asymmetry we observe.

A natural question about our empirical specification involves the use of the log of each state's population as a control. A point of potential interest is that the identifying variation in congressional representation is the variation that remains after residualizing with respect to this covariate. A feature of the data is that both the very smallest and the very largest states have positive residual representation after conditioning on log population. This raises the question of whether our estimates might be driven in part by large states. In Appendix table 7A.2 we run our 2SLS models on a sample of states that excludes the five largest by population. The estimates are very similar to the estimates presented in table 7.3, revealing that the estimates are not driven by the five largest states. This point was also clearly illustrated by the map presented in figure 7.2, as none of the most populous states enacted corporate tax cuts during this time period.

Our results are consistent with a scenario in which the income elasticity of demand for public goods exceeds the income elasticity of demand for private goods. This is consistent, for example, with the standard view of health care as a "luxury good." The same is also plausibly true of higher education. In such a scenario, additional grant receipt is disproportionately allocated to the public sector. Our finding is also consistent with models of retrospective voting in which voters cannot observe effort or rely on simple heuristics. In such models, elected officials in states that enjoyed particularly large federal transfers can coast to reelection without engaging in relatively high-variance policy competition efforts.

Whether a reduction in corporate tax competition is welfare-improving or -reducing once we aggregate over the states is not easily inferred, as discussed by Agrawal et al. (2022). Our brief analysis leaves ample room for future analyses of the effects of pandemic-era fiscal relief on state and local tax policy. These policy responses are likely to vary dependent on state characteristics, including industry mix, size, and concentration of economic activity in border areas. Anecdotally, state surpluses may have been dissipated in no small part through a mix of state-specific stimulus checks, personal income tax rebates, and other tax reductions. Indeed, the full budgetary incidence of pandemic-era fiscal relief may be of substantial interest. One could imagine that variation in policy choices had important consequences for the odds of survival of different firms and for the location choices of firms and households alike. Analyses of these additional tax and budgetary outcomes are beyond this chapter's purview.

## 7.5 Conclusion

In this chapter we have summarized some of the core insights from past research on intergovernmental relations and have provided an updated look at the institutions through which intergovernmental transfers are implemented in practice in the United States. We further discussed the prominent role of intergovernmental transfers in the context of the federal government's response to the COVID-19 pandemic, during which federal grants to state and local governments reached unprecedented levels, both in absolute terms and as a share of GDP. We conclude by discussing some dimensions of these issues that may be open for future research.

A first area for future work is opened by the prominent role of intergovernmental transfers in the context of the COVID-19 pandemic. Pandemic fiscal assistance opens a number of opportunities to investigate how fiscal institutions and alignments of interest groups shape the budgetary incidence of fiscal transfers. Large volumes of federal funds reached the budgets of cities, counties, school districts, and state governments, and much remains to be known regarding how funds were spent and the extent to which they impacted outcomes of interest. An understanding of how institutions shape these outcomes may be of use to policymakers going forward.

Second, we see substantial room for future research on the roles played by the elements of program design on which federal grants are conditioned (i.e., the "strings attached). Our review of the landscape reveals myriad strings attached to federal funds, and that these nonprice mechanisms for blunting the forces of tax and expenditure competition may, in many settings, be as important as thc associatcd federal block grants or matching grants. Further research to quantify the importance of such provisions and to understand the conditions under which alternative provisions exert greater or lesser influence would have high value. Additionally, the evidence base on the responsiveness of subnational governments either to matching grants or to the strings attached to federal grants remains less developed than the purely theoretical literature on the structure those grants might optimally take.

A third area that is ripe for additional research involves the effects of decentralization on how both the level of taxation and public services are selected and how they are targeted across beneficiary populations. One of the principal rationales for decentralization is to improve the extent to which public services cater to the preferences of the populations that finance them. As discussed above, however, a relatively limited empirical literature has addressed how decentralization shapes these choices and outcomes in practice. One noteworthy dimension of these issues is the question of how preferences within jurisdictions like US states relate to the preferences of the population as aggregated across the entirety of the federation, in particular as relates to matters of redistribution.

This question of the "optimality" of the system as reflected by the status quo relates quite directly to the processes through which the American system of fiscal federalism has evolved. Many of the largest changes to the system arose during or in the immediate aftermath of crises (wars, financial crises, pandemics). There is very limited clarity on why this has been the case. It may, for example, reflect reoptimization during periods in which elected officials have more room to maneuver. Alternatively, the history may reflect a so-called ratcheting phenomenon (Peacock and Wiseman 1961), whereby politicians refuse to let a crisis go to waste and make changes that in other times are highly persistent.

One recurring theme in our discussion of the US context specifically has been that much of the existing intergovernmental grants structure is focused on having the states administer antipoverty programs funded by and operated within parameters set by the federal government. On one level, this can be rationalized as an effort to limit tax competition and reduce policy competition of the race-to-the-bottom variety. But those objectives could also be accomplished if the federal government were to send more checks to households, as it does with the elderly. An open question therefore is why these programs are administered at the subnational level. There are a number of potential explanations. These include a desire to couple benefits with locally provided wraparound services (Evans et al. 2025); efforts by opponents of benefit programs to strategically create administrative burdens (Herd and Moynihan 2018); allowance for fine-tuning of program delivery to local preferences; constitutional constraints on federal mandates; the creation of space for the states to play their role as laboratories of democracy; and a view that program administration, in particular, benefits from more local mechanisms of political accountability and representation. The extent to which these and other explanations can account for the real-world patterns of fiscal federalism in the United States and the extent to which they reduce policy competition between subnational jurisdictions is not clear.

## Acknowledgments

We are grateful to Beatrice Lee for excellent research assistance, to David Agrawal and James Poterba for valuable suggestions during the manuscript's planning stages, and to David Agrawal, James Alt, James Capretta, Kevin Corinth, Laura Feiveson, Jeffry Frieden, Richard Geddes, Steven Hamilton, Robert Inman, Benedic Ippolito, Brian Knight, Pauline Leung, Byron Lutz, Eric Rasmusen, Sarah Reber, Ron Rogowski, David Wildasin, and Vinzenz Ziesemer for helpful comments on an earlier draft. We also benefited from comments and suggestions from attendees at the National Bureau of Economic Research meeting on Policy Responses to Interjurisdictional Tax Competition held in Cambridge, MA, on March 16–17, 2023. Clemens thanks the Hoover Institution for support in his capacity as a nonresident Visiting Fellow. For acknowledgments, sources of research support, and disclosure of the authors' material financial relationships, if any, please see https://www.nber.org/books-and-chapters/policy-responses-tax-competition/intergovernmental-grants-and-policy-competition-concepts-institutions-and-evidence.

## Appendix A

**Table 7A.1 Data appendix**

| Major grant category | Program name |
|---|---|
| **Health** | |
| | Salaries and Expenses |
| | Health Resources and Services |
| | Payments for Tribal Leases |
| | Contract Support Costs |
| | Disease control (Preventive health) |
| | National Institutes of Health |
| | Substance Use And Mental Health Services Administration |
| | Rate Review Grants |
| | Affordable Insurance Exchange Grants |
| | State Grants and Demonstrations |
| | Mental Health Parity Enforcement Grants |
| | Public Health and Social Services Emergency Fund |
| | Prevention and Wellness Fund, Recovery Act |
| | Payment to the State Response to the Opioid Abuse Crisis Account |
| | General Departmental Management |
| | Maternal, Infant, and Early Childhood Home Visiting Programs |
| | Health Resources and Services |
| | Substance Use And Mental Health Services Administration |
| | Cost-sharing Reductions |
| | Grants to States for Medicaid |
| | Children's Health Insurance Fund |
| | Child Enrollment Contingency Fund |
| | Pregnancy Assistance Fund |
| | Health Activities Funds |
| **Education** | |
| | Reading Excellence |
| | Education Jobs Fund |
| | Indian Education |
| | Impact Aid |
| | Safe Schools and Citizenship Education |
| | Chicago Litigation Settlement |

| Table 7A.1 (cont.) | |
|---|---|
| Major grant category | Program name |
| | Education Stabilization Fund |
| | Education Reform |
| | Education for the Disadvantaged |
| | School Improvement Programs |
| | State Fiscal Stabilization Fund, Recovery Act |
| | Innovation and Improvement |
| | English Language Acquisition |
| | Special Education |
| | Rehabilitation Services |
| | Special institutions for the handicapped |
| | Promotion of education for the blind |
| | Career, Technical and Adult Education |
| | Higher education (including college housing loans) |
| | Institute of Education Sciences |
| | Disaster Education Recovery |
| | Student Financial Assistance |
| | Disaster Education Recovery |
| **Transportation** | |
| | Supp Disc Grants for Natl Surface Transport System, Recovery Act |
| | National Infrastructure Investments |
| | National Culvert Removal, Replacement, and Restoration Grant Pro |
| | Strengthening Mobility and Revolutionizing Transportation Grant |
| | Safe Streets and Roads for All |
| | Grants-in-aid for Airports, Recovery Act |
| | Airport Terminal Program |
| | Airport Infrastructure Grants |
| | Payment to Grants-in-aid for Airports |
| | Grants for airports (Airport and airway trust fund) |
| | Grants for airports (federal funds) |
| | Federal-aid highways (trust fund) |
| | Other Federal fund aid for highways |
| | Other Trust fund aid for highways |
| | Motor Carrier Safety Grants, General Fund |
| | National Motor Carrier Safety Program |
| | Motor Carrier Safety |
| | Motor Carrier Safety Grants |
| | Border Enforcement Program |
| | Crash Data |
| | Supplemental Highway Traffic Safety Programs |
| | Highway safety grants |
| | Operating Subsidy Grants to the National Railroad Passenger Corp |
| | Northeast Corridor Improvement Program |
| | Emergency Railroad Rehabilitation and Repair |
| | Capital and Debt Service Grants to the National Railroad Passeng |
| | Restoration and Enhancement Grants |
| | Alameda corridor direct loan financing program |
| | Rail service assistance |

*(continued)*

**Table 7A.1 (cont.)**

| Major grant category | Program name |
|---|---|
| | Rail Safety Technology Program |
| | Railroad Safety Grants |
| | Grants to the National Railroad Passenger Corporation |
| | Local rail freight assistance |
| | Intercity Passenger Rail Grant Program |
| | Rail Line Relocation and Improvement Program |
| | Capital Assistance for High-Speed Rail Corridors and Intercity P |
| | Next Generation High-speed Rail |
| | Pennsylvania Station Redevelopment Project |
| | Alaska Railroad Rehabilitation |
| | Railroad Research and Development |
| | Conrail commuter transition assistance |
| | Northeast Corridor Grants to the National Railroad Passenger Cor |
| | National Network Grants to the National Railroad Passenger Corpo |
| | Federal-State Partnership for Intercity Passenger Rail Grants |
| | Consolidated Rail Infrastructure and Safety Improvements |
| | Northeast corridor improvement program |
| | Urban mass transportation grants |
| | Urban mass transportation grants |
| | Research and special programs (pipeline safety and other) |
| | Natural Gas Distribution Infrastructure Safety and Modernization |
| | Emergency Preparedness Grants |
| | Trust Fund Share of Pipeline Safety |
| | Port Infrastructure Development Program |
| | Merchant Marine Schools |
| **Income Security** | |
| | Total, 600 (Income Security) |
| **Other** | |
| | Total, 050 (National Defense) |
| | Total, 150 (International Affairs) |
| | Total, 270 (Energy) |
| | Total, 300 (Natural Resources and Environment) |
| | Total, 350 (Agriculture) |
| | Total, 370 (Commerce and Housing Credit) |
| | All other 400 (Transportation) |
| | Total, 450 (Community and Regional Development) |
| | All other 500 (Education, Training, Employment, and Social Services) |
| | All other 550 (Health) |
| | Total, 650 (Social Security) |
| | Total, 700 (Veterans Benefits and Services) |
| | Total, 750 (Administration of Justice) |
| | Total, 800 (General Government) |

**Table 7A.2** **Pandemic-related intergovernmental grants and corporate tax decreases excluding five most populous states**

| | Baseline (1) | Political (2) | COVID (3) | Combined (4) | Simple (5) |
|---|---|---|---|---|---|
| Total aid per resident (USD thousands) | −0.614*** | −0.431*** | −0.559*** | −0.382** | −0.617*** |
| | (0.157) | (0.165) | (0.159) | (0.185) | (0.181) |
| Log(Population) | −0.430*** | −0.213 | −0.424*** | −0.214 | −0.459*** |
| | (0.0942) | (0.137) | (0.106) | (0.141) | (0.113) |
| Share of population eligible for MLF | 0.253 | 0.285 | 0.0596 | 0.0583 | |
| | (0.394) | (0.454) | (0.366) | (0.397) | |
| Change corporate tax rate (2018–2019) | 6.822 | 4.571 | 8.312* | 13.30** | |
| | (4.634) | (5.337) | (5.018) | (6.684) | |
| Average OSI (March 2020) | 0.556 | −0.708 | −1.924* | −0.992 | |
| | (0.901) | (2.718) | (1.147) | (2.722) | |
| Average OSI (January 2022) | 1.748 | 1.725 | 3.275*** | 3.460*** | |
| | (1.232) | (1.113) | (1.059) | (0.943) | |
| Political controls | N | Y | N | Y | N |
| COVID-19 controls | N | N | Y | Y | N |
| Observations | 39 | 39 | 39 | 39 | 39 |
| R-squared | 0.301 | 0.384 | 0.447 | 0.529 | 0.194 |
| First-stage F-stat | 47.454 | 28.105 | 41.7849 | 20.6372 | 48.066 |

Note: This table uses data from Chidambaram and Musumeci (2021), Committee for a Responsible Federal Budget (2021), Federal Reserve Board (2021), Google LLC (2021), Hale et al. (2020), Lewis et al. (2021), Medicaid and CHIP Payment Access Commission (2021), MIT Election and Data Science Lab (2017), Tax Policy Center (2018, 2019, 2020, 2021, 2022), US Census Bureau (2021), US Department of the Treasury (2021a, 2021b), US Federal Transit Administration (2021), and US Office of Elementary and Secondary Education (2021) to estimate the following equations:

(1a) $$\frac{TotalAid_s}{Pop_{s,y\,2020}} = \alpha + \gamma_1\, RepsPerMillion_s + \gamma_2 X_s + \varepsilon_s$$

(1b) $$Corporate\ Rate\ Reduction_s = \alpha + \beta_1 \widehat{\frac{TotalAid_s}{Pop_{s,y\,2020}}} + \beta_2 X_s + u_s$$

where $TotalAid_s$ is the total federal aid per resident to state and local governments (USD thousands) in state $s$ pooled across all four major bills. It is scaled by $Pop_{s,y2020}$, state $s$'s 2020 official census population. In first stage equation (1a), ($TotalAid_s$ / $Pop_{s,y2020}$) is instrumented using $RepsPerMillion_s$, the number of representatives and senators per million residents for state $s$ in 2020. Estimates of equation (1b) are shown in Columns 1 through 5. $Corporate\ Rate\ Reduction_s$ is a binary variable indicating whether a state's maximum corporate tax rate decreased between 2019 and 2022. Column 1 reports the results of our baseline specification of equation (1b), which includes a set of state-level controls for state $s$ ($X_s$) including the log of 2020 official census population; the share of a state's population living in a town eligible for financing through the MLF; and the March 2020, end of March 2020, and January 2022 month averages of a state's Oxford Stringency Index. In Column 2, controls for share of votes cast for Donald Trump in the 2020 US presidential election in state $s$, and the percent change in retail mobility relative from January 2022 to a February 2020 baseline are added. In Column 3, controls for the number of new COVID-19 in January 2022, the cumulative number of COVID-19 deaths in January 2022, new COVID-19 cases in January 2022, and the cumulative number of COVID-19 cases in January 2022, are added. Column 4 presents results including both political and COVID-19 controls. Column 5 presents results of a simple specification controlling only for the log of 2020 official census population. Observations are weighted by area population of state $s$ and standard errors (in parentheses) are clustered by state. States that do not have a corporate tax rate (South Dakota, Wyoming, Nevada, Ohio, Texas, and Washington) are excluded from this analysis, as are the five most populous states not already excluded (California, New York, Florida, Pennsylvania, and Illinois).

**Table 7A.3 Bivariate regressions**

| | Decrease indicator (1) | Decrease size (2) |
|---|---|---|
| Total aid per resident (USD thousands) | −0.131*** | 0.00151** |
| | (0.0418) | (0.000672) |
| Constant | 0.589*** | −0.00611** |
| | (0.162) | (0.00251) |
| Observations | 50 | 50 |
| R-squared | 0.086 | 0.065 |

Note: This table uses data from Chidambaram and Musumeci (2021), Committee for a Responsible Federal Budget (2021), Medicaid and CHIP Payment Access Commission (2021), US Census Bureau (2021), US Department of the Treasury (2021a, 2021b), US Federal Transit Administration (2021a), US Office of Elementary and Secondary Education (2021), and Tax Policy Center (2018, 2019, 2020, 2021, 2022) to estimate the following equations:

(2a) $$Corporate\ Rate\ Reduction_s = \alpha + \beta_1 \frac{TotalAid_s}{Pop_{s,y2020}} + \varepsilon_s$$

(2b) $$Corporate\ Rate\ Reduction\ Size_s = \alpha + \beta_1 \frac{TotalAid_s}{Pop_{s,y2020}} + \varepsilon_s$$

where $TotalAid_s$ is the total federal aid per resident to state and local governments (USD thousands) in state $s$ pooled across all four major bills. It is scaled by $Pop_{s,y2020}$, state $s$'s 2020 official census population. Column 1 presents estimates of equation (2a), in which $(TotalAid_s / Pop_{s,y2020})$ is regressed on $Corporate\ Rate\ Reduction_s$, a binary variable indicating whether a state's maximum corporate tax rate decreased between 2019 and 2022. Column 2 presents estimates of equation (2b), in which $(TotalAid_s / Pop_{s,y2020})$ is regressed on $Corporate\ Rate\ Reduction_s$, a continuous variable indicating the magnitude of a state's corporate tax rate decrease between 2019 and 2022. Standard errors (in parentheses) are clustered by state $s$.

**Table 7A.4** **Table 1 and 2 from Dahlby (1996). Reprinted with permission from Bev Dahlby, "Fiscal Externalities and the Design of Intergovernmental Grants," *International Tax and Public Finance* <https://link.springer.com/journal/10797> 3(3): 397–412, 1996, Springer Nature**

Tax externalities

| Types of externality | Examples | Fiscal implications | Revenue matching grant rate |
|---|---|---|---|
| Direct horizontal | Tax Exporting: A hotel tax that is borne by visitors from other states. | Increased reliance on taxes where at least part of the burden is borne by residents of other jurisdictions. | $-\dfrac{\sum_{k=1}^{n} X_i^k - X_i^i}{\sum_{k=1}^{n} X_i^k}$ |
| Indirect horizontal | Tax Competition: A sales tax that causes consumers to purchase the taxed commodities in another state. | The potential mobility of the tax base leads to downward pressure on tax rates. | $\dfrac{\sum_{k=1}^{n} R_{t_{ij}}^k - R_{t_{ij}}^i}{R_{t_{ij}}^i}$ |
| Indirect vertical | Tax Base Overlap: Federal and state excise taxes on cigarettes | State governments, and possibly the federal government, will impose excessive tax rates on the shared tax base. Both levels of government could end up on the "wrong" side of the Laffer curve for total tax revenue. | $\dfrac{\tau_{0j}\epsilon_{jj}}{1 + \tau_{ij}\epsilon_{jj}}$ |

Where $X_i^k$ is the quantity of the good taxed by state $i$ and consumed by the residents of state $k$, $R_{t_{ij}}^k$ is the change in total revenue in state $k$ as a result of an increase in the tax on commodity $j$ by state $i$, $\epsilon_{jj}$ is the elasticity of demand for commodity $j$, $\tau_{0j}$ is the federal ad valorem tax rate on commodity $j$, and $\tau_{ij}$ is the state ad valorem tax rate on commodity $j$.

Expenditure externalities

| Types of externality | Examples | Fiscal implications | Expenditure matching grant rate |
|---|---|---|---|
| Direct horizontal | Benefit Spillovers: Pollution abatement activity that benefits the downstream residents of other states. | Underprovision of activities that generate beneficial externalities. | $\sigma_{g_i}(1 - \rho_{g_i})$ |
| Indirect horizontal | Spending Competition: Economic development grants that attract investment that would otherwise have occurred in other states. | Overprovision of activities that reduce the tax revenue of other state governments. | $\rho_{g_i} - \rho_{g_i}^i$ |
| Indirect vertical | Expenditure Interdependence: State education expenditures that increase the federal government's income, payroll, and sales tax revenues because of the increase in students' lifetime earnings. | Underprovision of activities that have a positive effect on the net revenues of other levels of government. | $\tau_0\phi(g_i)(1 + \eta)$ |

Where is the fraction of the direct benefits from the provision of a public service by state $i$ that accrue to nonresidents, $\rho_{g_i}$ is the additional revenue that accrues to all governments from an additional dollar spent on the public service by state $i$, $\rho_g^i$ is the additional revenue that accrues to state $i$ when it spends an additional dollar on the public service, $\tau_0$ is the federal tax rate on labor income, $\phi(g_i)$ is the increase in the wage rate when an additional dollar is spent on $g_i$ by state $i$, and $\eta$ is the uncompensated labor supply elasticity.

## References

Abramowitz, Alan I., and Steven Webster. 2016. "The Rise of Negative Partisanship and the Nationalization of U.S. Elections in the 21st Century." *Electoral Studies* 41: 12–22.

Adler, Loren, Matthew Fiedler, and Tim Gronniger. 2017. "Effects of the Medicaid Per Capita Cap Included in the House-Passed American Health Care Act." Brookings Institution.

Aghion, Philippe, and Jean Tirole. 1997. "Formal and Real Authority in Organizations." *Journal of Political Economy* 105 (1): 1–29.

Agrawal, David R., William H. Hoyt, and Tidiane Ly. 2024. "A New Approach to Evaluating the Welfare Effects of Decentralized Policies." *SSRN Electronic Journal.*

Agrawal, David R., William H. Hoyt, and John D. Wilson. 2022. "Local Policy Choice: Theory and Empirics." *Journal of Economic Literature* 60 (4): 1378–455.

Allers, Maarten A., and Wouter Vermeulen. 2016. "Capitalization of Equalizing Grants and the Flypaper Effect." *Regional Science and Urban Economics* 58: 115–29.

Alt, James E., and Robert C. Lowry. 1994. "Divided Government and Budget Deficits: Evidence from the States." *American Political Science Review* 88 (4): 811–28.

Asdrubali, Pierfederico, Bent E. Sørensen, and Oved Yosha. 1996. "Channels of Interstate Risk Sharing: United States 1963–1990." *The Quarterly Journal of Economics* 111 (4): 1081–110.

Atlas, Cary M., Thomas W. Gilligan, Robert J. Hendershott, and Mark A. Zupan. 1995. "Slicing the Federal Government Net Spending Pie: Who Wins, Who Loses, and Why." *American Economic Review* 85 (3): 624–29.

Aussenberg, Randy A. 2017. *A Primer on WIC: The Special Supplemental Nutrition Program for Women, Infants, and Children.* CRS Report R44115. Congressional Research Service.

Aussenberg, Randy A., and Kara Clifford Billings. 2020. *USDA Domestic Food Assistance Programs: FY2020 Appropriations.* CRS Report R46488. Congressional Research Service.

Baicker, Katherine. 2005a. "Extensive or Intensive Generosity? The Price and Income Effects of Federal Grants." *Review of Economics and Statistics* 87 (2): 371–84.

Baicker, Katherine. 2005b. "The Spillover Effects of State Spending." *Journal of Public Economics* 89 (2–3): 529–44.

Baicker, Katherine, Jeffrey Clemens, and Monica Singhal. 2012. "The Rise of the States: US Fiscal Decentralization in the Postwar Period." *Journal of Public Economics* 96 (11–12): 1079–91.

Baicker, Katherine, and Nora Gordon. 2006. "The Effect of State Education Finance Reform on Total Local Resources." *Journal of Public Economics* 90 (8–9): 1519–35.

Baicker, Katherine, and Douglas Staiger. 2004. "Fiscal Shenanigans, Targeted Federal Health Care Funds, and Patient Mortality." NBER Working Paper 10440.

Baicker, Katherine, and Douglas Staiger. 2005. "Fiscal Shenanigans, Targeted Federal Health Care Funds, and Patient Mortality." *The Quarterly Journal of Economics* 120 (1): 345–86.

Bailey, Michael A., and Mark Carl Rom. 2004. "A Wider Race? Interstate Competition across Health and Welfare Programs." *The Journal of Politics* 66 (2): 326–47.

Baker, Kendall. 2022. "1 Big Thing: The Fall of Favre." *Axios Sports*, September 27, 2022. https://www.axios.com/newsletters/axios-sports-629ad3ce-3d44-4118-86a2-66d13122c130.html.

Basurto, Maria Pia, Pascaline Dupas, and Jonathan Robinson. 2020. "Decentralization and Efficiency of Subsidy Targeting: Evidence from Chiefs in Rural Malawi." *Journal of Public Economics* 185: 104047.
Bayoumi, Tamim, Moms Goldstein, and Geoffrey Woglom. 1995. "Do Credit Markets Discipline Sovereign Borrowers: Evidence from U.S. States." *Journal of Money, Credit, and Banking* 27 (4): 1046–59.
Bernanke, Ben. 2020. "I Was Chairman of the Federal Reserve. Save the States." *New York Times*, July 15, 2020.
Berry, William D., Richard C. Fording, and Russell L. Hanson. 2003. "Reassessing the 'Race to the Bottom' in State Welfare Policy." *Journal of Politics* 65 (2): 327–49.
Berset, Simon, and Mark Schelker. 2020. "Fiscal Windfall Curse." *European Economic Review* 130: 103592.
Bianchi, Nicola, Michela Giorcelli, and Enrica Maria Martino. 2023. "The Effects of Fiscal Decentralisation on Publicly Provided Services and Labour Markets." *The Economic Journal* 133 (653): 1738–72.
Boadway, Robin. 2004. "The Theory and Practice of Equalization." *CESifo Economic Studies* 50 (1): 211–54.
Bohn, Henning, and Robert P. Inman. 1996. "Constitutional Limits and Public Deficits: Evidence from the U.S. States." *Carnegie-Rochester Conference Series on Public Policy* 45: 13–76.
Brang, Grace, Sewin Chan, and Travis St. Clair. 2024. "Fiscal Stimulus or Debt Relief: The Effect of Federal Pandemic Aid on State and Local Pensions." *SSRN Electronic Journal.*
Bruecker, Jan K. 2000. "Welfare Reform and the Race to the Bottom: Theory and Evidence." *Southern Economic Journal* 66 (3): 505–25.
Bucovetsky, Sam, and Michael Smart. 2006. "The Efficiency Consequences of Local Revenue Equalization: Tax Competition and Tax Distortions." *Journal of Public Economic Theory* 8 (1): 119–44.
Buettner, Thiess. 2006. "The Incentive Effect of Fiscal Equalization Transfers on Tax Policy." *Journal of Public Economics* 90 (3): 477–97.
Bundorf, M. Kate, and Daniel P. Kessler. 2022. "The Responsiveness of Medicaid Spending to the Federal Subsidy." *National Tax Journal* 75 (4): 661–80.
Calabrese, Stephen M., Dennis N. Epple, and Richard E. Romano. 2012. "Inefficiencies from Metropolitan Political and Fiscal Decentralization: Failures of Tiebout Competition." *Review of Economic Studies* 79 (3): 1081–111.
Caldeira, Emilie, Martial Foucault, and Gregoire Rota-Graziosi. 2015. "Decentralization in Africa and the Nature of Local Governments' Competition: Evidence from Benin." *International Tax and Public Finance* 22 (6): 1048–76.
Card, David, and A. Abigail Payne. 2002. "School Finance Reform, the Distribution of School Spending, and the Distribution of Student Test Scores." *Journal of Public Economics* 83 (1): 49–82.
Carlino, Gerald, Thorsten Drautzburg, Robert Inman, and Nicholas Zarra. 2023. "Partisanship and Fiscal Policy in Economic Unions: Evidence from US States." *American Economic Review* 113 (3): 701–37.
Cascio, Elizabeth U., Nora Gordon, and Sarah Reber. 2013. "Local Responses to Federal Grants: Evidence from the Introduction of Title I in the South." *American Economic Journal: Economic Policy* 5 (3): 126–59.
Cascio, Elizabeth U., and Ebonya Washington. 2014. "Valuing the Vote: The Redistribution of Voting Rights and State Funds Following the Voting Rights Act of 1965." *The Quarterly Journal of Economics* 129 (1): 379–433.
Case, Anne C., James R. Hines Jr., and Harvey S. Rosen. 1993. "Budget Spillovers and Fiscal Policy Interdependence: Evidence from the States." *Journal of Public Economics* 52 (3): 285–307.

Chidambaram, Priya, and MaryBeth Musumeci. 2021. "Potential Impact of Additional Federal Funds for Medicaid HCBS for Seniors and People with Disabilities." Kaiser Family Foundation, March 15, 2021. https://www.kff.org/medicaid/issue-brief/potential-impact-of-additional-federal-funds-for-medicaidhcbs-for-seniors-and-people-with-disabilities/.

Chirinko, Robert S., and Daniel J. Wilson. 2017. "Tax Competition among US States: Racing to the Bottom or Riding on a Seesaw?" *Journal of Public Economics* 155: 147–63.

Chorniy, Anna, and Christopher Mills. 2022. "More Money, Fewer Problems? The Effect of Foster Care Payments on Children's Quality of Care." Working paper.

Clemens, Jeffrey, Oliver Giesecke, Joshua Rauh, and Stan Veuger. 2024. "What Do States Do with Fiscal Windfalls? Evidence from the Pandemic." American Enterprise Institute Working Paper 2024–05.

Clemens, Jeffrey, Philip Hoxie, John Kearns, and Stan Veuger. 2023. "How Did Federal Aid to States and Localities Affect Testing and Vaccine Delivery?" *Journal of Public Economics* 225: 104972.

Clemens, Jeffrey, Philip Hoxie, and Stan Veuger. 2022. "Was Pandemic Fiscal Relief Effective Fiscal Stimulus?" NBER Working Paper 30168.

Clemens, Jeffrey, and Benedic Ippolito. 2018. "Implications of Medicaid Financing Reform for State Government Budgets." *Tax Policy and the Economy* 32 (1): 135–72.

Clemens, Jeffrey, Benedic Ippolito, and Stan Veuger. 2021. "Medicaid and Fiscal Federalism During the COVID-19 Pandemic." *Public Budgeting & Finance* 41 (4): 94–109.

Clemens, Jeffrey, John Kearns, Beatrice Lee, and Stan Veuger. 2023. "Spatial Spillovers and the Effects of Fiscal Stimulus: Evidence from Pandemic-Era Federal Aid for State and Local Governments." *Spatial Economic Analysis* 1–25.

Clemens, Jeffrey, and Stephen Miran. 2012. "Fiscal Policy Multipliers on Subnational Government Spending." *American Economic Journal: Economic Policy* 4 (2): 46–68.

Clemens, Jeffrey, Julia Payson, and Stan Veuger. 2024. "Aid for Incumbents: The Electoral Consequences of COVID-19 Relief." American Enterprise Institute Working Paper 2024–14.

Clemens, Jeffrey, and Stan Veuger. 2020a. "Implications of the COVID-19 Pandemic for State Government Tax Revenues." *National Tax Journal* 73 (3): 619–44.

Clemens, Jeffrey, and Stan Veuger. 2020b. "The COVID-19 Pandemic and the Revenues of State and Local Governments: An Update." *AEI Economic Perspectives* 2020–07.

Clemens, Jeffrey, and Stan Veuger. 2021. "Politics and the Distribution of Federal Funds: Evidence from Federal Legislation in Response to COVID-19." *Journal of Public Economics* 204: 104554.

Clemens, Jeffrey, and Stan Veuger. 2023. "Lessons from COVID-19 Aid to State and Local Governments for the Design of Federal Automatic Stabilizers." In *Economic Policy in a More Uncertain World*, edited by Melissa S. Kearney and Amy Ganz. Aspen Institute Press.

Collinson, Robert, Ingrid Gould Ellen, and Jens Ludwig. 2019. "Reforming Housing Assistance." *The Annals of the American Academy of Political and Social Science* 686 (1): 250–85.

Committee for a Responsible Federal Budget. 2021. "COVID-19 Money Tracker." Accessed on August 19, 2021. https://www.covidmoneytracker.org/.

Committee for a Responsible Federal Budget. 2022. "The Infrastructure Bill's Impact on the Highway Trust Fund." Committee for a Responsible Federal Budget Blog, February 3, 2022.

Corcoran, Sean, William N. Evans, Jennifer Godwin, Sheila E. Murray, and Robert M. Schwab. 2004. "The Changing Distribution of Education Finance, 1972–1997." In *Social Inequality*, edited by Kathryn M. Neckerman. Russell Sage Foundation.
Corinth, Kevin, and Amelia Irvine. 2023. "JUE Insight: The Effect of Relaxing Local Housing Market Regulations on Federal Rental Assistance Programs." *Journal of Urban Economics* 136: 103572.
Coyne, David. 2017. "Unmasking Local Fiscal Responses to Federal Tax Deductibility." *National Tax Journal* 70 (2): 223–55.
Cullen, Julie Berry, and Roger H. Gordon. 2008. "Deductibility of State and Local Taxes." Working paper.
Currie, Janet, and Firouz Gahvari. 2008. "Transfers in Cash and In-Kind: Theory Meets the Data." *Journal of Economic Literature* 46 (2): 333–83.
Dague, Laura, and Benjamin Ukert. 2022. "What Happens to Texans' Insurance Coverage When Medicaid and Marketplace Pandemic-Era Policies End?" Report Prepared for the Episcopal Health Foundation.
Dahlberg, Matz, Eva Mörk, Jørn Rattsø, and Hanna Ågren. 2008. "Using a Discontinuous Grant Rule to Identify the Effect of Grants on Local Taxes and Spending." *Journal of Public Economics* 92 (12): 2320–35.
Dahlby, Bev. 1996. "Fiscal Externalities and the Design of Intergovernmental Grants." *International Tax and Public Finance* 3 (3): 397–412.
Devereux, Michael P., Rachel Griffith, and Alexander Klemm. 2002. "Corporate Income Tax Reforms and International Tax Competition." *Economic Policy* 17 (35): 449–95.
Driessen, Grant A., Maggie McCarty, and Libby Perl. 2023. *Pandemic Relief: The Emergency Rental Assistance Program*. CRS Report R46688.
Duggan, Mark G. 2000. "Hospital Ownership and Public Medical Spending." *The Quarterly Journal of Economics* 115 (4): 1343–73.
Egger, Peter, Marko Köthenbürger, and Michael Smart. 2010. "Do Fiscal Transfers Alleviate Business Tax Competition? Evidence from Germany." *Journal of Public Economics* 94 (3–4): 235–46.
Eichengreen, Barry. 1992. "Should the Maastricht Treaty Be Saved?" *Princeton Studies in International Finance* 74. Princeton University Press.
Eriksen, Michael D., and Amanda Ross. 2015. "Housing Vouchers and the Price of Rental Housing." *American Economic Journal: Economic Policy* 7 (3): 154–76.
Evans, William N., Shawna Kolka, James X. Sullivan, and Patrick S. Turner. 2025. "Fighting Poverty One Family at a Time: Experimental Evidence from an Intervention with Holistic, Individualized, Wraparound Services." *American Economic Journal: Economic Policy* 17 (1): 311–61.
Federal Reserve Board (The Board of Governors of the Federal Reserve System). 2021. "Municipal Liquidity Facility," August 11, 2021.
Feiveson, Laura. 2015. "General Revenue Sharing and Public Sector Unions." *Journal of Public Economics* 125I: 28–45.
Feldstein, Martin S. 1975. "Wealth Neutrality and Local Choice in Public Education." *American Economic Review* 65 (1): 75–89.
Ganong, Peter, Pascal Noel, and Joseph Vavra. 2020. "US Unemployment Insurance Replacement Rates During the Pandemic." *Journal of Public Economics* 191: 104273.
Gaubert, Cecile, Patrick M. Kline, and Danny Yagan. 2021. "Place-Based Redistribution." NBER Working Paper 28337.
Goldin, Jacob, Tatiana Homonoff, and Katherine Meckel. 2022. "Issuance and Incidence: SNAP Benefit Cycles and Grocery Prices." *American Economic Journal: Economic Policy* 14 (1): 152–78.

Goldstein, Moms, and Geoffrey Woglom. 1992. "Market-Based Fiscal Discipline in Monetary Unions: Evidence from the U.S. Municipal Bond Market." In *Establishing a Central Bank: Issues in Europe and Lessons from the United States*, edited by Matthew B. Canzoneri, Vittorio Grilli, and Paul R. Masson. Cambridge University Press.

Goodman-Bacon, Andrew, and Lucie Schmidt. 2020. "Federalizing Benefits: The Introduction of Supplemental Security Income and the Size of the Safety Net." *Journal of Public Economics* 185: 104174.

Google LLC. 2022. "Google COVID-19 Community Mobility Reports," Accessed on April 14, 2022. https://www.google.com/covid19/mobility/.

Gordon, Nora. 2004. "Do Federal Grants Boost School Spending? Evidence from Title I." *Journal of Public Economics* 88 (9–10): 1771–92.

Gordon, Nora, and Sarah Reber. 2023. "Title I of ESEA: How the Formulas Work." All4Ed, January 24, 2023. https://all4ed.org/publication/title-i-of-esea-how-the-formulas-work/.

Gordon, Roger H. 1983. "An Optimal Taxation Approach to Fiscal Federalism." *The Quarterly Journal of Economics* 98 (4): 567–86.

Hackmann, Martin B., Juan S. Rojas, and Nicolas R. Ziebarth. 2024. "Creative Financing and Public Moral Hazard: Evidence from Medicaid Supplemental Payments." Working paper.

Hale, Thomas, Noam Angrist, Rafael Goldszmidt, Beatriz Kira, Anna Petherick, Toby Phillips, Samuel Webster, Emily Cameron-Blake, Laura Hallas, Saptarshi Majumdar, and Helen Tatlow. 2021. "A Global Panel Database of Pandemic Policies (Oxford COVID-19 Government Response Tracker)." *Nature Human Behavior* 5: 529–38.

Hart, Angela. 2023. "Prescription for Housing? California Wants Medicaid to Cover 6 Months of Rent" *Los Angeles Times*, March 20, 2023.

Hauk, William R. Jr., and Romain Wacziarg. 2007. "Small States, Big Pork." *The Quarterly Journal of Political Science* 2 (1): 95–106.

Helm, Ines, and Jan Stuhler. 2021. "The Dynamic Response of Municipal Budgets to Revenue Shocks." CESifo Working Paper 9083.

Hemel, Daniel. 2019. "The Death and Life of the State and Local Tax Deduction." *Tax Law Review* 72 (2): 151–96.

Hendren, Nathaniel. 2016. "The Policy Elasticity." *Tax Policy and the Economy* 30 (1): 51–89.

Hendren, Nathaniel, and Ben Sprung-Keyser. 2020. "A Unified Welfare Analysis of Government Policies." *The Quarterly Journal of Economics* 135 (3): 1209–318.

Herd, Pamela, and Donald P. Moynihan. 2018. *Administrative Burden: Policymaking by Other Means*. Russell Sage Foundation.

Hines, James R., and Richard H. Thaler. 1995. "The Flypaper Effect." *Journal of Economic Perspectives* 9 (4): 217–26.

Hoxby, Caroline M. 2001. "All School Finance Equalizations Are Not Created Equal." *The Quarterly Journal of Economics* 116 (4): 1189–231.

Hoyt, William H. 2017. "The Assignment and Division of the Tax Base in a System of Hierarchical Governments." *International Tax and Public Finance* 24: 678–704.

Inman, Robert P. 1971. "Towards an Econometric Model of Local Budgeting." *Proceedings of the 64th Annual Conference on Taxation*. National Tax Association.

Jacob, Brian A., and Jens Ludwig. 2012. "The Effects of Housing Assistance on Labor Supply: Evidence from a Voucher Lottery." *American Economic Review* 102 (1): 272–304.

Jackson, C. Kirabo, Rucker C. Johnson, and Claudia Persico. 2016. "The Effects

of School Spending on Educational and Economic Outcomes: Evidence from School Finance Reforms." *The Quarterly Journal of Economics* 131 (1): 157–218.
Janvry, Alain de, Frederico Finan, and Elisabeth Sadoulet. 2012. "Local Electoral Incentives and Decentralized Program Performance." *Review of Economics and Statistics* 94 (3): 672–85.
Keightley, Mark P. 2023. *An Introduction to the Low-Income Housing Tax Credit*. CRS Report RS22389.
Kirk, Robert S. 2021. *Federal-Aid Highway Program (FAHP): In Brief*. CRS Report R44332.
Kline, Patrick, and Christopher R. Walters. 2016. "Evaluating Public Programs with Close Substitutes: The Case of Head Start." *The Quarterly Journal of Economics* 131 (4): 1795–848.
Knight, Brian. 2002. "Endogenous Federal Grants and Crowd-Out of State Government Spending: Theory and Evidence from the Federal Highway Aid Program." *American Economic Review* 92 (1): 71–92.
Knight, Brian. 2008. "Legislative Representation, Bargaining Power and the Distribution of Federal Funds: Evidence from the US Congress." *The Economic Journal* 118 (532): 1785–803.
Kolbe, Tammy, Elizabeth Dhuey, and Sara Menlove Doutre. 2022. "More Money Is Not Enough: The Case for Reconsidering Federal Special Education Funding Formulas." The Brown Center Chalkboard, Brookings Institution. October 3, 2022.
Köthenbürger, Marko. 2002. "Tax Competition and Fiscal Equalization." *International Tax and Public Finance* 9: 391–408.
Köthenbürger, Marko, and Gabriel Loumeau. 2023. "Tax Responses in Local Public Finance: The Flypaper Effect at Work." CESifo Working Paper No. 10354.
Lafortune, Julien, Jesse Rothstein, and Diane Whitmore Schanzenbach. 2018. "School Finance Reform and the Distribution of Student Achievement." *American Economic Journal: Applied Economics* 10 (2): 1–26.
Lago, Manuel E., Santiago Lago-Peñas, and Jorge Martinez-Vazquez. 2024. "On the Effects of Intergovernmental Grants: A Survey." *International Tax and Public Finance* 31: 856–908.
Leduc, Sylvain, and Daniel Wilson. 2017. "Are State Governments Roadblocks to Federal Stimulus? Evidence on the Flypaper Effect of Highway Grants in the 2009 Recovery Act." *American Economic Journal: Economic Policy* 9 (2): 253–92.
Lee, Frances E. 1998. "Representation and Public Policy: The Consequences of Senate Apportionment for the Geographic Distribution of Federal Funds." *The Journal of Politics* 60 (1): 34–62.
Leung, Pauline. 2022. "State Responses to Federal Matching Grants: The Case of Medicaid." *Journal of Public Economics* 216: 104746.
Lewis, Jeffrey B., Keith Poole, Howard Rosenthal, Adam Boche, Aaron Rudkin, and Luke Sonnet. 2023. Voteview: Congressional Roll-Call Votes Database. https://voteview.com/.
Long, Cindy. 2023. "SNAP Emergency Allotments are Ending." USDA Blog, United States Department of Agriculture, February 8, 2023. https://www.usda.gov/media/blog/2023/02/08/snap-emergency-allotments-are-ending.
Lutz, Byron. 2010. "Taxation with Representation: Intergovernmental Grants in a Plebiscite Democracy." *The Review of Economics and Statistics* 92 (2): 316–32.
Mallett, William J. 2022. *Federal Public Transportation Program: In Brief*. CRS Report R47002.
Mauri, Nicola. 2024. "How Fiscally Autonomous are Local Governments? An Empirical Test." *Journal of Public Economics* 239: 105210.

Meckel, Katherine. 2020. "Is the Cure Worse than the Disease? Unintended Effects of Payment Reform in a Quantity-Based Transfer Program." *American Economic Review* 110 (6): 1821–65.

Meckel, Katherine, Maya Rossin-Slater, and Lindsey Uniat. 2023. "Efficiency Versus Equity in the Provision of In-Kind Benefits: Evidence from Cost Containment in the California WIC Program." *Journal of Human Resources* 58 (2): 363–92.

Medicaid and CHIP Payment Access Commission. 2021. "Annual Analysis of Disproportionate Share Hospital Allotments to States." US Department of Health and Human Services, March 2021.

MIT Election Data and Science Lab. 2023. "U.S. President 1976–2020." Harvard Dataverse, V6.

Musgrave, Richard A. 1971. "Economics of Fiscal Federalism." *Nebraska Journal of Economics and Business* 10 (4): 3–13.

Oates, Wallace E. 1972. *Fiscal Federalism*. Harcourt, Brace, Jovanovich.

Oates, Wallace E. 2008. "On the Evolution of Fiscal Federalism: Theory and Institutions." *National Tax Journal* 61 (2): 313–34.

Oates, Wallace E., and Robert M. Schwab. 1988. "Economic Competition among Jurisdictions: Efficiency Enhancing or Distortion Inducing?" *Journal of Public Economics* 35 (3): 333–54.

Office of Management and Budget. 2022a. "Table 12.1—Summary Comparison of Total Outlays for Grants to State and Local Governments: 1940–2027 (in Current Dollars, as Percentages of Total Outlays, as Percentages of GDP, and in Constant (FY 2012) Dollars)."

Office of Management and Budget. 2022b. "Table 12.3—Total Outlays for Grants to State and Local Governments, by Function, Agency, and Program: 1940–2023."

Olson, Mancur. 1969. "The Principle of 'Fiscal Equivalence': The Division of Responsibilities Among Different Levels of Government." *American Economic Review* 59 (2): 479–87.

Painter, William L. 2022. *The Disaster Relief Fund: Overview and Issues*. CRS Report R45484.

Peacock, Alan T., and Jack Wiseman. 1961. *The Growth of Public Expenditure in the United Kingdom*. Princeton University Press.

Peterson, Paul E., and Mark C. Rom. 1989. "American Federalism, Welfare Policy, and Residential Choices." *American Political Science Review* 83 (3): 711–28.

Peterson, Paul E., and Mark C. Rom. 1990. *Welfare Magnets: A New Case for a National Standard*. Brookings Institution Press.

Poterba, James M. 1994. "State Responses to Fiscal Crises: The Effects of Budgetary Institutions and Politics." *Journal of Political Economy* 102: 799–821.

Poterba, James M. and Kim Reuben. 1999. "State Fiscal Institutions and the U.S. Municipal Bond Market." In *Fiscal Institutions and Fiscal Performance*, edited by James M. Poterba and Jürgen von Hagen. University of Chicago Press.

Rodden, Jonathan. 2002. "Strength in Numbers? Representation and Redistribution in the European Union." *European Union Politics* 3 (2): 151–75.

Rogger, Daniel, and Ravi Somani. 2023. "Hierarchy and Information." *Journal of Public Economics* 219: 104823.

Rom, Mark Carl, Paul E. Peterson, and Kenneth F. Scheve Jr. 1998. "Interstate Competition and Welfare Policy." *Publius: The Journal of Federalism* 28 (3): 17–37.

Saavedra, Luz Amparo. 2000. "A Model of Welfare Competition with Evidence from AFDC." *Journal Urban of Economics* 47 (2): 248–79.

Shapiro, Jesse M. 2005. "Is There a Daily Discount Rate? Evidence from the Food Stamp Nutrition Cycle." *Journal of Public Economics* 89 (2–3): 303–25.

Shoag, Daniel, Cody Tuttle, and Stan Veuger. 2019. "Rules Versus Home Rule—Local Government Responses to Negative Revenue Shocks." *National Tax Journal* 72 (3): 543–74.
Shoag, Daniel, and Stan Veuger. 2016. "Uncertainty and the Geography of the Great Recession." *Journal of Monetary Economics* 84: 84–93.
Shoag, Daniel, and Stan Veuger. 2018. "Shops and the City: Evidence on Local Externalities and Local Government Policy from Big-Box Bankruptcies." *Review of Economics and Statistics* 100 (3): 440–53.
Shores, Kenneth A., Christopher A. Candelaria, and Sarah E. Kabourek. 2022. "Spending More on the Poor? A Comprehensive Summary of State-Specific Responses to School Finance Reforms from 1990–2014." *Education Finance and Policy* 1–28.
Skinner, Rebecca R. 2022. *The Elementary and Secondary Education Act (ESEA), as Amended by the Every Student Succeeds Act (ESSA): A Primer*. CRS Report R45977.
Skupnik, Christoph. 2014. "EU Enlargement and the Race to the Bottom of Welfare States." *IZA Journal of Migration* 3: 15.
Thompson, Steve. 2022. "1 in 4 Public Housing Units Sit Vacant During D.C. Affordability Crisis." *The Washington Post*, October 19, 2022.
Tiebout, Charles M. 1956. "A Pure Theory of Local Expenditures." *Journal of Political Economy* 64 (5): 416–24.
US Bureau of Economic Analysis. 2023. Personal consumption expenditures (implicit price deflator) [DPCERD3Q086SBEA], retrieved from FRED, Federal Reserve Bank of St. Louis; https://fred.stlouisfed.org/series/DPCERD3Q086SBEA, February 14, 2023.
US Census Bureau. 2021. "2020 Census Apportionment Results." April 16, 2021. Accessed on September 14, 2021.
US Department of the Treasury. 2021a. "Allocations for States, District of Columbia, and Puerto Rico." August 2021.
US Department of the Treasury. 2021b. "Coronavirus State and Local Fiscal Recovery Funds." Interim Final Rule. *Federal Register* 86 (93): 26786–824.
US Department of the Treasury. 2022. "Coronavirus State and Local Fiscal Recovery Funds." *Federal Register* 87 (18): 4338–454.
US Federal Transit Administration. 2021. "Fiscal Year 2021 American Rescue Plan Act Supplemental Public Transportation Apportionments and Allocations." US Department of Transportation.
US Office of Elementary and Secondary Education. 2021. "Emergency Assistance for Non-Public Schools." US Department of Education.
Volden, Craig. 2002. "The Politics of Competitive Federalism: A Race to the Bottom in Welfare Benefits?" *American Journal of Political Science* 46 (2): 352–63.
Wildasin, David E. 1984. "The Welfare Effects of Intergovernmental Grants in an Economy with Distortionary Local Taxes: A Simple General Equilibrium Analysis." *Journal of Public Economics* 25 (1–2): 103–25.
Wilde, Parke E., and Christine K. Ranney. 2000. "The Monthly Food Stamp Cycle: Shopping Frequency and Food Intake Decisions in an Endogenous Switching Regression Framework." *American Journal of Agricultural Economics* 82 (1): 200–213.
Wilson, John D. 1986. "A Theory of Interregional Tax Competition." *Journal of Urban Economics* 19 (3): 296–315.
Zodrow, George R. and Mieszkowski, Peter. 1986. "Pigou, Tiebout, Property Taxation, and the Underprovision of Local Public Goods." *Journal of Urban Economics* 19 (3): 356–70.

## Comment Brian Knight

In response to the recent COVID-19 pandemic, the federal government enacted an unprecedented fiscal stimulus program. This included substantial assistance to state and local governments, with federal grants to subnational governments increasing from 3.4 percent of GDP in fiscal year 2019 to 3.9 percent in 2020 and 5.5 percent in 2021, before dropping off again back to 4.8 percent in 2022.

Using this pandemic-induced shock to state and local budgets, this chapter investigates the relationship between intergovernmental grants and state tax policy. The identification strategy in this chapter involves the use of representatives in Congress per capita as an instrument for federal grants, and the authors document that states with more representatives per capita received more federal grants per capita. Based upon this first stage, the authors then examine the relationship between federal grants and tax competition, finding that, if anything, state governments that received more funding were less likely to reduce state corporate income tax rates. Thus, federal grants were associated with higher tax rates, meaning that this federal grant program tended to dampen tax competition between states.

Overall, this chapter contributes to three broad literatures in the areas of public economics and political economy: (1) tax competition, (2) the role of intergovernmental grants in federal systems, and (3) the role of representation of large states versus small states in Congress in terms of the distribution of federal funds.

### Tax Competition

Dating back to Zodrow and Mieszkowski (1986) and Wilson (1986), a literature has focused on the idea that tax competition can lead to economic inefficiencies in models with mobile capital and immobile labor. In short, when one state increases its tax rate, all else equal, this increases capital flows to other states and hence increases their tax base. To the extent that this cross-state externality is not internalized by state policymakers, then tax rates on capital will be too low in equilibrium. This empirical analysis of corporate tax competition between states yields new insights into the role of federal grants, which shift state budget constraints, in terms of the intensity of tax competition between states. Tying this finding back to the normative implications identified in this literature suggests that this COVID-19-induced federal grant program, by mitigating tax competition, might have been efficiency enhancing, at least along this particular dimension.

Brian Knight is a professor of economics at Brown University and a research associate of the National Bureau of Economic Research.

While this analysis pushes forward the empirical literature in this area via the use of an instrumental variables analysis, more research using causal inference methods is needed on this link between federal grants and tax competition. That is, does a marginal dollar in federal grants exacerbate or mitigate tax competition between state governments? One possible strategy, based upon Gordon (2004), involves using decennial census count shocks and their implications for federal grants distributed according to formulae, which typically include population.

## The Role of Intergovernmental Grants in Federalism

A long-standing literature on the flypaper effect has investigated state policy responses to federal grants. According to the median voter theorem and other political economy models of state policy formation, recipient state governments should reduce taxes when receiving additional federal assistance, as it relaxes their budget constraints and can be thus considered as a fungible resource to state policymakers. According to the flypaper effect, recipient states, by contrast, tend to not reduce their taxes and instead increase spending dollar for dollar when receiving external funds (Hines and Thaler 1995).

Based upon this disconnect between theoretical predictions and empirical findings, the literature then branched off in two directions. In the first direction, new theoretical analyses have attempted to develop models in which state policymakers with different objectives, such as budget maximization, might increase spending when receiving federal grants. A second direction has argued that the original empirical findings in this literature were largely based upon correlational analysis and thus not well identified. This second direction has instead attempted to develop stronger identification strategies. Using political instruments based upon, for example, committee representation in Congress, Knight (2002) finds that, consistent with standard political economy models such as the median voter theorem, the receipt of federal transportation funds does tend to reduce state contributions to highway spending and thus does not increase state budgets. Based upon shocks to Title 1 aid driven by census counts, Gordon (2004) finds that the receipt of Title 1 aid by school districts leads to a reduction in property taxation and thus does not increase education spending. Likewise, Lutz (2010), in the context of direct democracy in New Hampshire town meetings, finds that changes in state aid driven by school finance reform does not increase spending by local governments. In this chapter on tax competition, by contrast, the authors document an even stronger flypaper effect, with increased federal funding leading to increases in state corporate taxation, meaning that state government spending increases more than dollar-for-dollar. Again, more work using methods from causal inference is needed to understand the differences between these results and these settings and other results and other settings, and the extent to which this flypaper effect result is driven by the exceptional nature of the COVID-19 pandemic.

Another related literature on intergovernmental grants argues that federal grants (and progressive federal income taxation) can be used as a form of insurance against local business cycles. Asdrubali et al. (1996), in particular, estimate that 13 percent of state-level shocks are smoothed by the federal government during their sample period of 1963–1990. This empirical analysis sheds light on this issue via the analysis of state-level support provided by the federal government during a particularly severe economic downturn. To the extent that states respond to this aid by increasing corporate tax rates and to the extent that higher tax rates reduce private investment in the state, then this will reduce the role of the federal government in smoothing particularly severe business cycles. Additional work in this area could shed light on differences in federal policy over time; in particular, the role of the federal government in smoothing regional business cycles has presumably only increased since the 1963–1990 sample period examined in Asdrubali et al. (1996), given subsequent growth in the size of the federal government.

## Representation in Congress and the Geographic Allocation of Federal Funds

The authors provide convincing evidence that small states received more federal funding during the pandemic than large states on a per capita basis. That is, the smallest states, such as Wyoming, Vermont, and Alaska, received an additional $5,000–$6,000 in grants per capita, whereas the largest states, such as New York, Florida, Texas, and California, received roughly half of that amount, again on a per capita basis. The authors attribute this difference to, at least in part, Senate representation, under which every state has two senators, meaning that small states are overrepresented in the US Senate. In the US House, by contrast, representation is roughly proportional to state population. That is, while Wyoming, the smallest state, and California, the largest state, each have two senators, California currently has 52 representatives in the US House whereas Wyoming has only one. While this empirical finding of more COVID-19 funding to small states on a per capita basis is certainly consistent with Senate representation driving federal funding, there are also other possible explanations. In particular, it is difficult to separate the effects of representation from the effects of population itself. If there are economies of scale in the state provision of public goods, for example, then it might be efficient for the federal government to provide more funding per capita to small states. Likewise, if there are spillovers across states due to, for example, the interstate highway system, then again it might be efficient for the federal government to provide more funding per capita to small states.

Two papers have attempted to separate the effects of representation from the effects of population on the geographic allocation of funds. Knight

(2008) uses a database of projects that originated in House bills and projects that originated in Senate bills. Consistent with a small state bias in Senate representation, larger states tend to fare better in projects originally appropriated in House bills, whereas small states tend to fare better in projects appropriated in Senate bills. Likewise, while focused on the allocation of state funds, Ansolabehere et al. (2002) document that, following *Baker v. Carr*, which required regular reapportionment of state legislatures, previously underrepresented counties, which tended to be urban, witnessed an increase in state funding, whereas previously overrepresented counties, which tended to be rural, witnessed a decrease in state funding. Additional research in this area could examine other reforms to representation, with a focus on causal methods, and link these reforms to the distribution of funding across geographic areas.

For acknowledgments, sources of research support, and disclosure of the author's material financial relationships, if any, please see https://www.nber.org/books-and-chapters/policy-responses-tax-competition/comment-intergovernmental-grants-and-policy-competition-concepts-institutions-and-evidence-knight.

## References

Ansolabehere, Stephen, Alan Gerber, and Jim Snyder. 2002. "Equal Votes, Equal Money: Court-Ordered Redistricting and Public Expenditures in the American States." *American Political Science Review* 96 (4): 767–77.

Asdrubali, Pierfederico, Bent E. Sørensen, and Oved Yosha. 1996. "Channels of Interstate Risk Sharing: United States 1963–1990." *The Quarterly Journal of Economics* 111 (4): 1081–110.

Gordon, Nora. 2004. "Do Federal Grants Boost School Spending? Evidence from Title I." *Journal of Public Economics* 88 (9–10): 1771–92.

Hines, James R. Jr., and Richard H. Thaler. 1995. "Anomalies: The Flypaper Effect." *Journal of Economic Perspectives* 9 (4): 217–26.

Knight, Brian. 2002. "Endogenous Federal Grants and Crowd-Out of State Government Spending: Theory and Evidence from the Federal Highway Aid Program." *American Economic Review* 92 (1): 71–92.

Knight, Brian. 2008. "Legislative Representation, Bargaining Power and the Distribution of Federal Funds: Evidence from the US Congress." *The Economic Journal* 118 (532): 1785–803.

Lutz, Byron. 2010. "Taxation with Representation: Intergovernmental Grants in a Plebiscite Democracy." *The Review of Economics and Statistics* 92 (2): 316–32.

Wilson, John D. 1986. "A Theory of Interregional Tax Competition." *Journal of Urban Economics* 19 (3): 296–315.

Zodrow, George R., and Peter Mieszkowski. 1986. "Pigou, Tiebout, Property Taxation, and the Underprovision of Local Public Goods." *Journal of Urban Economics* 19 (3): 356–70.

# 8 Intermunicipal Cooperation in France and Related Tax Issues

Marie-Laure Breuillé and Pascale Duran-Vigneron

## 8.1 Introduction

### 8.1.1 Growing Intermunicipal Cooperation Around the World and Its Bases

This chapter focuses on intermunicipal cooperation as a policy response to tax competition. Intermunicipal cooperation enables several (usually nearby) municipalities to jointly provide public goods and services, possibly financed by autonomous tax collection. This practice is very widespread in Europe (Teles and Swianiewicz 2018). Even in the United Kingdom, where intermunicipal cooperation was referred to as the "missing ingredient" (Kelly 2007), it emerged in the 2010s and became quasi-generalized (Dixon and Elston 2020). Intermunicipal cooperation also shapes relations between municipalities in OECD countries outside Europe (OECD 2019), as well as in other developed and developing countries (e.g., in Brazil, Silvestre et al. 2020; Ecuador, Villalba Ferreira et al. 2020; El Salvador, Muraoka and Avellaneda 2021; and South Africa, Leck and Crick 2020).

The softest forms of intermunicipal cooperation consist of single or multipurpose shared-service agreements, which may be the exclusive collaborative practice among local councils, as in the United Kingdom and several former British colonies (such as Australia, Ireland, and New Zealand) or coexist with stronger forms of integration, as in France. Partnerships in the United Kingdom, for instance, may concern back-office administration or shared service programs devoted to health and social care, housing, high-

Marie-Laure Breuillé is research director at the INRAE, the National Research Institute for Agriculture, Food and Environment.

Pascale Duran-Vigneron was a research fellow at the French research institute Bureau d'Economie Théorique et Appliquée when this chapter was written.

ways, culture, regulation and planning, or waste management (Dixon and Elston 2020). On the other side of this spectrum of collaboration, intermunicipal cooperation can lead to the creation of supramunicipal authorities with delegated competencies (e.g., France, Portugal, Spain). As pointed out by OECD (2019), France is the "only OECD country that has systematically set up public institutions for intercommunal cooperation with taxing powers, i.e., able to raise their own sources of tax revenue." This makes it a particularly interesting country to analyze.

Economies of scale are the main driver for intermunicipal cooperation.[1] Greater efficiency is thought to arise from providing public goods and services on a larger scale regarding the population served. In countries characterized by a high degree of territorial fragmentation with small municipalities and a strong attachment to local entities—whose attempts to merge have often failed—intermunicipal cooperation appears to be a fallback solution in order to circumvent the drawbacks of municipal boundaries. Historical divisions are usually no longer appropriate to provide bundles of public goods in present-day societies characterized by communication technologies, more service-sector jobs, and interdependent territories due to increasing mobility. Furthermore, small municipalities, which lack the critical size and financial resources necessary to exercise certain competencies alone, reinforce their capacity or improve service quality through intermunicipal cooperation. It also proves to be a horizontal equalization mechanism by reducing the financial disparities caused by the unequal distribution of resources over the territory. Finally, intermunicipal cooperation may influence management practices in member municipalities and favor coordination on other policies.

Beyond these benefits, intermunicipal cooperation is characterized by potential risks and limitations, such as coordination costs (a fortiori when political decision-makers belong to different political parties), slower decision making, duplication of personnel due to bureaucratic inertia, democratic deficit, governance issues, reduced accountability, and free-riding.

### 8.1.2 State of the Art of the Literature on the Effects of Intermunicipal Cooperation

Since the most frequent motive for cooperation among local authorities is to achieve economies of scale, most academic papers evaluating the impact of intermunicipal cooperation have focused on local government's efficiency in the provision of public services, or on the amount of spending in the absence of data on costs and/or techniques such as nonparametric methods for estimating production frontiers (Moradi-Motlagh and Emrouznejad 2022). Although we cannot directly compare results in order to draw clear-

1. See Bel and Sebő (2023) for an extensive review of the main factors that drive in practice the choice of intermunicipal cooperation.

cut and universal conclusions about the benefits and limitations of intermunicipal cooperation, as papers adopt different methods (e.g., estimation of municipal spending choice using panel data and spatial econometrics, fuzzy regression discontinuity design, difference-in-differences), for different periods and in countries characterized by different forms of intermunicipal cooperation, we provide a brief review of the state of the art of the literature. Luca and Modrego (2021) produced one of the rare papers based on the computation of technical efficiency (thanks to a robust data envelopment analysis), finding no significant effect of intermunicipal cooperation on municipal efficiency in the provision of public goods in Italy. Estimating a stochastic cost frontier for Dutch municipalities, Niaounakis and Blank (2017) identify a significant relation between intermunicipal cooperation and cost efficiency through scale only. Frère et al. (2014) found no significant effect at all of intermunicipal cooperation, whether on municipal spending or interactions. More recently, Paty and Ubeda (2021) confirm the absence of a negative effect on spending from the joint provision of public goods for almost all competencies. However, other papers identify clear benefits of intermunicipal cooperation on expenditures and/or the associated costs, e.g., Silvestre et al. (2018) for a metareview focusing on the water and wastewater industries, Silvestre et al. (2020) for Brazil, and Ferraresi et al. (2018) for Italy.

Bel and Sebő (2021) explain these divergent outcomes by conducting a metaregression analysis. According to their results, population size and governance are key determinants of the role of intermunicipal cooperation in reducing service delivery costs. For instance, focusing on waste collection in Spain, Pérez-López et al. (2016) identified that intermunicipal cooperation is most effective in smaller municipalities (up to 20,000 inhabitants). In addition, the literature has revealed that benefits differ according to the type of public goods provided. In New York State, the multivariate assessment of the effect of cooperation by Aldag et al. (2020) reveals (1) cost reductions for solid waste management, roads and highways, police, library, and sewerage services; (2) higher costs in elder services and in planning and zoning; and (3) no significant effect for economic development, ambulance/EMS, fire, water, and youth recreation. Finally, the benefits may differ according to the timing of the adoption of intermunicipal cooperation, as shown by Tricaud (2021) for France.

Very few studies have investigated the effects of intermunicipal cooperation on other dependent variables, such as local public sector size (Jaaidane and Larribeau 2023), firm creation (Binet et al. 2022), peer effects through budgetary decisions (Breuillé and Le Gallo 2017), and taxation, which is the key focus of this book. The paucity of papers on the subject of taxation is explained by the extremely small number of countries or regions in which establishments for intermunicipal cooperation (EIMCs) benefit from tax autonomy. Beyond the collection in some countries such as Germany of taxes related to a specific public service such as waste administration (Silva and Puey 2018), or to interlocal industrial parks (Bischoff and Kosfeld 2021), France is a notable case because of the ability of EIMCs to levy taxes in addition to or in place of the municipal authorities to finance the whole bundle of public goods and services. In a sample limited to French urban areas, Charlot et al. (2015) find an increase in the local business tax rate when municipalities fully transferred business tax powers to their EIMC, which can be explained as the consequence of a decrease in the number of jurisdictions levying the business tax rate, which reduces the intensity of tax competition and thus confirms Hoyt (1991)'s theoretical predictions. Breuillé et al. (2018) extend the analysis to all municipalities and the four local direct tax rates by evaluating the causal impact of intermunicipal cooperation on tax rates. They estimate that the creation of EIMCs led to an increase in the four (municipal plus intermunicipal) tax rates, which accounts on average for 35 percent of the increase observed by the taxpayer, and exacerbated the tax disparities between the EIMC member municipalities. Intermunicipal cooperation also affects the fierceness of tax competition, strategic interactions among peer members of the same EIMC being less intense than strategic interactions with municipalities outside of the cooperative unit, as shown by Agrawal et al. (2020), due to less strategic interactions within the EIMC.

While the aim of reducing tax competition has never driven intermunicipal cooperation, tax externalities may be crucially affected by the type of funding scheme, the tax architecture (i.e., which tier taxes which tax base), and the share of competencies within member municipalities of the EIMC.

In this chapter, we will first describe collaborative practices among municipalities in one of the countries (if not the country) with the most integrated form of intermunicipal cooperation, France. By theoretical formalization, we will then analyze channels through which intermunicipal cooperation affects tax competition in a two-tier setting with two tax bases.

## 8.2 Spectrum of Intermunicipal Cooperation in France: The French Institutional Context

Inherited from the French Revolution, around 44,000 municipalities were created in 1789[2] (often replacing tax communities or ecclesiastical parishes) to build a new society governed identically throughout the country, in line with the abolition of privileges. In their wake, an upper level consisting of departments (*départements*) was created.[3] It was not until the mid-20th century that early forms of a third tier composed of regions (*régions*) appeared.

2. Decree of December 14, 1789, related to the constitution of "assemblies" (a term that will turn into "communes" from 1793). The number of assemblies is estimated at 43,915.

3. The *départements* were created by the Law of December 22, 1789, and their number, i.e., 83, was defined by the Decree of February 26, 1790.

Municipalities, departments, and regions are the three levels enshrined in the French constitution (Article 72) as territorial authorities of the Republic.

In practice, a fourth tier consisting of EIMCs has gradually emerged. With the first forms created in 1890 of EIMCs formed by municipalities that freely decided to group together, EIMCs had become increasingly widespread until they became mandatory in 2014. As coined by Hertzog (2018), intermunicipal cooperation in France is a "continuous reform." EIMCs have the status of administrative public establishments, which implies that they have legal personality, financial autonomy, and leeway to recruit their own staff. Their administrative decisions are subject to the control of legality exercised by the prefect and the jurisdictional control of the administrative court.

France has undergone several waves of intermunicipal cooperation, with roughly three different forms of intermunicipal cooperation. The most flexible one takes the form of "associative" cooperation through the formation of syndicates without tax powers. At the other extreme, some municipalities can voluntarily merge, often in response to financial incentives. In between emerged in the second half of the 20th century "project-based" or "federative" form of cooperation through the formation of establishments for intermunicipal cooperation with their own tax powers (EIMCs).

## 8.2.1 The Least Integrated Form of Cooperation: The Syndicates

### *8.2.1.1 The Three Types of Syndicates*

#### *8.2.1.1.1 Single-Purpose Intermunicipal Syndicates*

Intermunicipal cooperation dates back to the Law of March 22, 1890, which created the single-purpose intermunicipal syndicate (SIVU) status consisting of an association of municipalities that pool resources to produce a unique public good that they could not have produced alone or to generate scale economies. A SIVU can employ its own personnel and possess equipment. The first SIVUs were devoted to the development of electrification and water networks. The potential areas of intervention have since been considerably enlarged, and the competences of SIVUs may now cover the collection and treatment of household waste, the development of tourism and culture, public transportation and school transport, or the management and protection of natural parks, for example. In 2023, there were 4,738 SIVUs in France.

#### *8.2.1.1.2 Multiple-Purpose Intermunicipal Syndicates*

The multiple-purpose intermunicipal syndicate (SIVOM), created by the Ordinance of January 5, 1959, is similar to the SIVU, with the exception of being responsible for several competences rather than a single one. Since 1988, the membership conditions have been more flexible with the introduction of "à la carte" formulas, each municipality being free to join for a single subset of competences. In 2023, there were 1,214 SIVOMs, which EIMCs are gradually replacing.

##### *8.2.1.1.3 Mixed Syndicates*

Syndicates may also be "mixed" (*syndicats mixtes*) by including various partners. In addition to municipalities, the Decree-Law of October 30, 1935, enabled departments, establishments for intermunicipal cooperation with their own tax powers (EIMCs) and private bodies such as chambers of commerce to join forces. This status is particularly well suited to providing major public facilities (e.g., underground railway systems) or developing business parks. A distinction should be made between the closed mixed syndicate, which only associates municipalities and EIMCs, and the open mixed syndicate. In 2023, there were 1,964 closed mixed syndicates and 806 open mixed syndicates.

#### *8.2.1.2 Financing Aspects and Trends Toward Rationalization*

These three types of syndicates have no tax powers, and are funded either by contributions from their member municipalities (the share of which is fixed by the statutes of the syndicate) for administrative public services, or by fees and prices for industrial and commercial public services. Some exceptions are the funding of the household waste competence, for which the household waste removal tax can be levied, and the contribution to the function of transportation. The number of syndicates remains very high, despite several attempts to rationalize their mapping through their absorption by EIMCs (based on the design of the intermunicipal cooperation schemes described below) or mergers of syndicates. The French Court of Auditors published a critical report (Cour des comptes 2016) pointing out a large number of small syndicates and an inefficient overlapping of boundaries, and advocating the pursuit of rationalization.

Since syndicates have no tax powers and are usually poorly integrated, we will omit them from the rest of this chapter and focus on the other form of intermunicipal cooperation, EIMCs, which have their own tax powers. However, the historical formation of syndicates proves to be a relevant instrument for explaining the current membership of these EIMCs without reference to current tax decisions, as used by Agrawal et al. (2020).

### 8.2.2 The Most Integrated Form of Cooperation: Mergers of Municipalities

#### *8.2.2.1 Largely Unsuccessful Attempts to Reduce the Number of Municipalities from the French Revolution to the Twenty-First Century*

Just a few months after the creation of the 44,000 municipalities, the laws of August 12 and 20, 1790, voted by the Revolutionary Assembly, urged the merger of very small municipalities with fewer than 250 inhabitants. This first attempt to reduce the number of municipalities had very limited effects, like all the others that followed in the 19th and 20th centuries. A major flop was the Marcellin Law (1971), which encouraged the adoption of a "merger-association" status and included the right to reverse the decision in order to ease the fears of certain municipalities. Only 838 mergers occurred between 1971 and 1977, involving 2,045 municipalities (Tellier 2017). Some of the "Marcellin municipalities" were subsequently dismantled, leading to a limited decline in the number of municipalities from 37,700 to 36,400.

#### *8.2.2.2 The Most Recent Attempt: The Communes nouvelles*

After the failure of the Marcellin law, which had enshrined the negatively connoted term of "fusion" (merger) in the minds of local politicians, the Réforme des Collectivités Territoriales law[4] of 2010 (RCT law) has brought the term *commune nouvelle* ("new municipality") to the forefront. After being initially shunned, with only 25 creation of *communes nouvelles* within the first four years, the financial incentives of the Pélissard-Le Roux law[5] of 2015 prompted more municipalities to create a *commune nouvelle*. Between 2010 and 2023, 795 *communes nouvelles* were created by the amalgamation of 2,553 municipalities, leading to a 5 percent reduction in the number of French municipalities, which has now dropped below the symbolic 35,000 mark.

However, the "Inspection générale de l'administration" has recently published a critical report entitled "New Communes: A Disappointing Assessment, Uncertain Prospects" (Acar et al. 2022). Essentially, this report criticizes the low number and small size of the *communes nouvelles*, in addition to their lack of real added value.

#### *8.2.2.3 A Lack of Critical Mass for the Vast Majority of French Municipalities in Comparison to Most of Their European Counterparts*

In comparison, most European countries have made great strides on this issue over the last 70 years. Table 8.1, for instance, shows that 25 percent of German municipalities, 66 percent of UK municipalities, and 87 percent of Swedish municipalities have been abolished. Despite a reduction of 10 percent, the bottom-most tier in France still consists of 35,000 municipalities, which corresponds to 40 percent of the total number of municipalities in all European Union countries.

As shown in figure 8.1, both the number of inhabitants per municipality

4. See LOI n° 2010–1563 du 16 décembre 2010 de réforme des collectivités territoriales (1), https://www.legifrance.gouv.fr/loda/id/JORFTEXT000023239624.

5. See LOI n° 2015–292 du 16 mars 2015 relative à l'amélioration du régime de la commune nouvelle, pour des communes fortes et vivantes (1), https://www.legifrance.gouv.fr/loda/id/JORFTEXT000030361485.

**Table 8.1** **Comparison of changes in the number of municipalities with some other European countries**

| Country | N° of municipalities in 1950 | N° of municipalities in 2021 | Change (%) |
|---|---|---|---|
| Germany | 14,338 | 10,792 | −25 |
| Austria | 4,039 | 2,095 | −48 |
| Belgium | 2,359 | 581 | −75 |
| Bulgaria | 1,389 | 264 | −81 |
| Denmark | 1,387 | 98 | −93 |
| Spain | 9,214 | 8,131 | −12 |
| Finland | 547 | 309 | −44 |
| **France** | **38,800** | **34,965** | **−10** |
| Hungary | 3,032 | 3,155 | 4 |
| Italy | 7,781 | 7,904 | 2 |
| Norway | 744 | 356 | −52 |
| Czech Republic | 11,459 | 6,258 | −45 |
| United Kingdom | 1,118 | 379 | −66 |
| Sweden | 2,281 | 290 | −87 |

Source: Balladur (2009) and OECD (2021).

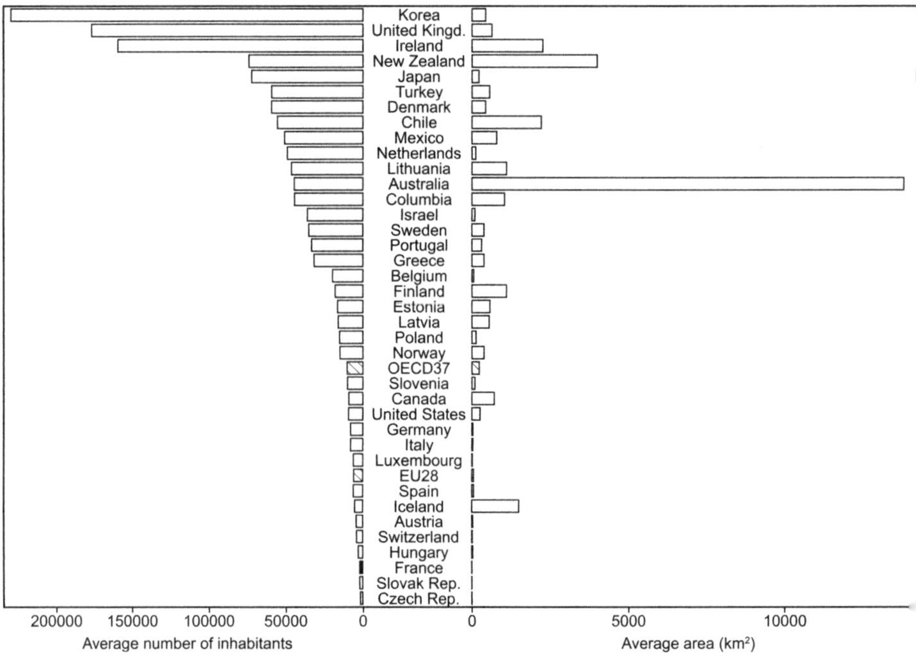


**Fig. 8.1 Average number of inhabitants and area in OECD countries in 2019**
Source: Authors from OECD (2021).

and the average surface area per municipality are among the lowest in the OECD. Half (49.6 percent) of France's 35,000 municipalities have fewer than 500 inhabitants, and 71.6 percent have fewer than 1,000 inhabitants.

### 8.2.3 Intermediate Forms of Intermunicipal Cooperation: EIMCs with Their Own Tax Powers

Contrary to syndicates, EIMCs must group municipalities together in a single block and without an enclave. In addition, a municipality must belong to a single EIMC (as multiple memberships are not permitted to avoid the overlapping of competences) while simultaneously being a member of one or more syndicates. The creation or extension of an EIMC can sometimes lead to the dissolution of a syndicate if the EIMC acquires a competence that was formerly managed by the syndicate. This is a more integrated form of cooperation than via syndicates, with the collective management of local projects financed by autonomous tax collection, which is our primary focus.

EIMCs are governed by two principles: (1) the principle of specialty, according to which EIMCs only intervene in the field of competences that have been transferred to them and within a territory restricted to the scope of member municipalities; and (2) the principle of exclusivity, which ensures that EIMCs are the only ones to intervene in the fields related to the competences they exercise. In addition, they only exercise competences qualified as being of "community interest." We distinguish between four types of EIMCs, which together cover the entire French territory.

#### *8.2.3.1 The Four Types of EIMCs*

##### *8.2.3.1.1 Communities of Communes* (Communautés de Communes)

The smallest and least integrated form of EIMC is the community of communes, created by the Law of February 6, 1992. They often group together municipalities of sparsely populated areas with a low population density. Since the NOTRe Law of August 7, 2015, an EIMC must contain at least 15,000 inhabitants (unless specific derogations apply). Another unit—the "community of cities"—was also created in 1992 and has since disappeared (due to its lack of success, with only five creations) after being integrated into agglomeration communities. Creating communities of communes was a cornerstone in intermunicipal cooperation by instilling a project dimension, whereas the sole vocation of the SIVU or the SIVOM is to manage equipment or infrastructures. Communities of communes exercise both compulsory competences and optional competences of community interest on behalf of member municipalities (see table 8.2).[6] To finance them, they can freely opt for an additional taxation regime or a single professional tax

6. For the exhaustive list of competences for communities of communes, see https://www.legifrance.gouv.fr/codes/article_lc/LEGIARTI000045213277/.

**Table 8.2** **Range of competencies by legal status**

| | Communities of communes | Agglomeration communities |
|---|---|---|
| Law | 1992 | 1999 |
| Number in 2023 | 992 | 227 |
| Minimal population threshold | 15,000 | 50,000 |
| Tax regime | FPU or additional taxation | FPU |
| Competencies | * ***Compulsory competences***:<br>−Urban planning<br>−Economic development actions<br>−Management of aquatic environments and flood prevention<br>−Reception areas for members of traveler communities<br>−Collection and processing of household and similar waste<br>−Wastewater treatment<br>* ***Optional competences of community interest***:<br>−Protection and enhancement of the environment<br>−Highways<br>−Cultural and sports facilities and preelementary and elementary education facilities<br>−Social welfare<br>−City policy<br>* ***By agreement with the department***, some or all powers in the social welfare field | * ***Compulsory competences***:<br>−Urban planning<br>−Economic development actions<br>−Management of aquatic environments and flood prevention<br>−Reception areas for members of traveler communities<br>−Collection and processing of household and similar waste<br>−Social balance of housing<br>−City policy<br>* ***Optional competences of community interest*** *(at least 3 of the 7 competences):*<br>−Protection and enhancement of the environment<br>−Highways<br>−Cultural and sports facilities<br>−Social welfare<br>−Wastewater treatment<br>−Water<br>−Public service centers<br>* ***By agreement with the department***, some or all powers in the social welfare and highways fields |

Source: Authors from legifrance.gouv.fr.

regime, which will be defined later. In 2023, there are 992 communities of communes.

*8.2.3.1.2 Agglomeration Communities* (Communautés d'Agglomération)

The Chevènement Law of 1999 created the new status of agglomeration communities for more urbanized areas. They encompass more than 50,000 inhabitants (or 30,000 inhabitants if they include the prefecture of the department) within the area around a central city of more than 15,000 inhabitants (or the prefecture or largest city of the department). On behalf of their member municipalities, agglomeration communities exercise both

| Urban communities | Metropoles |
| --- | --- |
| 1966 | 2010 |
| 14 | 21 (including Paris and Marseille) + Lyon |
| 250,000 | 400,000 |
| FPU | FPU |
| * ***Compulsory competences***:<br>–Economic, social, and cultural development and planning (activity zones; economic development actions; cultural, sociocultural, socioeducational, and sports facilities; high schools and colleges; tourism; support for higher education and research establishments)<br>–Urban planning (including mobility plan, highways)<br>–Local housing policy and social balance of housing<br>–City policy<br>–Management of public-interest services (wastewater treatment, water, cemeteries, slaughterhouses, fire and rescue services, energy transition, urban heating, public electricity and gas supplies, charging infrastructures for electric vehicles)<br>–Environmental protection (household and similar waste collection, measures to control air pollution and noise pollution, actions to control energy demand, management of aquatic environments and flood prevention)<br>–Reception areas for members of traveler communities<br>* ***By agreement with the department***, some or all powers in the social welfare and highways fields. | * ***Compulsory competences***:<br>–Economic, social, and cultural development and planning (activity zones; economic development actions; cultural, sociocultural, socioeducationa,l and sports facilities; high schools and colleges; tourism; support for higher education and research establishments)<br>–Urban planning (including mobility plan, highways including department-level roads, railway stations)<br>–Local housing policy and social balance of housing, improvement of the housing stock<br>–City policy<br>–Management of public-interest services (wastewater treatment, water, cemeteries, slaughterhouses, fire and rescue services, energy transition, urban heating, public electricity and gas supplies, charging infrastructures for electric vehicles)<br>–Environmental protection (household and similar waste collection, measures to control air pollution and noise pollution, actions to control energy demand, management of aquatic environments and flood prevention)<br>–Reception areas for members of traveler communities<br>* ***By agreement with the department***, some or all powers in the social welfare field, highways, allocation of aid under the solidarity fund for housing, integration program, assistance to young people in difficulty, specialized prevention actions for young people and families in difficulty, elderly people, *collèges* (middle schools), tourism.<br>* ***By agreement with the State***, some of its competences |

compulsory competences and optional competences of community interest that must be chosen from several groups of competences provided for by the law (see table 8.2).[7] In 2023, there are 227 agglomeration communities.

*8.2.3.1.3 Urban Communities* (Communautés Urbaines)

The urban community is the oldest form of EIMC, created by the Law of December 31, 1966. The first four urban communities (around Bordeaux,

7. For the exhaustive list of competences for agglomeration communities, see https://www.legifrance.gouv.fr/codes/article_lc/LEGIARTI000037666796/2018-11-25.

Lille, Lyon, and Strasbourg) were imposed as a means of narrowing the gap between administrative and economic realities. Those that followed were created on a voluntary basis by mayors. The minimum population threshold has been lowered by law to reach 250,000 inhabitants since the MAPTAM law of 2014 (unless specific derogations apply). In addition to compulsory competences, they are authorized to intervene in some of their department's fields of competence by agreement (see table 8.2).[8] In 2023, there are 14 urban communities.

*8.2.3.1.4 Metropoles* (Métropoles)

The metropole, created by the Law of 16th December, 2010, is the most integrated form of EIMC. In addition to the fields of competence of urban communities, they are also authorized to exercise competences legally attributed to the department or even the State, subject to concluding an agreement (see table 8.2).[9] In 2023, there are 21 metropoles, including Paris and Marseille, which have special status. Lyon, although a metropole in name, is not an EIMC but a territorial authority with a special status due to the merger of the urban community of Lyon and, within its territory, the department of Rhône in 2018.

### *8.2.3.2 EIMCs' Governance*

EIMCs are administered by their own body, the EIMC Council. Seats on the EIMC council are allocated to the municipalities according to their population (proportional representation at the highest average), with at least one seat per municipality. In communities of communes and agglomeration communities, seats can be distributed differently if municipalities conclude a local agreement, which must respect strict conditions. In particular, the share of seats allocated to a municipality may not differ by more than 20 percent from the share of its population in the total population of the EIMC. EIMC councilors must be municipal councilors.

The means of appointing EIMC councilors depends on the size of the member municipality. Since the 2014 elections, in municipalities with more than 1,000 inhabitants, voters have simultaneously voted for municipal councilors and EIMC councilors who represent the municipality within the EIMC by submitting a single ballot paper with their choice of candidate for the municipal election on the left-hand side and candidate for election to the EIMC on the right (who must necessarily come from the list of municipal councilors on the left-hand side). A proportional voting system with a 50 percent majority for the list that comes first applies. This dual ballot system is based on the model used in Paris-Lyon-Marseille, where borough

8. For the exhaustive list of competences for urban communities, see https://www.legifrance.gouv.fr/codes/section_lc/LEGITEXT000006070633/LEGISCTA000006192470.

9. For the exhaustive list of competences for metropoles, see https://www.legifrance.gouv.fr/codes/id/LEGISCTA000023245477.

(*arrondissement*) councilors and city councilors are elected at the same time. This election by direct universal suffrage, although linked to municipal elections, recognizes the increasingly important role played by the EIMCs in the territorial landscape and marks a further step toward territorial authority status. Before 2014, EIMC councilors who represented a municipality were appointed by the municipal council.

In municipalities with fewer than 1,000 inhabitants, EIMC councilors are appointed from among the members of the municipal council according to their status, i.e., first the mayor, then the deputy mayors according to the order of their election, followed by the other municipal councilors if necessary (depending on the limit of the number of seats allocated to the municipality on the EIMC council).

### *8.2.3.3 Tax Regimes of EIMCs*

To finance the competencies transferred by member municipalities, EIMCs have the ability to levy their own taxes on the four main local direct tax bases, which are:

1. the residential tax on secondary homes and other furnished premises not used as a main residence (*taxe d'habitation sur les résidences secondaires*), which is the remaining part after the gradual abolition of the residential tax on main residences from 2020 to 2023;
2. the property tax on developed land (*taxe foncière sur les propriétés bâties*);
3. the property tax on undeveloped land (*taxe foncière sur les propriétés non bâties*); and
4. the territorial economic contribution (CET), consisting of the *cotisation sur la valeur ajoutée des enterprises—CVAE* over which municipalities and EIMCs have no power to set rates and the business property tax (*cotisation foncière des enterprises—CFE*) based on property rentals.

Figure 8.2 charts the co-occupation by the four tiers of subnational jurisdictions (municipalities, EIMCs, departments, and regions) of the main local tax bases throughout the reforms. 2011 was a pivotal year due to a substantial reduction in the number of tiers sharing common tax bases, with potential consequences regarding vertical externalities. Tax revenues collected by municipalities and/or EIMCs from these four main local tax bases account for 55 percent of their tax revenues (even 62 percent if we add revenues from CVAE).

Two tax regimes exist for EIMCs.[10] The first one, introduced from the earliest days of intermunicipal cooperation, is the additional tax regime (*régime de fiscalité additionnelle—FA*), in which EIMCs have the authority

10. A zonal tax on the business property tax base can also be collected in an economic activity zone.

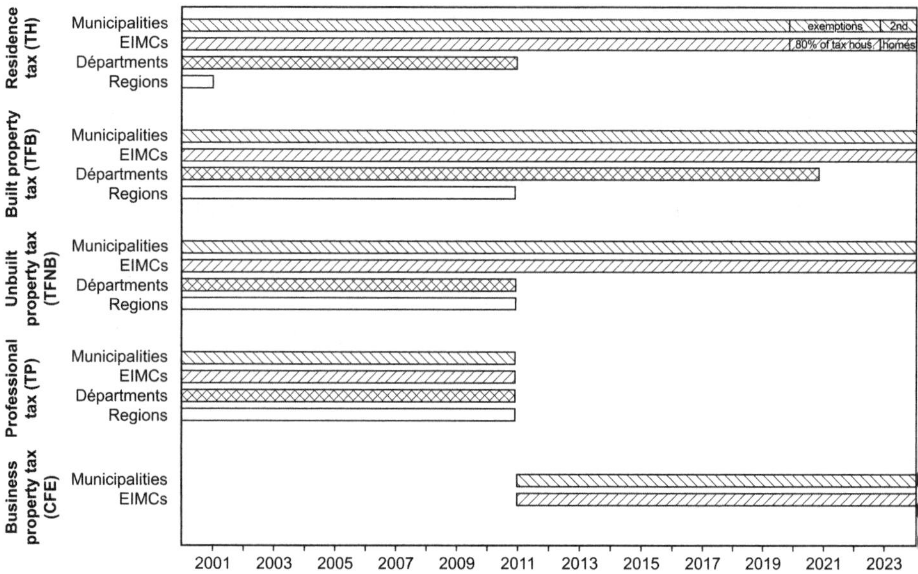


**Fig. 8.2 Who taxes what? Co-occupation throughout the reforms of the main tax bases on which subnational authorities have a tax-setting power**
Source: The authors.

to levy an additional tax on each of the four main direct tax bases, in addition to municipal taxes. In other words, EIMCs and member municipalities share the four tax bases, i.e., both the EIMC and the municipalities can set the tax rates for each of the four tax bases. In this case, the cumulative tax paid by residents (firms or households) corresponds to the intermunicipal tax plus the municipal tax for each tax base.

The second regime is the single professional tax regime (*régime de fiscalité professionnelle unique—FPU*) for which only the EIMC collects the business property tax instead of its member municipalities. A single tax rate is therefore applied to the municipalities' pooled business tax bases within the EIMC. While municipalities continue to levy a tax on secondary homes, a property tax on developed land, and a property tax on undeveloped land, the EIMC also sets additional rates for each of these taxes as under the additional tax regime.[11] This regime is inherited from the single business tax regime in which the EIMC only levied the business tax, which was introduced in 1983 with several objectives. First, the tax specialization characterizing this regime was intended to limit the tax inflation arising

11. EIMCs also levy the flat-rate network taxes (*imposition forfaitaire des entreprises de réseaux*), whose components are wholly or partially paid by the local authorities, and the tax on commercial floor space (*taxe sur les surfaces commerciales—TASCOM*). They can adjust the CFE rate and the TASCOM multiplier coefficient.

**Table 8.3** **Tax architecture under the two tax regimes**

| | | | | |
|---|---|---|---|---|
| **Additional tax regime (FA)** | | | | |
| Municipal tax rates | $t^B$ | $t^R$ | $t^{PD}$ | $t^{PU}$ |
| Intermunicipal tax rates | $T^B$ | $T^R$ | $T^{PD}$ | $T^{PU}$ |
| Cumulative tax rates | $T^B + t^B$ | $T^R + t^R$ | $T^{PD} + t^{PD}$ | $T^{PU} + t^{PU}$ |
| **Single professional tax regime (FPU)** | | | | |
| Municipal tax rates | | $t^R$ | $t^{PD}$ | $t^{PU}$ |
| Intermunicipal tax rates | $T^B$ | $T^R$ | $T^{PD}$ | $T^{PU}$ |
| Cumulative tax rates | $T^B$ | $T^R + t^R$ | $T^{PD} + t^{PD}$ | $T^{PU} + t^{PU}$ |

B = business property tax; R = residence tax; PD = property tax on developed land; PU = property tax on undeveloped land.

from a tax-base sharing system. Second, the single business tax regime was supposed to reduce inequalities arising from the highly unequal distribution of the tax base—80 percent of the tax base is concentrated in 5 percent of the municipalities—and to limit the tax competition between municipalities induced by the mobility of firms. Third, this tax regime was designed to promote the coordination of fiscal policies between EIMCs and member municipalities, since EIMCs are reliant on only one direct tax (the business tax). However, the limited tax autonomy of EIMCs led to the creation of a mixed taxation regime in 1999: by allowing EIMCs to set additional tax rates on municipal direct taxes, this tax regime provided EIMCs with the means to address potential financial difficulties.[12]

All metropoles and—except for six derogations—all urban and agglomeration communities are automatically subject to the single professional tax regime.[13] Among the communities of communes, which have the ability to choose their tax regime, 82.1 percent of them currently have a single professional tax regime.

### *8.2.3.4 Equalization Among EIMCs*

Since 2012, a horizontal equalization mechanism, the national fund for the equalization of intermunicipal and municipal resources (Fonds national de péréquation des ressources intercommunales et communales—FPIC), has set out to reduce the disparities in local resources. A measure of the aggregate financial potential (*potential financier agrégé—PFIA*) is calculated for the intermunicipal bloc made of the EIMC and its member municipalities by aggregating their financial potential. The national fund is financed by the

12. The reform of the business tax (2009) ended the distinction between the single business tax regime, where the EIMC only levies the business tax, and the mixed taxation regime, where the EIMC levies both the business tax instead of member municipalities and additional taxation on the three other tax bases.

13. See https://bofip.impots.gouv.fr/bofip/8316-PGP.html/identifiant%3DBOI-IF-COLOC-10-20-10-20220421.

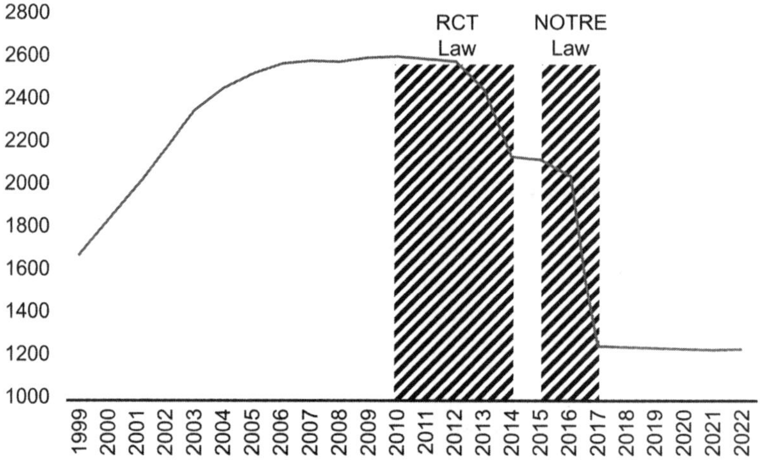


**Fig. 8.3 Changes in the number of EIMCs**
Source: The authors from BANATIC data.

contributions of intermunicipal blocs whose PFIA exceeds a certain threshold. The redistribution of the fund's resources then depends on the rank determined according to a synthetic index that accounts for their resources, their inhabitants' average income, and their tax effort, enabling the fund's resources to be redirected toward less favorably endowed intermunicipal blocs. It should be noted that municipal and intermunicipal authorities are granted considerable leeway in the sharing of levies or repayments within the intermunicipal bloc. This equalization scheme now exceeds €1 billion.

### *8.2.3.5 A Recent Rationalization of Intermunicipal Cooperation*

In the 2010s, France actively engaged in generalizing and rationalizing the intermunicipal map, supported mainly by two laws.

#### *8.2.3.5.1 Law Reforming Local Authorities of December 16, 2010 (the "RCT Law")*

The RCT law became a cornerstone of intermunicipal cooperation by requiring by early 2014 the nationwide coverage of France by EIMCs.[14] This law removed any isolated or landlocked municipalities, which numbered almost 2,500 in 2009. It also rationalized the boundaries of EIMCs by introducing a minimum threshold of 5,000 inhabitants and improving their spatial coherence, which explains the sharp drop in the number of EIMCs in figure 8.3 from 2,595 in 2010 to 2,127 in 2014.

In addition, attempts were made to reduce the number of syndicates,

14. Inner suburbs of Paris are exempted, as they would be integrated into the future Greater Paris Metropole.

possibly by transferring their competencies to EIMCs. The *préfet* (the representative of the state at the department level), assisted by the Departmental Commission on Intermunicipal Cooperation (Commission départementale de coopération intercommunale), was given a key role in this rationalization process with the power to modify boundaries and merge or dissolve syndicates. This law also created "metropoles" in order to meet the needs of large conurbations and improve regional competitiveness and cohesion. Finally, it improved local democracy with the election of the (previously appointed) councilors of EIMCs.

##### *8.2.3.5.2 Law on the New Territorial Organization of the Republic of August 7, 2015 (the "NOTRe Law")*

The aim of rationalizing the intermunicipal map and giving EIMCs a more important role as drivers of planning and development was reaffirmed by the NOTRe law, which increased the minimum population threshold of EIMCs from 5,000 to 15,000 inhabitants (with some exemptions depending mainly on the density of both the EIMC and the department). Through a series of mergers, the number of EIMCs dropped from 2,115 in 2015 to 1,254 in 2023, as shown in figure 8.3. In addition, the integration of municipalities within the EIMC was reinforced by adding two new items (tourism promotion and the management of reception areas for travelers) to the set of compulsory competences for communities of communes. Their optional competencies were also extended.

## 8.3 Channels Through Which Intermunicipal Cooperation Affects Tax Cooperation in a Two-Tier Setting with Two Tax Bases

### 8.3.1 The Theoretical Setting

We propose a theoretical framework to analyze the influence on tax externalities of the type of intermunicipal cooperation. We consider a model of capital tax competition in a two-tier setting like Wrede (1997) and Breuillé and Zanaj (2013). Our country comprises two subnational tiers with $n > 1$ identical EIMCs, indexed by $i = 1, \ldots, n$, and within each EIMC, $m > 1$ identical municipalities, indexed by $j = 1, \ldots, m$. These two tiers can potentially raise tax revenues through taxes on two tax bases, $x$ and $y$. Let $t_{i,j}^k$ be the proportional tax rate levied by municipality $j$ in EIMC $i$ on its tax base $k$, and $T_i^k$ be the proportional tax rate chosen by EIMC $i$ on its tax base $k_i$, with $k = x, y$. By construction, the EIMC tax base $k_i$ is the sum of the member municipalities's tax bases, i.e.,

$$k_i = \sum_{j=1}^{m} k_{i,j}$$

with $k = x, y$.

### 8.3.1.1 *Horizontal Tax Externalities Through the Taxation of a Municipal Mobile Tax Base*

Let us first consider that the tax base $y$ is immobile (e.g., land rents) and taxed by EIMCs only. The other tax base is a mobile production factor (e.g., labor) on which only municipalities can levy a tax rate. Tax base $x$ in municipality $ij$ is thus a function of municipality $ij$'s tax policy, $t^x_{i,j}$, the tax policies of neighboring municipalities belonging to the same EIMC $i$, $\boldsymbol{t}^x_{i,-j}$, and the tax policies of other municipalities belonging to other EIMCs, $\boldsymbol{t}^x_{-i,j}$.

The implicit demand function for factor $x$ is $x_{i,j}(r^x_{i,j})$, where $r^x_{i,j}$ is the after-tax return for factor $x$:

$$r^x_{i,j} = \rho^x + t^x_{i,j}$$

with $\rho^x(t^x_{i,j}, \boldsymbol{t}^x_{i,-j}, \boldsymbol{t}^x_{-i,j})$ being the equilibrium net return for factor $x$ implied by perfect mobility across the country. We assume nonatomistic jurisdictions, meaning that their tax choices have an impact on the welfare in other jurisdictions, i.e., jurisdictions have market power.[15] *Horizontal tax externalities* among municipalities occur through the taxation of the factor $x$. An increase in the tax rate levied on the factor by a municipality $ij$ induces an outflow of the factor from the municipality $ij$ and thus an inflow to all other same-tier municipalities. Municipalities do not usually take the positive horizontal tax externalities into account, only the distortive effect of taxation on their own tax base, i.e., $\varepsilon^{x,SH}_{mun} = (\partial x_{i,j} / \partial r^x_{i,j})(\partial r^x_{i,j} / \partial t^x_{i,j}) < 0$. The standard result is a race to the bottom, i.e., inefficiently low tax rates (Wilson 1986; Zodrow and Mieszkowski 1986). No externalities are generated by intermunicipal taxation due to tax base immobility.

### 8.3.1.2 *Vertical Externalities Add Through the Co-occupation of a Mobile Tax Base*

Now, suppose that EIMCs set an additional tax rate on the mobile factor $x$. As a result of this co-occupation, the tax base in municipality $ij$ also becomes a function of its EIMC's tax policy, $T^x_i$, and tax policies of other EIMCs, $\boldsymbol{T}^x_{-i}$.

The after-tax return $r^x_{i,j}$ is increased by the EIMC tax rate

$$r^x_{i,j} = \rho^x + t^x_{i,j} + T^x_i \qquad (1)$$

with $\rho^x(t^x_{i,j}, \boldsymbol{t}^x_{i,-j}, \boldsymbol{t}^x_{-i,j}, T^x_i, \boldsymbol{T}^x_{-i})$ the equilibrium net return for factor $x$. In addition to horizontal tax externalities at the municipal level and horizontal tax externalities at the EIMC level, *vertical tax externalities (SV)* also arise due to tax base sharing. An increase in the tax rate levied on factor $x$ by a jurisdiction induces an outflow of this factor from the jurisdiction(s) sharing the

15. See Agrawal et al. (2022) for more insights on the comparison between atomistic versus strategic (game-theoretic) tax competition.

same tax base in the other tier and thus an inflow to all other jurisdictions of this other tier. Vertical externalities induced by municipal taxation are *bottom-up* and the ones induced by EIMC taxation are *top-down*. Objective functions in the literature are specified in such a way that municipalities usually internalize only a proportion of the vertical bottom-up negative externalities imposed on the tax base of their EIMC, which are denoted by $\varepsilon_{mun}^{x,SV}$, as they only care about the welfare of their own inhabitants:

$$\varepsilon_{mun}^{x,SV} = \frac{1}{m}\sum_{h=1}^{m}\frac{\partial x_{ih}}{\partial r_{ih}^{x}}\frac{\partial r_{ih}^{x}}{\partial t_{ij}^{x}} < 0.$$

On the contrary, EIMC authorities usually fully internalize the negative vertical top-down externalities imposed on their members' tax base, which are denoted as $\varepsilon_{EIMC}^{x,SV}$, since they care about the welfare of all their members' citizens:

$$\varepsilon_{EIMC}^{x,SV} = \sum_{j=1}^{m}\frac{\partial x_{ij}}{\partial r_{ij}^{x}}\frac{\partial r_{ij}^{x}}{\partial T_{i}^{x}} < 0.$$

In this setting, horizontal and vertical externalities reinforce each other, which results in inefficiently low municipal and intermunicipal tax rates.

#### 8.3.1.3 *Same-Base and Cross-Base Horizontal and Vertical Tax Externalities*

Finally, let us suppose that tax bases $x$ and $y$ are both mobile and co-occupied by municipalities and EIMCs. For instance, these two tax bases may be two factors firms use for their production. Crucially, one factor's mobility may impact the other, i.e., they may be interdependent. The interdependence is expressed by the demand functions: $x_{i,j}(r_{i,j}^{x}, r_{i,j}^{y})$ and $y_{i,j}(r_{i,j}^{x}, r_{i,j}^{y})$. In the event of complementarity between the two tax bases, a higher cost of factor $x$ in jurisdiction $ij$ reduces demand for factor $x$, i.e., $(\partial x_{i,j} / \partial r_{i,j}^{x}) < 0$, as well as demand for factor $y$, i.e., $(\partial y_{i,j} / \partial r_{i,j}^{x}) < 0$. In contrast, the substitutability between tax bases implies that a higher cost of factor $x$ in jurisdiction $ij$ reduces demand for factor $x$ while increasing demand for factor $y$, i.e., $(\partial y_{i,j} / \partial r_{i,j}^{x}) > 0$.

The after-tax return is defined as in equation (1) for each tax base

(2) $$r_{i,j}^{x} = \rho^{x} + t_{i,j}^{x} + T_{i}^{x}$$

with $\rho^{x}(t_{i,j}^{x}, \boldsymbol{t}_{i,-j}^{x}, \boldsymbol{t}_{-i,j}^{x}, T_{i}^{x}, \boldsymbol{T}_{-i}^{x})$ being the equilibrium net return for factor $x$, and

(3) $$r_{i,j}^{y} = \rho^{y} + t_{i,j}^{y} + T_{i}^{y}$$

with $\rho^{y}(t_{i,j}^{y}, \boldsymbol{t}_{i,-j}^{y}, \boldsymbol{t}_{-i,j}^{y}, T_{i}^{y}, \boldsymbol{T}_{-i}^{y})$ being the equilibrium net return for factor $y$.

Therefore, the factors' interdependence affects the factors' demand but not their return.

This interdependence between tax bases generates cross-base tax externalities (in addition to same-base tax externalities). This is what Keen (1998) defines as effective concurrency. Although there are two different taxes and thus no formal concurrency between the taxes, the tax choices for one tax base do affect the tax choices for the other tax base: interdependence leads to effective concurrency. As Keen points out, "it seems hard . . . to conceive of federal tax arrangements that do not involve some degree of effective concurrency." *Cross-base horizontal tax externalities (CH)* occur when an increase in the tax rate set by a jurisdiction on a factor affects the amount of the other factor available to all other same-tier jurisdictions. As for same-base horizontal externalities (SH), a jurisdiction usually only cares about the cross-base externality on its tax base, respectively $\varepsilon_{mun}^{k,CH}$ for municipalities and $\varepsilon_{EIMC}^{k,CH}$ for EIMCs, and neglects the externalities imposed on the tax base of the other same-tier jurisdictions, respectively $\varepsilon_{mun}^{k,CH}$ and $\varepsilon_{EIMC}^{k,CH}$:

$$\varepsilon_{mun}^{k,CH} = \frac{\partial(-k)_{i,j}}{\partial r_{i,j}^{k}} \frac{\partial r_{i,j}^{k}}{\partial t_{i,j}^{k}}, \quad \varepsilon_{EIMC}^{k,CH} = \sum_{j=1}^{m} \frac{\partial(-k)_{i,j}}{\partial r_{i,j}^{k}} \frac{\partial r_{i,j}^{k}}{\partial T_{i}^{k}} \text{ with } k = x, y$$

and $-k$ is the other tax base. The sign of the cross-base horizontal tax externalities depends on the nature of the interdependence between the two tax bases. The externality on the jurisdiction's own tax base is negative, pointing in the same direction as the same-base horizontal externality when tax bases are complementary, i.e., $\varepsilon_{mun}^{k,CH} < 0$ and $\varepsilon_{EIMC}^{k,CH} < 0$, while it is positive, pointing in the opposite direction to the same-base horizontal externality when the tax bases are substitutable, i.e., $\varepsilon_{mun}^{k,CH} > 0$ and $\varepsilon_{EIMC}^{k,CH} > 0$.

The interdependence of factors combined with tax base sharing also generates *cross-base vertical tax externalities (CV)*, an increase in the tax raised by a jurisdiction on a factor affecting the amount of the other factor available to the other-tier jurisdictions. In the case of complementarity, the externalities correspond to an outflow of factors from the jurisdiction(s) sharing the same tax base to all other jurisdictions. In contrast, in the event of substitutability, the externalities correspond to an inflow of factor to the jurisdiction(s) sharing the same tax base. These externalities are cross-base *vertical bottom-up externalities* when arising from municipal taxation and *cross-base vertical top-down externalities* when arising from EIMC taxation.

As for same-base vertical externalities, municipalities usually internalize a proportion $1/m$ of the cross-base vertical bottom-up externalities imposed on their EIMC, denoted by $\varepsilon_{mun}^{k,CV}$, and EIMCs internalize all cross-base vertical top-down externalities, denoted by $\varepsilon_{EIMC}^{k,CV}$, imposed on their member municipalities:

$$\varepsilon_{mun}^{k,CV} = \frac{1}{m} \sum_{h=1}^{m} \frac{\partial(-k)_{i,h}}{\partial r_{i,h}^{k}} \frac{\partial r_{i,h}^{k}}{\partial t_{i,j}^{k}}, \quad \varepsilon_{EIMC}^{k,CV} = \sum_{j=1}^{m} \frac{\partial(-k)_{i,j}}{\partial r_{i,j}^{k}} \frac{\partial r_{i,j}^{k}}{\partial T_{i}^{k}} \text{ with } k = x, y$$

and $-k$ is the other tax base.

The sign of the cross-base vertical tax externalities depends on the nature of the interdependence between the two tax bases. The cross-base vertical tax externalities internalized by jurisdiction are negative, pointing in the same direction as the same-base vertical ones when tax bases are complementary, i.e., $\varepsilon_{mun}^{k,CV} < 0$ and $\varepsilon_{EIMC}^{k,CV} < 0$, while they are positive, pointing in the opposite direction to the same-base vertical externalities when tax bases are substitutable, i.e., $\varepsilon_{mun}^{k,CV} > 0$ and $\varepsilon_{EIMC}^{k,CV} > 0$.

### 8.3.2 Externalities Associated with Each Type of Intermunicipal Cooperation

Tax externalities can therefore be defined along two dimensions: (1) horizontal *versus* vertical externalities, i.e., externalities among authorities at the same tier *versus* externalities among authorities at two different tiers, (2) same-base *versus* cross-base externalities, i.e., externalities due to the migration of a tax base $k$ arising from a modification of a tax rate on this base ($t^k$ or $T^k$), *versus* externalities due to the migration of a tax base $k$ arising from a modification of the tax rate on the other tax base ($t^{-k}$ or $T^{-k}$). Cross-base externalities only occur when $F_{xy}^{ij} = F_{yx}^{ij} \neq 0$, i.e., when the demand for one factor is affected by the taxation of the other factor.

We investigate which type of these externalities are at work depending on the form of the EIMC and its tax regime. *Syndicates* are likely not to change tax externalities existing among municipalities before cooperation, provided that the provision of public goods and services delegated to the syndicates is now financed by municipal transfers funded by tax revenues previously collected. Only same-base and cross-base horizontal tax externalities at the municipal level, i.e., $\varepsilon_{mun}^{k,SH}$ and $\varepsilon_{mun}^{k,CH}$, occur. However, achieving scale economies through larger-scale supply could reduce the overall envelope and thus contribute to lessening the tax burden for all municipalities.

*Mergers* of municipalities by creating "communes nouvelles" amounts to considering only $n$ jurisdictions rather than $nm$ jurisdictions. As shown by Hoyt (1991), the merger of same-tier jurisdictions leads to increased tax rates and, therefore, public goods provision as the number of jurisdictions decreases. This results from the reduction in both same-base and cross-base horizontal tax externalities. When a *commune nouvelle* increases its tax rate, the tax base inflow to other *communes nouvelles* diminishes. Decreasing the number of jurisdictions reduces the change in the tax base; increasing the jurisdiction's tax rate is, therefore, less harmful for that jurisdiction.

*EIMCs with single professional tax regime (FPU)*—assuming no additional taxation on the other tax base—generate same-base horizontal externalities at the EIMC level on the professional tax base and same-base horizontal externalities at the municipal level on the other tax base. Since each tier only taxes one specific tax base, cross-base horizontal tax externalities and same-base vertical externalities are ruled out. However, vertical externalities still occur when tax bases are interdependent. Therefore, exclusive tax bases do not preclude vertical tax externalities.

Finally, *EIMCs with additional tax regime (FA)* generate all types of externalities since both tax bases are co-occupied by municipalities and EIMCs.

**Table 8.4** **Externalities at work for each type of EIMC**

| | Same-base | Cross-base |
|---|---|---|
| Horizontal externalities | Mergers, FA, FPU | Mergers, FA |
| Vertical externalities | FA | FA, FPU |

FA = EIMC with additional tax regime; FPU = EIMC with single professional tax regime (assuming no additional taxation on the other tax base).

Table 8.4 summarizes the externalities at work for each type of EIMC. With the exception of syndicates, all other forms of cooperation impact tax competition. In the absence of further assumptions regarding the share of competences among tiers and the degree of complementarity versus substitutability between tax bases, we cannot rank forms of intermunicipal cooperation regarding their ability to reduce the perverse effects of tax competition. Breuillé and Duran-Vigneron (2023) show that there exists a level of expenditure decentralization such that EIMC with an additional tax regime is better than mergers in terms of welfare, whatever the degree of interdependence between the tax bases. In addition, for a sufficiently high degree of substitutability between the tax bases, EIMC with single professional tax regime can lead to the lowest welfare.

### 8.3.3 Empirical Evidence of the Impact of EIMC Tax Regimes on Taxation

We empirically investigate, for France, whether the evolution of cumulative tax rates—which are the sum of municipal and intermunicipal tax rates—changes on average in accordance with EIMC tax regimes. In figure 8.4, we plot over the period 1994–2005 the average evolution of each one of the four cumulative tax rates (the residence tax, property tax on developed land, property tax on undeveloped land, and business tax) for the restricted sample of municipalities that joined an EIMC for the first time in 2003[16] (the EIMC may already exist), for an overall total of 2,189 municipalities. We track the trend of average tax rates for the three tax regimes: (1) the single business tax regime (FPU/TPU, with triangles, with 921 municipalities), where the EIMC levies the business tax and the municipalities levy the other three taxes; (2) the additional taxation regime (FA, empty circles, with 1,239 municipalities), where EIMCs and member municipalities share the four tax bases; and (3) the mixed taxation regime (black circles, with only 29 municipalities) in which a single business tax is levied by the EIMC and the three other tax bases are taxed by both the EIMC and its member municipalities. The last curve, the dotted line, corresponds to the average tax rate of municipalities that joined an EIMC created from 2006 onward.

16. 2003 is chosen to be soon enough after the Chevènement Law of 1999, which led to the creation of numerous EIMCs.

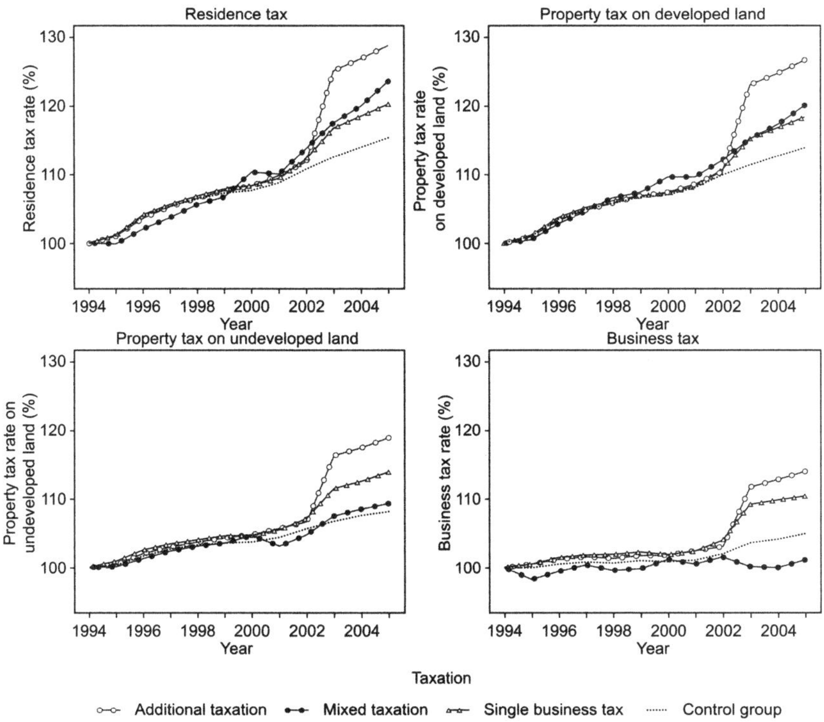


**Fig. 8.4 Average changes according to the tax regime in cumulative tax rates for municipalities that joined an EIMC for the first time in 2003 (base 100 in 1994)**

Before a municipality joins or creates an EIMC, the trends of the average cumulative tax rates are very similar, irrespective of the chosen tax regime. In the first year of membership (2003), we systematically observe a strong surge, except for the mixed taxation regime, for which we observe no change in the trend. On each dial, i.e., considering each tax independently, we observe the strongest increases for the additional tax regime and lower increases for the single business tax regime. These heterogeneous trends in accordance to the tax regime are consistent with the results of Breuillé et al. (2018), except for the mixed taxation regime. However, no direct comparison can be made with figure 8.4 because only 29 municipalities that joined an EIMC in 2003 adopted a mixed taxation regime. Beyond showing that intermunicipal cooperation led to an increase in the cumulative tax rates, the results of Breuillé et al. (2018) reveal a higher increase in cumulative tax rates when the municipalities and their EIMC share the same tax base, i.e., for all tax rates in an additional taxation regime and, to a lesser extent, all tax rates but the business tax rate for the mixed taxation regime (the estimated parameters are almost twice as small as those in the additional taxation

**Table 8.5** **Impact of IMC on taxation according to the tax regime from Breuillé et al. (2018). Interaction with tax regimes**

| | B | R | PD | PU |
|---|---|---|---|---|
| $\Delta Coop_{it}$ | 0.245*** | 0.076*** | 0.127*** | 0.488*** |
| | [0.027] | [0.013] | [0.023] | [0.078] |
| $\Delta Coop^*_{it}$ add. taxation | 0.360*** | 0.649*** | 1.051*** | 2.180*** |
| | [0.035] | [0.018] | [0.031] | [0.105] |
| $\Delta Coop^*_{it}$ mixed taxation | −0.116 | 0.364*** | 0.546*** | 1.213*** |
| | [0.087] | [0.042] | [0.073] | [0.195] |
| Control variables | Yes | Yes | Yes | Yes |
| Total effect of add. taxation | 0.605*** | 0.725*** | 1.178*** | 2.668*** |
| Total effect of mixed taxation | 0.129 | 0.440*** | 0.673*** | 1.701*** |
| F-test for eq. of interaction terms | 31.66*** | 45.92*** | 48.01*** | 25.05*** |
| Observations | 134,289 | 134,360 | 134,360 | 134,360 |
| F-Stat. | 89.14 | 341.28 | 323.83 | 149.17 |

Notes: *** indicates statistical significance at 1%, ** at 5%, and * at 10% level. B = business tax; R = residence tax; PD = property tax on developed land; PU = property tax on undeveloped land. Cluster-robust standard errors are in brackets. All estimations include time fixed effects, municipal fixed effects and linear municipality-time trends. F-test for equality of the interaction terms gives the F stat of the test of equality of coefficients between $\Delta Coop^*_i$ Add. Taxation and $\Delta Coop^*_i$ Mixed taxation. Reprinted from Marie-Laure Breuillé, Pascale Duran-Vigneron, and Anne-Laure Samson, "Inter-municipal cooperation and local taxation." *Journal of Urban Economics* 107: 47–64. Copyright © 2018, with permission from Elsevier.

regime). Table 6 in Breuillé et al. (2018) reports a significant correlation between the effect of the EIMC's tax regime and the effect of cooperation.

These results align with the theoretical literature on same-base vertical tax externalities, which predicts that tax-base sharing will increase tax rates (Breuillé and Zanaj 2013; Keen 1998; Keen and Kotsogiannis 2002). Further investigation would be required to identify the differentiated influence of cross-base horizontal and vertical externalities with respect to tax regimes.

## 8.4 Conclusion

With its long history of intermunicipal cooperation (over a century old), the large spectrum of forms it may take, and its total coverage of the territory, the French case is a laboratory for both practitioners and researchers. The number of EIMCs, the number of member municipalities, the share of competencies that are delegated to EIMCs, and the choice of tax regime are all factors that have major repercussions on the tax externalities at work and, consequently on the tax burden. The construction of a theoretical model thus enables—by isolating transmission channels that reinforce or offset each other—a more specific analysis of the link between intermunicipal cooperation and tax competition, a link that needs to be estimated empirically. This would complement the existing estimates, which show the inflationary impact of the creation of EIMCs on local tax choices. Beyond that, this chapter points to the need for future research on intermunicipal cooperation, both theoretically and empirically, through the use of causal inference methods exploiting quasi-natural experiences to enable practitioners to specify the size of EIMCs, and tax and spending assignments across municipalities and EIMCs in order to reduce tax externalities and increase the efficiency of the provision of local services, governance arrangements and democratic control.

## Acknowledgments

We thank David Agrawal, James Poterba, and Owen Zidar for their stimulative initiative on tax competition as well as the participants at the NBER Conference on "Policy Responses to Tax Competition," Spring 2023, and especially David Agrawal and Stefanie Stantcheva for their enlightened feedback. We also acknowledge Camille Grivault's very valuable support. For acknowledgments, sources of research support, and disclosure of the authors' material financial relationships, if any, please see https://www.nber.org/books-and-chapters/policy-responses-tax-competition/intermunicipal-cooperation-france-and-related-tax-issues.

# References

Acar, Bruno, Patrick Reix, and Virginie Giudici 2022. *Les communes nouvelles: un bilan décevant, des perspectives incertaines*. IGA Report n°22014-R.

Agrawal, David R., Marie-Laure Breuillé, and Julie Le Gallo. 2020. "Tax Competition with Intermunicipal Cooperation." Available at SSRN 3560611.

Agrawal, David R., William H. Hoyt, and John D. Wilson. 2022. "Local Policy Choice: Theory and Empirics." *Journal of Economic Literature* 60 (4): 1378–455.

Aldag, Austin M., Mildred E. Warner, and Germà Bel. 2020. "It Depends on What You Share: The Elusive Cost Savings from Service Sharing." *Journal of Public Administration Research and Theory* 30 (2): 275–89.

Balladur, E. 2009. *Comité pour la réforme des collectivités locales—"Il est temps de decider"—Rapport au Président de la République*. La Documentation française, Fayard.

Bel, Germà, and Marianna Sebő. 2021. "Does Inter-Municipal Cooperation Really Reduce Delivery Costs? An Empirical Evaluation of the Role of Scale Economies, Transaction Costs, and Governance Arrangements." *Urban Affairs Review* 57 (1): 153–88.

Bel, Germà, and Marianna Sebő. 2023. "26. Intermunicipal cooperation: an assessment of drivers and effects." In *Handbook on Local and Regional Governance*, edited by Filipe Teles. Edward Elgar.

Binet, Marie-Estelle, Ewen Lebrun, and Matthieu Leprince. 2022. "Does Intermunicipal Cooperation Favor Higher Firm Creation? French Evidence from a Natural Experiment." *The Annals of Regional Science*, 1–20.

Bischoff, Ivo, and Reinhold Kosfeld. 2021. "Does Inter-Local Cooperation Reduce the Intensity of Tax Competition? Evidence on Inter-Local Industrial Parks in Germany." MAGKS Joint Discussion Paper Series in Economics.

Breuillé, Marie-Laure, and Pascale Duran-Vigneron. 2023. "Decentralization When Tax Bases Are Interdependently Mobile: Shared or Exclusive Tax Bases?" Working paper.

Breuillé, Marie-Laure, Pascale Duran-Vigneron, and Anne-Laure Samson. 2018. "Inter-municipal Cooperation and Local Taxation." *Journal of Urban Economics* 107: 47–64.

Breuillé, Marie-Laure, and Julie Le Gallo. 2017. "Spatial Fiscal Interactions among French Municipalities within Inter-municipal Groups." *Applied Economics* 49 (46): 4617–37.

Breuillé, Marie-Laure, and Skerdilajda Zanaj. 2013. "Mergers in Fiscal Federalism." *Journal of Public Economics* 105: 11–22.

Charlot, Sylvie, Sonia Paty, and Virginie Piguet. 2015. "Does Fiscal Cooperation Increase Local Tax Rates in Urban Areas?" *Regional Studies* 49 (10): 1706–21.

Cour des comptes. (2016). *La carte des syndicats intercommunaux (SIVU, SIVOM, SMF): une rationalisation à poursuivre*. https://www.ccomptes.fr/fr/publications/la-carte-des-syndicats-intercommunaux-une-rationalisation-poursuivre.

Dixon, Ruth, and Thomas Elston. 2020. "Efficiency and Legitimacy in Collaborative Public Management: Mapping Inter-Local Agreements in England Using Social Network Analysis." *Public Administration* 98 (3): 746–67.

Ferraresi, Massimiliano, Giuseppe Migali, and Leonzio Rizzo. 2018. "Does Intermunicipal Cooperation Promote Efficiency Gains? Evidence from Italian Municipal Unions." *Journal of Regional Science* 58 (5): 1017–44.

Frère, Quentin, Matthieu Leprince, and Sonia Paty. 2014. "The Impact of Intermunicipal Cooperation on Local Public Spending." *Urban Studies* 51 (8): 1741–60.

Hertzog, Robert. 2018. "Inter-Municipal Cooperation in France: A Continuous Reform, New Trends." In *Inter-Municipal Cooperation in Europe: Institutions and Governance*, edited by Filipe Teles and Pawel Swianiewicz, 133–55. Palgrave Macmillan.

Hoyt, William H. 1991. "Property Taxation, Nash Equilibrium, and Market Power." *Journal of Urban Economics* 30 (1): 123–31.

Jaaidane, Touria, and Sophie Larribeau. 2023. "The Effects of Inter-Municipal Cooperation and Central Grant Allocation on the Size of the French Local Public Sector." *European Journal of Political Economy* 76: 102271.

Keen, Michael. 1998. "Vertical Tax Externalities in the Theory of Fiscal Federalism." *Staff Papers* 45 (3): 454–85.

Keen, Michael J., and Christos Kotsogiannis. 2002. "Does Federalism Lead to Excessively High Taxes?" *American Economic Review* 92 (1): 363–70.

Kelly, Josephine. 2007. "The Missing Ingredient: Inter-Municipal Cooperation and Central-Local Relations in the UK." In *Inter-municipal Cooperation in Europe: Institutions and Governance*, edited by Filipe Teles and Pawel Swianiewicz, 193–210. Palgrave Macmillan.

Leck, Hayley, and Florence Crick. 2020. "Beyond Urban-Rural Boundaries: Encouraging Inter-Municipal Collaboration for Climate Change Adaptation in KwaZulu-Natal, South Africa." In *Planning Across Borders in a Climate of Change*, edited by Wendy Steele, Tooran Alizadeh, Leila Eslami-Andargoli, and Silvia Serrao-Neumann, 59–73. Routledge.

Luca, Davide, and Felix Modrego. 2021. "Stronger Together? Assessing the Causal Effect of Inter-Municipal Cooperation on the Efficiency of Small Italian Municipalities." *Journal of Regional Science* 61 (1): 261–93.

Moradi-Motlagh, Amir, and Ali Emrouznejad. 2022. "The Origins and Development of Statistical Approaches in Non-parametric Frontier Models: A Survey of the First Two Decades of Scholarly Literature (1998–2020)." *Annals of Operations Research* 318 (1): 713–41.

Muraoka, Taishi, and Claudia N. Avellaneda. 2021. "Do the Networks of Intermunicipal Cooperation Enhance Local Government Performance?" *Local Government Studies* 47 (4): 616–36.

Niaounakis, Thomas, and Jos Blank. 2017. "Inter-municipal Cooperation, Economies of Scale and Cost Efficiency: An Application of Stochastic Frontier Analysis to Dutch Municipal Tax Departments." *Local Government Studies* 43 (4): 533–54.

OECD. 2019. *OECD Multi-level Governance Studies Making Decentralisation Work: A Handbook for Policy-Makers*. OECD.

OECD. 2021. *Subnational Governments in OECD Countries*. OECD.

Paty, Sonia, and Morgan Ubeda. 2021. "Inter-municipal Cooperation and the Provision of Local Public Goods: Economies of Scale, Fiscal Competition or 'Zoo' Effect?" Working Papers 2121, Groupe d'Analyse et de Théorie Economique Lyon St-Étienne (GATE Lyon St-Étienne), Université de Lyon.

Pérez-López, Gemma, Diego Prior, José Luis Zafra-Gómez and Ana María Plata-Díaz. 2016. "Cost Efficiency in Municipal Solid Waste Service Delivery. Alternative Management Forms in Relation to Local Population Size." *European Journal of Operational Research* 255 (2): 583–92.

Silva, Patrícia, and Esther Pano Puey. 2018. "Striving for Local Governance Capacity in Portugal and Spain." In *Inter-Municipal Cooperation in Europe: Institutions and Governance*, edited by Filipe Teles and Pawel Swianiewicz, 79–104. Palgrave Macmillan.

Silvestre, Hugo Consciência, Rui Cunha Marques, and Ricardo Corrêa Gomes. 2018. "Joined-Up Government of Utilities: A Meta-Review on a Public–Public Partnership and Inter-Municipal Cooperation in the Water and Wastewater Industries." *Public Management Review* 20 (4): 607–31.

Silvestre, Hugo Consciência, Rui Cunha Marques, Brian Dollery, and Aldenísio Moraes Correia. 2020. "Is Cooperation Cost Reducing? An Analysis of Public–Public Partnerships and Inter-Municipal Cooperation in Brazilian Local Government." *Local Government Studies* 46 (1): 68–90.

Teles, Filipe, and Pawel Swianiewicz. 2018. *Inter-Municipal Cooperation in Europe*. Palgrave Macmillan.

Tellier, Thibault. 2017. "La constitution d'un nouveau modèle d'action publique territoriale: la loi Marcellin de 1971 et la fusion de communes." *Revue française d'administration publique* 2: 253–66.

Tricaud, Clemence. 2021. "Better Alone? Evidence on the Costs of Intermunicipal Cooperation." CESifo Working Paper No. 9000.

Villalba Ferreira, Mario Emmanuel, A. Geske Dijkstra, Laura Quadros Aniche, and Peter Scholten. 2020. "Towards a Typology of Intermunicipal Cooperation in Emerging Metropolitan Regions. A Case Study in the Solid Waste Management Sector in Ecuador." *Cogent Social Sciences* 6 (1): 1757185.

Wilson, John D. 1986. "A Theory of Interregional Tax Competition." *Journal of Urban Economics* 19 (3): 296–315.

Wrede, Matthias. 1997. "Tax Competition and Federalism the Underprovision of Local Public Goods." *FinanzArchiv/Public Finance Analysis*, 494–515.

Zodrow, George R., and Peter Mieszkowski. 1986. "Pigou, Tiebout, Property Taxation, and the Underprovision of Local Public Goods." *Journal of Urban Economics* 19 (3): 356–70.

## Comment Stefanie Stantcheva

### Introduction

The chapter "Intermunicipal Cooperation in France and Related Tax Issues" by Marie-Laure Breuillé and Pascale Duran-Vigneron delves into the world of intermuncipal cooperation—an approach that towns and cities adopt to deal with tax competition. Intercity cooperation takes several forms and involves nearby municipalities joining forces to provide public services and share funds raised from taxes. This practice has garnered significant attention in Europe, where it has evolved into a prevalent approach, and beyond, influencing OECD countries and even making inroads into developed and developing nations such as Brazil, Ecuador, El Salvador, and South Africa.

From soft collaborations like shared-service agreements to more integrated forms like the creation of supramunicipal authorities, intermunicipal cooperation comes in various shapes. The focus of Breuillé and Duran-Vigneron is on exploring this cooperation in France, a unique setting with different forms of collaboration and tax raising powers by local entities.

The typical driving force behind municipal collaboration is economies of scale: offering services to a larger population to achieve greater efficiency. Particularly in regions with numerous small municipalities, intermunicipal cooperation acts as a solution to overcome the challenges of municipal boundaries and historical divisions. With communication technologies, service-sector jobs, and increased mobility reshaping societies, intermunicipal cooperation can be expected to evolve substantially over the coming years.

I will first summarize, provide some intuition for, and put into context the key theoretical results from the chapter and summarize its empirical findings adapted to the French setting. I will then discuss the issue of intermunicipal tax competition and cooperation with the help of a stylized model of coordinated and uncoordinated tax policy and offer some further thoughts.

### Key Findings and Discussion

I start by providing a summary and discussion of the chapter's main setting, theoretical results, and findings.

#### The French Setting

The chapter focuses on France, where intermunicipal cooperation comes in three distinct shapes, with varying levels of integration. It is useful to

Stefanie Stantcheva is the Nathaniel Ropes Professor of Political Economy at Harvard University, a faculty research fellow at the Centre for Economic Policy Research, and a research associate of the National Bureau of Economic Research.

describe them briefly because they provide an idea of the range of possible arrangements that can exist and coexist regarding municipal cooperation.

*Syndicates*

The least integrated form of cooperation are syndicates: single-purpose intermunicipal syndicates (SIVU), multiple-purpose intermunicipal syndicates (SIVOM), and mixed syndicates. SIVUs enable municipalities to collaborate and pool resources for specific public goods, such as electrification and water networks. SIVOMs expanded on this concept by allowing cooperation on multiple competences. Mixed syndicates involve diverse partners, including municipalities, departments (a higher-tier jurisdiction in France), and private bodies, to collaborate on larger projects like public facilities and business parks. Funding for these syndicates generally comes from member municipalities' contributions or fees for industrial and commercial services. Syndicates do not have taxing powers, which is why the chapter does not focus on them in its analysis.

*Municipal Mergers*

The most integrated form of municipal cooperation is mergers between municipalities. The chapter describes multiple historical attempts at integrating municipalities in France through mergers, but with limited success. The emergence of *communes nouvelles* ("new cities") in a 2010 reform, which aimed to promote integration with financial incentives, resulted in a 5 percent decrease in the total number of French municipalities. Yet a critical report highlighted concerns about the small size and limited benefits. In comparison to other European countries, France's municipal integration progress has been slower, with half of all municipalities having fewer than 500 inhabitants and almost three-quarters having fewer than 1,000 inhabitants.

*Establishments for Intermunicipal Cooperation*

Establishments for intermunicipal cooperation (EIMCs) with their own tax powers are a more integrated form of cooperation than syndicates, but less integrated than mergers. They adhere to two governing principles: the principle of specialty, where they operate only in the competences they are entrusted with and within the member municipalities' scope, and the principle of exclusivity, ensuring EIMCs are the sole entities intervening in their designated fields of competence.[1]

1. The chapter describes four types of EIMCs: (1) "communities of communes," typically incorporating municipalities from sparsely populated areas. These communities manage both compulsory and optional competences of community interest on behalf of member municipalities, with financial options such as additional taxation; (2) "agglomeration communities," formed in urbanized regions, encompassing over 50,000 inhabitants around a central city manage various competences and aim to foster urban development and coordination; (3) "metropolitan areas," consisting of a central city and surrounding areas that focus on strategic plan-

EIMCs are managed by their own governing body, known as the EIMC council. Seats on this council are allocated to member municipalities based on their population, with proportional representation, ensuring at least one seat per municipality.

These jurisdictions can impose taxes on four main local direct tax bases to fund the responsibilities they take over from member municipalities. These bases encompass the residential tax on secondary homes, the property tax on developed and undeveloped land, and the territorial economic contribution, which includes the business property tax and the value-added tax on businesses.

Importantly, there are two tax systems for EIMCs. In the "additional tax regime," both EIMCs and municipalities set rates on the four main tax bases, resulting in residents paying both intermunicipal and municipal taxes. In the "single business tax regime," the EIMC is allowed to collect the business property tax instead of its individual member municipalities. In addition, while municipalities retain their authority to impose taxes on secondary homes, developed land, and undeveloped land, the EIMC *also* has the capacity to determine supplementary rates for each of these taxes, mirroring the approach of the additional tax regime.

## Theoretical Results

To put the theoretical results into context, consider two key optimal policy results established in the literature regarding multi-tier tax competition. The first result suggests that more mobile tax bases should be allocated to the highest administrative tier to minimize distortions caused by taxing mobile factors within larger jurisdictions. The second optimal policy outcome suggests limiting the co-occupancy of tax bases among different tiers to avoid inducing vertical tax externalities.

However, when tax bases are interdependent (i.e., complementary or substitutable), there is a more nuanced picture. Specifically, a complex array of elasticities must be considered, including those within the same and across different bases, both horizontally and vertically. This complex issue forms the focus of an earlier paper by the authors (Breuillé and Duran-Vigneron 2021) and the basis for their adapted investigation in the chapter.

To understand the core of the model, let me summarize the main effects verbally.

### *Horizontal and Vertical Externalities*

Imagine, first, that there is only one factor $x$ that is mobile across municipalities. Horizontal tax externalities, i.e., externalities among municipalities,

ning, sustainable development, and economic growth; (4) "metropolitan urban communities," which are larger-scale entities created most recently (2014), concentrating on more extensive development projects and region-wide interests.

occur because an increase in the tax rate levied on the factor $x$ by a municipality induces an outflow of this factor from that municipality and, thus, an inflow to all other same-tier municipalities.

When there are two jurisdiction tiers, say, municipalities and EIMCs, there are also vertical externalities. An increase in the tax rate on factor $x$ by a jurisdiction triggers an outflow of this factor from jurisdictions within the other tier sharing the same tax base, resulting in an inflow to all other jurisdictions in that tier. Thus, a mobile tax base co-occupied by two tiers adds vertical tax externalities to the horizontal ones.

These externalities stemming from municipal taxation are termed "bottom-up tax externalities," while those from EIMC taxation are referred to as "top-down tax externalities." In general, municipalities internalize a portion of the negative vertical bottom-up externalities imposed on their EIMC's tax base, as their concern is primarily for the well-being of their own residents. Conversely, EIMC authorities fully internalize the negative vertical top-down externalities impacting their members' tax base, as their focus is on the welfare of all their members' constituents.

*Same and Cross-Base Externalities*

Consider now a scenario where tax revenue originates from two co-occupied bases, which could represent factors utilized by firms for production. These bases may be interdependent, with one's mobility affecting the other. In cases of complementarity, higher costs for factor $x$ in a jurisdiction lead to reduced demand for both factors $x$ and $y$. On the contrary, substitutability between tax bases results in higher factor $x$ costs leading to decreased demand for factor $x$ but increased demand for factor $y$.

The interdependence between these tax bases gives rise to cross-base tax externalities, alongside same-base tax externalities. Cross-base horizontal tax externalities arise when a jurisdiction's tax rate adjustment on one factor impacts the availability of the other factor for other same-tier jurisdictions. Typically, jurisdictions primarily concern themselves with the cross-base externality affecting their own tax base, overlooking externalities affecting the tax base of other same-tier jurisdictions.

The direction of cross-base horizontal tax externalities hinges on the interdependence nature between the two tax bases. For complementary tax bases, the externality on a jurisdiction's own tax base is negative, aligning with the same-base horizontal externality. Conversely, for substitutable tax bases, the externality is positive, opposing the direction of the same-base horizontal externality.

The interplay between interdependent factors and shared tax bases also gives rise to "cross-base vertical tax externalities." In scenarios of complementarity, these externalities result in a flow of factors from jurisdictions sharing the same tax base to other jurisdictions. In contrast, substitutability leads to an inflow of factors to jurisdictions sharing the same tax base. These externalities are referred to as "cross-base vertical bottom-up externalities" for municipal taxation and "cross-base vertical top-down externalities" for EIMC taxation.

Similar to same-base vertical externalities, municipalities internalize a fraction of cross-base vertical bottom-up externalities imposed on their EIMC, while EIMCs internalize all cross-base vertical top-down externalities imposed on their member municipalities.

*Earlier Theory Findings*

In their earlier theory paper (Breuillé and Duran-Vigneron 2021), the authors derived the following key results. In scenarios with independent but mobile tax bases, same-base horizontal and vertical externalities result in lower tax rates compared to those chosen by a social planner, leading to a race-to-the-bottom effect.

The authors discuss how the complementarity of tax bases exacerbates downward tax rate distortions caused by cross-base externalities aligning with same-base externalities. On the contrary, substitutability reduces these distortions, as cross-base externalities counteract same-base externalities.

Interestingly, partial decentralization with exclusive tax bases under certain decentralization levels might lead to inefficiently high tax rates, contrary to expectations. Furthermore, the authors conclude that while full centralization is always superior to partial decentralization in a single state scenario, this no longer holds true when multiple states are involved, as partial decentralization could be a more favorable approach.

*Current Theory Findings*

In the chapter, the authors derive the following theoretical predictions: syndicates should have little effect on tax externalities since they are financed by municipal transfers funded by tax revenues collected on the municipalities usual tax bases. In this context, only same-base and cross-base horizontal tax externalities at the municipal level occur, although scale economies from larger-scale supply could alleviate the tax burden for all municipalities. Municipal mergers instead can lead to increased tax rates and public goods provision as jurisdiction numbers decrease, due to reduced same-base and cross-base horizontal tax externalities.

Within the context of the EIMC using the single business tax regime and assuming no additional taxation on the other tax base, same-base horizontal externalities arise at the EIMC level on the business tax base and at the municipal level on the other tax base. Cross-base horizontal tax externalities and same-base vertical externalities are excluded, yet vertical externalities persist with interdependent tax bases. Finally, EIMCs operating under the additional tax regime generate all types of externalities due to the co-occupation of all tax bases by municipalities and EIMCs.

*Empirical Findings*

The empirical findings of the chapter confirm these theoretical predictions. When municipalities join or create EIMCs, there is a significant surge in tax rates. The exception is the single business tax regime, in which the residence and property taxes remain under sole municipal control. In this case, only the business tax sees a small increase. Notably, the additional tax regime sees the highest overall tax increases, as can be expected given that all tax bases are now co-occupied by both municipalities and EIMCs.

## Discussion of Tax Competition and Cooperation

I would now like to offer a much simpler, stylized framework to think about optimal taxation with tax cooperation and competition. This model is adapted to the intermunicipal setting from Kleven et al. (2020).

### A Simplified Model

Imagine two cities, A and B. We consider optimal tax policies under two scenarios: uncoordinated tax policy (i.e., tax competition) and coordinated tax policy (i.e., tax cooperation). The coordinated policy can be viewed as the one arising under a higher-tier jurisdiction that sets tax policy, such as an EIMC with full taxing powers in the French setting, and when municipalities can no longer impose taxes in a competitive way. The uncoordinated policy is what happens when there is no municipal cooperation.

*Uncoordinated Tax Policy*

Starting with uncoordinated tax policy, municipality A sets its nonlinear tax rate $T^A$ without considering the welfare impacts on other municipalities. Assume fixed earnings $y_i^A$ for residents in city A after accounting for residence. A symmetric situation holds for city B.

Let $P^A(c\,|\,y^A)$ denote the count of residents earning $y^A$ when disposable income is $c$, where $c = y^A - T(y^A)$. Let $g^A(y)$ denote the welfare weight on those earning $y$ in city A, which captures how much the city's government "cares about" those earning $y$. In other words, the function $g^A$ captures the inequality aversion and redistributive preferences of city A. Formally, $g^A = (\Sigma_{i\in A} g_i y_i^A)/(\Sigma_i g_i y^A)$ is the average, income-weighted welfare weight over all people $i$ in city A.

The migration elasticity to taxes, $\eta^A(y)$, plays a pivotal role in determining optimal tax policies. It is defined as

$$\eta^A(y) = \frac{\partial P^A(c\,|\,y)}{\partial c}\frac{y - T^A(y)}{P^A(c\,|\,y)}.$$

In this setting, the optimal tax for city A is given by

$$\frac{T^A(y)}{y - T^A(y)} = \frac{1}{\eta^A(y)} \cdot [1 - g^A(y)].$$

The formula shows that, as is standard, the tax rate is lower at income level $y$ when the weight on those earning $y$, $g^A(y)$ is higher. More interestingly, the optimal tax is lower when the elasticity $\eta^A(y)$ is higher. This migration elasticity depends on several factors. It is higher if the city is smaller (easier to move out) or if there are close, substitutable neighboring cities (i.e., people do not have strong attachment to a given city). Thus, cities that are larger and have many amenities and other attractive advantages may be able to tax more despite facing tax competition.

*Coordinated Tax Policy with Differentiated Policies*

Assume now that a central tax authority—for instance, the EIMCs above—is setting tax rates in both cities A and B. To simplify the analysis, we focus on the case of linear taxes $\tau^A$ and $\tau^B$. We exclude direct spillover effects from foreign immigration on the behavior of domestic agents or the local economy. There are two cases to consider, which sometimes are conflated together: a case in which policy is coordinated but can be differentiated by city (i.e., different cities can have different tax rates even if they cooperate) and a case in which policies are constrained to be uniform.

Let us start with the case of differentiated policies. Within this coordinated framework, we introduce the aggregate incomes $y^A$ and $y^B$ for cities A and B respectively, which are functions of both cities' net-of-tax rates with $y^A = y^A(1 - \tau^A, 1 - \tau^B)$ and $y^B = y^B(1 - \tau^A, 1 - \tau^B)$.

We define $\eta^A = [dy^A(1 - \tau^A)]/[y^A(1 - \tau^A)]$ to be the elasticity of migration (or income, since incomes are assumed to be inelastic to taxes) in city A to changes in $(1 - \tau^A)$, while $\eta^B_A[dy^B(1 - \tau^A)/y^B(1 - \tau^A)]$ represents the cross-elasticity. The average value to the social planner of transferring one unit of income to individuals in region A is denoted by $g^A$.

In this setting, the optimal coordinated, differentiated tax for city A is

$$\tau^A = \frac{1 - g^A - \tau^B\eta^B_A \cdot y^B / y^A}{1 - g^A + \eta^A} \tag{1}$$

A symmetric formula to((1)) holds for city B, namely,

$$\tau^B = \frac{1 - g^B - \tau^A\eta^A_B \cdot y^A / y^B}{1 - g^B + \eta^B} \tag{2}$$

A few key results emerge. Relative to the uncoordinated policy, the coordinated policy internalizes the spillovers from one region to the other. This is as suggested in the chapter, where the EIMC (the higher-tier jurisdiction) internalizes its top-down tax externalities on each municipality. Here, externalities are purely tax externalities, but other ones might be taken into account too (such as positive spillovers on productivity from migration). All else equal, this internalization will tend to make taxes higher in both regions and represent a move away from "beggar-thy-neighbor" tax competition policies.

The formulas also illustrate the value of differentiated tax policy. Importantly, cooperation and coordination need not (always) mean uniform policies. This means that different cities, because of different income distributions and preferences, as embodied in $g^A$ and $g^B$, or because of different mobility responses, as embodied in the elasticities, may choose to have different tax rates and levels of redistribution.

However, both the degree of progressivity and the divergence between the tax rates of the two cities is limited by mobility responses captured by the elasticities. The elasticities will be lower when the jurisdiction is larger, when there is more tax coordination, or when people's mobility is restricted due to nontax factors, such as strong location preferences, the availability of amenities, or other personal or professional concerns.

*Coordinated Tax Policy with Uniform Policies*

A case in which policy is coordinated and constrained to be uniform could be viewed as a deeply integrated intermunicipal cooperation that does not allow for differentiated tax policies across members.[2] If the policy is constrained to be uniform, we need to impose $\tau^A = \tau^B = \tau$, and the optimal, common tax is

$$(3) \quad \tau = \frac{1 - \alpha^A g^A - \alpha^B g^B}{1 - \alpha^A g^A - \alpha^B g^B + \alpha^A \eta^A + \alpha^B \eta^B} \quad \text{where } \alpha^A = 1 - \alpha^B = \frac{y^A}{y^A + y^B}.$$

Thus, the common coordinated tax is set to a level that reflects the average income-weighted welfare weight and migration elasticities. When policies are constrained to be uniform, they cater to the "average" city and are not optimal for any individual city.

Overall, these formulas illustrate that cooperation is more beneficial when there are large mobility responses that create spillovers, and that the uncoordinated policy does not internalize. While differentiation is always weakly better than nondifferentiation, political or other constraints may impose uniform policies. In that case, the benefits from cooperation are larger, all else equal, if the uncoordinated tax rates are not too different, i.e., if the cities' fundamentals are not too divergent.

## Conclusion: Future Avenues for Research

Both the chapter and the simple model above miss some key ingredients that are policy relevant and important in practice. These would be important avenues for future research on the theoretical and empirical sides.

2. A municipal merger would effectively result in such a tax too, but would also involve full integration of all other municipal activities.

First, one could imagine that there could be different configurations of cooperation in raising taxes and in spending revenues. It is possible to coordinate taxes without coordinating spending, for instance. Similarly, there can be coordination or cooperation only for some types of taxes and some spending categories, as is the case in the various schemes described above for France. Thus, cooperation and competition are not an all-or-nothing proposition and instead can be done to varying degrees for different types of taxes and activities.

Second, economies of scale in either tax administration or spending and program administration are key justifications for such cooperation in practice. These could be substantial, especially for smaller cities, and could be fruitful to explore.

Third, there could be specific political economy constraints and considerations that both shape the formation of cooperation and also affect its impacts. On the one hand, smaller cities might be prone to more informal dealings, corruption, and lobbying, which might be relieved once a higher-tier jurisdiction takes over. On the other other hand, larger jurisdictions with multiple layers of governance may also be less transparent and prone to misuse of funds. Depending on the electoral systems, officials in power may oppose or support more integration, which is another way in which political economy considerations come into play.

Fourth, spillovers other than tax spillovers could be important to take into account when thinking about intermunicipal cooperation and competition. Migration between cities can bring productivity benefits and agglomeration effects. At the same time, negative spillovers could stem from congestion effects and increases in pollution or noise.

Finally, there are fairness concerns that could come into play, as shown clearly in Stantcheva (2021) in the context of income tax. People may consider money raised at the level of different jurisdictions to carry different fairness implications and have different preferences on how it should be spent. Such preferences might be difficult to reconcile in larger jurisdictions with heterogeneous groups of people. Equity concerns could also make differentiated coordinated policies infeasible and push toward uniform policies.

For acknowledgments, sources of research support, and disclosure of the author's material financial relationships, if any, please see https://www.nber.org/books-and-chapters/policy-responses-tax-competition/comment-intermunicipal-cooperation-france-and-related-tax-issues-stantcheva.

## References

Breuillé, M.-L., and P. Duran-Vigneron. 2021. "Decentralization When Tax Bases Are Interdependently Mobile: Shared or Exclusive Tax Bases?" Technical report.

Kleven, H., C. Landais, M. Munoz, and S. Stantcheva (2020). "Taxation and Migration: Evidence and Policy Implications." *Journal of Economic Perspectives* 34 (2): 119–42.

Stantcheva, S. 2021. "Understanding Tax Policy: How Do People Reason?" *The Quarterly Journal of Economics* 136 (4): 2309–69.

9

# Minimum Tax Rates and Tax Competition
## Evidence from Property Tax Limits in Finland

Teemu Lyytikäinen

## 9.1 Introduction

The coordination of tax policy and the use of tax rate limits imposed by higher-level governments on lower-level governments has received significant attention in recent years. This trend is exemplified by the EU's recent introduction of a minimum corporate tax rate, which is intended to combat harmful tax competition. National governments have even greater power to constrain the tax policies of lower-level subnational governments. In addition to restricting the range of tax instruments available to local governments, central governments often impose limits on tax rates as well. Understanding how these limits on taxation powers affect local policy choice is important for policy design.

The focus of this chapter is on property taxes on business and residential real estate, which are an important source of revenue for local governments in many countries. This chapter sheds light on the effects of minimum property tax rate increases, and provides insights into how tax competition shapes local tax policies. I use panel data from Finland and a quasi-experimental research design to study horizontal fiscal interaction triggered by changes in minimum property tax rates. Additionally, the chapter considers vertical tax competition between central and local governments as a cause of minimum tax rates set by central government.

In Finland, municipalities choose property tax rates for different types of real property within tax rate bounds set by the central government. The government has raised the minimum and maximum tax rates several times

Teemu Lyytikäinen is an associate research professor and research leader in the research area of local public finance and provision of public services at the VATT Institute for Economic Research.

over the past 30 years, and the current lower limits are above the initial upper limits. This study analyzes the effects of these changes on the directly affected municipalities and on nearby municipalities. First, I describe the developments in the tax rate distribution over time as the bounds for the tax rates change. Second, I construct a measure of forced tax rate increases resulting from the minimum tax rate hikes, and use it as a treatment variable in an Event Study type regression framework to investigate how the affected municipalities and their neighboring municipalities responded to the forced tax rate increases.

The results indicate that when municipalities are forced to increase their property tax rates on business properties, the tax rates of their neighbors do not not change when a strong tax base equalization system is in place. However, I find some indication of a positive effect of forced increases on the tax rates of nearby municipalities after a reform of the tax base equalization system, which strengthened the incentives to compete for the tax base. On the other hand, forced increases in the residential property tax rate appear to lead to lower tax rates in nearby municipalities four years after the reforms.

Property tax limits in Finland have been analyzed previously by Lyytikäinen (2012), who used increases in the lower bounds of property tax rates in the year 2000 as a quasi-experimental setting to study strategic tax competition among local governments. No evidence of tax rate interaction was found. I revisit the 2000 reform, but extend the analysis to previously overlooked outcomes (tax base and tax revenue) and later increases in the property tax limits in 2010, 2015, and 2017. Moreover, this chapter uses a transparent Event Study approach and estimates reduced form effects of minimum rate increases, rather than a spatial instrumental variables strategy as used by Lyytikäinen (2012) to estimate tax policy reaction functions. Since the year 2000, there have been two important changes in the institutional setting that may affect competition in property taxes. First, the property tax base was removed from the tax base equalization scheme in 2012. Second, the number of municipalities has decreased by roughly 30 percent through municipality mergers. These changes have altered the context of local tax policy decisions, and the results suggest that they may have affected strategic interaction among municipalities.

The discussion on the Finnish institutional setting documents justifications for increases in property tax limits found in government law proposals. In contrast with the current discussion on international tax coordination, concern over inefficiently low tax rates through race-to-the-bottom tax competition does not seem to be the main justification for increases in minimum property tax rates. Horizontal tax competition among local governments was not discussed in the proposals, but it was mentioned in a committee report preparing the introduction of the Finnish property tax system in 1993. The law proposals suggest that the increases in minimum tax rates were to some extent motivated by vertical tax competition between central and local governments on labor income and corporate taxes, although the tax capacity of central government is not explicitly mentioned. When analyzing the direct effects of forced tax rate increases empirically, I find that forced increases have a clear and lasting effect on property tax revenue in the affected municipalities, which implies that the potential revenue of central government from other tax bases likely increases as intended.

This chapter forms part of a growing branch of quasi-experimental empirical work on strategic tax competition among local governments. A number of earlier studies have estimated tax rate reaction functions of spatially close jurisdictions using spatial econometrics tools, generally finding that a tax increase in one jurisdiction leads to increases in nearby jurisdictions (see Brueckner 2003 for a review). The critique of standard spatial econometric approaches by Gibbons and Overman (2012) has been influential in the emergence of quasi-experimental tax competition literature utilizing plausibly exogenous variation in tax rates due to policy reforms by upper-level governments or close elections, or close to jurisdiction borders. Examples of studies using quasi-experimental approaches include Agrawal (2015, 2016), Baskaran (2014), Eugster and Parchet (2019), Isen (2014), Lyytikäinen (2012), Mast (2020), and Parchet (2019). The results of these studies have challenged earlier findings of overwhelmingly positively sloped reaction functions, and lead to a more nuanced view of tax rate interdependence. As predicted by theoretical models, reaction functions can also be flat or negative.

Theoretical and empirical literature on local policy choice in the presence of fiscal externalities is reviewed extensively by Agrawal et al. (2022). They emphasize that the slope of reaction functions found in empirical studies is not informative of the welfare effects of tax competition, or of the existence of a race to the bottom, which both depend on the fiscal externalities associated with tax competition. Minimum tax rates have been analyzed theoretically by Keen and Konrad (2013). In a setting with two jurisdictions and mobile tax base, they find that a minimum tax rate set between unconstrained equilibrium rates increases tax rates in both jurisdictions. The only empirical studies I am aware of are Lyytikäinen (2012) and Buettner and Poehnlein (2021), who analyze local business tax limits in Germany. Köthenbürger (2002) analyzes theoretically the effects of equalization schemes on the distortion of tax competition, which arises because each jurisdiction ignores the external impact of its tax policy on the tax base of other jurisdictions. Tax base equalization internalizes this fiscal externality by compensating jurisdictions for the loss of their tax base due to a tax increase.[1] Egger et al. (2010) find empirical evidence that fiscal equalization alleviates business

1. Bucovetsky and Smart (2006) find that optimal equalization is weaker when the size of the capital stock is affected by taxes, and Kotsogiannis (2010) finds that the presence of vertical tax competition further reduces optimal equalization. Matsumoto (2022) studies equalization in the presence of multiple tax instruments (capital and labor taxes).

tax competition among German municipalities. Regarding the impact of mergers on tax rate interaction, Hoyt (1991) finds that equilibrium tax rates (and welfare) increase as the number of competing jurisdictions decreases.

The chapter is organized as follows. Section 9.2 discusses the role of property taxes in the Finnish local public finance system. Section 9.3 discusses the likely relevance of potential sources of horizontal fiscal interaction in the Finnish setting. Section 9.4 describes the data and provides a descriptive analysis of the evolution of property tax bounds and the distribution of property tax rates. Section 9.5 lays out the estimation strategy, and Section 9.6 presents the empirical results. Section 9.7 concludes.

## 9.2 Institutional Setting

### 9.2.1 Local Public Finance System

During the study period ending in 2022, local governments (municipalities) in Finland were responsible for several key public services, including elementary schools, health care, day care for children, and elderly care.[2] Local public expenditure is roughly 20 percent of GDP, funded through grants from central government and own tax revenue, consisting of local income tax, municipalities' share of corporate tax, and property taxes. Figure 9.1 presents the development of average real tax revenue per capita from different sources, as well as central government grants, from 1998 to 2019. The graph on the left shows that local income tax is the main source of own revenue, and, together with central government grants, covers the bulk of local public expenditure. Property taxes are relatively unimportant in terms of revenue, but the graph on the right shows that their share of revenue has increased over time. During this period property tax revenue per capita has increased by 142 percent in real terms while income tax revenue has grown by less than 10 percent.

The next section describes the Finnish property tax system in more detail. The main alternative to property taxes as a source of own revenue is local income tax. This is a residence-based flat rate tax on earned income (labor income) but a deduction set by central government means that it is applied to labor income above a threshold (currently roughly 16,000 EUR/year). There are no restrictions on the local income tax rate, which currently varies between 17 percent and 23.5 percent. Central government taxes earned income with a progressive schedule. Capital income is taxed separately from labor income by central government at a mildly progressive tax rate. Additionally, municipalities receive a portion of national corporate tax revenue. Central government has adjusted this share up and down several times. In

2. This changed in 2023 when social and health services were taken over by new middle-tier governments called "well-being services counties."

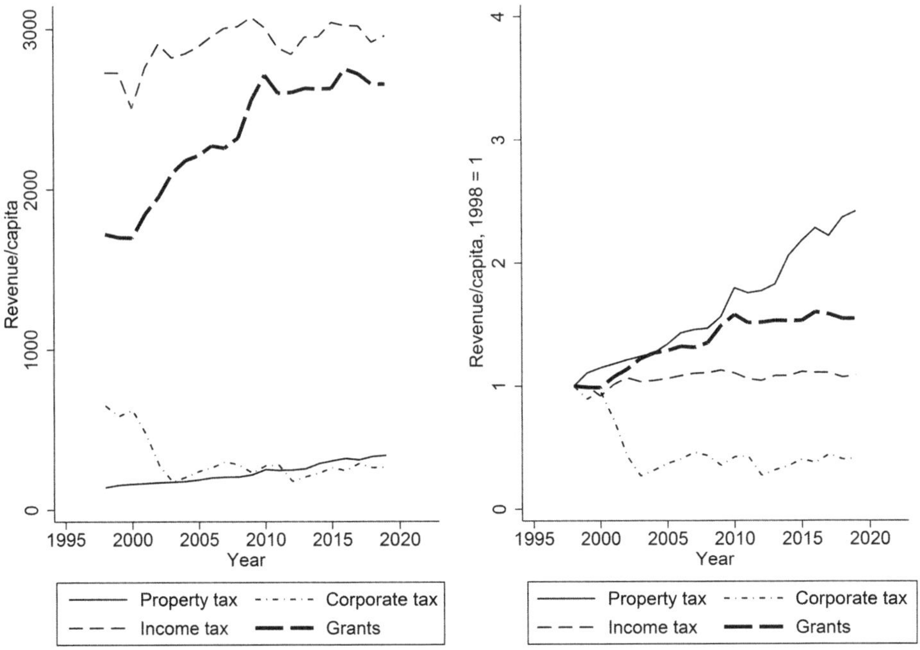


**Fig. 9.1 Average tax revenue and grants per capita in real terms 1998–2019**

Notes: The figure shows the average tax revenue and grants per capita in Finnish municipalities in 1998–2019 in real terms (in 2019 euros). The left graph presents the level of revenue. The right graph presents the development relative to 1998.

recent years, municipalities' share has been around one third of corporate tax revenue.

### 9.2.2 The Property Tax System

Local property taxes were introduced in Finland in 1993 to replace a disintegrated system of various national and local taxes and fees on real property.[3] The property tax rate can vary by type of property. The two main components of the property tax system are the general property tax (GPT) and the residential property tax (RPT), which apply to different types of real estate and have different allowed ranges.[4] The Finnish Tax Authority is responsible for the assessment of property values, and the same method is applied throughout the country.

3. The property tax system replaced a tax on imputed rental income and wealth tax (both had low revenue due to deductions and concessions that narrowed the tax base) and some local fees and charges.

4. In addition, the municipalities have the option to apply higher (than GPT) tax rates on vacation homes, power stations, and undeveloped lots, and they can exempt nonprofit organizations.

The GPT is applied to land and nonresidential buildings. The taxable value of land is based on the estimated market value of a similar undeveloped site, regardless of whether the site is actually developed.[5] Hence, the taxable value of land is independent of the development decisions of the land owner, and the GPT is a neutral land tax, to the extent that it is applied to land (Lyytikäinen 2009). However, the GPT is also levied on commercial and industrial buildings, valued at the estimated construction cost less depreciation. The part of the GPT that falls on buildings makes investment less profitable and may cause capital to relocate, implying a lower tax base in the long run. Hence, municipalities may use the GPT as a means to attract business capital.

Residential buildings are taxed at a separate tax rate, which has a lower allowed range than the GPT. The assessed value of residential buildings is based on estimated construction costs less depreciation, similar to business buildings. A higher residential building tax rate, other things constant, makes housing investment in a municipality less profitable and may lead to a lower tax base over time. Therefore, the RPT could be used as an instrument in the competition for housing capital. Section 9.3 also discusses other potential sources of fiscal interaction.

### 9.2.3 Stated Aim of Minimum Tax Rates

As both the GPT and RPT have the potential to give rise to horizontal tax competition, one possible reason for changes in minimum allowed tax rates is the prevention of harmful tax competition. In addition, increases in the lower bounds of property tax rates could be driven by vertical tax competition between central and local governments. Both levels of government tax labor income, and the revenue from corporate tax is divided between them. Therefore, central government could use increases in minimum property tax rates to force municipalities to collect additional revenue from other tax bases than labor income, and to alleviate the pressure to increase municipalities' share of corporate tax revenue, thereby improving the revenue capacity of central government.

This section discusses briefly the stated justifications for the minimum tax rates based on government proposals for the introduction of property taxes in 1993 and subsequent changes in the minimum tax rates in 2000, 2010, 2015, and 2017. The purpose is to find out if horizontal or vertical tax competition was explicitly mentioned in the proposals as a rationale for minimum tax rates, or whether there are implicit indications of tax competition being one reason behind minimum tax rate increases.

5. The target taxable value of land is 73.5 percent of the market value, but in practice the assessed values of land follow market values sluggishly, and assessed values have lagged behind target.

### 9.2.3.1 *Introduction of the Property Tax in 1993*

The government proposal for the law on local property taxes in 1992 did not discuss horizontal or vertical tax competition. However, the increased international mobility of other tax bases (business profits, labor income, and consumption) in the context of deepening international economic integration[6] was seen as an important rationale for the introduction of the property tax.

The government proposal did not consider a system without tax rate limits as an alternative, likely because a committee preparing the reform had proposed uniform national property tax rates, following the Swedish example.[7] The committee proposal for a uniform tax rate did mention that the possibility of competition among municipalities could have detrimental effects for local governments overall. Also, the committee considered that differential tax rates could in certain cases affect the location of new construction. Thus, concerns regarding the mobility of the tax base and horizontal tax competition seem to be one reason behind the committee's proposal for uniform tax rates. Hence, it seems that horizontal tax competition did play a role in the introduction of the property tax system and likely affected the initial property tax limits, although tax competition was not discussed in the government's proposal.

### 9.2.3.2 *Minimum Tax Rate Increases in 2000*

The government proposal for increases in minimum property tax rates in 2000 did not refer to horizontal tax competition, suggesting it was not seen as an important reason for the reform. The explicit aim of the reform was to prevent increases in local income tax rates. This can be interpreted as evidence of vertical tax competition, although the taxation capacity of central government was not explicitly mentioned in the bill. An alternative interpretation is that the government was concerned about negative labor supply responses to income taxation.

### 9.2.3.3 *Minimum Tax Rate Increases in 2010*

The reform of 2010 was at least partly motivated by the weakening outlook for municipalities' finances due to the financial crisis. The government wanted to increase the weight of the property tax in municipal finances, because the property tax was seen as providing a stable source of revenue free of cyclical shocks as compared to the corporate tax in particular. The reasoning that the property tax is better suited for municipalities than the

6. Finland became a member of the EU in 1995.

7. The property tax committee also proposed that 5 percent of the revenue should go to central government, but the government decided that all of the revenue would go to the municipalities.

corporate tax seems to suggest that vertical tax competition played a role in the reform. Previously municipalities' share of the corporate tax had often been adjusted upward to support municipalities when they faced negative shocks. As in the reform of 2000, the increase in tax rate limits was also seen as a tool to reduce pressure on taxing labor income, which can be seen as another indication of vertical tax competition between central and local governments. The government saw the property tax base as "immobile," suggesting that the possibility of construction investment responding to property taxes was not considered. Hence, horizontal fiscal interaction did not seem to be an important justification for the reform.

#### *9.2.3.4 Minimum Tax Rate Increases in 2015 and 2017*

The stated aims of the reforms of 2015 and 2017 were very similar to earlier reforms. The proposals paint a picture where the property tax base is seen as immobile, and therefore provides a good and stable source of revenue for municipalities. Increases in property taxes are also thought to prevent hikes in local labor income taxes.

#### *9.2.3.5 Maximum Tax Rates*

The rationale for maximum tax rates appears to be the prevention of large regional differences in property taxes. It seems likely that an upper bound was introduced in 1993 also to improve the political feasibility of the reform by alleviating concerns regarding excessive or even confiscatory tax hikes.

### 9.2.4 Fiscal Equalization

The local government grant system includes a tax base equalization component that transfers resources from rich to poorer municipalities. The system suppressed incentives to compete on the property tax base until 2012, when property taxes were removed from the equalization system. This implied that the mobility of the property tax base across municipalities has become a more relevant concern for municipalities.

The equalization system is based on imputed revenues per capita that are calculated by applying the average municipal income tax rates and property tax rates to the actual tax base of the municipality and adding corporate tax revenue. Municipalities above an equalization limit (in 2000, roughly 90 percent of average imputed per capita revenue) give up about 60 percent of their imputed revenue exceeding the limit and this revenue is used to raise the imputed revenues of poorer municipalities to the equalization limit.[8] The system weakens incentives to attract tax base, but municipalities above the limit still benefit from a higher tax base as they can keep 40 percent

8. In 2015, there was a grant reform that altered the limits and the functional form of the equalization system.

of the increase in imputed revenues due an increase in the tax base. For a municipality below the limit, an increase in the tax base may have little direct effect on revenues, but it may benefit from higher business capital indirectly through, for example, better employment opportunities.

Public discussion on municipal finances around the equalization reform suggested that there is a widespread misunderstanding that the equalization system applies to actual tax revenue rather than imputed revenue. Hence, some municipalities may erroneously make tax policy choices assuming that a change in revenue due to a tax rate change affects their equalization transfer. Baskaran (2014) argues that there is a similar pervasive wrong belief among German municipalities that choosing a tax rate multiplier smaller than a certain reference value of the equalization system will directly result in lower transfers, although the transfer is based on the tax base. It is not clear how common these kinds of misperceptions are among municipal decision-makers, but these considerations suggest that local tax policy may not always be based on very sophisticated reasoning and full understanding of the incentive structure.

### 9.2.5 Municipality Mergers

Figure 9.2 shows that the number of municipalities has decreased through municipality mergers throughout the study period. In 2009, there was a large merger wave due to a central government policy program that offered incentives for mergers (see e.g., Saarimaa and Tukiainen 2015). The motivation

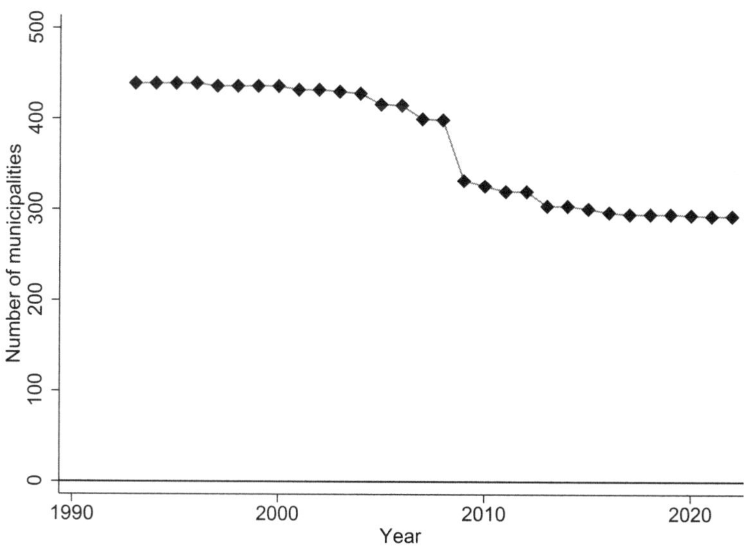


**Fig. 9.2 Number of municipalities 1993–2022**

for the program was to improve the efficiency of public service provision through economies of scale. The number of municipalities decreased by roughly 30 percent during the period, which may have affected the extent to which municipalities make tax choices strategically.

In the empirical analysis I omit municipalities that disappeared during the event window around each reform due to mergers. Larger merger partners that retain their initial municipality ID are included in the analysis.

## 9.3 Sources of Tax Rate Interaction

Three main sources of local government fiscal interaction identified in the literature are expenditure spillovers, competition on mobile tax base, and yardstick competition of local politicians. This section discusses the relevance of these mechanisms for the Finnish setting, largely following Lyytikäinen (2012) but adding new perspectives, such as the role of tax salience and the implications of changes in the institutional context (equalization reform and municipality mergers).

Expenditure spillovers arise if residents of a jurisdiction can benefit or are harmed by services provided by other jurisdictions (e.g., Case et al. 1993). Expenditure spillovers are possible in the Finnish setting, but, arguably, they are unlikely to be an important source of fiscal interaction since the bulk of services provided by the municipalities are publicly provided private goods. Competition for tax base and politically motivated yardstick competition are more potential sources of spatial interdependence in tax rates in Finland.

In the competitive versions of tax competition models, there are many relatively small jurisdictions that take the net return of capital as given, and hence strategic behavior is absent (Zodrow and Mieszkowski 1986). If jurisdictions are sufficiently large to affect the net rate of return, tax rates are set strategically taking into account tax rates in other jurisdictions (Wildasin 1988). For the purposes of empirical work on local taxes, it is important to note that strategic tax competition among jurisdictions in the same region requires that capital is not fully mobile but to some extent fixed to the region. Brueckner and Saavedra (2001) combine heterogeneous preferences of mobile households and a locally fixed tax base and show that, in a model with two jurisdictions competing for a fixed amount of capital, the relationship between capital tax rates in the jurisdictions may be positive or negative (or flat). Municipalities that are atomistic with respect to capital markets could also react to neighboring tax changes if they are linked in local labor markets and have market power in the labor market resulting in strategic interactions (Agrawal et al. 2019).

The property taxes studied in this chapter fall partly on business and housing capital. This implies that a higher property tax rate lowers the profitability of investment in the municipality and may cause capital to locate in other municipalities, which makes competition on tax rates in an attempt to attract capital possible.[9] As discussed above, the sign of tax rate interaction due to the tax base competition mechanism is ambiguous a priori. Lyytikäinen (2009) finds evidence that property tax incentives affect housing starts, suggesting that tax base mobility is a relevant concern for local politicians.[10] Changes in the Finnish institutional setting imply that fiscal competition may have changed over time. The removal of property taxes from the tax base equalization scheme in 2012 increased incentives to compete on the tax base (see section 9.2.4). Also the reduction in the number of municipalities through mergers (see Section s.2.5) in the study period may have strengthened fiscal interaction. When there are fewer municipalities in the region, strategic interaction is more probable.

So-called yardstick competition or tax mimicking arises if the true costs of providing public services are known only by the local government and not observed by voters, while tax rates are common knowledge (Besley and Case 1995). In this setting, voters may utilize the fact that the costs of providing services in their jurisdiction are likely to be correlated with other jurisdictions in the area to assess the performance of their government. Relatively high taxes may indicate that the government is inefficient or rent seeking and should be voted out of office. As a result, governments are forced to imitate their neighbors in order to stay in office.

Yardstick competition may be relevant to the Finnish case since Finnish municipalities are governed by elected councils. Information on tax rates is easily available, but comparing the efficiency of service provision across municipalities is difficult. Municipalities provide a wide range of services, and there are no commonly used performance rating systems. Hence, voters may use tax rates as a benchmark when evaluating the performance of their council relative to other councils in the area. One can of course question the relevance of forced tax increases due to the actions of central government for yardstick competition among local politicians. On the other hand, voters may be unaware of the exact causes of the tax increases they observe. Moreover, property taxes are a highly salient form of tax for property owners and often rank as the most hated tax in surveys, which could make property taxes more important for yardstick competition than income taxes.[11]

As the observed patterns of tax rate interaction in Finnish data are likely to be a combination of tax base competition (sign ambiguous), yardstick

9. Municipalities have a zoning monopoly, which they can use to influence land use to attract certain types of households or businesses.

10. The evidence of the negative effect of property taxes on housing starts is based on an analysis of the surcharge on undeveloped lots, which created a large incentive to develop. The point estimates of the effect of the residential property tax are also negative but imprecise.

11. Income taxation is highly automated in Finland through a withholding system and prefilled tax returns. Property tax bills are sent by mail to the property owners each year and paying the tax requires more effort and attention than with income tax. Cabral and Hoxby (2012) provide evidence that a more salient form of the property tax system is associated with stronger opposition toward property taxes.

**Table 9.1** **Summary statistics for 1996–2020**

| | Mean | Std. dev. | Min | Max |
|---|---|---|---|---|
| GPT rate % | 0.731 | 0.242 | 0.2 | 1.9 |
| RPT rate % | 0.338 | 0.122 | 0.1 | 0.9 |
| GPT base, EUR/capita | 9,049 | 6,171 | 1,574 | 100,700 |
| RPT base, EUR/capita | 15,247 | 3,641 | 8,102 | 28,192 |
| GPT revenue, EUR/capita | 72.6 | 66.3 | 3.8 | 921.3 |
| RPT revenue, EUR/capita | 54.8 | 31.1 | 9.2 | 220.9 |
| Population | 14,268 | 39,618 | 233 | 653,835 |

Notes: The table shows summary statistics for the main variables used in the empirical analysis. Sample size is 8,904.

competition (positive) and possibly expenditure spillovers (ambiguous), the expected effect of a tax rate change of one municipality on nearby municipalities is ambiguous. It should also be noted that the empirical strategy based on variation generated by forced increases is not necessarily informative of responses to voluntary increases.

## 9.4 Data and Descriptive Analysis

I use panel data on property tax rates in Finnish municipalities[12] from 1993 to 2022, and other municipality charateristics for varying shorter periods. The Event Study analysis on the impacts of forced tax rate increases uses data from 1996 to 2020. Summary statistics for key variables in this data set are reported in table 9.1. During this period GPT rates range from 0.2 percent to 1.9 percent and RPT rates vary between 0.1 percent and 0.9 percent. There is huge variation in the GPT base and revenue, while the RPT base and revenue vary less. This is likely due to regional differences in land values, which influence the tax base of the GPT, but differences in the stock of business buildings may play a role too. The same kind of residential buildings have the same taxable value everywhere, and therefore the tax base of the RPT varies less. There is large variation in the size of municipalities. The population ranges from a few hundred to over 650,000 in the city of Helsinki.

Figures 9.3 and 9.4 present the evolution of the statutory bounds for the general property tax rate and the residential property tax rate, together with the distribution of tax rates and the mean tax rate in 1993–2022. The size of the circles indicates the number of municipalities in the cell.

Figure 9.3 shows that the reforms raised the allowed ranges for the GPT and RPT substantially, and the current lower limit to GPT is above the

12. Municipalities in the partly autonomous region of the Åland Islands are dropped due to missing data and differences in the institutional setting.

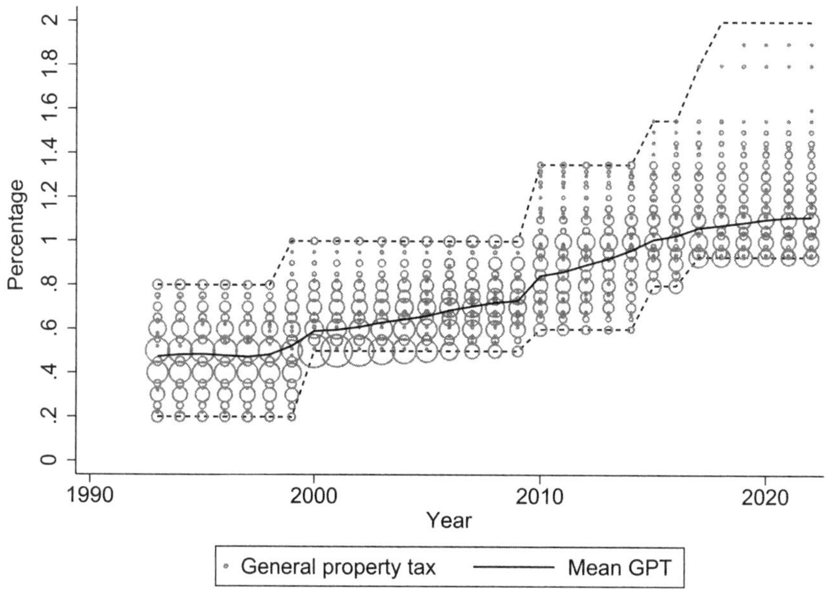


**Fig. 9.3 General property tax rates in 1993–2022**

Notes: The figure shows the statutory bounds for the general property tax rate, the distribution of tax rates, and the mean tax rate in 1993–2022. The size of the circle indicates the number of municipalities in the cell.

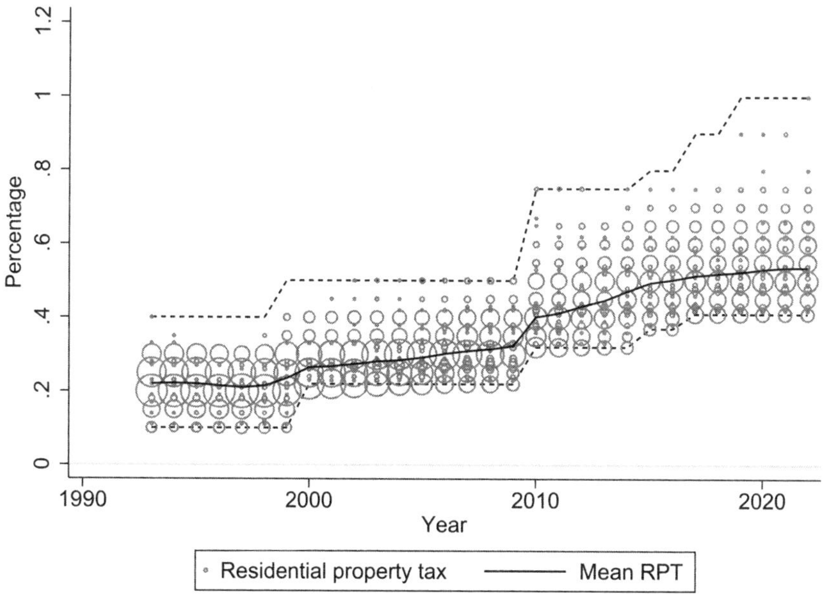


**Fig. 9.4 Residential property tax rates in 1993–2022**

Notes: The figure shows the statutory bounds for the residential property tax rate, the distribution of tax rates, and mean tax rate in 1993–2022. The size of the circle indicates the number of municipalities in the cell.

**Table 9.2** **Summary statistics for the reforms**

| | 2000 reform | | 2010 reform | | 2015–2017 reform | |
|---|---|---|---|---|---|---|
| Minimum GPT rate | 0.2% -> 0.5% | | 0.5% -> 0.6% | | 0.6% -> 0.8% -> 0.93% | |
| | Own | Neighbors' mean | Own | Neighbors' mean | Own | Neighbors' mean |
| Mean forced GPT increase | 0.052 | 0.051 | 0.007 | 0.008 | 0.038 | 0.038 |
| Share treated | 0.374 | 0.759 | 0.083 | 0.344 | 0.329 | 0.820 |
| Minimum RPT rate | 0.1->0.22 | | 0.22% -> 0.32% | | 0.32% -> 0.37% -> 0.41% | |
| | Own | Neighbors' mean | Own | Neighbors' mean | Own | Neighbors' mean |
| Mean forced RPT increase | 0.018 | 0.017 | 0.023 | 0.023 | 0.009 | 0.008 |
| Share treated | 0.461 | 0.833 | 0.549 | 0.917 | 0.200 | 0.563 |
| N in reform year | 436 | | 326 | | 295 | |

Notes: The table shows mean forced tax rate increases due to the reforms and the share of municipalities with nonzero forced increases.

initial upper limit. Before the reform of 2000, the mean GPT was flat at about 0.5 percent. The increase in the lower bound in 2000 was binding for a large share of municipalities. After the reform of 2000, the number of municipalities at the lower bound decreased gradually and the mean GPT increased through voluntary tax hikes. There was a clear upward shift in the mean GPT in 2010 when the bounds were raised again, and the upward trend continued after the reform. The upward trend continued through the reforms of 2015 and 2017 until 2020, after which it flattened. The bounds for the RPT (figure 9.4) were lower than for the GPT throughout the period, and there are only a few observations at the upper limit of the RPT.

Table 9.2 reports how binding the reforms were. In the empirical analysis of the effects of minimum tax rates, I use a measure of forced tax rate increases, which is the change in the tax rate required to meet the new minimum after the reform. The table presents the mean forced tax increase and the share of municipalities experiencing a forced increase after each reform. I present these statistics for own forced increases and neighbors' average forced increases separately. The reforms differ significantly in the amount of municipalities affected. The increase in the lower bound of the RPT in 2010 affected the majority of municipalities while the GPT reform in the same year was binding for only 8.3 percent of municipalities. The mean forced tax rate increase was highest in the GPT reform of 2000 (0.05 pp) and lowest in the GPT reform of 2010 (0.007 pp).

For the interpretation of the findings on the effects of the reforms in section

**Table 9.3 Occurrence and overlap of forced increases in different reforms**

| | General property tax | Residential property tax |
|---|---|---|
| No forced increases | 0.481 | 0.285 |
| Forced increases | 0.519 | 0.715 |
| –of which: | | |
| *Only 2000 reform* | 0.159 | 0.108 |
| *Only 2010 reform* | 0.014 | 0.193 |
| *Only 2015_17 reform* | 0.136 | 0.034 |
| *2000 and 2010 reforms* | 0.017 | 0.214 |
| *2000 and 2015_17 reforms* | 0.132 | 0.010 |
| *2010 and 2015_17 reforms* | 0.010 | 0.034 |
| *2000, 2010 and 2015_17 reforms* | 0.051 | 0.122 |

Notes: The table shows the share of municipalities that experienced forced increases from different combinations of reforms. The data is from 2017 and includes only municipalities that existed during all three reforms.

9.6, it is of interest to analyze whether the same municipalities were affected by multiple reforms. If the set of municipalities forced to increase property taxes differs vastly across the reforms, differences in the estimated effects of the reforms may be affected by heterogeneous responses by different municipalities, in addition to changes in the institutional setting. Table 9.3 uses data from 2017 and shows the share of municipalities experiencing different combinations of forced increases due to the reforms. There were no forced GPT increases in 48 percent of municipalities, and there is substantial overlap in the groups affected by different GPT reforms. For example, we see that out of the 33 percent with forced GPT increases in 2015–17 (see table 9.2), only 13.6 percent were affected solely by this reform. The remaining roughly 20 percent also experienced forced increases in 2000 or 2010 or both. The share of muncipalities without forced RPT increases is lower (28.5 percent), and again, there is substantial overlap in forced increases across the reforms. However, the turnover in the group facing forced increases is quite substantial too, indicating that differences in the effects of different reforms may be partly driven by differences in the composition of the treated municipalities.

Figures 9.5 and 9.6 illustrate the spatial distribution of property tax rates in 1997 before the first reform of the tax rate limits, and in 2017 after the last reform studied here. There is clearly positive spatial correlation in both years for the general property tax rates (left) and the residential property tax rates (right). All maps have clusters of high and low tax rate municipalities. This spatial correlation could arise due to interdependence in the tax rate setting, but spatial correlation in other determinants of tax rates is an alternative explanation. Variation due to increases in the minimum tax rates helps to disentangle between these explanations.

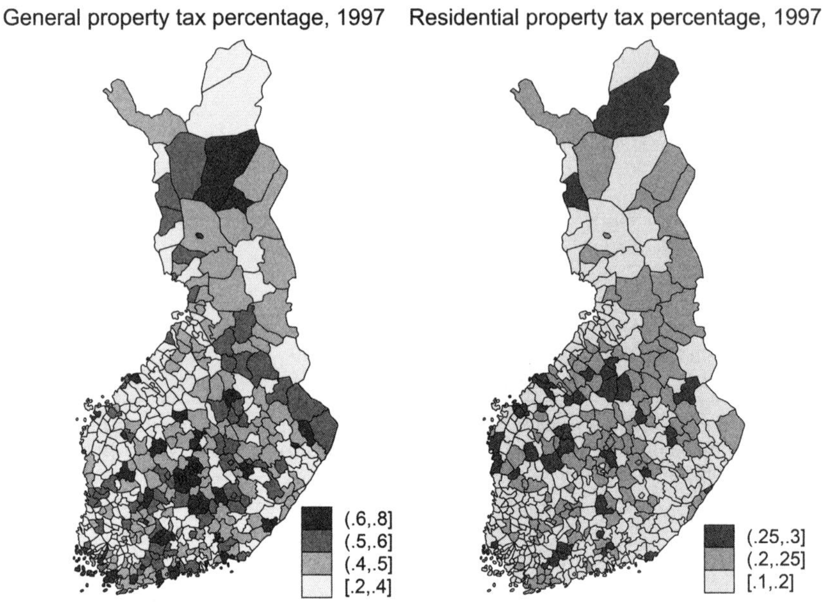


**Fig. 9.5 Property tax rates in 1997**

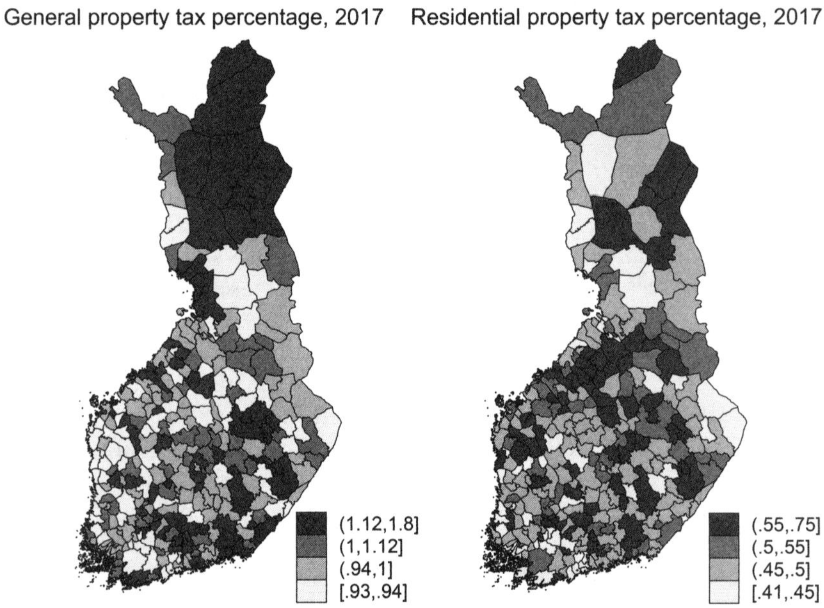


**Fig. 9.6 Property tax rates in 2017**

## 9.5 Empirical Strategy

Increases in the minimum property tax rate force municipalities where the limit is binding to increase their tax rates. The purpose of the empirical analysis is to test how these tax policy shocks affect their neighbors' tax rate choices, as well as their own tax rate, revenue and tax base.

Drawing on Lyytikäinen (2012), I construct a measure of forced increases in the property tax rates due to the reforms. The forced increase ($Z_{it}$) is the difference between the new lower bound $\underline{T}_t$ for the property tax rate $T$ in year $t$ and the tax rate in year $t-1$ for municipalities with a tax rate below the new lower bound. For municipalities above $\underline{T}_t$ in $t-1$, the forced increase is zero. The forced increase is written as

(1) $$Z_{it} = D(\underline{T}_t > T_{it-1})(\underline{T}_t - T_{it-1}).$$

For example, a municipality with a general property tax rate of 0.2 percent in 1999 was forced to increase its GPT by at least 0.3 percentage points in 2000 when the lower bound for GPT was raised to 0.5 percent, and thus $Z_{i2000} = 0.3$ for this municipality. Forced increases do not necessarily translate one-to-one into changes in actual tax rates because the municipality might also have increased its tax rate in the absence of the reform, or the municipality can increase its tax rate by more than the minimum required amount.

Because the reforms of 2015 and 2017 were close to each other and rather small in magnitude, I combine these reforms by summing up the forced increases in these years into one ($Z_{i2015\text{–}17} = Z_{i2015} + Z_{i2017}$). The reforms of 2000 and 2010 are analyzed separately.

I use the forced increase as the treatment variable in Event Study type two-way fixed effects regressions. The forced increase for each municipality is held constant within the event window around the reform. Our interest lies in the interaction of the forced increase with the year dummies. The model for the impact of own forced increases on outcome $Y$ is

(2) $$Y_{it} = \beta_t Z_i + \kappa_i + \lambda_t + u_{it}.$$

The parameter of interest is $\beta_t$, which measures the impact of a one percentage point forced tax rate increase relative to the base year (one year before the reform). Municipality fixed effects $\kappa_i$ and year fixed effects $\lambda_t$ control for time-invariant municipality characteristics and common time effects, and $u_{it}$ is the error term. Standard errors are clustered at the municipality level.

When analyzing spatial interaction in tax rate setting, the treatment variable is the weighted average of forced increases in nearby municipalities. I use a simple nearest neighbors weighing matrix where all municipalities that share a border with municipality $i$ get equal weights $1/N_i$ (where $N_i$ is the number of *i*'s neighbors) and other municipalities get zero weight.[13] The spatial interaction model is written as

$$(3) \qquad Y_{it} = \beta_t \sum_{j \neq i} (w_{ij} * Z_j) + \kappa_i + \lambda_t + u_{it},$$

where $w_{ij}$ denotes spatial weights. Again, the year before the reform is the base year, and controls include municipality fixed effects and year fixed effects. This model differs from Lyytikäinen (2012), who used neighbors' forced increases as an instrument for actual tax rate changes (1- to 4-year differences) to estimate tax competition reaction functions. Here the purpose is to estimate a reduced form model examining the effects of forced tax increases without making assumptions about whether the estimates are informative of responses to tax changes due to other factors.

I estimate a separate model for each reform and use data for four years before and four years after the reform years 2000 and 2010. For the 2015–2017 reforms, the event window is 2011–2020.

## 9.6 Results

### 9.6.1 Own Forced Tax Rate Increases

Before analyzing the spatial strategic interactions caused by the reforms, I will examine how own forced tax increases affect the actual tax rates, tax base, and tax revenues of municipalities. Alas, there is not enough statistical power to study the effects on several other interesting outcomes, such as local spending or the local income tax rate, because property taxes are still a relatively unimportant source of revenue, although their importance has increased, as shown in section 9.2. I will present the results in the form of graphs that plot the Event Study coefficients for each outcome variable for all three reforms.

Figure 9.7 shows the effect of own forced GPT (top) and RPT (bottom) increases on actual tax rates, for the 2000 reform (left), the 2010 reform (center), and the 2015–2017 reform (right). A coefficient of 1 would mean that a forced increase leads to an equally large increase in actual tax rate.

Starting from the GPT reform of 2000, the estimates for the impact of a forced GPT increase are between 0.8 and 0.9 after the reform. Before the reform there is a slight downward trend, indicating that GPT lagged behind other municipalities in municipalities that had large forced increases in 2000. This downward pre-trend is not surprising, as municipalities with low tax rates in 1999 cannot have raised tax rates in recent years. The negative pre-

13. Lyytikäinen (2012) tests for the robustness of his results to population weights or the inclusion of neighbors' neighbors. The findings regarding tax rate interaction are not sensitive to alternative weighing schemes.

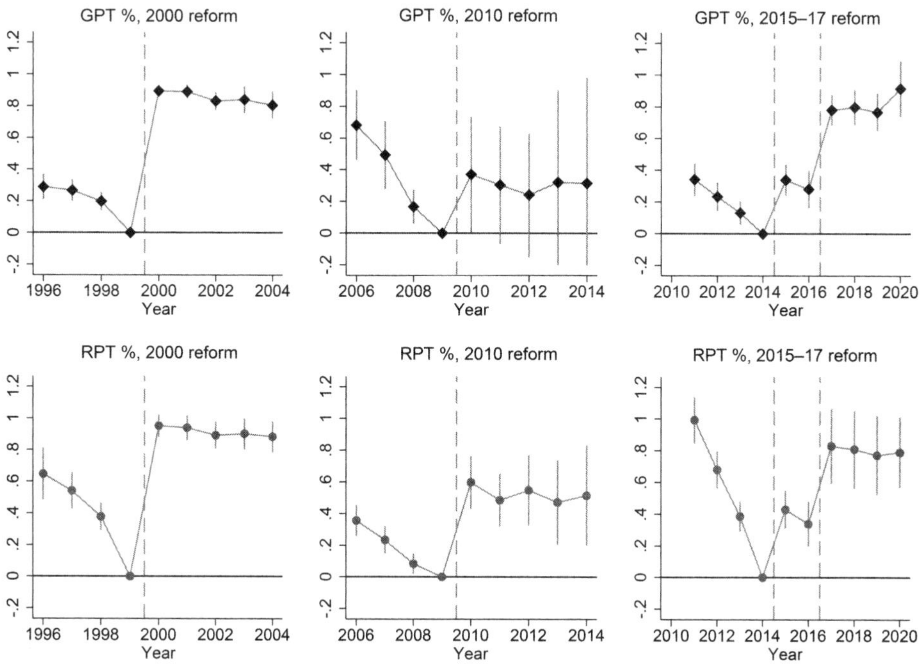


**Fig. 9.7 Own forced increases and own actual tax rate**

Notes: The figure plots the coefficients of the interaction of forced tax rate increases and year dummies for the general property tax (upper panels) and the residential property tax (lower panels) for the reforms of 2000 (left), 2010 (center), and 2015–2017 (right). The spikes indicate 95% confidence intervals (clustering at municipality level). The controls include municipality fixed effects and year fixed effects. The sample excludes municipalities for which the upper limit to the tax rate was binding one year before the reform and municipalities that dropped from the sample due to mergers during the period.

trend is even stronger in the GPT reform of 2010, and the impact of the forced increases on actual tax rates is less pronounced than 10 years earlier. The confidence bands are large because the reform was small in magnitude. Forced GPT increases due to the 2015 and 2017 reforms were related with a relative decline in GPT before the reform and large increases after the reform.

Turning to the residential property tax, the figure shows that own forced RPT increases led to clear increases in actual tax rates, especially after the 2000 reform. After the reform of 2010, the effect is less pronounced than the other reforms, and there is a strong negative pre-trend in the RPT reform of 2015–2017.

Figure 9.8 examines the impact of forced increases on the tax base. The dependent variable is the log of tax base per capita, and hence the estimates are semielasticities of the tax base per capita with respect to the tax rate. There is no clear evidence of deterioration of the tax base due to a forced

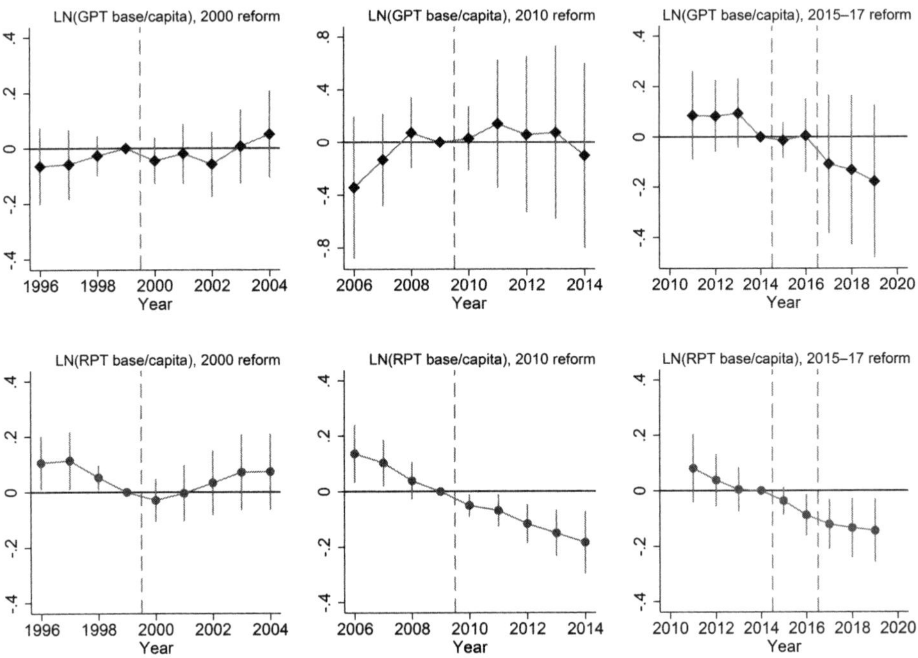


**Fig. 9.8 Own forced increases and tax base**

Notes: The figure plots the coefficients of the interaction of forced tax rate increases and year dummies for the general property tax (upper panels) and the residential property tax (lower panels) for the reforms of 2000 (left), 2010 (center), and 2015–2017 (right). The spikes indicate 95% confidence intervals (clustering at municipality level). The controls include municipality fixed effects and year fixed effects. The sample excludes municipalities for which the upper limit to the tax rate was binding one year before the reform and municipalities that dropped from the sample due to mergers during the period.

GPT increases in the upper panels, but the standard errors are quite large especially after the 2010 and 2015–2017 reforms, and economically significant effects can not be ruled out.

The lower panels of Figure 9.8 present the tax base effects of forced RPT increases. The estimates are not consistent with a decrease in the tax base. There is a downward trend in the tax base associated with forced increases before all the reforms, which continues after the reforms of 2010 and 2015–2017, but is reversed after the reform of 2000.

Overall, there is no clear evidence of detrimental effects on tax the base leading to a loss of revenue four years after the reforms. This is perhaps not surprising as the stock of housing and business buildings can adjust only gradually through new construction and demolition. The limited time horizon and nonnegligible statistical uncertainty mean that I cannot rule out economically significant tax base effects in the longer run.

The results for tax revenue are presented in figure 9.9. The combined effect

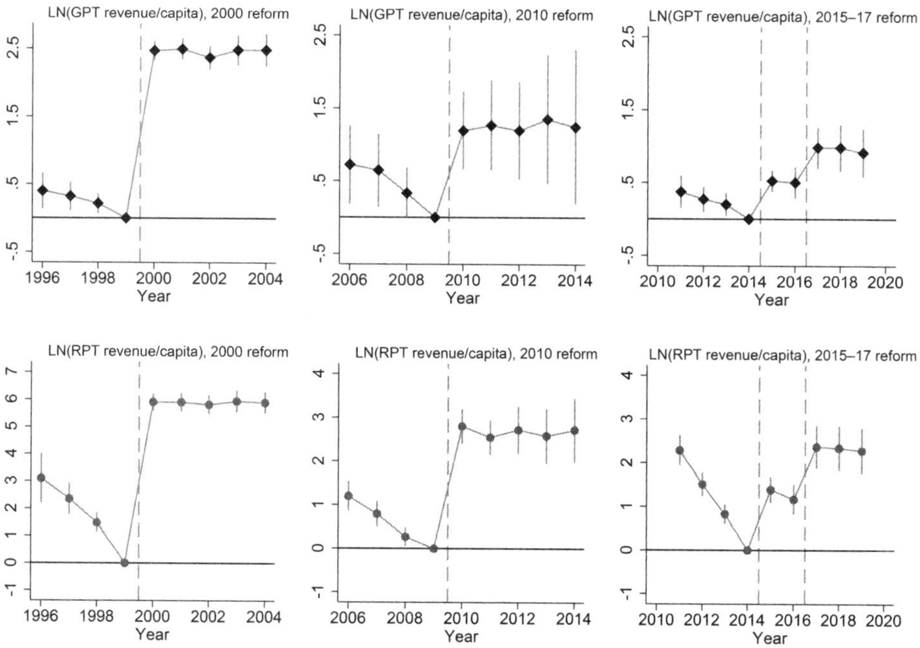


**Fig. 9.9 Own forced increases and tax revenue**

Notes: The figure plots the coefficients of the interaction of forced tax rate increase and year dummies for the general property tax (upper panels) and the residential property tax (lower panels) for the reforms of 2000 (left), 2010 (center), and 2015–2017 (right). The spikes indicate 95% confidence intervals (clustering at municipality level). The controls include municipality fixed effects and year fixed effects. The sample excludes municipalities for which the upper limit to the tax rate was binding one year before the reform and municipalities that dropped from the sample due to mergers during the period.

of tax rate increases and tax base effects is that forced GPT increases lead to clear and lasting increases in revenue after all three reforms. Similar to the GPT, the results for tax revenue from the RPT in the lower panels show clear and persistent increases in revenue due to forced tax increases.

## 9.6.2 Fiscal Interaction

Next I analyze spatial interaction in tax rates triggered by the minimum tax rate increases. To assess whether forced increases caused significant variation in actual spatially weighted average tax rates, I first estimate a model where the spatially weighted actual tax rate is the outcome variable. Figure 9.10 shows the results for both the GPT and the RPT and for all the reforms.

Starting from the GPT, neighbors' forced tax increases in the 2000 (top-left) and 2015–2017 (top-right) reforms lead to clear and persistent shocks in their tax rates. The 2010 reform (top-center), which increased the mini-

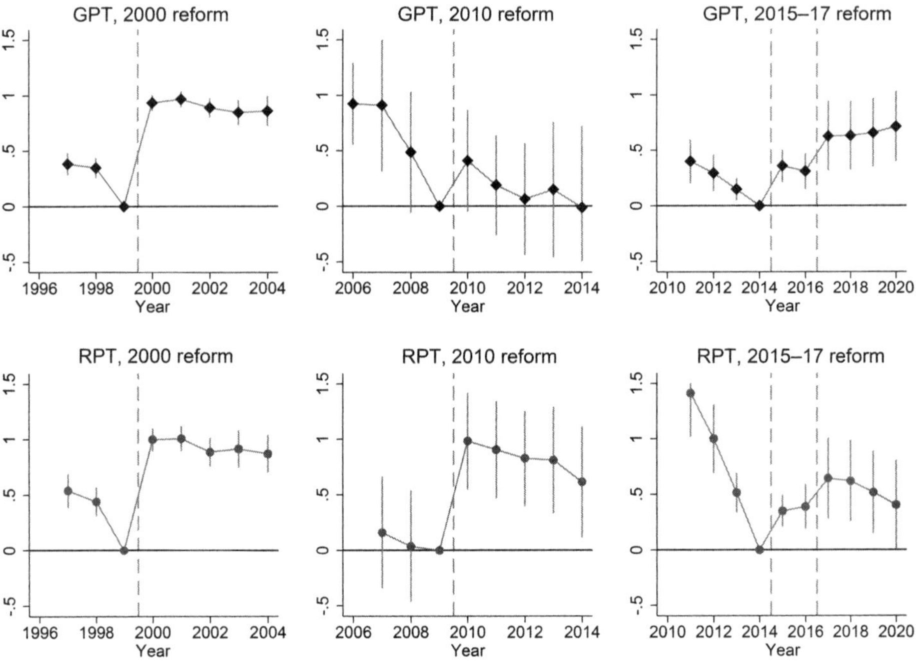


**Fig. 9.10 Neighbors' forced increases and neighbors' actual tax rates**

Notes: The figure plots the coefficients of the interaction of neighbors' average forced tax rate increases and year dummies for the general property tax (upper panels) and the residential property tax (lower panels) for the reforms of 2000 (left), 2010 (center), and 2015–2017 (right). The spikes indicate 95% confidence intervals (clustering at municipality level). The controls include municipality fixed effects and year fixed effects. The sample excludes municipalities with own forced increases in the reform year, municipalities for which the upper limit to the tax rate was binding one year before the reform, and municipalities that dropped from the sample due to mergers during the period.

mum GPT rate by a mere 0.1 pp, did not cause as clear shocks in neighbors' actual GPT rates as the other reforms, and the standard errors are large. The lower panel of Figure 9.10 presents the findings for the RPT. Forced RPT increases lead to clearly visible shocks to neighbors' actual tax rates after all the reforms. Before the 2015–2017 reform, there is a strong negative pre-trend.

Figure 9.11 presents the findings on how the choice of property tax rates is affected by neighbors' forced tax increases. The first important observation from the figure is that trends in property tax rates prior to the reforms are flat in all six panels, which increases confidence in the results being informative of the causal impacts of neighbors' forced tax increases. The results for the GPT reform 2000 indicate that GPT rates were unaffected by forced increases in nearby municipalities. This is in line with the findings of Lyytikäinen (2012) for the same reform. The results for the relatively

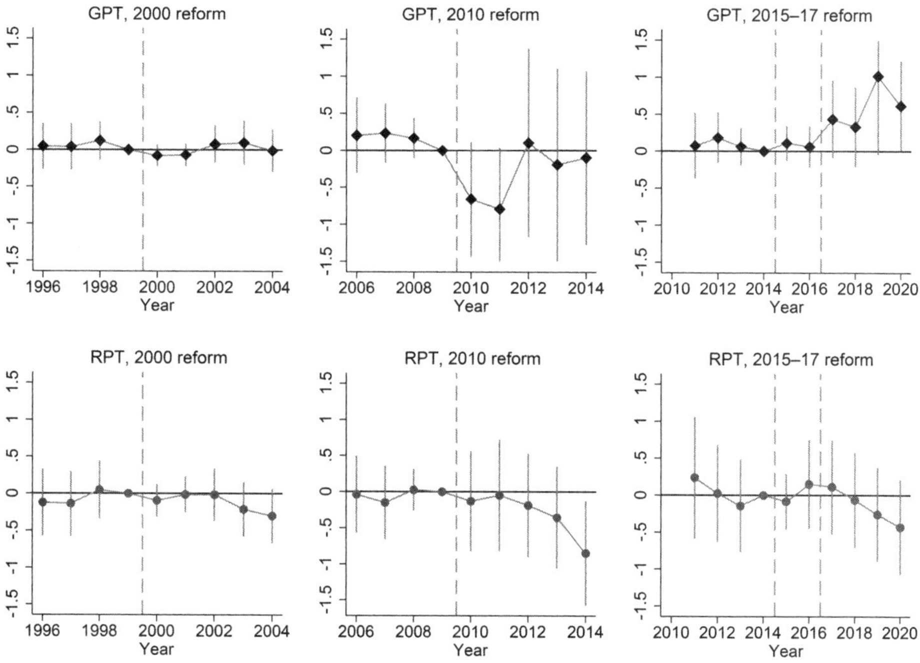


**Fig. 9.11 Tax rate interaction.**

Notes: The figure plots the coefficients of the interaction of neighbors' average forced tax rate increases and year dummies for the general property tax (upper panels) and the residential property tax (lower panels) for the reforms of 2000 (left), 2010 (center), and 2015–2017 (right). The spikes indicate 95% confidence intervals (clustering at municipality level). The controls include municipality fixed effects and year fixed effects. The sample excludes municipalities with own forced increases in the reform year, municipalities for which the upper limit to the tax rate was binding one year before the reform, and municipalities that dropped from the sample due to mergers during the period.

small GPT reform in 2010 are too imprecise to be informative, because the reform did not generate sufficient variation in neighbors' tax rates (figure 9.10). Forced GPT increases due to the reform of 2015–2017 seem to lead to tax increases in neighboring municipalities. A possible reason for the difference between the findings for the 2000 reform and the 2015–2017 reform is the equalization reform, which removed property taxes from the tax base equalization scheme. The decrease in the number of municipalities may also have increased strategic interaction. It should, however, be noted that the estimates have large standard errors, and we cannot rule out economically insignificant or zero effects with a large degree of confidence. Moreover, table 9.3 showed that the group of municipalities affected by the 2000 and 2015–2017 reforms differed substantially. This means that heterogeneous responses by different municipalities can be an alternative explanation for the different point estimates for these reforms.

Turning to the analyses of RPT in the lower panels, the estimates show a similar pattern after all three reforms. Neighbors' forced tax rate changes seem to lead to a gradual decline in RPT rates three to four years after the reform, and there is a significant negative coefficient four years after the reform of 2010. This consistent pattern points toward neighboring municipalities' RPT rates being strategic substitutes.[14] A potential mechanism could be that municipalities expect their neighbors' forced RPT increases to lead to an increase in their tax base, and they can therefore lower their RPT without losing revenue. The point estimate is more negative in the two latter reforms. A possible explanation could be intensified strategic interaction when the number of municipalities shrinks over time due to mergers. Also, the equalization reform could amplify expected tax base effects and strategic interaction. The confidence bands in the latter two reforms are, however, quite broad, implying that differences to the 2000 reform may be a coincidence. Again, heterogeneous responses by different municipalities affected by different reforms may be an alternative explanation.

#### *9.6.2.1 Vertical Fiscal Externalities*

The reforms analyzed above did not generate enough variation to estimate the impact of forced property tax increases on local income tax rates with reasonable statistical precision. Therefore, whether and to what extent the reforms caused vertical fiscal spillovers to the tax capacity of central government remains an open question. It should also be noted that Event Study analysis of the impact of minimum property tax increases on local income taxes would neglect any equilibrium effects on municipalities that were not directly affected by the reforms.

One can, however, calculate a rough upper bound estimate for the potential impact of the reforms on local and national income taxes by making the extreme assumption that in the absence of the reforms, all municipalities would still apply the tax rates of 1998 prior to the first increase in tax limits since the introduction of the property tax. This scenario assumes that the overall rise in property tax rates is fully attributable to changes in tax rate bounds. Further, I assume that all of the increase in property tax revenue was used to lower local income taxes, and municipal expenditure was unaffected. Finally, I assume away any responses to tax rates that would affect tax bases. This is a highly unrealistic thought experiment, but it is useful for determining a rough upper limit for the impact of changes in property tax limits on income taxes.

When actual property tax revenues in 2019 are compared with hypothetical revenues obtained by applying 1998 property tax rates to the tax bases in 2019, it is found that actual GPT revenue in 2019 is 75 percent higher

14. The results for the RPT reform of 2000 are consistent with Lyytikäinen (2012), where the estimate for the slope of the reaction function four years after the reform was –0.16 but insignificant.

than the hypothetical revenue, and actual RPT revenue is 144 percent higher than hypothetical revenue. Total property tax revenue in 2019 was 95 percent higher than hypothetical revenue in the absence of tax hikes. In monetary terms, the contribution of tax rate increases between 1998 and 2019 to property tax revenue in 2019 was €870 million. In the same year, municipal income tax revenue was €18.9 billion, and the income tax revenue of central government from the same tax base was €5.5 billion. Thus, in the absence of property tax revenue attributed to tax rate increases, local income tax would have to be 4.6 percent higher to cover municipal expenditure in 2019. Central government would have to cut its labor income tax revenue by 15.9 percent to keep the overall labor income tax burden constant. This simple calculation suggests that economically relevant vertical spillovers are possible, even though we lack the statistical power to estimate the magnitude.

## 9.7 Conclusions

The Finnish government has increased minimum property tax rates several times during the past 30 years, and the current lower limits are above the initial upper limits. This chapter analyses empirically the effects of these changes in minimum property tax rates using panel data and an Event Study research design.

I find that neighbors' forced increases in general property tax rates did not trigger responses after the reform of 2000. This is consistent with the findings of Lyytikäinen (2012) for the same reform using a somewhat different estimation strategy. The reforms of 2015 and 2017 indicate that forced increases lead to GPT increases in nearby municipalities. This would be consistent with intensified competition for business real estate after the removal of property taxes from the tax base equalization scheme in 2012. Regarding the spatial interaction of residential property tax rates, I find some indication that neighbors' forced increases in RPT rates led to lower tax rate choices by their neighbors four years after each of the reforms studied, even though the estimate is statistically significant only after the 2010 reform. These findings contribute to the growing quasi-experimental tax competition literature.

It should be borne in mind that the empirical results in this chapter concern strategic responses to neighbors' tax rates. Although the evidence on interaction among neighboring municipalities is limited, tax competition may still exist. In the standard model, jurisdictions that are negligible in size in the capital market compete, but the reaction functions are flat. The equilibrium may still be inefficient because fiscal externalities exist.

The empirical results for municipalities' own forced tax rate increases reveal that forced increases have a clear and lasting effect on own property tax revenue in the affected municipalities, as the tax rates rise and the tax base is largely unaffected in the short run. This suggests that the tax capacity of central government in regard to other tax bases likely increased. Interestingly, analysis of government bills on tax rate bounds suggests that the increases in minimum tax rates were at least partly motivated by vertical tax competition between central and local governments on income and corporate taxes. The impact of forced property tax increases on local income taxes cannot be estimated due to lack of statistical power, but a simple back of the envelope calculation assuming all property tax increases can be attributed to changes in tax rate bounds suggests that the impact on local income tax rates and revenue capacity of the central government can be economically significant.

**Acknowledgments**

I would like to thank David Agrawal, Leah Brooks, and the participants at the NBER Policy Responses to Tax Competition Conference for their insightful comments, and Oskari Harjunen, Erkka Silvennoinen, and Reetta Varjonen-Ollus for sharing their data. Funding from the Academy of Finland is gratefully acknowledged (grant no. 315591). For acknowledgments, sources of research support, and disclosure of the author's material financial relationships, if any, please see https://www.nber.org/books-and-chapters/policy-responses-tax-competition/minimum-tax-rates-and-tax-competition-evidence-property-tax-limits-finland.

## References

Agrawal, D. R. 2015. "The Tax Gradient: Spatial Aspects of Fiscal Competition." *American Economic Journal: Economic Policy* 7: 1–29.

Agrawal, D. R. 2016. "Local Fiscal Competition: An Application to Sales Taxation with Multiple Federations." *Journal of Urban Economics* 91: 122–38.

Agrawal, D. R., W. H. Hoyt, and J. D. Wilson. 2019. "Tax Competition with Mobile Labor, Residents, and Capital." Available at SSRN 3394617.

Agrawal, D. R., W. H. Hoyt, and J. D. Wilson. 2022. "Local Policy Choice: Theory and Empirics." *Journal of Economic Literature* 60: 1378–455.

Baskaran, T. 2014. "Identifying Local Tax Mimicking with Administrative Borders and a Policy Reform." *Journal of Public Economics* 118: 41–51.

Besley, T., and A. Case. 1995. "Incumbent Behavior: Vote-Seeking, Tax-Setting, and Yardstick Competition." *The American Economic Review* 85 (1): 25–45.

Brueckner, J. K. 2003. "Strategic Interaction among Governments: An Overview of Empirical Studies." *International Regional Science Review* 26: 175–88.

Brueckner, J. K., and L. A. Saavedra. 2001. "Do Local Governments Engage in Strategic Property-Tax Competition?" *National Tax Journal* 54: 203–29.

Bucovetsky, S., and M. Smart. 2006. "The Efficiency Consequences of Local Revenue Equalization: Tax Competition and Tax Distortions." *Journal of Public Economic Theory* 8: 119–44.

Buettner, T., and M. Poehnlein. 2021. "Tax Competition Effects of a Minimum Tax Rate: Empirical Evidence from German Municipalities." Available at SSRN 4081854.

Cabral, M., and C. Hoxby. 2012. *The Hated Property Tax: Salience, Tax Rates, and Tax Revolts*. Technical report, National Bureau of Economic Research.
Case, A. C., H. S. Rosen, and J. R. Hines Jr. 1993. "Budget Spillovers and Fiscal Policy Interdependence: Evidence from the States." *Journal of Public Economics* 52: 285–307.
Egger, P., M. Koethenbuerger, and M. Smart. 2010. "Do Fiscal Transfers Alleviate Business Tax Competition? Evidence from Germany." *Journal of Public Economics* 94: 235–46.
Eugster, B., and R. Parchet. 2019. "Culture and Taxes." *Journal of Political Economy* 127: 296–337.
Gibbons, S., and H. G. Overman. 2012. "Mostly Pointless Spatial Econometrics?" *Journal of Regional Science* 52: 172–91.
Hoyt, W. H. 1991. "Property Taxation, Nash Equilibrium, and Market Power." *Journal of Urban Economics* 30: 123–31.
Isen, A. 2014. "Do Local Government Fiscal Spillovers Exist? Evidence from Counties, Municipalities, and School Districts." *Journal of Public Economics* 110: 57–73.
Keen, M., and K. A. Konrad. 2013. "The Theory of International Tax Competition and Coordination." *Handbook of Public Economics* 5: 257–328.
Köthenbürger, M. 2002. "Tax Competition and Fiscal Equalization." *International Tax and Public Finance* 9: 391–408.
Kotsogiannis, C. 2010. "Federal Tax Competition and the Efficiency Consequences for Local Taxation of Revenue Equalization." *International Tax and Public Finance* 17: 1–14.
Lyytikäinen, T. 2009. "Three-Rate Property Taxation and Housing Construction." *Journal of Urban Economics* 65: 305–13.
Lyytikäinen, T. 2012. "Tax Competition among Local Governments: Evidence from a Property Tax Reform in Finland." *Journal of Public Economics* 96: 584–95.
Mast, E. 2020. "Race to the Bottom? Local Tax Break Competition and Business Location." *American Economic Journal: Applied Economics* 12: 288–317.
Matsumoto, M. 2022. "Tax Competition and Tax Base Equalization in the Presence of Multiple Tax Instruments." *International Tax and Public Finance* 29: 1213–226.
Parchet, R. 2019. "Are Local Tax Rates Strategic Complements or Strategic Substitutes?" *American Economic Journal: Economic Policy* 11: 189–224.
Saarimaa, T., and J. Tukiainen. 2015. "Common Pool Problems in Voluntary Municipal Mergers." *European Journal of Political Economy* 38: 140–52.
Wildasin, D. E. 1988. "Nash Equilibria in Models of Fiscal Competition." *Journal of Public Economics* 35: 229–40.
Zodrow, G. R., and P. Mieszkowski. 1986. "Pigou, Tiebout, Property Taxation, and the Underprovision of Local Public Goods." *Journal of Urban Economics* 19: 356–70.

## **Comment** Leah Brooks

Before launching into bigger-picture thoughts about how Teemu Lyytikäinen's work can help us consider the open important questions on tax competition, let me take a moment to describe the strengths of his chapter.

Leah Brooks is a professor in the Trachtenberg School of Public Policy and Public Administration at George Washington University.

Lyytikäinen's manuscript asks us to engage with the consequences of forcing low property tax rate municipalities to increase those low rates. We are interested in the consequences of this policy change for both for the targeted municipalities and for municipalities neighboring targeted ones. We learn that Finnish municipalities do what they are told: when instructed to increase tax rates, municipalities do so. Predictably, this leads to an increase in local property tax revenues. Sadly, the data are not sufficiently powerful to explain what happens to total local revenues. Such an analysis would help us understand whether this policy generates a net increase in local revenues, or instead a shift from one base to another.

Of particular interest to this volume, Lyytikäinen explores what happens to tax rates and revenues in municipalities neighboring those municipalities forced to increase rates. The bottom line is "not much." Neighboring municipalities show no substantive change in their tax rates or revenue collection in response to neighbors' forced tax rate increases.

There is a lot to enjoy in this chapter. For a US audience, the context and politics are radically different from our institutional setting. In the US, it is very rare for any government to mandate minimum tax rates from one level to another, so the mere existence of such a policy is quite novel. While tax rate maximums, such as the maximum local option sales tax—the maximum sales tax a state allows a local jurisdiction to levy—are common, minimums are few and far between (Burge and Piper 2012; Burge and Rogers 2018). Further, while the US has piecemeal policies, such as school finance equalization schemes, that may substitute for the role of equalization in Finland, we have no direct equalization between levels of government in the way that the Finnish government does.

Beyond this context, the chapter gives a wealth of critical institutional details that help us understand why actors behave as they do or fail to change behavior much at all. We learn that the property tax is a very small—though growing—share of revenues for Finnish municipalities. We also learn that the government has other tools to mitigate competition among municipalities. One such tool, prevalent over the period Lyytikäinen studies, are "encouraged" municipal mergers. Unlike the tax increases, these mergers are not mandated. Instead, the government tries to make an offer the municipalities can't refuse. This is more than a nudge, but less than a mandate. Municipal mergers internalize the competitive pressures that Lyytikäinen studies via tax rate competition.

And we also learn through Lyytikäinen's close reading of the lawmaking process that the increases in property tax rate minimums were likely driven by vertical tax competition, rather than fears of horizontal tax competition. Indeed, the national government feared that municipalities were gobbling up too much of the income tax and hoped that pushing them to collect more property tax would lessen these municipalities' dependence on the shared base of the income tax.

Finally, Lyytikäinen makes the very salient point that any shifts in the tax base potentially caused by these tax policy changes should be very slow. We look forward to Lyytikäinen's update in another decade on the impacts of raising the tax rate floor in 2000, the largest of all the policy changes, on the property tax base.

Lyytikäinen's study gives a generous launching pad to consider multiple big issues in tax competition: who we compete with, which jurisdictions force the competition, and when such a minimum tax rate policy can succeed. The chapter, like virtually all work in this literature, looks locally for tax competitors. It is easy to believe that municipalities compete with their geographic neighbors. Tiebout (1956) tells us that, within a metropolitan area, mobile households should drive policy packages of taxes and services. Local comparisons may also be particularly salient for voters.

But it is hard to believe that tax competition is limited to geographic neighbors, particularly for larger municipalities. For example, Wikipedia tells me that Finland's capital of Helsinki, population 657,674, sits next to three municipalities: Espoo, population 292,913, Vantaa, population 237,231 and Sipoo, population 21,693. Will those in Helsinki really bother to react to what citizens of tiny Sipoo do? I would hazard that those in Helsinki are at least as bothered about what happens in the other Nordic capitals of Stockholm, Copenhagen, and Oslo as they are about the behavior of Sipoo.

When I suggested at the conference for this volume that the spatial margin for tax competition was just one of many relevant margins, Jim Hines said that this was surely true but that there is no theory to guide us on other dimensions of competition. So let this be a call to arms—or at least to the keyboard! Other margins along which municipalities could compete include the income of residents, the size of the municipality, or the extent or type of specialty industries. In countries where equalization is valuable and salient, we may also see competition for jurisdictions near an equalization cut-off.

Where might such nongeographic competition be most fierce? My guess is that as an empirical matter it might be most obvious when jurisdictions compete for specialized industries. For example, consider the economic literature about film tax credits (Sewordor and Sjoquist 2016; Workman 2021). This seems like an area particularly well suited to analyze nongeographic tax competition. When the city of Atlanta offers tax breaks for film shoots, it is not competing with the suburb of Decatur: it is competing with Los Angeles and Vancouver and Toronto. This type of clearly defined competition, in conjunction with a well-posed theory, could let empiricists test which types of competition hold the most sway and under what circumstances.

In part to understand what the key dimensions of competition are, and in part to better understand how policies that seek to limit tax competition will be received, it is also useful to understand which jurisdictions set the agenda in the tax competition space. In Lyytikäinen's framework, these potential chief competitors would be the tax laggards. In the international case, tax competition is also usually driven by jurisdictions with low rates or by those with very permissive tax administration.

In a domestic context, it may not be so easy to clearly guess the characteristics of tax laggards—casting no aspersions on the state of Delaware, which makes its hospitality to incorporation crystal clear. Lyytikäinen helpfully tells us (see table 9.3) that in Finland, the government forces almost three-quarters of municipalities to raise residential property tax rates during one of the four reforms. Furthermore, roughly one-third of municipalities are repeat offenders, ordered by the government to increase rates in more than one rate-raising episode. However, only about half of municipalities end up in the government's crosshairs for the general property tax, and an even lower one in eight municipalities are general property tax repeat offenders. Why is this? And who are these laggards? Are they small? Do they specialize in some way?

Most broadly, if we believe that government funds can sometimes be used to improve people's lives, we are very interested in how they can be collected at the lowest possible cost. When governments collect tax revenues from the same base, they face a classic problem of collective action akin to fishermen foraging out of a common pool with a finite stock of fish. While total welfare increases when the fisherman limit fishing, each individual fisherman has a strong incentive to fish more than his allotted amount while the others observe the rules. Like the fisherman, tax collectors from different levels of government (or different countries) face a strong incentive to fish more than is socially optimal. In the world of fishing, some institutional solutions have been successful in minimizing overfishing (Olson 1965; Ostrom 1990). These solutions require incentives, trust, and monitoring.

The binding minimum tax rates that Lyytikäinen studies are one institutional solution to the problem of overfishing tax revenues. The Finnish context offers municipalities few direct incentives for compliance, but perhaps does not need to. The Finnish national government is an all-present monitor, assessing property, collecting taxes, and sending revenues to local governments.

Should we view Finland's system as a successful institutional arrangement limiting overfishing? And does it have implications for the more general problem of tax competition? As we look to the Organization of Economic Cooperation and Development's implementation of a binding minimum corporate tax rate, this is of central policy interest. Given the data's inability to establish evidence of tax competition before the Finnish policy, nor a competition response afterward, it is difficult to brand this policy as either a success or failure.

But if there is some success here, it gives us a launching pad to think about the context of when minimum tax rates succeed in stemming tax overfishing. The first obvious reason that minimum tax rates succeed here is that they are levied by a national government to a subnational government. Clearly, a national government has substantially more power over local governments than international organizations have over sovereigns.

But there are other possible reasons that a binding minimum may limit overfishing in Lyytikäinen's context. The tax at issue here—the property tax—has a relatively immobile base of durable capital. While capital can move—no one who has seen the long and continuing march of manufacturing around the world can doubt this—its movement is slow and costly. Additionally, Lyytikäinen points out that in his case, while property tax rates are both visible and salient, the level of services that a municipality offers with the tax revenues is less easily evaluated. Here, at least, this net impact yields little competition.

Finally, in the particular case here, Finland has an equalization scheme that may help compensate any losers from forced tax rate increases. This form of national insurance should make enacting difficult policy requirements somewhat easier. Is there any international analogue for this kind of "hold (a little bit) harmless" provision? Who would provide it? When might it be politically feasible?

Looking forward, economists should feel certain that problems of tax competition will remain fertile ground for decades to come. Many critical margins for competition beckon the research community, and the efficient tax collection it helps generate should yield benefits for all.

For acknowledgments, sources of research support, and disclosure of the author's material financial relationships, if any, please see https://www.nber.org/books-and-chapters/policy-responses-tax-competition/comment-minimum-tax-rates-and-tax-competition-evidence-property-tax-limits-finland-brooks.

## References

Burge, Gregory S., and Brian Piper. 2012. "Strategic Fiscal Interdependence: County and Municipal Adoptions of Local Option Sales Taxes." *National Tax Journal* 65 (2): 387–415.

Burge, Gregory S., and Cynthia L. Rogers. 2018. "Do State Sales Taxes Crowd Out Local Option Sales Taxes?" *B.E. Journal of Economic Analysis and Policy* 18 (3): 1–9.

Olson, Mancur, 1965. *The Logic of Collective Action: Public Goods and the Theory of Groups*. Harvard University Press.

Ostrom, Elinor, 1990. *Governing the Commons: The Evolution of Institutions for Collective Action*. Cambridge University Press.

Sewordor, Emefa, and David L. Sjoquist. 2016. "Lights, Camera, Action: The Adoption of State Film Tax Credits." *Public Budgeting and Finance* 36 (2): 5–25.

Tiebout, Charles M. 1956. "A Pure Theory of Local Expenditures." *Journal of Political Economy* 64 (5): 416–24.

Workman, Alec, 2021. "Ready for a Close-Up: The Effect of Tax Incentives on Film Production in California." *Economic Development Quarterly* 35 (2): 125–40.

10

# Competition, Harmonization, and Redistribution
## Corporate Taxes in Switzerland

Marius Brülhart, Marko Köthenbürger, Matthias Krapf, Raphaël Parchet, Kurt Schmidheiny, and David Staubli

### 10.1 Introduction

Taxable profits are ever more mobile. There is broad-based international agreement, therefore, that corporate taxation requires a degree of supranational coordination. Profit sheltering in low- or zero-tax jurisdictions has been recognized at least since the launch of the OECD's Base Erosion and Profit Shifting (BEPS) initiative in 2013 as a harmful practice for all nations bar a few tax havens. That practice has been estimated to deprive corporate host-country governments of more than US$200 billion in annual tax revenue (Beer et al. 2020; OECD 2017). According to Tørsløv et al. (2023), eliminating purely tax-motivated profit shifting would increase the corporate tax base by up to 20 percent in the European Union, 10 percent in the United States, and 5 percent in developing countries. In contrast, the corporate tax base of tax havens would contract by 55 percent.[1] Even if unchecked tax competition implies efficiency losses overall, coordination inevitably creates

Marius Brülhart is a professor of economics at HEC Lausanne, University of Lausanne.
Marko Köthenbürger is a professor of economics in the Department of Management, Technology, and Economics at ETH Zürich.
Matthias Krapf is an economist at the Swiss Federal Tax Administration.
Raphaël Parchet is a professor of economics at the Institute for Economic Research and the Institute of Economics at the Università della Svizzera italiana.
Kurt Schmidheiny is professor of economics and applied econometrics at the University of Basel.
David Staubli is an economist at the Swiss Federal Tax Administration.

1. These are inevitably rough estimates, and they abstract from indirect fiscal effects and behavioral responses. For instance, firms in high-tax countries could convert some of their tax savings on shifted profits into higher wages, dividends or R&D expenditure, which in turn would have positive fiscal effects (see e.g., Fuest and Neumeier 2023; Hines 2010; Hines and Rice 1994).

losers as well as winners and therefore implies challenging institutional and political tradeoffs.

Policy coordination in this area boils down to four essential dimensions: (1) harmonization of tax bases, (2) jurisdictional apportionment of tax bases, (3) harmonization of tax rates, and (4) redistribution of tax revenue. The OECD BEPS negotiations have so far involved dimensions (1) to (3). Proposals also exist for cross-country revenue sharing (dimension 4), e.g., among member states of the European Union (European Parliament 2021).

As a federal country that had started out as a loose confederation of cantons and became integrated, gradually and democratically, Switzerland could be considered as something of a model for international coordination. Corporate taxation is a case in point. As this chapter aims to document, many of the issues that are currently being negotiated at the international level have been disputed within Switzerland as well, and most have been settled within stable and widely supported institutional structures and informal arrangements.

In this chapter, we thus seek to provide an overview of corporate taxation in Switzerland, organized around the four essential dimensions of policy coordination. We describe and discuss current institutional arrangements and the scientific public-finance literature that exists on them. We moreover trace the emergence of those arrangements and the political and economic forces that helped them into being. In a concluding discussion, we tentatively draw parallels with ongoing supranational coordination efforts.

The chapter is divided into four main sections. Section 10.2 provides a cross-canton and historical overview of the corporate tax base, tax rates, and tax revenue, based on newly collected data series reaching back as far as 1949. In section 10.3, we discuss various pieces of evidence of corporate tax-base mobility and tax competition among cantons. In section 10.4, we describe the historical emergence of codified tax base definitions, a central plank of corporate tax coordination across fiscally autonomous cantons. Section 10.5 describes and discusses fiscal equalization, the main instrument designed to mitigate potential inequalities arising from decentralized tax setting. A concluding discussion is provided in section 10.6.

## 10.2 Corporate Taxation in Switzerland: Key Figures

### 10.2.1 Swiss Fiscal Federalism: Three Layers of Government

Switzerland has three main layers of government, each with its own legislative and executive branch: the Confederation (henceforth "federal government"), 26 cantons and, as of 2025, 2,121 municipalities. Cantons are the member states of the Swiss Confederation, similar to states in the United States or provinces in Canada. All three jurisdictional layers raise taxes on corporate profits.

The cantons were historically—and by some measures have remained—the most important layer of government in matters of taxation: they are administratively in charge of collecting income taxes for the three jurisdictional layers, and they continue to raise the largest share of taxes on personal income, the main tax base.

In terms of corporate taxation, however, the federal government has a more prominent role. It formally raises half of consolidated revenue, with the cantons raising about a third and the municipalities less than a fifth. As the federal government rebates around a fifth of its receipts directly to the cantons, total revenue from the corporate tax base is effectively split roughly evenly between the federal and canton layers, each absorbing around 40 percent.[2] This is a relatively recent state of affairs. From the introduction of federal-level corporate taxation in 1916 up until the mid-1990s, the cantons' corporate tax revenue had exceeded that of the federal government. Cuts in canton-level tax rates have been associated with a steady erosion of cantonal corporate tax revenue relative to that of the federal government (see section 10.2.3).

The legal framework is quite particular as well. According to the federal constitution, the cantons are sovereign to the extent that their sovereignty is not explicitly limited by that same constitution. This means that the cantons may levy any tax they wish, as long as it is in accordance with constitutional principles. Without a constitutional basis, the federal legislator may not enact any law that restricts cantons' tax policies. The cantons have levied corporate taxes since the middle of the 19th century. Federal taxing rights were given a constitutional underpinning only in 1959. To this day, the federal government's constitutional right to raising its own taxes on corporate and personal income is subject to a sunset clause. That right was last confirmed in a nationwide referendum in 2017 and will expire again in 2035.

Municipalities' right to tax profits originates in the cantonal constitutions. Their ability to set tax rates and schedules is severely circumscribed by cantonal law. They typically are allowed to raise a top-up tax on the cantonal rates by applying a multiplier on the cantonal rate schedule.

### 10.2.2 The Corporate Tax Base

Taxable profits and capital are distributed very unevenly across the cantons, and this distribution has changed considerably over time.[3]

In figure 10.1, we show the evolution of taxable profits since 1949 (black dashed and solid lines). A trend break is evident around the mid-1990s: profits, measured in constant prices, increased strongly between 1949 and the early 1970s, then stopped growing until the mid 1990s, to more than

2. The remaining 20 percent are absorbed by the municipalities. Until 2019, the share of federal tax receipts returned to the cantons was 17 percent. That share was increased in 2020 to the current 21.2 percent.

3. On the legal definition of the corporate tax base and its gradual harmonization, see section 10.4.

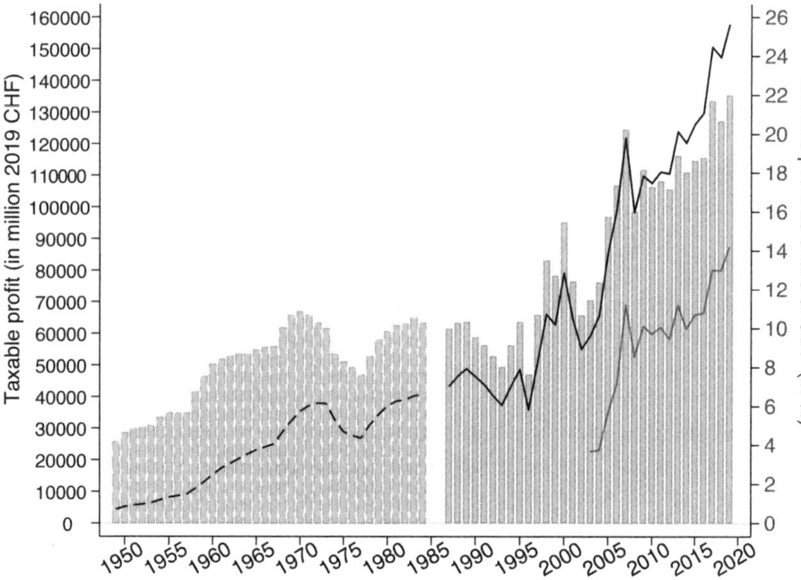


**Fig. 10.1 The evolution of total taxable profit in Switzerland**

Notes: The figure shows the evolution of nationwide taxable profits in CHF million at constant 2019 prices (black dashed and solid lines, left scale for total profits; gray solid line, left scale for profits reported by firms subject to privileged taxation), and the evolution of the nationwide taxable profits in % of GDP (bars, right scale). The data prior to 1987 do not correct taxable profits for deductions due to the firms' shareholdings in other firms, which could imply some upward bias due to double counting. Data for 1985 is missing. Source: Own calculation based on Federal Tax Administration (2022a).

quadruple since.[4] In 2019, 426,174 firms reported a total of CHF 158 billion of taxable profits (one CHF was worth around one USD in 2019). This corresponds to some CHF 18,300 per capita, or 22 percent of GDP—up from 10 percent of GDP in 1990 (gray bars in figure 10.1).

The main driver behind the recent growth in the corporate tax base were profits reported by tax-privileged "status" firms, whose profits are mainly foreign sourced (gray line in figure 10.1): those taxable profits increased by fully 271 percent between 2003 and 2018. Status firms were exempt from canton and municipal corporate taxes on income earned abroad. In contrast,

4. The growth acceleration of taxable profits after the mid-1990s roughly coincides with intensifying worldwide cross-border profit shifting in those years, documented by Wier and Zucman (2022). According to that study, the global rise in the share of shifted profits came to a halt in the 2000s. In Switzerland, however, taxable profits kept increasing strongly. Some of the disproportionate increase in tax-privileged declared profits may be due to internationally active firms switching from regular to privileged taxation. Cantons had a stronger incentive to treat firms as status firms after a reform of the fiscal equalization scheme in 2008 (see section 10.5 and A.4.3 for details).

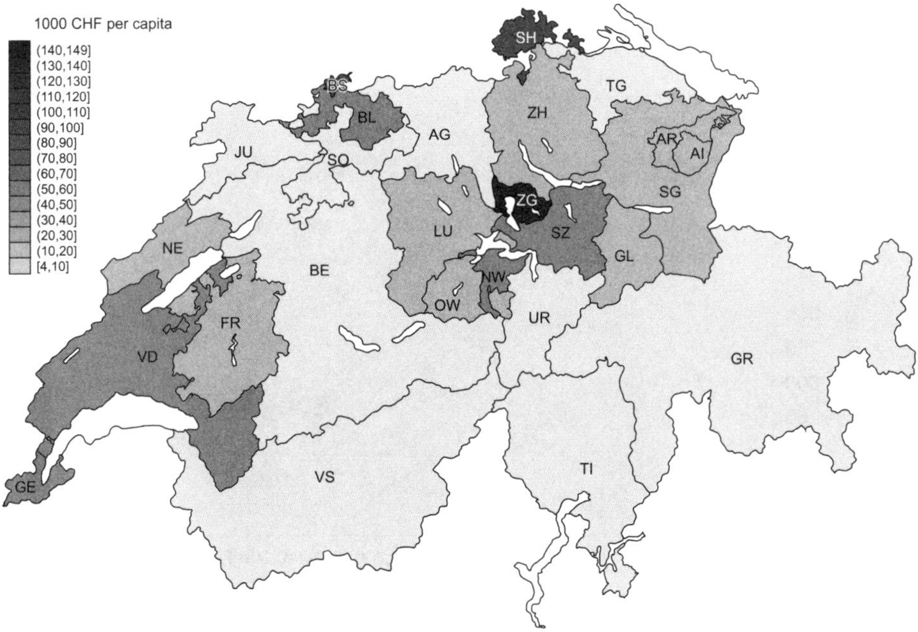


**Fig. 10.2 Taxable profits per capita, 2019**
Notes: Source: Own calculations based on Federal Tax Administration (2022a).

profits declared by domestically oriented firms subject to regular taxation rose by a comparatively modest 93 percent over the same time period.

Taxable profits have been highly concentrated among relatively few large firms throughout our sample period. In 2019, the top 1 percent of firms in terms of profits, reporting CHF 32 million per firm on average, accounted for 85 percent of total taxable profits—up from 68 percent in the early 1970s (see Appendix figure 10A.1). At the other end of the spectrum, 55 percent of registered firms reported zero taxable profits.[5]

Corporate profits are strongly concentrated also in the spatial dimension. Figure 10.2 maps 2019 per capita taxable profits by canton. Profits range from some CHF 4,000 per inhabitant in the mountainous canton of Valais (VS, population 353,000 in 2021) to CHF 149,000 in the small, semiurban, and centrally located canton of Zug (ZG, population 130,000 in 2021). Tax-

5. This analysis defines firms as tax units. These are individual legal entities, some of which are part of corporate groups (Federal Tax Administration 2022a). Profits of parent firms that stem from subsidiaries in Switzerland or abroad and were already subject to a corporate income tax are not taxed again at the parent level, and have thus been subtracted in the data since 1986 to avoid double counting. This is why we show a break in the series in that year for both figure 10.1 and Appendix figure 10A.1.

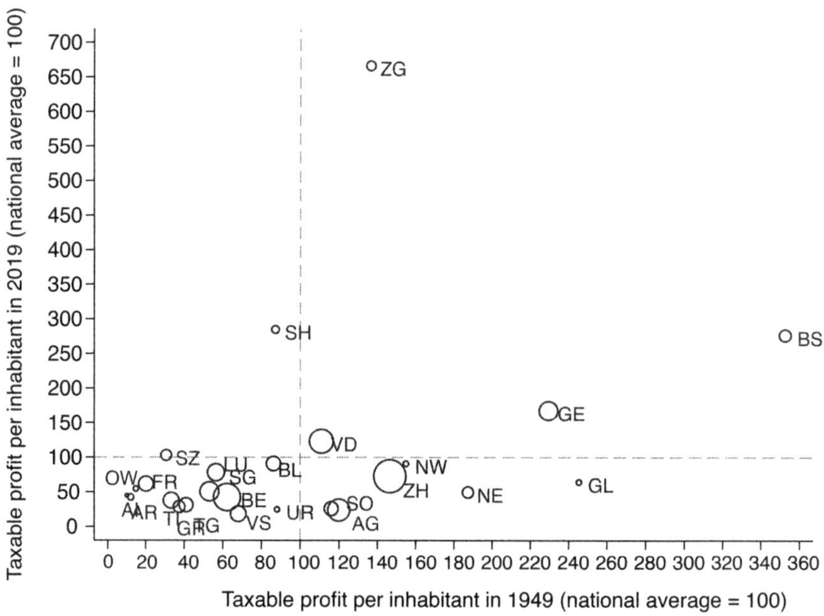


**Fig. 10.3 Taxable profits per capita, 1949 and 2019**

Notes: The figure shows per capita taxable profits in the Swiss cantons for 1949 (x-axis) and 2019 (y-axis). Variable scales are percentage deviations from the national average in the given year. The dotted lines denotes the respective national averages. Circle sizes are proportional to the 2019 canton population. Taxable profits in 1949 are not corrected for deductions due to the firms' shareholdings in other firms. Source: Own calculations based on Federal Tax Administration (1971) and Federal Tax Administration (2022a).

able profits thus differ by a factor of 37 between the least well endowed and the best endowed canton.

The geography of corporate profits and of corporate taxation has changed substantially over time. Figure 10.3 presents per capita taxable profits by canton in 1949 and 2019. Looking at the spatial distribution of profits in 1949 ($x$-axis), it appears that Switzerland emerged from World War II with relatively modest spatial disparities. Basel-Stadt (BS), home to a strong pharmaceutical cluster, had per capita taxable profits 3.5 times above the national average, while Geneva's (GE) per capita profits were 2.3 times above the average. In total, 10 of the then 25 cantons were host to above-average taxable profits, scaled to population. That spatial distribution changed dramatically over subsequent decades. Zug (ZG), whose per capita corporate tax base had been close to the national average in 1949, was host to per capita profits 6.6 times above the national average by 2019 ($y$-axis). Only six cantons had above-average per capita corporate profits in 2019. Were it not for the strong increase in Zug, the spatial dispersion of profits would now look rather similar to that observed 70 years ago. We explore the role of tax policy in the emergence of Zug as such an attractive location for firms and their taxable profits in section 10.3.3.

### 10.2.3 Corporate Tax Rates

Corporate profits are taxed by all three government layers, and corporate equity capital is taxed by cantons and municipalities.[6] The federal government has been raising a constant 7.8 percent on all taxable profits since 1998.[7]

Given the variety of corporate tax schedules across cantons and municipalities, we report consolidated effective statutory tax rates for a representative firm. By "consolidated" we refer to the sum of tax bills across the three layers of government. By "effective statutory" we mean the combined statutory tax amount of the profit and the capital tax, and we account for the fact that profit taxes are deductible from their own base.

#### *10.2.3.1 Regular Firms*

We first consider domestically oriented firms, subject to regular taxation already prior to the 2020 reform that abolished preferential taxation. They account for around half of the corporate tax base. In order to compare tax rates across cantons and over time, we take the definition used in available data: an imaginary firm with CHF 2 million of equity capital and profits of CHF 240,000. Such a firm is subject to the top corporate tax rate in most cantons.[8]

Figure 10.4 maps these tax rates across cantons in 2018, i.e., immediately prior to the recent reform and its associated tax cuts (see figure 10.5). Rates ranged from 12.7 percent in Nidwalden (NW) and 13.6 percent in Zug (ZG), to 25.6 percent in Basel-City (BS).[9] Switzerland is probably unique in the world for having such a large variance of corporate tax rates within such a small territory (1.5 times the area of Massachusetts).

In figure 10.5, we show the evolution of these corporate tax rates since 1949. Starting from a range of 19.4 percent to 36.4 percent in 1949, one can observe a general downward movement in tax rates, and a narrowing of tax differentials—consistent with predictions of tax competition models and

6. Federal-level taxation of corporate equity capital was abolished in 1998.

7. Strictly speaking, the commonly cited 7.8 percent federal profit tax rate is an upper-bound approximation of the true effective federal tax rate. The reason is that in Swiss corporate tax law, taxes are themselves deductible from the tax base. The headline federal tax rate is 8.5 percent. Considering that the tax payment itself can be deducted, and assuming away subfederal taxes, this implies an effective tax rate on pretax profit of 7.83 percent. When subfederal taxes are added, and themselves deducted from pretax profits, then the effective federal tax rate will fall below 7.83 percent. In what follows, we abstract from this subtlety and refer to the federal tax rate as amounting to 7.8 percent.

8. This is also the firm type for which the Swiss Federal Tax Administration provides tax rate data that is closest to the representative firm used by Krapf and Staubli (2025).

9. There is also variation within cantons across municipalities, but this variation is much smaller than the one across cantons shown here (see Krapf and Staubli 2025).

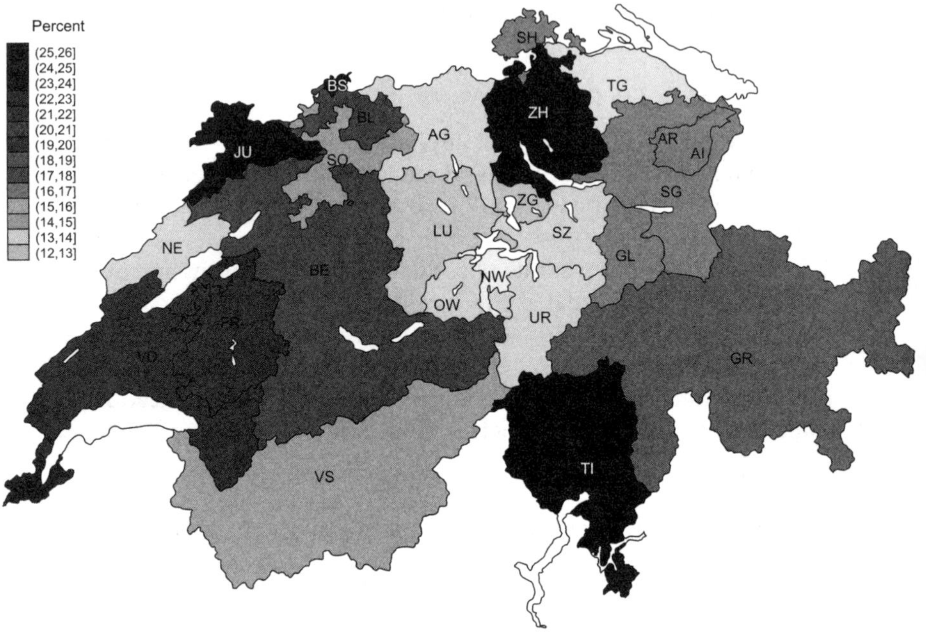


**Fig. 10.4 Consolidated effective statutory corporate tax rates on regular firms, 2018**

Notes: This figure shows the 2018 consolidated effective statutory corporate tax rate on regular firms in the cantonal capital municipalities. The rate is the consolidated (federal + cantonal + municipal) tax bill for a firm with CHF 2 million capital and CHF 240,000 profit, expressed as a share of that profit. Source: Tax rates from Federal Tax Administration (2018c).

with trends observed at the international level (e.g., Fuest and Neumeier 2023).

The long-run downward trend in corporate tax rates is even more starkly apparent in figure 10.6, where we track three different cross-canton averages. Irrespective of weighting, three main phases of corporate tax cutting emerge: the 1980s, the 2000s, and the most recent period since 2019. Average tax burdens weighted by population or by total profits have been above the unweighted average since 2000, suggesting that smaller cantons have cut corporate taxes particularly strongly in the last two decades—again consistent with models of (asymmetric) tax competition.

In figure 10.7, we illustrate the correlation between changes in tax rates and changes in tax bases, where causation may of course run both ways. Specifically, we show the long-run change in effective corporate tax rates on the two axes, and we draw the symbols proportional in size to the increase in cantons' per capita taxable profits over the same time period 1949–2018 (just before the most recent round of canton-level corporate tax reforms).

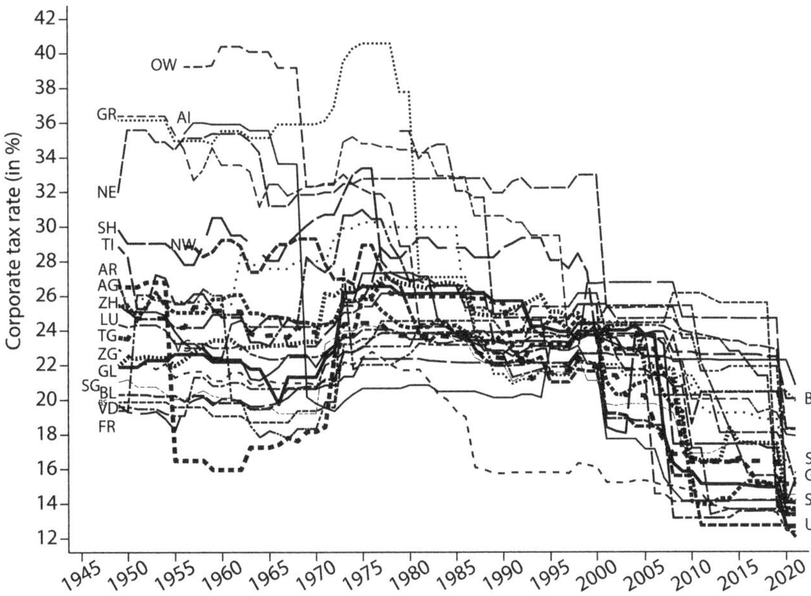


**Fig. 10.5 Effective statutory corporate tax rates on regular firms by canton, 1949–2021.**

Notes: The figure shows consolidated effective statutory corporate tax rates in the canton capital municipalities from 1949 to 2021 for a firm with CHF 2 million of equity capital and CHF 240,000 in domestically earned profits. Tax rates for the period 1949–1982 were reconstructed using the case of a firm with CHF 1 million of equity capital and CHF 100,000 in domestically earned profit, and linking it to the baseline representative case, for which data are available since 1983. The two series were linked by using the change in tax rates between 1982 and 1983 for the closest case for which the tax rates were available in both years (capital of CHF 100,000 and profit of CHF 20,000). Source: Tax rates from Federal Tax Administration (1949–2021).

Cantons with below-average corporate tax rates in 2018 turn out on average to have enjoyed somewhat larger increases in taxable profits, a pattern once again most starkly evident for the canton of Zug (ZG). This regularity, however, is not universal. The most notable difference is that the three cantons hosting the largest urban areas, Zurich (ZH), Geneva (GE), and Basel-Stadt (BS), have experienced above-average increases in their per capita corporate tax base despite having moved from the group of cantons with below-average corporate tax burdens in 1949 to the group of cantons with the highest corporate tax burdens in 2018.[10]

10. This observation is consistent with theory and evidence in economic geography, suggesting that urban agglomeration economies imply taxable rents (e.g., Brülhart et al. 2012). It is also consistent with the finding in Krapf and Staubli (2025) that the corporate tax base reacts less strongly to changing tax rates in urban centers than in more rural jurisdictions.

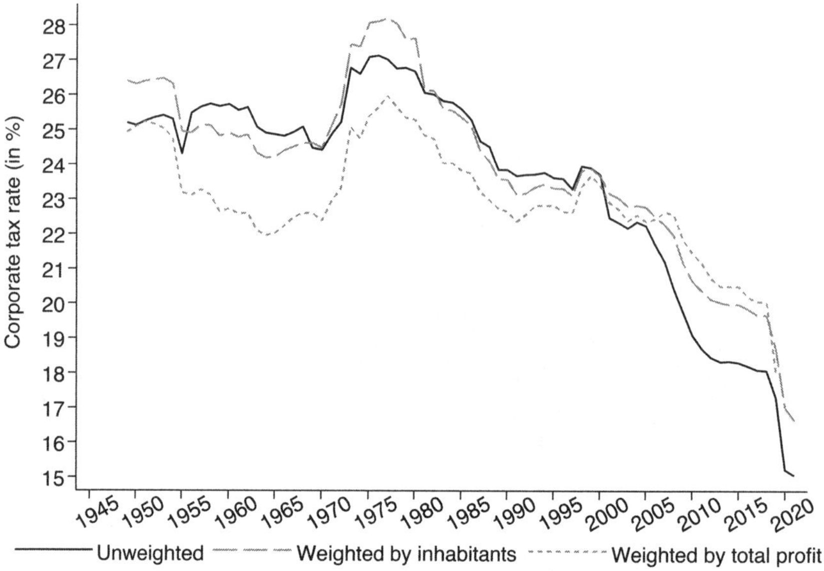


**Fig. 10.6 Averaged effective statutory corporate tax rates on regular firms, 1949–2021**

Notes: The figure shows three different averages of consolidated effective statutory profit tax rate across cantonal capital municipalities from 1949 to 2021, for a representative firm with CHF 2 million of equity capital and CHF 240,000 in domestically earned profits. Tax rates for the period 1949–1982 were reconstructed using the case of a firm with CHF 1 million of equity capital and CHF 100,000 in domestically earned profit, and linking to the baseline representative case, for which data are available since 1983. The two series were linked by using the change in tax rate between 1982 and 1983 for the closest case for which the tax rates were available in both years (capital of CHF 100,000 and profit of CHF 20,000). Source: Tax rates from Federal Tax Administration (1949–2021).

#### *10.2.3.2 Tax-Privileged Firms*

Up until the 2020 reform, an important lever of cantons' strategic tax policy had been special tax privileges granted to firms whose profits were earned mainly or solely abroad: so-called status firms. Those included pure holding and domiciliary firms and "mixed" firms, which report some domestically generated profits and a large share of foreign-sourced profits. Their taxable profits accounted for roughly the other half of the nationwide corporate tax base.

Pure holding firms were—and still are—not taxed by any government layer on the part of profits that they derive from their shareholdings in other firms, a common practice by international standards. More interesting is the case of the so-called domiciliary and mixed firms. Domiciliary firms were fiscally resident in a canton but did not carry out any business activities in Switzerland. Their foreign-sourced income was taxed normally by the federal government but largely exempt from cantonal and municipal cor-

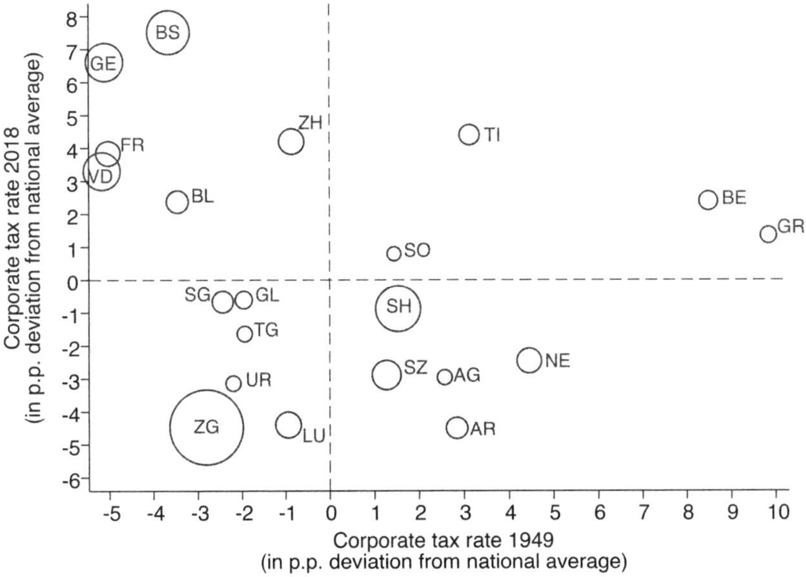


**Fig. 10.7 Consolidated effective statutory corporate tax rates on regular firms, 1949 and 2018**

Notes: The figure shows the statutory profit tax rate in the cantonal capital municipalities for 1949 and 2018. Tax rates in 1949 are for a firm with CHF 1 million of equity capital and CHF 100,000 in domestically earned profit. Tax rates for 2018 are for a firm with CHF 2 million of equity capital and CHF 240,000 in domestically earned profit. Tax rates are reported in percentage-point deviations from the national average in the respective year. The size of symbols is proportional to the increase in canton-level per capita taxable profit between 1949 and 2018. Note that tax rates in 1949 are missing in the official statistics for four cantons (AI, NW, OW, and VS), because these cantons hosted less than 5 percent of all corporations nationwide (Federal Tax Administration 1949, 63). Source: Tax rates from Federal Tax Administration (1949–2021); per capita taxable profits: own calculations based on Federal Tax Administration (1971) and Federal Tax Adminisration (2022a).

porate taxes.[11] "Mixed" firms were allowed to have some profit-generating business activity in Switzerland. For those firms, only the foreign-sourced part of consolidated profits could qualify for exemption from cantonal and municipal corporate taxes. At the federal level, profits of domiciliary and mixed firms were taxed at the standard rate. This has represented an effective backstop to the taxation of foreign-sourced profits at a rate of 7.8 percent (since 1998).

Tax privileges for domiciliary firms have a long history. According to van Orsouw (1995, 41), they first emerged in 1903, in the canton of Glarus (GL). The exact definition, e.g., whether domiciliary firms were allowed to

11. Domiciliary firms were, however, subject to taxes on equity capital, and the part of worldwide profits that was attributed to administrative activity in Switzerland was also subject to canton-level taxation. The tax rate on equity capital was lower than for firms subject to regular taxation.

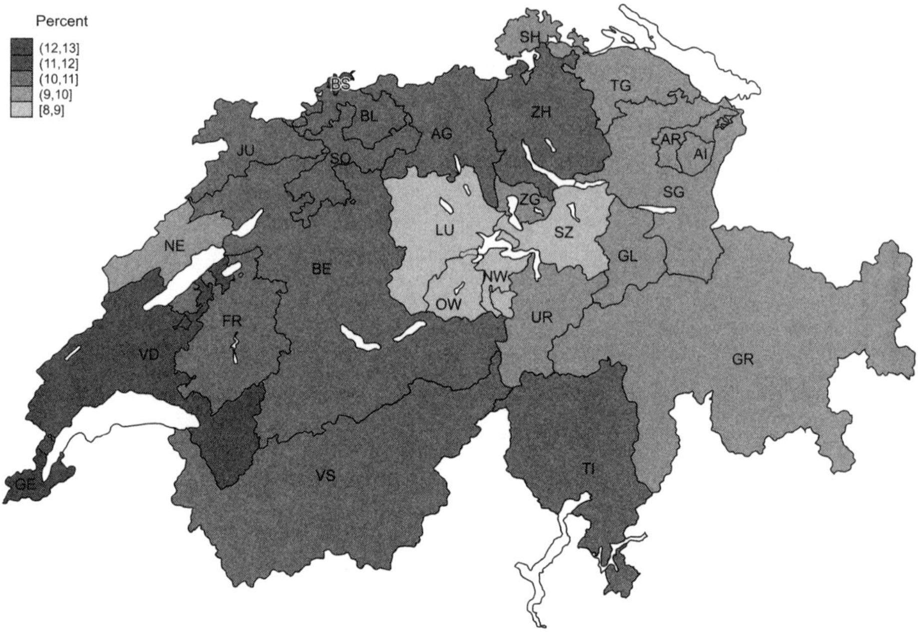


**Fig. 10.8 Consolidated effective corporate tax rate on privileged firms, 2016**

Notes: The figure maps the 2016 consolidated effective special corporate tax rate in the cantonal capital municipalities. The rate shown is the consolidated (federal + cantonal + municipal) rate for a "mixed" firm with CHF 10 million of equity capital, a 50% rate of return on equity, and 95% of foreign-sourced profits. Source: Federal Tax Administration (2018b).

have offices and employees, as well as the extent of tax privileges, differed from canton to canton.[12] These special tax regimes were harmonized in the 1990s (see section 10.4).

Figure 10.8 maps corporate tax burdens on a representative multinational firm in 2016, i.e., prior to the recent abolition of such privileges. The scale of the tax rates shown, ranging from 8.7 percent to 12.1 percent, makes it clear how attractive those privileges were, in both national and international comparison. Recall that regular rates were up to twice as high, ranging between 12.7 percent and 25.6 percent (figure 10.4). Differences across cantons in consolidated tax rates on multinational profits were considerably smaller than those in regular tax rates—which is partly a mechanical effect of the 7.8 percent federal tax rate that imposed a nationwide floor. Like the regu-

12. Appendix table 10A.3 provides a list of all rules governing taxation of holding and domiciliary firms in the Swiss cantons in 1947. The status of "mixed" firms appeared later, unofficially first in Zug (ZG), and then spread to other cantons through tax-base harmonization, see sections 10.3.3 and 10.4. All cantons bar Appenzell Innerrhoden (AI) and Uri (UR) have long granted special tax treatment to holding firms, either in the form of deductions in proportion to their shareholdings in other firms or by applying a special tax on equity capital.

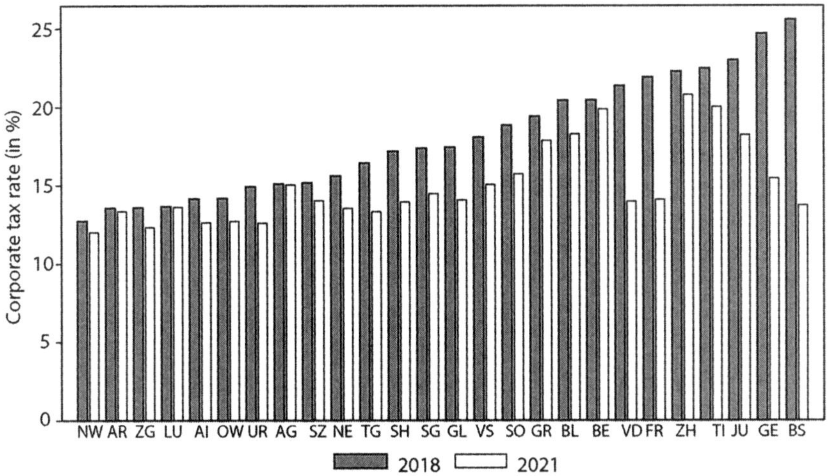


**Fig. 10.9 Consolidated effective statutory corporate tax rates on regular firms before and after the 2020 reform**

Notes: This figure shows the 2018 and the 2021 consolidated effective statutory corporate tax rate in the cantonal capital municipalities. The rate is the consolidated (federal + cantonal + municipal) tax bill for a firm with CHF 2 million of equity capital and CHF 240,000 of taxable profit, expressed as a share of that profit. Source: Tax rates from Federal Tax Administration (2021b, 2018c).

lar rates, low preferential rates were concentrated among mostly smallish cantons in central Switzerland, whereas the highest preferential rates were applied in the urban cantons of Geneva (GE) and Basel (BS).[13]

Tax privileges aimed at multinational profits conducive to cross-border shifting were abolished in 2020, following a nationwide referendum in 2019 (for details, see Appendix A.3). The impetus for this reform came from outside of Switzerland, through political pressure from the OECD and other supranational bodies. As a response, most cantons further lowered their regular corporate tax rates between 2019 and 2021 (figure 10.9), in line with the prediction of tax competition models (e.g., Keen 2001).[14]

13. Differences in privileged rates stemmed entirely from differences in regular rates (from which status firms were partly exempt). There were no legal differences in privileged tax regimes across cantons, but administrative practices could have varied.

14. In addition, new tax instruments were introduced that are internationally accepted while allowing to keep effective rates low on some particularly mobile segments of corporate income. The main instruments are patent boxes and additional deductions for R&D expenditure. See Appendix A.3. An interesting detail is that while the urban cantons of Geneva (GE) and Basel-Stadt (BS) reduced their regular rates strongly, Zurich (ZH), the largest urban canton, did not do so (see figure 10.9). This appears to be motivated by Zurich needing to maintain a high tax rate in order to be able to introduce an allowance for corporate equity (ACE) that favors its large financial services sector. Despite largely harmonized tax bases (see section 10.4), cantons' policy toolkit continues to contain instruments beyond the statutory tax rate, allowing them to optimize in different ways.

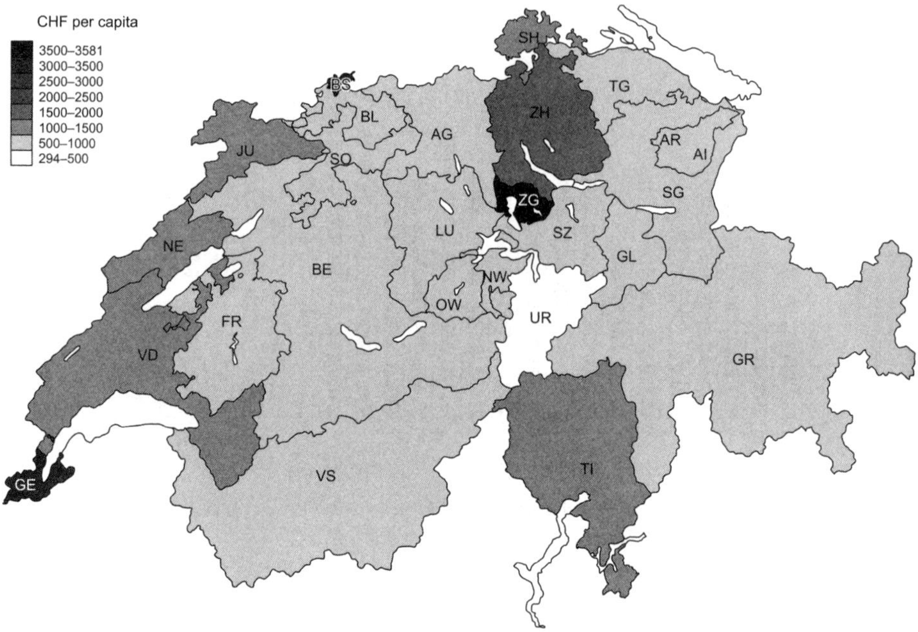


**Fig. 10.10 Sub-federal corporate tax revenue, 2020**

Notes: The map shows consolidated cantonal plus municipal revenue from profit and corporate equity capital taxation in 2020. Source: Federal Department of Finance (2023b).

### 10.2.4 Corporate Tax Revenue

We map the geography of per capita subfederal corporate tax revenues in figure 10.10. These revenues are the result of multiplying corporate tax bases (section 10.2.2) with the relevant corporate tax rates (section 10.2.3). The large intranational variance once more becomes apparent: per capita corporate tax revenues in the highest-revenue canton (Zug, ZG) exceed that of the lowest-revenue canton (Uri, UR) by a factor of 12. The geography of revenues does not, however, correlate particularly well with the geography of tax rates (figures 10.4 and 10.8). The historically relatively high-tax urban cantons of Basel-Stadt (BS), Geneva (GE) and Zurich (ZH) all collect above-average per capita corporate tax revenues—evidence again consistent with taxable urban agglomeration rents.

Revenue from corporate taxation has been steadily increasing in recent decades, both in per capita real terms (figure 10.11) and as a share of total tax revenue (figure 10.12). The revenue-share perspective of figure 10.12 is particularly interesting. It shows that, scaled by total tax revenues, the income from subfederal corporate taxation has overall been flat. Hence, the mechanical revenue loss from falling tax rates (figures 10.5 and 10.6) was roughly compensated by the expansion of the corporate tax base (figure 10.1).

A very different pattern emerges at the federal level. Despite an unchanged effective 7.8 percent corporate tax rate since 1998, federal per capita corpo-

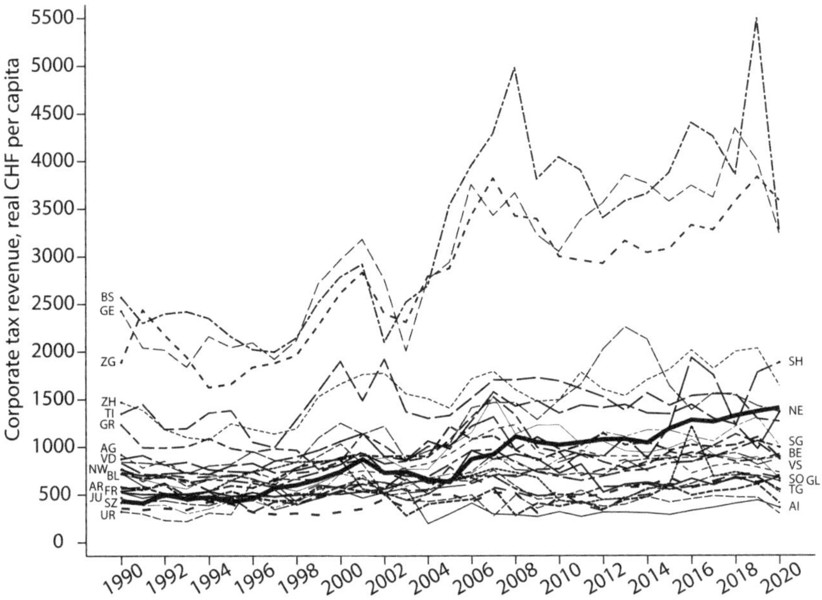


**Fig. 10.11 Corporate tax revenue per capita, 1990–2020**

Notes: The figure shows consolidated cantonal plus municipal revenue from corporate taxation in constant CHF per capita (2015 prices). The thick black line shows federal-level corporate tax revenue. Source: Swiss Federal Finance Administration (2023b).

rate tax revenue has more than doubled since then (increase of 140 percent, see the thick black line in figure 10.11). As a result, the share of corporate taxes in total federal tax revenue has almost doubled over the same period (increase of 87 percent, see the thick black line in figure 10.12). In purely fiscal terms, the main beneficiary of the expanding tax base, therefore, has been the federal government.

Federal-level corporate taxation has acted as a backstop to a race to the bottom in cantonal taxes. It did so mechanically, by raising the floor of the consolidated corporate tax rate, and perhaps also strategically, by lessening the incentives for additional canton-level tax cuts. Such an incentive effect can arise from the vertical externality in a federation with tax-base cohabitation by more than one government layer. In such a system, lower-level jurisdictions may not internalize tax-base effects on the federal government and therefore will not push down tax rates on mobile bases as far as in the absence of a federal government layer (Keen and Kotsogiannis 2002). According to that logic, the cantons would have lowered their corporate tax rates even more in a counterfactual scenario without a federal government.[15]

15. A more carefully specified empirical analysis of Swiss subfederal taxes suggests that the predictions of models with vertical tax externalities hold also in the Swiss context (Brülhart and Jametti 2006).

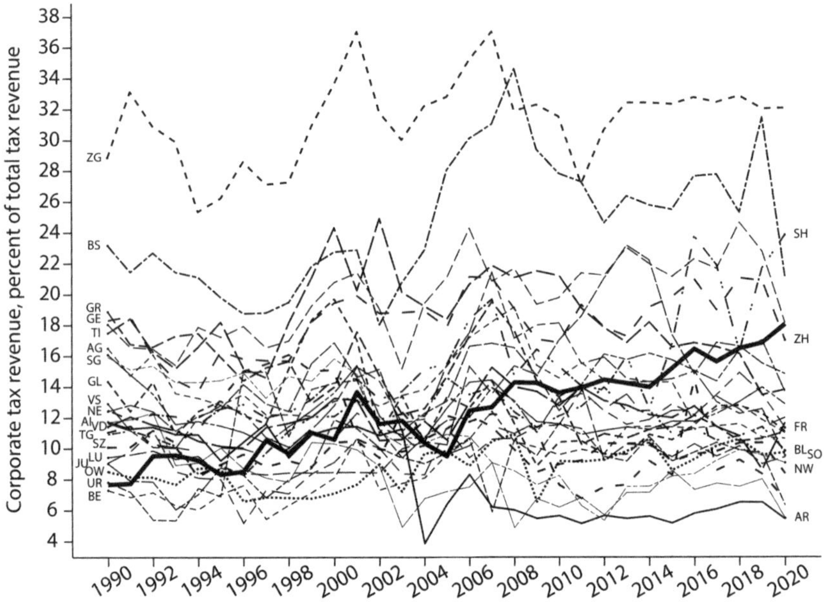


**Fig. 10.12 Corporate tax revenue as a share of total tax revenue, 1990–2020**

Notes: The figure shows consolidated cantonal plus municipal revenue from corporate taxation as a share of total tax revenue. The thick black line shows federal-level corporate tax revenue as a share of total federal tax revenue. Source: Swiss Federal Finance Administration (2023b).

## 10.3 Tax Competition Among the Cantons

Switzerland is often thought of as a sort of fiscal microcosm, especially with respect to tax policy choices by jurisdictions that compete for mobile tax bases. But is tax competition really a plausible driver of the fiscal landscape we observe in the Swiss cantons? After all, competition is not a directly observable mechanism. We therefore seek evidence on the importance of tax competition to cantons' policy choices.

Several patterns already documented in section 10.2 are consistent with corporate tax competition: (1) Cantons have gradually lowered their corporate tax rates, but the (much larger) federal government has not. (2) Smaller/rural cantons lowered their corporate tax rates more than larger/urban cantons. (3) Cross-canton differences in corporate tax rates have narrowed over time. (4) Cantons reacted to the abolition of privileged taxation of particularly mobile multinational profits in 2020 by cutting their regular corporate tax rates sharply.

Below, we provide three additional pieces of evidence on this issue: estimates of the elasticity of the corporate tax base, estimates of spatial tax reaction functions, and a case study of the fiscally particularly successful canton of Zug.

### 10.3.1 The Elasticity of Canton-Level Taxable Profits

The key parameter determining optimal corporate tax policy in a small open jurisdiction is the elasticity of taxable corporate income. Loosely speaking, the greater the elasticity and the more it is driven by mobility, the stronger are the pressures of tax competition.

Krapf and Staubli (2025) have estimated this elasticity using data for Swiss cantons and municipalities. They find the elasticity to be large in remote locations and essentially zero in cities. This finding is in line with previous research that found agglomeration economies to attenuate tax-base elasticities in Switzerland (Brülhart et al. 2012; Luthi and Schmidheiny 2014).[16]

In the following, we take a closer look at the experience of the canton of Lucerne, which cut its corporate tax rate by more than one-third in the early 2010s.[17] Figure 10.13 shows the evolution of corporate tax rates in Lucerne and in a group of comparison cantons used to form a "synthetic control group." Lucerne lowered its corporate tax rate by 7.6 percentage points between 2010 and 2012 (top panel of figure 10.13), which corresponds to an increase in the net-of-tax rate of 9.6 percent (bottom panel).[18]

Figure 10.14 shows that the reform was followed by a significant increase in taxable profits. Given the cumulative increase in the consolidated net-of-tax rate by 9.6 percent, the observed response by 2012 implies a net-of-tax-rate tax-base elasticity of around 5, or an elasticity with respect to the tax rate of −1.4. This is close to the break-even elasticity, estimated for Lucerne to have been around −1.5.[19] In other words, the corporate tax base may have grown sufficiently for the Lucerne corporate tax cut to have been revenue neutral—especially if revenue effects through other cantonal taxes, e.g., on personal income, were added to the calculation. This example shows that,

16. Estimating a distributed-lag model on a panel including the universe of Swiss municipalities, Krapf and Staubli (2025) find that an increase in a jurisdiction's corporate net-of-tax rate by 1 percent results in an increase in aggregate corporate taxable income of around 3.5 percent. This effect becomes small and insignificant if they weight by initial tax base, which is large in cities.

17. For details, see Krapf and Staubli (2025).

18. Lucerne's tax cut seems not to have been endogenous to (anticipated) changes in the corporate tax base. In the spirit of Romer and Romer (2010), Krapf and Staubli (2025) analyze the official information booklet provided to voting citizens by the Lucerne government prior to the referendum that sanctioned the proposed tax cuts. They find no evidence that the government reduced tax rates in response to prior increases in taxable profits or because they anticipated an increase in profits which enabled them to lower tax rates.

19. This estimate accounts for the floor imposed by the federal corporate tax rate, whereby a given percentage reduction in the cantonal tax rate results in a proportionally smaller reduction in the overall consolidated corporate tax rate. It also reflects the deductibility of taxes from the tax base, implying that a reduction in the cantonal tax rate increases the tax base for both cantonal and federal levels of government.

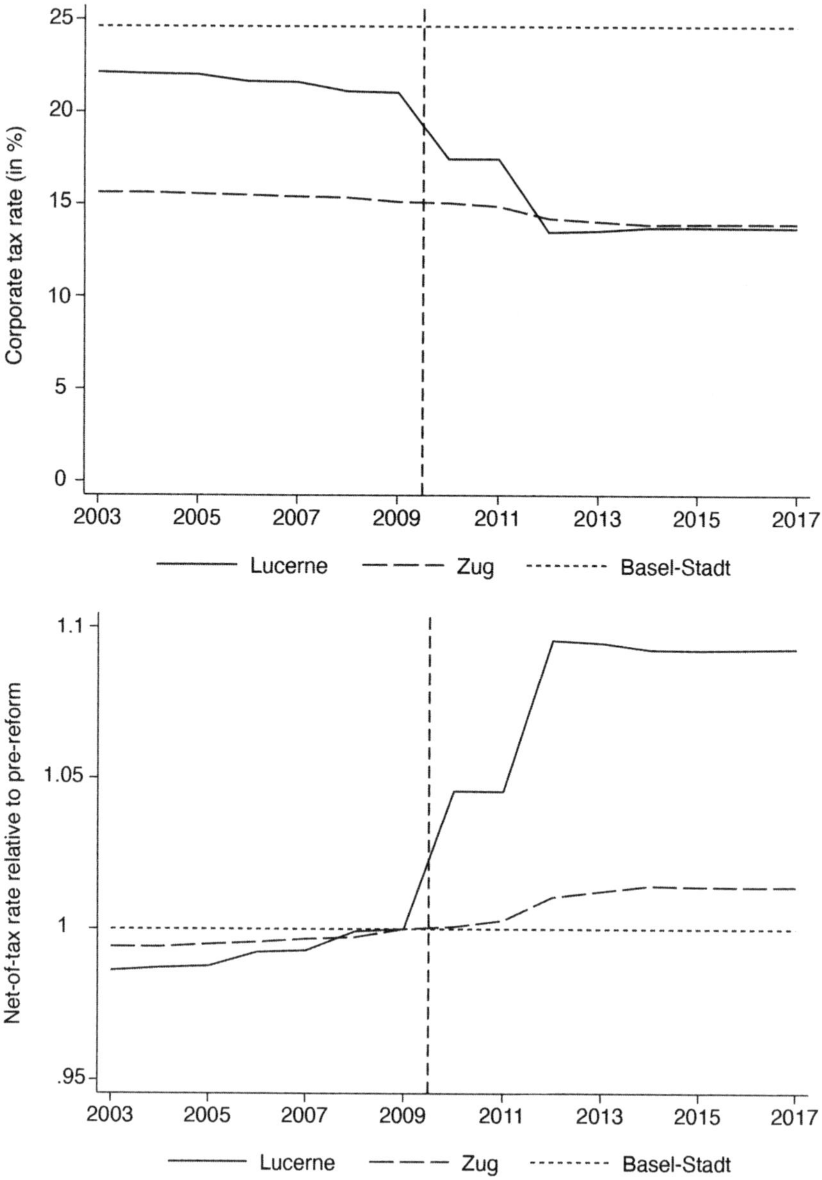


**Fig. 10.13 The treatment: Lucerne vs. comparison cantons**

Notes: The figures show evolutions of the consolidated (federal + cantonal + municipal) effective corporate tax rates (average across municipalities weighted by profits) and the corresponding net-of-tax rates in the treatment canton Lucerne and in the comparison cantons used to construct synthetic controls for the two experiments.

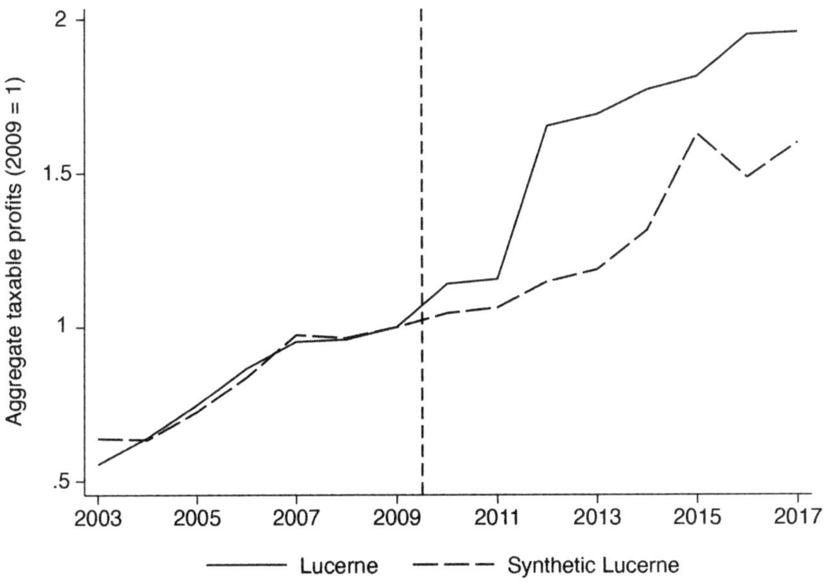


**Fig. 10.14 Treatment effects: Lucerne vs. comparison cantons**

Notes: The figure shows aggregate taxable profits in the treated canton Lucerne vs. the synthetic counterfactual relative to the pre-reform year 2009. "Synthetic Lucerne" consists of the cantons of Zug (75.4%) and Basel-Stadt (24.6%).

from the point of view of an individual canton, the corporate tax base can be highly elastic.

### 10.3.2 Tax Reaction Functions

Estimated spatial tax reaction functions can serve as another indirect indicator of competition over a mobile tax base (see e.g., Brueckner 2003). The idea is straightforward: if cantons' tax policy were indeed driven at least in part by competition over a mobile tax base, we would expect their close neighbors to respond more strongly than cantons located further away, because firms likely consider proximate cantons as closer locational substitutes than distant cantons (see e.g., Agrawal 2015).

Results for panel regressions of canton-level corporate tax rates on lagged neighbor-canton tax rates are shown in table 10.1. These estimates are based on a rather small dataset, and it is therefore not surprising that the estimates are somewhat imprecise, especially when we condition on time fixed effects and other controls. However, we note that all coefficients that pass statistical significance tests at conventional levels are positive. In other words, this evidence is consistent with neighbor-canton corporate tax rates being strategic complements. We also note that spatial correlations of tax rates on regular firms are more positive after 2008, i.e., subsequent to the introduction of

**Table 10.1** **Tax reaction functions across cantons, 2004–2011**

| | Regular firms | | | Tax-privileged firms | | |
|---|---|---|---|---|---|---|
| | [1] | [2] | [3] | [4] | [5] | [6] |
| Tax rate neighbor in $t-1$ | −0.327 | −0.139 | 0.118 | −0.056 | 0.304* | 0.341 |
| | (0.334) | (0.233) | (0.227) | (0.117) | (0.168) | (0.223) |
| Tax rate neighbor in $t-1$ x Post 2008 | 0.383*** | 0.241 | 0.023 | 0.268*** | −0.010 | −0.100 |
| | (0.132) | (0.158) | (0.188) | (0.096) | (0.059) | (0.091) |
| Canton fixed effects | yes | yes | yes | yes | yes | yes |
| Time fixed effects | yes | yes | yes | yes | yes | yes |
| Canton-specific trends | no | yes | yes | no | yes | yes |
| Controls | no | no | yes | no | no | yes |

Notes: Panel regression with $N = 208$ observations (26 cantons, 8 years). Dependent variable is the effective consolidated (federal + cantonal + municipal) profit tax rate for a firm with CHF 2 million equity capital and CHF 160,000 taxable profit and for a "mixed" firm with CHF 10 million equity capital, a 50% rate of return on equity, and 95% of foreign-sourced profits. The explanatory variable is the average profit tax of all adjacent cantons for the previous year. The interaction with a dummy variable for 2008 and thereafter stands for the introduction of a new fiscal equalization scheme. Controls are population in logs, real estate price index, crime rate, share of nonworking population, share of foreigners, share of underage population, and share of older population. Robust standard errors robust clustered at the canton level. R2 after partialing out canton effects. Significance levels: * $p < 0.10$, ** $p < 0.05$, *** $p < 0.01$. Source: Brülhart and Schmidheiny (2013).

a new nationwide fiscal equalization system (which we discuss in detail in section 10.5).

Distance-based spatial interaction functions rest on the assumption that neighboring jurisdictions are fiercer competitors than jurisdictions located far from each other. Therefore, they are informative about strategic interactions only to the extent that firms' locational preferences, conditional on local corporate tax rates, are distributed smoothly in space. In reality, however, those preferences may be highly irregular, with firms seeking to colocate in clusters (e.g., in financial services) or requiring certain exogenous locational amenities. The canton of Zug, which we analyze next, is a case in point.

### 10.3.3 The Interesting Case of the Canton of Zug

The small canton of Zug (population 130,000) is known within Switzerland for its low statutory tax rates (figure 10.7) and its exceptionally large per capita taxable profits (figure 10.8). How did Zug become this economically highly successful low-tax location? In figure 10.15, we track the evolution both of corporate tax rates and of per capita taxable profits over the last seven decades.[20]

20. These are new data series compiled from recently digitized archival documents kept by the Swiss Federal Tax Administration.

Zug emerged from World War II with per capita taxable profits close to the national average. Taxable profits then suddenly more than doubled in the late 1950s, and continued to increase until 1980, by which time they had reached a level equivalent to 10 times the national average. In a ranking of cantons by per capita taxable profits, Zug jumped from eighth in 1950 to first in 1959, a position it has held ever since (see also figure 10.2).

Could tax policy explain this evolution? Zug has indeed been cutting its corporate tax rate by about half since 1949 (dashed line in figure 10.15). As shown in section 10.2, Zug was not alone in cutting corporate taxes (see

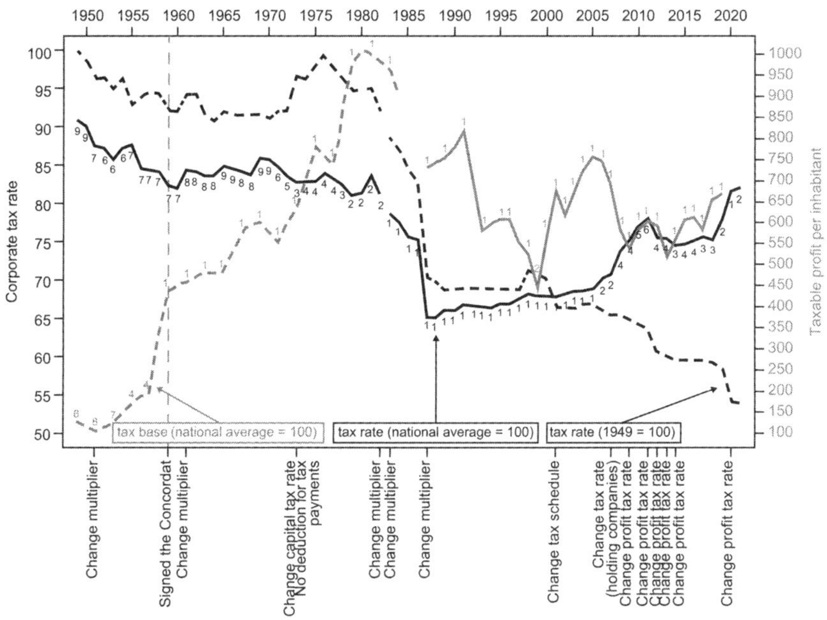


**Fig. 10.15 Tax reforms and per capita taxable profits in Zug, 1949–2021**

Notes: The figure shows the evolution between 1949 and 2021 of the consolidated effective statutory profit tax rate in the capital municipality of the canton of Zug (left scale, black solid line: in percent of national average; black dashed line: in percent of 1949 level), and of the per capita canton-level corporate taxable profit (right scale, solid gray line: with deduction for shareholdings in other firms; dashed gray line: without deduction for shareholdings in other firms). The tax rate for 1949–1982 corresponds to the statutory tax rate for a firm with CHF 2 million of equity capital and CHF 240,000 in profits. Tax rates for the period 1949–1982 were reconstructed using as baseline the case of a firm with CHF 1 million of capital and CHF 100,000 in profits, and combining it with the above-mentioned case available for the period 1983–2019. The two series have been combined by using the change in tax rate between 1982 and 1983 for the closest case for which the tax rates were available in both years (equity capital of CHF 100,000 and profit of CHF 20,000). Numbers next to lines refer to the rank among all cantons. The main changes to the corporate tax code are reported below the x-axis. Source: Tax rates from Federal Tax Administration (1949–2021). Per capita taxable profit: own calculations based on Federal Tax Administration (1971) and Federal Tax Administration (2022a).

figure 10.5). However, its tax-rate reductions were stronger than the average, moving it from the ninth-lowest tax rate in 1949 to the lowest in 1983 (solid black line in figure 10.15).

Interestingly, however, figure 10.15 shows that Zug's taxable profits soared before the main tax cuts were enacted. We observe dramatic increases in the corporate tax base in the late 1950s and throughout the 1970s, with a largely unchanged level since 1980 (in percent of the national average). Yet, Zug's corporate tax rate fell more strongly after 1980 than before—both in absolute terms and relative to the other 25 cantons. The main statutory tax cuts were enacted around 1985, at a time when growth of the corporate tax base had already peaked. It therefore appears that, at least in the sense of Granger causality, tax cuts were a consequence rather than a cause of soaring taxable profits.

An additional indication that low statutory corporate taxes were not the main determinant of Zug's success as a host for taxable profits can be found when considering the post-2000 period in figure 10.15. Because of corporate tax cuts in other cantons, Zug lost its status as the canton with the lowest corporate tax rate around 2005, and temporarily slid to 6th place. This notwithstanding, taxable profits booked in Zug do not seem to have shrunk, and Zug has maintained its position as the canton with the highest per capita profits.

What, then, were the causes for Zug's success in attracting profitable firms, considering that strategic cuts to statutory tax rates do not seem to be a plausible explanation? Was Zug lucky, perhaps by dint of its geography (close to Zurich), and was its fiscal policy more reactive than strategic? It turns out that the initial jump in taxable profits of the late 1950s occurred shortly before Zug signed a "concordat" of consenting cantons to rule out individual tax deals and to exchange information (see section 10.4.1 below). A possible explanation for the sudden increase in corporate profits could be favorable individual tax deals granted shortly before they became illegal. Another (complementary) explanation is the practice of privileging so-called mixed (domiciliary) firms. Cantons defined domiciliary firms very differently, but all of them would forbid any business activity within Switzerland. In the late 1950s, Zug was the first canton to allow domiciliary firms to have up to 20 percent of domestic turnover (van Orsouw 1995, 112).[21] Only a quarter of the income generated abroad by such firms was subject to tax, while the income generated in Switzerland was taxed in full. This practice arguably attracted many domiciliary firms to the

21. Van Orsouw (1995, 65–69) documents extensive lobbying by Zurich-based corporate lawyer Eugen Keller-Huguenin as early as the 1920s. Keller-Huguenin argued that it would be politically impossible to confer tax privileges to domiciliary and holding firms in a canton as large and socially divided as Zurich (van Orsouw 1995, 56). Zug, as a small canton within commuting distance of the city of Zurich and having an attractive lakeside location, seemed more suitable to him. van Orsouw (1995, 104) argues that a "service-oriented attitude of the cantonal tax administration," a favorable political environment, and the presence of specialized lawyers and trustees were other reasons for Zug's eventual success.

canton of Zug, thereby growing the tax base and allowing rates to be cut.[22] The neighboring canton of Schwyz subsequently also adopted this practice. In both cantons, however, there was no written documentation and no legal basis other than a generous application of the domicile privilege (van Orsouw 1995, 113). This practice was later codified and spread in all cantons through the formal harmonization of cantonal tax laws. We take a closer look at the history of (corporate) tax harmonization in Switzerland in section 10.4.

In sum, it would appear that the emergence of Zug as a low-tax magnet for corporate profits was driven less by deliberate and transparent forward-looking policy on statutory tax rates and more by less-visible changes to important details of tax-base delineation and tax administration. Which in turn implies that attempts at coordinating corporate taxation among fiscally autonomous jurisdictions need to focus not only on statutory rate schedules but also—and perhaps more so—on statutory and applied definitions of the corporate tax base. This is the issue to which we turn next.

## 10.4 The Long Road to Tax Base Harmonization

A central feature of the current Swiss system is "formal" tax harmonization among the cantons: despite cantonal sovereignty, largely consensual agreement has been found over time to constrain intranational tax competition to statutory tax rates as the sole policy instrument. Tax bases were harmonized in two main steps: a voluntary "Concordat" first signed by consenting cantons in 1949 to rule out individual tax deals and to exchange information, and a landmark federal law mandating common tax base definitions for all cantons since 1993 (the Federal Tax Harmonization Act, FTHA).

In this section, we briefly describe the content and genesis of those two harmonization agreements, and we seek to identify the economic and political forces that gave rise to them.

### 10.4.1 Voluntary Cooperation and Its Limitations: The "Concordat"

Following sporadic but unsuccessful initiatives going back several decades, a group of canton-level finance ministers decided in the late 1940s to take joint measures against the proliferation of special deals granted by cantonal tax authorities to individual taxpayers.[23] Tailored individual agreements had become common, especially in order to facilitate the establishment of

22. Newspaper reports confirm that the Zug government repeatedly justified statutory tax cuts with higher-than-expected tax revenue (*Die Tat* 1955; *Neue Zürcher Nachrichten* 1977).

23. A discussion about harmonizing canton-level taxes first arose after the federal government introduced its own taxes on income and wealth in 1916. In 1920, the tax law professor Ernst Blumenstein prominently called for the cantonal tax laws to be harmonized with the federal tax law (Blumenstein 1932/33, cited in Cavelti and Greminger 2010). The idea was not taken up by policymakers at the time. After World War II, in 1945, the Canton of Zurich submitted a cantonal initiative (*Standesinitiative*), which called for the federal government to address tax

new businesses in economically lagging regions and to lower the tax burden on businesses in which the public sector held significant stakes. Other less transparent deals also seemed to be offered. Such agreements came to be viewed as fanning increasingly fierce competition among cantons to attract lucrative taxpayers, and as complicating tax administration.

A subset of cantons agreed to act collectively: the Conference of Cantonal Finance Directors (CCFD) sought a solution by way of a voluntary agreement, named the "Concordat." Thirteen of the then 25 cantons agreed on the Concordat in 1948, which came into force after approval of the Federal Council in 1949 (Federal Tax Administration 2018a; *Neue Zürcher Zeitung* 1949). Most of the initial 13 signatory cantons were majority Protestant and German speaking, with the Catholic dominated and non-German-speaking cantons joining later. Cultural and political allegiances would therefore seem to have been the main drivers of self-selection into the agreement, dominating economic and fiscal interests.

The national debate about canton-level individual tax deals continued and culminated in a constitutional amendment that authorized the federal parliament to enact legislation against individual agreements with "unjustified tax advantages." This amendment was passed in a nationwide referendum in 1958. The federal government announced that it would not take any measures against signatories of the Concordat, which prompted all remaining cantons to join by 1960.

Through the Concordat, the cantons committed to abstaining from concluding tailored agreements with individual taxpayers. However, full or partial tax holidays lasting to up to 10 years were still permitted for newly opened industrial plants deemed to be of broader economic interest. The Concordat moreover instituted an early form of tax information exchange: origin and destination cantons of relocating households and firms committed to sharing their respective tax assessments upon request.

In the 1960s, expert opinion came to perceive a remaining need for greater harmonization. According to *Neue Zürcher Zeitung* (1969), the impetus did not come from voters or lobby groups but from experts and canton-level policymakers, who recognized the increasing complexity of administering 25 different tax laws when an increasing number of firms and individuals had taxable income in multiple cantons.[24]

In 1971, an official working group proposed an intercantonal agreement to implement full harmonization of tax bases, and a new Concordat was drafted (*Neue Zürcher Zeitung* 1971). During those deliberations, the

harmonization (Swiss Radio and Television 1977). The federal government rejected this initiative, arguing that it would violate cantonal tax sovereignty (Federal Tax Administration 2022b).

24. "Important preparatory work" (Swiss Radio and Television 1971) had been carried out in 1967 under the supervision of Ernst Höhn at the University of St. Gallen. The study compared cantonal tax laws and brought to the attention of the public and of policymakers how confusing the Swiss tax system was. Swiss television summarized the study saying that "we not only have a hopeless tax mess, but also that the tax regulations of the cantons are moving further and further apart from each other" (Swiss Radio and Television 1977).

involved experts and canton representatives concluded that it was important also to align federal income taxes with the harmonized principles (vertical tax harmonization; Höhn 1973). However, already in 1969, doubts had been raised by experts that a voluntary agreement would be sufficient unless the federal government was given the competence to enforce it if necessary (*Neue Zürcher Zeitung* 1969). One reason was that a new Concordat would only allow horizontal but not vertical tax harmonization. A second reason was that joining the Concordat would be voluntary for the cantons, and that compliance by all was therefore not assured (Cavelti and Greminger 2010; Federal Council 1976).

### 10.4.2 Mandated Cooperation: The Federal Tax Harmonization Act

The legal definition of taxable profits and capital has been harmonized across all cantons as well as across the three government layers since 2001, based on a law adopted in 1990 and in force since 1993: the Federal Tax Harmonization Act (FTHA).[25]

#### *10.4.2.1 The Genesis of the FTHA*

The 1990 FTHA is a much more comprehensive set of rules than the agreement of the 1949 Concordat. It makes effective tax differentials across cantons highly transparent: since tax bases are harmonized by law, it now suffices to compare tax rates. The law was passed in 1990 by large parliamentary majorities (121 votes to 4 in the National Council, 35 to 2 in the Council of States). The law is based on a constitutional amendment approved in 1977 by 61.2 percent of voters nationwide (it had been adopted by parliament with 183 votes to 1 in the National Council, 22 to 3 in the Council of States).

The cantons had eight years after the federal law came into force in 1993 to bring their tax laws into line with the FTHA.[26] The law regulates tax liability, the tax object, the timing of assessment, the procedure, and the criminal tax law.[27] The FTHA obliges cantons to levy a tax on personal and corporate income and on personal wealth and corporate equity capital, among others.

25. Federal Law: Bundesgesetz über die Harmonisierung der direkten Steuern der Kantone und Gemeinden (FTHA) vom 14. Dezember 1990. Available at https://fedlex.data.admin.ch/eli/cc/1991/1256_1256_1256. Circulars by the federal tax administration, harmonizing details of implementation: Kreisschreiben und Rundschreiben der Eidgenössischen Steuerverwaltung seit 1980, bzw. 2004. Available at https://www.estv.admin.ch/estv/de/home/direkte-bundessteuer/fachinformationen-dbst/dbst-kreisschreiben.html and https://www.estv.admin.ch/estv/de/home/direkte-bundessteuer/fachinformationen-dbst/rundschreiben.html.

26. The FTHA is limited to income and wealth taxes (often referred to as "direct" taxes, as opposed to consumption taxes, referred to as "indirect" taxes). Not affected by harmonization, moreover, are a range of fiscally less important taxes such as inheritance and gift taxes and specific taxes on real estate and real-estate transactions.

27. This form of federal-level intervention in cantonal autonomy is referred to in Switzerland as "formal" tax harmonization—distinct from "material" or "substantive" harmonization, which would involve constraints on tax rate schedules. To this date, the Swiss constitution explicitly forbids "material" tax harmonization. Federal taxes also conform with the principles of the FTHA. The corresponding adjustments to the federal corporate and personal income tax came into force in 1995.

For these taxes, the law regulates how the tax base is to be determined.[28] To this end, the law contains rules on taxable income components and admissible deductions. The FTHA stipulates the principle that the income statement under commercial law also determines taxable profits, unless the tax law provides for a deviation.[29] The FTHA also generalized the rule that corporate taxes themselves should be deductible, and it standardized the privileges of status firms.

What were the economic and political forces behind this agreement, and could there be parallels to current discussions on corporate tax harmonization at the international level? We attempt to shed light on these questions by providing a selective summary of the genesis of the FTHA.

The initiative for the first concrete steps toward achieving tax harmonization beyond the Concordat came from canton-level finance ministers.[30] In 1968, the CCFD appointed a commission of practitioners and academics to craft a model law for the cantons (*Journal de Genève* 1973c; *Neue Zürcher Zeitung* 1973c; Swiss Radio and Television 1977).[31] The commission published its final report in 1972. As mentioned above, the commission and the CCFD came to share the viewpoint previously put forth by experts that a voluntary agreement would not suffice.

The text proposed by the commission and endorsed by the CCFD limited the competence of the federal government to the establishment of principles of taxation and explicitly left the determination of tax rates within the competence of the cantons. The constitutional article adopted by nationwide referendum in 1977 largely kept this wording. The provision was also incorporated into the new Constitution as part of the 1999 constitutional reform without relevant substantive changes (Cajacob and Yuan 2019/20).

Concurrently with the work by the cantons themselves, a number of initiatives were launched in the federal parliament, and two nationwide referenda were held.[32] None of these initiatives succeeded, and the cantons' own proposals—limited to tax-base harmonization but leaving the cantons' autonomy over rates untouched—ended up being adopted in the constitutional amendment of 1977. This represented a win not only for the cantons

28. An important aspect in terms of tax administration is that the FTHA prescribes one-year present-based tax assessment ("postnumerando"). This means that taxpayers owe taxes in a given year for income earned in that same year. Before the FTHA, biannual backward-looking tax assessment had been standard ("praenumerando"). This meant, for example, that taxpayers in 1993 and 1994 owed taxes for average income and wealth in 1991 and 1992.

29. Art. 24 paragraph 1 the FTHA states three adjustments that have to be made for tax purposes starting from the income statement: correct for expenses charged to the income statement that are not justified by the business (e.g., if the manager-owner's wage is higher than what is in line with market wages); add capital gains, liquidation gains, and revaluation gains not credited to the income statement; and add interest on hidden equity.

30. For further details, see Appendix A.4.2.

31. The commission was chaired by Willi Ritschard, then finance director of the canton of Solothurn and later minister of finance in the federal government. Hence the popular term "Ritschard commission."

32. See Appendix sections A.4.2 and A.4.2 for details.

but also for center-right political parties. Calls for the harmonization of tax rates had emanated mainly from members of left-of-center parties.

### 10.4.2.2 *Competing Arguments and Interests in the Debate About Tax Base Harmonization*

If we want to understand the economics and politics behind the FTHA and thus to gauge the external validity of processes at play among Swiss cantons in the 1970s and 1980s, we need to ask what arguments were invoked for and against different harmonization models, and by whom.

Most economists would probably view the main potential benefit of harmonization to arise from mitigating inefficient tax competition (e.g., Wilson and Wildasin 2004) and spatial dispersion in tax rates (e.g., Fajgelbaum et al. 2019). Even if constrained to tax bases, harmonization may limit horizontal fiscal externalities. However, partial coordination of tax instruments could also result in welfare losses (e.g., Cremer and Gahvari 2000), and tax competition could be a second-best optimal mechanism when governments are revenue maximizers (e.g., Brülhart and Jametti 2019).

In the Swiss policy discussions, more practical concerns took center stage. Advocates of formal tax harmonization emphasized two main advantages: administrative simplification for increasingly mobile and spatially connected firms and households, and the facilitation of federal-level tax and equalization policies. We briefly discuss each of them in turn.

#### 10.4.2.2.1 *Administrative Simplification*

With the increasing economic interconnections among cantons, the costs of administering structurally different tax systems gradually increased, for both taxpayers and tax authorities. Certain inconsistencies between cantonal tax codes also became more visible over time.[33]

A prominent issue was the time period of tax assessments (*Journal de Genève* 1973b). Suppose a taxpayer (firm or household) moved from canton $A$ to canton $B$ in year $t$. Suppose also that canton $A$ practised present-period annual taxation, whereby taxpayers pay taxes in year $t$ on income and assets as declared in $t$. Suppose, finally, that canton $B$ practiced backward-looking biannual taxation, whereby taxpayers pay taxes in year $t$ on average income and assets as declared in $t - 1$ and $t - 2$. For those years, however, the taxpayer had already paid taxes in $A$.[34]

33. Appendix table 10A.2 provides an overview of the main differences across cantons in 1947 related to the deductibility of tax payments, tax holidays for new firms representing an important economic interest, loss carry-forward rules, and the time period of tax assessments. These differences were largely harmonized through the FTHA.

34. A vivid example to illustrate such inconsistency is the relocation of his a private bank by wealthy businessman Martin Ebner. He moved his bank from Zurich to Schwyz in 1997 and, could thereby exploit an inconsistency in the timing of the tax assessment of declared profits (*Tagesspiegel* 1998). At that time, the canton of Zurich practiced backward-looking taxation, while the canton of Schwyz had a present-based tax system. Through the timing of the move, profits made in 1997 escaped taxation at the canton level. This case occurred after the FTHA

Such inconsistencies distorted location decisions. With increasing inter-cantonal mobility, they were perceived to occur more frequently and to make the tax system appear increasingly unfair and administratively burdensome.

Prior to formal tax harmonization, cantons furthermore used different tax declaration forms, often with different terminologies and information requirements. This placed a high administrative burden on multiestablishment firms subject to taxation in every canton in which they had a legal entity or a permanent establishment.

The lack of a harmonized tax base increased the administrative burden in particular in the case of tax apportionment. When apportioning tax liability across cantons, taxable profits were (and are) determined for the firm as a whole and then allocated between legal entities and/or permanent establishments (section 10.4.3). Whenever legal entities or permanent establishments were located in cantons with different definitions of the tax base, apportionment became very complicated. This was a burden on corporate tax planning as well as on tax assessment by the cantonal authorities.

To facilitate the taxation of firms operating in multiple cantons, Art. 39 of the FTHA (Swiss Parliament 1990a) regulates the exchange of information between jurisdictions' tax administrations. To our knowledge, this exchange of information works largely informally in practice, often via phone calls among tax officials.

The nonharmonized tax system had also prevented the establishment of nationwide case law that would have ensured legal certainty (*Journal de Genève* 1973b). Because cantonal tax laws used widely different terminology, a court decision on a case in one canton could not necessarily be applied to a similar case in another canton.

Overall, it appears that the benefits of administrative simplification for both firms and tax administrations was an important driver behind the push for harmonization. Business interests fighting harmonization to protect potential sheltering opportunities seem to have played a comparatively smaller role. This dynamic may well have been due to the smallness of cantons, which implies both a very high volume of cross-border economic activity and limited administrative resources. In that sense, the Swiss experience is likely to differ from the configuration of business and political interests at the international level.

#### *10.4.2.3 Facilitation of Federal-Level Policies*

Efficient implementation of federal-level policies also requires a degree of canton-level harmonization. Therefore, the presence of a tax-raising and

had been passed but not yet adopted by all cantons. Martínez et al. (2021) have exploited the transition from the backward-looking to the present-based taxation as a natural experiment to estimate taxpayers' intertemporal substitution elasticities.

revenue-distributing central government acted as a catalyst for harmonization in two main ways: because co-occupancy of tax bases by vertically nested layers of government raises the administrative cost of nonharmonization, and because equitable fiscal equalization requires that tax bases and tax burdens be comparable.

Co-occupancy of tax bases implies that work toward the FTHA was linked to the simultaneous drafting of a permanent legal basis for direct taxation of personal and corporate income at the federal level (Swiss Parliament 1990b). This process started in the 1950s and took decades.[35] When multiple vertically nested layers of government tax the same base, it is administratively easier for that base to be defined in the same way for all government layers. Conversely, the greater the divergence between those definitions, the greater the requirements for differentiated tax filings and tax assessments by government layer.

A case in point are loss carryforward rules: for federal taxes, losses from up to seven financial years preceding a given tax year can be deducted if in the firm's interest. Prior to the FTHA, this federal tax provision was more generous than the corresponding provisions of many cantons, which generated considerable complexity for tax planning and filing. The fact that the cantonal tax authorities collecting the federal tax were known sometimes to mistakenly apply their own loss-carryforward rules to the federal tax was a source of administrative complexity and irritation. Since 2001, those rules are the same everywhere.

The implementation of fiscal equalization across cantons provided another rationale for harmonization. In the post-War decades, fiscal equalization transfers from the federal government to the cantons were partly based on cantons' tax revenue from income and capital. Experts emphasized the importance of formal tax harmonization to enable accurate comparisons of cantons' fiscal situation (*Neue Zürcher Zeitung* 1969, 1970, 1973a). Because canton-level tax systems differed in many respects, it was often difficult to tell whether a canton had low tax revenue because of low effective tax rates or because of small effective tax bases, i.e., low fiscal capacity to generate tax revenues. A frequently stated aim for formal tax harmonization was therefore to create transparency in this respect and, thereby, to facilitate a fiscal capacity equalization system that only depends on the cantonal tax base (see section 10.5 for a detailed discussion).

The need for coordinating federal and subfederal tax rules is a feature of the Swiss context that does not fit with the international setting. In this respect, cantons are different from countries. As long as the EU does not

35. According to the Federal Council (1976, 1475), federal-level taxation had acted as a spur to canton-level harmonization even earlier: "The historically rooted differences in the design of the individual cantonal tax laws were somewhat mitigated under the influence of the federal legislation that began to take effect in this area from 1916 onward (in particular, the crisis levy from 1934–1940, the defense tax from 1941 onward), but they are still considerable today."

introduce supranational corporate taxes, for example, the Swiss experience cannot be taken as a small-scale version of ongoing international harmonization efforts. One might, however, interpret the provisions defining the corporate tax base for the application of the BEPS Pillar-2 top-up tax as equivalent to a supranational tax law. The Swiss experience suggests that those provisions might spur some harmonization of national corporate tax laws as well. Indeed, Switzerland might have an incentive to align its corporate tax-base rules with the "GloBE" standards of BEPS Pillar 2, which would be reminiscent of the forces at play within Switzerland several decades earlier.

10.4.2.3.1 *Opposition to Tax Harmonization*

Sifting through official documents and press reports, one is struck by how little open opposition to formal tax harmonization there was. Nonetheless, the process to the final adoption of the FTHA took more than two decades, which suggests that political hurdles needed to be overcome.

The most critical voices, to the extent that we can discern them in the available documentation, were not directed against formal tax harmonization per se, but against the idea of harmonizing tax bases as a "slippery slope" toward harmonizing tax rates as well (Swiss Radio and Television 1977). Material tax harmonization, they argued, would undermine cantons' sovereignty and ultimately lead to a general increase in tax rates because the disciplining effect of tax competition would be lost. This was the argument invoked by the free-market Liberal Party, one of the only two (smallish) parties who recommended a no vote in the 1977 constitutional referendum on tax harmonization.[36]

Experts later also pointed to the role of tax competition as a laboratory for innovation in tax policy, which was to some extent constrained by formal harmonization. Baur et al. (2010) cite as examples of such bottom-up innovations canton-level limits on the double taxation of profits (at the firm level and at the shareholder level), deductions for childcare costs, and the introduction of special tax regimes for holding firms.

What may seem surprising from a current vantage point is the apparent lack of opposition from business interests. The main nationwide employers' and business associations supported both the constitutional amendment in 1977 and the FTHA in 1990, as did the trade unions and all main parties from center-right to center-left. It would appear that for most of the business establishment, the gains in administrative efficiency outweighed any potential tax-saving opportunities through arbitrage among nonharmonized cantonal tax systems.

When digging deeper into official documents, some dissent can, however,

36. The other formally opposed party, the far-left Workers' Party, made exactly the reverse argument, claiming that to limit harmonization to tax bases would set back the cause of harmonizing tax rates and might even exacerbate tax competition.

be made out. According to the public consultation on the constitutional amendment (Federal Tax Administration 1975), for instance, the (small) Association of Holding and Finance firms did "not view federal-level involvement in tax harmonization as a policy priority" (p. 1773). Similarly, the tax authorities of the cantons of Geneva and Vaud expressed support for a weaker form of agreement without federal involvement, analogous to the Concordat. These two cantons have historically hosted a large share of internally mobile firms and wealthy individuals.

In the referendum of 1977, the main small-business organization did not issue a voting recommendation, which implies significant resistance among their ranks. We see two reasons for a status-quo preference by some small and medium-sized firms. First, a lack of harmonized tax laws might have shielded them to an extent from out-of-canton competition in sectors with a need for a physical presence (e.g., retail or hospitality). Second, owners of such businesses likely had the knowledge and political connections that allowed them to take advantage of complicated canton-specific legislation and/or they had higher relocation costs (Marceau and Smart 2003; see also Appendix A.4.1).

The dissenting voices suggest that certain business interests and some jurisdictions did expect to lose from reduced tax sheltering opportunities when tax bases were harmonized through federal law. Those dissenters, however, remained a minority throughout.

### 10.4.3 Allocation of Taxing Rights

Coordinated taxation among fiscally autonomous jurisdictions requires a system of rules for allocating taxing rights over profits of multiestablishment firms. This is a surprisingly noncontentious even though only partially codified area of tax policy in Switzerland.

Swiss tax rules conform with international principles that date back to the League of Nations' "1920s Compromise" on the taxation of cross-border activity. These principles comprise three main elements. First, according to the "single entity approach," every legal entity of a corporate group is taxable in the jurisdiction in which it is tax resident. The group itself is not taxable, only the legal entities of the group. Second, there can be no taxation without a permanent establishment. If a legal entity that is tax resident in one jurisdiction has a permanent establishment in another jurisdiction, the jurisdiction of the legal entity must cede part of its taxing rights to the jurisdiction of permanent establishment. Third, according to the arm's-length principle for transfer pricing, services exchanged among entities of the same group are valued for tax purposes using the price that independent third parties would be expected to agree on.

Based on these principles, two types of allocation of taxing rights can be distinguished: the allocation of taxing rights among legal entities, and the allocation of taxing rights among legal entities and permanent establishments.

#### *10.4.3.1 Allocation of Taxing Rights Among Legal Entities*

Legal entities maintain their own financial accounts, which allows them to be treated as independent firms for tax purposes. Profit is allocated via transfer prices in accordance with the arm's length principle.

Transfer pricing among legal entities within Switzerland is governed by the OECD's guidelines. It is rarely contentious. At the international level, however, this is a source of considerable conflict. To our knowledge, no research exists on this issue in Switzerland. Two explanations strike us as plausible. First, tax-rate differentials across cantons, while significant (see figure 10.4), are not as large as cross-country differentials. Tax-rates rarely vary by more than 10 percentage points across cantons, while they can vary by up to around 35 percentage points internationally. Second, Switzerland is small, with a consensus-oriented political and administrative culture. Canton-level finance minsters and tax officials know each other and their largest taxpayers, and they interact frequently. This likely contributes to potential conflicts over profit apportionment and taxing rights being settled at the technical-administrative level rather than in the political or judicial arenas.[37] These are, however, speculative explanations, as a scientific analysis of this issue is so far lacking.

#### *10.4.3.2 Tax Apportionment*

The allocation of taxing rights among legal entities and permanent establishments, or among establishments only, is referred to as *tax apportionment*. Since permanent establishments are not considered legal entities, they do not hold separate tax liability, and it is generally not possible to allocate profits based on transfers prices.

Two main methods are used for intercantonal tax apportionment. For "producing" (mainly manufacturing) firms, tax apportionment is usually based on labor and capital costs (physical capital, or capitalized rent and wages). For trading firms (e.g., retailers and wholesalers), tax apportionment is usually based on sales. These rules reflect a similar approach to the formulary apportionment proposed under Pillar 1 of the OECD-led global corporate tax reform. However, unlike under Pillar 1, a physical presence is required for the allocation of taxing rights within Switzerland.

37. There are, however, recorded cases of conflict. An example is a Federal Court decision of 2019 on transfer pricing for electricity (Federal Supreme Court of Switzerland 2019). Lowland cantons (e.g., Aargau and Solothurn) that host headquarters of large energy firms (e.g., Alpiq and Axpo) were in disagreement with Alpine cantons that host those firms' hydroelectric power plants. The Alpine cantons (e.g., Valais) sought to impose transfer prices based on market prices, but the Federal Court ruled in favor of the "cost-plus" method stipulated by OECD guidelines, because the only partially liberalized Swiss electricity market would not allow a market price to be properly determined. This ruling happened to favor the headquarter cantons.

These rules are coordinated by an association of canton-level and the federal tax administrations (the "Swiss Tax Conference") and published as semiformal circulars. These documents regulate specific cases on which the tax administrations recognize a need for harmonization or clarification. Seven circulars regulate issues specifically related to tax apportionment.[38] The rules in the circulars are not legally binding. However, since these rules are established by the cantonal tax administrations, they are widely respected and applied.

The apparent noncontentiousness of tax apportionment is similarly striking to that of transfer pricing, and would make for an interesting research topic.

## 10.5 Fiscal Equalization

The decentralized Swiss system is complemented by sophisticated equalization schemes designed to limit fiscal disparities across jurisdictions. Equalization policies have been implemented for a long time, both within and among cantons.[39]

Intercantonal equalization originally evolved through a piecemeal process. Numerous equalization grants were introduced in the form of matching grants, where the matching rate was higher for poorer cantons. Some payments were linked to canton's tax rates. Over time, discontent arose with this opaque and sometimes incoherent system of intergovernmental transfers (Frey et al. 1994). In particular, the jumble of measures did not follow the Tinbergen rule, whereby every policy goal should be addressed by a separate instrument. Different layers of government were involved in the provision of public services via a variety of fiscal instruments, which made it challenging for voters to see which governmental layer was responsible for each policy and to hold politicians of different government layers to account.

### 10.5.1 Intercantonal Equalization Since 2008

Based on a constitutional clause adopted by nationwide referendum in 2004, a codified and carefully calibrated system of fiscal intergovernmental relations has been in force since 2008. Federal rules define fiscal transfers among cantonal and federal governments and assign expenditure respon-

38. These circulars concern: (1) tax apportionment for real estate leasing firms, (2) tax apportionment for banks, (3) tax apportionment for the national postal service, (4) procedure in special cases affecting multiple tax jurisdictions, (5) tax apportionment for insurance firms, (6) taxation of concessionary transport and infrastructure firms, and (7) tax liability of health insurance firms.

39. Some rudimentary equalization system already existed from the middle of the 19th century onwards. The goal of fiscal equalization was enshrined in the Swiss constitution in 1958, and equalization transfers gradually increased thereafter (Rey 2017). In this paper, we focus on equalization among cantons. For a rich account of within-canton equalization schemes, see Rühli (2013).

sibilities. The total system annually redistributes public funds worth some 0.7 percent of GDP, of which around a third are paid by contributor cantons and two-thirds by the federal government.

Redistributive transfers aimed at reducing disparities in fiscal capacity are the main pillar of the equalization scheme. They are based on the notion of a representative tax system.[40] This means that transfers are determined by differences in per capita tax bases, and not by differences in per capita tax revenue. Tax bases considered in the calculation of cantons' fiscal capacity include taxable profits as well as personal income and wealth.

The different cantonal tax bases are aggregated into a canton-level fiscal capacity index.[41] This index relates a canton's aggregate tax base to the nationwide average per capita tax base, set equal to 100. Cantons with an index value above 100 pay into the system in proportion to the deviation. Cantons with an index value below 100 receive transfers according to a progressive schedule with a floor at an index value of 86.5.[42]

Figure 10.16 shows per capita equalization payments for 2021. The majority of cantons are recipients (in gray), with only eight of the 26 cantons being donors (lines and dots). Among the donor cantons, Zug (ZG) again stands out—in this case as by far the largest contributor in per capita terms. The 26 fiscal capacity indices are updated annually, but lasting changes in the recipient/donor status of a canton are rare.[43]

The equalization system receives its wide political support mainly based on equity arguments and on considerations of efficient public service delivery. The system is intended to level the playing field among cantons with different exogenous conditions while still allowing them to engage in fiscal competition.

Concerns that equalization transfers may have an effect on tax competition among cantons have been repeatedly voiced, in particular by donor cantons. Part of their concern is the potential fiscal response of transfer-receiving cantons: they might lower their tax rates rather than spending

40. In this respect, the Swiss system resembles those of other countries, including Canada and Germany. The other two pillars of the equalization scheme are targeted at disparities in geographical and topographical conditions that influence the cost of providing public services, and socioeconomic characteristics of cantons that influence the need for public services.

41. In the past, a certain amount of regular taxable profits was given the same weight in the calculation of the fiscal capacity as that same amount of taxable personal income. Starting in 2024, profits are gradually being weighted down, to reach a level currently estimated at around 33 percent by 2031, to account for their lower tax yield of corporate relative to personal income. The wealth tax base enters the calculation with a weight of approximately 1.5 percent.

42. Due to the progressivity of the equalization system for recipient cantons, cantons with a fiscal capacity index of 70 percent or lower are lifted to 86.5 percent, while cantons with a fiscal capacity index between 70 percent and 86.5 percent are lifted to more than 86.5 percent.

43. An exception is the small canton of Obwalden (OW), which switched from being a recipient to being a donor in 2018. This was likely the result of large tax cuts Obwalden had implemented in the late 2000s. These tax cuts were followed by significant growth of the tax base, pushing up the fiscal capacity index, but they likely nonetheless implied revenue losses for the canton (Martínez 2022).

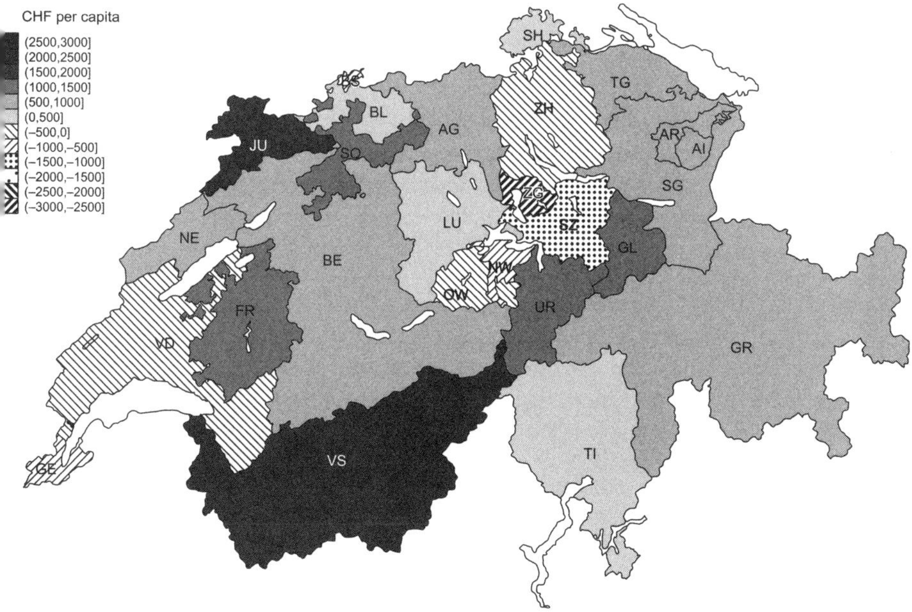


**Fig. 10.16 Fiscal equalization transfer payments 2021**

Notes: The figure shows per capita fiscal equalization payments of the Swiss cantons in 2021. Positive values (in gray) are transfers received by 18 recipient cantons; negative values (diagonal lines or dots) are transfers paid by 8 donor cantons. Source: Federal Department of Finance (2021).

transfers on public services.[44] While the evaluation of this hypothesis is empirically demanding, the literature on incentive effects can shed light on important aspects of the issue.

## 10.5.2 Incentive Effects

In general, equalization transfers can have income and substitution effects on canton-level policy choices. The income effect describes how the change in public resources influences tax and expenditure policies, whereby higher transfers might be "spent" in the form of tax cuts. Recent empirical work by Köthenbürger and Loumeau (2023) finds no evidence of such income effects.[45] An absence of income effects runs against the hypothesis that trans-

44. This is vividly illustrated in the following newspaper report (*Neue Zürcher Zeitung* 2023): "The finance minister of the canton of Zurich has long been irritated by the fact that some cantons that receive money from fiscal equalization and thus indirectly from Zurich use it to reduce their taxes and then poach firms or taxpayers from the canton [of Zurich]. This should not happen again."

45. Analyzing tax rate choices at the municipal level, they find transfers to have no effect on tax rates. Rather, transfer income is found to increase spending, and even to crowd in additional debt-financed spending.

fers will fuel tax competition. The available evidence is instead consistent with the flypaper effect, whereby transfers fully or even more than proportionally "stick" to the public budget they are sent to, and too small a share of transfers (if any at all) is passed on via lower taxes (Bradford and Oates 1971; Hines and Thaler 1995).[46]

Equalization formulas can also generate substitution effects.[47] Relative to a system that responds to actually collected tax revenues, a representative tax system such as the Swiss one has the advantage that cantons do not have an incentive to lower their tax rates to mechanically lower the measure of fiscal wealth that is used to allocate transfers. However, the tax bases included in the calculation of a canton's fiscal capacity index are a function of the respective canton-level tax rates. This creates incentives to increase the tax rate since any resulting loss of tax base is at least partially compensated by higher transfer payments (Köthenbürger 2002; Smart 1998). In a similar vein, public infrastructure spending that expands the tax base leads to a reduction in transfers, creating disincentives to spend on such items.

Incentive effects are typically quantified through the system's tax-normalized (or "effective") absorption rate, which takes account not only of the equalization formula but also of the tax rate actually applied by a given canton and its municipalities. This is illustrated in figure 10.17. The four panels show the revenue effect of a hypothetical CHF 1 million arrival of taxable profits from abroad.[48] The equalization system absorbs part of such an increase in the corporate tax base. The tax-normalized absorption rate measures the change in transfer payments relative to the change in tax revenue that follows from the inflow of taxable profits. An absorption rate above 100 implies that a tax base that grows faster than the national average is fiscally loss making for the canton concerned.

Absorption rates differ between donor and recipient cantons. Figure 10.17 shows the rates for 2018, when privileged tax regime for "status" firms were still in force, and for the year 2021, after the abolition of the old privileges. In all cases, absorption rates are higher for recipient cantons (fiscal capacity index below 100). This is in part due to the progressive nature of the equalization scheme. For instance, in 2018, the canton of Uri (UR) faced an

46. The reference point is the combination of spending increase and tax rate reduction that the population would prefer.

47. See Smart (2009) for an overview.

48. In computing tax-normalized absorption rates, we follow Leisibach and Schaltegger (2019) and account for adjustments in the different parameters and average values used in the equalization formula. We use fiscal capacity indices for 2018 (pre-2020) and 2021 (post-2020) from Federal Department of Finance (2018b, 2021), weights for privileged profits in 2018 from Federal Department of Finance (2018a), estimated weights for profits inside and outside the patent box after the 2020 reform from Federal Department of Finance (2020), corporate tax rates in the cantonal capitals in 2018 and 2021 as in figure 9 from Federal Tax Administration (2018c, 2021), corporate tax rates for privileged firms in 2016 from Federal Tax Administration (2018b) and cantonal tax rebates for profits in the patent box from Federal Department of Finance (2023a).

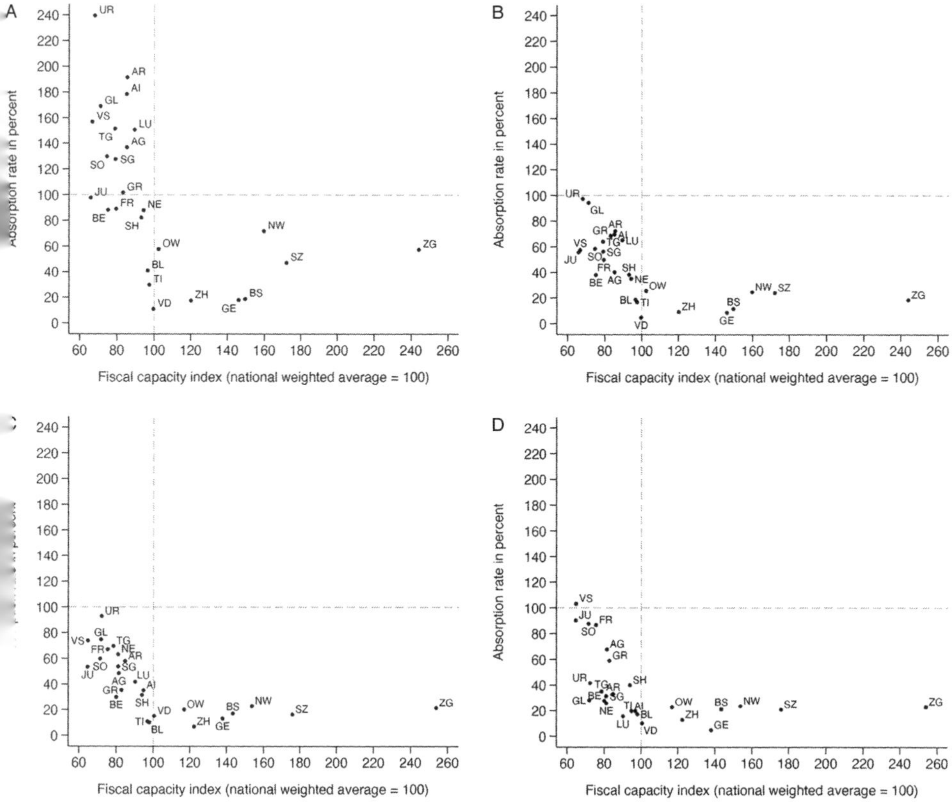


**Fig. 10.17 Tax-normalized absorption rates in the Swiss tax equalization scheme**

A: Taxable profits of regular firms, pre-2020

B: Taxable profits of tax-privileged firms, pre-2020

C: Taxable profits of regular firms, post-2020

D: Taxable profits in patent box, post-2020

Notes: The index on the horizontal axis measures the fiscal capacity of a canton based on all its different tax bases (personal income, wealth, profits). Cantons with an index value above the population-weighted average (= 100) pay into the tax equalization scheme while cantons with an index value below 100 receive transfers. Absorption rates express how much of the additional cantonal and municipal tax revenue due to attracting corporate profits is taken away by the equalization scheme. A rate above 100% means that the canton loses revenue when the tax base increases, and vice versa. We simulate the change in the tax equalization payments when a firm with taxable profits of CHF 1 million moves to the cantonal capital from abroad. Panels A and C show the equalization rates for regular firms before (panel A) and after (panel C) the 2020 corporate tax reform. Postreform equalization rates are computed based on system parameters as they will apply after the full phase-in period in 2032. The corresponding effective tax rates are shown in Figure 10.9. Panel B shows the equalization rate for a multinational firm subject to pre-reform privileged taxation, with tax rates shown in Figure 10.8. Panel D shows the equalization rate for post-reform patent-box profits. Data source: Own calculations based on Federal Department of Finance (2018a,b, 2020, 2021, 2023a) and Federal Tax Administration (2018b,c, 2021b).

absorption rate of 250 percent on regular profits (panel A of figure 10.17). This implies that following an inflow of taxable profits, incoming transfer payments would shrink 2.5 times more than the increase in corporate tax revenue. For privileged (multinational) profits, Uri faced an absorption rate of around 100 percent (panel B of figure 10.17). Hence, viewed through a purely fiscal lens, recipient cantons such as Uri had no incentive to compete for mobile firms and their profits. Absorption rates were considerably lower for donor cantons, leaving them with a stronger incentive to compete for mobile profits.

The 2020 tax reform abolished the privileged corporate tax regimes but introduced patent boxes, which offer lower corporate tax rates on qualifying income from intellectual property. At the same time, profits were down-weighted in the calculation of the fiscal capacity index. These changes are gradually being introduced over the phase-in period 2020–2031. We report projected posttransition incentive effects, i.e., with the parameters that will apply in 2032 but with fiscal capacity values and tax rates of 2021. As a result, absorption rates for regular taxable profits will fall as the the new rules are phased in (panels C and D in figure 10.17). This implies that intra-national competition over taxable profits might further intensify in coming years, as the fiscal penalties implied by the equalization scheme will be significantly lowered.

Some empirical evidence exists on the effect of changing absorption rates on policy choices: higher absorption rates are found to increase observed tax rates (Buettner 2006; Egger et al. 2010; Mauri 2023), and to reduce infrastructure spending (Hauptmeier et al. 2012). To the extent that corporate tax rates are inefficiently low with unfettered tax competition, and infrastructure spending is inefficiently high compared to public consumption spending (Keen and Marchand 1997), these findings are consistent with the idea that fiscal equalization enhances efficiency in addition to its redistributive effect. From this perspective, the equalization system might be seen as an implicit, and largely unintentional, tax coordination device.[49]

## 10.6 Concluding Discussion

It is tempting to look to the Swiss experience for clues on the possible future evolution of international tax policy. After all, Switzerland embarked on tax coordination about half a century ahead of the OECD-led international initiatives. The country started from similarly heterogeneous conditions to end up with a finely calibrated, democratically endorsed system that

49. The argument is not restricted to corporate taxation and also extends to personal income taxation and wealth taxation; the other two tax bases that enter the fiscal equalization scheme. These two tax bases significantly respond to tax rate changes. See Brülhart et al. (2022), and Köthenbürger et al. (2023), among others.

balances cantonal autonomy and tax competition with strong elements of coordination and equalization.

Until the early 20th century, the cantons had set their tax policies entirely autonomously, with no formal coordination. The federal government did not yet possess any general taxing powers. As we document in this chapter, a consciousness emerged toward the middle of the 20th century that greater coordination was needed, especially in the area of corporate taxation. The motivations echo some current-day concerns: increasing cross-border business activities calling for administrative harmonization, and targeted low-tax strategies by some cantons being perceived as unfair competition by others. As we also document, Switzerland shows the classic hallmarks of corporate tax competition:

- a mobile and thus elastic tax base,
- opportunistic low-tax strategies pursued by smaller jurisdictions and aimed at particularly mobile multinational profits,
- steadily falling first and second moments of the cross-cantonal distribution of corporate tax rates, and
- large, urban cantons sustaining comparatively high tax rates.

This configuration initially spurred bottom-up coordination efforts by a subgroup of cantons. In the 1949 Concordat, half of the cantons agreed to abstain from discretionary tax rulings and to practice a rudimentary form of tax information exchange. This voluntary process, however, did not seem to tend endogenously toward universal adoption, and it was through federal-level legislation that recalcitrant cantons ended up being pushed into joining. Similarly, the second big leap toward coordinated tax policy, the harmonization of tax bases negotiated in the 1970s and 1980s and implemented in the 1990s, was led by the federal government and parliament, albeit with broad support from the cantons themselves. This evolution toward gradually less decentralized coordination resembles the shift of emphasis at the international level: coordination based on bilateral double-taxation treaties is gradually being superseded by multilateral agreements backed by the influence of the OECD, the G20, and the Inclusive Framework. Although these bodies have no formal jurisdiction over their member states, the political and economic importance of their largest members gives them effective powers not unlike those of federal-level policymakers within Switzerland. An extrapolation from the Swiss experience would lead one to expect the importance of those (or similar) supranational bodies to increase further, at least in the area of tax policy coordination.

The main feature of tax harmonization among cantons is its limitation to tax-base definitions, without any direct bearing on tax rates. In that sense, the 15 percent minimum tax rate agreed under the OECD's Pillar 2 rules exceeds any coordinating measure ever implemented within Switzerland. Apart from the headline minimum tax rate, Pillar 2 rules also define corporate tax bases and reporting requirements. In that respect, they resemble the harmonization measures adopted within Switzerland in the 1990s quite closely.

Why did the Swiss cantons never agree on minimum tax rates, whereas such an agreement was feasible at the politically and economically much more heterogeneous international level? We see two particularly plausible reasons.

One possible explanation is that the federal corporate tax, with an effective rate of around 8 percent, has provided an effective floor to the race to the bottom. Of the federal tax revenue, 17 percent have been rebated to the cantons (21.2 percent since 2020) and thus effectively imply a canton-level minimum tax rate of some 1.4 percent. The remaining federal tax revenue was allocated to the federal general budget, allowing any one canton's success in attracting taxable profits to be shared by the entire nation. Fiscal equalization further contributed to spreading around the benefits from growth in the tax base of individual cantons. A political culture featuring strong cantonal allegiances and favoring low taxes and a limited role for the public sector, especially among the German-speaking majority, could also have limited the appetite for additional harmonization (see Eugster and Parchet 2019).

The other important factor is the country's small size: unlike, say, policy for the OECD as a whole, corporate tax policy of Swiss cantons is largely aimed at attracting mobile profits from outside their own grouping. As we have shown, preferential tax treatment of multinational profits has been associated with Switzerland serving as a popular location for multinational profit reporting. In that sense, canton-level corporate tax competition was a positive-sum process from the fiscal perspective of the country as a whole. The smallness of the country and resulting familiarity of canton-level decision makers probably also contributed to the relative noncontentiousness of profit apportionment and transfer-pricing decisions between cantons.

In a nutshell, the experience of the Swiss cantons confirms that tax-base harmonization, increasingly centralized coordination, and efforts at equalizing revenues, are natural corollaries of growing economic integration and mobility. At the same time, Switzerland as a whole has been a successful tax competitor in the international arena, which in turn has held in check its appetite for stronger internal harmonization measures, especially tax-rate harmonization. That external dimension, however, is less important for larger countries and for groupings such as the G20 or the OECD. Therefore, global political forces for further supranational harmonization may end up being even stronger than those for intranational harmonization have ever been in Switzerland.

## Acknowledgments

David Agrawal, James Poterba, and Owen Zidar have provided very helpful comments. We in addition thank Denise Aeberhard, Beatrice Aebersold,

Enea Baselgia, Fabian Baumer, Grégoire Bosson, Jan Brueckner, Martin Daepp, Christian Frey, Bruno Jeitziner, Nicola Mauri, Andreas Remund, Lukas Stähli, Thibaut Urbain, Nathanael Zahnd, Adrian Zimmermann, and NBER conference participants for helpful information and suggestions. We also thank Chiara Bigger, Adele Bortoletti, Gleb Kabakovitch, and Janos Majer for excellent research assistance. Marius Brülhart and Raphaël Parchet gratefully acknowledge funding from the Swiss National Science Foundation (grants 192546 and 182380, respectively). Any errors or inaccuracies are ours alone. For acknowledgments, sources of research support, and disclosure of the authors' material financial relationships, if any, please see https://www.nber.org/books-and-chapters/policy-responses-tax-competition/competition-harmonization-and-redistribution-corporate-taxes-switzerland.

# Appendix A

## 10A.1 Supplementary Figures

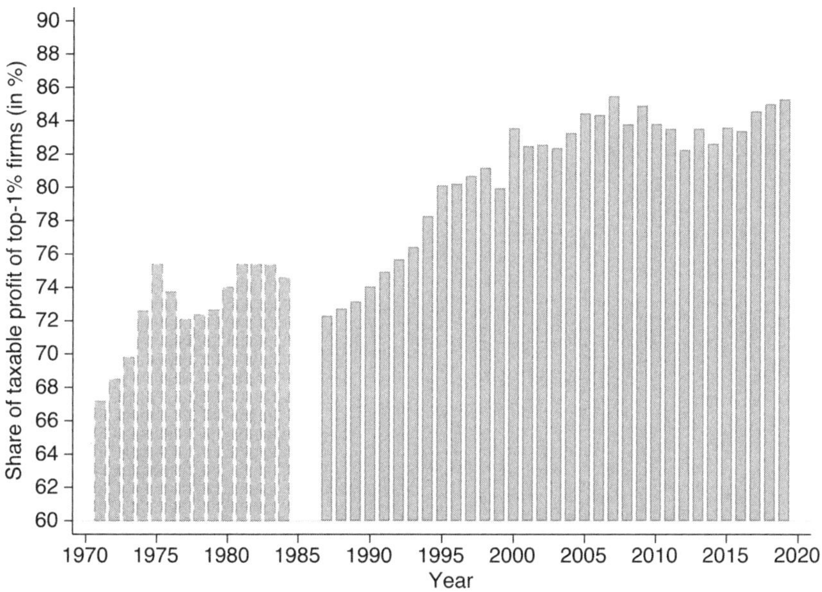


**Fig. 10A.1 Taxable profit from top 1% firms**

Notes: This figure shows the evolution of the share of total taxable profit in Switzerland accruing to the top 1% of firms. The figures before 1987 do not correct taxable profits for the deductions due to firms' participation in other firms. Source: Own calculation based on Federal Tax Administration (2022a).

## 10A.2 Supplementary Tables

**Table 10A.1 Municipal tax autonomy and maximum tax rates in 1947**

| Canton | Cantonal multiplier | Municipal tax autonomy | Minimum tax | Maximum tax |
|---|---|---|---|---|
| AG | No | No | Minimum profit tax rate given by tax schedule = 4.25% | Maximum profit tax rate given by tax schedule = 17% |
| AI | Yes | Yes, multiplier | No | No |
| AR | Yes | Yes, multiplier | No | No |
| BE | Yes | Yes, multiplier | No | No |
| BL | No | Yes, effective tax rate (same as for private households) | No | No |
| BS | No | No | Minimum profit tax rate given by tax schedule = 3% | Maximum profit tax rate given by tax schedule = 23% |
| FR | No | Yes, can choose among a multiplier or a proportional tax | | Municipalities cannot set a multiplier higher than 100%. Maximum cantonal and municipal tax rate = 14% |
| GE | Yes | Yes, multiplier | No | No |
| GL | Yes | No | Minimum profit tax rate given by tax schedule = 4.2% | Maximum profit tax rate given by tax schedule = 16.8% |
| GR | Yes | Yes, effective tax rate (base and tariff could be different from canton. Tariff cannot be more progressive than cantonal tax schedule) | No | No |
| LU | Yes | Yes, multiplier | No | No |
| NE | No | Yes, multiplier | No | Municipalities cannot set a multiplier higher than 200%. Maximum profit tax rate given by tax schedule and maximum multiplier = 36% |
| NW | Yes | Yes, multiplier | No | No |
| OW | Yes | Yes, multiplier | No | No |
| SG | Yes | No | Minimum profit tax rate given by tax schedule = 9.1% | Maximum profit tax rate given by tax schedule = 31% |
| SH | Yes | Yes, multiplier | No | No |
| SO | Yes | Yes, can choose among a multiplier, own progressive tariff or same tariff as for income of private households | No | No |
| SZ | Yes | Yes, multiplier | No | No |
| TG | Yes | Yes, multiplier | No | No |
| TI | No | Yes, multiplier | No | No |
| UR | No | Yes, effective tax rate (same base as canton) | No | No |
| VD | No | Yes, multiplier or effective tax rate (same base as canton) | No | Maximum cantonal and municipal profit tax rate = 20% |
| VS | Yes | Yes, effective tax rate | No | Municipal tax rate cannot exceed 3 per mil. |
| ZG | Yes | Yes, multiplier | No | No |
| ZH | Yes | Yes, multiplier | No | Municipalities cannot set a multiplier higher than 250% Maximum profit tax rate given by tax schedule and maximum multiplier = 36% |

Notes: The table reports the autonomy granted by cantons to their municipalities in setting a municipal corporate tax rate, as well as the minimum and maximum tax rates (if any) in 1947.

**Table 10A.2 Differences in tax practices across cantons in 1947**

| Canton | Deductibility of tax payments | Tax holiday for new firms | Loss carry forward | Taxation period | Period for tax base calculation |
|---|---|---|---|---|---|
| AG | No | No | n.a. | 1 year | Previous year |
| AI | No | No | No | 1 year | Previous year |
| AR | No | Yes | Yes | 2 years (also 1 year depending on size of firm) | Average of previous 2 years |
| BE | No | Yes | No | 2 years | Average of previous 2 years |
| BL | Yes | Yes | No | 1 year | Previous year |
| BS | Yes | No | No | 1 year | Previous year |
| FR | Yes | Yes | n.a. | 1 year | Previous year |
| GE | Yes | No | No | 1 year | Previous year |
| GL | Yes | No | No | 2 years | Average of previous 2 years |
| GR | No | No | No | 1 year | Previous year |
| LU | Yes | No | No | 2 years | Average of previous 2 years |
| NE | No | Yes | No | 1 year | Previous year |
| NW | No | Yes | Yes | 1 year | Previous year |
| OW | No | No | No | 4 years (also 2 years or 1 year depending on size of firm) | Average of previous 2 years or the previous year in case of a taxation every year |
| SG | Yes | No | No | 1 year | same as taxation period |
| SH | No | No | No | 1 year | Previous year |
| SO | No | No | No | 1 year | Previous year |
| SZ | Yes | Yes | Yes | 2 years | Average of previous 2 years |
| TG | Yes | No | No | 1 year | Previous year |
| TI | Yes | Yes | No | 1 year | Previous year |
| UR | No | No | No | 1 year | Previous year |
| VD | Yes | No | No | 1 year | Previous year |
| VS | No | No | No | 1 year | Previous year |
| ZG | Yes | No | Yes | 2 years | Average of previous 2 years |
| ZH | No | No | Yes | 1 year | Previous year |

Notes: The table reports the main differences in tax practices across cantons in 1947.

**Table 10A.3** **Tax treatment of holding, investment and domiciliary firms in 1947**

| Canton | Holding firms | Investment firms | Domiciliary firms |
|---|---|---|---|
| AG | Same as investment firms. Cantonal government may grant special tax reduction. | Firms that hold at least 20% of the capital of other firms. Profit from participation not taxed. Maximum reduction of 75%. | Not recognized. Taxed as regular firms. |
| AI | Not recognized. Taxed as regular firms. | Not recognized. Taxed as regular firms. | Not recognized. Taxed as regular firms. |
| AR | Profit and capital tax not levied. Proportional special tax of 0.03% on paid-in capital. Nonpaid-in capital, open and hidden reserves not taxed. No multiplier. | n.a. | Not recognized. Taxed as regular firms. |
| BE | Profit and capital tax not levied. Proportional special tax of 0.05% on capital. No multiplier. The Government Council may also grant special tax reductions. | Firms that hold at least 20% of the capital of other firms. Profit from participation not taxed. | Not recognized. Taxed as regular firms. |
| BL | Profit and capital tax not levied. Proportional special tax of 0.05% on paid-in capital and of 0.025% on nonpaid-in capital. Open and hidden reserves not taxed. | Not recognized. Taxed as regular firms. | The canton and the municipalities levy the same tax (set by the cantonal government. |
| BS | Profit and capital tax not levied. Proportional special tax of 0.1% on paid-in capital and on open reserves. Tax of 0.025% on nonpaid-in capital. Hidden reserves not taxed. | Not recognized. Taxed as regular firms. | Not recognized. Taxed as regular firms. |
| FR | At the request of the taxpayer, the ordinary profit and capital taxes are not levied. The cantonal government sets a special proportional tax on capital. | Not recognized. Taxed as regular firms. | Same as for holding firms. |
| GE | Profit and capital tax not levied. Proportional special tax of 0.1% on paid-in capital and on open reserves. Tax of 0.05% on nonpaid-in capital. Multiplier. | Not recognized. Taxed as regular firms. | Same as for holding firms. |
| GL | Profit and capital tax not levied. Proportional special tax of 0.05% on capital. Minimum tax of CHF 50. No multiplier. | Not recognized if employees in the canton. | Same as for holding firms. |

| | | | |
|---|---|---|---|
| GR | Profit and capital tax not levied. Proportional special tax of 0.1% on paid-in capital and on open and hidden reserves. Tax of 0.05% on nonpaid-in capital. No multiplier. | n.a. | Profit and capital tax not levied. Proportional special tax of 0.05% on paid-in capital and on open and hidden reserves. Non paid-in capital not taxed. |
| LU | Profit and capital tax not levied. Proportional special tax of 0.01% on paid-in capital and on open and hidden reserves. Nonpaid-in capital not taxed. No multiplier. | Firms that hold at least 20% of the capital of other firms. Profit from participation not taxed. Tax on capital as for regular firms. | Not recognized. Taxed as regular firms. |
| NE | Profit and capital tax not levied. Proportional special tax of 0.05% on paid-in capital. No multiplier. | Not recognized. Taxed as regular firms. | Not recognized. Taxed as regular firms. |
| NW | Special tax agreement possible. | Special tax agreement possible. | Special tax agreement possible. |
| OW | Profit and capital tax not levied. Proportional special tax on paid-in capital, open and hidden reserves. No multiplier. | Same as for holding firms. | Profit and capital tax not levied. Annual special tax, the type and amount of which shall be determined by the Government Council. No multiplier. |
| SG | Profit from participation not taxed. The capital tax can be replaced by a flat-rate tax to be determined by the cantonal government. | Same as for holding firms. | Not recognized. Taxed as regular firms. |
| SH | Profit and capital tax not levied. Proportional special tax of 0.05% on paid-in capital and on open and hidden reserves. No multiplier. | Firms that hold at least 40% of the capital of other firms. Profit from participation not taxed. No reduction for the capital tax. | Legal entities with head office in the canton, but no business operations. Profit and capital tax not levied. Proportional special tax of 0.01% on paid-in capital and on open and hidden reserves. No multiplier. |
| SO | Reduction of profit and capital taxes by a maximum of 80%. The cantonal government decides on the reduction individually for each firm. | Not recognized. Taxed as regular firms. | Not recognized. Taxed as regular firms. |

(*continued*)

**Table 10A.3** **(cont.)**

| Canton | Holding firms | Investment firms | Domiciliary firms |
|---|---|---|---|
| SZ | Firms that hold at least 20% of the capital of other firms. Profit from participation not taxed. Cantonal and municipal multipliers. | Same as for holding firms. | Not recognized. Taxed as regular firms. |
| TG | Reduction of 20% of the tax amount. No reduction for the capital tax. | Same as for holding firms. | Not recognized. Taxed as regular firms. |
| TI | Profit and capital tax not levied. Proportional special tax of 0.04% on the paid-in capital and of 0.02% on the nonpaid-in capital. Open and hidden reserves not taxed. No multiplier. | Not recognized. Taxed as regular firms. | Same as for holding firms. |
| UR | Not recognized. Taxed as regular firms. | Not recognized. Taxed as regular firms. | Not recognized. Taxed as regular firms. |
| VD | Reduction of 75% of the tax amount on profit and on capital. Special multiplier of 20% on the reduced tax amount. | Not recognized. Taxed as regular firms. | Not recognized. Taxed as regular firms. |
| VS | Profit and capital tax not levied. Proportional special tax of 0.05% on the paid-in capital and on open reserves. Cantonal multiplier. Capital tax for municipalities as for regular firms but can be reduced. | Not recognized. Taxed as regular firms. | Same as for holding firms. |
| ZG | Profit and capital tax not levied. The canton levies a special tax from 0.05% to 0.15% on paid-in capital. Rate decided on a case-by-case basis by the cantonal tax commission. No multiplier. | Firms that hold at least 20% of the capital of other firms. Profit from participation not taxed. Tax on capital as for regular firms. | Same as for holding firms. |
| ZH | Profit and capital tax not levied. Proportional special tax of 0.05% on paid-in capital, open and hidden reserves. Cantonal and municipal multipliers as for regular firms | Same as for holding firms. | The extension of the holding privilege to domiciliary firms decided on a case-by-case basis. |

Notes: The table reports the main differences in tax practices across cantons in 1947 for holding, investment, and domiciliary firms.

## 10A.3 The 2020 Corporate Tax Reform

Aiming to align its corporate tax law with international standards, Switzerland abolished privileged taxation for holding, domiciliary, and mixed firms as of 2020, based on a 66 percent majority vote in a 2019 nationwide referendum. These tax privileges had been qualified as "harmful tax practices" by the OECD under Action 5 of the "Base Erosion and Profit Shifting" (BEPS) project.

Taxable profits of multinational "status" firms that had been eligible for preferential taxation have been found to be significantly more tax sensitive than profits of firms that were subject to regular taxation (Brülhart and Staubli 2017; Daepp and Staubli 2018). New relief measures were therefore introduced, motivated at least in part by a desire to remain attractive for internationally active firms and their taxable profits. Those measures apply only to subfederal taxation, as did the former privileges. The federal government continues to levy an unchanged 7.8 percent effective tax on all taxable profits. The measures introduced by the 2020 Corporate Tax Reform include the following.

### 10A.3.1 *Patent Box*

Profits derived from patents and similar intellectual property rights are now partially exempt from subfederal corporate income taxation. Cantons are obliged by federal law to provide this tax relief. They can set the extent to which qualifying profits are exempt to no more than 90 percent. In the interest of practicality, a patent or a similar intellectual property right is typically both a necessary and sufficient prerequisite to qualify for the patent box. This framework is designed to conform with current international standards, particularly the OECD's modified nexus approach. Because they are obliged to by federal law, all cantons have introduced the patent box. More than half of them have set the maximum relief to the maximum 90 percent according to federal law. Geneva, Glarus, and Lucerne have set the maximum relief at 10 percent. They apparently do not want firms to use this instrument (cf. the comments below on the relief limitation).

### 10A.3.2 *Deduction for R&D Expenditure*

Cantons may offer firms the option to claim an additional deduction of up to 50 percent for R&D expenditure. This measure targets domestically conducted R&D (as does the patent box, given the nexus requirements). In the context of Swiss law, the definition of R&D is quite comprehensive, encompassing fundamental and applied research as well as knowledge-driven innovation. For the sake of simplicity, these deductions are calculated solely based on labor costs. However, to acknowledge other types of R&D expenditures, a supplementary uplift of 35 percent is provided. Most cantons have adopted this new deduction.

### 10A.3.3 *Allowance for Corporate Equity*

Cantons are given the right to grant an interest deduction on equity. This deduction aligns with the imputed interest on what is known as "security equity," which refers to the portion of taxable equity capital in Switzerland that surpasses the long-term business activity's required equity capital. To date, only the canton of Zurich has implemented such a provision.

### 10A.3.4 *Reduction in Subfederal Corporate Tax Rates*

While it was not formally part of the nationwide reform, most cantons lowered their corporate tax rates as a countermeasure to the tax rises resulting from the phase-out of status privileges. As we show in figure 10.9, most cantons cut their regular tax rates contemporaneously with the reform. Cantons that hosted a high share of firms with status privilege cut their tax rates particularly strongly (see Portmann and Staubli 2020).

### 10A.3.5 *Cap on Total Tax Relief*

The cumulative tax relief arising from the patent box, additional deductions for R&D, and the allowance for corporate equity is not allowed to exceed 70 percent of the taxable profit. Cantons may set this limit at a lower level. This means that, assuming the cantonal relief limit is set at $x$ percent, the corporate tax base will be determined by the greater of two values: taxable profit after tax relief, or $(1 - x)$ percent of taxable profit before tax relief. About half of the cantons have set the cap at 70 percent. Some cantons, however, set the cap at 20 percent or lower, such that it is unlikely to be worthwhile for firms to take on the administrative burden of claiming patent-box or additional R&D deductions.

At the time of writing, the data available on the aftermath of the reform are not yet sufficient for a rigorous ex post evaluation. This will be an interesting setting for empirical research in a few years' time. Some ex ante evaluation of the tax reform is provided in Chatagny et al. (2017).

## 10A.4 The Federal Tax Harmonization Act (FTHA)

The exact relationship between the direct federal tax and tax harmonization at the cantonal level is an open question. The discussion in section 10.4.1, however, suggests that voluntary cooperation without federal involvement would have been limited. We, therefore, first describe the history of the federal government and direct taxation before the FTHA, followed by a discussion of the emergence of the FTHA. We then discuss the relationship between the FTHA and cantonal fiscal equalization and, finally, some important implications of the FTHA for corporate taxation.

### 10A.4.1 A Brief History of the Fiscal Role of the Federal Government

#### *10A.4.1.1 Political Parties*

The Swiss Confederation as a federal state came into being in 1848 after a civil war. After this war and indeed throughout much of the 20th century, three political parties were relevant in Switzerland. These parties had different points of view in the run-up to the creation of a direct federal tax.

The socially conservative Christian Democratic People's Party[50] and related regional groups represented the Catholic minority. Having lost the civil war of 1847 that led to the creation of the federal state, Swiss Catholics were traditionally opposed to measures that strengthened the central government and to harmonizing legislation in Catholic cantons with legislation in Protestant cantons.

The party that long dominated the federal government (and even the parliament until electoral reform in 1918) was the liberal Free Democratic Party,[51] which represented the winners of the civil war of 1847. The Free Democratic Party's position toward a federal direct tax was ambiguous. The argument that taxes tend to be economically harmful did not feature as prominently in the Free Democratic Party as one would expect nowadays. There was even support for building a democratic state and centralized government, which included functioning taxation. However, the Free Democratic Party generally preferred indirect taxes. One stronghold of anticentralism besides Catholics were French-speaking cantons and their Free Democratic Party representatives who feared domination by a German-speaking majority (see e.g., Freiburghaus and Buchli 2003, 35).[52]

The Social Democratic Party, and the labor movement more broadly, have always favored centralization. They had been pushing for (permanent) direct federal taxes since World War I (Grossmann 1943, 274–75), which was crucial for the legislation that would eventually happen. The main motivation for the Social Democratic Party's position does not seem to have been a negative stance toward tax competition. Two other reasons can be documented

50. The party united with the Conservative Democratic Party of Switzerland and changed its name to The Centre in 2021.

51. The party united with the Liberal Party and changed its name to FDP–The Liberals in 2009. "FDP" was the acronym of the Free Democratic Party (Freisinnig-Demokratische Partei).

52. In October 1959, for example, *Neue Zürcher Zeitung* (1959) reports that member of the National Council Piot of the Free Democratic Party urged fellow party members from the French-speaking cantons to abandon their opposition against direct federal taxation arguing that "our national defense must not be guided by Khrushchev's smiles or tantrums." Arguments concerning national defense had previously already been decisive for reforms leading to increased centralization, especially in the run-up to the constitutional reform of 1874, as a result of which the military was largely placed under the control of the federal government (Freiburghaus and Buchli 2003, 33).

from contemporary sources. First, the Social Democratic Party wanted to abolish indirect taxes, which in their view disproportionately burdened the workforce. Second, they primarily associated the fractionalization of Swiss tax laws with rent-seeking behavior of local authorities at the expense of working-class people and thought that, at the national level, organized labor would be better able to protect them.

The congress of the Social Democratic Party in 1916, for example, decided that they would not approve of any federal tax reforms that did not include direct taxes (*Solidarität* 1916). They also wanted to replace tariffs, a form of indirect taxation as argued by Robmann (1918), with direct taxes. As a compromise between the political camps, both direct and indirect taxes would eventually be introduced.[53]

These party-specific differences seem more salient during the period until the 1950s, during which federal direct taxation was still controversial. Afterward, when a consensus had been reached, this appears not to have been that much of an issue anymore.[54]

### 10A.4.2 Direct Taxation in the Cantons Until the 1940s

Swiss cantons have been making use of direct taxation since the mid-19th century. Until then tariffs had been their major source of tax revenue. In 1848, after the war that led to the creation of a federal state, cantons lost the right to impose tariffs, which implied a substantial decrease in overall revenue because many cantons had not yet developed the capacity to rely on direct forms of taxation. It took cantons much time to build fiscal capacity.

Eugen Grossmann (1879–1963), professor of public finance at the University of Zurich, paints a bleak picture of the situation in the cantons until the 1940s. Quoting Grossman (1945), Tanner (2012, 33) argues that not a single canton had a "reasonably up-to-date tax administration" before World War I. Wage statements, lists of securities and debt documents were "unknown concepts." Seligman (1914, 358) discusses shortcomings of wealth taxation in Swiss cantons and a widespread culture of underreporting, arguing that the income tax might "work just as badly" or even be "still more unsuccessful than the general [wealth] tax." Tanner (2012, 33)

53. An extensive article in *Rote Revue* (1926), a party newspaper of the Social Democratic Party, discussed the common theme of harmonization and direct federal taxation. The article not only addressed the context of Swiss history and constitutional considerations but also came up with international examples. A reform in the course of the French Revolution, in which a single direct tax was introduced instead of a multitude of both regional and indirect taxes, is mentioned as an inspiration for the Social Democratic Party's policy proposals. The article cites a 1920 reform in the German Empire as an example that similar tax unification can succeed in a federal state.

54. A fourth party that initially emerged from mostly urban-rural divisions within the Free Democratic Party and became powerful later on during the 1990s is the euro-skeptic and fiscally conservative Swiss People's Party. The Green Party and Green-Liberals became influential after the turn of the millennium.

notes that there was "a veritable proliferation of cantonal and municipal tax concessions." Referring to Grossmann (1935, 107–8), Tanner (2012, 44–45) argues that, as late as the 1930s, the taxation procedure was "completely outdated." Many cantons thought "that they were able to master the problem of taxation almost without any legally and economically trained civil servants." Information asymmetries that favored politically connected taxpayers abounded.

The practice of basing the personal and corporate income tax on the previous (two) years' income, referred to as "praenumerando method," is one example of cantons' inability to adequately administer taxation. Lacking the capacity to assess taxable income in time, under praenumerando, cantonal administrations would make the assumption that taxable income was the same as (a mean of) previous years' taxable income. Federal Council (1983, 14) mentions that during the 1930s, there were three cantons (Schwyz, Aargau, Thurgau) that used a six-year period as base years. Many cantonal tax administrations claimed that the praenumerando method reduced bureaucracy because taxpayers only had to fill out tax returns every two years. In numerous cases, however, cantonal tax administrations had to make interim assesments due to sharp fluctuation in income or changes in tax liability, which according to Federal Council (1983, 15) more than nullified this advantage.

Hürlimann (2015, 37–38) discusses knowledge transfers between the cantonal and federal tax administrations. She explains that, while after the federal government first introduced direct taxes in 1916, it benefited from cantonal expertise (specifically expertise from the canton of St. Gallen). During the late 1940s the establishment and expansion of the Federal Tax Administration led to a surge in professionalization in many cantons.[55] Relatedly, Tanner (2012, 35) mentions that data and estimates published by the federal government in the course of collecting the war tax after 1915 differed substantially from declared wealth as assessed by the canton of Zurich's tax administration. The canton subsequently expanded its tax administration starting in the late 1910s.

### 10A.4.3 Direct Taxation at the Federal Level Before 1959

Eugen Grossmann laid the intellectual foundations for a direct federal tax in Switzerland, sometimes referring to Edwin R. A. Seligman (Grossmann 1943, 278). Seligman's writings had previously influenced the legislation that followed the adoption of the 16th Amendment, which allowed for a progressive federal income tax in the United States (e.g., Seligman 1893).

55. van Orsouw (1995, 82–99) discusses one example where, following the example of the federal government in 1934, the canton of Zug switched from taxing earned income to taxing broadly defined income in 1947. The canton of Basel-City had pioneered the taxation of broadly defined incomes during the 19th century.

Direct taxation at the federal level only emerged after, as a consequence of World War I, tariff revenue collapsed at the federal level. In a referendum on June 6, 1915, a vast majority of Swiss voters (and cantons) voted in favor of a progressive one-time "war tax" (*Kriegssteuer*) levied on personal wealth and earnings as well as on corporate equity capital (Hürlimann 2015, 32–33). Grossmann (1943, 274–75) emphasizes the influence of the labor movement and social democracy, at whose urging this vote came about. The union newspaper *Gewerkschaftliche Rundschau* (1915) called for a "war profits tax" that went beyond this and provided estimates of the expected revenue.[56]

After the introduction of the one-time war tax, the Social Democratic Party came up with a proposal for a permanent federal direct tax, which was voted down by 54 percent of the electorate in a popular referendum in 1919 (Tanner 2012, 36). Even more strikingly, 87 percent of Swiss voters voted against a Social-Democrat proposal for a one-time capital levy to finance the burden of World War I in December 1922 (Tanner 2012, 36–37). The war tax, originally intended to be a one-time tax, was, however, renewed in 1919 during an economic crisis, maintained until 1932 and subsequently replaced with a "crisis levy" (*Krisenabgabe*; Hürlimann 2015, 33, 36).

A federal-level tax on corporate income was first enacted in 1933 during the Great Depression and was only supposed to last for four years (1934–37). When World War II began and the economy did not improve, these temporary laws were repeatedly extended or replaced with laws that similarly allowed for direct taxation in 1938 and 1941. Since 1941, there has been a "direct federal tax" (*direkte Bundessteuer*), which until 1983 was referred to as "defense tax" (*Wehrsteuer*). In addition, the government introduced a sales tax as a political compromise (*Warenumsatzsteuer*; Hürlimann 2015, 36–37). Swiss voters voted down a proposal for a permanent direct federal tax in 1950. Eugen Grossmann had played a leading role in drafting this failed tax reform. Instead, the electorate decided to retain the existing regulation until 1954.

An attempt (prepared by Social Democratic Party member of the Federal Council Max Weber, who subsequently resigned) to introduce a definitive new regulation failed in another referendum in 1953 (Freiburghaus and Buchli 2003, 47). Since then and until today, Switzerland has been in a state of "permanent provisionalism," in which the federal government has the right to levy taxes, but this right must be confirmed in a national referendum at regular intervals.

56. World War I, which brought widespread poverty and social tensions culminating in a strike in 1918, was a turning point for Swiss politics more generally. After electoral reform was agreed upon in 1918, the ruling Free Democratic Party lost its absolute majority in the Swiss Parliament. Also, the war led to the implementation of "Bismarck-style" social reforms, although to a limited extent only (see, e.g., Freiburghaus and Buchli 2003, 40–41; Hürlimann 2015, 35; Lengwiler and Leimgruber 2018).

#### 10A.4.4 A Turning Point: Constitutional Basis for Federal Direct Taxes

In 1958, the federal direct tax was constitutionally enshrined in the Federal Financial Code (Bundesfinanzordnung; Hürlimann 2015, 29). In May, the electorate approved a "federal decree on the constitutional reorganization of the federal financial budget" (Bundesbeschluss über die verfassungsmässige Neuordnung des Finanzhaushalts des Bundes). At the same time, federal wealth taxes were abolished as a concession to the cantons (Hürlimann 2015, 39).

This initiated a long-standing legislative mandate for the federal government: "Since 1959, the Federal Government has had the constitutional task of transforming the . . . defense tax decision [*Wehrsteuerbeschluss*] . . . into ordinary statutory law." (Federal Council 1983, 6). A process of 25–30 years began, during which various politicians, political commissions, and government agencies drafted legislative bills.

### 10A.5 The Development of the FTHA

#### 10A.5.1 The Federal Direct Tax Act (FDTA) and the Federal Tax Harmonization Act (FTHA)

Although it remains unclear whether cantonal taxes would have been harmonized in the absence of federal direct taxes, in practice, the drafting of the Federal Tax Harmonization Act (FTHA; Swiss Parliament 1990a), was closely linked to the simultaneous drafting of legislation on direct taxation of personal and corporate income at the federal level (FDTA; Swiss Parliament 1990b). This process lasted almost a quarter of a century until 1983. It then took another seven years until the Swiss Parliament approved the FTHA in 1990. Key references on the process that led to the FTHA and the FDTA are the draft legislation published by the federal government (Botschaften des Bundesrates) in 1977 and 1983 to convince both chambers of Switzerland's national parliament (Bundesversammlung) of the new legislation drafted by the federal government (Federal Council 1976, 1983).

#### 10A.5.2 Initiatives by the Cantons

Following the principle of subsidiarity, cantonal finance directors first tried to harmonize taxes without conferring a new competence on the federal government. All efforts by the cantons to harmonize taxes were limited to tax base harmonization ("formal tax harmonization"). At no time was harmonization of tax rates an option for the cantons ("material tax harmonization").

In 1968, the Conference of Cantonal Finance Directors (CCFD) appointed a commission of practitioners and researchers. The mandate was to craft a model law for the cantons (*Neue Zürcher Zeitung* 1973c). This so-called Ritschard commission was chaired by Willi Ritschard, at the time finance director of the canton of Solothurn and later member of the Federal Council (federal government).[57] The Federal Department of Finance (FDF) already previously installed a commission under the leadership of Lucerne cantonal member of government Bühlmann (Christian Democratic People's Party) to prepare preliminary legislative drafts on federal direct taxation. This commission presented its legislative proposals in 1970.

In 1970, Federal Councilor Nello Celio and the CCFD agreed to coordinate the legislative proposals on a direct federal tax and on a model law on the direct taxes of the municipalities and cantons (Höhn 1973; Ritschard 1972). As a result, the FDF and the CCFD established a joint "Coordination Commission for Tax Harmonization" in November 1970, consisting of members of the aforementioned commissions. This commission, which was initially chaired again by Willi Ritschard, should draw up joint legislative proposals for the FTHA and the FDTA. The Coordination Commission started drafting legislation for the FDTA basically from scratch, considering the Bühlmann Commission's drafts were written in technical language that was difficult to understand.[58]

In 1971, a working group headed by Ernst Höhn, then professor at the University of St. Gallen, proposed an intercantonal agreement (concordat) as one possibility to realize tax harmonization.[59] The CCFD subsequently mandated the Ritschard commission to draft a concordat based on the draft of the model law (*Neue Zürcher Zeitung* 1971). At the end of 1972, the Ritschard commission completed its work.

57. Federal Councilors Willi Ritschard and Otto Stich (both serving as finance ministers) played key roles in the legislative process between the late 1960s and mid-1980s. Both had already been involved in drafting legislative proposals for tax harmonization before their time in the Federal Council. While both were Social Democrats, they each got into the Federal Council through votes from the bourgeois majority and against Social Democratic Party election nominations.

58. After his election to the Federal Council in 1974, he was succeeded by Wolfgang Lorétan (CSPO, a regional Catholic party), a member of the Valais cantonal executive and president of the CCFD. Other chairmen of the coordination commission, which was active until 1980, were the Zurich cantonal executive Albert Mossdorf (Free Democratic Party) and the Lucerne cantonal executive Carl Mugglin (Christian Democratic People's Party).

59. in previous academic work, Höhn had documented and quantified differences in taxation in the individual cantons. The Ritschard Commission began its work only after the emergence of Höhn's studies, which it drew upon extensively (Ritschard 1972, 103). In Höhn (1971, 8–9), Höhn explains why he thought harmonization was necessary at this point. Different tax rates in different cantons did not necessarily constitute an injustice, as circumstances in the cantons differed in other respects as well. With regard to the differences in deductibility documented by Höhn, for example, between pension contributions and pension benefits, however, the situation was different. Additionally, Höhn (1968, 269) mentions that tax harmonization within the European Economic Community (EEC), which was advanced during the 1960s, could serve as a model for cantonal tax harmonization in Switzerland (Ritschard 1972, 101, mentions this argument, too). He also quotes statements of Federal Councilor Nello Celio (Free Democratic Party), who emphasized the need of adapting Swiss laws to EEC legislation (Höhn 1968, 275–76).

The concordat solution proposed by Höhn was ultimately not pursued (Ritschard 1972, 104). As early as 1969 Höhn had himself already raised doubts that a concordat would be sufficient, unless the federal government was given the competence to enforce it if necessary (*Neue Zürcher Zeitung* 1969). The CCFD later also came to this conclusion. One reason was that a concordat would only allow horizontal but not vertical tax harmonization. A second reason was that joining the concordat would be voluntary for the cantons (Cavelti and Greminger 2010; Federal Council 1976). But if not all cantons were on board, then the goal of tax harmonization was not achieved. See also section 10.4.1 for the limitations of voluntary cooperation among cantons without involvement of the federal government.

At a meeting on June 14–15, 1973, the CCFD declared its support for the creation of a constitutional amendment for the creation of a tax harmonization law. It also suggested a wording for the new constitutional article (*Journal de Genève* 1973a, 1973d; *Neue Zürcher Zeitung* 1973b), which limits the competence of the federal legislative body to the establishment of principles of taxation (formal tax harmonization) and explicitly leaves the determination of tax rates within the competence of the cantons. This CCFD proposal prevailed in the subsequent political process along its broad lines. The constitutional article largely corresponds to the wording proposed by the CCFD at the time. Furthermore, on June 14–15, 1973, the CCFD approved the revised model law and recommended it "as a basis for further work on tax harmonization among the cantons, for revisions of cantonal tax laws and for the enactment of the future federal law on direct federal taxation" (*Neue Zürcher Zeitung* 1973b).

### 10A.5.3 Initiatives by Members of the Federal Parliament

There were numerous proposals from members of the federal parliament. In contrast to the initiatives from the cantons, they focused from the beginning on creating a constitutional basis that would give the federal parliament the authority to legislate in the area of tax harmonization. Some of these initiatives went beyond formal tax harmonization including varying degrees of material tax harmonization. There was a lively debate in federal parliament, also in connection with referenda (see section 10A.4.2), about how far harmonization should go.

There are several kinds of proposals, which members of parliament can submit. The most important ones are motion, postulate, and parliamentary initiative. They can all be approved or rejected by parliament. A motion mandates the Federal Council to draft legislation. A postulate mandates the Federal Council to examine and report on the appropriateness of preparing draft legislation or other measures to be taken. With a parliamentary initiative, a member of parliament may propose a draft legislation.

The proposals in parliament relating to tax harmonization included:

- December 3, 1968, postulate submitted by Max Weber, member of the National Council (Social Democratic Party, Bern): The Federal Council should evaluate the possibility to transfer the right to corporate taxation to the federal government. The postulate was approved by the National Council on March 13, 1969.
- March 1969, two identical motions submitted by Hans Conzett (March 12), member of the National Council (Swiss People's Party, Zurich) and Heinrich Herzog (March 20), member of the Council of States (Swiss People's Party, Thurgovia): they requested the Federal Council to evaluate the undesired consequences of the disharmonized tax system in Switzerland. The Federal Council agreed with the general principles of the proposals and requested that the motions be converted into postulates. They were approved as postulates by the National Council (June 12, 1969) and by the Council of States (June 17, 1969).
- November 26, 1969, a committee of the Council of States submitted a motion that demanded that the Federal Council draw up a constitutional reform bill to harmonize income and wealth taxes in Switzerland. The corresponding committee of the National Council submitted an identical motion. Both the National Council and the Council of States accepted the proposals on June 24, 1970. The motion was submitted in connection with the deliberations on the amendment of the Federal Financial Code, which was later voted down in a referendum.
- March 11, 1971, motion submitted by Walter Biel, member of the National Council (of the now defunct party Landesring, Alliance of Independents, Zurich): he requested that the Federal Council draft a reform proposal to introduce a federal tax on both individuals and firms that would replace cantonal taxes. Within a certain margin, the determination of the tax allowances may be left to the cantons. This proposal asked for full formal tax harmonization and far-reaching material tax harmonization, i.e., harmonization of tax rates and schedules.[60] The Federal Council opposed the proposal but agreed to take it on board as a postulate. It was approved as a postulate by the National Council (March 19, 1973). Ultimately, the motion was not successful (Hürlimann 2015, 44).
- March 17, 1971, parliamentary initiative submitted by Otto Stich, member of the National Council (Social Democratic Party, Solothurn; later he was elected a member of the Federal Council and assumed the role of minister of finance). He proposed a constitutional amendment that

60. Biel's arguments quoted in Swiss Radio and Television (1976) primarily relate to personal income taxes. They are, however, similar to the arguments discussed today in the context of the OECD reforms. For example, Biel addresses the fact that high-income taxpayers can minimize their tax burden by moving to a different municipality. He also mentions that municipalities with relatively low-income taxpayers often provide more public goods because they charge higher taxes.

allowed the federal parliament to legislate "in order to promote tax harmonization among the cantons." The initiative was mostly limited to formal tax harmonization, but it included all taxes (not only on income and wealth). By allowing the federal parliament to prescribe a uniform regulation of the taxation of holding and domiciliary firms, however, the initiative provided for an element of material harmonization. As outlined in the report of the Commission of the National Council (1975), Otto Stich justified his proposal also with the large differences in the tax burden in the cantons, even though his proposal was largely about formal harmonization. He further argued that the taxation of holding and domiciliary firms differed greatly across cantons. In some cantons it was sufficient for taxation at the preferential rate that the assets consisted mainly of participations. Other cantons had stricter regimes giving rise to distortions and huge differences in tax rates across cantons. The legislative work was assigned to the committee of the National Council. In the report released on March 17, 1975, the committee rejected the initiative and proposed a constitutional amendment that was very close to the one drafted by the Ritschard commission.

- September 1972, identical motions submitted by Hans Letsch (September 18), member of the National Council (Free Democratic Party, Argovia) and Ulrich Luder (September 19), member of the Council of States (Free Democratic Party, Solothurn): The motions proposed delegating a mandate to the Federal Council to draft a constitutional amendment that would facilitate formal tax harmonization among the cantons. However, this harmonization would explicitly exclude the harmonization of tax rates. The Federal Council agreed with the general principles of the proposals and requested that the motions be converted into postulates. They were approved as postulates by the National Council (Letsch's proposal, March 19, 1973) and by the Council of States (Luder's proposal, March 7, 1973).
- September 28, 1972, postulate submitted by Albert Rüttimann, member of the National Council (Christian Democratic People's Party, Argovia): The postulate asked the Federal Council to prepare a constitutional amendment that allows for federal legislation prohibiting unjustified tax deals and granting the authority to prescribe to the cantons, if necessary, a minimum tax for certain income categories. The postulate, which also comprised elements of harmonization of tax rates, was approved by the National Council (December 4, 1972).
- December 1973, parliamentary initiative by Laurent Butty (Christian Democratic People's Party, Fribourg): He proposed a constitutional amendment that would transfer the authority to levy personal income and wealth taxes to the federal government. At most 25 percent of the revenue would go to the federal government, and at least 75 percent would be distributed among cantons (proportional to the population).

The cantons could still add a surcharge on the federal tax and keep the revenue. Corporate taxation would remain within cantonal sovereignty. This initiative therefore provides for a far reaching harmonization, both formal and material, of personal income and wealth taxation. Very much like Otto Stich, he justified his proposal with the large differences in tax burdens across cantons. He argued that a formal tax harmonization would not lead to a convergence in tax rates (Commission of the National Council 1975). The legislative work was assigned to the committee of the National Council. In the report released by the commission on March 17, 1975 it also rejected this initiative.

The most important result from the list of political proposals was the report of the committee. The report that was released by the committee on March 17, 1975, was the result of deliberations from 1971 to 1975. The committee examined the parliamentary initiatives of Stich and Butty and the proposal of the CCFD (prepared by the Ritschard commission) and formulated its own proposal, which was substantively very close to the CCFD proposal. A public consultation was held on all these options. Based on the responses to the consultation, the committee revised its proposal editorially but left it substantively largely unchanged. Following the CCFD proposal, the committee's proposed wording limits the competence of the federal government to the establishment of principles of taxation (formal tax harmonization) and explicitly leaves the determination of tax rates within the competence of the cantons. Furthermore, also following the CCFD, the tax harmonization would only apply to direct taxes. The committee refrained from a material tax harmonization, because it wanted to hold on to the financial and tax sovereignty, and therefore the federal law "has to respect the regional differences in the population and economic structure."

#### 10A.5.4 Popular Initiatives

There were two popular initiatives for tax harmonization in the 1970s. Both initiatives went beyond formal tax harmonization and included at least elements of material tax harmonization. They were voted down, the first on March 21, 1976, and the second on December 4, 1977. For both initiatives the rejection rate was between 50 percent and 60 percent. The rejection rate was thus surprisingly low, considering that both initiatives called for a fundamental overhaul of the Swiss tax system and aimed at eliminating tax competition completely or to a large extent.

A popular initiative is a democratic right prescribed in the constitution. It allows 100,000 citizens to sign an initiative for a constitutional amendment and to bring it to the ballot (50,000 signatures were required until September 25, 1977). In most cases, the constitution is not directly applicable. For instance, a constitutional provision conferring on the federal legislator the right to levy an income tax is not a sufficient legal base to collect taxes. For this purpose, the legislature must first implement the constitutional provision in a law. The aim of a popular initiative is therefore to instruct the legislature to enact a law in accordance with the constitutional provision according to the initiative.

As Dubach (2010a) argues, the two initiatives were launched in the wake of deteriorating federal finances, providing a fertile ground for popular initiatives on the tax system. At the beginning of the 1970s, federal finances fell into deficit, partly because of growing federal subsidies to the cantons and the social security system. The situation worsened with the global economic crisis as of 1974. We base our summary of the two popular initiatives on Dubach (2010a, 2010b), which appeared in a collection that summarizes all referendums in Switzerland from 1948 to 2007.

#### *10A.5.4.1 Initiative "For a Reform of the Tax System (Fairer Taxation and Abolition of Tax Privileges)"*

The referendum was initiated by the Alliance of Independents and took place on March 4, 1976. It called for a uniform tax system throughout Switzerland and to abolish tax privileges. The initiative's goal was to replace the cantonal tax laws with a uniform federal law. The federal law would regulate both the tax base and the tax rates. The initiative did not define tax rates, but it prescribed a progressive tax schedule for personal income and a proportional tax for corporate income (flat rate without exemption level). The cantons would have received part of the revenue to cover their financial needs. The initiative allowed cantons to levy an extra revenue by applying multipliers to the federal tax.

The initiative was rejected with 57.8 percent of the votes and 24 out of 25 cantons at the time. It got very little support from political stakeholders. The left-of-center parties and the trade unions did not issue a voting recommendation. The Federal Council and the Parliament rejected the initiative together with the center-right parties and business associations.

Opponents argued that the initiative disregarded the federal structure of the country and that it undermined the ongoing, urgently needed and more adequate tax reform efforts. The proponents argued that material tax harmonization is fairer emphasizing the negative effects of tax competition (Swiss Radio and Television 1976).

#### *10A.5.4.2 Initiative "For Tax Harmonization, Greater Taxation of Wealth and Relief for Lower Incomes (Taxation of the Wealthy Initiative)"*

The referendum was initiated by the Social Democratic Party and took place on December 4, 1977. It called for formal tax harmonization and for higher tax rates for high-income and high-wealth individuals. For corporate taxation it called for both formal and material harmonization. The demand for formal tax harmonization was substantively the same as what had already been passed in the June referendum earlier in 1977 (see appendix supplementary tables). This demand had thus become redundant. The initiative went further, however, by calling for greater progressivity in income and wealth tax. For the federal income tax, incomes below CHF 40,000 were to be exempt. For incomes of CHF 100,000, the tax rate should be at least 6 percent; for incomes of CHF 200,000, at least 10 percent; and for incomes of CHF 1 million, at least 14 percent.

For the cantons, the initiative called for minimum tax rates. This is a material intervention in cantonal tax policy, which would not be possible without such a constitutional amendment. For the cantonal income taxes, incomes up to subsistence level should remain tax-free. For incomes of CHF 100,000, the tax rate should be at least 21 percent; for incomes of CHF 200,000, at least 27 percent; and for incomes of CHF 1 million, at least 33.4 percent.

For corporate taxation, the initiative sought full formal and material harmonization, i.e., harmonization of both tax bases and tax rates. The taxation of corporate income and corporate capital would have been transferred entirely to the federal government. According to the initiative, the cantons would receive at least one-third of the revenue. On corporate income, the initiative left the determination of tax rates to the federal legislature.

The initiative was rejected with 55.6 percent of the votes and 22 out of 25 cantons at the time. It got support from the left-of-center parties and from part of the trade unions. The Federal Council and the Parliament rejected the initiative together with the center-right parties and business associations.

Opponents of the initiative argued that the initiative would weaken capital formation and investment activity. This weakening of competitiveness would ultimately also put jobs at risk. Furthermore, the initiative would not respect the diversity of the cantons. The proponents emphasized that higher taxation of the wealthy and the tax reliefs for lower incomes would increase tax justice and eliminate tax evasion and tax competition between the cantons.

### 10A.5.5 Harmonization of Tax Bases Only or Also of Rates and Schedules?

Although all efforts to harmonize tax rates across cantons failed in the end, such proposals did play a role in public discussions. In a 1972 article, Ritschard (1972, 106–7) wrote that, in his opinion, a majority of the population probably favored material harmonization at the time. However, Ritschard saw practical obstacles and considered formal harmonization as a necessary precondition for harmonization of tax rates. According to Ritschard, the per capita GDP in the then richest canton of Basel-Stadt (CHF 17,410) exceeded that of the then poorest canton of Appenzell-Innerrhoden (CHF 7,635) by a factor of 2.3. If each canton had continued to levy its taxes independently, harmonization of tax rates would have meant that either tax revenues would have increased immensely in Basel-Stadt, or that they would have decreased sharply in Appenzell-Innerrhoden. Ritschard considered tax base harmonization as a prerequisite for better financial equalization as a prerequisite for a necessary reduction of intercantonal income differences.

In retrospect, things have not turned out as Ritschard had intended. Tax competition may even have intensified after tax bases had been harmonized. And while fiscal equalization may work better today, the FTHA has not helped level intercantonal differences, either. According to the latest figures for 2020, per capita GDP in Basel-Stadt, still the canton with the highest per capita GDP (CHF 189,354), is 3.4 times higher than in Valais (CHF 55,313), now the canton with the lowest GDP per capita, and 2.9 times higher than in Appenzell-Innerrhoden (CHF 64,358).[61]

### 10A.5.6 The Position of Business Associations and Representatives on Tax Harmonization

Both Höhn (1971, 8) and Ritschard (1972, 101) mention the difficulties that firms face in operating their business in several cantons as a main motivation of why they thought tax harmonization was necessary.

"Big business" as a consequence was emphatically in favor of tax harmonization. Swiss corporate union economiesuisse endorsed harmonization. SGV/USAM, representing mostly smaller businesses, on the other hand, neither formally endorsed nor opposed it.

Tax harmonization made it easier for larger corporations, especially in retail, to scale their operations and operate in multiple cantons. The growth of these larger businesses, such as supermarket chains, that were able to operate at lower costs than local businesses allowed for welfare gains.

The increased competition could have been to the detriment of remote jurisdictions if not only the tax bases but also the tax rates had been harmonized. The results of Krapf and Staubli (2025) suggest that economic activity would be more concentrated in urban centers today if tax rates had been harmonized in addition to tax bases (see section 10.3.1).

If there was any interest group for whom the preharmonization situation was beneficial, then it was probably small businesses that only operated in one canton. We see two reasons: First, lack of harmonized tax laws shielded them to an extent from competition by larger corporations that operated in multiple cantons. Second, owners of these small businesses likely had the knowledge and political connections (as opposed to working-class people) that allowed them to take advantage of complicated legislation in the can-

61. See Kantonales Bruttoinlandsprodukt (BIP) pro Einwohner, from the Federal Statistical Office, https://www.bfs.admin.ch/bfs/de/home/statistiken/volkswirtschaft/volkswirtschaftliche-gesamtrechnung/bruttoinlandprodukt-kanton.assetdetail.23526480.html.

tons. Tax harmonization curtailed smaller local businesses of this edge that they previously had and may have forced some of them out of the market.

### 10A.5.7 Completion of the Legislative Procedures

On June 12, 1976, a vote was held on federal resolutions on the one hand on a "reorganization of the sales tax and direct federal tax," and on the other hand on tax harmonization. Although the electorate rejected the bill on direct federal tax, it voted in favor of the tax harmonization bill. This vote was preceded by parliamentary initiatives by the two national councilors, Otto Stich (Social Democratic Party, Solothurn) in 1971 and Laurent Butty (Christian Democratic People's Party, Fribourg) in 1973, which differed in how far the harmonization should go and whether, for example, it should include only direct taxes or all taxes. A committee of the National Council decided against the two parliamentary initiatives and decided instead, in coordination with the CCFD, to submit proposals of the Ritschard Commission to the electorate for vote. This vote led to the new Article 42 quinquies in the federal constitution, which mandated the federal legislator, in cooperation with the cantons, to harmonize direct federal, cantonal, and municipal taxes. After a phase as a cantonal executive in the canton of Solothurn, National Councilor Otto Stich would succeed Willi Ritschard as Federal Councilor in the FDF from 1984 to 1995.

In 1983, the federal government proposed a law on tax harmonization, i.e., the unification of cantonal legislation with regard to tax bases in particular. It was part of this proposal that the tax itself not be part of the tax base. Moreover, the federal government proposed to abandon the progressive schedule it had applied to corporate income in favor of a proportional tariff. It took seven years until this law on tax harmonization (FTHA) was approved of in 1990. The FTHA became effective in 1993.

## 10A.6 The FTHA and Fiscal Equalization

At the time of the discussion on the introduction of formal tax harmonization, the financial equalization between the cantons was structured differently than it is today. The cantons received money from the federal government for specific projects (e.g., for the construction of infrastructure or a school building).

How much financial support cantons received from the federal government depended on the so-called financial capacity of a canton. The financial capacity was determined by, among other things, the amount of tax revenue of the canton. A canton with low per capita tax revenue tended to receive more money from the federal government, a canton with low per capita tax revenue tended to receive less money from the federal government.

Numerous media reports (*Journal de Genève* 1973b, 1973c; *Neue Zürcher*

*Zeitung* 1969, 1970, 1973a) emphasized the importance of formal tax harmonization to enable the comparison of cantons' fiscal capacity for purposes of the financial equalization scheme. There were concerns that recipient cantons would deliberately reduce their revenues by lowering taxes and then requesting financial support from the federal government. According to the *Neue Zürcher Zeitung* (1973c), "it is unacceptable that a canton deliberately manipulates the elements used to determine financial capacity in such a way that it is placed in the group of financially weak cantons and accordingly receives high federal funds." Federal Council (1976) describes the leitmotiv according to which the cantons should first "try to help themselves with all possible means before asking for solidarity from others."

However, because the tax systems in the cantons were completely different, it was practically impossible to gauge the actual financial needs of a canton. In other words, it was often unclear whether a canton had low tax revenues because of low taxes or because of little financial capacity. Formal tax harmonization was meant to create transparency in this respect. Cantonal tax laws would differ only in the tax rates. Other provisions, like the way the tax base was determined or the frequency with which tax holidays were granted, ceased to play a role. Thus, the harmonization of the tax base would allow the federal government to tell whether a canton used all the reasonable measures to raise sufficient public funds on its own.

As mentioned above, some actors assumed or hoped that a more efficient financial equalization would lead to a reduction in differences in per capita income and eventually in tax rates across cantons (Ritschard 1972, 106–7). Others saw it as an indirect path to some degree of harmonization of tax rates in the cantons. When Leo Weber, the Rapporteur of the Committee, spoke to the National Council on June 22, 1976, he said that the Commission had explicitly ruled out direct material harmonization. However, formal tax harmonization should indirectly path the way to convergence in tax rates via financial equalization (loosely translated) (Commission of the National Council 1975).

These arguments were criticized for being somewhat unclear. At that time, there was no concrete plan on how to solve the identified problems in fiscal equalization after tax harmonization had been realized. *Journal de Genève* (1977) noted that the situation remains very unclear as to how to improve the financial equalization scheme subsequent to tax harmonization. This main argument for tax harmonization, that it would enable more efficient and fairer financial equalization, never manifested itself to any relevant extent. In any case, a revision of the financial equalization system was prepared in the 1990s, so that contributions to and from the cantons no longer depended on how much the cantons utilize their fiscal capacity. The reform of financial equalization came into force in 2008, two years after the transition period for the cantons to implement tax harmonization in cantonal law had ended.

## 10A.7 The FTHA, the FDTA, and Corporate Taxation

### 10A.7.1 Specific Implications of the FTHA for Corporate Taxation

Four components of the FTHA draft of 1983 were of particular importance for corporate taxation (e.g., Federal Council 1983, 5):

1. The FTHA stipulated that the taxes themselves should be deductible from the tax base. This had previously been handled very differently by the cantons. Also, there was some controversy around this with some cantons trying to make deductibility of the tax itself optional in the FTHA (Federal Council 1983, 53).
2. The cantons should retain sovereignty over tax rates (Federal Council 1983, 54–59). It was also discussed whether the FDTA should include measures to mitigate the economic double burden of corporate tax. However, the Coordination Commission ultimately rejected this (Federal Council 1983, 54–58).
3. At the federal level, the three-tier schedule was replaced with a proportional schedule (Federal Council 1983, 53–54 and 78–79).
4. The cantonal privileges for holding and domiciliary firms were to be standardized (Federal Council 1983, 61–63).

In 1998, the federal tax on corporate capital was abolished. Cantons still tax corporate capital. Following the lead of the federal government, most cantons have, however, moved toward proportional schedules on taxable profits as documented in Portmann and Staubli (2020).

### 10A.7.2 Praenumerando Versus Postnumerando

Plans to eliminate the practice of basing income tax on previous years' incomes were a central albeit the most controversial component of the efforts that led to the FTHA. The federal government considered the "standardization of temporal assessment" to be one of the "important goals of harmonization" and "an explicit objective of the constitutional mandate" (Federal Council 1983, 17–20). There was opposition from the cantons, but less in relation to corporate tax and more in relation to personal income tax. The federal government had already drafted a legislative proposal in 1973, but the cantons decided to delay arguing that standardization should coincide with the introduction of direct federal taxation. In 1980, the Conference of Cantonal Finance Directors (CCFD) even decided by a majority to uniformly apply the system with a two-year tax period and past assessment for personal income tax. Cantons that had already switched to the one-year tax period (BS, GE, NE, SO) and present assessment (BS) were to be obliged to reverse reforms. The federal government thought it could break the fierce opposition from some cantons by including the standardization of the time-based assessment in its bill for the FTHA of 1983. The version of the FTHA that was approved in 1990, however, prescribed past assessment and left cantons the choice between one- or two-year assessment period. In the late 1990s and early 2000s, however, Swiss cantons still moved toward a standard system with one-year tax period and present assessment. A revised version of the FTHA, which reflects this new reality, has been in force since 2014.

#### 10A.7.3 Tax Loss Carryforward

The provision in the FDTA (Swiss Parliament 1990b, Art. 31) regarding losses carried forward continues a practice that has existed since 1978 (Federal Council 1983, 96–97). According to this practice, losses from the seven financial years preceding the tax period can be deducted if they could not be taken into account in the calculation of the taxable income of these years. It should, however, be mentioned that, especially prior to the FTHA, the cantons, out of convenience, often applied their own legal regulations to the federal tax, which they are in charge of collecting, as well. This provision in the federal tax was initially more generous than it was in many cantons before the introduction of the FTHA, which often provided for less than seven years. While the drafts in the FTHA were therefore oriented toward the FDTA with regard to loss carryforwards, they did not provide for an obligation to adopt the regulations of the FDTA. The draft legislation for the FTHA, which allowed loss carry-forwards for up to seven years, left the cantons the option to follow the rules applicable to the federal direct tax (Federal Council 1983, Art. 28 Abs. 2, 301). Since a change in the law in 2001, the FTHA, however, uses the same rule as the FDTA (Swiss Parliament 1990a, Art. 25 Abs. 2).

## References

Agrawal, David R. 2015. "The Tax Gradient: Spatial Aspects of Fiscal Competition." *American Economic Journal: Economic Policy* 7 (2): 1–29.

Baur, Martin, Martin Daepp, and Bruno Jeitziner. 2020. "Die formelle Steuerharmonisierung im Lichte okonomischer Theorien." *Die Volkswirtschaft*, March 1, 2020.

Beer, Sebastian, Ruud de Mooij, and Li Liu. 2020. "International Corporate Tax Avoidance: A Review of the Channels, Magnitudes and Blind Spots." *Journal of Economic Surveys* 34: 660–88.

Blumenstein, Ernst. 1932/33. "Ein schweizerisches Steuersystem." *Archiv für Schweizerisches Abgaberecht (ASA)*.

Bradford, David F., and Wallace E. Oates. 1971. "Towards a Predictive Theory of Intergovernmental Grants." *American Economic Review* 61 (2): 440–48.

Brueckner, Jan. 2003. "Strategic Interaction Among Governments: An Overview of Theoretical Studies." *International Regional Science* Review 26: 175–88.

Brülhart, Marius, Jonathan Gruber, Matthias Krapf, and Kurt Schmidheiny. 2022. "Behavioral Responses to Wealth Taxes: Evidence from Switzerland." *American Economic Journal: Economic Policy* 14 (4): 111–50.

Brülhart, Marius, and Mario Jametti. 2006. "Vertical Versus Horizontal Tax Externalities: An Empirical Test." *Journal of Public Economics* 90 (10): 2027–62.

Brülhart, Marius, and Mario Jametti. 2019. "Does Tax Competition Tame the Leviathan?" *Journal of Public Economics* 177: 104037.

Brülhart, Marius, Mario Jametti, and Kurt Schmidheiny. 2012. "Do Agglomeration Economies Reduce the Sensitivity of Firm Location to Tax Differentials?" *Economic Journal* 122 (563): 1069–93.

Brülhart, Marius, and Kurt Schmidheiny. 2013. "NFA, Steuerwettbewerb und Mobilität der Steuerzahler." Studie zum Zweiten Wirksamkeitsbericht NFA, University of Basel and University of Lausanne.

Brülhart, Marius, and David Staubli. 2017. "Die optimale Unternehmenssteuerreform: Auf drei Variablen kommt es an." Working paper.

Buettner, Thiess. 2006. "The Incentive Effect of Fiscal Equalization Transfers on Tax Policy." *Journal of Public Economics* 90 (3): 477–97.

Cajacob, Meret, and Karolina Yuan. 2019/20. "Die Steuerharmonisierung in der Rechtsetzung: Eine Auslegeordnung mit Fokus kantonaler Gestaltungsspielraum und Steuerfreibeträge." *Archiv für Schweizerisches Abgaberecht (ASA)* 88 (9): 681–714.

Cavelti, Ulrich, and Bernhard Greminger. 2010. "10 Jahre Steuerharmonisierung." *Archiv für Schweizerisches Abgaberecht (ASA)* 79 (5): 445–78.

Chatagny, Florian, Marko Köthenbürger, and Michael Stimmelmayr. 2017. "Introducing an IP License Box in Switzerland: Quantifying the Effects." *International Tax and Public Finance* 24 (6): 927–61.

Commission of the National Council. 1975. "Parlamentarische Initiativen betreffend Steuerharmonisierung: Bericht der vorberatenden Kommission an den Nationalrat." Report of the preliminary advisory commission to the National Council and the Federal Council, March 17, 1975.

Cremer, Helmuth, and Firouz Gahvari. 2020. "Tax Evasion, Fiscal Competition and Economic Integration." *European Economic Review* 44 (9): 1633–57.

Daepp, Martin, and David Staubli. 2018. "Dynamische Schätzung der Einnahmeeffekte der Steuervorlage 17." *Eidgenössische Steuerverwaltung*.

*Die Tat*. 1955. "Budgetberatung in Zug." January 29, 1955.

Dubach, Roswitha. 2010a. "'Kantönligeist' obsiegt gegen 'Klassensteuer': Wohlhabende bleiben verschont." In *Handbuch der eidgenössischen Volksabstimmungen 1848–2007*, edited by Wolf Linder, Christian Bolliger, and Yvan Rielle, 367–68. Haupt.

Dubach, Roswitha. 2010b. "Unerwartet knappes Nein zu einer Steuervereinheitlichung." In *Handbuch der eidgenössischen Volksabstimmungen 1848–2007*, edited by Wolf Linder, Christian Bolliger, and Yvan Rielle, 345–46. Haupt.

Egger, Peter, Marko Köthenbürger, and Michael Smart. 2010. "Do Fiscal Transfers Alleviate Business Tax Competition? Evidence from Germany." *Journal of Public Economics* 94 (3–4): 235–46.

Eugster, Beatrix, and Raphaël Parchet. 2019. "Culture and Taxes." *Journal of Political Economy* 127 (1): 296–337.

European Parliament. 2021. *Reform of the EU Own Resources*. Policy report, European Parliament, Policy Department for Budgetary Affairs.

Fajgelbaum, Pablo D., Eduardo Morales, Juan Carlos Suárez Serrato, and Owen Zidar. 2019. "State Taxes and Spatial Misallocation." *Review of Economic Studies* 86: 333–76.

Federal Council. 1976. "Botschaft des Bundesrates an die Bundesversammlung über die verfassungsmässige Neuordnung des Finanz- und Steuerrechts des Bundes." Botschaft des Bundesrates, March 24, 1976.

Federal Council. 1983. "Botschaft zu Bundesgesetzen über die Harmonisierung der

direkten Steuern der Kantone und Gemeinden sowie über die direkte Bundessteuer (Botschaft über die Steuerharmonisierung)." Botschaft des Bundesrates, May 25, 1983.
Federal Department of Finance. 2018a. "Aggregierte Steuerbemessungsgrundlage 2018; Bemessungsjahr 2014 (Excel Spreadsheet)." https://www.efv.admin.ch/ efv /de/home/themen/finanzausgleich/zahlen.html.
Federal Department of Finance. 2018b. "Ressourcenausgleich 2018 (Excel Spreadsheet)." https://www. efv.admin.ch/efv/de/home/themen/finanzausgleich/zahlen .html.
Federal Department of Finance. 2020. "Erläuterungen zu den massgebenden Gewinnen im Rahmen der STAF." https://www.efv.admin.ch/dam/efv/de/dokumente /finanzausgleich/rechtsgrundlagen/erlaeuterungen-gewinn-staf.pdf.download. pdf /erlaeuterungen-massgebende-gewinne-staf-d.pdf.
Federal Department of Finance. 2021. "Ressourcenausgleich 2021 (Excel Spreadsheet)." https://www.efv.admin.ch/efv/de/home/themen/finanzausgleich/zahlen .html.
Federal Department of Finance. 2023a. "Ermässigte Besteuerung von Gewinnen aus Patenten und vergleichbaren Rechten (Patentbox)." https://www.estv.admin .ch/dam/estv/de/ dokumente/estv/steuersystem/steuermaeppchen/patentbox-jp -de-fr.pdf.download. pdf/patentbox-jp-de-fr.pdf.
Federal Department of Finance. 2023b. "Open Government Data: Financing Statement by Nature and Function." https://www.efv.admin.ch/efv/en/home/themen /finanzstatistik/daten.html.
Federal Supreme Court of Switzerland. 2019. "Urteil vom 27. Mai 2019."
Federal Tax Administration. 1949–2021."Steuerbelastung in der Schweiz." https:// www.estv.admin.ch/estv/de/home/die-estv/steuerstatistiken-estv/ steuerbelastung -schweiz/belastung-kantonshauptorte.html.
Federal Tax Administration. 1971. "Eidgenössische Wehrsteuer 14. Periode. Steuerjahre 1967/68. Juristische Personen."
Federal Tax Administration. 1975. "Parlamentarische Initiativen betreffend Steuerharmonisierung Bericht der vorberatenden Kommission an den Nationalrat und den Bundesrat (Vom 17. März 1975)." https://www.fedlex.admin.ch/eli/fga/1975 /2_1748_1764_1691/de.
Federal Tax Administration. 2018a. "Interkantonales Konkordat über den Ausschluss von Steuerabkommen." https://www.estv.admin.ch/dam/estv/de/dokumente/estv /steuersystem/ dossier-steuerinformationen/a/a-interkantonale-konkordat.pdf .download.pdf/a-interkantonale-konkordat.pdf.
Federal Tax Administration. 2018b. "Unterschiede in der Steuerbelastung natürlicher und juristischer Personen 2004–2016." https://www.estv.admin.ch/dam/estv /de/dokumente/ estv/steuerpolitik/berichte/2018/steuerbelastungsunterschiede -2004–2016.pdf. download.pdf/Steuerbelastungsunterschiede_2004–2016.pdf.
Federal Tax Administration. 2018c. "Steuerbelastung in der Schweiz." https://www .estv.admin. ch/estv/de/home/die-estv/steuerstatistiken-estv/steuerbelastung -schweiz/ belastung-kantonshauptorte.html.
Federal Tax Administration. 2021. "Steuerbelastung in der Schweiz." https://www .estv.admin. ch/estv/de/home/die-estv/steuerstatistiken-estv/steuerbelastung -schweiz/ belastung-kantonshauptorte.html.
Federal Tax Administration. 2022a. "Individuelle Steuerveranlagungen der juristischen Personen [Individual corporate tax returns], 1973–2019." Unpublished confidential data.
Federal Tax Administration. 2022b. "Steuerharmonisierung." In "Steuerinformation," Schweizerische Steuerkonferenz.
Freiburghaus, Dieter, and Felix Buchli. 2003. "Die Entwicklung des Föderalismus

und der Föderalismus-diskussion in der Schweiz von 1874 bis 1964." *Swiss Political Science Review* 9 (1): 29–56.
Frey, René L., Andreas Spillmann, Bernard Dafflon, Claude Jeanrenaud, and Alfred Meier. 1994. *Der Finanzausgleich zwischen Bund und Kantonen.* Technical report, mandated by the Federal Finance Administration and the Conference of Cantonal Finance Ministers, Bern.
Fuest, Clemens, and Florian Neumeier. 2023. "Corporate Taxation." *Annual Reviews of Economics* 15: 425–50.
*Gewerkschaftliche Rundschau.* 1915. "Besteuerung der Kriegsgewinne" 7 (10): 150–51. https://www.e-periodica.ch/digbib/view?pid=grs-001:1915:7::467#166.
Grossmann, Eugen. 1935. "Das Problem der Steuerlast, mit besonderer Berücksichtigung der Schweiz." *Swiss Journal of Economics and Statistics,* 83–109.
Grossmann, Eugen. 1943. "Gestaltende Kräfte im bundesstaatlichen Finanzausgleich." *Swiss Journal of Economics and Statistics* 4 (1): 269–79.
Grossmann, Eugen. 1945. "Moral und Technik in der schweizerischen Finanzpolitik." In *Die Schweiz. Ein nationales Jahrbuch,* edited by Neue Helvetische Gesellschaft Zürich, 96–107.
Hauptmeier, Sebastian, Ferdinand Mittermaier, and Johannes Rincke. 2012. "Fiscal Competition over Taxes and Public Inputs." *Journal of Public Economics* 42 (3): 407–19.
Hines, James R. 2010. "Treasure Islands." *Journal of Economic Perspectives* 24 (4): 103–26.
Hines, James R., and Eric M. Rice. 1994. "Fiscal Paradise: Foreign Tax Havens and American Business." *Quarterly Journal of Economics* 109 (1): 149–82.
Hines, James R., and Richard H. Thaler. 1995. "The Flypaper Effect." *Journal of Economic Perspectives* 9 (4): 217–26.
Höhn, Ernst. 1968. "Die Steuerharmonisierung in der EWG und ihre Bedeutung für das schweizerische Steuerrecht." *Archiv für Schweizerisches Abgaberecht (ASA)* 37 (6–7): 257–76.
Höhn, Ernst. 1971. "Die Steuerharmonisierung in der Schweiz." *Bulletin/Schweizerische Kreditanstalt* May: 8–11.
Höhn, Ernst. 1973. "Die Harmonisierung der direkten Steuern des Bundes und der Kantone." *Archiv für Schweizerisches Abgaberecht (ASA)* 42: 119–28.
Hürlimann, Gisela. 2015. "Schweizerische Steuerwelt(en). Dic Bundessteuerpolitik im Kontext von Föderalismus, Gerechtigkeits- und Verteilungsfragen." *Archiv für Schweizerisches Abgaberecht (ASA)* 84(1–2): 29–48.
*Journal de Genève.* 1973a. "Fiscalité: les directeurs cantonaux des finances admettent l'ediction d'une loi cadre fédérale." June 18, 1973.
*Journal de Genève.* 1973b. "Harmonisation fiscale en Suisse: de nombreux problèmes subsistent." March 8, 1973.
*Journal de Genève.* 1973c. "Harmonisation fiscale intercantonale" September 20, 1973.
*Journal de Genève.* 1973d. "Une base à l'harmonisation globale des fiscs." June 27, 1973.
*Journal de Genève.* 1977. "Une harmonisation fiscale qui prétend se borner à la manière d'imposer." June 8, 1977.
Keen, Michael. 2001. "Preferential Regimes Can Make Tax Competition Less Harmful." *National Tax Journal* 54 (4): 757–62.
Keen, Michael, and Christos Kotsogiannis. 2002. "Does Fiscal Federalism Lead to Excessively High Taxes?" *American Economic Review* 92 (1): 363–70.
Keen, Michael, and Maurice Marchand. 1997. "Fiscal Competition and the Pattern of Public Spending." *Journal of Public Economics* 66 (1): 33–53.

Köthenbürger, Marko. 2002. "Tax Competition and Fiscal Equalization." *International Tax and Public Finance* 9 (4): 391–408.
Köthenbürger, Marko, and Gabriel Loumeau. 2023. "Tax Responses in Local Public Finance: The Flypaper Effect at Work." CESifo Working Paper 10354.
Köthenbürger, Marko, Costanza Naguib, Christian Stettler, and Michael Stimmelmayr. 2023. "Income Taxes and the Mobility of the Rich: Evidence from Us and UK Households in Switzerland." CESifo Working Paper 10376.
Krapf, Matthias, and David Staubli. 2025. "Regional Variations in Corporate Tax Responsiveness: Evidence from Switzerland." *European Economic Review*, 171, 104891.
Leisibach, Patrick, and Christoph A. Schaltegger. 2019. "Zielkonflikte und Fehlanreize: Eine Analyse der Anreizwirkungen im Schweizer Finanzausgleich." *Perspektiven der Wirtschaftspolitik* 20 (3): 254–79.
Lengwiler, Martin, and Matthieu Leimgruber. 2018. "Im Schatten des Landesstreiks: Sozialpolitik nach dem Ersten Weltkrieg." *Soziale Sicherheit: CHSS* 2018 (3): 27–30.
Luthi, Eva, and Kurt Schmidheiny. 2014. "The Effect of Agglomeration Size on Local Taxes." *Journal of Economic Geography* 14 (2): 265–87.
Marceau, Nicolas and Michael Smart. 2003. "Corporate Lobbying and Commitment Failure in Capital Taxation." *American Economic Review* 93: 241–51.
Martínez, Isabel Z. 2022. "Mobility Responses to the Establishment of a Residential Tax Haven: Evidence from Switzerland." *Journal of Urban Economics* 129: 1034–41.
Martínez, Isabel Z., Emmanuel Saez, and Michael Siegenthaler. 2021. "Intertemporal Labor Supply Substitution? Evidence from the Swiss Income Tax Holidays." *American Economic Review* 111 (2): 506–46.
Mauri, Nicola. 2023. "Fiscal Equalization Pushes Up Local Tax Rates: Evidence from Switzerland." Working paper.
*Neue Zürcher Nachrichten*. 1977. "Zug senkt Steuern." January 28, 1977.
*Neue Zürcher Zeitung*. 1949. "Konkordat über den Ausschluss von Steuerabkommen." October 11, 1949.
*Neue Zürcher Zeitung*. 1959. "Zukunft gestalten—Freiheit erhalten: Kundgebung des Schweizer Freisinns in Luzern." October 4, 1959.
*Neue Zürcher Zeitung*. 1969. "Harmonisierung der kantonalen Steuersysteme?" August 24, 1969.
*Neue Zürcher Zeitung*. 1970. "Die Verwirklichung der Steuerharmonisierung." September 7, 1970.
*Neue Zürcher Zeitung*. 1971. "Für die Harmonisierung der Steuerordnungen in der Schweiz." August 6, 1971.
*Neue Zürcher Zeitung*. 1973a. "Der Bundesrat zur Steuerharmonisierung." June 22, 1973.
*Neue Zürcher Zeitung*. 1973b. "Die Finanzdirektoren zur Steuerharmonisierung." June 27, 1973.
*Neue Zürcher Zeitung*. 1973c. "Die Vorarbeiten für eine Steuerharmonisierung." April 3, 1973.
*Neue Zürcher Zeitung*. 2023. "Wie starkt profitiert die Schweiz von Leistungen des Kantons Zürich?" January 16, 2023.
OECD. 2017. *Background Brief: Inclusive Framework on BEPS*. Policy report, OECD.
Portmann, Marco, and David Staubli. 2020. *Entwicklung der Unternehmenssteuerbelastung in der Schweiz von 2003 bis 2020: Analyse auf Gemeindeebene*. Policy report, Swiss Federal Tax Administration.

Rey, Alfred. 2017. "Finanzausgleich." In "Historisches Lexikon der Schweiz (HLS)," Version 13 March. Accessed February 27, 2023. https://hls-dhs-dss.ch/de/articles/013760/ 2017-07-13/.
Ritschard, Willi. 1972. "Notwendigkeit und Mühsal der Steuerharmonisierung." *Schweizer Monatshefte: Zeitschrift für Politik, Wirtschaft, Kultur* 52 (2): 101–8.
Robmann, Agnes. 1918. "Die direkte Bundessteuer." *Die Vorkämpferin* 13 (5): 3–4. https://www.e-periodica.ch/digbib/view?pid=vor-001:1918:13::67#331.
Romer, Christina D., and David H. Romer. 2010. "The Macroeconomic Effects of Tax Changes: Estimates Based on a New Measure of Fiscal Shocks." *American Economic Review* 100 (3): 763–801.
*Rote Revue*. 1926. "Ein Beitrag zur Frage der Steuervereinheitlichung." 5 (8): 252–59. https://www.e-periodica.ch/digbib/view?pid=ror-001:1925:5::539#254.
Rühli, Lukas. 2013. *Irrgarten Finanzausgleich*. Avenir Suisse.
Seligman, Edwin R. A. 1893. "The Theory of Progressive Taxation." *Political Science Quarterly* 8 (2): 220–51.
Seligman, Edwin R. A. 1914. *The Income Tax: A Study of the History, Theory and Practice of Income Taxation at Home and Abroad*, 2nd ed., rev. and enlarged with a new chapter. Macmillan.
Smart, Michael. 1998. "Taxation and Deadweight Loss in a System of Intergovernmental Transfers." *Canadian Journal of Economics* 31: 189–206.
Smart, Michael. 2009. "The Incentive Effects of Grants." In *Intergovernmental Fiscal Transfers- Principles and Practice*, edited by Richard Boadway and Anwar Shah, 203–23. World Bank.
*Solidarität*. 1916. "Sozialdemokratischer Parteitag in Zürich." 2 (24): 1–2. November 18, 1916. https://www.e-newspaperarchives.ch/?a=d&d=VHT19161118–01.2.4& e=———-de-20—1—img-txIN————0——-.
Swiss Parliament. 1990a. "Bundesgesetz über die Harmonisierung der direkten Steuern der Kantone und Gemeinden (Steuerharmonisierungsgesetz, StHG)." https://www.fedlex.admin.ch/eli/cc/1991/1256_1256_1256/de.
Swiss Parliament. 1990b. "Bundesgesetz über die direkte Bundessteuer (DBG)." https://www.fedlex.admin.ch/eli/cc/1991/1184_1184_1184/de.
Swiss Radio and Television. 1971. "Schweiz: Steuerharmonisierung, Angleichung der Strukturen der Steuererhebung in den einzelnen Kantonen." July 7. 1971. https://www.srf.ch/play/tv/rundschau/video/steuerharmonisierung?urn= urn:srf:video:2746baa3-f22d-43a9–91e3–217ee07b22f4.
Swiss Radio and Television. 1976. "Kontroverse über materielle Steuerharmonisierung." June 26, 1976. https://www.srf.ch/audio/samstagsrundschau/kontroverse-ueber-materielle-steuerharmonisierung?uuid=3e44e894–425a-44b2-8aef-2c60b81dc8f5.
Swiss Radio and Television. 1977. "Steuerharmonisierung." June 4, 1977. https://www.srf.ch/audio/samstagsrundschau/themen-finanzplatz-schweiz-steuerharmonisierung?uuid=30cb7e42-be75–4f22–9101-ad929a19c250.
*Tagesspiegel*. 1998. "Wirtschaft: Martin Ebner: Steuerjongleur, Wanderprediger und Rattenfänger." February 12, 1998.
Tanner, Jakob. 2012. "Der totaldemokratische Minimalstaat: zur Geschichte des Steuerstaates in der Schweiz." In *Steuern und Umverteilen: Effizienz versus Gerechtigkeit?* edited by Gisela Hürlimann and Jakob Tanner, 27–54. Vdf Hochschulverlag.
Tørsløv, Thomas, Ludvig Wier, and Gabriel Zucman. 2023. "The Missing Profits of Nations." *Review of Economic Studies* 90 (3): 1499–534.
van Orsouw, Michael. 1995. *Das vermeintliche Paradies–Eine historische Analyse der Anziehungskraft der Zuger Steuergesetze*. Chronos Verlag.

Wier, Ludvig, and Gabriel Zucman. 2022. "Global Profit Shifting, 1975–2019." UNU-WIDER Working Paper 2022 (121).
Wilson, John D., and David E. Wildasin. 2004. "Capital Tax Competition: Bane or Boon." *Journal of Public Economics* 88 (6): 1065–91.

## Comment Jan K. Brueckner

This chapter provides an interesting study of corporate taxation in Switzerland. The study is descriptive and thus contains few "results" in the usual sense, but the multitude of tax-structure details that it provides should be of great interest to any public finance economist and especially to those working on corporate taxation.

Although the chapter says little about it, Switzerland is a tax haven. This status can be seen from Figure 1 in Wier and Zucman (2022), which shows pretax corporate profits by country as a percentage of local employee compensation. If a country is the domicile of many multinational firms with little physical presence but substantial worldwide profits, this percentage will be large. Wier and Zucman's figure shows that Ireland, a well-known tax haven, ranks second or third in the world on this measure for the years 2015 and 2019. But Switzerland ranks fourth or fifth. While the measure shown in their figure may be imperfect in capturing tax-haven status, it remains highly suggestive. Further evidence of Switzerland's status can be seen in figure 10.1 from the chapter, which shows taxable profit as a share of GDP rising dramatically in the post-1990 era of globalization.

Switzerland's appeal to firms seeking to limit their tax burden has two sources. First, the country's federal tax rate is relatively low, at around 8 percent since 1998. Second, "domiciliary" firms, which have no physical presence in the country, were exempt from corporate taxes at the cantonal and municipal levels until 2020. Since the combination of the two subfederal tax rates appears to have been at least as large as the federal rate until recently, exemption from these taxes is an important source of Switzerland's appeal as a tax haven.

While the chapter offers impressively detailed discussion of the social and political underpinnings of Switzerland's tax structure, it is silent about the reasons for the asymmetric treatment of domiciliary firms at the federal and subfederal levels, although that logic could be interesting. If the tax exemption had been granted at the federal level instead of the subfederal level, multinational firms would have faced a wide variety of subfederal tax

Jan K. Brueckner is Distinguished Professor of Economics at the University of California, Irvine.

rates across cantons, complicating their choice of a domicile. Given this tax variety, a successful push for tax-haven status might have precluded exposure to the country's complex subfederal tax environment, achieved via an exemption to these taxes instead of the federal tax.

With a national population of only 8.7 million, the average population of the country's 26 cantons is only 335,000, about half the population of an average California county. With autonomy in setting a wider variety of tax rates than in a typical US county (personal income and property as well as corporate rates), it is natural to expect a degree of tax competition, possibly in all the separate tax rates, among Switzerland's cantons. The chapter argues that corporate tax competition is likely responsible for the long secular decline in cantonal corporate rates, which is especially notable since 1980 in figure 10.5. Evidently, the end of multinational firms' exemption from subfederal taxes in 2020 could enhance the incentives for tax competition, as cantons would now compete to attract these firms. On the other hand, the limited physical investments made by such firms may attenuate this incentive.

In table 10.1, the chapter provides empirical evidence on tax competition by estimating tax reaction functions. If cantons are competing among one another for corporate investment, the expectation is that tax rates in neighboring cantons will affect a given canton's tax choice. As a result, the neighbors' average tax rate appears as an explanatory variable on the right-hand side of the regression. Theory does not pin down the sign of this tax rate's coefficient, which could be either positive or negative. Although the coefficients on the uninteracted tax variables are mostly statistically insignificant, table 10.1 shows several significantly positive coefficients for a variable that interacts the neighbor tax rate with a post-2008 dummy, which is designed to capture a new equalization scheme after 2008. Thus, the coefficients in the table say that interaction was mostly absent prior to 2008 but was stronger after 2008 under the specifications in columns 1 and 4. Further tests would be required, however, to test whether interaction was actually different from zero in this latter period (a significance test on the sum of the uninteracted and interaction coefficients is needed).

With tax rates jointly determined under tax competition, the neighbor tax rate must be treated as endogenous. Table 10.1 takes only a partial step in dealing with this endogeneity by using a lagged tax rate on the right-hand side. A superior approach is to use an instrumental-variables approach to control for endogeneity of the neighbor rate. The literature in this area contains criticisms of commonly used instruments, but in a noteworthy 2009 paper, one of the current authors (Raphaël Parchet) offers an approach that surmounts these criticisms, relying on data from Switzerland.

Parchet's paper investigates tax competition among municipalities (not cantons) in setting their personal income-tax rates. Parchet argues that the neighboring tax rate that matters is the *combined* municipal and cantonal tax rate, which will determine the neighboring cantons' attractiveness taxwise as places to live. In the regression, this combined rate, along with the own-municipality's cantonal income-tax rate, help to determine the own municipal rate. The neighbor's combined tax rate is endogenous because of tax competition in its municipal component, but Parchet's innovation is to use the neighbor's *cantonal* rate, which can be treated as exogenous, as the instrument for its combined rate. When doing so, Parchet finds significant tax interaction, with a significantly positive coefficient for the neighbors' combined rate in the estimated reaction function. This clever exercise is possible only because of the richness of the Swiss tax structure. Note that, since the chapter estimates tax reaction functions for cantons, not municipalities, Parchet's approach is not applicable.

The chapter surveys a decades-long effort to achieve corporate tax-base harmonization in Switzerland, starting in 1948 and culminating in the Federal Tax Harmonization Act of 1993. A fascinating detail is that initial efforts were partly spurred by a desire to eliminate special tax deals designed to attract investment, a goal that persisted as efforts continued. Evidently, these deals sometimes involved favorable, targeted adjustments in the tax base for particular firms. Base harmonization was designed to prevent such adjustments and thus to limit the scope for special deals. Harmonization also simplified tax computations for firms operating across multiple cantons, which had faced a variety of different base definitions.

Special state-level deals designed to attract big investments (commonly auto assembly plants) are rife in the United States, and they are often viewed as a governmental transfer from taxpayers to firms with little allocative effect. The logic of this view is that, with multiple states offering similar deals, they cancel one another out, thus leaving firms to select an investment site based on its innate labor-force and transport-access characteristics. Taxpayers lose because the large cost of these deals (usually in excess of $200 million) diverts money from being spent on public goods and services. More recent deals, such as those designed to attract a second Amazon headquarters or microchip production facilities, are the most costly to date.

Recognizing its costliness and possible ineffectiveness, many state governments would evidently prefer that deal competition were eliminated. However, a voluntary agreement among states is likely to prompt defections that cause its collapse, suggesting that federal intervention would be required. As in the Swiss case, tax base harmonization might provide one way to limit the special deals, although many of the components of these deals in the US do not involve corporate taxes. Instead, they often include abatement of sales taxes on inputs, state-paid abatement of local property taxes, and subsidies for worker training and transportation improvements. Therefore, federal intervention that bans such arrangements would probably be needed to stop the competitive process.

Although a broad voluntary agreement to stop competing for investment via special deals would probably be unsustainable, a more limited agreement between two neighboring states exists and appears to be working. The agreement involves the states of Kansas and Missouri, each of which contains a portion of the Kansas City metro area. Through various deals, the two states over the years had attempted to attract firms from one side of the metro area to the other, a competition that the press described as a "corporate-welfare border war" (Brown 2019) and that was formally analyzed by Kim (2023). In 2019, Kansas and Missouri agreed to stop this competitive process through legislation and executive orders, and the agreement appears to be stable. The approach would be applicable in other cases where a US metro area crosses state borders.

Although Switzerland's alternate harmonization approach to outlawing special deals appears promising, there is in fact a loophole. Although the base is harmonized, corporate tax holidays as long as 10 years are allowed at the cantonal level for new industrial firms. These holidays resemble the various tax abatement schemes practiced in the US, and they leave the door open for special deals despite the efforts to close it.

For acknowledgments, sources of research support, and disclosure of the author's material financial relationships, if any, please see https://www.nber.org/books-and-chapters/policy-responses-tax-competition/comment-competition-harmonization-and-redistribution-corporate-taxes-switzerland-brueckner.

## References

Brown, Marcia. 2019. "Kansas and Missouri Call a Truce in Corporate-Welfare Border War." *American Prospect*, August 6, 2019. https://prospect.org/economy/kansas-missouri-call-truce-corporate-welfare-border-war/.

Kim, Donghyuk. 2023. "Economic Spillovers and Political Payoffs in Government Competition for Firms: Evidence from the Kansas City Border War." *Journal of Public Economics* 224, article 104941.

Parchet, Raphaël. 2019. "Are Local Tax Rates Strategic Complements or Strategic Substitutes?" *American Economic Journal: Economic Policy* 11: 189–224.

Wier, Ledwig, and Gabriel Zucman. 2022. "Global Profit Shifting, 1975–2019." United Nations University World Institute for Development Economics Research Working Paper 121.

# Author Index

# Subject Index

Note: Page numbers followed by *f* or *t* refer to figures or tables, respectively.